E.J. PRATT

Letters

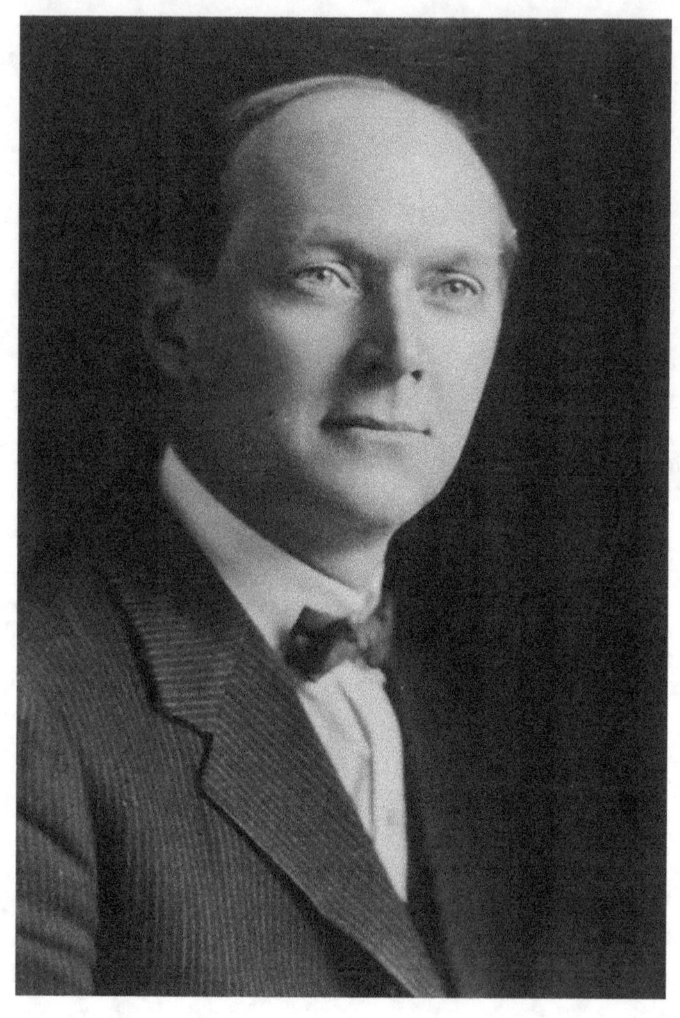

E.J. Pratt, 1930
(Bursar's Office fonds, Special Collections,
E.J. Pratt Library, Victoria University, Toronto)

E.J. PRATT

Letters

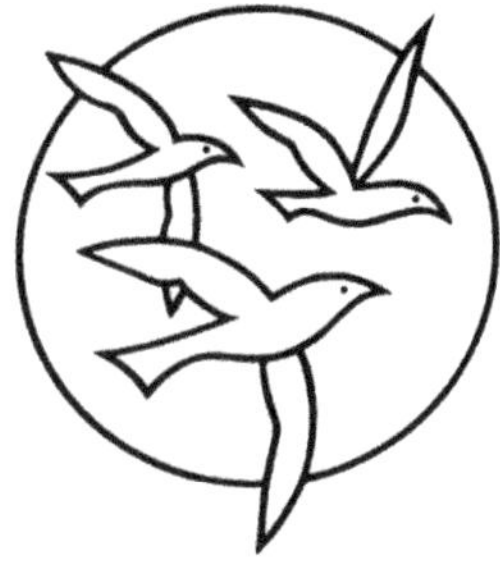

Edited by Elizabeth Popham and David G. Pitt

UNIVERSITY OF TORONTO PRESS
Toronto Buffalo London

Toronto Buffalo L ondon
www.utppublishing.com

ISBN 978-1-4426-5023-7

Collected Works of E.J. Pratt

Library and Archives Canada Cataloguing in Publication

Pratt, E.J. (Edwin John), 1882–1964
[Correspondence. Selections]
E.J. Pratt : letters / edited by Elizabeth Popham and David G. Pitt.

(Collected works of E.J. Pratt)
Includes bibliographical references and index.
ISBN 978-1-4426-5023-7 (cloth)

1. Pratt, E.J. (Edwin John), 1882–1964 – Correspondence. 2. Poets, Canadian (English) – 20th century – Correspondence. I. Popham, Elizabeth A., editor II. Pitt, David G. (David George), 1921–, editor III. Title. IV. Title: Letters. V. Title: Correspondence. – Selections. VI. Series: Pratt, E. J. (Edwin John), 1882–1964. – Works (Series)

PS8531.R23Z48 2017 C811'.54 C2016-904280-4

This book has been published with the help of a grant from the Federation for the Humanities and Social Sciences, through the Awards to Scholarly Publications Program, using funds provided by the Social Sciences and Humanities Research Council of Canada.

University of Toronto Press acknowledges the financial assistance to its publishing program of the Canada Council for the Arts and the Ontario Arts Council, an agency of the Government of Ontario.

Canada Council for the Arts
Conseil des Arts du Canada

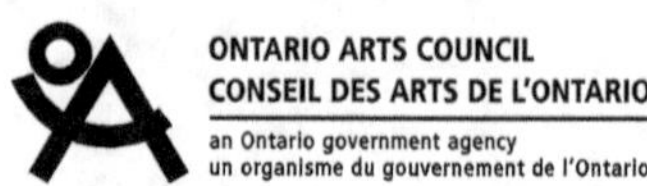

Funded by the Government of Canada
Financé par le gouvernement du Canada

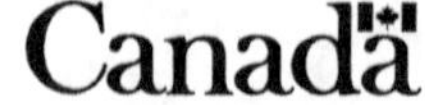

Contents

THE COLLECTED WORKS OF E.J. PRATT

GENERAL EDITORS: SANDRA DJWA, W.J. KEITH, ZAILIG POLLOCK.

The aim of this edition is to present a critical annotated text of the collected works of E.J. Pratt – complete poetry; selected prose and correspondence.

BOOKS IN THIS SERIES

E.J. Pratt on His Life and Poetry, ed. Susan Gingell (1983)

Complete Poems, ed. Sandra Djwa and R.G. Moyles (1989)

Pursuits Amateur and Academic: The Selected Prose of E.J. Pratt, ed. Susan Gingell (1995)

Selected Poems, ed. Sandra Djwa, W.J. Keith, and Zailig Pollock (1998)

E.J. Pratt: Letters, ed. Elizabeth Popham and David G. Pitt (2017)

In addition, with the cooperation of the E.J. Pratt Library at Victoria College (Toronto) and the University of Toronto Press, the E.J. Pratt Publication Project has supplemented print publication with digital resources on *The Hypertext Pratt* website (www.trentu.ca/pratt).

Introduction

As for my own letters and correspondence generally, I haven't preserved a syllable – not a letter. I have never had a 'proprietary' interest in my own compositions apart from my manuscripts of poetry.

E.J. Pratt to H. Pearson Gundy, Librarian, Queen's University, 24 October 1961

I think he had more control over his persona than most people have. We all decide on what we would like, the face we would like to show the world, but we don't have as much control over it as he had.

Claire Pratt to Lila Laakso, Librarian, Victoria College, 1964

E.J. Pratt occupies a unique place in the history of Canadian literature. From 1925 to 1964, he was arguably Canada's foremost poet, and he had an unprecedented run as one of our first literary celebrities – a very public cultural figure at a time when the cultural identity of the nation was taking shape. The letters in this volume will confirm many aspects of the public face of E.J. Pratt, but there are also some glimpses behind the curtain. The correspondence shows him negotiating the chasms between academic and popular audiences, and Victorian and modern sensibilities. He rejected the late romanticism of the 'Confederation' poets early in his career, aspired for a time to the modernism of the McGill Group, but ultimately went his own way. Although he published several volumes of lyrics with convincing 'modernist' credentials, his most characteristic poems were meticulously researched epics which anticipated both the fascination of later Canadian poets with the 'long poem' and the 'documentary' impulse in Canadian writing and film. Repeatedly in his letters, Pratt made it clear that his poetry was intended to be populist as well as intellectual, both in its sound – which blends the cadence of Pratt's native Newfoundland with the metric discipline of Shakespearean blank verse – and in its subject matter – which was often ripped from the headlines or the history books. He engaged with the moral and spiritual concerns of his theological education as a Methodist seminarian, the complexity of human perception and motivation being illuminated by the emerging discipline of psychology, and the potential – for violence and destruction, and for evolutionary growth – of science and technology. The resulting poems were ironic without being cynical, epic in their expansiveness, and elegiac in their focus on suffering and endurance in the face of apparently insurmountable obstacles. In short, they affirmed – and helped to create – the Canadian myth of creative moral engagement with a hostile environment.

As often happens with personal documents, particularly when the author lives in the midst of an active community, Pratt's correspondence mentions matters which we would consider of vital significance only in passing: his membership in PEN Canada; his affiliation with associations advocating for free speech and civil liberties; his participation in the Canadian-Soviet Friendship Council from its inception in 1943 to the outbreak of the 'Cold War'; and the events of both world wars, about which he writes so powerfully in his verse. For the most part, the letters in this volume are the day-to-day record of a carefully managed literary career. He started late, but once he began to write, Pratt produced a volume of verse every one to five years over three decades. Not surprisingly, much of his correspondence reflects his aims and ambitions as a poet. Perhaps because he earned immediate critical and public approval, letters written during his period of apprenticeship between 1918 and publication of *Newfoundland Verse* in 1923 contain no expressions of doubt in his abilities, but provide evidence that a small group of Pelham Edgar's protégés – Pratt, Arthur Phelps, and Herbert Greaves – regularly critiqued each other's verse. His subsequent letters to publishers, editors, and critics provide a record of his efficient negotiation of the publication and reception of his work. Throughout his career, he monitored reviews, writing letters of acknowledgment to reviewers and editors, even for mixed reviews; and he maintained a carefully planned publication schedule.[1] Correspondence related to his activities as a member of the Canadian Authors Association and editor of the CAA-sponsored *Canadian Poetry Magazine* (1936–43) shows him consciously taking on the task of 'making' Canadian culture as part of a collaborative enterprise, as well as personally as a poet and a mentor for other writers. In his letters to fellow writers and critics who supported his work, and were therefore invariably adopted as 'friends,'[2] we see him constructing a supportive community. As an established writer, his responses to scholars about his inspirations, philosophy, and technique provide a retrospective assessment of his own writing. The portrait that emerges is of a man who viewed writing poetry as his 'profession.' However, it is the letters to Viola and Claire Pratt that most clearly provide what Gérard Genette calls 'a more or less organized tour of the "workshop"' of an active and successful writer, 'uncovering the ways and means by which the text has become what it is.'[3] Although he claimed that he had not 'preserved a syllable' of his correspondence when asked by H. Pearson Gundy to consider placing his letters in the archival collection at Queen's University (letter to Gundy, 24 October 1961; p. 657), Pratt's wife and daughter saw themselves as caretakers of his memory, and preserved practically everything. Taken as a whole, the letters in this volume complicate Pratt's performed identity as professional poet by showing us the man, the husband and father, the cultural worker, and the disciplined writer collecting data and anxiously experimenting with poetic form.

Those readers familiar with David Pitt's biography of the poet will find confirmation in the letters on which the biography was based (and others discovered after its publication) of his portrait of 'Ned Pratt' as a profoundly social man – the inveterate host of 'stag' parties at one or the other of Toronto's clubs, gathering around him the best and brightest of the bright young men, as well as influential older ones from the worlds of culture, business, and politics. This was Pratt's public face. For decades, Pratt was at the centre of a group of extraordinary gentlemen who were (or would become) the movers and shakers of Canadian culture. His wide-ranging acquaintance included Frederick Varley of the Group of Seven, former prime minister Arthur Meighen, future prime minister Mike Pearson, mogul Sir Ellsworth Flavelle, medical scientist Sir Fredrick Banting, career soldier and founder of the Dominion Drama Festival Colonel Henry Osborne, and Leonard Brockington, first president of the Canadian Broadcasting Corporation. When he was a fledgling writer, his mentors were Pelham Edgar of Victoria College, who encouraged his move from clinical psychology to literature, and Lorne Pierce of Ryerson Press, who published his first collection, *Newfoundland Verse* (1923), while others like Duncan Campbell Scott – to whom he wrote a fan letter on 18 January 1918 (pp. 9–10) – and Charles G.D. Roberts, the dean of Canadian poetry in the 1920s and '30s, offered encouragement by example. His contemporaries were fellow Victoria College student and apprentice poet Arthur Phelps, who went on to a distinguished career as an academic and radio personality; print journalist and cultural commentator William Arthur Deacon; and his great 'enemy,' rival poet Wilson MacDonald.[4]

As he came into his own as a writer, his literary circle expanded to include his publisher, Hugh Eayrs of Macmillan; critic W.E. Collin, author of *The White Savannahs* (1936); and the poets of the McGill Group – Frank Scott, Leo Kennedy,

A.M. Klein, and A.J.M. Smith – who enlisted the older, more established poet in the enterprise of producing the first anthology of Canadian modernist poetry, *New Provinces* (1936). As founding editor of *Canadian Poetry Magazine* (1935–43), he entered into extended correspondence with George Herbert Clarke, long-time editor of *Queen's Quarterly*, and Leo Cox of the Montreal Branch of the Canadian Authors Association, as well as communicating with hundreds of other Canadian poets – whether in detailed commentaries on poems accepted for publication or brief notes of rejection. His students included Northrop Frye, Douglas Bush, Earle Birney, Claude Bissell, Ernest Sirluck, and Desmond Pacey; and his protégés included younger colleagues like Marshall McLuhan at St Michael's College and Gordon Roper at Trinity, as well as anthologists Ralph Gustafson (*Anthology of Canadian* Poetry [1942]) and A.J.M. Smith (*The Book of Canadian Poetry* [1943]). He cultivated the approval of reviewers – particularly those like John Collings Squire of *London Mercury* and William Rose Benét of the *Saturday Review of Literature* – who could provide access to the potentially lucrative English and American markets. And, whether or not he agreed with their conclusions, he was immensely appreciative of the scholarly attention of Lorne Pierce (*An Outline of Canadian Literature* [1927]); W.E. Collin (*The White Savannahs* [1936]); E.K. Brown (*On Canadian Poetry* [1943]); Henry W. Wells and Carl Klinck (*Edwin J. Pratt: The Man and His Poetry* [1947]); John Sutherland ('E.J. Pratt: A Major Contemporary Poet,' *Northern Review* [1952] and *The Poetry of E.J. Pratt: A New Interpretation* [1956]); and Desmond Pacey (*Ten Canadian Poets: A Group of Biographical and Critical Essays* [1958]).

The highest endorsement his literary or academic acquaintances could receive in his letters was the promise to 'gather the boys together' for a dinner when the object of his approbation was next in Toronto. On 23 January 1934, in the midst of the negotiations about the selection of poems for the modernist anthology *New Provinces*, he wrote Frank Scott, suggesting that they try to schedule a 'stag' during his upcoming visit to Toronto, or at the very least 'celebration dinner when [Leo Kennedy] and Klein & Smith can be present' (p. 120). On 8 April 1941, he conspired with A.J.M. Smith to gather together E.K. Brown, and W.E. Collin from London, for a dinner when he visited Toronto in August (p. 203), and on 29 January 1954, he wrote to his daughter Claire, then working in Boston,

> I am having my birthday stag a week from tomorrow (Saturday). It will be much the same gang at the York Club – Knox, McLuhan, Goudge, Corbett et al. After dinner we do nothing but chin, chin, chin till we have exhausted all the stories. I enjoy such an evening and the boys say such stags are the highlights of existence. (pp. 553–4)

Pratt's letters to Pelham Edgar in October 1945 outlining arrangements for Edgar's return to Victoria University to give an address at Alumni Hall (letters of 10 and 23 October; *EJP: Web*) show the care with which these evenings were constructed: coordinating the guest list, planning the menu in consultation with the chef at the York Club, appointing the 'chairman' and planning of the speeches, and (implicitly) orchestrating the conversation. He was pleased (and clearly relieved) when, having been appointed chairman of the Board of the Toronto Branch of the Ontario Division of the Canadian Mental Health Association after his retirement in 1953, he found that his chief duty would be to gather together potential donors at dinner meetings (letters to Claire Pratt, 4 and 15 September 1953; pp. 537–9). Finally, as Viola explained to his long-time friend Murdo MacKinnon, when quite literally on his deathbed, he declared that he was 'waiting till he was better to see his friends. He never wanted to see anyone when he was sick – but only a few days before he died he said, As soon as I get up I am going to give a bang-up dinner at the York Club' (20 March 1964; p. 668). Almost on a par were the private parties at his own home such as the dinner in 1945 for visiting poet John Frederick Nims (letter to Claire Pratt, April 1945; pp. 327–8) and receptions during the Second World War for members of the Russian embassy (letter to Carl Klinck, 7 January 1946; *EJP: Web*).

He was not only an extraordinary host but the most appreciative of guests. It was the ceremony of these formal dinners that Pratt loved, and he took great pleasure in carving at table and presiding over discussion by a lively and creative group of acquaintances. However, it becomes evident in his letters that his enjoyment came not so much from hedonism as from a feeling of responsibility for others – with the dinners providing an opportunity for mentoring and networking. Indeed, as poet Ronald Everson recalled, although he was concerned with his own finances and ability to support his adult daughter should she need assistance, 'Ned ran an unofficial Canada Council, using his own money and bits from some others of us, to help deserving unknown poets and shaky little magazines.'[5] This was the 'Ned' Pratt for whom the café at Victoria College is named – the hospitable man who firmly believed that intellectual community needed to be fostered by gathering around a table, sharing food and drink. And, although Pratt's mentorship of young men – writers and critics – is well known, his support of the careers of young female writers can be set in the balance against his participation in the 'old boys' network' of the Toronto cultural scene of clubs and dinners. There are letters to, or in support of, Dorothy Livesay, Anne Wilkinson, P.K. Page, Doris Ferne, Eugenie Perry, and, although always with a paternalistic concern for her health, Margaret Avison. He even provided encouragement to Audrey Alexandra Brown, a favourite of his mentor, Pelham Edgar, although he did so with a touch of resentment for her affected speech and superior attitude.

A similar spirit of community infused his poetry. Today, it is common for writers to give readings of their work – particularly in conjunction with the marketing of books. However, this is a relatively recent phenomenon. It is evident from the correspondence that, from the start of his career, both performance and publication were essential parts of Pratt's artistic process, and he was increasingly open to experimentation with media. This most 'social' of poets honed his writing in recital, and in his letters we see his need to *voice* his poetry – to *hear* it in the public space – in order to assess it, as well as his anxious need for the approval of an audience. On 6 August 1929, Pratt wrote to his mentor Pelham Edgar that *The Roosevelt and the Antinoe* was progressing, and 'I am awfully anxious to go over it with you. I would much prefer to read it to you personally as a whole than send a fragment by mail' (p. 86). Meanwhile, he was working to 'get the poem in shape' for its public debut on 17 October – prior to publication by Macmillan in February – at 'my Recital at Hart House Theatre' (p. 86). The letters are full of references to 'recitals,' sometimes with extraordinarily large audiences. For example, Pratt wrote to Edgar on 26 August 1932 that at his recent recital in Halifax, there were 'nearly a thousand people' and he 'had a gorgeous time' (p. 100). While the number was reduced to 'seven hundred' in a subsequent report to William Arthur Deacon (4 September 1932; p. 102), it is difficult to imagine this large an audience for a poetry reading today. In letters arranging speaking engagements, Pratt typically offered a range of topics from which his hosts might choose, often with 'A Poetry Recital' or 'Readings of Miscellaneous Poems' as the final offering,[6] and it is evident as the years go by that this option was by far the most popular. *The Roosevelt and the Antinoe*, 'The Great Feud,' 'The Cachalot,' and *The Titanic* are all clearly performance scripts, and while 'They Are Returning' was commissioned by Arthur Irwin for publication in *Maclean's*, it was subsequently adapted for radio before finally being published as a 'pamphlet.'

Pratt claimed in a letter to Desmond Pacey on 20 October 1954 that the evolution of this poem taught him how to write for the burgeoning medium of radio (p. 583), but *Brébeuf and His Brethren* most clearly demonstrated to Pratt the potential of moving into different media and working in partnership with other artists, when composer Healey Willan suggested the possibility of their collaboration on 'a Canadian Passion Play or Oratorio' (letter to Ellen Elliott, 28 October 1940; p. 198).[7] (Pratt and Willan presented plans for regular performances at the Martyrs' Shrine in Midland when trying to raise financial support for a full-scale oratorio, but this grand scheme was never realized.) By the mid-1940s, the correspondence confirms that multiple stages of publication, in a variety of media, were part of his planning for *Behind the Log*, a poem which is very much a 'master work' both in terms of its execution and the conditions contributing to its composition. Pratt was at the peak of his skills and reputation at this point in his career. He had recently published *Still Life and Other Poems* (1943), and *Complete Poems* volumes had been published in Canada by his long-time publisher Macmillan (1944) and in the United States by Alfred A. Knopf (1945). His potential as a 'public poet,' capable of shaping the national consciousness, was acknowledged in the most satisfying ways when he was commissioned by the Royal Canadian Navy to write a poem about the North Atlantic convoys – in the same spirit in which the government had engaged artists to provide a visual record of the war.[8] Once the narrative had taken shape, Pratt performed the poem in recital, revised it in collaboration with Earle Birney for publication in *Canadian Poetry Magazine*, revamped it for a CBC radio production, and finally collaborated with Navy war artist Grant Macdonald[9] to produce the book published by Macmillan in 1947.

Writing to Earle Birney on 14 April 1946, Pratt shared his insights on the advantages of working in different media: 'I think you should take every opportunity of enlarging your public platforms and radio and magazines' (p. 375). And, once published, his poems were available for collaboration after the fact in the form of performance by others, including Birney and Alan Crawley, who frequently read Pratt's poems on CBC, and actress and elocutionist Cécile de Banke (alone or with her students) in concert and on radio.[10] Pratt proudly informed E.K. Brown on 4 November 1941 that his patriotic poem 'Dunkirk' had been read on air on Armistice Day by Lionel Brockington, then special assistant to Prime Minister William Lyon Mackenzie King (p. 215), and boasted to Lorne Pierce on 13 April 1949 that the final verse of his 'Newfoundland Seamen' was read by both Prime Minister Louis St Laurent and Lionel Brockington (then president of the Canadian Broadcasting Corporation) in their broadcasts welcoming Newfoundland into Confederation in 1949 (pp. 430–1). Full-scale dramatic performances of Pratt's long poems were a staple on the CBC, in part because of the educational market,[11] but also because – especially during the Second World War – they fulfilled the patriotic mandate of the national network.

From the first, Pratt clearly considered recitals to be an integral part of his role as a poet, as well as a supplementary source of income. On 4 May 1925, he wrote to Bill Deacon that he had '[j]ust come back from London where I gave an address and reading on Newfoundland' (p. 58). In the 1940s, end-of-term recitals of his poetry were a regular feature of his routine as a teacher in the summer schools at Halifax and Kingston. On 29 July 1940, he wrote to Viola about his first public reading from the manuscript of *Brébeuf* at Grant Hall, with an audience that 'ran to 350': 'I got through the half hour all right. Really not long enough to do justice to the subject but quite long enough for the heat and the attention of the audience. It gave me some idea of what passages to read and what to explain in prose' (p. 190). On 28 July 1945, he wrote from Halifax, where he had been teaching a class at the Convent of the Sacred Heart, 'I am getting ready now for my recital tonight to the sweet penguin-dressed sisters' (p. 359), and on 1 August, he sent his daughter Claire a cheque for $25: 'I received my pay for the Summer School recital last Thursday night' (p. 360). In addition to visits to regional CAA groups in Ontario and Quebec, he was enlisted to give series of talks and recitals across Canada in 1927–8 by the Association of Canadian Clubs (letters to Lorne Pierce, 15 July and 10 August 1927; pp. 72 and 74), and during the Second World War visited American venues in a tour sponsored by the Wartime Information Board (WIB) (letters to E.K. Brown, 11 May and 14 September, 1943; pp. 254 and 262).[12] At the high point of his career, after the publication of his *Collected Poems* in Canada and the United States, he was in constant demand as a speaker. On 3 February 1946, he wrote to William Rose Benét that he had been invited 'to give the Morris Gray lecture-recital at Harvard this year' (p. 371), and on 14 April, writing to congratulate Earle Birney on his Governor General's Award, he reported that he had just returned "from Texas, of all places" where he had given "a poetry-recital" – the last in 'a series of five trips during the last two months, Rochester, Buffalo, Harvard, Columbia and Houston. If this sort of thing had come ten years ago, how welcome it would have been' (p. 375).

Recognizing public interest in his exotic heritage, Pratt worked up lectures on Newfoundland language and culture. On 31 July 1947, he wrote to Albert Hatcher, president of Memorial College in St John's, that he would be unable to accept his invitation to return to Newfoundland that year, but that his brother Cal had been organizing a series of 'addresses and recitals' for the fall of 1948. He asked whether the college would be willing to sponsor the trip, saying 'During the time in St. John's I could give three lectures (excluding the two special ones) on subjects related to my own work, say, provisionally, "Poetry of the Sea," "The technique of the dramatic narrative," "the *Titanic* as a study in irony," or kindred subjects that would let me work in some readings and some references to Newfoundland life' (p. 402). In the end, he did not make the trip home until January 1949, when he was asked by the St Andrew's Society to preside at the annual Robbie Burns dinner and took the opportunity to combine his speaking engagements with research for a book on Sir John Franklin's final expedition in 1845–7.[13]

In the 1950s, especially after his official retirement in 1953, Pratt suffered from a number of minor but debilitating ailments and was no longer writing,[14] but he remained an active performer of his work. Performances were stripped down, and he asked for reassurance that he would not be required to stand for any length of time or cope with a question period. On 22 March 1952, he wrote to Father V.J. Guinan, president of the University of St Thomas in Houston to modify his earlier acceptance of an invitation to speak:

> There is just one qualification which I discussed with Father McCorkell. I like giving lectures, but Floor discussion is a bit uncongenial, partly because an ear infection this winter has made me slightly deaf, and partly because controversy from the Floor has always been a nervous exaction for me. I don't mind small groups where there is a sit-around intimacy and informality and everyone is at ease. (p. 489)

Despite these handicaps, he thrived on performance, volunteering to supplement his main talk with 'as many "talks" and lecture-recitals as desired, inside or outside your city, the same as on the previous trip' (p. 489).

However, in interviews with his wife and daughter following his death, and in Claire Pratt's portrait of her father in the final chapter of her family history *The Silent Ancestors*,[15] another side of Pratt emerges. While publicly he was the antithesis of the 'poet in the garret,' this too was part of his artistic process – both literally and figuratively. Several of his long poems were researched and composed – at least in part – in Mrs Cartwright's rooming house (125 University Avenue in Kingston) during summer session at Queen's University, or in residence rooms at Dalhousie, and his daughter recalled that, when she was a child, '[e]venings and weekends, when he was not playing golf, saw him in his den in a huge chair beside the fire, filling black notebooks with a tiny stub of pencil ... In the summer, the setting would change to our cottage at Bobcaygeon in what was then deep country stillness where he would settle comfortably, feet up, on a chair on the screened-in verandah, or the green den he had built for himself fifty yards from the cottage and nearer the lake where there was nothing to disturb him but the occasional crow' (p. 171). At the opening of the E.J. Pratt Room of Contemporary Poetry in the Victoria College Library in 1964, Claire Pratt commented that 'his absent-mindedness ... his being hail fellow well met, and stag parties ... was only a garment that he put on.' At home, sheltered from his busy public life, '[s]ilence was absolutely necessary to him. There was no way he could function without it. There was no way we could not provide it for him. And we did. The house was always quiet. Although we had people, we had people in and out of the house all the time – guests coming to stay – but no noisy ones, at least if they were, they quickly lost their noisiness when they got there! ... People just knew what he wanted and they fitted in with him' (VLP,

VUL, box 39, file 16). His letters are full of complaints about noise – crows in a letter to Claire on Christmas 1949 (p. 447); cars near the new house on Glencairn Avenue on 27 June 1953 (p. 532); radiators, anonymous 'snoring,' and inconsiderate boarders in 'the [G.B.] Harrison house' during a teaching exchange in Kingston on 12 March 1945 (p. 322). In a letter to Claire on 26 September 1956, he declared that an extended visit by a very talkative family friend 'had me on the floor just slumped with inertia' (p. 628).

His family was called upon to support both the public persona of the poet and the private discipline required to produce his poems, and one of the most intriguing aspects of the Pratt correspondence is the evidence of his partnership in both respects with his extraordinary wife, Viola Leone Whitney Pratt. Viola was a career woman at the centre of a cultural circle of her own, focused on her work as founding editor of the international children's magazine *World Friends* (1929–55) and the numerous women's clubs that defined the intellectual and social life of educated women in Toronto: the University Women's Club, the Heliconian Club, the Canadian Club, and the 'Talents,' a service club founded by Viola and Claire Pratt to provide help to those ineligible for assistance from social agencies. (The degree of gender segregation in the cultural community of the time may surprise some readers.) It was Viola who had first introduced Pratt to the informal poetry class held by Pelham Edgar on Monday evenings at Victoria College, and she recognized and supported the public obligations and private discipline integral to her husband's double role as university professor and poet. As a young wife and mother, she accepted the necessity for a writer-scholar to take his grand tour of Britain;[16] as the partner of a successful writer at the height of his career, she acted as hostess, research assistant, and sounding board for work in progress; as the mature wife of an infirm retired man, she assisted with the freelance editing assignments that augmented their income, even while she maintained her own career; in his final years, she was both his nurse and his conduit to the outside world.

Most significantly, Viola and later Claire, herself a talented artist and poet, were E.J. Pratt's chief correspondents. The main reason we have such a comprehensive record of Pratt's 'workshop' is that he was so often separated from his family. The carefree days when, as a bachelor or young married man, Pratt could retreat to Bobcaygeon in the summer months to write disappeared by 1937 when he pre-emptively (and without consulting his wife) sold the summer property. Claire had contracted poliomyelitis in the autumn of 1925 and required surgeries throughout her life to treat associated illnesses and infections.[17] Both E.J. and Viola Pratt took on extra work in order to carry the financial burden associated with Claire's medical condition and had been less and less able to make use of the cottage.[18] Starting in 1931, Pratt taught in Summer Sessions at Dalhousie, the University of British Columbia, and Queen's, while

Viola's position as editor of *World Friends* and other contract work often kept her in Toronto. There were medical bills to be paid, and Pratt was anxious to set up an annuity in case his daughter should be unable to support herself financially as an adult. His concern for his daughter's health and financial security is palpable in his letters to his wife, and later to Claire herself when she moved to New York to study at Columbia University in 1944 and to Boston in 1953. As he approached retirement, and then embarked on his post-retirement career as a fundraiser and freelance editor, he frequently voiced concerns about both his inadequate pension and her financial needs. However, Viola Pratt bore the brunt of hands-on care for Claire when her husband was away at summer school and when Claire was undergoing major surgeries and convalescences in New York and Cambridge.

Separated from his wife and daughter for months at a time, Pratt wrote long, chatty letters, full of accounts of his meetings and conversations, his research for the latest of his poems, and their early reception in recital. We meet the private man, who was, among other things, an inveterate sports enthusiast. As a golfer, he was thrilled to be able to attend the British Open in 1924 and the Vancouver Jubilee Open, played on the Shaughnessy Heights Golf Course in 1936 (letters to Viola Pratt, 22 June 1924 and 24 July 1936; pp. 41 and 148). He was proud of his success in the annual Cataraqui Golf Club tournaments in the 1930s and 40s (letter to Viola Pratt, 28 July 1939; p. 175), and as late as 1950 wrote that, although he could not play in 'the great Tournament at the Cataraqui Course ... it will be a pleasure to sit under a tree and watch the 496 scratch players approaching the 18th green' (letter to Viola Pratt, 12 August 1950; *EJP: Web*). In retirement, when walking was difficult, his old friend and golfing buddy Malcolm Wallace convinced him to take up lawn bowling (letter to Claire Pratt, 8 October 1954; p. 581). But he was also an avid boxing fan and (surprisingly) once blithely declared that the ice capades 'is my favourite out-door pastime' (letter to Viola Pratt, 22 Jan. 1955; p. 612).

When he taught summer school, he was freed from the heavy workload of the regular academic session (during which he also regularly took on overload teaching for the School of Dentistry or Department of Extension) and from the social obligations that accompanied his professional life, and was able to devote more of his energy to writing. In some respects the solitude suited him. For example, on 5 July 1939, he wrote to Viola from Queen's University, describing his complete immersion in research for *Brébeuf and His Brethren*: 'I just stayed in my room with coat and shirt off all the afternoon and with the thirty-third volume of the Jesuit Relations in my hands trying to get some shape to the new idea. It is going to be a tremendous task, perhaps too big, but I imagine the hardest is getting started. Should it take shape and go, it ought to hit a clip, but it's a gamble' (*EJP: Web*). And on 20 July, he confessed to Claire that he was relieved to find out that he could not possibly finish the poem in time for the three hundredth anniversary of the massacre, because now he could take his time 'ploughing … through the thousands of pages and find out just what material is suitable' (p. 175). In the summer of 1945, Pratt's research for the poem that would become *Behind the Log* is of a different sort, and his letters convey his excitement at the degree of the Navy's cooperation with the project: tours of navy vessels, interviews with officers, ratings, and common seamen, access to still restricted information about sonar and other naval technologies, and VIP treatment at every turn. On 26 June, he wrote to his wife: 'It is certainly going to be a difficult job learning the ways of the ship and her instruments – bigger even than I anticipated and I'll take the necessary time' (p. 343). That summer and the following autumn as the poem took shape, Pratt wrote enthusiastically to Pelham Edgar, Douglas Bush, E.K. Brown, and Earle Birney, often exaggerating both the duration of his tours of naval vessels and the level of access he had been given for the sake of a good story. For example, he wrote to Bush on 1 July 1945 that '[t]he Admiralty Board at Ottawa offered me access to the ships of the Navy for the Summer for the purpose of getting a poem "done" on the operations in the North Atlantic. The Board wants records in verse as well as in documentary prose' (p. 346), but went on to say that 'I have spent the last two weeks out to sea in the Micmac, a tribal destroyer' (pp. 346–7) when he had been in Halifax for one week and spent only one day on the ship.[19] The almost daily letters to 'Vi' in July provide a more accurate, if more pedestrian, record of his investigations.

In the case of *Towards the Last Spike*, his last great documentary poem, that record is enlivened by his bantering correspondence with his daughter Claire, whom he always felt an obligation to entertain. Pratt had conducted preliminary research for his 'railway saga' (letter to E.K. Brown, 17 November 1950; p. 462) while teaching at the summer school in Kingston and in September embarked on a CPR-sponsored trip to Alberta and British Columbia with Viola, who acted as his 'amanuensis' and research assistant.[20] On 9 September 1950, he sent his daughter a detailed list of some of the questions he had prepared for an interview with George Dalmage, a government geologist: '(1) Would fossils be discovered in the midst of the mountain tunnels several thousand feet below the summit?' '(2) Are they found along the river beds?' '(3) What makes the Kicking Horse River so chalky white, a dirty chalky?' (p. 453), and so on. The next day, he wrote to Viola, who had gone to visit her brother in Red Deer while her husband conducted research in Vancouver, announcing jubilantly that the information provided by Dalmage would support the central metaphor of his poem:

> I have also learned what muskeg is exactly – a lake of water over which vegetation has grown particularly caribou moss (the food of caribou) and – what I had hoped

> for – it covers the pre-Cambrian rock – so it can be made part of the 'lizard,' perhaps a leg or a flipper such as an alligator might have. This lizard I expect will be fearfully and wonderfully made, perhaps grotesquely made, before the beast is finally carved out. (p. 455)

And later the same day, he wrote to Claire with a detailed report on his findings about fossils, concluding with a humorous attempt to bond with his artistic daughter:

> The trilobite is like a crab. I shall give evidence of my draughtsmanship by drawing one from a verbal description given me by Mr Dalmage ...
>
> Almost human isn't it? I have known people whose faces resembled that. I could mention a few but my artistic modesty forbids elaborating on the resemblance for if you knew whom I had in mind you would say that I was seeking a compliment on my achievement. Suffice it to say that I have looked like that occasionally when a poem went bad or when I was turning over in bed vainly trying to get to sleep on the CPR. (p. 456)

Here, as always, Pratt's writing process for his long poems involved intensive research, followed by journalistic investigation. On 2 August 1945, he responded to a series of questions from Pelham Edgar, who was writing an article for an issue of the Quebec journal *Les Gants du Ciel* devoted to English Canadian writing, lamenting that, in the case of the 'new' poem, *Behind the Log*, 'I haven't written a line yet, have nothing but data, data, data. The task of selection and elimination is tremendous. I may get at it in early fall' (p. 363). In the same letter, he reminded Edgar of the process of composition of the first of his documentary poems, *The Roosevelt and the Antinoe*, recalling how Edgar solicited funds from wealthy patrons so that he might 'spend a week on the steamer and get all the details from the officers and crew,' investigate 'the funeral service held in the saloon of the R on the night of the storm when the two sailors Heitman and Wertanen were drowned,' and ascertain 'the exact messages transmitted from the Antinoe to R and from R to A. A wireless officer described the sounds of the dots & dashes and I made up my own metaphors, etc.' (p. 362). In the case of *Brébeuf*, in addition to documentary research, he interviewed priests on 'the matter of ritual,' walked the site, and surveyed local fauna (p. 362).

Pratt's lyric poetry involved a different process. Lyric was the mode of his apprenticeship, and in a letter to John Sutherland on 21 May 1954, he described *Rachel* – his first publication – as having been 'written in a flat Wordsworthian (Michael) style,' acknowledging that he did not find his 'characteristic vein' until *Witches Brew*, published nine years later (p. 566). On

25 November 1954, in answer to Desmond Pacey's query about 'influences' on his writing,[21] Pratt wrote, 'I admired (and still admire) the Carman, Lampman, Roberts, D.C. Scott group. But, as far as I know, there was no influence, for I reacted in the early '20s against the landscape prepossessions, regarding 'scenery' mainly as backdrop to human endeavour' (p. 600). He went on to declare, 'As Canadian poetry had its fill of pastoral and amorous treatment, I got a bit fed up with it. As you say, I didn't feel drawn to it. I abhor sticky sonnets particularly' (p. 601). In fact, Pratt's early lyrics share defining features with the modernism of F.R. Scott and A.J.M. Smith in this prejudice against romanticism, as well as in their impersonal voice, stripped down imagery, vernacular diction, and experimentations with poetic form. Yet many of his comments on modernism and its practitioners are distinctly ambivalent – occasionally even hostile. On 8 July 1933, teaching summer school in Halifax, he wrote to his wife, '[t]he nuns are as cordial as ever – I had them laughing over modernistic poetry yesterday' (p. 109). And on 1 August 1945, teaching summer session at Queen's University, he took great delight in telling his daughter an anecdote about 'a couple of chaps at Harvard who decided to put over a fast one on the critical cults in poetic criticism' by submitting nonsense verse to 'an exclusive magazine which printed it with the comment that the poem opened up a new epoch in American poetry,' and then publishing it 'in the form of a small book with brilliant format and fine printing' to critical acclaim (p. 360).

However, although he repeatedly asked, 'To what depths has the school of obscurity sunk?' (p. 360), he was also anxious for acceptance – for inclusion in the category of 'younger' poets. On 5 August 1941, having finally – after years of trying – had his verse accepted for publication in *Poetry* (Chicago), he wrote what amounts to a fan letter to editor George Dillon to say 'how much I love your Magazine':

> With the exception of a few lean years of oatmeal fare, I have been a subscriber since 1916, and have been an unofficial publicity agent for Poetry in Canada. I used to get the odd letter from 'Harriet' and the not-so-odd rejection slip with its little P.S. – 'I liked your "Erosion" or your "Magnolia Blossoms," but we are dreadfully overcrowded. It *nearly* got in.' I owe Harriet an immense debt if for no other reason than she taught me how to palliate blows at unfortunate contributors, during my own editorial term of office.
>
> Those were great days – Sandburg, Lindsay, Frost, Yeats falling into my lap every month or so. They did so much for me in my callow twenties. And I am sure that you have brought back the old glories. Jeffers, MacLeish, Fearing, Rukeyser lay hold upon my soul. I liked 'Quiz' of Ruth Lechlitner. I should like to meet Babette Deutsch. She's a honey! If you should manage to come up to Toronto, Brown and

> I will put on a partridge dinner for you. He was most enthusiastic about you. Floreat 'Poetry' (p. 206)

Here and elsewhere, Pratt aligned himself with the modernist generation, claiming to be in his 'callow twenties' in 1916, when he was actually thirty-four, and claiming the poets currently being published in *Poetry* as his contemporaries. In the Canadian context, Pratt literally was of two generations. His true contemporaries were Robert Service, Marjorie Pickthall, and Kenneth Leslie, but he did not begin to write until he was thirty years old, and the publication dates of his first books – *Rachel* (1917) and *Newfoundland Verse* (1923) – placed him in the company of younger writers. In 1934, when he was asked to contribute to the anthology of 'new poetry' that would become *New Provinces*, there is little doubt that his chief qualifications for inclusion in Scott and Smith's anthology were that he (together with Robert Finch) would provide geographic balance to the Montreal group and – as one of the best-selling poets in Canada – he would guarantee a broader audience for the collection. When *New Provinces* and W.E. Collin's *The White Savannahs* were published in 1936, he was fifty-two (born in 1882), while F.R. Scott was thirty-five (b. 1899), Robert Finch thirty-four (b. 1900), A.J.M. Smith thirty-two (b. 1902), Leo Kennedy twenty-seven (b. 1907), and A.M. Klein the youngest at twenty-five (b. 1909).

His attempts to fit into this company of younger poets were somewhat endearing. In the letters to and from F.R. Scott in which the selection of poems was being negotiated, Scott acted as contact for the Montreal writers, and Pratt for himself and Finch in Toronto, each to some degree attempting to soften the sometimes blunt critiques of Smith and Finch. Pratt typically attempted to build a sense of community. For example, on 9 January 1934, he conveyed Finch's suggestion that 'we be known as the "group of six" as a publicity matter,' and proposed a dinner 'as a celebration of the birth of the volume' (p. 117), concluding, rather anxiously, 'This group is to continue in perpetuity, isn't it so?' (p. 117). However, awkwardness becomes distinct discomfort in his attempts to negotiate the matter of Smith's famously 'suppressed' preface. In his letter of 11 January 1934, Scott declared his intention to 'introduce a touch of political radicalism somewhere' in the anthology, and Smith's political agenda was evident in the rejected preface in which he argued that the modern poet 'must try to perfect a technique that will combine power with simplicity and sympathy with intelligence so that he may play his part in developing mental and emotional attitudes that will facilitate the creation of a more practical social system.'[22] Pratt certainly agreed with, and 'embodied ... in his own practice,' much of what Smith had to say about the need for a 'substantial renovation of poetic technique,'[23] and in many of his letters – especially once he had taken on the editorship of *Canadian Poetry Magazine* and was soliciting poems from members of the *New Provinces* group – he expressed similar sentiments about 'the products of the "Maple Leaf" Milling Co.' (9 October 1940; p. 197) and the unbearable 'sweetness' of the verse so heavily represented in anthologies like John W. Garvin's *Canadian Poets* (1916, 1926).[24] However, while he echoed modernist rhetoric in the correspondence about Smith's preface, he had an older – and more conservative – man's sense of decorum in matters both poetic and political.

On 20 December 1935, he wrote to Scott:

> I went over the ms. and read for proof, then took it over to Finch who did likewise. Finch feels very strongly that the Preface ought to go. He doesn't like the tone of it and the general impression which will be left on the public mind that Canadian literature had to wait for us to get its first obstetrical success. We talked it over with Eayrs who likes the verse but is very dubious about the prologue. He calls it 'nose-tweaking.' (p. 137)

Hugh Eayrs had agreed to publish the anthology because of Pratt's track record with Macmillan – although with conditions to protect the press financially. Although Finch also found the essay unacceptable, it was Eayrs's discomfort that most swayed Pratt to his opinion that a one-page statement of 'point of view' by Scott (letter to Scott, 14 January 1936; p. 138) should replace Smith's colourful tirade against 'the great dead body of poetry laid out in the mortuary of the *Oxford Book* or interred under Garvin's florid epitaphs.'[25] Here, as in his position as editor of *Canadian Poetry Magazine*, Pratt walked a middle path. On 5 December 1935, he wrote to Dorothy Livesay, accepting 'Day and Night' for publication in the first number, but adding a word of caution about the accessibility of modernist verse to potential readers:

> Dee, I think a little punctuation in the short-lined verses might clarify poetic intention. I am aware of some of the changes going on in that direction, but I am afraid the public might put the newer styles down to oversight in proof-reading. I do not like too much punctuation myself, but I think the verses are a trifle scant in this case. (p. 135)

And, on 23 February 1936, with the fate of *New Provinces* still uncertain, he wrote to Scott:

> Say, supposing I went through the carbon copy of New Provinces, which I have, would I be at liberty to take the odd poem at the regular ridiculous rates. I need

> you fellows for stiffening, – where my own personal taste lies. But I am supposed to give a representative collection and not ignore the traditional schools, though I am keeping out the scarlet maples and the beaver dams wherever possible. (p. 141)

In the aftermath of *New Provinces*, Pratt's continuing support for Kennedy, Klein, Scott, and Smith – and for Smith's anthology project – was counterbalanced by a sense of personal resentment of the next wave of young Montreal writers – 'the Anderson Scott Page Ruddick gang' (letter to Smith, 28 January 1944; p. 276)[26] and the 'angry penguins'[27] of the contentious Montreal CAA chapter (letter to Claire Pratt, 13 October 1944; p. 274). However, the issue was less disdain for modernism than revulsion at their shockingly bad manners. On 28 January 1944, he was outraged that Neufville Shaw 'acted like a shit' in his review of A.J.M. Smith's *The Book of Canadian Poetry* in *Preview*:

> I didn't mind the criticisms so much as the prejudice. It was so blatantly obvious that the whole article was a build up for the Preview editorial coterie. After damning all Canadian literature up to the present, there came in the last paragraph a eulogy of the Anderson Scott Page Ruddick gang. The new Light had arisen now and Poetry had just been stalling for those bastards to rise in their effulgence. I don't know Shaw but he gave his case away by that last paragraph. Only a goddamn imbecile could have been guilty of such patent self-infatuation. All of the great ones listed were Preview Editors except Watson. The only notable omission was Preview – Ruddick.
>
> … All we want is a discriminating criticism, severe at times as it may be, – not a self-interested extermination. They ought to have been thankful that an anthology had come out which was catholic enough to admit the old and the new, the traditional and the experimental. Shaw & Ruddick were mad they weren't included. (pp. 276–7)

Despite such outbursts, Pratt ultimately maintained an uneasy neutrality in the poetry wars, aligned with the modernists but unwilling to dismiss the traditionalists entirely, and writing the long poems that ultimately defined his career. As Brian Trahearne has observed, Pratt's *The Titanic* (like his other book-length poems) is 'characteristic of the poet but not of his or her era, and the relation … to modernism is fruitfully debatable.'[28]

What is not debatable is Pratt's status as a shaper of Canadian consciousness – as Canada's epic poet. There is, of course, some irony here, as for much of his life Pratt was not 'Canadian.' He was born and raised in another country – Newfoundland – which did not enter Confederation until 1949. As he explained to Duncan Campbell Scott on 18 January 1918, his early verse 'springs out of the sea-faring life of Newfoundland, my native home' (p. 10), and largely owing to the efforts of his brother Cal, who assured that every library in Newfoundland received a copy of each of his books[29] and eventually commissioned David Pitt to edit the anthology *Here the Tides Flow* (letter to Pitt, 2 February 1958; p. 639), Pratt became and has remained Newfoundland's undeclared poet laureate. Regarding his position as a defining Canadian voice, Pratt himself was sceptical, writing in a letter to Desmond Pacey on 25 November 1954, 'Nationalism was never very strong. The only poems which might be called 'Canadian' are *Brébeuf* and certainly the *Spike*. The subject is tremendously dramatic, and I had the additional advantage of being able to *go over the ground*' (p. 601). On 17 November 1950, he wrote to E.K. Brown about *Towards the Last Spike*:

> I've come to the conclusion that the C.P.R. was built not so much by the chaps who did the technical and physical work, indispensable as they were, but by the fellows with the gift of gab, the talkers and the wranglers and argufiers. 'In the beginning was the Word' – and so to the end, to the last spike. Does that strike you as a perverse way of viewing the thing? I sometimes take a cockeyed view of things, as you are well aware. But I think I am sound on this.' (p. 462)

Elsewhere, he described *Towards the Last Spike* as 'an objective poem on the First Canadian transcontinental – objective in the sense that it is neither pro nor con politically' (letter to John Sutherland, 15 November 1951; p. 479). This was typical of Pratt's resistance to making overtly political statements, another way in which he was distinguished from the modernist poets. F.R. Scott expressed the difference very clearly when he asked in 'All Spikes but the Last,' 'Where are the coolies in your poem, Ned? … who has sung their story?' (ll. 1, 6).[30] However, the subjects of his poems – natural disasters, martyrdom, wartime heroism, the building of the transcontinental railway – were (and are) focal points for patriotic or nationalistic feeling, and while Pratt's treatment focused on psychological and moral testing rather than social or political issues, his work resonated with a nation struggling to define itself. His poems of Newfoundland authorize regional identity; his war poems – *Dunkirk*, *They Are Returning* (which he planned to subtitle 'A Canadian Poem') (letter to Ellen Elliott, 7 July 1945 (p. 349)), and *Behind the Log* – trace a national coming of age through global conflict; *Titanic*, *Brébeuf and His Brethren*, and *Towards the Last Spike* resonate with the geographic immensity of Canada and the imagination and will of those confronting it. 'In the beginning was the Word.'

We tend to associate the rise of cultural nationalism in Canada with the period following the Second World War: the report of the Royal Commission on National Development in the Arts, Letters, and Sciences (the Massey Report) in 1951; the founding of the National Library in 1953; the Canadian Writers Conference at Queen's University in 1955;[31] the establishment of the Canada Council in 1957; and the first issue of *Canadian Literature* in 1959. However, the correspondence of E.J. Pratt demonstrates how the ground was laid for these developments by the activities of the Canadian Authors Association to encourage Canadian writers and publishers in the 1930s and '40s; the establishment in 1935 of *Canadian Poetry Magazine*, the first journal devoted to Canadian poetry; the founding of the Canadian Broadcasting Corporation in 1936; the institution of the Governor General's Awards for literature in 1937; and the emergence of a new nationalism in and through Canadian participation in the Second World War. Pratt's letters provide a view of the enterprise from its very centre – from the perspective of the foremost literary figure of his time.

NOTES

1 For example, on 15 June 1945, he wrote to Ellen Elliott at Macmillan about 'They Are Returning': 'One reason why I should like to have it produced is that I may not have another book for two or three years. This is the only poem I have written in two years, and the one now projected on the convoys and the R.C.N. generally, will take me two years or more from now' (p. 337).

2 His letter to anthologist Ralph Gustafson on 19 September 1956 is typical: 'It is always grand to get a word of appreciation from a man like yourself whom I admire and love. You have ever been a great friend of mine and (apart from it) when you come to Toronto I shall put up a real "stag" for you at the York Club with your friends to "circle" you at the dinner table, if the geometry of the room allows the"circling" ' (p. 627).

3 *Paratexts: Thresholds of Interpretation*, trans. Jane E. Lewin (Cambridge: Cambridge University Press, 1997), 401.

4 The designation was MacDonald's rather than Pratt's. In the 1930s, the two were considered by many to be Canada's best poets, which fuelled their rivalry. On 20 November 1935, Pratt had written to MacDonald to acknowledge his letter of congratulations on the publication of *Titanic* (pp. 133–4). In the bottom margin, MacDonald scrawled 'This is from Pratt – my life-long enemy.'

5 Ronald G. Everson to David G. Pitt, 1 May 1967. See the letter to John Sutherland, 29 September 1955 (p. 621).

6 See the letters to Margaret Furness MacLeod, 22 September 1941 (pp. 211–12) and Father V.J. Guinan, 22 March 1952 (pp. 488–90).

7 A musical and dramatic version of *Brébeuf* composed by Healey Willan was performed at the CBC studios on 26 September 1943, with Ettore Mazzoleni

conducting the orchestra and James Finlay producing the broadcast. The first public performance – by the Mendelssohn Choir and the Toronto Symphony directed by Sir Ernest MacMillan – was on 18 January 1944 at Massey Hall; in 1947, Willan adapted the script for performance by choir and organ. A version was performed under his direction at the Timothy Eaton Memorial Church in 1967.

8 In the First World War, artists (including Frederick Varley, A.Y. Jackson, and Wyndham Lewis) were commissioned by the Canadian War Memorials Fund to depict Canada's participation in the war. In the Second World War, the Canadian War Records Programme seconded artists serving in the armed forces, including Lawren Harris, Charles Comfort, and Alex Colville.

9 See 'Grant Macdonald: The Artist, the Protagonist and the War at Sea,' *Fresh Water – A Journal of Great Lakes Marine History* 6, no. 1 (1991).

10 See, for example, the letters to Cécile de Banke, 24 December 1941 and 21 November 1942 (pp. 217–18 and 241).

11 Pratt's poems were staples in textbooks for the Ontario schools: *Heroic Tales in Verse* (1941) and *Poems for Upper School 1956–57* (1956), which included *The Roosevelt and the Antinoe*; *Poems for Senior Students* (1950), *Poems for Upper Schools* (1953), and *Poems for Upper Schools 1958–59* (1958), which included *The Titanic*. Both *Ten Selected Poems* (1947) and *Here the Tides Flow* (1962), edited by David G. Pitt for the Newfoundland market, included substantial selections of Pratt's verse.

12 The CAA had set up a Writers' War Committee, of which Pratt was a member, to work in conjunction with the WIB, to 'channel more effectively contributions of Canadian writers toward the War effort at home and abroad.' Brown coordinated a brief tour of American sites, including Cornell University, where he was teaching.

13 The principal source of information about the never-completed Franklin project is Pratt's report to the Humanities Research Council in spring 1949 (pp. 428–30). Shortly afterward, Pratt shifted his attention to the building of the transcontinental railroad, publishing *Towards the Last Spike* in 1952.

14 Pratt made the first of many references to problems with his right eye in a letter to John Sutherland on 12 May 1953 (p. 527), and finally admitted to 'chronic eyestrain' on 12 November 1956 (p. 632). On 18 February 1958, he wrote to Pacey, 'Neuritis set in all through my left foot necessitating a wheel chair in the house' and 'my hand is shaky with neuritis' (p. 640).

15 In *The Silent Ancestors: The Forebearers of E.J. Pratt* (Toronto: McClelland and Stewart, 1971), Claire Pratt described her father's subtle enforcement of the 'discipline' of silence on both children and adults: 'by some osmosis that many of us would give our eye-teeth to understand, the message came unmistakenly through that there was to be *no noise* nor disturbing commotion … Guests at a dinner party, if they did not know when to go home, were often minus a host by a certain hour, and no hard feelings. In fact, people took it for granted' (171–2).

16 On 7 August 1924, he wrote to Lorne Pierce: 'I have been to every great literary centre since I came over and have drunk deeply. I shall end that sentence right there so as to leave your imagination free scope for figurative exercise' (p. 51).

17 See *EJP: TY*, 72–4.

18 Several letters to friends confirm arrangements for their rental of the cottage. See, for example, the letter to Lorne Pierce of 30 January 1932 (pp. 95–6), and letters to William Arthur Deacon of 3 June 1926 (p. 66) and 4 September 1932 (pp. 101–2).

19 He later wove similar tales around his preparation to write *Brébeuf and His Brethren*, claiming in a letter to Henry Wells that 'I lived for a year practically with the Jesuits, attended Mass, spent hours and days in the Cathedrals before the altars, became almost a Catholic to get inside Brébeuf' (26 February 1945; p. 320). When the statement was echoed in the manuscript of *Edwin J. Pratt: The Man and His Poetry* (1947), Pratt corrected the exaggeration in a letter to Karl Klinck on 21 November 1945: 'I deleted "became almost a Catholic." I might be taken up on that literally. It is strong enough as it stands' (p. 320).

20 Pratt wrote his wife on 18 September 1950 with instructions to 'keep your eyes open for any kinds of trees, flowers, moss etc. that the CPR tracks might go over in their first laying. I don't know what use I can make of them yet but I am sure that they will be helpful some time' (p. 462). Viola kept a 'CPR journal' containing this and other information and Pratt integrated her catalogue of cotton grass, orchids, sphagnum moss, bladder-wort, sweet-gale, and pitcher plants into his depiction of the Precambrian shield (*TLS*, ll. 1269–75; *CP2*, pp. 239–40).

21 Pacey was writing a book of critical essays on major Canadian poets, published as *Ten Canadian Poets* in 1958.

22 A.J.M. Smith, 'A Rejected Preface,' *Canadian Literature* 24 (Spring 1965): 9.

23 Brian Trahearne, 'Afterword,' *Canadian Poetry 1920 to 1960* (Toronto: McClelland and Stewart, 2010), 435.

24 On 17 September 1941, Pratt wrote to Smith to congratulate him on receiving support from the Guggenheim Foundation to create an anthology of Canadian poetry: 'I think it is a great national blessing that the Foundation recognized you as the man for the job. The Garvin tradition is alive only in the drawing-rooms and the cross-road churches' (p. 210).

25 Smith, 'A Rejected Preface,' 7.

26 In a letter to Deacon on 10 July 1946, he expresses a similar opinion of the 'inflated exhibitionism' of 'the Anderson, – Layton – Souster gang,' and the hope that '[t]hey may grow out of it in time' (p. 379).

27 An allusion to the Australian avant-garde journal *Angry Penguins*. See the note to 'a fast one on the critical cults of poetic criticism' in the letter to Claire Pratt, 1 August 1945 (p. 360).

28 Trahearne, 'Afterword,' 444.

29 On 29 September 1955, Pratt wrote to John Sutherland that his brother was ordering one hundred copies of the *Northern Review* issue devoted to his work: ‘He intends contributing two copies to each of the 28 libraries in Nfld. and taking the balance for personal gifts’ (p. 620). This was typical of Cal’s support.

30 *F.R. Scott: Selected Poems* (Toronto: Oxford University Press, 1966), 64

31 See *Writing in Canada: Proceedings of the Canadian Writers’ Conference, Queen’s University, 28–31 July, 1955*, ed. George Whalley (Toronto: Macmillan, 1956).

Editorial Procedures

Principles of Selection

The letters collected by David G. Pitt in the course of his biographical research form the bulk of this anthology of E.J. Pratt's correspondence; Elizabeth Popham has been responsible for the collection of additional letters, textual editing, and annotation. With the gradual acquisition of the papers of E.J. Pratt's contemporaries by archival collections, the number of letters to and from Pratt available for study continues to grow. As of the date of publication, the editors have collected just under 1,200 letters from E.J. Pratt to family, friends, and professional contacts. All of these will be included in the hypertext edition of the *Complete Letters of E.J. Pratt* (www.trentu.ca/pratt/) as of potential interest to scholars of Canadian literature, and this electronic edition will continue to expand over the years as new letters are identified. Owing to the duration, volume, and nature of his very active correspondence, this print volume in the *Complete Works* series is a selection – although a carefully expansive one.

This volume contains only letters from E.J. Pratt, with the other side of the correspondence cited in explanatory notes where it is available and useful in deciphering Pratt's meaning. Much of Pratt's letter writing is 'incidental,' consisting of brief, rather cryptic notes confirming appointments or conveying congratulations to colleagues and friends. In the early decades of the twentieth century before telephones and then computers took their place on every desk and in every home, such correspondence was commonplace. The current equivalent is the standard email message: a brief written communication presented without context which nonetheless makes perfect sense to the writer and the recipient. These have been omitted from the print collection, unless the context or the personal connection is judged to hold special significance to scholars of Canadian literature and culture.

In addition, three main blocks of correspondence have been winnowed, with care to provide sufficient indications of the nature of Pratt's activities and relationships.

1 From 1930 to 1952, Pratt taught summer school in Halifax, British Columbia, or Kingston, and carried on an almost daily correspondence with his wife and daughter in which he detailed his activities and (when a poem was in the offing) his research. Where the letters recount research – for example, for *Brébeuf and His Brethren* in Kingston the summer of 1939 or *Behind the Log* in Halifax in the summer of 1945 – they are included; but where they simply focus on arrangements for family outings, they are 'selected.'
2 From January 1936 to August 1943, during which time Pratt served as the founding editor of *Canadian Poetry Magazine*, much of his correspondence consists of solicitation of material or brief indications of acceptance of a poem. Representative selections have been made. Appreciation or constructive criticism is rare but has been retained when it occurs.
3 Finally, in 1945 when Claire Pratt attended graduate school in New York, and again after his retirement in 1953 when her career took her to Cambridge and Boston, the mass of correspondence is with his absent daughter. It provides an extraordinary picture of the relationship between proud and anxious father, and his intellectually ambitious and physically frail daughter, but like many familial conversations it is often concerned with minute and highly repetitive rehearsal of details of daily life. Representative examples have been retained.

For the convenience of readers, and to emphasize the evolution of the implied narrative embodied in the letters, the correspondence has been presented in eight chronological groupings roughly corresponding to major divisions in David Pitt's two-volume biography of the author:

I Peregrinations: 1903–1925
II A Taste of National Acclaim: 1925–1932
III Prospect and Promotion: 1932–1939
IV Historical Fact and Epic Construction: 1939–1944
V Steering between Extremes: 1944–1948
VI Knockings at the Door: 1948–1953
VII Accepting the Years: 1953–1955
VIII As Good as Any Old Horse My Age: 1955–1964

Sources and Locations

The substantial volume and range of letters making up this edition in its print and electronic versions is owing to three main factors.

1 The first is Pratt's extraordinary self-confidence as a writer. He had a late start – not seriously attempting to write until 1914, when, at the age of 32, he fell under the influence of Pelham Edgar and his poetry group at Victoria College. However, he never doubted that he would be a good or even great poet. His letters indicate periodic wrestling with subject, technique, research, or revision, and frequently demonstrate concerns about how to reach a wider readership to gain prestige or greater financial returns by finding British or American publishers, but they reflect no crises of faith in his own abilities. With the exception of two early efforts – *Clay* and *Rachel* – Pratt preserved his manuscripts, while Viola and then Claire Pratt carefully preserved the letters written to them during Pratt's frequent absences from home.

2 The second factor is Pratt's close connection from the beginning of his career with Victoria University at the University of Toronto. Responding to a request from Charles D. Abbott, Director of Libraries at the University of Buffalo, for manuscripts for the Modern Poetry Collection of the Lockwood Memorial Library, Pratt acknowledges 'technical difficulties here at my own University,' specifically 'a tacit understanding with the President and Librarian of Victoria College to pass over the manuscripts to the Library some time in the future' (28 January 1945). In the same letter, he also, in a (somewhat disingenuous) excuse for his appalling handwriting, claims that the manuscripts of his poems are nearly indecipherable because,

> [i]n writing a poem I never conceived the possibility that anyone would ever be interested in the original; hence the chaos. Any reader or student would at once infer that the author had creeping paralysis. And again, the composition is mixed up in the same book with drafts of speeches, letters and lectures. However, I shall take a look through them and see if anything is available. I shall have to consult the College in any case. (p. 312)

Victoria College evidently held him to the 'tacit understanding,' and in 1946–7 Pratt made an initial donation of manuscripts, inaugurating the Pratt Collection. However, the volume of early material indicates that the possibility had been broached with him much earlier in his literary career, for he and his family habitually saved both manuscripts and copies of his letters from the time of the publication of *Newfoundland Verse* in 1923.

Further material was purchased by Victoria University from Viola Pratt in 1967–8, with additional donations from Mrs Pratt in 1978, and from Viola and Claire Pratt in 1985 and 1988. The family correspondence from this later period (after 1946) is frequently edited (i.e., photocopied with pieces of white paper covering sections of text – often a few lines at the beginning or ending of the letters). However, Claire Pratt's papers, which came to the library at her death in 1995, contain both additional letters and unedited originals of letters previously included as photocopies in the E.J. Pratt Collection. Almost without exception, the material excised from Pratt's letters by the family included either self-deprecating stories by Pratt of his own absent-mindedness or ineptitude, or specific details of Claire Pratt's medical condition and her father's attempts to make financial arrangements for her treatment and future maintenance.

Over the years, Victoria University Library has extended the collection to include letters from Martha Eugenie Perry (acquired in 1979 from the Provincial Archives of British Columbia), E.K. and Margaret Brown (acquired in 1980 from Margaret Brown), and Irving Layton (photocopies of the Concordia University Library, 1980).

In addition, the letters of several of Pratt's principal correspondents are preserved in the collections of such institutions as the Thomas Fisher Rare Book Library at the University of Toronto (Earl Birney, William Arthur Deacon and the Canadian Authors Association, and A.J.M. Smith), Queen's University (George Herbert Clark, Frederick C. Gullen, Lorne A. Pierce), McMaster University (Hugh Eayrs, Winnie Eayrs, Ellen Elliott, John M. Gray, and other employees of Macmillan Canada), the University of New Brunswick (Desmond Pacey and Charles G.D. Roberts), the University of Waterloo (Jenny and Newton Pincock), the University of Saskatchewan (Ralph Gustafson), and Library and Archives Canada (Charles Clay, A.M. Klein, F.R. Scott, and several others). A few letters remain in the private collections of scholars (most notably David G. Pitt and Sandra Djwa). A complete list of these sources is included in the digest of abbreviations used in this volume ('Abbreviations,' pp. 673–6).

3 The third major source of material derives from David G. Pitt's decades of research for his award-winning biography, *E.J. Pratt: The Truant Years* and *E.J. Pratt: The Master Years*. In interviews with Pratt's family, friends, and colleagues, copies or transcriptions of letters were offered in evidence of tales told by Leo Cox, Arthur Phelps, and others. In some cases, the originals remain with the correspondent or his family. In other cases, additional letters have been shaken loose by the biographer's interest that were unavailable at the time of his research – the most notable examples being several letters to Arthur Phelps from the early days of their acquaintance and literary

apprenticeship (1918–27) and several to Ronald G. Everson from the 1950s, when he was mentored by Pratt on resuming writing verse. These are now housed with their papers in the University of Manitoba and McMaster University archives respectively. There is no doubt that the publication of Pratt's biography sensitized owners of letters to their value to students of Pratt's life and work.

Presentation and Textual Notes

The editorial approach in this volume is very conservative. Pratt's correspondence is almost always handwritten. It is seldom formal, and is expressive, jovial, and opinionated, resulting in an idiosyncratic style. So as not to dilute the colloquial effect, features such as Pratt's erratic capitalization and the progressive indentations of his complex closings have been retained. However, obvious inconsistencies in spelling and punctuation have been corrected.

Correction of accidentals is made without notation. For example, punctuation at the end of lines is frequently replaced with a line break. In these cases, the comma or period has been provided. Typographical standardization has also been applied to some of Pratt's distinctive habits of penmanship. For example, 9th has been recorded as 9th; M^{rs} and $M^{\underline{rs}}$ as Mrs; indications of the hour as 1.30 or 1^{30} as 1:30; and $\$2^{00}$ as $2.00.

In addition, the following categories of accidentals have been regularized in accordance with the 'house' style of the University of Toronto Press: quotation marks (single, with double quotation marks for interior quotes) and ellipsis points (triple throughout). Canadian spelling conventions have been followed throughout.

The exception to the general practice of silent correction of accidentals is Pratt's misspelling or mistaken recording of the names of persons, organizations, or books. Because they frequently elicit comment or correction in subsequent correspondence (often from Pratt himself), these have been left uncorrected in the text of the letters. These are indicated in explanatory notes by [*sic*], with the correct form supplied.

Substantive emendations have been made only when a passage is incoherent as it stands – usually because a word or punctuation mark has been left out – and the correct alternative is obvious. All substantive emendations are indicated in endnotes. Interpolations are made where sense requires and are indicated by square brackets, [ ]. The editorial notation [*sic*] is used in notes to indicate apparent inconsistencies and errors; it has not been used within the text of the letters themselves.

There are no editorial annotations in the main text. Indecipherable words are indicated by brackets enclosing ellipsis points, each corresponding to a letter: e.g., 'in the [.....] these days.' Uncertain words are followed by a question mark in brackets: e.g., 'has much weighting[?].' Likely constructions are indicated within square brackets: e.g., 'betel[geu]se hea[ve]nly.'

Where text has been blocked out by the family before photocopying a letter for inclusion in the Pratt Collection, [ ] indicates the deletion. An indication of the size of the deletion (e.g., approximately four lines) has been made in the textual notes.

The only editorial ellipsis in this volume is designed to reduce repetition of return address. Return addresses provided by Pratt in handwriting or type are considered to be part of the text of the letter. However, the vast majority of Pratt's correspondence is written from Victoria College on stationery with variations on the college letterhead. These and other frequently used letterheads – *Canadian Poetry Magazine* and personal addresses – are indicated in abbreviated form in the textual notes. Unique or infrequently used letterheads are indicated in full.

Where letters are not dated or where dates are partially indicated, the presumed date is included in square brackets: e.g., '[late April/early May 1922]' or 'Monday 23 [March 1918].'

Explanatory Notes

The primary function of the explanatory notes is to gloss obscure terms and references, and to identify persons, events, and texts. Full annotation of the identities of people addressed or named in the letters is made once, usually when their name first appears. Where subsequent references to a person are not clear (for example, where only a first name or a common last name is used in a letter), an explanatory note will clarify his or her identity and/or the specific context of the reference. The hypertext edition of the letters contains an exhaustive index of every person, organization, and institution mentioned in Pratt's letters.

Citations to Pratt's published writings are to the *Complete Works of E.J. Pratt* (University of Toronto Press), except where references are to specific editions or drafts of Pratt's poems.

The main sources of information are:

- David G. Pitt, *E.J. Pratt: The Truant Years 1882–1927* (University of Toronto Press, 1984) and *E.J. Pratt: The Master Years 1927–1964* (University of Toronto Press, 1987)
- Lila Laakso, 'Descriptive Bibliography,' in *E.J. Pratt: Complete Poems*, ed. Sandra Djwa and R.G. Moyles (University of Toronto Press, 1989), 2:373–497

- Material in the Victoria University Library (Toronto, Ontario), including the E.J. Pratt Collection, the Claire Pratt Collection, and *Acta Victoriana.*

Because the choice to publish in Canada, the United States, or England is at issue in Pratt's lifetime and letters, all bibliographic notes include the place of publication.

Appendix

The appendix (pp. 665–9) includes letters written by Viola Pratt on Pratt's behalf toward the end of his life when he could write few letters himself, and several written shortly after his death on 26 April 1964.

In addition, for the convenience of scholars, some Pratt family letters that provide a sense of Pratt's early life in Newfoundland, and a complete index to the hundreds of letters which do not appear in this volume, including source and/or location as well as a brief indication of their contents, can be found at: www.trentu.ca/pratt/ (*EJP: Web*). The hypertext edition also houses a master index to these and other documents in the form of a 'Timeline' keyed to all letters, manuscripts, and printed editions of Pratt's work.

Acknowledgments

The process by which this volume of letters has come into existence began in the final years of E.J. Pratt's life when David Pitt first approached the poet about writing a biography. Along with scores of interviews with Pratt, his family, colleagues, and friends, Pratt's letters provided the foundation for the award-winning two-volume biography *E.J. Pratt: The Truant Years 1882–1927* (1984) and *The Master Years 1927–1964* (1987). Despite Pratt's insistence in 1961 to H. Pearson Gundy, head librarian at Queen's University, that 'I haven't preserved a syllable – not a letter' (24 October 1961), his frequent requests that letters be returned to him, and the extensive collection of original and photocopied letters housed with Pratt's manuscripts in the Canadiana collection of the E.J. Pratt Library at Victoria College, University of Toronto, indicate that he had developed the habit of retaining at least some of his correspondence – a habit no doubt encouraged by the avid interest of librarians and academic colleagues at Victoria College. The careful stewardship of Pratt's archival memory has been continued over the years by the staff of the E.J. Pratt Library, particularly bibliographer Lila Laakso and recently retired chief librarian Dr Robert Brandeis, a fact appreciated by Pratt's daughter Claire, who passed on her role as literary executor to Victoria College on her death in 1995, along with numerous letters and other papers to which the family had previously restricted access.

That so many of his correspondents retained Pratt's letters is indicative of his many sociable and professional relationships with key figures involved in the 'making of Canadian culture' in the 1920s, '30s, '40s, and '50s. When David Pitt was amassing witnesses and documentary evidence for his biography, many of Pratt's friends and associates were generous enough to share these letters in the form of original manuscripts, photocopies, transcriptions, or tape-recorded readings. The biographical process encouraged Viola and Claire Pratt to add their papers to the archival collections at Victoria College, and made other correspondents aware of the significance of their keepsake letters, many of which have since come into archival collections across Canada.

For an indication of the extraordinary number of contributors to David Pitt's biographical research, we refer readers to his prefaces to *E.J. Pratt: The Truant Years* and *E.J. Pratt: The Master Years*. Most notable among the many who helped bring that project to completion was, of course, Marion Pitt with her extraordinary facility at reading Pratt's quite extraordinarily bad handwriting. In that research and in Elizabeth Popham's subsequent search for additional letters, the staff of libraries and special collections across Canada and the United States have provided invaluable assistance. (See "Abbreviations," pp. 673–6, for a complete list.) In particular, we would like to acknowledge the assistance over the years of the staff of the E.J. Pratt Library at Victoria College, most recently Robert Brandeis, Lisa Sherlock, Agatha Barc, Colin Deinhardt, and Halyna Kazar. All of the images that appear in this volume are used by permission of Victoria University (University of Toronto).

In the editorial process, Elizabeth Popham is grateful for the advice of David Pitt and the support of other members of the Pratt Editorial Committee (Sandra Djwa, Susan Gingell, W.J. Keith, Lila Laakso, Perry Millar, and Zailig Pollock) and Advisory Board (David Bentley, Claude Bissell, Robert Brandeis, Peter Buitenhuis, Michael Darling, Douglas Lochhead, Jay Macpherson, Malcolm Ross, David Staines, and Brian Trahearne). The hypertext edition has been developed by Elizabeth Popham in close cooperation with the editors of *E.J. Pratt: Selected Poems* (2000) and the hypertext *Complete Poems* (1998–), particularly Zailig Pollock, the foremost textual editor at work in Canada today. Research assistance to Elizabeth Popham was provided over the years by Trent University students Jennifer Bistolas, Catherine Downey, Luke Tromly, Daphne Uras, and Sarah Miller, and assistance with the initial design of the hypertext edition by Christine Rudin and Jason Verbovski.

Finally, the editors wish to acknowledge the assistance of the editorial team at the University of Toronto Press, especially Siobhan McMenemy and Frances Mundy. The financial assistance provided to the Pratt Publication Committee by the Social Sciences and Humanities Research Council of Canada was invaluable in the preparation of this edition, as was funding for student assistance provided by the Editing Modernism in Canada (EMiC) Project, under the direction of Dean Irvine. Publication was assisted by a grant from the Awards to Scholarly Publications Program of the Federation for the Humanities and Social Sciences, using funds provided by the Social Sciences and Humanities Research Council of Canada.

Biographical Chronology

1882	Born 4 February at Western Bay, Newfoundland; third child of eight of the Rev John Pratt, Yorkshire-born clergyman, and Fanny Pitts Knight, daughter of a Newfoundland sea captain
1888–1902	Educated in outport schools and at the Methodist College, StJohn's, with a three-year intermission, 1897–1900, as a clerk in a dry-goods store
1902–4	Teacher at Moreton's Harbour, a fishing village in Notre Dame Bay
1904–7	Probationary minister in the Methodist ministry at Clarke's Beach-Cupids and Bell Island-Portugal Cove
1907–11	Student in philosophy, Victoria College, University of Toronto; BA, 1911
1912	Received MA degree, University of Toronto
1913	Received BD degree; ordained into the Methodist ministry
1913–20	Demonstrator-lecturer in psychology, University of Toronto; assistant minister in a number of churches around Streetsville, Ontario
1917	Received PhD from University of Toronto. His thesis, *Studies in Pauline Eschatology and Its Background*, was published in Toronto; *Rachel: A Sea Story of Newfoundland in Verse* was printed privately in New York
1918	Married Viola Whitney (BA, Victoria College, 1913), 20 August
1920	Joined Department of English, Victoria College
1921	Birth of only child, Mildred Claire, 18 March
1923	*Newfoundland Verse*, first commercially published book of poems
1925	*The Witches' Brew* published in London
1926	*Titans* published in London, *The Witches' Brew* in Toronto
1927	*The Iron Door (An Ode)* published in Toronto
1930	Appointed professor, Department of English, Victoria College; elected fellow of the Royal Society of Canada; *The Roosevelt and*

	the Antinoe published in New York; *Verses of the Sea*, with introduction by Charles G.D. Roberts, published in Toronto
1930–52	Taught summer school at Dalhousie, Queen's, and the University of British Columbia
1932	*Many Moods* published in Toronto
1935	*The Titanic* published in Toronto
1936	One of the founders and first editor, from January 1936 to August 1943, of *Canadian Poetry Magazine*
1937	*The Fable of the Goats and Other Poems* published in Toronto, winner of the Governor General's Award
1938	Appointed senior professor, Victoria College
1940	*Brébeuf and His Brethren* published in Toronto, winner of the Governor General's Award; awarded the Royal Society's Lorne Pierce Gold Medal for distinguished service to Canadian literature
1941	*Dunkirk* published in Toronto
1943	*Still Life and Other Verse* published in Toronto
1944	*Collected Poems* published in Toronto
1945	*Collected Poems*, with introduction by William Rose Bénet, published in New York; *They Are Returning* published in Toronto; received DLitt from University of Manitoba, first honorary degree (others: LLD, Queen's 1948; DCL, Bishop's 1949; DLitt, McGill 1949; DLitt, Toronto 1953; DLitt, Assumption 1955; DLitt, New Brunswick 1957; DLitt, Western Ontario 1957; DLitt, Memorial 1961)
1946	Created Companion of the Order of St Michael and St George in the King's Honours List
1947	*Behind the Log* and *Ten Selected Poems* published in Toronto
1952	*Towards the Last Spike* published in Toronto, winner of the Governor General's Award; awarded the University of Alberta Gold Medal for distinguished service to Canadian literature; member of the editorial board, from 20 December 1952 to 13 September 1958, of *Saturday Night*
1953	retired from Victoria College; appointed professor emeritus of English
1955	elected honorary president of the Canadian Authors Association
1957	received Canada Council Award on seventy-fifth birthday
1958	*The Collected Poems of E.J. Pratt*, 2nd ed., edited by Northrop Frye, published in Toronto
1959	received Civic Award of Merit from the City of Toronto
1961	received the Canada Council Medal for distinction in the field of literature
1963	elected honorary member of the Empire Club of Canada; elected first honorary member of the Arts and Letters Club
1964	died in Toronto, 26 April

LETTERS

I Peregrinations, 1903–1925

... exploring the country to find out the chances

E.J. Pratt to Reverend Charles E. Manning, 8 July 1908

TO THE EDITOR, *THE COLLEGIAN*[1]

Moreton's Harbour

[Sept. 1903]

Dear Sir,

Would it be too much to ask you to reckon me as one of your candidates, and to put my name amongst the others in the list of undergraduates in the Collegian. I got through wholly and absolutely upon the strength of the 1902 and previous year's grinding.

Yours truly,
Edwin J. Pratt

1 A monthly publication of the Methodist College, St John's, Newfoundland. Pratt was a student there from 1900 to 1902, when he completed his Junior Matriculation (Grade XI, then known as 'Associate of Arts'). In the summer of 1903 he passed the external matriculation examinations of the University of London, and wrote this letter to *The Collegian*.

TO BARBARA BRETT[2]

Clarke's Beach
Conception Bay

Sept. 22nd/04

My dear Barbara,

I must congratulate you upon gaining such a high place in the first division of Preliminary.[3] I quite expected that you would pass and secure Honours in some subjects. Everyone of the seven Preliminaries that went in passed, but you have gained first place.

Both Nina & Ida have also passed in Primary.[4] I suppose you have seen the Exam. list.

You have gained Honours in both French & English. If you had a few more marks you would have gained your $4 prize for English.

Emily French also has 2 Hons. One in French & one in Hygiene.

Hettie Burt has Hons. in French.

The three boys have passed, & Clara in 2nd division.

But I am really delighted with your work. I knew all the year by your close attention to your work that you would figure a good place in the Exam. list. Don't forget to keep up your English & French. Have you a teacher yet this year?

Poor little Flossie.[5] How much she would have wished to have taken the Exams. I suppose by this time you have got tired of Holidays, and want to get at your studies again.

I have not heard much of Moretons Hbr. School since Sept. and would like to know how things are working along.

I want you to write me and let me know, especially if the marks have come, and get them copied off to send me.

Honours in the Hygiene came to Emily. I know you were not far behind in that subject.

2 Brett (1890–1983) was one of Pratt's students when he taught at Moreton's Harbour (1902–4). She earned a BA from Mount Allison University and taught for forty years in Newfoundland schools, including Grand Falls Academy.

3 Grades 7 and 8.

4 Grade 6. (Public examinations were held in all grades from Primary to Junior Matriculation.)

5 Barbara's cousin Flossie Brett died in the winter of 1904.

Anyway go on, continue to study as you have in the past and there won't be much chances of failure with you.

A girl that keeps to her work and doesn't put pleasure and amusement before it will always succeed. Don't fail to write this return mail.

I remain
Yours very sincerely
E.J. Pratt

P.S. Give my congratulations to Emily, Hettie & Clara & the boys. Remember me to Hedley,[6] your mother & father and your cousins.

E.J.P.

TO WILLIS PIKE[7]

Victoria University
Toronto

January 26th 08.

Dear Uncle Billy,

How are you getting along at all? Still at the plant I suppose and getting almost sick of it EH! Do you ever have any muscles and pigs tongues now-adays? They don't know how to cook things like that up here in Toronto. If you ever do get a bit of cabbage it is no good because it is not boiled in Pork. But, however, I have no reason for complaint as I can get all the fruit I want at a low cost. I often think of the fun I used to have when about seven or eight o'clock I would go down and have an hour's chat at your house. I often think of the Bill Roost and the J.S.[8] I fancy I can hear dear little Mumu[9] saying it now, 'I give ow the Bill oost' the dear little thing. I would so much like to see her again and take her out for a little walk. And Gladdie and Maisie. I suppose they go to school all along. How is Mrs Pike? Mother often mentions her ever since the time she saw her at her house. She knows all about our duck supper and laughs a lot when I tell her of it. I eat so

---

6 Barbara's older brother.

7 A Bell Island resident. Pratt frequently visited Pike and his wife and three daughters in 1905–7 when he was a probationary minister on the Portugal Cove-Bell Island Methodist circuit.

8 Possibly local boats.

9 Muriel.

much that night I thought I could hardly get home afterwards. I saw hobgoblins and ghosts all night in my sleep after it.[10] OH! these were good times. I suppose your new couch is getting worn a little bit by this time. Is the pump working satisfactorily, and have you got your Masonic flag up yet?

Does Mr Alty[11] go in to see you very often? I suppose things are going ahead as usual. Did you get the photograph I sent you some time ago. I sent one to Mrs Whiteway and addressed it 2 Monroe Street. I do not know if she had changed house at that time or not.

I am living here[12] with a Mr & Mrs Hanna just across from the University. Will Pike[13] & Soper[14] are here with me in the same house. I am very fond of the work. I am taking an Arts Course and like it immensely. If I knew the address of your brother I should go to see him. There are several friends of mine here in Toronto whom I should have gone to see but I haven't got their address. It is such a big city that a person may become lost in the different streets if he doesn't take care. You should see the three of us sometimes getting supper. We go out to a restaurant for dinner. But sometimes we get hungry about 10 o'clock in the night and I put the kettle over the gas jet and make a grand cup of cocoa with milk. We have everything like that here. OH for a roast duck or a dish of pigs tongues. I only wish that Mrs Pike could take a peep in at us once in a while. I know that she would laugh.

Give my best regards to her, and give Mumu and Maisie and Gladdie I suppose if she hasn't got too big by this time, a good kiss for me.

I remain
yours Sincerely
E.J. Pratt

P.S. I've got out of the J.S. luck altogether since I came here.

---

10 According to Viola Pratt, Pratt's poem 'The Pursuit' (*MM*, 48; *EJP: CP* 1.290) was based on his recollection of a nightmare 'caused by a surfeit of roast duck when he was a student minister in Newfoundland.'

11 Thomas Alty, the student minister who succeeded Pratt at Bell Island when he left to attend Victoria College, Toronto in 1907.

12 A boarding house on St George Street, Toronto, where Pratt lived during his first year at Victoria College.

13 William H. Pike (no relation to Willis Pike), another Newfoundland-born probationary minister, friend and classmate of Pratt. Ordained in 1911, he served ethnic missions in western Canada.

14 Samuel Soper, also a Newfoundland-born probationer, friend, and classmate of Pratt. He served for many years after his ordination as a missionary of the Methodist (later United) Church in China.

TO REVEREND CHARLES E. MANNING[15]

Turner
Macoun
Saskatchewan

July 8th 08.

Dear Mr Manning,

I thought I might drop you a line to give you a brief idea of the Mission work out here in Estevan West. I arrived at Estevan about the 20th of June and got out to my Mission on the following day. I spent the first three weeks exploring the country to find out the chances of establishing a good Mission Centre, and at last decided upon Turner, a farming district as my headquarters. I visited all the homesteads within a radius of 20 miles and arranged for three appointments every Sunday. The morning appointment is at Shire's about 7 or 8 miles South. I hold the service in a large shack, then drive back[16] to Magoons'[17] and hold the afternoon service at that place after which I drive across the Country about 20 miles and take the third appointment at the small town of Hitchcock on the railway line. The meeting there is held in the schoolhouse and the congregation has been growing continually until last Sunday night the building was filled. I am delighted with the work, especially as the farmers take such an interest in the cause, some leaving their homesteads in the evening and coming as much as fifteen miles in the round trip in order to attend the service. The district is an entirely new one, eighty per cent of the homesteaders having come within the last three or four years. Cash is at present scarce on that account, but the crops give every indication of a good harvest and the financial prospects are therefore encouraging. With regard to the question of travelling expenses from Toronto as far as Winnipeg and back, if the people here are willing to pay all those expenses incurred by my coming to the Mission, that is refund what I have already paid out of my own pocket for my trip to Winnipeg as well as the remainder which, it

15 Secretary of the Home Mission Board of the Methodist Church. Pratt was writing from his student mission field in southeastern Saskatchewan.

16 By horse and buggy.

17 That summer Pratt boarded with homesteader William Magoon and his family. According to his daughter, Esther (Magoon) Bailey, he was the first to call Pratt 'Ned.' For several years Magoon managed a generally unproductive farm to which Pratt acquired mortgaged title in the summer of 1908. Pratt disposed of the farm in 1911, exchanging it for real estate in Toronto.

has already been agreed, shall be paid, would there be any objection to receiving it? Several have mentioned the fact to me, that it would not be difficult to raise enough by a special collection if the crops are good, to defray the total expenses from and back to Toronto, while if there was then a surplus it would of course go into the common fund. I said I should write and get instructions from you.

I shall a little later forward on the repayment of the loan of $40.00 you so kindly lent me in May and wishing your every success in your work.

I remain
yours sincerely
E.J. Pratt

TO VIOLA WHITNEY (LATER MRS E.J. PRATT)[18]

159[19]

Thursday
July 5, 1917

My dearest,

I have just finished typewriting 'Rachel,'[20] and am now sending a copy of it to your dear self.

---

18 Viola Whitney Pratt (1893–1984) was born in Atherley, Ontario, and was a graduate of Victoria College and the Ontario College of Education. She married Pratt in August 1918, and was the efficient manager of their very busy household. In addition to being her husband's first reader and assisting with research for his books, she was an editor for the United Church Publishing House (Toronto) and founding editor of the United Church's children's magazine *World Friends* (1929–55). She wrote and published several books, including *Famous Doctors: Osler, Banting, Penfield* (Toronto: Clarke Irwin, 1956) and *Journeying with the Year* (Toronto: The Women's Missionary Society of the United Church of Canada, 1957), a collection of short pieces for young readers, mostly her own. Intensely interested in the study of comparative religions, a social activist and popular public speaker, she was awarded an honorary Doctorate of Sacred Letters by Victoria College for her 'outstanding literary contributions and ... rare combination of intellect, temperament, and faith.'

19 159 Cumberland Street, Toronto

20 *Rachel: A Sea Story of Newfoundland in Verse* (*EJP: CP* 1.20) was Pratt's first long narrative and first Newfoundland poem. Begun in 1916 after a brief visit to Newfoundland, it was printed privately in 1917. A portion of the poem appeared in *NV*, but it was not published in its entirety until 1962 in *HTF*.

I am also this morning sending one to Dr Edgar[21] at Camp Kapuskasing.[22] I am anxious to see what he has to say. Shall send you his report just when I see it.

Am going back to Streetsville[23] this afternoon, but will be in the city for a day or two early next week.

Lovingly
Ned

TO DUNCAN CAMPBELL SCOTT[24]

Victoria College
Toronto, Ont.

Jan. 18th 18.

Dear Mr Duncan Campbell Scott,
Ottawa.

Dear Mr Scott,

I am taking the liberty of sending you a little message of appreciation although unknown to you personally.[25] I had the pleasure last week of spending an evening at the home of Dr Edgar, an esteemed friend of yours, and no less beloved of mine. In the course of the evening by the fire, he read to me selections from 'Lundy Lane,'[26] particularly, that magnificent 'Height of Land.' I had known the poem for a considerable time, but its growing beauty was so vividly impressed

---

21 Oscar Pelham Edgar (1871–1948) was born in Ottawa and educated at Upper Canada College, the University of Toronto, and Johns Hopkins University. He was appointed to Victoria College to teach French, but in 1902 became head of its Department of English, a post he held until his retirement in 1938. He was a distinguished scholar and author, and mentor to many noted scholars and writers, including Pratt, whom he appointed to the English Department in 1920.

22 An internment camp for prisoners of war and 'enemy aliens' near the northern Ontario town of Kapuskasing. Edgar was on duty there for the War Department in the summer of 1917.

23 A community on the western outskirts of Toronto, now part of Mississauga. Pratt served there as a 'summer supply' minister in 1917.

24 (1862–1947). Ottawa-born poet Duncan Campbell Scott served for many years in the federal Department of Indian Affairs. His books include *The Magic House and Other Poems* (Ottawa: J. Durie, 1893) and *Lundy's Lane and Other Poems* (1916), *Beauty and Life* (1921), and *The Poems of Duncan Campbell Scott* (1926), all published by McClelland & Stewart.

25 Shortly thereafter, Pratt met Scott at Pelham Edgar's home and recited some of his verse for him.

26 An error for *Lundy's Lane and Other Poems*, Scott's most recent book of verse.

upon me as he read it, that I asked him if you would not think it presumptuous, were I to write you and express my appreciation directly. He replied that you would be glad to get a line from any lover of poetry, and especially from one who had read and loved your own work. As such conditions are most thoroughly fulfilled in my case, I feel at liberty to write.

Three or four years ago, Arthur Phelps[27] – a college class-mate of mine – and I undertook to make a special study of Canadian poetry, and we soon found our interest mainly centered in Archibald Lampman,[28] Marjorie Pickthall[29] and yourself. 'The Height of Land' and the 'Lines to Edmund Morris' just thrilled us, and I frankly confessed to a slight feeling of jealousy, when Phelps told me that you had written him, and occasionally had sent him some of your poetry. He is naturally enthusiastic over it. Whenever we fall out upon any point, we pay each other back our grudges by bombarding each other with sonnets, etc., each seeking to inflict upon the other the greater injury, – a phase of ballistics unknown to any theory of militarism.

If your health is good, Mr Scott, could you stand an attack? I should dearly love to submit a few poems under separate cover for your examination. I wanted to send some last year but could not muster up sufficient courage. Dr Edgar, however, gave me a new faith. Most of the verse springs out of the sea-faring life of Newfoundland, my native home.

And could you once in a while send me a poem of your own, – a new one? I should indeed be very proud.

Sincerely yours
E.J. Pratt.

27 Arthur Leonard Phelps (1887–1970) was born in Columbus, Ontario. He was ordained a Methodist minister in 1913, but left the ministry to teach English at Cornell College in Iowa (1920–1), Wesley College, later the University of Winnipeg (1921–45), and McGill University (1947–53). He published two slim books of verse, *Poems* (Mount Vernon, IA: The English Club of Cornell College, 1920) and *A Bobcaygeon Chapbook* (Lindsay, ON: Author 1922), but his chief literary work was as a critic and commentator on Canadian affairs in various CBC radio series. He and Pratt were lifelong friends.

28 Archibald Lampman (1861–99) was perhaps the most significant poet of the group known as the 'Confederation Poets.' Employed in the Post Office Department in Ottawa, he published several collections including *Among the Millet* (Ottawa: J. Durie, 1888) and *Lyrics of Earth* (Boston: Copeland and Day, 1885).

29 Marjorie Pickthall (1883–1922) was a librarian at Victoria College. Born in England, she lived in Toronto from 1890 to 1912. Before her early death, she published two books of poetry – *Drift of Pinions* (Montreal: University Magazine, 1913) and *The Lamp of Poor Souls* (Toronto: S.B. Gundy, 1916) – as well as the verse drama *The Woodcarver's Wife* (Toronto: McClelland & Stewart, 1922), 200 short stories, and three novels, two for children.

TO ARTHUR PHELPS

Victoria College

Aug. 9th 18

My dear Art,

We had it planned to go up to Bob[30] on the Wed. Hincks,[31] Hube[32] & I. Hincks was taken down with severe grippe, and I have a funeral on at Shatwells.[33] We were disappointed because the balance of our time in August is so restricted. The wedding takes place on next Tuesday week[34] and if I knew that you & Lal[35] would be in Bob up to the [...] week in Sept., I would bring the girl up then. If not, I will try to get a run up next week probably Wed, but I am not sure, on account of the small event coming on so soon and the thousand and one things to look after. Let me hear from you soon. In the last couple of weeks financial prospects have rather unexpectedly follow[ed] a rather clouded turn, and I shall have to wait until things are definite before I dare take too much upon myself. Then I would like to run up at any rate, and see you both again.

Write soon.
Ned

30 Bobcaygeon, a small town in the Kawartha Lakes region about eighty miles northeast of Toronto.

31 Clarence ('Clare') Hincks (1885–1964) was a medical doctor and a prominent mental health specialist. In 1918, he and Dr C.K. Clarke (assisted by Pratt, then working as a demonstrator in psychology at the University of Toronto) founded the National Committee for Mental Hygiene (later the Canadian Mental Health Association) of which he was a director until 1952.

32 W. Hubert Greaves was an American of independent means who taught public speaking at Victoria College. He and his wife Cornelia often hosted Pratt at the elegant home 'upon the Humber's crested dome' celebrated in Pratt's lyric 'In a Beloved Home (To W.H.G.)' first published in *NV* (114; *EJP: CP* 1.111), and at their summer retreat near Kingston, Ontario. Greaves moved to Yale University in 1929. (See the note to 'a funny article in the Telegram' in the letter to Viola Pratt, 6 August 1945 [*EJP: Web*].)

33 Although he had completed his doctoral studies in 1917, Pratt still worked part-time as a minister.

34 Pratt had been engaged to Viola Whitney since 1914, but their marriage was delayed by Pratt's doctoral studies and difficulties finding full-time employment. They were married on 20 August 1918. Clare Hincks served as best man. (See the note to 'poor old Bob' in the letter to Phelps, 18 September 1918 [p. 13].)

35 Lila ('Lal') Irene Nicholls married Arthur Phelps in 1915.

TO ARTHUR PHELPS

Victoria College
Toronto, Ont.

Sept. 18th 18

Dearest old Art & Lal,

Your letter brought joy to me as all your letters do. Please do not talk about the time I gave you at Conway.[36] You gave me a rare, rich week[37] that I will not and can not forget. God bless your dear souls.

I was sorry I couldn't finally see my way clear for that Bob investment. But, as you say, the lot is in the family anyway, and whatever happens, Vie & I will see you & Lal often. If you can make Toronto in the fall, sure as guns, our apartments are yours, and all the salads, meats, chicken pies, etc. that a gas range can cook.

Hube was saying that he received six excellent sonnets from you which he will read to me when next we get together. Art, old man you must start writing again. Bring on your old-time spurts and inspirations and keep the muse ever by your side. You have genius – foster it. Bobcaygeon will be your Parnassus yet.

Let us know when you can come to Toronto, do.

I wonder what the fall is like at Conway. The hues will be turning in a week or so won't they? Have you & Lal got your coal in for the winter, to come down to earth for a minute. And has Lal started in on that school yet! My! But it will be grand if you two can spend the following year in Toronto. In the meantime, save! Save! With that end in view.

Vie & I had a splendid time at the Muldrew Lakes[38] – just got back last night. The devil of a job it is getting curtains, furniture, etc. No end to it. The men up at the Lakes were good to us beyond praise. We must have gained about five pounds each of solid pork over the three weeks. That is all my frail anatomy can stand. More than that and I would become corpulent – and I hate a paunch.

36 A vacation spot on Lake Ontario in the Adolphus Beach area.

37 Pratt had spent a few days in Bobcaygeon with his friends before his wedding on 20 August. (See the letter to Phelps, 9 August 1918 [p. 11].)

38 The Pratts' honeymoon was spent in the Muldrew Lakes, near Muskoka.

Poor old Bob[39] is over that concern now. He is making some improvement but slow – infernally slow.

Love to yourself & Lal,
From Vie and myself.
Ned.

TO ARTHUR PHELPS

Sept. 21st 18

Victoria College

Dearest old Art,

Your sonnet sequence warmed and throbbed my heart. Hube had spoken several times to me of their finality in fairly rapturous terms and we had it arranged to spend an hour or so over them. I love the very form of them as they stand under their numbers I, II, III, etc. The sentiment throughout is philosophically profound, but what caught my eyes most was the subtly-phrased contrast between the drab and the crimson, the world that is and the world we all hope for, ending up with the exquisite figure of the goldfinch. Hubert compares them to Mrs Browning's sonnets. I shall turn elsewhere for relationships. I am not a devotee of Elizabeth Barrett anyway, and I do not think her sonnets are equal to these.

The parts I like best are the opening lines of the first with the lure of that fireplace of yours, the fall of the withered crimson leaf into the pool, in the second, the sestet of the III especially the last four lines (these are among the best of any lines you have written), the extension and elaboration of the leaf simile in the 4th, and especially the closing sonnets the finesse of the six in structure, I think.

39 Robert LeDrew ('Bob') was a native of Brigus, Newfoundland, where Pratt had known him as a boy. When he came to Toronto in 1915, he and Pratt lived together in one of several houses they had built as part of a joint venture in real estate in 1916–17. In August, LeDrew was hospitalized for Hodgkin's disease and was replaced by Clare Hincks as best man at Pratt's wedding. He died in 1919.

Art, so right it is old boy. You have got the sonnets swing as none of the rest of us have. 'Thoughts,'[40] 'Cherries,' 'A perusal of a leaf etc. (the 'Poetry' sonnet),' and several others are among the best I have seen in many years of reading.

Greaves and I are going to spend a good hour over a pipe in the company of the last six.

For a little lyric of betel[geu]se hea[ve]nly, however, commend me to Sea Beauty. It is a given.

With best love to yourself and Lal
Ned

TO ARTHUR PHELPS

Victoria College

[late Apr./early May 1922]

Dear Art,

Here's the Forum with the 'Ice-Floes.'[41] It has been almost completely re-done since the summer, and looks very good I think. I worked like a devil on it and think it the *very best* I am capable of doing at the age of forty years. If it don't go over, well – ! I will soon hear I daresay. In the Forum there's also a thing by Doug Bush,[42] a corker. I went into convulsions of merriment over it. You'll do the same I think. Hoping to see yourself before long. The best to Lal.

Ned.

40 Published in *Poems* (Mount Vernon, IA: The English Club of Cornell College, 1921), 9.

41 Pratt's poem 'The Ice–Floes' (*EJP: CP* 1.58) was first published in *CF* 2 (April 1922): 591–3.

42 Literary historian and critic Douglas Bush (1896–1983), who went on to have a distinguished career at Harvard University, was still a student at the University of Toronto. The 'thing' was an essay entitled 'A Plea for Original Sin' (*CF* 2 [April 1922]: 589–90), a Swiftian satire on the stultifying effects of Canadian mores on Canadian writing. The essay influenced Pratt's 'The Witches' Brew' written in the summer of 1923.

TO WILLIAM ARTHUR DEACON[43]

Bobcaygeon, Ont.[44]

Monday morning [18 Sept. 1922]

Dear Billy,

Would you like to run up to Bobcaygeon on a holiday for one, two, three or four days as your time would permit. Art Phelps and wife have just left for Winnipeg. My wife and bairn[45] are in Toronto and I am left alone in my cottage for one whole week ending Sept. 23rd. I have just shot two wild black ducks less than an hour ago. What am I going to do with them? They won't keep till my return and I can't eat them all by myself. Could you run up early in the week. The train leaves Toronto 9:05 a.m. and 5 p.m., and leaves Bobcaygeon 6:45 a.m. and 2:45 p.m. So good connections. Great sleeping here out in the open air and thoroughly screened in. Not a footstep day or night to disturb dreams. I have a little garden containing, at present, sweet corn, beans, tomatoes, squash and so on, clamouring for your stomach. An open fire place with pine stumps! Evening Smokes! Fresh Cream! Bass!!

Can you come? J.V. MacKenna[46] had arranged to come but was suddenly called to New York and so had Ernie McCullogh,[47] but he had, likewise, to cancel the trip.

If you can make it let me know by wire: Ned Pratt, Bobcaygeon and I will meet you, with canoe, at the station. Bring some of your stuff with you to while away an evening. Enjoyed 'Angels'[48] very much and several other articles.

Sincerely
Ned Pratt

43 (1890–1977). A classmate of Pratt and Phelps at Victoria College, who completed a law degree at the University of Manitoba, Deacon was literary editor of *Saturday Night* (1922–8), the Toronto *Mail and Empire* (1928–36), and the *Globe and Mail* (1936–60). A prolific freelance reviewer, critical essayist, and letter writer, he was Pratt's long-time friend, though their friendship vacillated from time to time because of Deacon's temperament.

44 Phelps bought a cottage in Bobcaygeon in 1919 and helped Pratt acquire one adjacent to his in 1921. The Pratts spent parts of fifteen summers there.

45 The Pratts' daughter, Mildred Claire, had been born in March 1921.

46 Unidentified.

47 A prominent Toronto physician.

48 An article by Deacon published in *Saturday Night*, 29 July 1922.

TO ARTHUR PHELPS

Victoria College

Oct. 26, 22

Hi there! You old bees-wax!

Hi there! you of the golden aureole!

How are ye? How are ye?

Why the Sam Hill, Art have I not received a line from you since your sail from Bobcaygeon? Here Lal has written Vi twice most devotedly, most voluminously, but ne'er a chirp from you.

I had a chat with Flint[49] the other day. The Chancellor,[50] Pro[vo] and *I* ate dinner together. Flint spoke most glowingly of you and your work as teacher and writer, the Chancellor himself chiming in in unison. Bowles says to Flint. Here's Pratt – Phelps' bosom chum. I smiled sweetly at the compliment and returned with an account of your efficient and vital activities in the Department of English hit at in medley.

Art, send me a sheaf of your stuff at once. We left you know without arranging our plans. I should like to submit a few to the Forum so they can select. Now do this at once, or I will absolutely refuse to write another letter. In fact, I will make subsequent correspondence subject to that condition. I had your chapbook[51] uppermost on my desk. Several of my friends have been interested in it, and some warm appreciation rendered. Hubert[52] likes the Spenserians[53] very much. In fact they are the favorites here with the Bob bits[54] coming a good second. How are things moving along? Anything new. W.G.[55] was here during

49 Charles W. Flint was president (1915–22) of Cornell College, a small Methodist institution in Mount Vernon, Iowa. In 1921, Phelps had left Cornell to take up a position in the Department of English at Wesley College in Winnipeg.

50 Reverend Richard Pinch Bowles (1864–1960), born in Ontario and a graduate of Victoria College, was its president and chancellor from 1913 to 1930.

51 Phelps had recently published *A Bobcaygeon Chapbook* (Lindsay, ON: Author, 1922).

52 W. Hubert Greaves.

53 A poetic sequence in the chapbook: 'Prelude and Invocation: Prefacing a Tale Told in the Spenserian Stanza.'

54 'Bits from Bobcaygeon,' a poem in the chapbook.

55 W.G. (William George) Smith (b. 1873) taught experimental psychology in the Department of Philosophy at the University of Toronto (1905–21) before moving to Wesley College (Winnipeg) as vice-principal and professor of philosophy and sociology in 1921. He had been Pratt's overseer in the psychology laboratories and supervisor of his dissertation research. Their relationship was one of 'chronic antagonism.' (See *EJP: TY*, 149, 152–4.)

Seniors Conference. Turned down all along the line I understand, excepting Bland[56] and Endicott[57] who spoke in favor of the right of the professor with a gu[arantee] to a hearing.[58] Nothing further than that. I didn't see him at all except at the Alumni Dinner.

Am plunged in work up to the crop. Enjoying it immensely. Have not done any writing, nor do I expect to get a chance this year. Must wait till next summer. I showed Hube my summer stuff.[59] He did not care very much for any of that realistic dialogue. I guess it smelled too much of the tar and fish and oil – too local in its flavor. The Scholar and the Salt too much Earth Earthy, or of the Sea, Sea-y. Didn't like much John Jones, not enough discussion. He says he likes the graver, more sombre and elevated lines. Liked Newfoundland very much and the Toll of the Bells & Magnolia Blossoms,[60] but nothing else. In fact he lamented my lapse into Realism. I told him that I felt my heart strangely warmed toward these old salts and their ways and meant to do more of it ... when time permitted. I told him how I liked your Knock Rovey and the *stick stick stick*.[61] He can't see it. I have not submitted anything to the Forum of my

56 S.G. (Salem Goldworth) Bland (1859–1950) was a leader of the social gospel movement. He had taught New Testament and Church History at Wesley College from 1903 until his forced retirement on economic grounds in 1917. Like Smith, he had challenged his dismissal. (See Horn, *Academic Freedom in Canada: A History* [Toronto: University of Toronto Press, 1999], 50–2).

57 Norman Endicott, a professor of English at University College, Toronto. Pratt, for reasons unknown, is said to have 'heartily disliked him.'

58 Earlier in 1922, Smith had been dismissed from his position as vice-principal of Wesley College, ostensibly for voicing heretical opinions. However, it is more likely that he was removed for attempting to introduce academic programming in keeping with the Social Gospel – a radical change only four years after the Winnipeg General Strike. The appeal court of the Methodist Church had refused to hear his appeal. (See Horn, *Academic Freedom in Canada*, 80–2 and Stephen Harold Riggins, "'A Square Deal for the Least and the Last': The Career of W.G. Smith in the Methodist Ministry, Experimental Psychology, and Sociology," *Newfoundland and Labrador Studies* 27, no. 2 [2012]: 179–222.)

59 Many of the poems included in *NV* were written in the summer of 1922.

60 'Newfoundland' (*NV*, 887-90; *EJP: CP* 1.99); 'The Toll of the Bells' (*NV*, 15–16; *EJP: CP* 1.68); 'Magnolia Blossoms' (*NV*, 18–19; *EJP: CP* 1.69).

61 Phelps's poem 'Knock Rovey' has a very aggressive metre. In the preface to *A Bobcaygeon Chapbook*, Phelps records Pratt's friendly appreciation of his work, and this poem in particular: 'Ned Pratt (Dr. E.J. Pratt, Victoria College, Toronto, who of a morning comes down through his raspberry patch, climbs the line fence, and makes me swing my legs back across the breakfast bench to turn and say "well, but Ned ..."), Ned Pratt should be publishing a chapbook this summer. He has too much dignity and reticence. He embarrasses me by making me notice my lack of too much. All being Well he'll publish a real chapbook of quality next summer. That's why I am happy when he says he likes KNOCK ROVEY and the lines [from 'Prelude and Invocation'], "teaching a vagrant line to match / A pacing moment that fine eloquence."'

own yet except John Jones[62] which was liked quite heartily. It may come out through the winter.

Have not had an opening yet to show Pelham[63] any of it. I am waiting for the chance to come from him both for you and for myself. He is somewhat reticent this year for some reason. Verbally he is still akin to Canadian things as a result of [...] atmosphere and wines. Brown [...] [...] when read. Neither did Hube like the Bird of Paradise, or at least he maintained silence on it after being shown that amorous effusion. He liked your People with the exception of the line – 'from that bed get up'.[64] (By the way, send on any subscription to the Forum, Brody's[65] at al.) Hube is smitten with *Louise*.[66] Can't read anything else now till the epidemic is over. Still the v[ai]n boy is as friendly with me again as if nothing had ever occurred. God moves in a mysterious way. Did you get any comments from Pierce[67] on the stuff? Or did he sniff cod liver oil too heavily?

Write. Write Write.
Ned.

---

62 'The History of John Jones' appeared in *CF* 3 (January 1923): 110.

63 Pelham Edgar.

64 Another poem from *A Bobcaygeon Chapbook*. The offending lines read in full 'She knew the thing that I knew / I should never from that bed get up.'

65 Unidentified.

66 Unidentified.

67 Phelps had sent a copy of the chapbook, and Pratt the 'summer stuff' alluded to in this letter, to Lorne Pierce at Ryerson Press. In Fall 1922, Pierce accepted Pratt's first collection of poems which was published as *Newfoundland Verse* (1923).

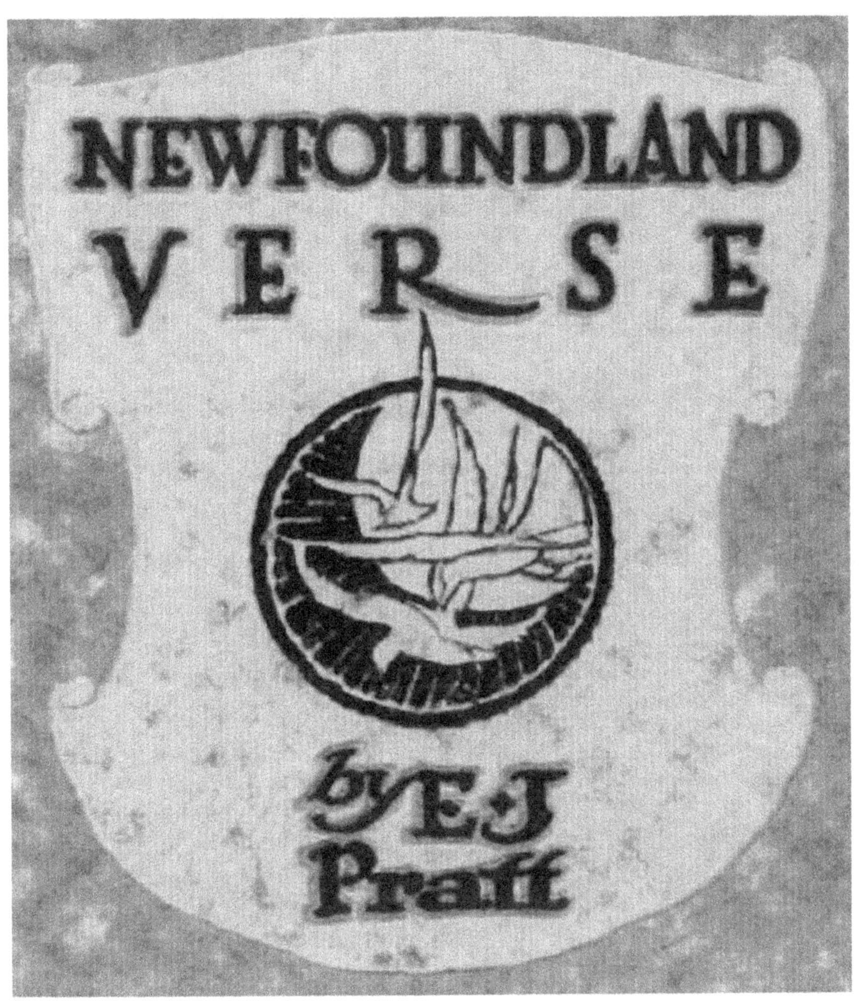

Newfoundland Verse (Ryerson 1923) was designed by Pratt's friend Frederick Varley.

TO LORNE PIERCE[68]

Victoria College

Jan. 16, 23

Dear Dr Pierce,

Mr Varley[69] tells me that he will finish those designs absolutely by the end of this week. I think he is counting upon having an interview with you to-morrow or next day. I intimated to him that I would prefer a design having the quality of spaciousness befitting ocean themes than those too closely-woven patterns with their intricacy of detail that MacDonald[70] works out though, of course, with his own peculiar finish. Varley agreed with the suggestion.

Will you let me know what negotiations you make with outside firms? I should like an English imprimatur on the volume as understood in our first interview.

In any publicity given to the book will you kindly see to it that such an ugly, stiff term as 'Professor' is absolutely excluded: first, because the title is at present technically incorrect and, secondly, the term is sufficient to stultify any poetic claims which a writer may, in all modesty, put forth. Just plain E.J. Pratt, or Mr Pratt if the formality demands it.

---

68 Lorne A. Pierce (1890–1961) was editor-in-chief of Ryerson Press (formerly the Methodist Book Room) from 1920 to 1960, making it one of the most productive publishing houses in Canada. An ardent literary nationalist, Pierce both encouraged and published Canadian authors, and books and pamphlets on Canadian literary, educational, and religious subjects. In 1926, he endowed a prize – the Lorne Pierce Medal – to be awarded by the Royal Society 'in annual recognition of achievement in imaginative and critical literature.' After Pierce accepted Pratt's first collection of poems, *NV*, in 1922, he and Pratt were good friends and frequent correspondents for many years.

69 Frederick H. Varley (1881–1969) came to Canada from Sheffield, England, in 1912 at the urging of Arthur Lismer, and joined the Grip design firm, where he worked with Tom Thomson. In 1920, he was a founding member of the Group of Seven. At Pratt's request, Ryerson Press engaged Varley to design the endpapers and decorations for *NV*.

70 Wilson MacDonald (1880–1967), born at Cheapside, Ontario, had made a name for himself as a poet, pen-and-ink artist, and magician. He published a dozen books of mostly romantic, traditional verse, often decorated with his own 'closely-woven' pen-and-ink drawings. In the 1920s and 1930s, he mounted frequent and extremely popular recital tours. Deacon for a time regarded him as Canada's most promising new poet, but neither Pierce nor Pratt considered him a good poet or a pleasant acquaintance.

Finally a suggestion from a friend. Look after your health and get some sleep. We don't want 'Ryerson Press' to revert to 'Wm Briggs'[71] because of the early 'demise' of the new literary manager.

More power to your elbow.

Sincerely,
E.J. Pratt

TO WILLIAM ARTHUR DEACON

25 Tullis Drive[72]

Friday noon [27 Apr. 1923]

Dear Bill,

The Review[73] tended to restore my collapsed heart more effectively than digitalis. What impressed me more favourably than anything else was the expression of your own critical integrity where side by side with your own valued appreciation you were not backward in stating an adverse judgment upon inferior work.

It's your intellectual candour no less than your literary insight that is making your column[74] live to-day. Put the petrol on us and apply the match when necessary. There is a lot of dead timber to be consumed. God himself has special uses for flames, and a self-complacent poet makes excellent roasting material.

Thanks Bill, anyway, old thing, for the generous space you gave the volume in your paper. It was more than I deserved.

---

71 As Book Steward of the Methodist Church of Canada (1879–1918), Reverend William Briggs was responsible for the Methodist Book Room press, which published under the imprint of his name. In 1919, Reverend Samuel Fallis (or Follis) succeeded him as book steward and changed the name to Ryerson Press to commemorate Egerton Ryerson, founder in 1830 of the original Methodist Press in Canada.

72 The Pratts had recently moved to a house at 25 Tullis Drive, Toronto, after having lived for two years with Viola's widowed mother in a house on Davenport Road.

73 Deacon had given *NV* a generally enthusiastic review in *Saturday Night* on 21 April 1923.

74 Besides editing the book review section in *Saturday Night* and writing many of the reviews, Deacon had a weekly column under the pen name 'Candide' entitled 'Saved from the Waste-Basket,' a potpourri of snippets from correspondence, literary gossip, and personal tidbits.

I am lying on my back in bed and may have to remain here for two more weeks – slow heart convalescence after flu.[75] But anytime you and your beloved wife feel like straying up this way for an evening chat – and let us hope it will be very soon – the door is wide open. There is still a little sherry left and a humidor for John Cotton[76] and a *great deal* of welcome.

Ned.

TO LORNE PIERCE

May 16, 23

Hello, old globe-trotter:

I called in to see you this morning but you were *not* as Job might say.[77] I trust your health has improved since our two hearts, a month ago, beat as one.[78] Mine is gradually taking on normal speech though still afflicted with sibilants.

Are you getting a little time to yourself, and could you next week run up with me for a day or two to Bobcaygeon and help me plant my Irish Cobblers?[79] Think over this question with prayer and fasting and let me know in good time.

How is Newfoundland Verse swimming? I have just received word from my brother[80] who said that S.E. Garland, a leading bookseller in St. Johns, thinks that the sale down there ought to be 'considerable.' I suppose the Wholesale Department is in touch with the Nfld. market.

This is what I should like to say, old thing. When the time comes for a Second Edition,[81] or a first English or American Edition, I'd like to make a few small but important corrections. 'Magnolia Blossoms' must certainly be

---

75 Pratt had been ill since early April with a reputed mild 'heart seizure' aggravated by influenza. He remained in bed until 5 May, by which time he had fully recovered from the 'heart attack he may never have had,' to quote Viola Pratt, who always doubted the diagnosis.

76 A brand of pipe tobacco.

77 An allusion to Job 7:21: 'thou shalt seek me in the morning, but I shall not be.'

78 See the letters to Pierce, 16 April 1923 (*EJP: Web*) and William Deacon, 27 April (pp. 21–2). Pierce's heart condition had indisposed him for several weeks concurrently with Pratt's reputed 'heart seizure.'

79 Potatoes.

80 Calvert C. Pratt (1888–1963), the youngest of Pratt's surviving brothers was a prominent St John's businessman, president or director of a number of commercial firms and widely known for his philanthropy. He was named to the Canadian Senate in 1951.

81 There was no second edition of *NV*.

integrated.[82] 'Newfoundland' must have its last stanza spatially articulated to the body of the poem. Two or three mis-spellings and some punctuations must be corrected. Wherever the errors are due to my oversight in proof, I shall gladly put up the coin.

And now apart from business, are you going to take a good holiday this summer? I do not like the idea of your spending the vacation in dusty New York archives. Your stimulating articles in the 'Christian Guardian'[83] do not need any extra polish from undue research, and remember the medical definition of a 'pericardium.' 'The pericardium is a very *thin*, if elastic, membrane surrounding the heart and enclosing a liquor which prevents the surface of the heart from becoming *dry* by its continual motion.'

Verb. Sap.[84] (no slang implications in the latter word)

Pratt.

TO LORNE PIERCE

Wednesday p.m. [23 May 1923]

My beloved Mephisto,[85]

If *pro*spects be realised we shall hold our Saturnalia in the back-yards of the Allobroges[86] at – I hope – a no very far distant date. Thanks for your most kindly remarks in the Guardian this week.[87]

---

82 'Magnolia Blossoms' (*NV*, 18–19; *EJP: CP* 1.69) consisted of a pair of sonnets, the second of which had been divided into two distinct parts in the volume.

83 A weekly newspaper of the Methodist Church of Canada, published by the Methodist Book Room (and later Ryerson Press).

84 *Verbum sat sapienti (est)*: 'a word to the wise is sufficient.' Pierce, replying to Pratt's letter on 21 May, responded:

> I had been expecting you for a long time to confessional. I suppose your long spell of prayer and fasting has left you with little of the taint of sin to confess about.
>
> The Wholesale advise me that 'Newfoundland Verse' has excellent prospects – the 'pro' meaning 'on ahead.' Don't book your passage for Tahiti before you learn just how you stand, not in spectral sovereigns but in actual dollars …
>
> The reviews are all salubrious, both east and west, and that's something. If you do not get a lift toward the Chancellorship because of this it will have been a miscarriage of justice.

85 Mephistopheles. Pratt had been reading Goethe's *Faust*, which influenced his writing of 'The Witches' Brew' in the summer of 1923.

86 An ancient Celtic tribe inhabiting what is now Dauphine and Savoy and remembered chiefly for their saturnalian rites. Pratt refers to himself and Phelps as members of that tribe.

87 Pierce had reviewed *NV* in the *Christian Guardian*, 23 May 1923, 22.

I am enclosing the corrections referred to in my last letter.[88] Some or most of them *may* be due to mine own omissions in reading proof. Wherever that is the case I shall gladly abide by contract. I am also inserting in brackets an explanatory dedication under the title of the sonnets 'Magnolia Blossoms.' Edgar[89] who is very fond of this poem suggested some addition, on the ground of the 'subtlety of the lines.' I am inserting (To a Certain Magdalen).

Yours fraternally,
Faust.

Corrigenda.
1) Page 14 *has* for hast in 'Majestically *hast* cast'
2) Page 18 Magnolia Blossoms
(a) (To a Certain Magdalen)
(b) ironic for irenic
Page 19 (c) omit III before last six lines
3) Page 39 omit period after depart 'ere I depart.'
4) " 89 Bring forward one-half of the last section on page 90 to page 89 as the poem looks now as if it ended with the line 'guard too well.'
5) " 103 omit ; after the line 'on the frozen air' and omit accent over e in formed.
6) 114 *blenching* for *blending* in the line 'which, blending as of night's austerity.'
7) 134 *sips* for *sits* in line 'where sits the lily of the morning dew.'
8)[90] 74 *of a* for *in* in line
might cool this hell *in* Paradise
9) 105 Before an altar on one page.
10) 71 New paragraph with 'His mates had never heard'

TO LORNE PIERCE

Thursday am. [24 May 1923]

88 Since *NV* was not reissued, his full page of 'Corrigenda' was never used. Corrections were made, however, in the poems selected from the book for inclusion in *CP1* and *CP2*.

89 Pelham Edgar.

90 Pratt initialled the page opposite the eighth point in his list of corrections.

Dr Lorne Pierce

Ryerson Press.

Say old thing,

I forgot to mention in my letter of yesterday that my job of correcting proof ceased with the galleys that morning when Wilson MacDonald came into your office. I didn't see any page proofs at all. I assumed that the hurry of printing in order to get the books into the stores by Easter made it impossible to get final revision done.

But don't do any unnecessary worrying about the matter.

Yours
E.J. Pratt.

Excuse pencil. Have lost pen.

P.

TO WILLIAM ARTHUR DEACON

Bobcaygeon, Ont.

June 19, 1923

My Dear Bill,

There must be telepathic affinities between us. I was on the point of writing you when your missive arrived. I have since opened up communications with the President of the Immortals[91] inquiring why procrastination, that human failing, should also be present in the Councils of the Gods. Have not yet had a reply but certain vibrations intimate to me that Juno and Hebe are both plucking at the beard of Jove.[92] Well, here's hoping, old dog, that all your wishes concerning weight, health, and gender may soon be realised. Vi is sending along a little token for good luck. Let us know developments.

---

91 Thomas Hardy's description of Fate, or 'the Power that rules our destinies,' in his novel *Tess of the D'Urbervilles.*

92 In Roman mythology, Juno was the wife of Jove or Jupiter; Hebe was their daughter and the cup-bearer to Jove. Pratt refers to the expected birth of the Deacons' first child, a son who was named William Herbert.

We were fearing, after we left your place that night, that the baby carriage would be in a rather musty condition not having been attended to for over a year. As long as you can make it snug there will be some good long sleep in it.

With regard to Moore,[93] since reading your letter, the atmosphere of the cottage has been sulphurous. Sacré bleu! Sapristi! Ciel![94] Damnation without Redemption! That fellow would alter the Codex Bezae[95] if he happened to get hold of it, on the ground of archaic lettering. I am glad the Authorized Version happened to be complete before he was born and that Hebrew vowel points were constructed before anyone thought of asking the cooperation of E.J.M. Verdammit! Did you ever read in cold print of such presumption. Not satisfied with altering Petrarchan sonnet forms he must unearth the bones of sacred Herrick;[96] change constructions, punctuation! He knows as much about style as a second engineer in a Kansas elevator. Pierce is away just now, I understand, but before he left he wrote me – in answer to a letter in which I protested against any fifth-rate amanuensis tinkering with my stuff – that he was going to make a rigid investigation into the various responsibilities of the house. Since the Varley episode[97] he could bite off a six-inch spike. Moore evidently is so sore over the readjustments of a couple of years ago[98] that the only way he can release his feelings is by chewing up other people's manuscripts.

Well Bill, if you and Mrs Deacon can manage to run up any time during the summer there is a bedroom, lots of fresh air and lots of welcome. Week ends or whole weeks as often as you can manage it. Thanks ever so much for your inclusion of Newfoundland Verse in the list of holiday books.

Vi sends love to Mrs Deacon in which of course I join.

Ned

---

93 E.J. Moore was advertising manager at Ryerson Press. He also did some editorial work, and Deacon had accused him of making unauthorized changes in the text of his book *Pens and Pirates*, then in press. Pratt now suspected that Moore had been responsible for the errors and alterations that had crept into *NV*.

94 Mild expletives in French: roughly translated, 'Holy Mary! For God's sake! Heavens!'

95 A fifth-century Graeco-Latin manuscript of the four gospels and the Acts of the Apostles.

96 A poem by the seventeenth-century English poet Robert Herrick, quoted by Deacon in his book, had been mutilated in transcription, and Moore had been blamed. In his letter of 21 June, Deacon wrote to Pratt: 'I am getting along splendidly with Moore, who is not a bad fellow at heart, when you go at him easy. He swears that he did not make the alterations but that a new proof-reader did. He is having it all put back for me as it was in the beginning.'

97 Frederick Varley's designs for the endpapers of *NV* had been printed with light brown ink on beige paper and did not appear to good effect. Pierce, Varley, and Pratt were very annoyed by the mistake, and Moore was blamed, at least by Pratt.

98 In 1920, when Ryerson Press was reorganized, Lorne Pierce became editor-in-chief.

TO LORNE PIERCE

Friday [23 Nov. 1923]

Hello, old thing,

I had my mind made up a dozen times, I suppose, to drop you a line during the last month, but somehow or other the thousand and one duties intervened. I wanted to write, all the more, because I thought you were upset over a conversation which Deacon, Cornell[99] and I had with the chief. As Deacon possibly informed you it was the first intention to go to you direct but some friend of his advised him to go to Fallis[100] as you would probably veto any action being taken to the chief. Deacon and Cornell asked me to go along and also Wallace[101] as we belonged to the younger group that the Ryersons were encouraging. We were divided between solicitude for you and mistrust of some one else before we came to a decision. We explained to F.[102] that you were utterly ignorant of our action, that we had every confidence in F. and yourself, in your policies, in your soundness of motive, in your outlook generally but we felt that apathy if not antagonism from a certain quarter was neutralising your efforts. At the time I had no special grievance, as I told F., beyond the fact that I knew our whole group was being blocked by adverse criticisms. Certain positively impudent remarks which M.[103] had made to Cornell as well as the prolonged delay in getting 'Lantern Marsh' on the market were specially mentioned and F. expressed in no uncertain terms his opinion of M's doings. He gave you highest appreciation, admired your writing and your point of view and promised to keep his eyes open for untoward developments. Perhaps our action was ill-advised. We would not have done anything to give you anxiety or increase your cares but if we were going to meet with continuous opposition from the (as far as we are concerned) most critical part of the whole machinery – the Advertising and Publicity

99 Beaumont S. Cornell (1892–1958) was a medical researcher, a colleague of Frederick Banting, as well as an author. Ryerson Press had recently published his second novel, *Lantern Marsh* (1923).

100 The 'chief' was Reverend Samuel Fallis, managing director of Ryerson Press. Pierce wrote in his diary on 15 October 1923, 'I was chagrined the other day when E.J. Pratt, Beaumont Cornell and W.A. Deacon all lined up and called on Dr. Fallis to complain about the sale of their books. I suppose no three men have had more done for them.'

101 Paul A.W. Wallace had published *The Twist and Other Stories* with Ryerson in 1923.

102 Samuel Fallis.

103 E.J. Moore. See the letter to Deacon, 19 June 1923 (p. 26).

Department – then we were going to govern our future contacts accordingly. I realise you have done your d–est for us and I am grateful for the enthusiastic encouragement you have given 'Newfoundland Verse.' But I should like to know why M. has consistently ignored that volume in his otherwise exhaustive list of new publications. I was not mentioned in the successive issues of the Canadian Bookman or the Canadian Magazine, the Saturday Night, or any place outside of the 'Guardian' where the special reference to the volume by *outside* writers gave all the publicity there that it needed. I have always noted your unfailing interest in it and you have given it, in your 'Corner,'[104] many very appreciative references, but in the general literary magazines and periodicals it was ignored and that fact was pointed out to me many times by my friends. 'If the Ryerson Press published your work, then at least they might [..] advertise it.' 'In a list which apparently aims to be inclusive why isn't Newfoundland Verse mentioned?'

The only thing I want to know, old chap, is – Do you candidly think that personal prejudices are working against us? You need not commit yourself if you do not want to, but all of us think that that fat-head in the East of the building is out 'to get us' by inertia if not by positive obstruction.

Well now I have got that off my chest and that's all I shall say except to reiterate my confidence in you and my admiration for your own work.

I have a poem finished[105] in which you might be interested. Both Edgar and Hooke[106] of Victoria think it is unquestionably the best single thing I have done and are very confident as to its selling qualities. It would make a little volume of about fifty pages. If you would care to see it I will send it along at once.

Pardon this outburst and will you burn the screed when read.

Ned Pratt.

---

104 The book column which Pierce wrote in the *Christian Guardian.*

105 'The Witches' Brew.'

106 Samuel H. Hooke (1874–1968) had come to Victoria College in 1913 as associate professor of Oriental languages and literatures. He also taught modern history and was a founder of the university magazine *The Rebel* (1917–20), which had evolved into *Canadian Forum.*

TO LORNE PIERCE

Dec. 1/1923

Dear old thing,

Your letter[107] with its manliness and straight-forwardness came into my paws a few minutes ago. It has confirmed the impressions I have always had of your Highness. I note with much gratification the prospect of having you and your family as neighbours in the near future.

With regard to Newfoundland Verse I have learned of the prominence you gave it in the recent Exhibits[108] and I believe that the demand even if it does not partake of the character of sky-rocketing is steady and growing. Since I saw you last I have received many personal letters of warm appreciation – urging further literary activity – from prominent critics, notably Morgan-Powell[109] and Bernard McEvoy[110] of the Vancouver Daily Province.

The main thing I want to consult you about is this: – I referred in my last note to a new poem which I have recently finished. Its subject and treatment are entirely new – 'The Witches' Brew or the Immortals' Night Off,' in tetrameters with prose insets. In a day or two as soon as I can get a typed copy – I shall submit it to you.

There are a few points I should like to raise.

I should like it to be tried out upon one or two American and English Publishers first – firms of a more aggressive character that take hold of young men. If they undertake to publish it then the Ryerson Press, if it so desired, could handle it for Canadians. I am not particularly anxious for Canadian publication alone for reasons I will state later. I can understand the difficulties in getting my first volume upon a foreign market. An American publisher naturally likes to

107 On 29 November, Pierce had replied to Pratt's letter of 23 November (pp. 27–8), defending his firm and its policies, and appearing to take no offence from the actions of the three authors. He expressed an interest in Pratt's new poem, about which he had heard 'from several quarters.'

108 Pierce had reported that *NV* had been given 'prominence' at 'Libraries and Retail Stores' during the recent Canadian Book Week. (See the letter of 23 November [p. 28].)

109 Samuel Morgan-Powell (1867–1962) was for many years literary editor of the *Montreal Star*. He reviewed *NV* for the *Star* (5 May 1923, 15). He was a devotee of Pratt's poetry and a casual friend. Pratt wrote a foreword to a book of his verse, *Down the Years* (Toronto: Macmillan, 1938).

110 McEvoy (1842–1932) had worked ten years for the Toronto *Mail and Empire* before moving to the Vancouver *Daily Province*. He published several books of verse, but is best known for *From the Great Lakes to the Wide West* (Toronto: Briggs, 1902).

see a prospective Canadian volume justify itself in its homeland by review and sale before taking risks, and perhaps when a fair circulation has been reached here, – possibly a second edition, – the foreign market may lose some of its tightness and fear. However, Newfoundland Verse in actual print together with review clippings and account of sales might be sent as bona fide 'collateral' to authenticate the 'Witches' Brew.' A certain publisher from abroad staying over in Toronto as a guest of Pelham Edgar was shown the manuscript by Edgar and was convinced of its value and tentatively suggested that it might be open for negotiation. I did not act on the suggestion as I felt the importance of my own contact with you and your generous treatment of my first volume and your greatly appreciated belief in my humble self. Edgar, Hooke, Kennedy,[111] Phelps and others think it is the best, at least the most vital single thing I have done, certainly the most original. A few of the more conservative men felt a little dubious about the theme, – whether some controversy might not arise from it, but all agree as to impact and grip.

Professor Alexander[112] is having an evening at his home next week, where I am to present it to the staff and a few outside picked University men interested in poetry, some of whom have already seen it.

Now I know your own progressive and almost radical outlook on life and literature and I do not feel any hesitation on that score, but I want you to tell me if the Ryerson Press might feel any qualms about its publication, or whether the Canadian Constituency would be interested in it. I may be raising questions without any basis whatsoever. The poem has been 'tried out' on a half-dozen of the Vic staff and they entered whole-heartedly into the mood of it and were willing to back it.

But in any case, if you feel disposed – you might try to make some outside contacts first as a 'try-out.' All who have seen it suggest fantastic decoration or illustration in harmony with the framework of witchcraft in which the theme is set. It might be a work of above fifty pages which could easily sell for one dollar but I think illustration would be very desirable. I will send the manuscript along in a day or two.

With the best of good luck
Ned Pratt

111 William P.M. Kennedy (1879–1963), associate professor of modern history at the University of Toronto, and later professor of law and dean of the Toronto School of Law, was the author of numerous works on constitutional, industrial, and social law.

112 Browning scholar William John Alexander (1855–1944) was professor and head of the Department of English Literature at University College, Toronto from 1889 to 1926.

TO LORNE PIERCE

April 5, 1924

Hello, old Lucifer,

Your note received. Thanks very much for your efforts to place 'The Witches Brew.'[113] I suppose, after all, publishers are the best judges of the market, and perhaps I had better keep the poem on the shelf until I publish my next volume when I may include it at the end. Edgar is so confident about it that he has sent it off to Constable, England.[114] I understand though, that the bottom has fallen out of the world market for books, so, I can only wait.

I suppose 'Newfoundland Verse' may get in England as soon as it enters upon a Second Edition here. There was a good reference to it in 'The British Weekly' in February, in a literary survey of modern poetry. It is a pity that it couldn't be placed in some way or other on the British stalls just for a try out. At least, it would have the chance of being reviewed in the English magazines over there. I know that you are doing your damnest any way. I expect to get across to England this coming summer if the banks are merciful.

Hope you are keeping well, and that the world, the flesh and their boon companion are not pursuing you too persistently. Will be in to see you next week.

Yours sincerely,
E.J. Pratt.

TO LORNE PIERCE

April 12, 24

Once again, old thing,

A delightful little tidbit came into my hands a few days ago which it would be selfish to keep to my self, so I am passing it on to you. It concerns our mutual

113 Having read 'The Witches' Brew,' Pierce decided that publishing a poem with its alcoholic elements was too great a risk for Ryerson Press with its close ties to the Methodist Church. He agreed to try to 'place' it with other firms, primarily in the United States, but was unsuccessful. (See the letter to Pierce, 1 December 1923 [p. 30].)

114 Constable and Company, a British publishing house.

friend Wilson MacDonald and Pelham Edgar. Pelham came in to my office last Thursday with a letter in his hands from W.M. – a most abusive letter in which the said W.M. asserted that when he gets back to the Queen City there is going to be war to the death between himself and the dignified Professor of English Literature of Victoria College. Edgar said to me, 'Why Pratt, I do not even know the *names* of the people he is talking about or *what* he is talking about. It is enough by half to commit the fellow to a lunatic asylum.' The names of Bothwell,[115] Salverson,[116] were repeated often, and MacDonald claimed that if Edgar said one word of commendation about such a disreputable brood then MacDonald would open his seventeen inch batteries when he got back. 'Do you know what they are saying about you out here?' he asks Edgar. 'They hate you Edgar, they call you a fop, a nobody, a - - - - - - - -.' He blames Bothwell for a dirty prank that he played on him a little while ago. Bothwell knew MacDonald for a vegetarian yet ordered a beefsteak for him at a dinner in his honour. And several of the 'literary lights' out West refuse to recognize him as equal to Shelley or Keats. Edgar adds 'The name Shakespeare is just as easy to pronounce as Shelley … Why does not the damn fool bring in the Almighty as well?' Edgar did not know whether to laugh or swear when he read the letter. MacDonald is going to shake the dust of Canada off his feet, a nation of *ingrates* & ! ? : " " ! ! Edgar is getting heartily sick of him.

Well, I shall try to get on to see you next week some time. I met Locke[117] yesterday and he showed me his Catalogue of Canadian books which is going to be placed in Exhibit in England this summer.[118] I appreciated his inclusion of N.V. especially when the poetic section had to be limited. Are there any arrangements for an English supply at publishing firms or book stores in case of a demand, however slight, resulting from the Exhibit. I expect to be in England myself about the first of June. Do you think there is any chance of my being able

---

115 Austin McPhail Bothwell (1885–1928), the first Rhodes Scholar from Saskatchewan, was editor of the *Bulletin* of the Saskatchewan Teachers' Alliance. He had taught German at Wesley College in Winnipeg and, after the First World War, English literature at Central College Institute in Regina.

116 Laura Goodman Salverson (1890–1970), a protégée of Austin Bothwell, had just published her first novel *The Viking Heart* (Toronto: McClelland & Stewart, 1923), based on the experiences of Icelandic pioneers in Manitoba. Her six subsequent novels were less successful, but her autobiography, *Confessions of an Immigrant's Daughter* (Toronto: Ryerson; London: Faber and Faber, 1939), is one of the best Canadian examples of the genre.

117 George H. Locke (1870–1937), long-time chief librarian of Toronto Public Libraries, was the author of several works on Canadian history and a founding member of the Canadian Authors Association.

118 An exhibition of books from around the British Empire at the 1924 Wembley Exhibition.

to give a few readings in clubs or Churches? I should like to be able to introduce it if the avenues were open. I thought of asking Dr Trevor Davies[119] to give me a note of introduction to some of his overseas friends. What do you think? I trust that your old heart is pounding more rhythmically now-a-days. Are you going to have a few holidays this summer?

Yours till the last wave breaks
Ned

P.S. I have a faint suspicion that you might regard this haphazard and inconsequential effusion as in the mad category as well.

TO VIOLA PRATT

Friday 8 pm. [23 May 1924][120]

Well, old darling,

We have just passed under the Quebec Bridge and finished a most marvellous dinner. The four of us[121] sit together and we have an Immense time – the weather is perfect. We spend hours on deck walking around, cultivating an appetite and the roast beef & capons disappear like magic. The steamer is very comfortable even luxurious, just suits my tastes. I am feeling tip-top only a bit lonesome for yourself & Clare. What kind of a time did you have today? Did Art & Lal[122] stay over? I hope you have a real good time with lots of leisure on your hands. Take care of yourself and don't be afraid to spend a bit of gink[123] once in a while to keep the days humping.

---

119 Born (1871) in Wales, Davies was superintendent minister of Timothy Eaton Memorial Methodist Church, Toronto.

120 On board the *Montclare*, the Canadian Pacific liner on which Pratt was travelling to England.

121 Making the voyage with him were R.S. ('Bobby') Knox (1887–1975) and Herbert Davis (1893–1967), both in the Department of English at University College, Toronto, and both British-born. Knox remained at University College until his retirement, but Davis moved to Cornell University as head of the Department of English, and later to Smith College in Massachusetts, where he was president. Davis was accompanied by his wife, making up 'the four of us.'

122 Arthur and Lila Phelps.

123 Money; loose change.

Just now I am writing this in the smoking room. Bobbie is out in the next room writing to Freda[124] who sent a great? basket of the richest fruit on board grapes & black cherries etc. etc. We – that is the four of us – have to go in to Davis' Cabin to *eat* at nine o'clock. Just imagine. It is now eight p.m. and dinner just over. However, between appetites and pills no jaundice is likely to happen.

Bobbie catches me hold by the arm and promenades with me around the deck speaking in the most endearing terms. I can't solve the riddle exactly as the old rapprochment of which we have spoken so often is not nearly as intimate as we considered it. Bobbie's procrastination has very much weakened the tie on the other side. I understand from Davis that things might have been different a year ago *if things had been different*, as Irish as that remark may be.

Well in about an hour or two the Montclare will be in Rimouski and this letter will be returning to you Westward. No land before getting into Liverpool. Weather conditions are excellent and the prospect is ideal.

Well old sweetheart give yourself and Claire a dozen hugs for me. Tell Claire Daddy is gone to England to get her a doll's carriage and will be back by & bye.

Love
Ned.

TO VIOLA PRATT

Liverpool,
Melville Chambers
50a Lord Street

Thursday 5 [June 1924]

Dearest Vi,

Well, it is just ten o'clock and I have finished breakfast. Knox has left his brother's place in the suburbs of Liverpool and gone to up to Aberdeen for a rather extended visit to his own home. Olmstead[125] arrived two days ago, stayed with us a day and now is gone to Wales to recuperate after a very sea-sickly voyage. He lost eight pounds in as many days, poor chap. To-morrow I intend going up to Durham and Barnard Castle[126] spending a few days there before proceeding

124 Freda Maud Woodman, whom Knox married in 1926.

125 Unidentified.

126 A town on the Durham side of the River Tees; the birthplace of Pratt's father, the Reverend John Pratt (1839–1904).

North to Aberdeen to spend a time with Knox. Knox, Olmstead and I will probably go to Alyth where Knox's brother-in-law has a country cottage mid agisting[127] sheaves and grouse preserves. I am to collect sufficient [....] for supplies and to cook the grub.

That's as far as my plans extend for the present.

I spent an hour or so yesterday in the Liverpool Art Gallery, saw the originals of two of our pictures, Hope and Dante & Beatrice,[128] in fact a third too, the one in the dining room of the death of Beatrice.[129]

At night Knox and Mrs Cumming his sister, Art, Maud and I went at the invitation of Knox to the Theatre where we saw Zack a play by Brighouse,[130] a comedy which you must see if it ever comes to Toronto – Brighouse is the author of Hobson's Choice. It's too bad we missed that – they say it's worth making an effort to see.

Liverpool is a comparatively uninteresting city – quite industrial and I am anxious to get away. I should like to go hike Wales for a few days, but I think I'll defer that till I come back from the North. Knox says I must go to Chester which is only twelve miles from [*missing page*]

I have been wondering just how you have been getting along these last two weeks, you two old chumps. Did the Browns[131] get in to the house all right? and are the examination results out yet? Tell me all the news old dearie, and when I get up to Durham I'll drop you all the information and instruction necessary for the good of your soul, & I'll send some picture cards to Clare.

Love,
Ned.

127 A misuse of the word, which refers to 'the taking in to pasture' of livestock (*OED*).

128 'Hope' is undentified; 'Dante and Beatrice' is probably Dante Gabriel Rossetti's *The Meeting of Dante and Beatrice in Paradise* (1852, watercolour).

129 Probably Rossetti's *The First Anniversary of the Death of Beatrice* (1853–4, watercolour).

130 Harold Brighouse (1882–1958), born and educated in Manchester, England; the author of some seventy plays between 1909 and 1952, including *Hobson's Choice* and *Zack*.

131 During Pratt's absence, Viola and Claire were staying with Viola's mother at 889 Davenport Road, and 25 Tullis Drive was rented to the Brown family.

TO VIOLA PRATT

June 10, 1924

Dearest Vi,

I have just finished dinner at the above-named hotel.[132] It is now half-past eight and I am a bit sleepy and tired after a very long walk. The last two or three days since coming here have been somewhat full of incidents. As soon as I arrived I looked up a man whose name was Pratt, the only person in this little town of 4000 who possessed that name. He was no relative at all but he gave me the name of a man here – Sunter, who he claimed knew all the old inhabitants. As soon as I told Sunter who I was, he almost fell upon my neck, crying out – 'Are you actually Johnny Pratt's son?' He took me into his house and told me that my father and all the Pratt kin had removed to a little village called Gunnerside about seventeen miles from Barnard Castle, and he doubted whether any of them might be found there as the old folks were dead and the young ones had moved out. However, yesterday morning I started off at 9 a.m. to walk over the beautiful hills and dales to Gunnerside. It took me until 5 pm. to reach the place all tuckered out, but all the inhabitants made a great fuss over me when I disclosed my identity. They took me to the house where he was brought up, a house made of stone, (in fact all of the houses here are made of stone) and over one hundred & fifty years old. I met Miss Coates, a lady of more than 80 yrs who knew not only my dad but his dad, James Pratt. She was a sister of Calvert Coates, Father's friend and name sake of Cal. I went inside of the Church where dad used to hold forth, visited the cemetery where the Pratts for generations were buried, chatted to several indigenous nonagenarians and did all kinds of queer stunts, getting back to Barnard Castle about an hour or so ago. I will not walk that distance any more. Five miles a day is enough for me after this. I will remain here another day and if I get word from Knox to go up north I will go for a week.

Living has not been very costly so far. I am keeping well within my allowance per diem. I suppose later on in the summer when I get down to Wembley[133] the expenditure will go a little higher.

132 The King's Head Hotel, Barnard Castle.

133 *NV* was to be included in a display of Canadian books at the Wembley Exhibition. (See the letter to Lorne Pierce, 12 April 1924 [pp. 32–3].)

This last week I have been feeling about as lonely as that Zanzibar cat on the top of the parapet before he sprang into the Pacific.[134] I wish you could come across in an aeroplane in twenty-four hours. I begin already to look forward to the time passing to board the Montcalm.[135]

Next week if I do not go north I shall take a visit to the Lake District. I want to get to the Yorkshire Coast sometime as well. This Yorkshire county, especially these dales are so beautiful that they cannot be described. I never beheld any village more charming in its situation as Gunnerside.

On the way over today I plucked one leaf of holly, one forget-me-not and one blue-bell, and am enclosing them in this letter. They will be pretty badly crushed when you get them but you may be at least able to identify them. The forget-me-not is for Kaky, a little reminder of her doll's carriage when I get across. The rest you can put away with other things that I will send from time to time.

I notice by your letter that you corrected the proof.[136] Thanks very much. Keep a copy of the magazine when you get it. You may get an additional copy, for me from Billy Little when you see him. Send me the Examination results, or I suppose by this time, they have been forwarded. Address all mail to Art as you did your first letter.[137] It is safest and Art can forward it on wherever I am.

Well old sweetheart, have a good time, and be good to yourself. Claire's head drawn by Daddie.[138]

lovingly
Ned.

---

134 'Tom the cat from Zanzibar' in Pratt's 'The Witches' Brew':

And so this wild-cat, now bereft
Of all of life's amenities,
Took one blood-curdling leap and left
Magellan's for the vacant seas. (ll. 555–8)

135 Pratt frequently misidentified the *Montclare*, the Canadian Pacific liner on which he travelled, calling it variously the *Montcalm*, the *Montfort*, and the *Montrose*.

136 Of an essay, 'Thomas Hardy,' which Pratt published in the *Canadian Journal of Religious Thought* 1 (May-June 1924): 239–47.

137 The word 'second' has been scored out.

138 A crude drawing of a head and arms appears here in the text.

TO VIOLA PRATT

June 22, 1924

My dearest Vi

I wrote you last from Alyth[139] on my way back from Glenisla (the county home of Knox's brother-in-law).

Olmstead, Knox and I arrived at Glasgow the day before yesterday. Olmie went on to Edinburgh to spend a couple of days before proceeding to Europe; Knox stayed at Glasgow with his brother and I left immediately for Ayr to spend a day looking up the monuments and memorials of Burns. Ayr is a town of good size about one hour's run from Glasgow. I immediately went out to Alloway, three miles away and 'ransacked' the Cottage in which Burns was born, and the museum attached. The cottage is still the same, thatched, and the rooms, kitchen, 'ben,'[140] barn and bedroom have been preserved with all the relics that the curators have been able to assemble. His bed where he was born, the old clock, dish platter, spinning wheel, etc. etc. in the cottage, and practically all of his manuscript poems and letters in the adjoining museum. They were all open beneath glass cases. There was the big ha' bible[141] owned by his father and registering the births of the family, Robert's name first. Most interesting. A little farther on was the brig of Doon, and the statue and monument of Burns in a well-cared for garden overlooking the Doon. I spent two days there moping about by myself, saw the grave of Wm Burns, Robert's father. Burns himself is buried in Dunfries. It seems that Ayr *just* keeps itself going by tourists visiting the place. When the visit was over I had a game of golf on the Ayr links, so you see I am keeping myself fairly well in trim for next fall.

The next trip I made was one day's sail down the Clyde to Rothesay and Dunoon,[142] – two islands. It took me the day and I arrived back at Glasgow by 8 pm. and here I am writing the old girl.

---

139 Alyth is a small town in Perthshire, Scotland; Glenisla is 15 kilometres north of Alyth in County Angus.

140 An inner room or parlour (Scots dialect).

141 'The great Bible that lay in the *ha'* or principal apartment' (*OED*).

142 Rothsay is in County Bute, and Dunoon in County Argyll; both are on the west side of the Firth of Clyde.

To-morrow I go to Edinburgh for two days. I meet Knox there who will show me around, will visit the castle, Melrose and Abbotsford,[143] the Scottish National Gallery in the city and then probably I will go back to Liverpool for a few days while the world contest in golf[144] is being held. I would like to see it.

My money is holding out pretty well, having lived so far well within my contemplated expenditure.

Davis is still in Germany. Mrs D., poor woman, came out of the trip worse, the lung has opened again, and there is no chance of her coming back to Toronto. The doctor says it will mean a straight year and a half to get her right again if at all. Davis may not come back either if she is no better. Hard luck isn't it? Possibly my trip with him to the South of England is off on account of it.

If I go to Liverpool in a few days I shall stay there for a very short time. I would like to get my Wales trip in soon and it would be more convenient for me to take it from that close centre. I have not yet been through the Lake District, leaving that for the first part of July. Nor have I been to London. Perhaps later in the summer will be best for there.

I was glad to get your letter of June 2nd, enclosing your excerpts. I suppose by this time you have received the Committee's cheque. How are you off for funds. See Mac[145] if you are short. He can let you have a hundred dollars. I hope Burnette[146] sent you the cheque instead of to me. I will not need it, at least according to present prospects. How are the Browns[147]?

I have not heard anything further about Floss's[148] coming to England. I hope she hasn't got cold feet on it. Art[149] is expecting her and will be greatly disappointed if she doesn't take the trip.

I suppose by this time you will have received about a dozen letters and postcards etc. from your humble servant. I am giving you a daily account of my Iliad so you can see my geographical movements. I have decided though most

143 Melrose is a medieval Cistercian gothic abbey 60 kilometres southeast of Edinburgh, the reputed burial place of the heart of Robert the Bruce; Abbotsford is a mansion on the Tweed 5 kilometres west of Melrose, the home of Sir Walter Scott from 1812 until his death in 1832.

144 The British Open.

145 Newfoundland-born Mac Burden, Pratt's lawyer.

146 Unidentified.

147 The Browns were renting 25 Tullis Drive while Pratt was in England.

148 'Floss' or 'Poss' was Florence Sophia Pratt (1892–1984), one of Pratt's three sisters. She never married and at the time was living with her mother in St John's. She lived most of her adult life in Toronto.

149 Arthur Milligan (Art) Pratt (1886–1961), E.J. Pratt's brother. In 1924, he lived with his new wife, Maud, in Liverpool, where he was in business. Pratt made their home his headquarters during his visit to Britain.

emphatically that I will not take any extended trip again without your Majesty and the little Princess. It is too gol darned lonely without you. However, we will have a great time next September. I sent Claire a postcard yesterday. I hope she got it all right. Her letter to me was splendid Hindustani. I can imagine her sitting up at the table drawing those marks, bless her little neckie.

Well it is now ten Lal, etc. etc. an o'clock or after and I must hie off to bed. Best regards to your mother, Mr & Mrs Powell, Leila, John, Art, Lal[150] and much love to yourself.

Ned

TO VIOLA PRATT

Melville Chambers
50 a Lord St.
Liverpool Eng.

Sunday June 29 [1924].

Dearest Vi,

Here I am back in Liverpool after being three weeks away in the North. I spent two days in Edinburgh after returning from Ayr and met Knox again, Olmstead having gone to the Continent. I never visited a more beautiful city in my life than Edinburgh. It is built on or around seven hills like Rome. As soon as I arrived there I went to Holyrood and Edinburgh Castles, visited the famous Banqueting Hall of the Scottish Kings, saw the Crown jewels, – the Crown, the Sceptres, and Stones possessed by the kings for many centuries back. Queen Margaret's Chapel stood almost intact, a thousand years old nearly. A gun that was forged in the fourteenth century was mounted on the top with a great hole in it caused by an explosion in a battle circa 1500. At another side of the parapet was fired the one o'clock gun, keeping up an ancient practice. Close at hand was an iron crate many centuries old used for signal fires. The last one was lit in 1805 on the expectation of an invasion from Napoleon. The red guide raced through his explanation with great self-assurance and dignity. In the afternoon I took a char-a-banc[151] trip down to the Ford Bridge. This is the largest bridge

150 The Powells are unidentified; Leila and J.D. (John) Robins (1884–1952), a colleague in the Department of English at Victoria College; Arthur and Lal Phelps.

151 Motor coach.

in the world, almost a mile long and equal to three Suspension Niagara Bridges all in one. The following morning, Knox and I had the inevitable golf game. He allowed me nine bisks of a handicap[152] an eighteen hole course. A bisk means a shot at any hole you like. I had nine of them and we evened. That is, you see, he had a margin of nine of a superiority. Excuse the elaboration but I know your aversion to technical terms. Before Knox came I went out by myself to play around the course. Fortunately I met an Edinburgh medical student who was glad to get a partner. He was, as I soon discovered an 'eighty' man, – almost a professional, and he likewise took me to be one during the *first* three holes when I beat him on two and tied with him on one. In one hole I secured a 3. One shot less than bogey. That awakened his respect temporarily but the balance of my play showed eights and nines and even one ten. Tell John[153] that I will take him on when I get back with a handicap of six strokes, the handicap of *course* being in my favor. The *next time he presents you with a rose.*[154]

The next day I returned to Liverpool to witness the world championship game at Hoylake. I followed the champions and ex-champions for the two whole days, saw Hagan, Taylor, Duncan, Sarazen and the rest.[155] Hagan beat by one stroke in four rounds – 301.[156] Hoylake has never had less than 300 at any time. But the last year's champion – Havers took 3 shots to get in to the hole on the green with a distance of 5 feet. Just imagine the luck. I have cussed many a time at exactly the identical luck. Tell John I am acquiring a deadly brassey,[157] deadly to the brassey.

What do you say to a foursome next September. John, Leila, you and I. I must get you a set of clubs and initiate you, if you promise not to hit the ball back of you too often. Ha! ha!! I intend making Claire a first class golfer in her early teens.

Well, I am now at Liverpool for a few days. Floss arrived yesterday feeling fine and will remain in England until October. We may all go to London

152 The word 'three' has been crossed out and replaced with 'nine.'

153 J.D. (John) Robins (1884–1952) was a lecturer in German at Victoria College from 1919 to 1925. He joined the Department of English as an associate professor in 1925.

154 Pratt and Robins had an agreement that the loser of their golf games presented a rose to the winner's wife.

155 Walter Hagan won the British Open tournament four times in his career (1922, 1924, 1928, and 1929); John H. Taylor had won at Hoylake in 1913, and George Duncan at Deal in 1920; Gene Sarazen, the great American champion, did not win a British Open until 1932 at Sandwich. Arthur G. Havers (mentioned later) would win in 1923 with a score of 295.

156 Over the four rounds of tournament play, Hagan shot 77-73-74-77, one shot over the course record.

157 Or 'brassy' – 'a wooden club shod in brass' (*OED*).

together for a few days and *see* Wembley.[158] Nellie[159] is staying home in St. John's until Floss returns. Shortly I shall go to the Lake District for a week and then go to Oxford where I shall meet Dale[160] who is studying there.

I was so glad to get your letters this week, one dated June 4, the other, 14th. The examination results were interesting. I am expecting the First and Second years any time now, perhaps to-morrow.

I trust you have received your cheque from the National Committee[161] by this. I was hoping Burnette would have sent his to you.[162] It hasn't come to me yet. When it comes I will return it forthwith as I will not need it. I will be well within my allowance and will have a balance I think when I get back. If you are short after the 15th of July go to Billy Little[163] and he will advance one hundred dollars on my August cheque. You can give him an I.O.U. for the 15th of August. In any case Mac can advance you whatever you need. But don't go short. Wasn't that $2.00 cheque a joke? Don't tell anyone about it for goodness sake; it is too funny.

I haven't seen anything in the English Reviews yet.[164] Possibly there will be something in the July numbers that will be out in a few days. If there's anything I will send it on to you.

I suppose by now you will be out on the Uplands. Tell old Hube[165] I will write him in a few days. I suppose he in feeding up his hens. I would like to see the old boy in his shirt sleeves roaming around his estate.

Tell Claire that the very day I get to Toronto I will take her down to get her doll's carriage.

With the best of love,
Ned

Floss is going to write you soon.

158 The Wembley Exhibition, where *NV* would be part of a display of Canadian books.

159 His sister, Nellie Beatrice Pratt.

160 Ernest Abel Dale (1884–1952) had lectured at Victoria College from 1912 to 1916, and now taught Latin at University College,Toronto.

161 Viola Pratt was a member of the National Committee for Mental Hygiene, the forerunner of the Canadian Association for Mental Health.

162 See the previous letter to Viola Pratt, 22 June 1924 (p. 39).

163 Reverend William J. Little (Billy) (1890–1951), bursar at Victoria College.

164 Pratt had arranged for review copies of *NV* to be sent to major English periodicals and was hoping for a response. (See the letter to Lorne Pierce, 7 August 1924 [p. 51].)

165 Viola and Claire Pratt were visiting Cornelia and Hubert ('Hube') Greaves at their summer retreat, Cragmoor Farm, near Kingston, Ontario.

TO VIOLA PRATT

Wednesday July 2 [1924]

Dearest Vi,

Your letter of the 18th June came yesterday morning just as I was on the point of leaving Liverpool for the North-West. It seems strange that you did not receive a letter three or four days after I wrote my first Liverpool one. No week has passed yet when I have not written at least two or three times.

I spent last week-end in Liverpool and then started for Furness Abbey – a good base for the exploration of the Lake District. Today I am taking the whole twelve hours by train, steamer and motor through the Wordsworth county. It was a lovely cruise down or rather up & on Lake Windermere, twenty miles in length, to Ambleside, then a gorgeous motor trip along the road skirting Rydal Water and Grasmere. We stayed for ten minutes in the neighbourhood of Wythburn Church that Wordsworth speaks of as the smallest church in England. I went inside. It might hold fifty people at the most, an old white-washed church with beams so old that they seemed to be falling down. Outside were old graves dating back into the last century and into the century before. I am sending you a photograph of it. Rydal Water with its small islands and reeds looks just like the description of it.[166] Leaving that we motored up to the summit of the high road passing Helvelyn on the way and then down in to the loveliest region I have yet seen, surpassing Windermere and Grasmere, – Derwentwater. I am also sending a photo of this place surrounded by very high hills or fells,[167] – high meaning about three thousand feet. Derwentwater is lovelier I think than even Lock[168] Lomond or Katrine.

On the way we passed the Swan Hotel with Wordsworth's allusion engraved over the door – 'who does not know the famous Swan.'[169]

When I got in to Furness Abbey Hotel I met a young fellow, a rural teacher at the lunch hour. We decided to 'do' the Lake District together. It was quite fortunate for me as he undertakes to look after tickets, hours of departure and arrival of trains & buses and he has a store of technical information that suits

166 Wordsworth moved from Dove Cottage to Rydal Mount in 1813, living there until his death in 1850. He describes Rydal Mere often in his verse.

167 He sent a postcard with a picture of Derwentwater this same day, with the note 'Keep this card.'

168 Pratt's misspelling of 'Loch.'

169 'The Waggoner,' canto 1, line 88.

me very conveniently. We have yet to visit Wastwater a very inaccessible lake near Scawfell the highest English peak, and also the Carmel Priory which will finish up the Lake tour. That might be the week after which I will go back again to Liverpool previous to my Oxford visit. Going back to Liverpool is a great convenience and saves considerable expense.

I am in tip-top condition as to health, not having a headache since I came here, the only indisposition being loneliness which will be over in a couple of months or so, please goodness. I was only thinking as I was returning to the Abbey Hotel last evening what I would give if some fairy could transport you and duckins to the road about one hundred yards distant. Wouldn't we have one hullabaloo of a time? However we must plan our next trips in the spring together, through Quebec, or down to New York, a week at a time let us say, with one or two hundred dollars to blow up without any compunction. You received the cheque from the Forum.[170] By all means if any money comes in from any source nab it, and use it. I will not want any more. I do hope you have not gone short. You do not need to. The College will advance …

Sometime this month I intend paying a visit to Wales, two or three days or so. It is likely that Art & Floss will go too.

If you get wind of that High School book on Literature[171] coming out, try to get a copy and see how the 'Ice Floes' looks in it. I have not done any writing since I left, – too busy I guess getting up material for lectures from my trips.

Well, old sweetheart, take the greatest care of yourself.

Love
Ned.

TO VIOLA PRATT

July 3 [1924]

Dearest Vi,

I came back to this hotel last night about nine o'clock from Keswick and the Grasmere district. I wrote you at Keswick, but on the return trip the motor bus stopped a few minutes at the village of Grasmere and I had the opportunity of visiting the grave of Wordsworth, an incident not described in my letter. There is a little rail enclosure containing the graves of the whole Wordsworth family,

170 For his poems 'The Last Survivor' (*CF* 4 [June 1924]: 274; *EJP; CP* 1.128) and 'The Drag-Irons' (*CF* 4 [July 1924]: 301; *EJP: CP* 1.128).

171 *Shorter Poems*, edited by W.J. Alexander (Toronto: T. Eaton, 1924).

father, Wm W, Mary, Dorothy and several others. It is a very modest looking place, no *costly* monuments, or *tomb* stones, but just a large slab. The enclosure is in a remote and unnoticed part of the cemetery.

The cottage itself is back a few yards from the road and has none of the striking approaches that mark the birth-place of Burns. (New ink)

Well, we returned as I said about nine o'clock, my friend (whose name I don't know, though we have travelled together for three days) and I. Supper of cold roast duckling was served to us, he taking only a small portion, I a second heap, after which I went to bed and slept the sleep of the full and the just.

This morning it was my intention to take a shorter trip to Wastwater and Mount Scawfell but as the weather looked a little threatening I stayed at the Hotel and went to the Golf Course and beat my last record by five strokes on nine holes. My Brassey is improving though my mid-iron is getting weaker I think. There is some damnable compensation about this great and ancient game. If you improve on one club you correspondingly go back on another. If I could manage to use all my clubs simultaneously I might accomplish something. This afternoon it poured cats and dogs and I did not move from the lounge in the Hotel. A number of Americans are here now taking the same trip through the Lake District.

Well, I am expecting a letter from you by to-morrow-morning, – perhaps two. Art is forwarding all mail. I am going to stay here over the week-end as I like the quietness and the comfort of this hotel and place.

Most lovingly
Ned

TO VIOLA PRATT

Long Buckley
Rugby

Wednesday, 16 [July 1924]

My dearest Vi,

Here I am at Long Buckley with Davis.[172] The place is a little village about twenty miles or less from the town of Rugby. I have been here for two or three days having a very peaceful time visiting small country estates and churches and playing golf in the intervals. Mrs Davis is a wee old lady of seventy-three years

172 Herbert Davis.

of age, a semi-invalid who lives with an unmarried cousin a Miss Jones – about her own age. They have a garden full of strawberries, raspberries, red currants and green peas, and I have been fed (not fed up) with very substantial desserts. The night before last a friend of Davis and Hooke,[173] Mr Hollister, took us out in his car for ten miles in the Midlands to Naseby ridge where Cromwell defeated Charles I. A obelisk had been erected to commemorate the battle. I could imagine Cromwell's Ironsides storming down the hill on the fat Shire horses overwhelming Rupert's Spanish cavalry[174] with sheer weight. I had a beautiful view of the Midland Country from the heights which serve as the watershed for three rivers. It is slightly undulating with fields and clumps of trees and shrubs everywhere; not at all like the Yorkshire moors, or Scotland.

To-day we leave Long Buckley for Oxford arriving there about noon. Oxford is only about forty miles from here. Knox is to meet us there and he has arranged for lodgings in students' quarters at a cheap rate, some thing less than two pounds a week. So this week will be an economical week. Knox & Davis are trying to arrange an evening with Professor Gordon of English.[175] If that comes off I will give you a full account of it. I am anxious to see the place, the buildings, the library and to meet a few of the Professors.

I received, through Davis, the June and July Canadian Forums[176] yesterday. The July number with MacDonald's sketch on the cover[177] looks fine, a great improvement on the old covers I think. Davis is now preparing a review of 'The Continuity of Letters' by John Bailey[178] for a subsequent number.

I am eagerly expecting a letter from you. I wrote Art yesterday to remit all mail to my new Oxford address. As soon as I get there and get settled I will communicate the incidents to your most esteemed and beloved Highness. Tell Cakey she is going to get in addition to her doll's carriage, a Jack in the Box.

Best love
Ned.

173 Samuel J. Hooke.

174 Prince Rupert was the younger brother of the deposed monarch, Charles I.

175 George Stuart Gordon (1881–1942), Merton Professor of English at Oxford University, and later professor of poetry and vice-chancellor of the university. He was author of *Companionable Books* and *Lives of Authors* (London: Chatto & Windus, 1927 and 1950 respectively).

176 Each contained a poem by Pratt: 'The Last Survivor' in *CF* 4 (June 1924): 274 (*EJP: CP* 1.128), and 'The Drag-Irons' in *CF* 4 (July 1924): 301 (*EJP: CP* 1.128).

177 Thoreau MacDonald (1901–99), son of Group of Seven artist J.E.H. MacDonald, specialized in linocuts and wood engravings for book illustration. His work frequently appeared in the *Canadian Forum* in the 1920s.

178 Pratt misspells the name. John Baillie (1881–1963) was a Scottish theologian who taught at Victoria College in the 1920s.

TO VIOLA PRATT

Oxford

July 21 [1924]

Dearest Vi,

Here I am at last in the Home of Learning. Davis and I arrived here first, then Knox came along and the three of us are staying at a private house where Davis lodged when he was studying at Oxford. It is naturally a very interesting place. I have been busy since, going the rounds of the College buildings. I went into St. Mary's Church where Keble preached his sermon on National Apostasy 1833, – and started the Oxford Movement.[179] I climbed up Dr Samuel Johnson's stairs went in to his room. They tell the story that old Samuel was so poor that his shoes were worn through to his feet. A student seeing them outside of his door in the early morning took pity on him and displaced the shoes by a new pair. Johnson was furious when he discovered it, sought out the fellow and fired the new shoes at his head.

I saw Shelley's memorial, a beautiful marble statue representing him as he was brought to shore when drowned. I also visited the Bodleian Library saw old manuscripts by Milton, Queen Elizabeth letters, old Bibles, the first book printed in England, etc. etc. But the most memorable evening I have had since coming here, was with Professor Gordon, Professor of English Literature – Knox's and Davis' Professor.

We stayed till half-past two and I read the Witches' Brew. It went off splendidly. He said the verse was 'simply magnificent.' The prose parts though he didn't like because they dealt with a particular issue – Prohibition, which damaged the universality of the rest of the narrative. He wants a copy revised and he will submit it to the London Mercury – Squire.[180] It may be yet too long for publication perhaps but there is a good chance when it is sponsored by the biggest man in Academic Letters in England. Don't say anything about this yet. That is the Mercury – until I hear later. I am busy now revising it. I will cut out the Milton episode and many of the minor comments, keep the feast and the Cat above all. I will acquaint you with all developments as soon as I hear.

---

179 British cleric John Keble (1792-1866) was professor of poetry at Oxford from 1831 to 1841, mainly on the strength of his popular collection of verse, *The Christian Year* (1827). Keble's famous sermon on 'National Apostacy' instigated the Oxford Movement, an attempt to restore 'primitive and Catholic principles' to the Church of England.

180 Poet and historian John Collings Squire (1884–1958) was editor of the influential monthly periodical *London Mercury* from 1919 to 1934.

Yesterday when I was going down town who should I meet on High Street but Marjorie Millman.[181] She was on her way through the country, touring with a couple of girl friends. She is the only Toronto or Canadian person I have yet met on my travels. I am going back to Liverpool in a day or two and perhaps by the last of July I will go to London.

Your letter of July 6 came the day before yesterday. So Claire is growing fast. She wanted a slipper spanking. She will get one when daddy returns. I am glad you are enjoying the art course. I expect to be 'skitched off' next September. I weighed myself at Professor Gordon's house the other night. Just imagine – 150 pounds. Greatest weight of all. I think the scales flattered me a little. But still they couldn't be much out.

Best love,
Ned.

TO VIOLA PRATT

July 24, 1924

Stratford on Avon

My dearest Vi,

I wrote you, Monday morning I think it was, from Oxford. For three days now I have been at Stratford and the time is passing more quickly. I visited Shakespeare's birthplace, saw a original copy of the First Folio worth £7500, a number of quartos, his will, a number of conveyances, in the original, of property and a great many relics. In the corner was a chair owned by him about the only piece of authentic property in the room. Later I visited the Stratford Church, a beautiful building, and in the most prominent place before the altar; four slabs covering the graves of Shakespeare, Anne Hathaway, Susanna, and Nash.[182] At night I went to the Memorial Theatre and saw Othello played by the Stratford Players with Balliol Holloway; a marvellously fine actor who is making a name for himself. The next night I saw The School for Scandal by the same players.

---

181 A Toronto acquaintance.

182 Thomas Nash of Stratford-upon-Avon was the first husband of Shakespeare's granddaughter, Elizabeth Hall, daughter of Susanna. He is not to be confused with the Elizabethan poet and playwright Thomas Nash.

Yesterday I took an eight mile trip to Warwick and spent the whole afternoon in the Castle. Many fine originals by Holbein, Van Dyck, & Rubens were hanging on the walls. The Castle is eight hundred years old though of course much altered and added to in the course of time. Following that I visited Kenilworth, Leicester's place – in complete ruin with grass growing on the top of the turrets and walls. Did I tell you that while at Oxford, I saw in the Bodleian Library a latin exercise written by Queen Elizabeth. I wondered how her tutor praised it when he saw it. The script was perfect in legibility, etc. I did not see any marks indicating errors. Probably the Latin master knew better than run a red pencil through it.

This is a place where you must come on our next trip. If the Witches Brew goes, – and I have not lost hope of an English publication yet – we will have a royal time. To-morrow morning I go back to Liverpool where I expect a letter and news from your dear old self. I may spend two or three days in Wales and then start for London which yet I have not seen.

By the way, speaking of mail, did you get an early letter written sometime in June[183] containing two or three flowers I picked on the Yorkshire moors, a forget-me-not, a blue bell and a little leaf of holly. I flattened them out to fit in the envelope. You did not mention it and I wondered if the letter reached you. It seems likely that some letters have miscarried. Burnette's has not turned up. I wonder if I had not better write him or wait till I return – Possibly the latter would be the better.

Well much love to you & Cakey.

Ned.

TO VIOLA PRATT

50A Lord Street

July 30 [1924]

Dearest Vi,

Your two letters just came in and two days ago I received another with the Second Year results. I was greatly charmed with all the news, especially the little note at the end of your last to the effect that the Phelpses have a daughter and

183 See the letter to Viola Pratt, 10 June 1924 (pp. 36–7).

heiress to the Bobcaygeon Estate.[184] Isn't it just grand? I was feeling a bit anxious but you can never tell results. Give my best congratulations to them. I wrote Art only two days ago.

I was also glad to know that you received the National cheque.[185] That will help you along and in all be a fine contribution to the Home Exchequer generally.

So your art course is progressing well. You have undoubtedly learned a lot about the nature and History of Art, in addition to gaining proficiency in the practical side of it. *Mind you* I want a charcoal sketch of my profile when I get back and one of Claire. I bet you could do it well after a few months though mine may be the means of making the pencil brittle and breakable.

Well, the time is passing isn't it? Here it is the end of July and in six weeks I pack up for the return. Just think of it? I am looking forward to 25 Tullis Drive, to you and Cakey enormously. This week I am at Liverpool. Saturday the 2nd of August I start off to London for probably three weeks.

I met a Catholic Priest on the golf links yesterday and became his partner in a couple of rounds. I took such a fancy to him or he to me that he has asked me to go with him and spend two or three days at his palace near Chester sometime late in August. He will show me Chester and all the historic remains there etc. A good old scout and a rare old sport. I may go when I return from London if I have time.

Floss and Art went up to Burnley[186] yesterday to see a cousin of ours. They found her an old lady of 64 mind you, a niece of father's. She said she was father's favourite niece. She is living with her daughter. Her other four children are scattered; one is a clergyman in some remote part of the world. She was wonderfully excited to see any of her hitherto unknown relatives.

Well, as soon as I land in London I will write and tell you all the happenings. Tell Mac[187] I shall file a strict report to him as my financial advisor of my expenditures and let him pass on them as to whether they are excessive or not.

With great love,
Ned.

---

184 Ann, daughter of Arthur and Lila Phelps (later Mrs J.D. Hamilton of Toronto), had just been born.

185 A dividend from a small investment in the National Trust Company.

186 Burnley is in northeastern Lancashire, about 60 kilometres from Liverpool. The cousin was a daughter of John Pratt's sister, Sarah Ann.

187 Mac Burden.

TO LORNE PIERCE

Aug. 7, [192]4

Hello old Beeswax,

How are you? Here I am at London having toured this God-intoxicated country from the Grampians[188] to this famous Capital. Much have I voyaged since I struck this silvern isle and my peregrinations are still to continue until September 12th when I set my jibs for Canada and the Queen City.

What kind of a summer have you had at all? I trust your health has been good but you must take a good holiday or by Jove (bah Jove) when I get back I'll take your corpus in hand my self. I have been to every great literary centre since I came over and have drunk deeply. I shall end that sentence right there so as to leave your imagination free scope for figurative exercise.

By the way old thing, are you sure those copies of Newfoundland Verse were sent to the specified English papers & Reviews? I haven't seen any hare of it, not even in the columns of 'Books Received.' Would you mind keeping your weather eye peeled for hypothecatives,[189] etc. etc.

I had one grand evening at Oxford. Dinner at the home of Professor Gordon of English Literature at Oxford where I was the guest. I read the Witches Brew. He was unreservedly enthusiastic and asked for a copy, suggesting its publication over here. He said it was a Julianesque[190] production and felt certain of its success if I revised it a bit cutting out the prose explanations and digressions relating to Prohibition. I have since done so, abridging it quite a bit. He liked the *Cat* very much calling it a zoological marvel. I will tell you more of it later when I see you. Tolkein,[191] Professor at Leeds, also wants a copy. I had dinner also with him .

188 A mountain range in northeastern Scotland.

189 Properties pledged (usually as a security), but not actually transferred. He suggests that copies of *NV* may not have been sent to British periodicals. Pierce replied on 20 August: 'Regarding review copies ... Mr Moore assures me that they have been sent. I recall distinctly on one occasion I had enquired and they had told me that these had gone out.'

190 After Julian the Apostate, the Roman emperor (331–63) who attempted to resist the advance of Christianity by encouraging paganism. The word here means 'joyously pagan in spirit.'

191 [*sic*] J.R.R. Tolkien (1892–1973), author of the *Lord of the Rings* trilogy. In 1924, he was reader of English at Leeds University; however, in 1925, following the publication of his translation of *Sir Gawain and the Green Knight*, he was appointed professor of Anglo-Saxon literature at Oxford University.

Has the Ontario High School text book[192] come out yet with the 'Ice Floes.' That ought to help circulation of N.V. I think.

Will you drop me a line when you get this.

Address
50a Lord St.
Melville Chambers
Liverpool.

I am leaving Liverpool 12th of Sept.

Ned.

TO VIOLA PRATT

Aug. 23 [1924]

My dearest Vi

Back again in old England after nearly a week in Paree. I had a whirlwind of a time in that famous city. I think I gave you a mere skeleton or two on three post-cards, but so many incidents were thronged into so short a time that I shall need the calm hours after dinner and coffee next fall to do them adequate justice. Floss stayed with me for two or three days then went back to Liverpool. I remained on for the balance of the week to fill out a programme of travel with a group from London. I found a good companion in a man from Scotland a Scot of Scots, and an architect. He and I stayed close together all the time, visited all places that make Paris famous from the Louvre down to a wild spot called *Ciel et Enfer* where Mephisto and his imps acted as guides to dark and sulphurous corridors and rooms. Dickson, the man just named, was a brawny Scot, with a Jack Dempsey pair of arms, and I felt quite re-assured all the time.

We left last night and spent some hours crossing the Irish Channel[193] during which time I slept less than thirty minutes. Just now I am going to bed. It is eight thirty, – to make up for practically a week's loss of slumber. I expect to remain in my comfortable bed in this hotel until ten-to-morrow morning.

During the month I have not had one round of golf, – a whole month mind you. I did not even bring my clubs along as I, with great strength of volition, decided that they might possibly interfere with the sight-seeing etc.

---

192 See the note to 'that High School book on Literature' in the letter to Viola Pratt, 2 July 1924 (p. 44).

193 An error for the *English* Channel.

To-morrow I start off on a char-à-banc[194] trip to Dorsetshire. It will last about three days and then within a fortnight, I pack my trunk & grips for Toronto. I am just about crazy to get back, the admitted pleasures of home notwithstanding.

Much love old thing. Your two letters of the 7 & 11th of August just came in today. Delighted.

Neddilius

TO VIOLA PRATT

50A Lord St.
Liverpool

[29 Aug. 1924]

Dearest Vi

Back once more to my central location and now within two weeks of embarking for Canada and Toronto Hoorah!

I have just come back from the South of England having visited Dorsetshire. I had my headquarters at Bournemouth about twenty miles from Southampton. From there on the first day I went to Salisbury to see the famous cathedral. On the next to Wells and to Cheddar. The last place was one of the most picturesque sights I have yet seen. The route lay between exceptionally deep gorges and at the bottom we entered the Cheddar Caves, vast underground corridors running for nearly half-a-mile. These were discovered less than fifty years ago and inside were lime and oxide or iron stalactites long icicle-looking things hanging down from the vaults formed by the slow action of water. It was lit up by electricity and looked like Aladdin's Cave. In fact one chamber was so called.

The next day I went through New Forest and through the Dorset moors, saw Wellbridge Manor chosen by Hardy as the scene of Tess's marriage.[195] I spent five days altogether in that district and arrived at Liverpool last night pretty nearly stranded. I just about finished up my supply of funds; so for the next fortnight I must act like a very economical husband if I am to land in Montreal with enough to get to Toronto.

I am sending a little Maltese hand-made handkerchief for Cakey, bought at

---

194 Motor coach.

195 In Thomas Hardy's *Tess of the D'Urbervilles*, the name undergoes a slight metamorphosis from Wellridge to Woolbridge Manor.

the Exhibition at Wembley. She can blow her little nose with it at her next cold which I hope will not be for some time yet.

Lovingly
Ned

TO VIOLA PRATT

Sept. 5, 1924

My dearest Vi,

Just think of it. A week from today I board the Montrose.[196] By the time you get this note I shall be nearing the coast of Newfoundland or possibly steaming up the St. Lawrence. And the days can't move too quickly now. I once thought of moving my date of sailing back to the 5th instead of the 12th, but the rush for tickets was so great that it couldn't be done with convenience. However, I am spending the balance of the time in and around Liverpool getting in an odd game of golf. I expect Knox in next week. He will spend a few days with his sister in Blundell Sands a suburb of this city. John Line[197] is due to sail today. I am now waiting at Art's office for him, just to wish him good day.

Congratulations upon your successful emergence from the Art Examination. I knew it in advance. I expect the instructors must have had a high opinion of your work if they only would reveal their minds. Mind now I must be drawn in profile with Claire next fall.

I am glad you have had such a nice time by the Lakes[198] this Summer. We might plan for a little trip for a few days to Bob or Windermere[199] when I get back. The steamer will probably get into Montreal about the 20th, and then a day's run into Toronto. If I get in at night, you must stage a meeting with Claire in the morning. If in the morning, then I must hide behind the door when I get up to the house and let her sniff me out.

I shall get those table napkins to day. Floss will help me select them.

---

196 An error for the *Montclare*.

197 British-born John Line (1885–1970) had been Pratt's classmate at Victoria College. He was an ordained Methodist minister but taught in the Faculty of Theology at Victoria College until his retirement in 1950.

198 Viola and Claire had been staying at the Greaves's summer place near Kingston.

199 'Bob' is Bocaygeon; Windermere is a village on Lake Rousseau in the Muskoka region where Viola's relatives had a summer cottage.

Did you say that you only received one letter from me in two weeks? If you did then his majesty's mails must have run on the rocks. I never passed a week without writing at least twice, sometimes more, letters and cards.

And didn't Hubert[200] get my letter either, written at Stratford on July 23rd. I wrote him a long letter, only one indeed but a long one in addition to a number of cards. I am absolutely positive about it, and I wrote Art[201] at the same time. I can't imagine where the letters have gone to if they didn't reach their destinations.

I am looking over my finances for the summer. I find that I ran over my allowance somewhat on account of my London and Paris trips. I had to borrow from Art.[202] If I had received Burnette's cheque I would have been all right. I wonder if he sent it and it went astray. I must write to him immediately upon my return.

Besides I have bought a suit of clothes, a mackintosh etc. My one and only suit had become threadbare and clothing's cheap over here.

Well old lover; by the 21st we'll –

Most lovingly
Ned.

TO LORNE PIERCE

Sept. 24, 1924

Dear old thing,

Here I am back again in the Queen City of Diabolus. Would like to have a psychic interview with your Satanic self. I suppose by this time you have heard from Selwyn & Blount to the effect that they will act as English Representatives of Newfoundland Verse. They are asking for Review copies for England, twenty I think, and intend pushing the volume. They suggested that their imprint be placed upon the opening page, as the London firm.

I submitted also the Witches Brew which they accepted instantly. They will publish one thousand copies, cloth cover with illustrations.[203] Professor Gordon of Oxford wrote enthusiastically about it and sent a copy of it to Squire of the

---

200 Hubert Greaves.

201 Arthur Phelps.

202 His brother Art.

203 When Selwyn & Blount went out of business a few years later, Pratt jokingly ascribed its failure to the rash decision to publish *WB*.

Mercury.[204] Squire may print it in parts. In any case it took well wherever it was presented, both in London, Oxford and Leeds. Selwyn & Blount were to write you to see if you would represent it over here.[205] The volume will sell for one half-crown, (60 cents). Let me hear from you old cheese very soon.

With loving remembrances.
Ned Pratt

TO LORNE PIERCE

Dec. 18, 1924.

My Lord and Editor,

Your Epistle just received. Sorry that the vintage proved a little too stimulating for regular consumption.[206] I understand the situation in which you are placed, as a firm, by reason of ecclesiastical affiliations. I think that Gundy[207] would be willing to handle it. All I want is its appearance on such book stalls as would be interested in it. I am positive that there would be an immediate demand for a

204 See the letter to Viola Pratt, 21 July 1924 (p. 47).

205 On 1 October, Pierce replied: 'I am happy to hear that Selwyn and Blount are taking your Witches's Brew. As soon as the book is finished I hope that they will send me page proofs, together with quotations, and we shall discuss with them the matter of taking a Canadian edition. Before your letter had arrived we had already received, during my absence, an order from Selwyn and Blount for *NV.* They ordered fifty copies, the order to depend upon our willingness to send them ... 25 copies for review purposes.'

206 Pratt had sent Pierce the page proofs of *WB* from Selwyn & Blount on 8 December (*EJP: Web*), hoping that Ryerson Press would publish the book in Canada. However, Pierce replied on 16 December as follows: 'Your *Witches' Brew* has been passed around the Book Room and both Dr Fallis and the management generally have taken copious draughts from its sparkling rim. The general feeling is that a publishing house so closely connected with the Methodist Church could not very well act as Canadian distributor for it. Personally, I should like very much to be able to do something for you with this book not because it is endorsed by the Oxford Regius Professor of English [George Gordon was actually Merton Professor] but for your own sake. I hope the timidity of our house is not prevalent among the other publishers in town and that you may be more successful with them. I do not see that it is necessary to have the imprint of a Canadian publisher on it at all. Some one would likely handle it for you. There is only one change I would make if I were you. On page two I would strike out your name and on page 9 I should do the same kind service.' Pierce was advising him to publish it anonymously.

207 S.B. Gundy, a Toronto literary agent and publisher. Unable to reach a satisfactory arrangement with Gundy or other firms he approached, Pratt turned to Hugh S. Eayrs, the new president of Macmillan of Canada, who readily agreed to be the Canadian publisher of *WB.*

few hundred copies at least by what I have been informed. Almost that number of people have been inquiring about it already.

Would be delighted to have lunch with you soon. Could you come to the Arts & Letters at noon Monday the 22 inst.[208]

Yours Bacchanally,
Ned Pratt

TO *SATURDAY NIGHT*

[Apr. 1925]

Literary Editor, SATURDAY NIGHT,[209]

Dear Sir,

In view of Mr. Wilson MacDonald's generous inclusion of my name in one phase of the comparisons instituted by his article,[210] there may be a touch of indelicacy on my part in making any contribution to the discussion. But disclaiming, in advance, any pretensions to rank with the well-known names quoted, I feel that his general statement is a healthy tonic for Canadian literary criticism. One of the dangers into which we are drawn today is the complacency with which we take accepted classifications. We have not gone far enough yet to satisfy ourselves with

208 Pierce did not meet him. A cooling of their friendship ensued, mainly because of Pratt's insistence on publishing the book – under his own name. Pierce disapproved of the direction which Pratt's poetic inclinations seemed to be taking him. Their friendship was restored two years later, after Pratt published 'The Great Feud' in *Titans* and commenced writing 'The Iron Door.' But Ryerson Press published no more of Pratt's books. Macmillan was his publisher until his death – and after.

209 Pratt's letter was published (with others) in *Saturday Night*, 25 April 1925, under the heading 'Is Carman Supreme?'

210 'Is Carman Supreme?' *British Whig* (Kingston, ON: 11 March 1925). The article had initiated what has been called 'The Carman Controversy of 1925.' At a dinner given him on 7 March by the Toronto branch of the CAA, Charles G.D. Roberts, newly returned to Canada after seventeen years abroad, had declared his cousin Bliss Carman 'the greatest living lyric poet with the possible exception of Mr. W.B. Yeats.' MacDonald's article had refuted Roberts's pronouncements and declared the claims of other Canadian poets to equal recognition with Carman. Deacon, in *Saturday Night*, 28 March 1925, reprinted the article with a provocative preface of his own in which he supported MacDonald's views. A series of letters to the press ensued, most of them pro-Carman and anti-MacDonald. Pratt's contribution, which Deacon had probably urged him to make, was the letter included here. It went unanswered, though the debate continued in the press for another six weeks.

unassailable titles, and the moment we refuse to regard any writer in our midst as a legitimate problem for critical examination, we are drifting into very stagnant waters. We are all prone to the manufacture of myths about our favourite authors, but granting, as we might very honestly and truthfully do, a considerable basis upon which the legend might ferment, in the case of Bliss Carman, yet, as you pointed out in your preface to the letter, much injustice may be done to the work of less known but equally significant writers. It might be considered sacrilege to question the place of a deity in our little world, still it must be remembered that our throne is one we build with our own hands.

E.J. Pratt.

TO WILLIAM ARTHUR DEACON

May 4, 1925.

Dear Bill,

Just came back from London where I gave an address and reading on Newfoundland.[211] As you haven't a phone I thought I'd drop you a line to tell you how much they appreciated your visit.[212] After the address they whisked me off to the home of Grace Blackburn[213] where a number of the London Branch of the C.A.A. had gathered. I never experienced more kindness anywhere; and we got talking about you and your work. Miss Fiddler[214] (I think that's how you spell it) said you held them spell-bound for 2 hrs, Grace Blackburn wanted to

---

211 On 1 May Pratt had spoken at the Victoria Public School, South London, on the subject 'The Seafaring Life' and read from *NV*, including 'The Ice-Floes,' which had been reprinted in a standard high school textbook, *Shorter Poems*, edited by W.J. Alexander (Toronto: T. Eaton, 1924). On the same day 'Fanfan' in the London *Free Press* had reviewed the book at great length.

212 Deacon had addressed the London branch of the CAA a few weeks earlier on the subject of Ontario writer Peter McArthur (1866–1924).

213 Literary and theatre critic for the *London Free Press*, of which her father Josiah Blackburn was proprietor and editor. She wrote under the nom de plume 'Fanfan.'

214 Jennie Fidlar (not 'Fidler' as Pratt spells it) was secretary-treasurer of the Western Ontario (London) branch of the CAA.

be most warmly remembered to you and Seaborn (the Doctor)[215] said that Fox's appreciation[216] amounted to enthusiasm. You must have had an extraordinary good time even better than you thought. They told me how you stayed over on the following day missing train after train. Miss Seaborn intended answering your letter but there was sickness or something in the Family at the time that pressed her for time. All thought your visit well worth while for them & your treatment of Peter[217] a cracker-jack of exposition.

A more magnetic and charming personality than Grace Blackburn I have rarely met. Thought I would just tell you. In haste.

Ned.

TO WILLIAM ARTHUR DEACON

Bobcaygeon, Ont.

August 10 [1925]

Dear Billy,

We are planning on one gorgeous week-end here next Saturday, 15th inst. Could you get, by hook or by crook, Roberts[218] and MacDonald[219] to come up with you and MacInnes[220] again if he can make it. Glad Phelps[221] is going to invite some of her petites blondes for a few days and it's quite possible a little moonlight dance could be executed on the grounds outside of the cottage. Art[222] is inviting you

---

215 Edwin Seaborn (1872–1951) was a medical doctor and occasional author. He published *The March of Medicine in Western Ontario* (Toronto: Ryerson, 1944).

216 In 1925, William Sherwood Fox (1978–1967) was professor of classics and dean of arts at the University of Western Ontario. He would serve as president of the university from 1927 to 1947. In 1949, Pratt wrote a short foreword to his (and Wilfrid Jury's) *Saint Ignace, Canadian Altar of Martyrdom* (Toronto: McClelland & Stewart, 1949).

217 Peter McArthur. See the note to 'your visit' above (p. 58).

218 Charles G.D. Roberts (1860–1943), the New Brunswick–born poet and prose writer, had recently settled in Toronto after seventeen years abroad.

219 Wilson MacDonald.

220 Tom MacInnes (1867–1951) was born in Ontario and spent most of his life in Vancouver. He published seven books of poetry, including *Complete Poems* (Toronto: Ryerson, 1923). He had recently returned from an extended sojourn in China, poor in health and low on funds. Pratt had entertained him for several days at the Bobcaygeon cottage earlier that month.

221 The sister of Arthur Phelps; her name was Welsh and was actually spelled 'Gwlad.'

222 Arthur Phelps.

as well. Between our two cottages we could accommodate all comers. Do try to make it, and *get* Roberts & Mac[223] by all hazards. I can look after all the males.

Ned.

TO WILLIAM ARTHUR DEACON

Bobcaygeon

Tuesday [18 Aug. 1925]

Dear Billy,

Art and I both enjoyed the style (Deaconian or Deaconal – which?) of your 'Glorious Present.'[224] It re-touched for us the hoary issue of literary evaluations. Your third section I considered the best. It is almost staggering to think that one's destiny is suspended by so slight a thread, and life and death separated by almost microscopic boundaries. I like to think of you as a literary diagnostician percussing thoracic and abdominal walls for unusual sounds before passing the cases over to a public surgeon. May your fingers never lose their sensitiveness.

I shall be charmed to send you an original copy of 'Tatterhead'[225] as soon as I get within reach of a typewriter.

Love to the family,
Ned.

---

223 'Mac' likely refers to MacInnes rather than MacDonald.

224 An essay in *Saturday Night*, 15 August 1925. In it, Deacon muses on reading and books, particularly how some books survive while others quickly die: 'Sometimes the thinnest of margins separates the book that is immortal from its twin that goes to utter oblivion.'

225 A short poem Pratt had written that summer (*EJP: CP* 1.165). It was first published in *AV* 50 (January 1926), 13–14, and was later included in *MM*. Pratt had given Tom MacInnes a copy, which he had shown to Deacon, who, 'greatly taken with it,' wrote on 13 August to ask for a copy.

TO MRS HORACE PARSONS[226]

Bobcaygeon

Tuesday 22 [Sept. 1925]

Dear Mrs Parsons,

Many apologies for the mistake of enclosure. It was so stupid of me. I am returning to the city tomorrow and will telephone you after eight p.m.

Thanks also for your kindness in returning letter. I can now get in touch with the *other* mystified correspondent.

Sincerely,
E.J. Pratt

226 An amusing Prattian anecdote is attached to this short note. Writing from Bobcaygeon simultaneously to Mrs Parsons, secretary of the Toronto branch of the CAA, and Clark Locke, a close friend, he had somehow interchanged the enclosing envelopes. Locke had received a letter about CAA matters, while the astonished Mrs Parsons had received a short missive saluting her as 'Dear old Thing' (a common salutation of his for close friends) and enquiring whether, 'since I am to be in town overnight and my house is rented out, could I spend the night with you?' Sensing a grave error, she returned the note with a discreet enquiry. This is Pratt's reply.

II A Taste of National Acclaim, 1925–1932

It was quite gratifying to get, really for the first time … a taste of national acclaim.
– E.J. Pratt to Arthur Phelps, 3 January 1926

TO MRS HORACE PARSONS

Oct. 29./25

Dear Mrs Parsons,

I think the Hygeia House[1] will suit splendidly. I am only too glad to leave everything of that nature to your own excellent judgment.

I am delighted that Dr Roberts can take the Presidency.[2] I trust he will find it convenient to be present at our meetings.

Regarding Book Week, we might suggest Kirkconnell's[3] points at our next meeting.

Very gratefully,
E.J. Pratt

---

1 For a social evening of the Toronto branch of the CAA.

2 Paul Wallace, president of the Toronto branch of the CAA, had recently resigned, and Pratt, as 'First Vice,' would normally have assumed the post. He hoped to evade the responsibility by suggesting that the post be offered to Charles G.D. Roberts, who had recently moved to Toronto. Unfortunately, although Roberts accepted, he was on tour until late December, and Pratt had to shoulder the additional workload.

3 Watson Kirkconnell (1895–1977) was a prolific author and translator from Ukrainian, Hungarian, and other European languages. He taught classics and English at Wesley College and English at McMaster University and later served as president of Acadia University (1949–64). An early member of the CAA, he held all of its national executive offices.

TO WILLIAM ARTHUR DEACON

Monday a.m. [Oct. 1925]

Dear Billy,

I sent off my order for marked copies of the American Mercury last week. Two copies go to Newfoundland. I am enclosing 'Tatterhead' to *you*. Also inserting a few small ones new and unpublished which you might look over. They may be a little too sombre for a Christmas Review[4] and they do not adjust themselves to space. If that is so, *do not hesitate* to exclude them. The short one 'Waiting'[5] might be the only one that might fit into a corner.

Ned.

TO ARTHUR PHELPS

25 Tullis Drive

January 3, 1926

Dear Art,

Sorry I didn't get around to answering your note before. Yes, 'The Cachalot'[6] went over well. Sold out the *CF* I am told. I was positively inundated with congratulations and the most enthusiastic expressions of delight from all sorts of people. It was gratifying to get, really for the first time as you say, a taste of national acclaim. Like Byron, I felt I was suddenly 'famous overnight.'

Little Claire is much improved now, though still a cause for worry.[7] The paralysis fortunately was relatively mild, but her foot is affected and may need corrective surgery. It has been an anxious time.

Thanks for the book. And best wishes for the New Year to you all.

Ned

4 None of the poems submitted with this letter was published in Deacon's *Saturday Night* Christmas review.

5 The title was changed to 'A Lee Shore,' and later to 'The Lee-Shore' (*EJP: CP* 1.204).

6 The poem was published in *CF* 6 (November 1925): 47–51 (*EJP: CP* 1.150).

7 Claire Pratt, age four, had been afflicted with poliomyelitis in her right leg in the autumn of 1925, shortly after she and Viola returned from Newfoundland.

TO AUSTIN BOTHWELL[8]

March 12, 1926

My dear Mr Bothwell,

I want to thank you very much indeed for your kind words about the Witches' Brew in the recent number of the Canadian Bookman.[9] I make it a point of never getting in touch with a reviewer in anticipation of a review but when the deed is done I would be less than human if I did not feel kindly disposed towards a sympathetic and appreciative critic. Your name is quite familiar to me through a number of incisive letters and articles published but I never had the good luck to meet you personally. Last week I had dinner with a number of friends, Eayrs[10] and Edgar[11] among them, and Eayrs was talking about you very cordially, that you were a kind of a lonely leviathan out in the West and remote from much that you loved in the East.

It is too bad that a few of us separated by distance and probably by the 'financial situation' cannot meet and fraternize once in a while.

I know I would love to meet you, and please accept my genuine thanks for your kind words.

Yours sincerely
E.J Pratt.

8 See the note to 'Bothwell' in the letter to Lorne Pierce, 12 April 1924 (n. 115, p. 32).

9 *CB* was the official voice of the Canadian Authors Association.

10 Hugh Smithurst Eayrs (1894–1940) joined Macmillan of Canada in 1917 and by 1921 was president of the company, a post he held until his death. He and Pratt had become close friends after Eayrs agreed to publish *WB* in Canada in the summer of 1924.

11 Pelham Edgar.

TO ARTHUR PHELPS

April 8 [1926]

Dear old Art,

Just a line to let you know that we won't be seeing much of Bob[12] till late July. Pelham[13] has asked me to motor down to Chicago with him in June – for two or three weeks from the 8th on.

Have had a busy winter. Claire is much improved, the paralytic effects scarcely noticeable in one foot only, which will probably need an operation or special treatment.

I have almost finished the pre-historic allegory poem[14] – quite a battle in more senses than one. Perhaps it's too crazy – in a different way from the Brew. I've kept in a touch of comedy. It needed a chuckle of humour now and then; otherwise it would have been much too ghastly and grim. As you know it was that motion picture[15] I saw last spring that got me going, that and 'The Cachalot' which gave me the form and technique. Of course I'd read the book long before, as I have everything or almost by Sir Arthur C-D. Anyway it's nearly done, but it remains to be seen how it goes over. I'll read it to you in July.

Love to all.

Yours till the dinosaurs return.
Ned.

12 His cottage in Bobcaygeon.

13 Pelham Edgar.

14 Shortly afterward titled 'The Great Feud: A Dream of a Pleiocene Armageddon' (*EJP: CP* 1.168). The poem was first published with 'The Cachalot' in *Titans* (Toronto: Macmillan, 1926).

15 *The Lost World*, the 1924 film version of Sir Arthur Conan Doyle's 1912 'pre-historic novel' of the same title. The movie featured very realistic dinosaurs and other pre-historic creatures.

TO WILLIAM ARTHUR DEACON

Thursday am. [3 June 1926]

Dear Bill,

Arrived in from Bob last night where I was spending three or four days gardening. Have made the verandah fool proof respecting mosquitoes. And I have a little strip of shore 50 X 20 feet wired in, with nine loads of sand dumped, making it ideal for tumbling about. The deepest part is less than 18 inches. The wharf will have to be barricaded an easy matter. Claire played in the water & sand all day.

I would make this suggestion![16] –

I have just received word from the government of my appointment[17] till the 20th of July. Hence I will not be able to go to the cottage till that date. From the 15th of June until July 20th it is at your disposal. Why not send Mrs Deacon and the Kiddies up there on the earlier date, you going, say, week ends till your vacation starts. The Phelpses are next door and will give her all the advice re food and other desirables. By then the lettuce will be up and by July the peas ought to be forming. The strawberries look promising.

If Mrs. Deacon could get a little girl to assist her and help look after kids, there is room, of course. I would advise that. She might get a Bobcaygeon girl if she couldn't lay her hands on a city one. Phelpses will suggest possibly.

So it makes no difference which fortnight you decide on as I am compelled to remain in Toronto hard at it through the most of July.

Ned.

16 Deacon had written to Pratt on 30 May asking to rent Pratt's cottage 'outright' from 5 June to 21 July, and offering his house in town in exchange. In spite of Pratt's counter-proposal here, Deacon's suggestion was adopted: the Deacon family were in residence at Bobcaygeon on 7 June. Deacon's wife was pregnant and his children (Bill and Deidre) had been sick with whooping cough. He was reluctant to bring the family to Bobcaygeon to recuperate, as Pratt had apparently suggested, for fear of contaminating Claire.

17 He had been appointed to the Ontario High School Examination Marking Board.

TO WILLIAM ARTHUR DEACON

25 Tullis Drive

Monday [7 June 1926]

Dear Bill,

Off to Chicago tomorrow.[18] I have lost a cheque for $30 somewhere, and have wondered whether I left it in my inside pocket of the coat put into the suitcase over the kitchen door.[19] Cheque made out by MacLean's Magazine in my favor. It was attached to a note by a clip and is inside of an envelope. I may have left it in my coat (black with white pin stripe). There are two suitcases strapped up on top. Would you mind opening them up and examine the coat. If you find it send it to Vi 25 Tullis Drive. If you can't find it there it may be on one of the shelves in the living room. If not there I guess I may have lost it in transit as I had my coat off on train. Hope you are having a good time. Get all the rest you can.

Love to all
Ned.

TO WILLIAM ARTHUR DEACON

Bobcaygeon, Ont

Sept. 9 [1926]

Dear Billy,

I had this review[20] up to four hundred words but by a second pruning I managed to get it down to 335. I hope it will do though I don't think it is 'any great shakes,' as I can only accomplish anything worth while when I have the impulse to *let myself go*.

---

18 Pelham Edgar had arranged for Pratt to give a recital at a conference in Chicago. Pratt then returned to Toronto through July to work for the Marking Board, while Edgar stayed on in Chicago to teach summer school. (See the letter to Phelps, 8 April 1926 [p. 65].)

19 At the cottage in Bobcaygeon, where the Deacons were staying for most of June and July.

20 Deacon had asked Pratt to review Flora Jewell Williams's *New Furrows: A Story of the Alberta Foothills* (Ottawa: Graphic Publishers, 1926) for the Fall Supplement of *Saturday Night*, 4 December 1926.

I am glad to see that your Poteen is ready for the market. I received a notice from the Graphic P but I intend buying a couple of copies from the Toronto book stores when I get back. I want your autograph on. Don't bother about a complimentary copy, old man, as you will have expense enough in sending around the inevitable ones. We are looking forward to seeing the whole damn family on our return. Procreation is a wonderful natural gift.[21]

Ned

TO ARTHUR L. PHELPS

Nov. 9 [1926]

Dear Art,

I had the pleasure of proposing (and Deacon seconding) your name for membership in the P.E.N.[22] the other day, and yesterday the ballot recorded your selection. It is going to be very exclusive. I think you were the only one accepted out of seven nominations. You got a good 'blowing up' all round. Members present – Edgar (Chairman), Wrong,[23] MacInnes,[24] Heming,[25] Macdonald,[26] Allain,[27] myself. It is going to be the most exclusive literary thing in Canada probably limited to 25 all told. Galsworthy[28] is president of the International

21 A reference in Deacon's letter of 22 August to 'us five' had reminded Pratt of the Deacon baby born that summer in Bobcaygeon.

22 International PEN was founded in England in 1921 to represent 'Poets, Essayists, and Novelists.' Early members included John Galsworthy (its founding president), Joseph Conrad, George Bernard Shaw, and H.G. Wells. The first Canadian PEN centre was established in 1926 in Montreal. In 1983, the English-language centre, PEN Canada, moved to Toronto, with the French-language Centre Québécois du PEN remaining in Montreal.

23 George MacKinnon Wrong (1860–1948) was an Anglican priest who lectured on ecclesiastical history at Wycliffe College, Toronto. He was head of the Department of History at the University of Toronto from 1894 to 1927.

24 Tom MacInnes.

25 Arthur Heming (1870–1940) was a prominent painter, illustrator, and writer internationally known for his depictions of the Canadian north in *The Heming Paintings of Northern Life* (1923), and for accounts of his own experiences in *Spirit Lake* (Toronto: Macmillan, 1907), *The Drama of the Forests: Romance and Adventure* (New York: Doubleday, 1921), and *The Living Forest* (New York: Doubleday, 1925).

26 Wilson MacDonald.

27 Unidentified.

28 British novelist and playwright John Galsworthy (1867–1933), who won the Nobel Prize for Literature in 1932, is principally remembered as the author of *The Forsyte Saga* – consisting of six novels, two interludes, and a collection of short stories. His work critiques the social injustices of the class system.

P.E.N. and it is international in the und[...] sense. Production of high rank is the qualification. Katherine Hale[29] and number of other women were hissed down and [...] men. Keep this under your hat. Deacon will notify you. Whenever any member travels he goes furnished with the P.E.N. credential.

You are the only western rep. outside of Mrs Adam Beach[30] of Vancouver.

Love to Lal & Nan
Ned

TO LORNE PIERCE

25 Tullis Dr.

Sun. [2 Jan. 1927]

Good Old Lorne,

I must reply at once to your very kind expression of deeply understanding sympathy and brotherly support on the recent passing of my much loved Mother.[31] It was good to have a few lines from you after so long.[32] Her passing wasn't unexpected; she had been in poor health for some time. So it wasn't a great shock, but saddening all the same. My sincerest thanks again for your kind words.

On the other matter you mention I agree entirely: 'both carping and insensitive' puts it mildly. I must admit that I believe for the first time I was hurt by a review.[33] I was not expecting anything eulogistic, but God above! – he came out with a diatribe full of cavils and sneers, and the merest appreciation – if it is that – of only the humour and such minor points. It's time Billy stopped playing lickspittle to that mischief-maker W. MacD.[34] A pity, because Bill has some good points about him. I can't say how happy I am that you are going, as you

---

29 'Katherine Hale' was the pseudonym of Amelia (Mrs J.W.) Garvin (1878–1956). Between 1914 and 1950, she wrote five books of verse, and a prose work, *Canadian Cities of Romance* (Toronto: McClelland & Stewart, 1928).

30 Unidentified.

31 Fanny Knight Pratt died in St John's on 22 December 1926.

32 Pierce's short, handwritten letter of 26 December 1926 was the first correspondence between them in two years. (See the note to 'Lunch … Monday the 22 inst.' in the letter to Pierce, 18 December 1924 [p. 57].)

33 W.A. Deacon had published a 'carping and insensitive' review of Pratt's *Titans* in *Saturday Night*, 18 December 1926, causing strain in his friendship with Pratt that lasted several months.

34 Deacon was still lauding Wilson MacDonald as 'Canada's leading poet.'

say, 'to show him a few things that he missed.'[35] Spoken like the Prince you are. I shall look forward.

When can we get together for a chat? There is so much I want to talk over with you. Again Old Man, my deepest thanks.

Ned

TO ARTHUR L. PHELPS

Jan.18, 1927

Dear Art,

Received word from Tom to give him some particulars about you. (Word came from DeWitt.)[36] I gave you your *career* at Cornell, and the rival bidding for you with Flint & Riddell,[37] Flint wanting to retain, Riddell to get you at any price. Your determination based finally on patriotism, your writing ability, lecturing enthusiasm, love of students, public recognition, civic reputation, broad reading of English literature dramatic, essay, poetry, etc. I stated your specialization was 19th Cent & contemporary *rather* than *Beowulf Chaucer etc.* I left it at that. You wanted to get East, your salary at present was $3500 but might make *small* sacrifices.[38] (This was to guard against big drops, and yet I didn't want to scare Tom as I had heard they were looking for an assistant. But Tamblyn[39] is rather old and there might be a good chance there in a few years. DeWitt said he wanted to know academic qualifications. I said in letter that I had known you from undergraduate days and that the B.L. did not hire any professor due[?]

---

35 In his letter, Pierce had promised to write a review of *Titans* which would be quite different from Deacon's 'diatribe.' (See Pratt's letter to Pierce, 20 January 1927 [p. 71].)

36 Phelps was again searching for an academic position in Ontario and was being considered by the University of Western Ontario. (See the letter to Phelps, 24 January 1925 [*EJP: Web*].) 'Tom' is unidentified. Norman Wentworth DeWitt (1877–1958) was professor of Latin at Victoria College from 1908 to 1945, and dean of arts and principal from 1924 to 1928.

37 Charles W. Flint, president of Cornell College, Iowa (1915-22), had hired Phelps to teach in the English Department in 1921. John Henry Riddell (1863–1952) was principal of Wesley College in Winnipeg from 1917 to 1938. Phelps had taught there since 1922.

38 Pratt had offered similar advice on salary negotiations in his letter of 24 January 1925 (*EJP: Web*).

39 William Ferguson Tamblyn (1874–1956) was professor of English at the University of Western Ontario from 1901 to 1949, and served as head of department for forty-three years.

to [...] qualifications. You were, however, in shouting distance of an M.A., needing finance and time to get it. But your teaching ability and your literary gifts were beyond the technical credentials.

You may hear. Would love to have you at London.

Ned

TO LORNE PIERCE

Jan. 20, 1927

Dear old Lorne,

Your review[40] went gloriously to my heart. It was the best account I have had. Edgar has just been reading it and remarked 'the more I read of that fellow the bigger he grows,' and talked about your intellectual richness. The wife said you were the only reviewer who got behind the 'Great Feud.' You stated exactly my own purpose especially at the conclusion. A small circle, *yourself*, *Edgar*, *Norwood* (of Varsity),[41] *Fairley*,[42] *Dennison*,[43] see the significance of it, apart from extravaganza. Thanks old dear for your magnanimity.

By the way do you know that MacDonald is circulating the report around that I wrote that article in the Canadian Forum[44] and used Bush's name as a pseudonym to glorify myself and belittle him? Of course no one around here would believe it, but what damage he could do in remoter places I can imagine. He's a desperately dangerous fellow. Some of my friends suggested a denial of it in the Forum, but I refuse because it would seem as if I took his slander seriously.

Best love to you again
Ned.

---

40 Pierce had sent Pratt a copy of his review of *Titans* in *New Outlook* 3 (19 January 1927): 26, inscribed, 'My dear Ned. It's it! Piscatorially yours.' (See the letter to Pierce, 2 January 1927 [pp. 69–70].)

41 British-born Gilbert Norwood (1880–1954) had come to the University of Toronto as professor of classics in the summer of 1926.

42 Barker Fairley (1887–1986), professor of German at University College from 1915 to 1957, was a founder and, for a time, editor of *Canadian Forum*. He was also an accomplished painter, with Pratt being one of his subjects. (See the frontispiece of *EJP: CP* 1.)

43 Merrill Denison, whose name Pratt habitually misspells as 'Dennison.'

44 Douglas Bush had published an article entitled 'Making Literature Hum' in *CF* (December 1926) which was complimentary to Pratt, and severely critical of Wilson MacDonald.

TO LORNE PIERCE

Victoria College
Toronto

July 15 [1927].

My dear Lorne,

I am sending you this poem[45] with my deepest affection. You are responsible for the 2nd and 3rd stanzas on page 4.[46] I have never written any thing which came so naturally from my heart.

Last night, a whole crew of people came up to my house to hear it read, – Hector Charlesworth,[47] Edgar, Eayrs, Jack Creighton[48] and others – and it was their common judgment that the ode was the best thing I had done by a long chalk. I only wish you could have come up, but your secretary said you were out of town. Eayrs is going to publish it immediately in book form and get the English Macmillans to publish it over there. I told Eayrs it had your backing and he values your judgment immensely. I will make it the chief item on the Western tour. I have to thank you also for your work with Spry.[49] He has sent me the itinerary for confirmation. When you return will you let me hear from you by letter. Address Victoria College which will forward it wherever I am.

You simply must make Bobcaygeon in August for a few days. Plan for it ahead and let me know when you are free.

Ned.

45 A typed manuscript of 'The Iron Door: An Ode' (*EJP: CP* 1.204). The poem was prompted by his mother's death in December 1926.

46 The stanzas begin 'One who had sought for beauty all his days' and 'One who had sought for truth, but found the world.' According to Viola Pratt, the stanzas had been included at Pierce's suggestion, the first representing Pierce himself, and the second Pratt, 'as he was when a student, searching for the truth about the Universe.'

47 Critic and journalist Hector W. Charlesworth (1872–1945) had been associate editor of *Saturday Night* from 1910 to 1926, and was beginning a six-year term as editor (1926–32). He is best remembered in Canadian cultural history for his severe criticism of the Group of Seven painters in the 1920s.

48 In 1927, John H. Creighton was a freelance writer and reviewer. He later taught at several universities, before becoming educational manager at Oxford University Press.

49 Graham Spry (1900–83) had a varied career in journalism, socialist politics, and business. In 1927, he was national secretary of the Association of Canadian Clubs and had invited Pratt to make a tour of the western provinces. In 1936, as chairman of the Canadian Radio League (1930–4), he would help found the Canadian Broadcasting Corporation.

TO LORNE PIERCE

Bobcaygeon, Ont.

August 4, 1927

My dear Lorne,

I wonderfully appreciate your cordial letter.[50] You are one of a half-dozen whose judgment I value most highly. I have often stated my own admiration for your own productivity and refinement of style backed by your scholarship. I am proud to have you as my friend because I believe there are deep strands of nobility in your character and general outlook on life.

I would so like to have you take a run up here sometime in August if you could manage it. I wrote Spry inviting him up any time between the 8th and 12th. I am keen to know how the itinerary is progressing. He is to be in Toronto for the 8th attending the Peace Conference.[51]

I am giving two lecture recitals at the Muskoka Assembly[52] the latter middle part of the month, then I come back to Bob until the second week in September. I hope you are taking a *restful* holiday though I daresay your notion of a holiday is an excursion through five centuries of Romance literature.

The very best
Ned.

---

50 Pierce had written enthusiastically about *ID*. (See the letter to Pierce, 15 July 1927 [p. 72].)

51 Probably one of several conferences sponsored by the Women's International League for peace and Freedom.

52 The meeting hall in Muskoka where the CAA was holding its second 'literary summer school.' The first was in 1926.

TO LORNE PIERCE

Bobcaygeon, Ont.

August 10 1927

My dear Lorne,

I sent Mr Spry a list of biographical details[53] about a month ago. I wonder if he received them or not. Really there isn't very much to say. Born and brought up in Newfoundland, my father John Pratt a Methodist Clergyman in that Country. My grandfather on my mother's side was Captain William Knight, a well known mariner associated with the sealing industry for more than forty years.

Left Newfoundland in the early twenties (age)[54] came to Victoria College, University of Toronto and graduated in Arts in 1911. Degree of Doctor of Philosophy 1917.[55] Now On the Staff in English Literature in Victoria College. Visited Newfoundland periodically in the summer vacation to be with his mother who has recently died.[56]

The rest you know – Leave out ecclesiastical lingo and *professor*, horrid word!

Ned.

TO WILLIAM ARTHUR DEACON

Bobcaygeon, Ont.

August 27, 1927

My dear Billy,

Your letter came this afternoon and I greatly appreciate your kindness and consideration.[57] It was your good old self that was writing. I have been looking into

53 For a publicity 'flyer' advertising his western tour of Canadian Clubs.

54 He was actually twenty-five at the time. He often implied that he was younger than he was, giving his birth year as 1883 instead of 1882.

55 Following this, 'Associate Professor' is scored through, perhaps to discourage organizers from referring to him as 'professor.' See the final paragraph.

56 He had visited St John's only twice between leaving for Toronto in 1907 and his mother's death in 1926 – in 1916 and 1925.

57 On 25 August, Deacon had written Pratt a long, generally conciliatory letter, requesting a poem for the Fall Literary Supplement to *Saturday Night* and enquiring about 'The Iron Door' (*EJP: CP* 1.204) of which he had heard rumours. It was the first correspondence between them since Deacon had written his harsh review of *Titans* in December 1926. (See letter to Lorne Pierce, 2 January 1927 [pp. 69–70].)

some short poems to select for your Supplement but most of them possess a tragic cast that would unfit them for your bright columns. You remember I submitted a few of them last year and you decided quite rightly, – with my concurrence, – that they were somewhat too sombre. I intend, in the future, (this of course as the mood strikes me) to indulge the lighter lyrical moments. I am, however, submitting one called 'Cherries'[58] not yet published in any form, nor offered for publication, but read at my recital last winter, which might fit in, but I am not sure of the length of its lines and stanzas as being adjustable to your space. If it does not so fit, feel perfectly at ease in sending it back, as I will understand.

I would like to deal with the Iron Door at some length. You remember in a couple of conversations last Spring, once in a walk down to your office, and again at a dinner with Burpee[59] that I had in mind the construction of a poem different from anything I had ever done. The theme came to me at the time of my mother's death last December. It originated in a dream where my mother, who was a woman of the profoundest faith in the life to come, was standing before a colossal door – the door of Death – and expecting without any fear of denial whatsoever, instant and full admission into the future state where she believed other members of her family had already entered. This was the nucleus of the poem. From there I elaborated it into a general conception of the problem of Immortality, starting with the feeling of despair and apparent inevitability which faces one at a grave-side. That is, from a particular experience, I tried to universalize the idea. In front of the door are gathered a vast multitude and a number of individuals emerge who present their cases to the Unseen Warders, or God or the Governor of the Universe whoever he may be, demanding some information of what is going on, on the other side. All but one – the last – are drawn from persons I had known in life. The last one, to my mind, sums up the problem, partly biological, partly environmental, of injustice and inequality in the moral order, and she presents the case in its glaring enigma.

The first case is that of the naive simplicity of a child who relies upon a father to unravel the knots. The second is that of a rugged seamen who with a stark sense of justice asks the 'unknown admiral' if the great traditions of the service might be fairly assumed to prevail on the wastes of the hinter sea, if such a sea might be assumed to exist. There is no cringing in his attitude whatsoever; he feels he has the right to ask and to demand it. The third – that of my own mother – represents a large number of people who believe implicitly in the essential soundness of the heart of the Universe and who impute to God only the

58 'Cherries' (*EJP: CP* 1.203) was published in *Saturday Night*, 1 October 1927, 1.

59 Lawrence J. Burpee (1873–1946) was a civil servant, but also director of the short-lived Graphic Press. A man of literary and historical interests, he is best known as the author of *The Search for the Western Sea: The Story of the Exploration of North-Western America* (Toronto: Musson, 1908). He was national president of the CAA in 1924-25.

same fair principles which they realise in their own honest natures. The next is a young man who gave up health and prime and life in a futile attempt to save an unknown life when there was not a human eye to stimulate or encourage the sacrifice. Then two more speak.[60] One a searcher after beauty in all its forms in this life who is puzzled that Death should apparently negate the value of the quest; and another a searcher after truth – a Hardyesque type (or Bertrand Russell type) – who meets with disillusion at the end, yet exhibits a noble stoicism when faced with what looks like extinction. Then comes the last with the most poignant and tragic appeal.

In order to make the psychological contrast as sharp as possible I put in a stanza or rather section describing the desolation of the world at this point – to give edge and relief to what follows. To my mind it would be a cardinal artistic and moral blunder to end it in complete gloom. The setting I think requires the conclusion, but I did not feel, on the other hand, that the requirements would be met by anything like a conventional heaven, harps or angels or such outworn paraphernalia. The only demand I make is that there shall be life and light with continued life effort on the other side. Hence I never see inside the door. I only judge by the reflection on the faces of human beings and by certain sounds which intermittently break through that there are vast stretches beyond. I do not aim at solutions. I only wanted to give an imaginative and emotional interpretation of what I feel my self because I have never done anything which put the same compulsion on me for expression. I do not know if I thoroughly succeeded. I simply wrote as I felt.

The reasons why I did not give you more details on my scheme are vaguely these. I only finished it a few days before I left for Bobcaygeon, that is in its entirety. The general conception was submitted to Macmillans who decided that they would publish it on the first draft. A few of my friends were interested in it and asked for a reading which I gave. They were somewhat enthusiastic about it and urged immediate publication with some changes of lines etc. I did not hand it to you at the time – though I would dearly love to have done so – because of a natural reticence against appearing to influence a reviewer and I know how you must be embarrassed with authors coming to your office in advance of publication.[61] I wanted you to make up your own judgment independently and I am writing this tonight because of your kindly interest expressed in your letter today. I had a very few typed copies, two of which went to the

60 These two characters represent himself and Lorne Pierce. (See the note to 'the 2nd and 3rd stanzas on page 4' in the letter to Pierce, 15 July 1927 [p. 72].)

61 In 1923, Deacon had chastised Pratt for bringing a copy of *NV* to him to be reviewed.

publisher's. In fact this one which I now send to you is the only one I have left and I gladly give it to you. The poem is in the galleys and I am not in immediate need of it. As for a section in the Supplement, I scarcely think a dozen lines could be taken out independently, though if some introduction could be given the sections from – *And at this darkest moment as I dreamed* to 'new lights and shadows leaped upon the dial' might conveniently be inserted. This of course at your own discretion.

Regarding the itinerary the developments are these: Nearly all the Canadian Club branches have ratified the arrangements of the Executive, though I am not yet in possession of the programme with dates etc. That will be in in a few days and I can let you have a copy. I start on the 11th of September beginning with Chapleau, going on to Keewatin, Winnipeg, Edmonton, Olds, Calgary, Revelstoke, Vancouver, Victoria, Kamloops, Moose Jaw, back to Winnipeg and other towns intervening. The trip is exclusively under the sponsorship of the Can. Club though in some cases the Authors' Branches have cooperated. The C.P.R. made out the itinerary and have granted transportation both for my self and Vi. I get back the first week in October. It is a poetry recital (my own).

So that's that, old boy. I expect to be in Toronto about the 6th and will see you.

The book appears sometime in late September in two Editions a limited autographed of 100 copies selling at 2.50 and a trade of 1.25. 1000 copies.

With best wishes to yourself, Sal
& family

from Vi and me.
Ned Pratt

P.S. The rush in September will probably prevent me from reviewing a book for the Section[62] but I will be ready for the next one if you wish it.

N.

62 Deacon edited the literary section of *CB*.

TO LORNE PIERCE

Vancouver

Oct. 2, 1927

My dear Lorne,

This has been the experience of my life.[63] Enthusiasm unbounded every where. Hospitality unparalleled. I gave the audience a good deal of ' Newfoundland Verse' to vindicate your own splendid cooperation. I shall never forget the fine idealism of your nature, and your most trusted friendship. 'The Iron Door' took the best of all at Calgary.[64] I did not [have] sufficient time at the luncheons to read it. But the few individuals to whom I read it thought it my best. You are greatly loved out here. Many remembrances of your visit. You are always welcome out West. And I came across many little tokens of your interest in me.

I am sending you a clipping from the Vancouver Star, an editorial. It's typical of the appreciations everywhere. I am glad for the sake of yourself and Spry. Spry knew it was an experiment and I am glad to have vindicated it to some extent.

I will be back by middle of October.

Affectionately
Ned P.

TO CHARLES G.D. ROBERTS

Dec. 15, 1927

Dear Old Charlie:

Come back to us soon. A stag the other night talked kindly of you and yearned for your spontaneity and full heartedness. Thanks for 'The Vagrant.'[65] I knew

63 Pratt had started his tour of Western Canada on 12 September. (See the letter to Deacon, 31 August 1927 for his itinerary [p. 77].)

64 In a previous letter to Pierce, 24 September (*EJP: Web*), he expressed delight at 'a capacity audience in the Palliser.'

65 *The Vagrant of Time*, a small book of Roberts's verse published that year by Ryerson Press.

most of the poems before, delightful and musical in the extreme. Here's luck to you in Vancouver.[66]

Boys send love.
Ned.

HARRIET MONROE[67]

Feb. 6, 1928

Miss Harriet Monroe,
Poetry,
Chicago.

Dear Miss Monroe,

I submitted a little batch of poems last year to 'Poetry' and your reply was – 'They nearly got in but we were dreadfully over-crowded.' This is hoping that the Mississippi has subsided a little.[68]

Yours sincerely
E.J. Pratt

66 Roberts, as national president of the CAA, was giving a series of lectures on Canadian literature at the University of British Columbia.

67 American poet Harriet Monroe (1860–1936) founded the influential Chicago-based *Poetry: A Magazine of Verse* in 1912 and edited it until her death. Often referred to as *Poetry* (Chicago), it provided an outlet for many modernist poets who felt compelled to break with established tradition. Pratt repeatedly submitted poems to *Poetry*, but none was accepted until 1941.

68 Monroe's reply to his latest submission was a scribbled note across this letter: 'Ret'd – but pretty good.'

TO LORNE PIERCE

March 5, 1928

My Dear Old Lorne,

I received this letter from your friend Ella Reynolds[69] yesterday. I had acknowledged her review of the Iron Door and had mentioned you to her. The enclosed is lovely isn't it?

I am now reading your Canadian Literature[70] and finding it extremely lucid and comprehensive. I advertised it everywhere during the last month of my itinerary,[71] and I am sure I secured many individual sales for you, in Sudbury, North Bay, Montreal, etc. etc. where I have been addressing Canadian Clubs. You have done a scholarly thing in your own *finished* style. Eayrs thinks you have a *real pen*. Thanks for the lovely page devoted to your humble servant.

By the way, Mrs Bothwell[72] has just written Eayrs in which she says that Bothwell's last message before death was: 'Tell Pratt that the Iron Door is opening for me.' He quoted many of the lines with his last breath. The news nearly overwhelmed me when I heard it.

Well, old chap, when am I going to see you again? I have had the most enthusiastic reception all over the cities of Ontario, even in places where I have had to clean up the dirt and smear of W.M.[73] He pursues you and me and Roberts like a hound. I strike against it in every place I go, but people are getting wise to his reptilian ways.

Ned

69 Ella Julia Reynolds (1881–1970) worked at the *Hamilton Spectator* from 1912 to 1945, writing music and theatre reviews as well as the book column 'Under the Study Lamp,' and a weekly feature, 'Wren's Nest,' under the pen name Jenny Wren.

70 Throughout the 1920s, Pierce had been using his position as editor of Ryerson Press to encourage the development of Canadian identity by publishing a series called *Makers of Canadian Literature* (1923), and most recently the essay *Outline of Canadian Literature (French and English)* (Toronto: Ryerson, 1927).

71 After his recital tour of the Canadian Clubs in northwestern Ontario and the western provinces in fall 1927, he was asked to complete the 'National circuit.' He had just returned from the first leg of his tour of eastern Canada (*EJP: MY*, 28–30).

72 The widow of Austin Bothwell, who had recently died at forty-two.

73 Wilson MacDonald had made a practice of spreading malicious rumours about perceived rivals and enemies. (See the letter to Pierce, 20 January 1927 [p. 71].)

TO LORNE PIERCE

April 11, 1928

My Dear Lorne,

I am sending you the manuscripts of a couple of poems with my brotherly affection. The first is the London Mercury one – 'The Decision,'[74] and the other I have just written called 'Blind.'

You remember my mother who was up in Toronto three years ago for an operation upon her eyes.[75] She spent the winter with me after the operation which really meant the removal of one and the practical closing of the other. I think 'Blind'[76] is one of the best short lyrics I have ever written. Anyway, old boy, I am proud to have you to send a copy to.

Yours sincerely
Ned Pratt

I am enclosing two letters of appreciation from Professor John MacNaughton[77] and Laurence Binyon.[78] Will you return them to me as they are valuable.

Ned.

74 (*EJP: CP* 1.67) First published in *AV* 48 (November 1923): 220; it appeared in *LM* 17 (January 1928): 244.

75 Fanny Pratt had been in Toronto for surgery of a cancerous tumour in one eye in the winter of 1922.

76 (*EJP: CP* 1.217) First published in *AV* 55 (December 1930), 23

77 MacNaughton (1858–1943) had come to University College, Toronto, as professor of classics in 1917 after teaching at Queen's University and McGill. He was known in the 1920s for his trenchant essays in defence of the humanities in *CF*.

78 Binyon (1869–1943) was keeper of Oriental prints and drawings at the British Museum from 1913 to 1933. He published several books of poetry and books on art, and is best known for his war elegy 'For the Fallen' (1914). The Pratts had entertained him in November 1926 when he lectured in Toronto on 'T'ang Art.' Pratt described him as 'one of the most solemn men of my acquaintance.'

TO RAYMOND KNISTER[79]

Oct 6, 1928

My dear Raymond,

I want to congratulate you upon that article in the Saturday Night Supplement this week.[80] I think it is sound and temperate and of the kind this country needs with all its log-rolling and ballyhoo. It is an antidote to the disease of thinking that every poem written in this land merits comparison with Shelley. Not one of us with our present out-put can be described as 'great,' in the *great* sense of the term. We need to put more fundamental brain work into the structures.

I trust your new volume[81] will bring in the shekels.

Yours sincerely,
Ned Pratt.

I am sending you my most recent volumes with my compliments.

N.

TO LORNE PIERCE

Dec. 12 1928

My Dear Lorne,

Exceedingly good of you old top to do this.[82] I am sending along a Liverpool Post Review[83] which you may return later.

79 Knister (1889–1932) was born in Kent County and attended the University of Toronto and Iowa State University. In the mid-1920s, while publishing verse and short stories in American magazines, he worked in Toronto as a freelance journalist. He wrote two novels, *White Narcissus* (Toronto: Macmillan; London: Cape, 1929) and *My Star Predominant* (Toronto: Ryerson, 1934) based on the life of John Keats which was published posthumously. He died by drowning – perhaps a suicide.

80 'The Poetic Muse in Canada,' *Saturday Night* 6 (October 1928).

81 Knister had edited *Canadian Short Stories* (Toronto: Macmillan, 1928).

82 Pierce was preparing a statement supporting Pratt's election to the Royal Society of Canada. He was not elected until 1930.

83 His brother Art in Liverpool was instrumental in having several of Pratt's books reviewed in the *Liverpool Post Review*.

You know of course that the 'Ice-Floes' is on the Newfoundland Curriculum[84] in 'Shorter Poems' edited by W.J. Alexander of U of T.

There is one thing only I wish to say. You know of course that The Witches Brew was *not* published in the London Mercury.[85] It was accepted by Squire for publication but on account of its great length it was postponed from time to time until the publishers went ahead and put it in book form. Squire as you know kept Scott's[86] poems three years late. You need not mention the Mercury matter as it might be misunderstood.

When am I going to see you again. Will you be at the A & L annual?[87]

Best of love
Ned.

TO PELHAM EDGAR

Bobcaygeon, Ont.

August 6 [1929].

Dear old boy,

I was delighted to get your letter yesterday, but mark ye, it was a heluva long delay. I put it down to New York humidity.[88] Glad to know you are feeling fit despite the torpors. I didn't know Robert[89] was with you. What luck! And still what luck if the three of us could get together for six weeks next summer with the sessions[90] covering our financial perplexities. I hope the two of you can work it for me and that you will be repeating. I feel confident that you are meeting with the same

84 Pratt was mistaken.

85 See the letter to Pierce, 24 September 1924 (pp. 55–6).

86 Duncan Campbell Scott.

87 The Arts and Letters Club's annual banquet, held in late December.

88 Edgar was teaching summer session at Columbia University.

89 American-born Robert Finch (1900–95) taught French at the University of Toronto from 1928 to 1968. He was an accomplished poet, painter, and musician. His early poems were published in magazines, as well as in *New Provinces* (1936), the first Canadian anthology of 'new poetry.' His first collection, *Poems* (Toronto: Oxford, 1946), won the Governor General's Medal. He later published several more volumes, including *Dover Beach Revisited* (Toronto: University of Toronto Press, 1961) and *Acis in Oxford* (Toronto: Macmillan, 1961), which also won the Governor General's Award. He was elected to the Royal Society in 1963 and received the Lorne Pierce Medal in 1968.

90 Summer school sessions.

success as at Chicago.[91] The 'personal touch' Pelham! I am going to try it myself: it saves night-sweats; though I do not hope to equal you in that respect.

My left foot is like Gibraltar.[92] It has been my one and only constant since I left you. My driver never has gone back on me, but as a damnable offset my mashie has become so abominable (even with the open face) that I am almost losing interest in the game. The other day I went out for a practice, put down fifty balls and sent at least twenty of them at right angles to my direction. Some of the buggers even went behind me – utterly inexplicable. I got so disgusted that I haven't been out since. Strange game!

Have spent most of the summer up here at the Cottage. Finished my Shakespeare.[93] The work was valuable to myself as I had to cover a lot of new ground, – comparatively new – and master it, even though the final presentation was somewhat elementary. I have soon to start on The Merchant.[94]

We have a maid here who comes mornings. That gives Vi a chance to do her editorial work. Did I tell you she had been appointed as Editor of a little Missionary paper called World Friends.[95] She likes it and is being paid a small honorarium for it. It takes her to Toronto every alternate week, so I am left with the two kids, Claire and Kathleen (the Fresh Air child).[96] Still the maid stays all day when Vi is gone, so it isn't so much a worry.

Yes, the publication of the Roosevelt[97] is postponed until February. That's too bad in a way though it won't interfere with the October 17 recital.[98] That will come off with the P.B.[99] in front seats at all costs. Here are the facts. First of all I haven't it completed yet as the editorial work and other things climbed on top of me in July. But Hughie[100] had mentioned my intentions to Harpers and to Macmillans of U.S., and they were anxious to take a look at the poem. I took a chance with the unfinished job though it was much against my grain to

91 Edgar had taught summer session in Chicago the previous year.

92 A reference to his golfing stance.

93 Pratt had been engaged by Hugh Eayrs of Macmillan Canada to assist in editing several plays by Shakespeare for use in high schools. Pratt wrote the general introductions.

94 Shakespeare's *The Merchant of Venice*.

95 A monthly publication of the United Church of Canada for young readers. Viola Pratt would edit the magazine for the next twenty-six years.

96 Children from the poorer districts of Toronto were placed in camps or private summer homes for summer vacations. The program was subsidized by the *Toronto Daily Star*'s 'Fresh Air Fund.'

97 His long poem, 'The Roosevelt and the Antinoë' (*EJP: CP* 1.219), had been scheduled for publication in the fall of 1929.

98 The event was actually scheduled for 16 October at Hart House.

99 'Poker Brethren,' a group of their intimate friends who gathered to play poker fairly regularly during the academic term.

100 Hugh Eayrs.

let a thing out prematurely as you know. The introduction and the conclusion weren't done and the main part was unrevised. However I sent it to Harpers[101] and another copy to Macmillans. Harpers (the Monthly Editor, the Publicity Editor and one associate) read it and made me an immediate offer for Spring publication as the Fall lists were out six weeks ago. Quite enthusiastic they were. Next week comes an offer from Macmillan. Brett[102] had sent the fragment on to his Reader – Edwin Arlington Robinson.[103] I saw Robinson's report two or three days ago – the most whole-hearted commitment I have ever received in my life. His first sentence was – 'The Roosevelt & the Antinoe knocked me on to my beam-ends,' and the rest of the page was without reserve. Macmillan before Robinson's report had offered 10% royalty. It was refused by Hugh. He next offered 10% on 2500, 12 ½ up to 5000, 15 thereafter. Hugh is now holding off to jockey Harpers against Macs. This is all done within the last three or four days. If you happen to see any of Brett's outfit down there don't mention anything as I am not supposed to know the Reader or his report yet.

In the meantime I am working to complete it. Did I tell you that I had a long interview with the American Consul at Toronto who gave me a lot of assistance most cordially. He wanted to know all about the design. He gave me the sea-articles signed by the seamen & master and I am working the oath of discipline etc. in with actual phrases taken from the articles underlined.[104] I think a strong

---

101 Harper & Brothers, an American publishing firm. In addition to books, it published *Harper's Magazine*, *Harper's Weekly*, and *Harper's Bazaar*.

102 George Platt Brett Sr. (1858–1936), president of the Macmillan Company in New York.

103 (1869–1935) American poet probably best remembered for his poem 'Miniver Cheevy.' Robinson won the Pulitzer Prize three times, for *Collected Poems* (1922), *The Man Who Died Twice* (1925), and *Tristram* (1928). His *Man against the Sky* (New York: Macmillan, 1916) may have influenced Pratt's *ID*.

104 The technique is used in the second verse paragraph of 'The Roosevelt and the Antinoë':

> In the Commissioner's room it was agreed
> Between the Master and the mariners,
> That as the men received *per month or run*
> Their wage in dollars and were guaranteed
> By statutes of the State that they might draw
> Their scale of rations – *bread and meat and water,*
> *Lemon and lime* and such *prescribed by law*,
> With *means of warmth in weather*; they, the crew
> Should pledge themselves to conduct, *faithful, true,*
> And orderly, in honest, sober manner;
> At all times in their duties diligent;
> To the Master's lawful word obedient,
> In everything relating to the vessel –
> Safety of passengers, cargo and sore,
> Whether on board, in boats, or on the shore. (ll. 13–27; *EJP: CP* 1.219–20)

dramatic point can be achieved there. Brett also offered to work out a special edition for the steamships (apart from trade).

So there it lies. I am putting other things aside now to complete it, at least to get it in shape for October 17. As it isn't to be published till early New Year, the final touching can be left till later. I am awfully anxious to go over it with you. I would much prefer to read it to you personally as a whole than send a fragment by mail. In any case I have nothing typed at hand yet.

Vi and I extend the most cordial invitation to you & Mrs P to visit us at Bobcaygeon on your return from Digby.[105] Will you let us know well in advance when we might expect you? Then I will order a duck dinner and we will put in some glorious nights. Will get special birch billets for the fire place. Could Robert come up then do you think? Will he be still holidaying?

Here's to you old darling.
Ned.

TO WILLIAM ARTHUR DEACON

'The Rookell and the Antinoe'

Oct. 11 1929

Dear Billy,

Would you accept a couple of complimentaries to my Recital in Hart House Theatre[106] Oct 16? Wednesday evening? I am presenting the new poem now finished 'The Roosevelt and the Antinoë.' It was too bad I couldn't get it completed in time for the fall lists, and the American Macmillans are publishing it in January. But the evening goes ahead. H.J. Davis of the English Dept. of the University is reading the Cachalot first, then a professional contralto singer, Miss Ruby Moss, is singing some sea-songs, then I come on with the R & A.

Yours sincerely,
Ned Pratt

105 The Edgars planned to spend a week or longer at Digby, Nova Scotia, their way home from New York.

106 Hart House is a student centre and residence on the campus of University College, University of Toronto.

TO LORNE PIERCE

[Oct. 1929]

The funeral service on the deck of the Roosevelt which is the climax of the poem had its germ in that little cabin in which you slept last summer.[107] This section takes 100 lines of the poem.[108]

Ned P.

TO WILLIAM ARTHUR DEACON

Oct. 21 [1929]

My dear Billy,

I want to tell you how much I appreciated your comments in the 'Mail' on Saturday.[109] It was sterling encouragement and it put heart into me for further work. It was people of your stamp that put the calibre in the audience the other night and I felt honoured by your presence. I am sending along a copy of my home paper.[110] You will notice how your article on 'Mechanisation,' Page 2, impressed the Editor. I hope your syndicated work[111] succeeds as it richly deserves.

Yours very sincerely,
Ned P.

107 Pratt had built a small 'summer house' as a place for quiet and seclusion for writing near the lakeshore on his Bobcaygeon property. It also contained sleeping accommodations.

108 See *RA*, ll. 544–633 (*EJP: CP* 1.235–8).

109 In spring 1928 Deacon had become literary editor of the Toronto *Mail and Empire*. On Saturday, 19 October, he had published a highly complimentary note on Pratt's Hart House recital of 16 October.

110 The *St John's Daily News* (12 October 1929) reprinted a column by Deacon entitled 'Declares the World Is Over Mechanised.'

111 Deacon had begun a national syndication of book reviews in the brief interval between being fired by *Saturday Night* in April and hired by the *Mail and Empire*.

TO PELHAM EDGAR

July 17, 1930

Dear old Pelham,

It was indeed refreshing to get your letter. Not a day has passed since you left but you have been in my thoughts. I missed you greatly last Wednesday evening. As you know I am lecturing in the Summer Session[112] and 'baching it' at the house. I felt rather lonely for my old friends so I drummed up a monster stag at my house, the largest ever. That afternoon I played in a foursome at York Downs[113] – Malcolm W,[114] J.S. MacLean,[115] Arthur Meighen[116] and I, and we decided to end up at 25 Tullis Drive. I rounded up post-haste fourteen men, two poker games of Seven – Edgar MacInnes,[117] Speakman,[118] J.H. MacDonald,[119] E.K. Brown,[120] Eric

112 At Victoria College.

113 A golf course in northwest Toronto. Pratt was a member.

114 Malcolm Wallace (1873–1960), born in Essex County, Ontario, and a graduate of the universities of Toronto and Chicago, was professor of English and head of department at University College, Toronto. His major scholarly work was his *Life of Sir Philip Sidney* (Cambridge: Cambridge University Press, 1915). He and Pratt were golf and stag-party cronies for more than thirty years.

115 James Stanley McLean (1876–1954), a graduate of the University of Toronto, was founder and long-time president of Canada Packers. He and Pratt were good friends, but never intimate 'cronies.' Here Pratt misspells his surname.

116 Meighen (1874–1960) held cabinet posts under Prime Minister Robert Borden before serving two brief terms as prime minister in the 1920s. Defeated by Mackenzie King in 1926, he quit politics until appointed to the Senate in 1932. He later settled in Toronto as a Bay Street financier.

117 Again Pratt misspells the name. McInnis (1899–1973) was professor of history at the University of Toronto. The author of many publications on historical subjects, he twice won the Governor General's Medal for non-fiction.

118 Horace B. Speakman (b. 1893 in Lancashire, England) was professor of zymnology (the science of fermentation) at the University of Toronto from 1919 to 1928, when he was appointed the first director of the Ontario Research Foundation.

119 The 'H' should be an 'F.' John F. MacDonald, born in 1878 in Huntington, Quebec and a graduate of Queen's and Chicago universities, was professor of English at Queen's (1908-25) and University College, Toronto (1925-48). He was one of several editors who worked with Pratt on the Macmillan Shakespeare series. (See the note to 'my Shakespeare' in the letter to Pelham Edgar, 6 August 1929 [p. 84].)

120 Edward Killoran Brown (1905–51) was born and educated in Toronto before attending the Sorbonne in Paris. He taught English at University College, Toronto (1929–35, 1937–41), the University of Manitoba (1935–7), Cornell University (1941–4), and the University of Chicago (1944–51). Author of several scholarly works, including the Governor General's Award–winning *On Canadian Poetry* (Toronto: Ryerson 1943), he was an editor of the *UTQ* from 1932 to 1941. He and Pratt were close friends for more than twenty years.

Arthur[121] and so on and so on. We didn't leave till 2 o'clock – the latest hour J.S. Mac spent away from home in months. We had a snack at midnight. O'Keefe's[122] & Sandwiches and lobster (Newfoundland). We sang the National Anthem, toasted you and several other absentees. One of the jokes of the evening was the fact that all the cars had to be parked up near Yonge St. The immortal red light still shining in front of Tullis Drive 'Road under repair.' It is still there and will be for the next ten years. Wallace remarked on turning the corner that he always knew Ned's street from the red light; he never had to look for the name on the corner stone.

Well here I am Summer Sessioning. Two lectures one in the morning & one from 3 to 4. It gives me a good deal of time for golf. My game varies, the score being in the late nineties. Nothing to crow over. I get up to Bobcaygeon every Friday evening, returning on the Sunday special. By August 12 the job will be over and I hike north for nearly a month. Claire is quite well now, having got rid of the last whoop about two weeks ago.[123] She has to face her ankle operation[124] next October I fear. It could be postponed till the spring but I see no advantage in that. I am grateful in any case for the improvement in her general health.

I am glad that you are enjoying Los Angeles.[125] The climate is ideal for you, fine weather and moderate temperatures with no rain. Are you finding time for your book?[126] I would like to see you through with it for your own financial well-being.

Most of the P.B.[127] are out of town. Hughie[128] is in England – He hasn't written me yet, the recreant! I wonder how our virile society will get along next year. I fear the horizon in a vague way; do you not? There is nothing startling to tell this time. It is the season for the doldrums.

Lovingly
Ned

---

121 Born in New Zealand and educated in England, Arthur (1898–1982) was professor of architectural design at the University of Toronto, and a member of the architectural firm Fleury, Arthur and Calvert.

122 A brand of beer.

123 Claire had whooping cough that spring.

124 To correct the effects of polio. (See the note to 'Claire is much improved' in the letter to Arthur Phelps, 3 January 1926 [p. 63].)

125 Edgar was teaching summer session at the University of California.

126 Edgar was doing research for a book which was published in 1933 as *The Art of the Novel: From 1700 to the Present Time* (New York: Macmillan).

127 'Poker Brethren.'

128 Hugh Eayrs.

TO NEWTON MACTAVISH[129]

Dec. 15, 1930

My dear Newton,

I intended writing two or three days ago but postponed it thinking I should have a chance to finish your manuscript and thereby include my judgment upon it within my general letter. But as I have been so rushed since my return I shall have to forgo now the pleasure which I know awaits me a little later on.

I want first of all to express my deepest appreciation, – which rises into affection, for your wonderful hospitality during the three days of my stay in Ottawa.[130] It was marvellous, and nothing less. Dear Kate and Maxine[131] might very well pose as models of grace and charm. How they entertained on Monday evening! They simply floated through the rooms. And Mackenzie King![132] Here on my desk this morning are two letters from him. What a personality! Your invitation of the ex-prime minister to dine was a great honour to me.

I have been sounding the praises of the MacTavish household ever since my return: in the University and without. Wait till you come to the city here in February. Have no breakfast or lunch on the day of the 'Stag.'

Thanks for the 'nightie.'[133] My wife roared when it came. I didn't tell her that I left it behind and when she opened the parcel and saw its contents the house rocked with mirth.

My trip to Perth was successful. I spoke twice there, once at the Commencement and the next morning at the Collegiate. I returned to Toronto Thursday evening, arriving just in time to get to the theatre before the rise of the curtain. My trip did me good. It will stand out as one of the great journeys of my Canadian life and so much of it was due to 'Sweet Kate,' Maxine & your beloved

129 (1877–1941). A journalist and art historian who wrote for the Toronto *Globe* (1898–1906) and edited the *Canadian Magazine* (1906–26) before becoming a member of the Canadian Civil Service Commission (1926–32). He was a founder of the Arts and Letters Club and a contributor to the *Encyclopedia of Canada* (6 vols, ed. William Stewart Wallace [Toronto: University Associates of Canada, 1935–7]).

130 Pratt had been on a speaking tour (8–11 December) to Ottawa and Perth, Ontario.

131 MacTavish's wife and daughter.

132 Liberal prime minister of Canada from 1921 to 1930 (except for three months in 1926), King lost the 1930 election to Conservative R.B. Bennett, but he would regain the office and serve from 1935 to 1948.

133 Pratt frequently slept in a homemade nightshirt.

Self. Hughie Eayrs and I had a stag chat with each other yesterday with you as the inspiring subject. He loves you.

With the best of joy peace love
and prosperity to the three of you.
Ned Pratt

TO AUDREY ALEXANDRA BROWN[134]

Jan. 30, 31

Dear Miss Brown,

I have just read your 'Laodamia'[135] in manuscript and have been so impressed by it that I decided to send you a word of appreciation. It contains more beautiful description to the page than anything I have seen in many a day. It is a poem of distinction and it ought to create a widespread interest upon its appearance from the publishers. I have followed your poems now for three or four years and it was no surprise to me to find your literary talent issue in 'Laodamia.' Again my appreciation and sense of delight.

Yours sincerely
E.J. Pratt

TO NEWTON MACTAVISH

June 3, 1931

Dear old Newton

This is to extend a most robust invitation to you to have a 'stag' with me some evening during the Authors Week June 22-29 in Toronto.[136] I do hope you will

---

134 Born in Nanaimo, BC, Audrey Brown (1904–98) had only four years of formal schooling and was largely self-educated. She began publishing poems at sixteen, finding a mentor in Pelham Edgar, and produced six collections of verse between 1931 and 1948, including *A Dryad in Nanaimo* (Toronto: Macmillan, 1931). In 1944, she was the first woman writer to receive the Lorne Pierce Medal for 'achievement in imaginative and critical literature.'

135 Her best-known poem, published in *A Dryad in Nanaimo*.

136 The annual convention of the CAA.

be able to be present part of the time at least. I am on the Entertainment Committee and I think of you as representing Authorship East of Toronto. Hughie[137] and Mell Hammond[138] et al will be on hand.

Saw your photo in the Star the other day with announcement of your election as President of Ottawa Branch. Your mug was rather austere in the picture as if you had sighted Currelly[139] in the offing.

Much love
Ned.

Affectionately to your wife and daughter.

N.

TO WILLIAM ARTHUR DEACON

Halifax Club
Halifax, NS.

July 11th, 1931

Dear Bill,

The Geographic[140] arrived all right. I enjoyed your article thoroughly. It was a Deacon issue and no mistake. Those cuts possessed a great deal of romance for me for I love rummaging away back into the past. I am enjoying my visit here very much – Two lectures a day one in Contemporary drama and one on Canadian literature. The Course lasts six weeks and the whole School is attended by no less than seven hundred students. I find Munro[141] an excellent fellow and I am already making a lot of friends. I find some time for writing and the very fact of having the ocean smell in my nostrils every day is worth

137 Hugh Eayrs.

138 Melvin O. Hammond (1876–1934) was literary editor of the Toronto *Globe* for many years, the author of several books, an accomplished photographer, and a collector of paintings and photographs.

139 Charles Trick Currelly (1876–1959), Methodist minister and professor of archaeology at the University of Toronto, was the first curator of the Royal Ontario Museum (1907–46).

140 *The Canadian Geographical Journal*, May 1931, 335–76) contained a long historical essay by Deacon entitled 'Toronto' which was illustrated with numerous photographic 'cuts.'

141 Dr Henry Fraser Munro, superintendent of education for Nova Scotia and director of the school, had given Pratt his appointment in the summer school.

three times the dustiness of home. It acts like strychnine. Best regards to Sal and family. Most sincerely

Ned.

TO WILLIAM ARTHUR DEACON

N.S. Summer School

July 17, 1931.

Dear Bill,

Thanks very much for the clipping, though I had read your article at the Halifax Club which subscribes to the 'Mail.'[142] I showed it to Chief Justice Chisholm[143] with whom I had dinner the other evening. His comment was: 'Now I know where to go for funds when I am down and out.' He thought it was an able presentation of the authors' case.

I read McFarlane's[144] letter to the Mail of the Tuesday issue and he intimates that he is a voluminous author – some twenty, I think, of publications. Does he mean novels? He was rather high-hat in his general indictment but you scored splendidly. I fear you placed my business sagacity on too high a level. I wish I had the bargaining touch personally. All the credit coming to me from that direction should rather go to my good friend Hughie[145] who worked both Harpers and Macmillans[146] when he was in New York with the manuscript. I would have accepted the initial terms on my own. He has been a wonderful advisor and a good friend, bless his fat stomach.

I am enjoying the trip here very much – meeting princely fellows all the time. Today I am going with a group of men to Antigonish and to the Marjaree[147] for a day's fishing.

---

142 The Toronto *Mail and Empire.*

143 Sir Joseph Chisholm (1863–1950), chief justice of Nova Scotia.

144 Leslie McFarlane (1902–77), born in Haleybury, Ontario, published many popular stories in journals, as well as books of juvenile fiction, in the Hardy Boys series under the pseudonym Franklin W. Dixon. He and Pratt met at the Toronto Writers' Club and became good friends. His letter to the *Mail and Empire* (14 July) was an attack on the Canadian Authors Association.

145 Hugh Eayrs.

146 See the letter to Pelham Edgar, 6 August 1929 (p. 85).

147 [*sic*]. The Margaree River.

Hope you are having a holiday yourself. You certainly need a vacation considering your close application to your work.

Congratulations again for your splendid protagonism of the craft.

Ned

TO GEORGE HERBERT CLARKE

Jan.12, 1932

Dear Clarke:

Thanks for your warm welcome note. I have been looking over my dates and I find Tuesday and Thursday Jan. 19 and 21, Feb. 2 and 4 available.[148] But as we are so badly understaffed it will be impossible for me to stay overnight. Auger[149] has gone to Chicago for the winter which puts extra lectures on me: hence I must leave on the 12.45 CNR. getting to Kingston at 5 and I must return on the 1 o'clock (*a m* damn) that same night. I understand I can get my berth early at 11 which will allow me to secure some sleep. But this is inevitable. I had wished I could spend a day or so but it seems I shall be able to take only the Poetry recital in the evening. Perhaps later on in the spring or early summer I may have a chance of running down to see you.

Most sincerely
Ned Pratt.

P.S. As soon as the Club decides on the date would the Secy. get in touch with our Extension Dept. immediately and make arrangements. You can tell the Director that any one of the above dates is suitable to me.

P.

148 See the letter to Clarke, 17 December 1931 (*EJP: Web*).

149 Charles Auger (1880–1935) was an associate professor of English at Victoria College.

TO LORNE PIERCE

[13 Jan. 1932]

Dear Lorne:

You are most welcome to consign these Eschatological monstrosities[150] to the everlasting flames where they should have gone in the first place.

I burned some fifty of them seven years ago and the house has remained hot ever since. I calculate that twenty tons of coal were saved thereby. This is your authorization to give them a hasty and fiery dispatch.

Ned

TO LORNE PIERCE

Jan. 30, 1932.

My dear Lorne:

I have recently been re-appointed to the Summer School at Halifax, so I shall take Vi and Claire with me. That will leave my cottage vacant from the first of July to August 20th. I intend putting the cottage up for rent during this period and if you wish to take it for your family you may have the first offer.[151] The rooms have been enlarged since you were up. There are six beds besides the one in the Den. The boat is an excellent one, and the raft which I had built last summer is large enough to hold eight persons. It really makes sport for the summer. The water never gets beyond three feet until it reaches the channel away out. As for the rental I may say that all cottages up there go for $100 a month. That is the price Phelps wanted for his and gets. I should be glad to let you have it for the whole seven weeks July l – Aug. 20 for the one hundred if you considered it a reasonable figure. It is completely furnished of course, oil stove with three burners, and the big open fire-place. There is sufficient wood there I think for the season, or nearly so.

---

150 Pierce had written asking permission to 'consign' the remaining copies of Pratt's doctoral thesis, *SPE* (published by Ryerson Press in 1917), 'to the Eschatological incinerator.' Only a few copies had ever been sold.

151 Pierce accepted the offer. See the letter to George Herbert Clarke, 7 April 1932 (*EJP: Web*).

Supplies are brought to the door and ice three times a week for the refrigerator. Will you let me know soon what your plans are?

I hear from Vi that you consider my photograph[152] a good reflection of a face flushed or distorted by a sequence of fiery Manhattans; pie-eyed and melancholy over the ills of this mortal coil. Well, you're another.

Affectionately
Ned.

TO GEORGE HERBERT CLARKE

Feb. 6, 1932

My dear Clarke:

I want to drop you this little note of appreciation and affection. I do not know when I enjoyed an evening more and your own companionship was the chief element in the enjoyment. I wish we could meet oftener and possibly in the future we may find the roads more open.

I have been dipping into your Hasting Day[153] to my great pleasure. You have such a variety of rhythms from the staccato Tenant of Time to the rolling 'Sun.' I love your dog-poems too. There is something at once noble and intimate about 'To the Memory of Toby.' I am going to read it from beginning to end – some of the verses I knew before.

I am submitting 'The Lost Cause'[154] for the Quarterly. This poem will be included in my next volume to be published in the fall.[155]

Most sincerely
Ned Pratt

152 Taken late in 1931 by Toronto photographers Pringle and Booth.

153 Clarke's book, *The Hasting Day: Poems* (London and Toronto: Dent, 1930).

154 (*EJP: CP* 1.217). Clarke was the editor of QQ, and Pratt's sonnet – which had already appeared in the *Canadian Journal of Religious Thought* 7 (September-October 1930) – was published in QQ 39 (May 1932).

155 *Many Moods* (Toronto: Macmillan, 1932).

TO GEORGE HERBERT CLARKE

June 30, 1932

Dear George:

I have just received your note and poem which I have read with great pleasure. Let me congratulate you, old chap, upon an acceptance from the 'Atlantic.'[156] Great stuff. I should like to see you do more of it. It is new to Canadian output and possesses what ninety-nine per cent. of our writers lack – prosocialist suggestion. It reminds me of what Eggleston[157] (our friend of the dinner party at Ottawa) said about your lecturing. He was most enthusiastic on the score of your philosophical interpretations.

Am awfully sorry you are in doubt about Halifax.[158] If you come be sure of a dinner and evening with me.

Affectionately
Ned. P.

TO HUGH S. EAYRS

24 Preston St.
Halifax, Ont[159]

July 9, 1932

Dear Hughie,

Your two letters came, one yesterday, the other just now.

Regarding the account,[160] I should have cleared it up before I left Toronto but as it happened, I had to deplete my bank credit to finance my Halifax trip as I

156 Clarke's poem 'Halt and Parley' appeared in *Atlantic Monthly*, October 1933.

157 Wilfrid Eggleston (1901–86), a graduate of Queen's University, was Ottawa correspondent for the *Toronto Daily Star*. He went on to be professor of journalism at Carleton University and author of several books on Canadian politics and policy, including *The Road to Nationhood: A Chronicle of Dominion-Provincial Relations* (Toronto: Oxford University Press, 1946).

158 Clarke had considered paying a brief visit to Halifax during Pratt's time as a summer session instructor.

159 [*sic*]. 'Ont.' should read 'N.S.' for Nova Scotia.

160 Pratt owed money to Macmillan of Canada for copies of *RA* which he had ordered for private presentation.

didn't get a pass this summer.[161] I intended, in fact, to wait until I received my first Munro cheque[162] which falls due at the end of July, but I have written Little of Victoria to put my August cheque to my credit at the Royal in advance. I am sure he will do it. I am enclosing $50.00 at present.[163] I would send it all but Newfoundland and Liverpool are getting their hands into my pocket during this depression pretty heavily.[164] Perhaps later on the 'contra' will help to 'allay' the balance. Optimism says you!!

Well dear old chap I'd love to put in an evening here with you and Dora.[165] There's so much to chat about. I'm beginning to make grand contacts here again. The classes are good and enthusiastic. I have no less than fifteen nuns in one class at the 'Convent of the Sacred Heart,'[166] who bow profoundly every time I come even within a mile of the Deity. If they see the Lord in the distance when I read a poem their knees begin to wobble. I don't know how I'll get through 'The Depression Ends'[167] when I read it. Fred Clarke[168] is a grand lad. I am having him in to dinner on Sunday with his daughter.

Munro has given me [...] ticket for the Halifax Club again. I haven't seen Chisholm[169] yet. Stanley[170] and I are the greatest of pals. Claire plays with his 12 year-old daughter and Mrs St. and Vi chum a lot. Stewart[171] has taken us all for a motor trip along the coast. Everybody is phoning us up wishing us welcome. I am expecting a really good time these six weeks. If you have any Macmillan suggestions to make other than what we have in common pass them on. One idea of mine is to have the Stanleys and the Bennetts in for a 'substantial dinner' one evening. It would greatly buck up Bennett.[172] I am passing on

161 The previous year he had a free pass for the railway trip east.
162 His summer school stipend: H.F. Munro, as director, paid the staff.
163 See the letter to Pelham Edgar, 26 August 1932 (p. 100).
164 His unmarried sisters in St John's and his brother Arthur in Liverpool, England, were in financial straits and needed help.
165 Dora Eayrs, Hugh's wife.
166 Classes at summer school were held in several locations, including Mount St Vincent, St Mary's, and Dalhousie universities. The convent was affiliated with Dalhousie University.
167 First published in *CF* 13 (October 1932), the poem was finished shortly before his trip to Halifax. (See the letter to Edgar, 26 August 1932 [pp. 100–1].)
168 Professor of classics at the University of Manitoba.
169 Chief Justice Joseph Chisholm, with whom he had become acquainted the previous year. (See the letter to Pelham Edgar, 17 July 1931 [p. 93].)
170 Carleton W. Stanley (1886–1971), a graduate of Victoria College and Oxford University, had taught English briefly at Victoria and later classics at McGill University. He served as president of Dalhousie University from 1931 to 1945.
171 Harold L. Stewart (1882–1953), professor of philosophy at Dalhousie University.
172 [*sic*]. Pratt misspelled the surname of Charles L. Bennet (1895–1980), a New Zealander and a graduate of Cambridge and Harvard universities, who was a professor and head of the English Department at Dalhousie and long-time editor of the *Dalhousie Review*.

your kind remarks about him. Stewart told me too he was making good as a lecturer. The Merkels[173] came over to see us this morning.

Now about the volume.[174] Vi and I are delighted with Sea Foam and Star Shine.[175] Cut the hyphens out by all means. Any other suggestions will be welcome. What about the book having a jacket without decoration but with a few comments on the earlier poetry. I should like to have P.C. Scott of the Manchester Guardian[176] somewhere in the advertisement. He wrote a gorgeous thing himself on the Roosevelt and on Titans. He is regarded (or was) as the greatest figure in journalism in the British Empire. I could send you some clippings later if you considered them desirable. However, I leave that matter to your judgment.

How is Dora? You said she was ill on your last trip. I trust that she has recovered.

Love to the last
Neddie

TO PELHAM EDGAR

Bobcaygeon, Ont.

Aug. 26, 1932

My dear Pelham,

I have been wondering a lot how you have survived the heat and the vexation of this summer. Dear old chap, that postponement of your 'Fiction'[177] has been almost as great a disappointment to me as to you. I have heard nothing since your letter to Halifax but I suppose there has been no change of plans or any sign of New York repentance.[178]

173 Andrew D. Merkel (b. 1884) was an occasional poet as well as Atlantic superintendent of the Canadian Press.

174 Pratt's forthcoming book of poems, *MM*.

175 This was Hugh and Dora Eayrs's suggestion for the title of the book.

176 Pratt reverses the initials of C.P. (Charles Prestwich) Scott (1846–1932), former editor of the *Manchester Guardian (1872–1929)* and one of the most celebrated journalists of his time. His review of *RA*, 'An Epic of the Sea,' appeared in *Manchester Guardian*, 5 August 1930.

177 Edgar had just finished his book, *The Art of the Novel*. (See the note to 'your book' in the letter to Edgar, 17 July 1930 [p. 89].)

178 The book would be published by Macmillan of New York in 1933.

What have you been doing since the session closed? You hinted that your stomach had gone back on you. I trust you are making good time from the few weeks holidays left and will be in some sort of condition at the opening of the term.

I looked in on you last Friday but your office was closed and I judged by the cramming of the letter box that you had decamped from the city. I spent but one day in Toronto and made at once for the cottage.

My Halifax trip was quite successful I think. The only trouble – and it was quite a considerable one – was Claire's neuritis. She had it every day and every night for the whole six weeks. Indeed Vi thought once of returning with her before the close of the term but Claire wanted to stick it out. It was the weather beyond any doubt – the sea moisture, for immediately we struck Ontario the rheumatism disappeared magically and not a twinge of it has come back thank God. If I go to Halifax next summer, and Munro has invited me – I shall go alone.

The expenses were very heavy. I used up my honorarium and half as much more. In fact a cheque for fifty dollars[179] which I sent Macmillans on account was returned N.S.F. from the Royal Bank of Canada, Bloor and Yonge Toronto. I didn't know how much I had with them. It turned out to be only seven dollars but the bastards should have carried me for a few weeks until Little deposited my monthly. I wrote and gave them hell – worded the remonstrations so strongly that they didn't reply. I shall try another bank next fall. Huckvale[180] of 70 Bond St. returned my cheque, then I had to borrow from Munro in order to send a certified draft from the Nova Scotia Bank.

I am counting a little upon my new volume but I have been so often disappointed financially that I am putting the bridle on my hopes. I submitted 'Sea and Sky'[181] to Hughie but he said it was used in another and recent volume. 'Many Moods' was finally decided on.

I gave a recital in Halifax[182] just before leaving with the University Gymnasium filled – nearly a thousand people. Had a gorgeous time. The Depression Ends and the Reverie on a Dog[183] went the best of them. I told them how you started

179 See the note to '$50.00' in the letter to Hugh Eayrs, 9 July 1932 (p. 97).

180 In 1932, Robert Huckvale was accountant and secretary of Macmillan of Canada in Toronto. From 1940 to 1946, he was acting president.

181 A possible title for his forthcoming book of poems.

182 On Sunday, 14 August.

183 The poem was written the previous winter and first published in *UTQ* 2 (October 1932): 40–8.

the Depression by your 'prognathic' suggestion.[184] One lyric which was very cordially accepted was 'From Java to Geneva.'[185]

I received a letter from Squire last week with the galley of my two poems – they appear in October.[186]

If I had a big break with a book I'd lift you out of your present morass.[187]

Love
Ned

TO WILLIAM ARTHUR DEACON

Bobcaygeon Ont

Sept. 4, 1932.

Dear Bill:

Many thanks indeed for your long and interesting letter received yesterday. I am glad to think that you and your family are having a much-deserved holiday,

---

184 Pratt gives several varying accounts of how 'The Depression Ends' (*EJP: CP* 1.261) 'sprang out of a word which was given me by Dr. Edgar. He called out to me one day as I was passing his office, "Ned, here's a word I've never seen in a poem and rarely in prose."' The word was 'prognathic' and Edgar asked him to write a poem embodying it. Uncertain of its meaning, they consulted a dictionary and found that it meant 'having a protruding jaw.' Consulting his wife, Pratt found that the word suggested to her 'a grand-mother who was always interfering with a mother in the bringing up of the children.' The image prompted a train of thought, but the picture which suggested itself to him was of 'a very stern governess in charge of an orphan asylum' whose severity and parsimony were manifested in her feeding her charges *prunes* and similar abominations. It was this, Pratt wrote, 'that gave me the idea of a dinner which I would give this orphanage. But the thing grew, of course, beyond all bounds.' [Unpublished script, *EJP*, *VUL*]. A variant of this account appears in *EJP: OHLP*, 88–9. The unlikely seminal word occurs only once in the poem, in line 146.

185 (*EJP: CP* 1.260) Later published under the tile 'From Stone to Steel,' the poem first appeared in the *Canadian Journal of Religious Thought* 9 (September-October 1932): 224.

186 'Sea-Gulls' (*EJP: CP* 1.218) and 'The Way of Cape Race' (*EJP: CP* 1.283) were published in the *LM* in December rather than October (lm 27 [December 1932]: 109).

187 Edgar had recently suffered financial losses as a result of investment failures due to the Depression.

but you should have left your portable[188] behind you, since your recreation ought to receive the same whole-hearted attention that you characteristically put into your routine work. Still I realise how necessitous the times are through which you are passing.

We have been here at 'Bob' now for two weeks and intend to return by Sept. 12 when Claire goes to school. The weather has been perfect – only two days of rain. The swimming has been delightful. I had a large raft built last summer capable of holding six persons before foundering, and Claire – who swims well – likes to take the neighbouring kiddies out about one hundred yards from the dock where they splash about for hours. You and Sal must bring along your troupe sometime for a couple of weeks. There are quite a few occasions when the cottage is empty for that period and Vi says she would rather see Sal getting the sunshine out of it than many another. Youngsters pick up here. When we came up I weighed Claire and Kathleen – a little fresh-air girl that we take up every season –. They have gained four pounds each already and I expect they'll go six by the time we leave. Kathleen was hit in a motor accident in June with bone fractures. She is now as fit as a fiddle.

We were pleasantly surprised two or three days ago when Jack Charlesworth[189] and wife blew in on us. They have a cottage on the other lake. We reminisced on the doings of the Writers Club. So Gordon[190] and Austin[191] regaled the boys in my absence. I wish I had been present. Both have eminently dramatic records. I think we ought some day to have Fred Griffin[192] talk about the Russian situation. I am very fond of Fred – the lad and his writing.

Well about my own activities. The Halifax trip was again an inspiration to me. I love the people there. I have been invited back for next summer. I gave a Sunday recital in the University gymnasium just before I left, more than seven hundred present. All new stuff, part of the content of the approaching volume, which I am

---

188 Typewriter.

189 John L. Charlesworth (b. 1896), after working on the Guelph *Daily Herald*, became editor of *Industrial Canada* in 1920. In 1931, he joined the public relations firm of Johnston, Everson and Charlesworth.

190 Gordon Sinclair (1900–84) joined the *Toronto Daily Star* in the early 1920s. He became one of Canada's most colourful journalists, broadcasters, and television personalities.

191 Austin Campbell (b. 1884) was a businessman for whom writing was a hobby. He wrote fugitive pieces for various journals, a novel (*The Rock of Babylon* [Ottawa: Graphic Press, 1931]), and a poetry chapbook (*They Shall Build Anew* [Toronto: Ryerson, 1944]).

192 Frederick Griffin was a leading journalist at the *Toronto Daily Star* who had been sent to Russia in 1931 to report on the progress of Communism. His book, *Variety Show: Twenty Years of Watching the News Parade* (Toronto: Macmillan, 1936), gives a colourful account of his experiences as a newspaperman.

calling 'Many Moods.' It ought to be out early autumn. I want to thank you for your suggestion which shows your warm and abiding interest in my work. Last fall you remember I had contemplated bringing out a book. I am glad now I didn't for two reasons: the market was untimely, and the production would have been somewhat lacking in variety. Again, a year has given me time to discard some stuff which at first I thought good but now feel is scarcely up to form.

The volume will have four or five long poems that is of more than 200 lines each, the best being in my judgment the leading one – A Reverie on a Dog, not too good a title perhaps but the best I could rummage up to indicate the composite nature of the content which is partly descriptive, partly reflective. It is somewhat of the Cachalot order but much more human. Another – 'Putting Winter to Bed' is a fantasy. Lismer,[193] last Christmas, did a lot of illustrations for it for the purpose of a seasonal offering, but here again I am pleased I didn't publish it separately as it was too slight.

I have been bucked up over the magazine reception lately, the University of Toronto Quarterly is publishing in full 'The Reverie'; the Dalhousie,[194] the Putting Winter to Bed; the Forum,[195] 'The Depression Ends'; the London Mercury, two lyrics, and the Manchester Guardian another,[196] all appearing in the October issues, with the possible late exception of the last. The Mercury took – 'Sea Gulls' and 'The Way of Cape Race.'

There are approximately fifty poems.

When I get back by the middle of the month I'll try to get down to College St. to see the boys.

Sincerely
Ned.

---

193 Arthur Lismer (1885–1969) was principal of the Victoria School of Art and Design in Halifax (1916–19) before becoming vice-president of the Ontario School of Art in 1919. A founder of the Group of Seven, he had a long and distinguished career as an artist, art educator, and lecturer.

194 *Dalhousie Review.*

195 *Canadian Forum.*

196 No poem by Pratt appeared in the *Manchester Guardian.*

TO O.J. STEVENSON[197]

Bobcaygeon, Ont.

Sept. 5, 1932

Dear Dr Stevenson:

I wish to thank you very much for your kind words about myself and my poetry, and I should be delighted to go to the O.A.C.[198] some time this fall or winter to give a lecture recital. In view of your long and honoured connection with the teaching of English Literature in this country, I regard your invitation as a great honour. I notice two of my friends from your letter-head, McLean[199] and Miss Masson.[200] I should be pleased to see them again.

I am bringing out a volume of verse this autumn, 'Many Moods,' through Macmillans. There are four or five new narrative poems in the collection though the main content is lyrical and dramatic. The leading poem – 'A Reverie for a Dog' – might suit your book if it isn't too late for you to make a decision. The poem was read last spring before the Royal Society of Canada and I think it is the best I have done since 'The Roosevelt and the Antinoe.'

However, the copyright is now owned by Macmillans and it is a matter for Mr H.S. Eayrs to decide. But if it is too late I thank you none the less for your generous appreciation.

Yours sincerely
E.J. Pratt

197 Stevenson, a professor of English at the Ontario Agricultural College in Guelph, was compiling a school text – *Poetry Anthology for Canadian Schools* (Toronto: Copp Clarke, 1932–4) – and had written to ask whether Pratt had an unpublished manuscript suitable for inclusion.

198 Ontario Agricultural College.

199 J. Alden McLean (1912–92) had been the first professor of animal husbandry at the Ontario Agricultural College and maintained his connection with the institution.

200 Unidentified.

TO HUGH S. EAYRS

Bobcaygeon, Ont

Sept. 5, 1932.

Dear Hughie.

I suppose by this time you are back in Toronto and feeling like a fighting-cock after Stanhope Beach.[201]

When you get the galleys of Many Moods I could rush the corrections. I expect to be in Toronto for good by Sept. 12 as Claire goes to school on the 13th. I hope you intend playing some golf this fall to keep the old corporation down within reasonable compass. My putting is simply infernal. I took *five* 5 putts on one green in my last game and I was on in 2. I had 52 putts on the course. I've gone flooey. I am enclosing this from Stevenson.[202] I wrote him saying it was a matter between him and you as to whether any poem in 'Many Moods' should be released. I am inclined to think he has his collection made anyway.

Hoping to see you old dear as soon as I return. Your face will be welcome again.

Ned[159]

201 Eayrs and his wife had taken a holiday at Stanhope Beach, Prince Edward Island.

202 See the letter to O.J. Stevenson, 5 September 1932 (p. 104).

III Prospect and Promotion, 1932–1939

I am thrilled with the prospect and will do anything to further promotion.
– E.J. Pratt to F.R. Scott, 9 January 1934

TO KATHERINE MACTAVISH

[Dec. 1932]

Dear Mrs MacTavish (Kate)

First of all let me wish you, Newton and Maxine the compliments of the season with the most affectionate greetings. It is my loss that I do not see much of you but nearly three hundred miles separate the MacTavishes and the Pratts.

It was so kind of you to get the Ottawa people interested in my poetry. I shall never forget your kindness and your marvellous hospitality when I was in your city.[1] And I want you now to accept as a Xmas present, however slight it may be, a copy of 'Many Moods.' I am simply startled at the way the book has gone so far. Out only three weeks and the first edition practically exhausted. It is getting splendid press and I am sending you along a few extracts as you kindly requested. Some time later would you return them as they are in demand for publicity.

'The Reverie on a Dog' gets the most attention from the Reviewers. 'Putting Winter to Bed,' 'Angelina,' come next and of the shorter poems, 'Blind' 'Old Age' 'From Stone to Steel' Erosion' and the 'Lee-Shore' have been specially commented on.

---

1 See the letter to Newton MacTavish, 15 December 1930 (p. 90).

The Roosevelt and the Antinoe' went into the third thousand, and this new book seems to be going faster still. Good for a time of Depression.

I would indeed love to see you all again – Perhaps next spring I may manage to stop over on my way East to Halifax.

Most sincerely,
E.J. Pratt (Ned Pratt)

'Sea-Gulls' and 'The Way of Cape Race' have just appeared in the London Mercury.[2]

Ned

TO WILLIAM DOUW LIGHTHALL[3]

June 13, 1933.

Dear Dr Lighthall:

It was very generous of you to write me about my work in connection with the C.A.A. trip to England.[4] To whom should I send the books? It would be unfair to you to burden you with such a task.

Still I am sending you a copy of my latest – 'Many Moods,' which is receiving some excellent and heartening reviews in England right now. 'The Reverie on a Dog' and 'The Depression Ends' with the lyrics are being specially noted.

The 'Roosevelt and the Antinoe' ran into nearly three thousand copies and is still selling.

Yours very sincerely
Ned Pratt

---

2 The poems appeared in *LM* (December 1932): 109.

3 Lighthall (1857–1954) was best known for his anthology *Songs of the Great Dominion* (London: W. Scott, 1889). He was a founder of the Canadian Authors Association, and its president in 1929–31. His collected poems, *Old Measures* (Montreal: A.T. Chapman), appeared in 1922.

4 A contingent of CAA members was leaving on tour of Great Britain on 1 July on the *Empress of Britain*. An exhibition of Canadian books was planned for various stops on the tour. Pratt did not make the trip.

TO VIOLA PRATT

July 8, 1933

Dearest Vi:

I suppose today or tomorrow you will be on your way to Toronto to get Claire's cast off.[5] I wonder how it will come out. Will you spend a few days in the city? I guess that will be the best thing – to keep it under observation.

It was a great relief to know that Karl[6] and the family would be with you. Claire must be thrilled at the prospect. If only now she will be in condition for swimming and rafting. I am sending something or other every second day, to keep her spirits up.

I have a nice room here with the Grants 2 Vernon St. Stewart[7] came in to see me last night after motoring me during the afternoon down to Hubbards.[8] He is a great friend of Dr Grant who died last year at the age of 95. My room is quiet and warm, though I do all my work at the Club and at the University. Clarke[9] is with me a lot. I haven't met Bennet[10] yet though I hope to do so in a few days. MacGillivary, the stately Dugald,[11] is away from Halifax. Settled down at Annapolis.

Do you know that I haven't played one game of golf yet. Rain, Rain, fog, fog everyday and yet Munro is still remarking, 'Oh, this is not really Halifax weather you know. Wait till August!' August!! It is so foggy now I can't see across the street at the Club. Dripping clammy fog. I suppose it will clear up *in time*.

I am feeling pretty well, except for those lightning movements in my left eye. There must be infection somewhere though I can't see where, as the suspected teeth (upper) are out.

---

5 Claire had been stricken with severe osteomyelitis, which particularly affected her left arm. It had been in a cast for several months.

6 Karl Whitney, Viola's brother. His home was in Francis, Saskatchewan.

7 Harold L. Stewart. See the letter to Hugh Eayrs, 9 July 1932 (p. 98).

8 A village 35 kilometres southwest of Halifax.

9 G.H. Clarke of Queen's University was also teaching in the summer session.

10 Charles L. Bennet. See the letter to Hugh Eayrs, 9 July 1932 (p. 98).

11 Superintendent of the Maritime and Newfoundland branch of the Canadian Bank of Commerce in 1920, and later manager of the Eastern Trust Company, Dugald MacGillivary was a member of the board of governors of Dalhousie University.

The nuns are just as cordial as ever – I had them laughing over modernistic poetry yesterday. The Mother Superior Hughill, still talks about the dear Cardinal (Newman) and wondering when in the course I shall be coming to him.

It is very hard to see how I can work him into a series on Shaw Galsworthy Somerset Maugham and Noel Coward. But the miracle *may* happen.

I didn't see the Star and the MacDonald list.[12] Could you send it on to me if you can locate it. I expect Deacon will answer it in the Mail. The Club takes the Globe & Mail but not the Star.

Well old dear, take care of yourself.

Love,
Ned

TO VIOLA PRATT

Tuesday morning. [25 July 1933]

Dearest Vi:

I wonder what is the best thing to do about the Masons.[13] I hardly know how to advise since it is a dilemma in any case. I think you had just be a bit cool and aloof with them so they will scent dislike of too close familiarity. Rather that than a blank refusal. Perhaps you might hint – 'What is wrong with the former premises?' I'd be chary of letting those two youngsters go scamping all over the place. I think I'd risk complete break rather than that. They have no manners whatever.

I am glad that you are getting some fish. Does Karl catch any? Or are the fish in the other lake mainly? I hope George[14] brings you some lunge once in a while.

Let Karl fix up the dock if it needs attention near the boat premises. But I wouldn't do anything to the large central portion as it is very rotten. Patching up would be useless. I guess it might go another year, though if it is dangerous as it stands now, Karl might fix it up for safety. My idea later would be to have a small good dock where the boat and raft are and then fill in the rest with rock and earth as the timbers there are sound and big to enclose it.

12 See the second paragraph of the letter to Lorne Pierce, 20 August 1933 (p. 111).
13 A noisy and quarrelsome family had rented the cottage next to the Pratts at Bobcaygeon.
14 George, local handy man, fished for muskellunge, a large game fish from the pike family.

Give Karl my winter overcoat by all means. It is a good one yet and all the more reason he should have it than if it were shabby. He could get two or three years out of it and it is the warmest coat I have ever had. I am only too glad that he should have it.

Fine that Claire is improving. The swimming is a godsend to her. It is the finest thing about Bobcaygeon and compensates for a lot of things. I trust that the infection in the hip will find its way out without an abscess.[15] I was hoping that by this time it would have absorbed. It may be the same way as the arm. Dr Norman[16] said absorption was the normal process.

I am enjoying the work here much more now than I did the first two weeks. The weather has decidedly improved: in fact the days are just about perfect for sunshine and for temperature. Our trip to Pictou and New Glasgow was just as pleasant as last year's tour. Munro is a pearl. I see Stewart a lot nearly every day and Chisholm. They all wish to be remembered to you and Claire. I agree with you that Mrs S.[17] is the best of them here.

I am sending Claire something today. The bracelet is a valuable one – bought at a jeweller's! So she's to take good care of it.

Lovingly
Ned

TO CLAIRE PRATT

July 28, 1933

Dearest Cakie:

Here are two five-dollar bills. You are to give one of them ($5.00) to Aunt Rita[18] and keep the other for yourself with this qualification. One dollar must be spent in things to be shared around the household. Anything you like: – pins, needles, clocks, collars, cushions (I mean pin-cushions), all day suckers, Esquimau pies, popsicles and icicles, ju-jubes, licorice drops and chocolate bon-bons, fire

15 In 1931–2, Claire had undergone operations to relieve the effects of osteomyletis in her left arm. The infection had now migrated to her left hip.

16 Dr James Norman, the Pratt family's doctor and a personal friend.

17 Probably the wife of Carleton Stanley, president of Dalhousie University. See the note to 'Stanley' in the letter to Hugh Eayrs, 9 July 1932 (p. 98).

18 Wife of Viola's brother, Karl Whitney.

crackers, nut-crackers, marshmallows, peanuts and pea-nut candy, dish mops and second hand brooms, bootees for Harvie,[19] and teddy bear for Kathleen,[20] one ice-cream cone and two prize packets (one cent ones).

There you have your list. The snaps were lovely. Send some more.

Daddy!

TO LORNE PIERCE

Victoria College

August 20, 1933

Hello, you old ink-slinger:

How the devil are you? I have just returned from Halifax and the Summer Session. I spent a week-end at Wolfville, gave a poetry recital at Acadia, stayed with the Rhodenizers[21] and had altogether a most enjoyable time. A good many of your friends there wished to be remembered to you. Your visit there some years ago is still most cordially recollected. Your speech and your behaviour generally. Miss Rosamond Archibald[22] particularly said, 'Oh, if you see Dr Pierce – tell him how much we love him in Acadia.' You must have knocked them cold (or hot) – if the slang may be reversed with delicacy of significance. Halifax remembers you likewise.

Did you notice that that Gorgonzola hunk (if I am not defaming a good cheese) W.M. published his Scribner classification[23] in the 'Daily Star' about a month ago. I didn't see the 'Star' but my friends wrote me about it when I was in the East.

Jack Elson tells me he expects to bring out through you a little manual on Canadian poets. I have an idea it should go across well market-wise. I am continually being written for biographical information and I should like to refer to

---

19 Son of Karl and Rita Whitney.

20 See the note to 'Fresh Air child' in the letter to Pelham Edgar, 9 August 1929 (p. 111).

21 Vernon B. Rhodenizer (1886–1968) was professor and head of the English Department at Acadia University from 1918 to 1954.

22 (1882–1953). Head of the English Department at Acadia Seminary from 1914 to 1926), and Horton Academy from 1926 to 1947.

23 Wilson MacDonald had published a list of major Canadian books recently published, but had omitted Pratt's *MM*.

some one else than that J.W.G. anthology.[24] I would get behind the book personally in my literature classes of Extension and could push the sales. I have a liking for Jack: he is a good-natured and decent fellow and trying to batter out a living for himself in a cold world. There are scores of literary (Canadian) clubs springing up every where, and the project looks good. Count on me for backing it up when it appears, if the book is moderate in cost.

Well, old boy, I am off to Bobcaygeon on Tuesday morning for ten days. Will be seeing you on return.

Affectionately
Ned.

TO WILLIAM ARTHUR DEACON

Oct. 31, 1933

Dear Bill:

It gives me a rare delight to know that the 'Vision'[25] has become a 'best seller.' You certainly deserve your success, old man, and I hope the book will go on selling for it is unique in this country. You know already my enthusiasm for you and for what you are doing. I might drop a sentence or two which would lend itself to quotation. You are perfectly free to use what you consider fit.

'The book over-rides the occasional prejudice against individual positions by the very momentum of the style, – the crisp, exhilarating manner in which the arguments are marshalled.'

'There is a prophetic glow in the writing, especially in the later chapters, which makes the issues take on the warmth and intimacy of a personal message. The book thoroughly justifies its title, in that, being compellingly alive and straightforward, it possess the qualities of *vision*.'

Most sincerely,
Ned

---

24 *Canadian Poets*, edited by John W. Garvin, was published by McClelland, Goodchild & Stewart in 1916. A revised edition in 1926 included a note on Pratt and several of his poems. Garvin (1859–1935) was by turns a teacher and insurance agent. He edited the *Collected Poems of Isabella Valency Crawford* (Toronto: William Briggs, 1905) and several other anthologies.

25 *My Vision of Canada* (Toronto: Ontario Publishing Company, 1933) was an outspoken political treatise.

TO WILLIAM ARTHUR DEACON

Sunday pm. [5 Nov. 1933]

Dear Billy:

Your tribute to Emily Murphy[26] was a beautiful thing. I do not know when you wrote a more lovely article, as fine and as touching as anything that ever appeared in the 'Mail.' It was read from beginning to end last night aloud and before a group of eight men. It hit us all right in the emotional ganglion. You must have loved her to write like that, and I realise that you write best when you feel deeply.

I will take any bet that thousands of the Mail readers appreciated it.

Affectionately
Ned.

TO WILLIAM ARTHUR DEACON

Thursday a.m. [16 Nov. 1933]

Dear Billy,

I have just sent off to Scott[27] a letter expressing my great appreciation of the Literary Section of the Mail. I was a constant reader of the paper; my interest increasing since your connection with it. Your columns gave the ablest, the most vital criticism in Canada. Then my own candid opinion of 'The Vision' as I have

26 Emily Murphy (née Ferguson) (1868–1933) had died on 27 October, and Deacon's 'tribute' appeared on 4 November. Born in Ontario, Murphy lived most of her life in western Canada, where she was a prominent writer (under the pseudonym 'Janey Canuck'), feminist, and social reformer, and the first female magistrate in the British Empire. Pratt had met her on his western tour in 1927.

27 On 15 November, Deacon had written Pratt an anxious letter. John Scott, the managing editor of the *Mail and Empire*, had received six letters of complaint about Deacon's article on Emily Murphy ('Janey Canuck'). (See the letter to Deacon, 5 November 1933 [p. 113].) The paper was already disturbed by the radical political views expressed by Deacon in *My Vision of Canada*. Deacon asked if Pratt and his colleagues might send some positive comments about his work to Scott. See the letter to Deacon, mid-November 1933 (*EJP: Web*).

stated it to you, – that in the circle in which I move I found genuine admiration and respect etc. etc.

Immediately got in touch with Fennel[28]: Bob says he will not only telephone but will personally see both Scott & Smith.[29] Smith he says he is a friend of his – a dinner friend and so forth. He will tell Smith (and Scott) that he thinks the literary exposition of the Mail without a rival in this country, and your book is in like vein.

Then I have just seen Edgar again. Edgar will see Smith whom he knows better than Scott and speak positively for you. I know he will do that.

I will scout about & get more fellows besieging the Mail.

Yours as ever
Ned

Forgive rush just now. Devil of a hurry!

TO GEORGE HERBERT CLARKE

Nov. 29, 1933

My dear George

I have a new sonnet just written which I should like to submit to the 'Queen's Quarterly' – *A Timeless Moment*.[30]

How are you anyway? Are you coming to Toronto through the Christmas vacation? If you do I can put you up at my house. We have moved into wider rooms[31]; there is a spare bed, and I shall see to it that roast goose from seven to eight will ensure sound sleep from eleven to nine.

Affectionately
Ned Pratt

28 Robert Fennel (b. 1891) was a prominent Toronto lawyer and corporate business manager, a member of the administrative boards of several major Toronto institutions, including the University of Toronto and the Royal Ontario Museum.

29 F.D.L. Smith, editor-in-chief of the *Mail and Empire*.

30 (*EJP: CP* 1.298). Not published in *QQ*, the poem appeared as 'To Any Astronomer' in *Saturday Night*, 24 March 1934, 2, and in *FG* (38).

31 In 1932, the Pratts moved from 25 Tullis Drive to 21 Cortleigh Boulevard.

TO AN UNKNOWN CORRESPONDENT

[Dec. 1933]

Thank you for your interest in the poem 'In Absentia.'[32] I did not have in mind a *particular* person whom I could call by name, but rather any teacher who was off on a fishing holiday, let us say sometime in late May when he was getting very tired giving lectures or marking exam papers. He may be assumed to be an ardent fisherman and the emotion that seized him when he hooked a 'big one' was so great that the whole life-span of seventy years (in fact the whole universe) is concentrated in the experience. The sun and the sky are mirrored in the water and are but minor features compared with that fish.

Obviously the man is a teacher of languages ('language-weathered face'). The whirling desk is the revolving trolling spoon. The asterisk or star attached to a subject in which a student has failed would bring an expression of excitement to the face of the student. I have transferred the expression to the face of the professor for there is the possibility of his failure to land the fish, but I have left it to the reader to regard that as momentary for the tug on the line indicates a pretty good hold.

May, the time of examinations, and September, the time of recommencing of lectures, are now not on the calendar for the fisherman.

32 The letter survives as a handwritten draft in one of Pratt's notebooks, in proximity to a rough version of stanzas for the poem 'Like Mother, Like Daughter' (*EJP: CP* 1. 292) which was written in fall 1933 and first published in the *Saturday Night* Christmas Supplement, 2 December 1933, 8. Hence the projected date. The letter is a reply to a request from a student or teacher for an explication of 'In Absentia' (*EJP: CP* 1.52) first published in *CF* 1 (June 1921): 271–2 and later in *NV* (35). His correspondent probably read the poem in *Verses of the Sea* (1930), which was widely used as a textbook. (See the letter to Wendy Jenks, 19 May 1956 [*EJP: Web*].)

TO F.R. SCOTT[33]

Victoria College, Toronto

Wednesday evening [3 Jan. 1934]

My dear Scott,

Your letter just came and I am rushing off my selections.[34] I have indicated the order, which is quite arbitrary, in the list of contents of 'Many Moods' presented to you with my compliments. Number one is a sonnet just written and unpublished – 'Credo quia non Intellego.'[35] I have specified twelve, any ten of which might be chosen according to your discretion or any rejected with your own substitutions drawn from the balance of the volume.

I have been going over your folio with the greatest interest and pleasure. It delights my heart to be in with this Montreal group, and what a thrill to meet Smith[36] in this novel manner of introduction!

I have but one little criticism of your own offerings. I think the prose addendum to your C.A.A. poem[37] detracts somewhat from the subtlety of the satire in the substance of the poem. The thing is complete in my judgment without it. However, my objection is not strenuous enough to it, if it meets with the accord

33 Francis Reginald, 'Frank,' Scott (1899–1985) was a professor at the McGill School of Law, a political activist – one of the founders of the Co-operative Commonwealth Federation (CCF) and a contributor to the Regina Manifesto – and a 'modernist' poet. His books of poetry include *Overture* (Toronto: Ryerson, 1945), *Events and Signals* (Toronto: Ryerson, 1954), *Signature* (Vancouver: Klanak; Montreal: McGill University Press, 1964), and *Collected Poems* (Toronto: McClelland & Stewart, 1981).

34 The correspondence that follows concerns an anthology of 'new' poetry proposed by Scott, A.J.M. Smith, Leo Kennedy, and A.M. Klein, all from Montreal, who through Scott had invited Pratt, and later Robert Finch, to join them. The anthology was entitled *New Provinces, Poems of Several Authors* (Toronto: Macmillan, 1936).

35 (Lat.) 'I believe what I do not understand.' This sonnet was published in *FG* under the title, 'The Mystic' (*FG*, 44; *EJP: CP* 1.299).

36 Poet and critic A.J.M. (Arthur James Marshall) Smith (1902–80) was born and raised in Montreal and attended McGill University, where he and F.R. Scott founded the *McGill Fortnightly*. After receiving his doctorate at Edinburgh University in 1931, he taught at several American universities before settling at Michigan State University in 1936. His books of poetry include *News of the Phoenix* (Toronto: Ryerson, 1943), *A Sort of Ecstasy* (East Lansing: Michigan State College Press; Toronto: Ryerson, 1954), *Collected Poems* (Toronto: Oxford University Press, 1962), and *The Classic Shade* (Toronto: McClelland & Stewart, 1978).

37 'The Canadian Authors Meet,' first published in the *McGill Fortnightly Review* (April 1927).

of the others. Raise the point with them. I shall see Finch[38] to-morrow and report immediately to you.

If you decide to return to Toronto let me know and my house is yours during your stay.

Best of luck,
Pratt

TO F.R. SCOTT

Jan. 9, 1934.

Dear Frank Scott,

I am sending along Finch's collection. He and I have agreed on ten of the twenty. These are marked 1 to 10 in order of excellence from our subjective standpoints. Finch has written quite a large body of poetry and I was simply delighted with much of it. He is a real one and a discovery like Kennedy.[39] He tells me he will go his share of the cash or subscription guarantee if needed. He can sell a lot of copies he says.

We have something I am sure to offer the critical readers. I am thrilled at the prospect and will do anything to further promotion. He suggests that we be known as the 'group of six' as a publicity matter, getting people piqued at the start. I will put on a dinner as a celebration of the birth of the volume, if Klein,[40] Leo, AJM., Scott, Pratt and Finch can meet in Toronto on a given date.

This group is to continue in perpetuity, isn't it so?

---

38 See the note to 'Robert' in the letter to Edgar, 6 August 1929 (p. 83).

39 Leo Kennedy (1907–2000) was born in Liverpool, England, and moved to Montreal in 1912. Though he attended Laval, Kennedy first published his verse in the *McGill Fortnightly Review* and became closely associated with the McGill group of poets which included Scott, Smith, and A.M. Klein. With Scott, he founded the *Canadian Mercury*, dedicated to replacing the romanticism of much Canadian verse with modernist poetics. His only book of verse, *The Shrouding* (Toronto: Macmillan, 1933), was published partly owing to the support of E.J. Pratt. In the late 1930s, he moved to the United States, where he worked in advertising and public relations.

40 Abraham Moses Klein (1909–72) was born in Ukraine and grew up in Montreal, attending McGill University. His early poems were published in magazines. His first book, *Hath Not a Jew* (New York: Behrman's Jewish Book House), appeared in 1940 and was followed by *Poems* (Philadelphia: Jewish Publication Society, 1944), *The Hitleriad* (New York: New Directions, 1944), and *The Rocking Chair* (Toronto: Ryerson, 1948), for which he won the Governor General's Award, and a novel, *The Second Scroll* (New York: Knopf, 1951). A lawyer, editor, and activist for Jewish causes, he suffered from mental illness in his later years, writing little after *The Second Scroll.*

I am submitting two other poems to take the place of those you Montrealers might not like. 'The Inexpressible'[41] and 'A Timeless Moment.'[42] Finch is strong for these. He does not care for 'The Prize Winner'[43] nor for the 'Prairie Sunset'[44] quite so much. On second reading I scarcely think they fit into the collection.

Pratt

TO F.R. SCOTT

January 16, 1934.

My dear Frank:

I would have answered your letter earlier but it is only today that I managed to see Finch who had been laid up for most of the week with laryngitis. We spent an hour or two going over our newest stuff and I am enclosing the contents of the Dragnet.[45] I suppose you couldn't find the time to run to Toronto for the week-end for a last revision. If you could, I would arrange to have Finch to come up to my place for dinner and the three of us would go through the poems. You could stay with me.

I really believe we are on to a big thing in this Anthology, but the first consideration is the material. We both have our doubts on the '6000'[46] as appropriate and much prefer 'Silences'[47] as the one 'longer' poem of the selection. You haven't seen this yet. I had at first thought of the 'Prayer Medley' (Canadian Forum December)[48] but you and Smith considered it too experimental. Probably it is.

Finch prefers '*The Drag-Irons*' of *Many Moods* to the Convict Holocaust. So do I as the latter needs a footnote which impairs the look of the poem. He has revised

---

41 An opaque sonnet on sexual love, never published in Pratt's lifetime (*EJP: CP* 2.368).

42 See the note to 'A Timeless Moment' in the letter to George Herbert Clarke, 29 November 1933 (p. 114).

43 Better known as 'The Prize Cat' (*EJP: CP* 1.301).

44 The poem had been published in 1932 in *MM* (11; *EJP: CP* 1.215).

45 Of the poems named here by Pratt, all but 'The Inexpressible' and 'But One Way' were published either in *MM* or *FG*. These two poems (*EJP: CP* 2.368 and 361) were not published in Pratt's lifetime. The poems eventually included in *New Provinces* are (in order of presentation), 'The Prize-Winner,' 'The Convict Holocaust,' 'From Java to Geneva' ['From Stone to Steel'], 'Man and the Machine,' 'Seen on the Road,' 'The Drag-Irons,' and 'Sea-Gulls.' 'The Text of the Oath' was added later.

46 Pratt's celebrated locomotive poem had appeared in *MM* (49; *EJP: CP* 1.257).

47 Appeared in *CF* 15 (March 1936): 9, and in *FG* (25–6; *EJP: CP* 2.3).

48 *CF* 14 (December 1933): 92–3 (*EJP: CP* 1.293).

his opinion as to the fitness of the *Prize-Winner*, and now agrees. But he is not so keen on '*Man and the Machine*.' I am also skeptical of that poem, metrically.

I am submitting the following with his approval: '*Seen on the Road*,' *Silences. Fire The Weather Glass Credo quia The Inexpressible But One Way. To Any Astronomer*

The common agreement as indicated by your letter is with (1) Stone to Steel[49] (2) The Prize-Winner, (3) Sea Gulls.

Finch would like two more included *Blind* and *A Legacy* in 'Many Moods.' I would agree here. Will you take a second look at these after you have examined the seven new ones.[50]

If you can come to Toronto for the week-end will you telegraph me to Victoria College.

Very sincerely
Ned Pratt.

Love to Leo[51]

TO F.R. SCOTT

January 23, 1934.

My dear Frank:

We are indeed making progress. I can see a group that will make poetry a life avocation. We are in it for keeps. This is only a beginning. And I agree with you and Leo[52] that the distinctive mark of this volume ought to be its salt rather than its sweetness. I have always fought sentimentality though I do not like to strip a poem bare of its emotional tones. I think, however, my later development will be more along the line of the stuff you have selected, that is, my mind has been running with 'Stone and Steel' and 'Silences' etc. I am glad you like these two and also the 'Seen on the Road' genre. Finch liked 'Blind' & 'A Legacy' but the 'affections' are too much played up there to suit this volume.

---

49 Published as 'From Java to Geneva' (*EJP: CP* 1.260).

50 Marginal notes indicate Scott's decisions: approval of 'Silences,' 'The Drag-Lines,' and 'Man and the Machine'; 'A Legacy' is marked as 'possible'; and 'Blind' is marked as 'No / F.R.S.'

51 Leo Kennedy.

52 Leo Kennedy.

No: I haven't seen 'The Orators'[53] but have seen it reviewed quite a bit by Leavis[54] and others. Do you know where I may find it?

Will you fellows get busy thinking of titles, programmes, manifestos and so on, that will furnish artistic integrity to our movement. Finch and I have a lot of fun speculating as to what we shall say to the critics and to our audiences – 'The distinctive flavour of this volume is – .'

I am delighted you can come up on the 10th & 11th. Can you not spend the three nights, Friday, Saturday, Sunday. The spare bed is there with clean sheets. Let me know which night would be best for you. I shall have a stag dinner and have the boys concerned. Could Leo come along? If he couldn't, then we must arrange later for a celebration dinner when he and Klein & Smith can be present.

We have yet to select a couple of additional poems – Finch and I. We could do that when you are here.

Very Sincerely
Ned Pratt

TO HUGH S. EAYRS

February 24, 1934.

Dear Hughie:

I am writing this note separately as it has confidential matter. Immediately upon receipt of Mrs. Booth's[55] letter about the Broadus anthology,[56] I went over across the park[57] to canvass the situation in as unobtrusive a manner as possible.

You remember that I put the sand in the gear of our halitosis friend[58] some time ago when the existing anthologies were being examined; hence, after the sifting of other inadequate handbooks there remained that of Broadus. I might say at the start that so far as the University is concerned the name of the author has an

---

53 *The Orators: An English Study*, an experimental mixture of verse and prose by W.H. Auden (London: Faber and Faber 1932).

54 (1895–1978). Acerbic English critic, author, and editor of the literary journal *Scrutiny*.

55 A secretary at Macmillan of Canada.

56 The *Book of Canadian Prose and Verse*, edited by E.K. (Edmund Kemper) Broadus (1876–1936), professor and head of the English Department at the University of Alberta, and his wife, E.H. (Eleanor Hammond) Broadus. The book had been published by Macmillan in 1923. Pratt had been asked for advice and assistance in producing a revised edition.

57 Queen's Park.

58 J.W. Garvin, whose anthology *Canadian Poets* (Toronto: McClelland & Stewart, 1916, 1926) was now outdated

independent market value apart from the content. Therefore, Miss Suttis[59] would have little interest side by side with Broadus. As it stands now, Broadus is accepted for the ensuing academic year beginning October. The book has become a text for the fourth year honour English classes. I find that the students are somewhat less than one hundred, so the sales would not be considerable from this one source, though it is practically certain that they would be repeated year after year as long as the prescription was retained.

I felt that if the book were placed on the Pass Course as well, then that 'hundred market' would be multiplied by two or three or even more, and I was also anxious that the Pass students should be familiar with it. I asked E.K. Brown if he would support me in the proposal to put it on, and he enthusiastically agreed – not for next October however, as the prescriptions are now already final, but rather for October of 1935. Hodgins and Simpson of Trinity[60] are also favourable.

But, all offered critical suggestions which, if met, would I am sure make the book the outstanding anthology, not merely for the University or universities, but for the general public, supplanting 'J.W.'s'[61] which I understand has run into many thousands. This (the Broadus) is a book able to sail in both seas. All were insistent upon thorough-going revision. Hodgins' remark was, 'I hope the price won't be any bigger.' Brown's was, 'The type is not very legible, hard on the eyes; the format is poor; title indistinct; paper very poor.' Could the book be made more attractive at this price? And so on.

But the weightier suggestions are these:

(1) There is much of the poetry, especially in the earlier part, which is of low order and should be abandoned;
(2) It should be made up-to-date with regard to the younger writers of the last ten years;
(3) The prose is the better part at present, but should be supplemented by the newer writers and the portion – a small one – of less important writers reduced;

59 Unidentified.
60 English instructors at Trinity College, University of Toronto.
61 J.W. Garvin's anthology; see the note to 'our halitosis friend' above (p. 120).

(4) I found that most of the staff favoured writers that were Macmillan's. They wanted Grove,[62] Mazo,[63] Morley,[64] Knister,[65] myself, Audrey[66] and Leo.[67]

The opportunity is excellent. I think the future for the book is enormous, as Reading Groups are always asking me what is the best Canadian Anthology. The little biographical sketches are helpful, too.

Can you get some selections from other publishers, like 'Chez Nous,'[68] 'Rock Bound' by Day[69] (Alexander gave it the Book of the Month decision some years ago and rang me up about it when so doing). Do you hold Redvers Dent,[70] Blake's 'Brown Waters'[71]? I would suggest Massey's speech[72] possibly, and so and so on.

If you would revise it, I would undertake to get the favourite authors, works and selections from the other members of the staff. Would Broadus consent to have the revision left in Macmillan hands and still allow his name, as at present? For very obvious reasons I want my own name, that is, if I do the revision, absolutely out of the job. I would be much freer to work behind the scenes. I

62 Frederick Philip Grove (1879–1948), born Felix Paul Greve in East Prussia, was a prolific writer of short stories, essays, and novels, including *Settlers of the Marsh* (Toronto: Ryerson, 1925) and *Master of the Mill* (Toronto: Macmillan, 1944).

63 Mazo de la Roche (1879–1961), Ontario-born author of the 'Jalna' or 'Whiteoak' series of novels chronicling several generations of a fictional Ontario family. The first of these, *Jalna* (Toronto: Macmillan; Boston: Little, Brown, 1927), won the *Atlantic Monthly* $10,000 prize for fiction.

64 Morley Callaghan (1903–90), Toronto-born author of more than a dozen novels and many short stories. His *The Loved and the Lost* (Toronto: Macmillan, 1951) won the Governor General's Award for fiction.

65 Raymond Knister.

66 Audrey Alexandra Brown.

67 Leo Kennedy, whose *The Shrouding* was published by Macmillan in 1933.

68 Unidentified.

69 Frank Parker Day (1881–1950), author of several regional novels. *Rockbound* (Garden City, NY: Doubleday, Dorn, 1928) told the story of the hard lives of Nova Scotia fishermen.

70 Walter Redvers Dent (1900–63), a freelance journalist in Vancouver, had written a novel, *Show Me Death!* (Toronto: Macmillan, 1930) about Canadians in the First World War.

71 William Hume Blake (1861–1924) was a lawyer and fishing enthusiast. *Brown Waters, and Other Sketches* (Toronto: Macmillan, 1916) was one of three books of essays in the tradition of Isaac Walton's *The Complete Angler*. Blake's translation of Louis Hemon's *Marie Chapdelaine* was published by Macmillan in 1947.

72 Toronto-born Vincent Massey (1887–1967) served at various times as Canadian ambassador in Washington, Canadian high commissioner to Great Britain, chancellor of the University of Toronto, and governor general of Canada (1952–9). His chief literary contributions were public addresses of considerable eloquence.

could get Bennet next summer behind it, and Lothian[73] and Sedgewick.[74] You understand this side of the question naturally.

Yours sincerely,
Ned

TO HUGH S. EAYRS

March 27th, 1934.

My dear Hughie:

I have just received your letter regarding the Broadus Anthology[75] and I think your suggestions are excellent. I remember very distinctly Wallace's four lectures upon A Liberal Education In A Modern World,[76] and portions of the book ought to be included. The seven pages you indicate would make a fine allocation. I shall examine them again shortly. Massey,[77] too, by all means.

So far, I have gone through the book mainly for the purpose of excision. The amount of lumber in the early part of the poetic section is appalling – unknown names and indifferent verse. I wonder how it got by Broadus. The only palliation is the developmental reason. I also scoured the prose division, and between the two eliminations I have taken out 130 pages, about one-quarter of the volume. That leaves us an adequate margin for inclusion. Grove should be represented by a selection from Prairie Trails. I find that there is fair unanimity upon this work on account of the purity of the style. The descriptions are picturesque and attractive. I would urge a good slice especially of that part where he works in crystallography so beautifully in his account of snow-drifts. Grove is in good favour academically. Mazo's 'foaling'[78] quite necessary especially at her time of life. You are agreed, eh, what? Callaghan's short story rather than a

73 J.M. Lothian, professor of English at the University of Saskatchewan and the University of Aberdeen.

74 Garnet G. Sedgewick (1882–1949), professor and head of the English Department at the University of British Columbia.

75 See the letter to Hugh Eayrs, 24 February 1934 (pp. 120–3).

76 These lectures by R.C. (Robert Charles) Wallace (1881–1955) had been published by Macmillan with the subheading *The Burwash Lectures Delivered at Victoria University Toronto* (1932).

77 Vincent Massey. See the letter to Eayrs, 24 February 1934 (p. 122).

78 An episode in chapter 19 ('A Variety of Scenes') of Mazo de la Roche's award-winning novel *Jalna* (pp. 256–62).

fiction excerpt. Redvers Dent? What about Merrill[79]? Brown[80] likes him. I mentioned once before Frank Day's Rockbound. But perhaps there are copyright difficulties and I am not sure that he is Canadian.[81] I shall look up this point.

I should exclude any verse from Mazo and Philip on the ground that they are primarily novelists and already represented in that capacity, their poetic effusions being merely casual offerings. Kirkconnell[82] is more of a translator than a poet. I should definitely put Clarke in. His stuff is good enough and it is valuable to have a friend at Queen's. He is a warm personal friend of mine and I intend personally to have a chat with him next May when the R.S.C.[83] meet at Quebec. The chances are excellent for an adoption as he is all powerful when it comes to the English curriculum. British Columbia might be represented by Dalton[84] and Brown.[85] Does Ryerson control Dalton?

I appreciate the copyright hurdle. But one heavy count against the Broadus book was that it did not represent Duncan Campbell Scott and was slim on Roberts,[86] and again, that Carman had minor poems in, instead of, say, Low Tide on Grand Pré. If the costs of purchase are too heavy, what do you think of this suggestion? Approach Duncan, explaining the inexorable character of copyright, but urging the desirability from his own point-of-view and from the standpoint of the Anthology, of his inclusion, and ask him if he could let you have a sheaf of his new unpublished verse. I don't think he would stipulate a price. Roberts might do the same, though here the bargain might possibly be on a different footing. If nothing could be squeezed from Carman, then we might let his selections stand as they are.

---

79 Merrill Denison.

80 E.K. Brown.

81 See the note to '"Rockbound" by Day' in the letter to Eayrs, 24 February (p. 122). Day was born in Nova Scotia. However, his academic career had taken him to the United States: before and after the First World War, he was head of the English Department at the Carnegie Institute of Technology, and later professor of English at Swarthmore College before becoming president of Union College (1928–33). In 1934, he had recently returned to Nova Scotia.

82 Watson Kirkconnell See the note to 'Kirkconnell's points' in the letter to Mrs Horace Parsons, 29 September 1925 (p. 62).

83 Royal Society of Canada.

84 Annie Charlotte Dalton (1865–1938) was born in England and lived most of her life in Vancouver. She published nine slim collections of verse, including *The Marriage of Music* (Vancouver: Evans and Hastings, 1910), *Flame and Adventure* (Toronto: Macmillan, 1924), and *Lilies and Leopards* (Toronto: Ryerson, 1935).

85 Audrey Alexandra Brown.

86 Charles G.D. Roberts.

Who owns Isabella Valancy Crawford[87]? If it is the Baron of Halitosis,[88] I would say 'let well enough alone,' but the two selections, particularly 'Malcolm's Katie' are poor. Her 'Helot' would be admirable, if available. I am thinking of her name as a drawing card for the public market principally.

Again, the Preface must be revised in view of these alterations. I have examined it and scored out contradictions springing out of the revisions. Would Broadus re-write it? I am keeping your suggestions on file and would you, as the ideas strike you, toss them off to me, as we want to make a definitive anthology which would throw into the shade all prospective competitors.

Neddie.

TO F.R. SCOTT

June 6, 1934

My dear Frank:

I have gone through the tome and find it good. I haven't been able to get hold of Finch yet for some reason, but I am sure he will approve the compilation. Now the next thing is to convince Eayrs whose marketing eye is exceedingly sharp. I suppose, you will be up to see him before long or you may write him about it, after which he will consult me. I know he has been turning down manuscripts lately or at least 'postponing' them, so the approach must be well laid.

Love to Leo,[89]
Ned

---

87 (1850–87). Born in Ireland, Crawford came to Ontario at an early age. She wrote numerous serialized novels, short stories, and poems for several Canadian and American publications, but published only one book of verse in her lifetime, *Old Spookes' Pass, Malcolm's Katie and Other Poems* (Toronto: J. Bain, 1884).

88 J.W. Garvin, the editor of Crawford's *Collected Poems*. See the note to 'our halitosis friend' in the letter to Eayrs, 24 February 1934 (p. 120).

89 Leo Kennedy.

TO F.R. SCOTT

Sept. 19, 1934.

Dear Frank:

Eayrs is in New York for ten days or so. He liked the idea of the anthology very much and was favourable to its publication but quite dubious over the market prospects. He does not 'see it as a seller'; hence he requires protection to some degree. However, he is not very keen about getting it before the public this fall as the book would not appear in the 'fall lists' and in his general advertising media. I think he feels the same way about Collin's book on modern poetry.[90] He accepts it but prefers to publish next year.

Eayrs holds all the copyright on my stuff. Personally I would release my material many times over for an anthology of this nature but Eayrs always has taken the stand that a fee, however small, should be paid.

The way out would be to publish poems of mine not yet under the Macmillan imprint. A few of these are already accepted but Smith evidently has turned down most of my new offerings like Silences and some of the short pieces. (Finch thinks, too, that Smith skimped him rather vigorously and that on very subjective grounds.) If a new examination of this stuff provided for a sufficient presentation there would of course be no expense as I control everything I have written since the publishing of Many Moods (two years ago).

'Tangents'[91] leaves itself open to quips on the part of hostile reviewers. What was wrong with 'New Provinces'? I thought we had decided on that title.

Do you think that a year's postponement would be a very serious matter? Would we not have a better 'cull' after the wait? I would prefer that Macmillans handled the book if arrangements could be properly effected – but I would enter into any plan the rest of you thought advisable.

Sincerely
Ned Pratt

90 W.E. Collin's *The White Savannahs*, a study of recent Canadian poets, including Pratt, F.R. Scott, A.J.M. Smith, and A.M. Klein. Like *New Provinces*, it was published by Macmillan in 1936.

91 A new title for the proposed anthology suggested by Scott.

TO LEO KENNEDY

Oct. 24, 1934.

My dear Leo:

I spent an hour with Eayrs last Saturday going over the manuscript and urging him to do the publishing at the 'least expense' to the contributors. He had been away in New York for a week before that, hence the delay.

I found him somewhat decisive against releasing my stuff for another house without fees. He has taken that stand on all other inclusions in anthologies etc., so I couldn't budge him. He owns outright all my verse.

I asked him to draw up a scheme under which he would agree to publish the volume and let me know as soon as possible so I could communicate with you. He is doing that.

There is no chance of a pre-Christmas publication and he is certain that no house would rush it out now without detriment to the book (lack of adequate listing, advertising etc.) I think though he would publish it after the new year. At least I got that partial admission from him. What I am after though is to get Macmillans to take most or all of the risk – without financial encumbrances on the bunch of us.

I will write you in a day or two,

Ned

TO F.R. SCOTT

Nov. 7, 1934

Dear Frank:

I have just received a letter from Hugh Eayrs of Macmillan stating that he is willing to publish the volume subject to certain conditions. I had had a long interview with him the week before, and this is now his official opinion. I am quoting a paragraph:

'We should like to be associated with this book. I don't see any way of our doing it unless in some sort the book is subscribed. I think we should definitely need a list of subscribers equalling $200 or $250, for which the return would be made in books to the subscribers, whether to the poets themselves or to those they name. The rest of the edition we should publish at our own risk paying the usual 10% royalty as the men would instruct us.'

There are six of us. Could we put up $35 each? I am sure Eayrs would stand by the smaller amount. He would publish after the New Year.

Eayrs also objects to the Preface.[92] He says it is unwise. It would stir up unnecessary antagonisms. Let the Scott Roberts group alone and let the volume stand on its own feet without the initial 'nose-tweaking' as he describes it. The book will get plenty of criticism apart from that, but the criticism should be offered in terms of the poetic content within and not centred upon a feature which is merely accessory.

'I think in the interests of the poets themselves they would be much better without any preface at all, or at the most four or five lines of simple explanation that they are aware that their forms and content are new or newer [....], and that they invite the public to look at them or not as they wish'! Quotation.

Say Frank, come along soon to Toronto. Ring me up and we'll see Eayrs and make arrangements.

Is Leo back yet?

Ned

TO F.R. SCOTT

Nov. 30, 1934

My dear Frank:

So Dent's terms[93] are similar to those of Macmillans.

I agree with Leo that we should not undertake the financing of the publishers, but what if that is the only recourse? Those publishers are, first of all, business men with their vision on sales and market conditions.

As for myself, I have not been able to persuade Macmillans to release my verse for another imprint without a financial obligation which I certainly would not want the group to incur. If you succeed in getting a House to take the stuff,

---

92 A.J.M. Smith had written a provocative preface critical of the older Canadian poets and the so-called 'Canadian tradition' represented by Duncan Campbell Scott and Charles G.D. Roberts. It was not published in *New Provinces*, and first appeared in *Canadian Literature* 24 (Spring 1965): 6–9. Pratt has usually been blamed for its rejection, but, as this letter and the letter to Scott of 20 December 1935 illustrate, both Hugh Eayrs of Macmillan Canada and Robert Finch were wary of offending readers and critics.

93 British publishers J.M. Dent and Sons had a branch house in Toronto.

I would withdraw from the collection and leave you a free hand. I would co-operate in every way after the publication to further the sale and the recognition of the volume.

Finch has been through the manuscript and strenuously protests against Smith's 'Hyacinth to Edith.'[94] He says it negates the very spirit of his Introduction, and exhibits no trace of originality. And don't you think that the middle part of 'Shadows There Are' is pretty flat? But the 'Hyacinth' should be plucked definitely.

Sincerely
Ned

TO F.R. SCOTT

Dec. 10, 1934

My dear Frank:

Vi and I extend the most hearty invitation to you to come and stay with us throughout your proposed visit to Toronto. We have at present a friend – Mrs Joliffe, occupying the spare room but she is leaving for Ottawa on December 21st and will remain there till after the new year. So if you can manage the trip between the 21st and the 3rd, the room is yours. I would try to plan a little 'stag' for you as before.

I have your two letters before me – Dent's and Ballantyne's.[95] Ballantyne looks favourable but a new publisher in these uncertain days needs some investigation regarding credit and assets etc. 'The Graphic'[96] and 'Carrier'[97] let their authors down badly. Still he is worth following up.

With regard to myself, it might be that between us we might fish out two or three substitutes for those published by Macmillans and make the charges less. I cannot allow the group to put up anything excessive for myself. I would take the bit in my own teeth first and get out.

On the other hand I want to be loyal to Eayrs. He is a great friend of mine, and my relations with the firm he represents have been of the most cordial

94 Smith's 'Shadows There Are' was included in *New Provinces*, but 'Hyacinth to Edith' was omitted.

95 An old Scottish publishing house with a small branch in Toronto.

96 Graphic Publishers, which advertised itself as 'an all-Canadian Company,' was established by Henry Miller in Ottawa in 1923 but went bankrupt in 1932, leaving many authors with little return for their work.

97 Montreal journalist Louis Carrier (1898–1961) had founded 'Louis Carrier and Company' in 1928 with offices in Montreal and New York. The firm went bankrupt in 1929.

kind. I know he has worked in my interest again and again, and I would stay with him as long as he is in control. I urged the release of these few poems but he has never yet departed from his policy of charging for Macmillan copyright. That is his principle and his business. Since he charges the same fee for a short poem as for a long one – why not exchange a couple of short ones for that 'No 6000' engine poem? – Leo wanted that in as it was modern in theme – away from maples and dog-tooth violets and so forth. Then we might find two or three others on which we might agree and substitute. Eayrs sticks to $25 per poem – too much altogether in my opinion. He might be induced to lower the total by an offer – In any case, I would defray most of the expense in which my contributions involved the group. But this is confidential to our group.

And remember, of course, that I have a personal sense of loyalty to Eayrs who has done many kind things for me in the past few years. I feel the situation somewhat of a dilemma and I do not want to saddle you fellows with it.

However, we can talk it over later. Let me know if you can come between the two dates referred to.

Yours very sincerely
E.J.P.

TO WILLIAM ARTHUR DEACON

April 8, 1935.

My dear Bill:

It was so lovely and so characteristic of you to write that letter. Saturday night was such an event for me because I made my first tentative presentation of the poem.[98] I had never read any portion of it before except with my own family, and it was a joy to read it before 'the boys' of the 'Kit Kat'[99] and receive such overwhelming responses. It was for me the perfect audience because I loved the fellows like brothers and none more, believe me, than your own good self. You have been a grand critical stimulus to me over the years, only one other

98 'The Titanic.'

99 A nickname for the Toronto Writers' Club, derived from a famous eighteenth-century writers' and painters' club named for its founder, Christopher Katt, at whose tavern it first met in 1703. The Toronto Writers' Club replaced a defunct Toronto Men's Press Club in 1923. It survived until 1943, when it collapsed because of the war. In the 1920s and 1930s, its membership comprised most of the writers in Toronto, who held regular, usually lively, meetings. Pratt and Deacon were faithful members throughout most of the club's existence: Deacon had been vice-president in 1930 and became president in October 1931.

person having a like influence and that's naturally my colleague and chief, P.E.[100] I have to thank you for the very bumps I received in my raw and amateurish days ten years ago.[101] I needed them as every 'youngster' does who is worth his beans. And through all your excellent criticisms there ran encouragement and confidence which have meant so much for me. And the appreciation is mutual, for I am honest when I say that I envy the prose style you have cultivated and attained over the years. Your 'Vision'[102] was a joy to me in sheer expression.

I have an ambition of my own, that if ever we get out of this depression and establish our finances at this College, to have a half-a-dozen of the Writers' Club deliver lectures before the classes here periodically, giving their own vital approaches to life to students. I would see to it that they got well paid too by God! That's a pipe dream but I believe there's tobacco behind the smoke, and if I could arrange for a series from you I should be proud.

To revert to the Titanic, I read only a half of the stuff I had in the book which again is only half of the total projected. I am simply swept away by the theme as I was in the Roosevelt[103] only to a vaster extent. It is so much more complex, involves so many more philosophic, economic and artistic issues that I don't want to hurry it too much. I hope to get right at it as soon as exams are over, expecting to finish it by September getting it out as a fall book. I shall delightedly send you a typed carbon well in advance and I shall be glad to get any advice upon the construction so I may make any necessary adjustments before it goes to proof.

The Roosevelt was a rescue of outright heroism simple in its texture. The Diapasons are all the time going in an event like that. But the alternations in the Titanic, the crescendos of cries and fears approaching panic, the terrible silences and innuendos, the tensions, the inward voiceless struggles that issued in decisions, the stark outlines of the iceberg remaining immovable while the ship takes her plunge, grim, alone, and triumphant – well, the subject is unique and will test every resource for the treatment. That's the reason why I intend taking time off closeted and concentrated, so as not to botch the task. I have Beesley, & Shaw and Lightoller (only surviving officer) and others.[104]

---

100 Pelham Edgar.

101 Pratt is recalling Deacon's review of *Titans* in December 1926. (See the letter to Lorne Pierce, 2 January 1927 [pp. 69–70].)

102 Deacon's book, *My Vision of Canada*. See the letter to Deacon, 31 October 1933 (p. 112).

103 'The Roosevelt and the Antinoe.'

104 Books relating the story of the *Titanic*: Lawrence H. Beeseley, *The Loss of the Titanic* (London: Allen, 1912); Captain Frank Shaw, *Famous Shipwrecks* (London: Matthews and Marrot, 1930); and Charles H. Lightoller, *Titanic and Other Ships* (London: Nicholson and Watson, 1935).

Again Bill, my true-hearted friend, thanks. If the book should ever happen to 'take' on a big scale I'll pension all the Writers of the Club when they become superannuated. But it has to be done first –

affectionately
Ned

TO F.R. SCOTT

Victoria College
Toronto, Ont.

Oct. 13, 1935

My dear Frank:

Have you heard of this new Quarterly[105]? Some Puck behind the intelligence of the C.A.A. prompted the suggestion of my Editorship. I accepted it on condition of my having a fairly free hand in selection of the general material. That was granted although the awards are contingent upon the judgment of *twenty representative persons on an Advisory Council.* Would you send me some of your stuff of that *ancient anthology*[106] & let me pick out one or two. Now that I have taken it over, I need your help and Leo's. But I know that the way ahead is rough.

Fraternally
Ned Pratt.

Address Victoria College – personal.

105 In 1935, *Canadian Poetry Magazine* had been established by the Canadian Authors Association in Montreal at their annual meeting. Pratt had been appointed as its first editor that summer and continued in the position until 1943.

106 *New Provinces*, still unpublished, eventually appeared in 1936.

TO GEORGE HERBERT CLARKE

Oct. 25 [1935]

Dear Herbie:

Thanks so much for your encouragement. I would like to get that Hymn[107] for the Magazine. Could you let me have it? I do not know yet just what the first issue will have, as a Board[108] has to decide, but I would like to see it in. Or if you have anything else before the end of November so we can take a look at it. Recent publications (except in book form) are eligible, so long as they are not more than one year's standing.

I have been so busy getting my Titanic out that I have no short stuff left, but maybe later on for the Quarterly.[109]

While all general correspondence goes to address below,[110] will you always write me *personally* so I will be sure of getting anything direct.

Ned

Try to interest Kingston in subscriptions will you.

TO WILSON MACDONALD

November 20th 1935.

My dear Wilson:

Thanks for your kindly letter with its good wishes.[111]

107 A poem by Clarke, 'Hymn to the Spirit Eternal.'

108 Only a few months into the project, Pratt's dissatisfaction with the arrangement, and the composition of the board, is already evident. The advisory board included, in addition to himself, Pelham Edgar, Sir Andrew Macphail, Sir Charles G.D. Roberts, Duncan Campbell Scott, and Mrs John Garvin (Katherine Hale).

109 Clarke had requested a poem for *QQ*.

110 The address of *CPM* appears as a footer: 'Post Office Box No. 491, Station F, Toronto, Ontario.

111 MacDonald had written to congratulate Pratt on the recent publication of *Titanic*. The good feeling is strained: MacDonald has written across the bottom of this letter: 'This is from Pratt – my life-long enemy.'

I know how a lecturing tour takes the energy out of one but I think that your absorption will not preclude you from the bit of leisure which is so necessary for writing. Any time you have a poem on hand, we shall be delighted to publish it though the payment – three dollars or so per page – is scarcely more than a receipt for a manuscript.

With cordial greetings.
E.J.P.

TO F.R. SCOTT

Nov. 29, 1935.

My dear Frank:

I am glad that progress is being made upon the New Provinces. Finch had thought the project was over and was welcoming the idea of the new Quarterly as a means of publishing the stuff over a period of time. I do not know what the publishing expense is going to be.[112] I trust it isn't great as my household bills through Claire's sickness have been devastating and another operation to come on in March. Still, if the costs are moderate, we shall go ahead.

Now about the Quarterly, I want 'the boys' to stand behind me particularly *you*, *Leo*[113] and *Finch*. I want the three of you in the opening issue. I am keeping myself out as I do not want to be open to the charge of exploiting myself. But send me along three or four so I may select one or two. The damn Quarterly is only 48 pages which must contain the selected grade of all contributions coming in from the Dominion. I have sent back 9/10 of the stuff submitted already, and I want a good deal of the *salt* sprinkled through it from the new group.

I am going to have difficulties. The C.A.A. controls it in a sense. They are raising the subscriptions and getting the guarantees (if any), so that the traditional interests will have to be represented. But certainly it is going to exhibit the principle of catholicity and be hospitable to the new and the young.

The pay will be small Frank, but at least it will be something – $2½ or $3 a page at first.

---

112 Hugh Eayrs had stipulated that, in order for Macmillan to publish *New Provinces*, it would have to be subsidized by the six contributors. See the letter to F.R. Scott, 7 November 1934 (pp. 127–8).

113 Leo Kennedy.

Are you coming up Christmas time? Claire is better now and going to school, so I shall have more opportunity to extend a bit of entertainment to you, a dinner or whatnot.

Yours sincerely
Ned Pratt

Leo sent me a couple of poems for the Quarterly. I am printing one if not two of them.

P.

TO DOROTHY LIVESAY[114]

Dec. 5, 1935.

My dear Dee:

'Day and Night' is a splendid bit of work. I will publish it in the opening issue.[115] This is one of the best things I have ever seen you do.

Dee, I think a little punctuation in the short-lined verses might clarify poetic intention. I am aware of some of the changes going on in that direction, but I am afraid the public might put the newer styles down to oversight in proofreading. I do not like too much punctuation myself, but I think the verses are a trifle scant in this case.

Would you send me a final copy so I might send it direct to the printer. I have to save my time in every possible way.

Thanks again Dee. I am more than delighted to have you in this start-up.

Yours
Ned Pratt

---

114 Dorothy Livesay (1909–97) was born in Winnipeg and educated at the universities of Toronto and Paris. Always a social activist, in the 1930s she joined the Communist Party and worked as a social worker and a teacher. Volumes of her poetry include the early modernist collection *Green Pitcher* (Toronto: Macmillan, 1928), *Day and Night* (Toronto: Ryerson, 1944), *Poems for People* (Toronto: Ryerson, 1947), *The Documentaries* (Toronto: Ryerson, 1968), and the retrospective collection *The Woman I Am* (Erin, ON: Porcepic, 1977).

115 It is the first poem in the first issue of the magazine – *CPM* 1 (January 1936): 8–13.

TO CHARLES CLAY

English Department

Dec. 14, 1935.

Dear Mr Clay:

Thank you very much for the copy of the 'Free Press' with its generous notice of the new Quarterly.[116] I also read a few days ago from the Saturday issue in the Common Rooms the review of the 'Titanic.'[117] It warmed my heart. The Free Press has always been most stimulating and encouraging.

There has been quite a bit of confusion in the mail since that Post Office Box address was given for the Quarterly. Some of the letters have gone 'across country' two or three times and some of them I never received. The Postmen are now getting their sense of location.

The response to the magazine requirements has been good, and the result is that we have the winter issue complete already. I should be glad if, when you get hold of any really good stuff, you would slip it along for examination by the Board. We want variety as many a good poem in its own right has to be excluded by reason of the magazine having too much of the same type.

Most sincerely,
Ned Pratt

TO F.R. SCOTT

Victoria College
Toronto Ont.

Dec. 20, 1935.

My dear Frank:

I am putting two poems of yours in the first issue O Tempora and the Epitaph for a Professor;[118] two of Kennedy's[119] and two of Finch's.[120] So the group are being well represented. I hope to feature you fellows right along if the magazine prospers.

116 *CPM*; 'New Poetry Magazine,' *Winnipeg Free Press*, 11 November 1935, 21.
117 'Sweeping Dramatic Poem Deals with The Titanic,' *Winnipeg Free Press*, 7 December 1935, 32.
118 'O Tempora' and 'Epitaph for a Professor,' *CPM* 1 (January 1936): 17.
119 'Loser Take All' and 'Frost,' *CPM* 1 (January 1936): 22.
120 'The Hammers' and 'Window-Piece,' *CPM* 1 (January 1936): 18.

I went over the ms.[121] and read for proof, then took it over to Finch who did likewise. Finch feels very strongly that the Preface ought to go.[122] He doesn't like the tone of it and the general impression which will be left on the public mind that Canadian literature had to wait for us to get its first obstetrical success. We talked it over with Eayrs who likes the verse but is very dubious about the prologue. He calls it 'nose-tweaking.'

Personally, I would feel more contented with a small foreword indicating the point of view.

Then why not, Frank, bring out a volume of your own? It is the most readable stuff of the batch. You have plenty of fine incisive material and a punch to get it across. Think it over.

Ned Pratt

TO GEORGE HERBERT CLARKE

Victoria College, Toronto

Dec. 28, 1935.

My dear George:

I have been wondering over the choice of the sonnet (P.E.I.)[123] or the 'Hymn' for the Quarterly.[124] The Hymn is unquestionably the bigger work in every way and I am not going to forfeit it. As it is over a hundred lines, it will take five pages or more, so I am going to propose it for the second issue and leave the first issue for younger and newer writers almost exclusively. Roberts, Scott[125] and I and two or three of the others agreed to keep our own names out at the start and go in later when convenient and advisable. The whole scheme of the magazine as outlined in the editorial is to go after the rising talent and keep the contributions of the more established poets as backlogs, so to speak, for successive issues.

The Hymn will give ballast to the spring number. Perhaps you and C.G.D. will represent us, then in the third perhaps Scott and another. I think this is the best plan. The other scheme is to put in your sonnet this time, but that would

---

121 Of *New Provinces*.

122 The dispute over A.J.M. Smith's preface to *New Provinces* had been going on for over a year. See the note to 'the Preface' in the letter to Scott, 7 November 1934 (p. 128).

123 'Brackley Beach.' See the letter to Clarke, 22 December 1932 (*EJP: Web*).

124 'Hymn to the Spirit Eternal' appeared in *CPM* 1 (April 1936): 33–7.

125 Sir Charles G.D. Roberts and Duncan Campbell Scott, both of whom were on the board of *CPM*, as was Clarke.

eliminate the Hymn for some time as we do not want to have any contributor appear in too rapid succession. Hence I shall withhold your longer work for the spring. Agreed?

Ned

TO F.R. SCOTT

Jan. 14, 1936

Dear Frank:

I took the manuscript[126] in to Eayrs ten days ago. It was handed over to the Estimates Department for a judgment upon costs.

I rang the office just now after getting your letter and Eayrs replied that he would write you very shortly as to terms. Eayrs is definite upon the exclusion of that Preface as it now stands. Finch suggested H.S. Davis,[127] an outsider though sympathetic to our aims, but I know your opinion on that. I then suggested to Eayrs that you write a short statement of point of view. Eayrs thinks that is admirable but it should be limited to a page.

'So uncle there you are – to the task.' Too bad there has been so much delay but at the bottom of it all was Eayrs' scepticism as to the marketability of the book to justify 'overhead.'

Once the printing is decided on, it would take very little time to put it into shape. Books of verse in this country do not get across in sales. I know it – damn it! If the stuff is of the sentimental type of Edna Jaques,[128] it sells but not otherwise. My Titanic has had a gorgeous press (thanks for your own kind review[129]) but in spite of the warm and cordial critical reception everywhere, the bloody thing scarcely meets costs. It's not the publishers' fault. They have done their damnedest! But this country will not buy verse. *To hell with it.*

Ned

---

126 Of *New Provinces.*

127 The middle initial is incorrect. Finch had suggested that Herbert John Davis be asked to write a foreword to the collection.

128 (1891–1978). A prolific writer of sentimental, mostly domestic verse published in newspapers, popular magazines, as well as over a dozen small volumes of verse.

129 Scott had reviewed *Titanic* in *CF* (January 1936).

TO GEORGE HERBERT CLARKE

2nd [Feb.], 1936

My dear Herbert:

Many thanks for the good words of commendation, etc.[130] The reception has been generally excellent, good reviews, and many warm expressions of appreciation. Sorry you didn't warm to the poker game.[131] I rather enjoyed that bit myself. But, then it's the reviewers prerogative – and as I've often said to you before, he ought not to hesitate to rap on the knuckles when he sees fit to do so. My thanks all the same.

Thanks for the poems you sent too. They are all first rate, especially the 'Hymn,'[132] which will be in next issue I expect, in April – if I can make the deadline. The editorial chores should settle down to a more reasonable temperature soon. So far they have been quite mad. As you are probably aware, the editor is the final work-horse and whipping-boy. I was somewhat unfortunate in the committee I was given, mainly by Edgar. He himself is a great help, of course, and close by for advice. But the others are not much benefit. Pelham promised me a formidable array of literary talent as a supporting committee, but look what I got. I only gave in on the strength of that promise.[133] What I got was Mrs Garvin,[134] poor old Scott,[135] Sir Andy,[136] and Sir Charlie[137] ... Of the lot Charlie is the most help, but a bit petrified in his tastes and erratic in his judgments.

I almost chucked it when the business of awarding prizes came up.[138] But I made it clear that while I was ready to take final editorial responsibility for the stuff that went in, I could not be responsible for such meticulous weighing of merit in such a mass of stuff as would be needed to make awards. Imagine

---

130 Clarke had reviewed Pratt's *Titanic* in *QQ* (January 1935–6): 557–8.

131 In his review Clarke had written of the poker game described in lines 505 to 570 of the poem: 'although zestfully presented and dramatically important, [it] develops some surplusage that, in the interest of balance and proportion, could perhaps be spared.'

132 'Hymn to the Spirit Eternal.'

133 That is, he agreed to edit *CPM*. See the letter to F.R. Scott, 13 October 1935 (p. 132).

134 Amelia (Mrs J.W.) Garvin.

135 Duncan Campbell Scott.

136 Sir Andrew Macphail (1864–1938) practised medicine in Montreal and taught the history of medicine at McGill University from 1907 to 1937. He was a prolific writer of non-medical books and essays.

137 Sir Charles G.D. Roberts.

138 Although the magazine paid only $3 a page to contributors, three or four cash prizes were awarded for poems of 'leading merit' in each issue. The first prize was $25.

being the sacrificial victim of all the outraged non-entities chucked out with the cullage! So now we have an Advisory Board to do the dirty work, though this has greatly multiplied the correspondence chores. You're on the Board, so you know what I mean. Well, we shall see what eventuates. I am not committing myself to any definite term of service. But I'm afraid both my golf averages and my verse output are going to drop like the present temperatures outside. Just wait and see what happens when a certain W. MacD.[139] doesn't win first prize. He and a few of his friends (he has a few, you know) could make a lot of nasty fuss if they chose to do so. But I am not going to lose any sleep. My idea is to keep genuine quality as the first criterion for every issue if possible.

I think we got off to a good resounding launching in the first number, with as much new, good, solid stuff aboard as we could stow under the hatches in forty-odd pages. We try to keep in mind the school of young sharks that lie in wait to snap our collective heads off the moment we show. As yet they don't seem to have broken the surface. But I dare say they will before long. I'm afraid I am in for a damnable procession of headaches, but I do not intend letting them descend to lower parts of the anatomy to afflict me as heartaches, bellyaches, or aches in other unnamed posterior regions. Your sage advice will be appreciated any time, old codger.

Ned

TO F.R. SCOTT

Feb. 23, 1936.

My dear Frank,

Herewith the forty dollar cheque.[140] The Preface is fine: suits the case admirably.[141] Sorry I couldn't see you and put up a party for you as once before.

The damned Magazine[142] is out and though I objected to the Maple Leaf on the cover it was put on. I trust you will appreciate the divergent interests and clashing points of view behind a project like this. I think on the whole that some mighty good stuff got inside; some indifferent material, and some poor, but you should see what we rejected. Lord of Judah! One and one half tons of stinking mackerel.

---

139 Wilson MacDonald.

140 Pratt's share of the cost of publishing *New Provinces*. See the letters to Scott, 7 November 1934 (pp. 127–8) and 10 December 1935 (pp. 129–30).

141 A short foreword by Scott replacing A.J.M. Smith's 'rejected' preface.

142 The first number of *CPM*.

Say, supposing I went through the carbon copy of New Provinces, which I have, would I be at liberty to take the odd poem at the regular ridiculous rates. I need you fellows for stiffening, – where my own personal taste lies. But I am supposed to give a representative collection and not ignore the traditional schools, though I am keeping out the scarlet maples and the beaver dams wherever possible.

Sincerely
Ned P.

TO GEORGE HERBERT CLARKE

March 27, 1936

Dear Herbert:

Your 'Hymn' has gone on to the printer with the rest of the contents.

With regard to the competition, the asterisk placed at the head of a poem indicates that the poem is *non*-competitive. That rule was made at the beginning to eliminate unfairness in a race, say, between a writer like Roberts and some new unknown youngster from a back concession. Of course it is entirely at the option of the contributor. Audrey Brown remained in with the first issue as she is young and needy, but she is starred in the present one because she won a prize in the first.[143] Theodore Goodrich Roberts,[144] Katharine Hale and I are appearing in the current number with asterisks but I think that not one of us with our short poems would win anyway.[145]

Your 'Hymn' would probably win first prize by a group of disinterested critics because it is so substantial and elevated in treatment but so many of the judges are looking for satire today and would be apt to favour that mode. It is all a gamble. Do what you feel like, Herbert. Any choice you make will be perfectly acceptable to me. I am so glad to have that Hymn anyway.

Ned

---

143 Brown's poem 'Penelophon' won first prize as the best poem in the first number of *CPM*. The first poem in the second number was her 'Lammastide' (pp. 8–11).

144 (1877–1953). Roberts, whose middle name is 'Goodridge' (not 'Goodrich' as Pratt has it here) was Charles G.D. Roberts's brother. Born and educated in Fredericton, he spent many years working as a journalist in the United States and Newfoundland. He published two books of poetry and thirty or more novels, mostly in a romantic vein. His 'April Weather' appeared in *CPM* 1 (April 1936): 12.

145 Hale's 'Rudyard Kipling' and Pratt's 'The Prize Cat' (*EJP: CP* 1.301) appeared in *CPM* 1 (April 1936): 15 and 23.

TO INA MCCAULEY[146]

May 8, 1936

My dear Ina:

Your letter came today with its lovely words of appreciation. I am so glad that you like the 'Titanic' and I am so pleased that you read it to your classes. I would be honoured to put my name in the copy when I get it.

Yes, the Californian saw the rockets but failed to come to the rescue of the Titanic. One of the officers came to the cabin of the captain and informed him that rockets (or what looked like rockets) were seen in the vicinity of the Titanic. Captain Lord sleepily asked 'Were they white?' The officer said, 'Yes, sir.' White rockets were definitely distress signals but Lord paid no further attention and went to sleep. When he was placed on the investigation stand in London under Lord Mersey, he gave as his lame excuse that he thought they were the signals of fishermen communicating with one another. The Commissioner condemned his conduct and Lord was stripped of his Command as a penalty. Sheer, gross neglect of a duty. The Californian was only about fifteen miles off and might have rescued all.

The Captain of the Carpathia was knighted for his Services – Sir Arthur Rostrum!

I was sorry to hear that you had been sick, Ina. I trust that you have recovered and that the trip abroad will put twenty pounds of health and weight on you or more, bless you!!

Vi is well, but Claire has a lot of trouble with her foot. She has to have an operation on it next fall and to go in a cast for five months. It is a great worry to us.

Well, the best of life to you.

Most sincerely,
E.J. Pratt

146 A friend of the Pratt family. Born in Belleville (ca 1895), she taught school for many years in London, Ontario. She had sent Pratt a number of questions about *Titanic*, which he attempts to answer here. (See the letter to McCauley, 2 May 1938 [pp. 166–7].)

TO VIOLA PRATT

Tuesday [7 July 1936]

Summer Session School[147]
U of BC.

Dearest Vi:

I have been wondering how you got along during the last three days of heat. The papers here have featured the hundreds all over the west and I have thought so much of Central Saskatchewan[148] – I hope you all stood it without too much ennui and exasperation.

I sent off a couple of little parcels for Claire yesterday which I suppose she will receive by the time she gets this letter.

This place is ideal residentially. It has only one drawback: it is so far removed from the city and the transportation is poor – a bus and a street car take nearly an hour to get down to the centre. I have a room on the top floor of Union College with three double windows opening on miles of land and water, overlooking Vancouver harbour with mountains in the distance. The University grounds are up hill all the way, so you can imagine the elevation and the prospect it commands. Principal Brown[149] is in charge and there are a dozen ministers here attending some church functions. I played golf on the University course today with three old ministers over seventy.

The University main building, few minutes walk from Union, houses the summer students and the lecturing. I lecture from ten to twelve having the afternoons free which is more satisfactory than Halifax. There are twenty-five students in my classes, a very nice group, mostly teachers who have come in from outlying towns. I haven't met any of the Professors whom I knew except Sage in History.[150] Sedgewick is not lecturing himself and Billy MacDonald[151] is on Vancouver Island marking matriculation papers.

---

147 Pratt was teaching summer session classes at the University of British Columbia and living in residence on the campus.

148 Viola and Claire Pratt were visiting Viola's brother, Karl Whitney, in Francis, Saskatchewan, about 50 kilometres southeast of Regina.

149 From 1927 to 1948, J.G. Brown was the principal of Union College, a United Church theological college affiliated with the University of British Columbia.

150 Walter Noble Sage (1888–1963) was professor and head of the History Department at the University of British Columbia.

151 Wilbert L. MacDonald (1879–1966) was a member of the Department of English at the University of British Columbia from 1919 to 1950.

Living here is much cheaper than in Halifax. Union rates are low – just two dollars a day, board and room, and five dollars gives one all his golf for a month. So you see, dearie, I can save to buy salads for you and cones for Cakie when I return.

Next week the 'Authors' come.[152] Pelham's picture almost life size, was in the Vancouver Daily Province yesterday, with a screed underneath describing him as 'Professor, Historian, Poet, Editor, Journalist and Man of Letters.' Pelham will probably buy a few hundred copies to send around. He was also called: – National President of the Association of Canadian Authors and President of the Association of Canadian Bookmen.

I have to read my paper some time next week[153] but I think I will hike back when it is over as I don't want to be drawn in to the discussions.

I wonder darlings how you are getting on. Is Claire enjoying herself? Are the nights cool? Is she taking her new pills and has the sciatica lightened up? I trust it is not going to give her too much bother.

Tell me what the crop prospect is at Francis. What a pity the heat should hit them again this way. Are they ever going to get one good year? How fortunate we are in Toronto comparatively. We must all help one another. In a little while when the first payment comes in I shall slip along a little bit of jink. Tell me how things are. How are your appetites? Have you weighed yourselves? Keep tab on all such matters as concern the frailty of the flesh.

I am sending Cakie her Saturday's allowance (one dollar) plus another one to distribute as she thinks fit. Bless you all – Hello Cakie!

Daddy
Neddie

TO LORNE PIERCE

Summer Session
University of British Columbia
Vancouver BC.

July 12, 1936

---

152 In 1936, the Canadian Authors Association held its annual convention in Vancouver and Victoria from 14 to 20 July.

153 See the letter to Viola Pratt, 16 July 1936 (p. 145).

My Dear Lorne:

Your letter reached me in a roundabout way today. It was forwarded on from Cortleigh Blvd to Francis, thence to Vancouver.

I haven't a single humorous poem[154] since the publication of Many Moods, and the complete copyright of all my stuff is exclusively in the Macmillan possession. Any negotiation, therefore, must be between Ryersons and Hughie. I leave everything of that nature in his hands. I have found him such a grand trustee that I leave copyright or its release to his judgment absolutely. If he feels inclined to give a poem or more, my own good will is behind it. 'The History of John Jones'[155] might be appropriate.

I am enjoying the lecturing at the Summer School immensely. Sedgewick and Billy MacDonald are awfully good to me. The CAA. meets tomorrow and I have to finish off a paper for them.

Very sincerely
Ned Pratt

TO VIOLA PRATT

Summer School
U. of BC.

Thursday am. [16 July 1936]

Vi ducks:

I read my paper yesterday and it was fairly well appreciated.[156] At any rate it's off my chest now. Today I have to speak to the Kiwanians on The Roosevelt & the Antinoe. Mr Dalton[157] is coming up to motor me down from the College. Mrs Dalton is a dear old lady stone-deaf, so for the hour I was there I had to write questions and answers on a pad, much the same way I do for Lorne Pierce. It is

154 Pierce had asked him for a poem suitable for inclusion in *Cap and Bells: An Anthology of Light Verse by Canadian Poets* (Toronto: Ryerson, 1936), edited by J.W. Garvin with a foreword by Pierce. Pratt's 'Jock o'the Links' from *MM* (44; *EJP: CP* 1.289) was selected.

155 (*EJP: CP* 1.63) Originally published in 1923 in *NV*.

156 His paper for the CAA convention was entitled 'Some Tendencies in Modern Poetry.' It was published in part in the *Canadian Author* (September 1936): 10.

157 Businessman William ('Willie') Dalton, husband of poet Annie Charlotte Dalton.

cute the way she peers over my shoulder when I put down a word and the way she infers the conclusion ahead of the last words. Some time she is wrong. The poor old soul had an operation on her spine eight years ago and she is an invalid.

To day I am sending a copy of the Vancouver Province with these funny Caricatures inside. The faces are a scream. The reporter got us all speaking. Look at my mouth, and McCrae[158] who was sitting next to me looks just like that. Exactly. So does Kennedy.[159] They overdid Pelham's eyebrows.[160] I laugh too at Roberts.[161] My, but I think the whole collection is enough to give everyone the jitters.

Nellie McClung[162] looks very efficient. I haven't seen her yet. It will be all over in a day or two. Some of the delegates may go to Victoria to attend a breakfast session, 10-12. I don't know if I can get away. If I do I will accept MacDonald's invitation[163] and spend a week-end with him.

I sent Claire a spoon yesterday with the Vancouver imprint on it. If I go to Victoria, I shall get another.

I hear the heat wave has broken for the East, and for the prairies. I sincerely hope so. A hundred plus must be bad enough even in the dry air of the province.

Love
Ned.

TO VIOLA PRATT

Monday am. 20th [July 1936]

Summer Session

---

158 A.O. McCrae, a Vancouver writer and president of its CAA branch.

159 Howard A. Kennedy (1861–1938), best known for his travel books, was national secretary of the CAA.

160 Pelham Edgar.

161 Sir Charles G.D. Roberts.

162 (1873–1951). Politician, suffragist, social reformer, and writer. Nellie McClung is best remembered for her role in the 'Persons Case' which saw women declared as 'persons' under the law in 1929. Her books included the novel *Sowing Seeds in Danny* (New York: Doubleday, 1908) and her two-volume autobiography, *Clearing in the West: My Own Story* and *The Stream Runs Fast: My Own Story* (Toronto: Thomas Allen, 1935 and 1945 respectively).

163 Wilbert L. (Billy) MacDonald. (See the letter to Viola Pratt, 27 July 1936 [p. 149].)

Vi dear:

Yours and Claire's just arrived from Qu'Appelle[164] on the 16th. I am just dropping this note to submit a proposition. I fancy the constant heat is having an enervating effect on both of you and that works against recuperation. I would suggest this. If I got a nice house for three weeks say from Aug 1 to 21 or later, with a garden and suitable environment would you and Claire come to Vancouver. I was just in at my banker's (Bank of Commerce manager) and he is writing the manager of the Bank of Commerce at Francis, to cash your cheque on your Royal Bank Toronto sufficient to get two return tickets from Regina to Vancouver. That would save time as my large cheque is not made out till Aug. 1. I will reimburse you later. We have the money and we might as well make use of it in the interests of health. The days are lovely here & the nights cool and refreshing. And Claire would sleep better and rest better. If when you get this, you find that the heat is a real burden, wire me Union Coll. stating day of departure and I'll try to get a good home. I need to know definitely if you are coming so I can negotiate which I will do immediately on receipt of a night lettergram from you. If you feel, however, that the weather is breaking for the cooler, and that Claire would prefer to remain where she is then of course we needn't make the change.

I think you would like it here and that three weeks would do you good.

Love
Ned

TO VIOLA PRATT

Summer School
U. of BC.

Friday am. [24 July 1936]

Vivey:

This paper[165] is explained by an examination which I am holding for my class this very hour. Your letter, July 21, was on my office desk when I entered and I am answering it in the intervals of watching and shepherding the class.

---

164 A small town in the Qu'Appelle River valley 50 kilometres east of Regina; a favourite vacation spot.

165 The letter is written on foolscap.

I was sorry that Poison Ivy got a hold on you again – I suppose it means two weeks or more before the plague ends and such a dose of it. Didn't you wash yourself with lots of soap after being in contact with it? It nearly ruins a holiday doesn't it?

I am so relieved that the heat is less now for you and that Claire can sleep out of doors without trouble. Sleep & cool fresh air will do a lot I am confident. No sciatica or temperature is a relief. Now if the back discharge gets less and does not give her any bother.

Letter addiction is a habit in the good direction. If she makes it a point to improve her style it will be fine for later composition. Let her work nature description into it, flowers & trees & shrubs and prairie effects as well as news.

My work is pleasant here but I am a bit lonely to get back to you and Claire. I find the time a little monotonous although I am preparing lectures for next term.

The life up here on the heights is removed from the city almost as much as a village in the country. I play golf with Dr Ramsay a Greek Professor of Saskatoon University[166] and Mr Myers, the Warden of Union College.

This afternoon and tomorrow afternoon I go to Shaughnessy Heights Golf Course to see the open golf game played.[167] It will be a treat to follow some of the world champions around. – Tony Manero,[168] Jimmy Thompson,[169] MacDonald Smith.[170] What a piece of luck to be here when such a game is in progress.

Too bad about Walter Knight[171] isn't it! He had an unfortunate life. Most of the Knight family were in straitened circumstances. If I knew where the sisters lived in Vancouver I would look them up. No one telephoned me.

I had an interesting time at the Victoria Convention which I will describe tomorrow in my letter. Audrey[172] was there with her abeots and deowns worse than at Mrs LeFevre's.[173] I will tell you more in the next. The students are beginning to look at the ceiling and gape so I had better watch them.

Love,
Ned.

166 The University of Saskatchewan at Saskatoon.

167 The Vancouver Jubilee Open, played at the Shaughnessy Heights Golf Club.

168 Winner of the United States Open Golf Tournament in 1936.

169 A British golfer, known as a long hitter, he was runner-up in the U.S. Open Championship in 1935 and the Canadian Open in 1936.

170 Winner of the Canadian Open in 1926 and many other tournaments, he was elected to the Professional Golf Association's Hall of Fame in 1954.

171 Pratt's first cousin, a son of his mother's brother, Allan Knight, who had settled in Regina many years before. Walter Knight had recently died.

172 Audrey Brown.

173 Mrs L.A. LeFevre was a wealthy octogenarian living on a large estate near the campus. Pratt was an occasional visitor there.

TO VIOLA PRATT

Summer School

July 27 [1936]

Vi dear:

Your letter and Cayke's came today, and I am so glad that things are more comfortable for you both, that your ivy business is getting less irritating.

Your account of John[174] is most interesting. I think I could make use of that dinner account in some form or other – just to show that writers are not like Wilson MacDonald, vegetarians and salad fiends. Would you amplify that famous dinner so I can include it in my notes or lectures. It is a scream.

Things are quieter here now since the Convention is over, though I was down to it only three times. The one at Victoria was the most interesting. It was a breakfast, at least announced as such. We went over to the Parliament Buildings at ten to see the archives, and saw letters of the 18th Century from explorers and judges and captains who visited Vancouver and Victoria. There was one letter to Queen Victoria which described a dispute over the name of a place on this Coast. The good Queen wrote diplomatically, taking neither side, rejecting both proposed names, and offered as her choice – New Westminster, the name adopted.

We returned at eleven for breakfast which lasted till one o'clock. Twelve people spoke or read. Edgar gave a fifteen minute address in his choice English, drawing 'exquisite' distinctions between prose and poetry. I read a few poems. Audrey Brown read 'Pilgrims' with five hundred 'abeouts' and 'teowns' till Pelham had to take a drink to solace his annoyance. She is a stuck up little thing, spoke about Nanaimo as claiming her and not Victoria. Yes siree she belonged to Nanaimo.

Mrs Doris Ferne[175] is a charming delicate little lady, the convenor of the Poetry Society. I met most of the contributors some of whom I liked and some I didn't – On the whole it was an attractive place and occasion. I had to leave before the 'brunch' was over as MacDonald[176] was fuming outside at the delay. Mac is a sweet old lad. He has invited me over again, probably next week-end or the next. It helps to relieve some of the monotony here to get the trip.

---

174 Unidentified.

175 Doris Maud Ferne (b. 1896) spent most of her life in Victoria. She wrote verse, stories, and reviews, and gave many radio broadcasts. In 1941, with Dorothy Livesay, Anne Marriott, and Floris McLaren, she co-founded the literary magazine *Contemporary Verse*, edited by Alan Crawley.

176 Pratt's host, Wilbert L. MacDonald.

I have my regular golf game almost every afternoon. Today I went out with three ministers, one of whom was Dr Kerr[177] minister of the biggest United Church in Montreal. He knew Lloyd Smith[178] but thinks Lloyd takes the world much too seriously.

So you are going to the Regina Fair. I guess Claire is keen on it. It will be a change. I hope she sees her friend.

On Friday or Saturday of this week I get my first cheque and I will send you a bit of money.

Excuse the pencil as I let my fountain pen fall and damaged the nib.

Tell Cayke I will send her the film, though perhaps the pictures will be a bit dull through the roll being left aside for a month. I discovered it in the suitcase.

Love
Ned

TO VIOLA PRATT

Thursday [6 Aug. 1936]

Darling Vi:

When I got your letter this morning with the suggestion of hurrying up the lectures for return I decided to telegraph that I would leave on Saturday night 7:15 Aug. 22nd. I had written before saying that I could scarcely get away till Monday night.

The Summer examinations are carried out here like the May exams in Toronto. The papers are printed and seats assigned with regular supervision. The exams are followed by a meeting of the staff with marks and results.

I asked the Dean if I could get relieved from the meeting so I could catch the Wednesday boat[179] at noon on the 26th. He said he thought it could be done if I could get my papers marked in time.

I rang up the C.P.R. and they told me that the train leaving here on Sunday 7:15 would connect with the boat on the following Wed. If I left Sat. night I would have a day at Francis. Would Claire be very much disappointed if I couldn't make the stay-over. It all depends if I can get my returns in. There are

---

177 Reverend F.W. Kerr (b. 1881) had been minister of St Andrew's United Church in Westmount, Montreal, since 1932.

178 A. Lloyd Smith (1890?–1962) had been Pratt's classmate at Victoria College and was now a United Church minister in Montreal.

179 The family was considering making part of their return journey home by lake steamer from Port Arthur to Toronto.

thirty five exams and I may be rushed to bits getting down to the train Sat. night as I am here quite removed from the station. Let me know what you think. If I left Sunday night I could pick you up at Regina without delay and go right on, but I would strain hard to go if Claire would be disappointed if I didn't spend the day there. I will have to come to a decision early enough to get berths, etc.

I have a lot of news to tell you next letter about the C.C.F.[180] activities in the University. What a place for Leila[181] to come to! Earle Birnie[182] whom I have got to like a lot is the most idealistic Utopian going, and some of his speeches and actions would make a cow laugh. You must know him and his friend when they return. My! but the sorrows and burdens of the world rest heavily upon him.

The weather is fine here, no rain for a month. Excuse the pencil. I broke my fountain pen twice and it's now in the pen hospital.

Love
Ned

I am having dinner with Mr and Mrs Dalton tomorrow night.

TO VIOLA PRATT

Monday am. [10 Aug. 1936]

Dearest Vi:

Your letter of August 7 just came in to my desk and it is always a delight to see your handwriting with the little Francis stamp. I shall get a few little articles for the family and for Claire. If I find I can't make the Sat. connection I shall send a few things by parcel post. I am so glad that Claire is sleeping well. When we get back we shall have a couple of weeks at Bobcaygeon and the weather will be at its best.

I have done a considerable amount of work on my new 4th yr Sh. lectures, more lecture writing than I have ever done in one summer. The place has been

---

180 The Co-operative Commonwealth Federation, a socialist political party organized in 1932. In 1961, it united with several labour bodies to form the New Democratic Party (NDP).

181 Leila Robins, the wife of Pratt's friend John Robins, was an ardent supporter of the CCF and the League for Social Reconstruction.

182 Pratt frequently misspells Earle Birney's last name. Birney (1904–95) was born in Calgary and educated at the universities of British Columbia, Toronto, California, and London. He taught English at the universities of Toronto (1936–41) and British Columbia (1946–63). In the 1930s he was strongly attracted to Marxism, but gradually abandoned his attachment. His first book of poetry, *David and Other Poems* (Toronto: Ryerson, 1942), won the Governor General's Award. He won a second Governor General's Award for *Now Is the Time* (Toronto: Ryerson, 1945), and many books of poetry as well as two novels followed.

ideal for work as there are few distractions and I am a lot by myself. This morning I had a phone call from a Mrs Ruth Crook or Cook who said she and her husband were living in Vancouver and they wanted me to come to see them. She is the daughter of our old family physician Dr Duncan of Cupids or Brigus Newfoundland. She is a great friend of Nellie's. I knew her mother quite well. I am to have dinner there next Tuesday.

To night I run over – a hundred yards or so from here – to Mrs Lefevre for dinner. You would like the dear frail old soul – over eighty –. She has a wonderful estate with conservatories and garden and lawn and groves. I go over occasionally to read under the trees. *And I am always sure of a mighty meal*, to contrast with the meals at Union.

To-morrow evening we go to the Dean's residence to a tea or garden party, after which I spend an hour or two at the Birnies', the Muscovites, or Marxists, extreme left wing but so idealistic. You must hear them talk next fall to get the low-down on what the world will be like in the future. University Professors are going to be the world's best paid men with honour & fame. They are to be the crowned heads of the world with enough crowns to go round and poets are sovereigns over the crowned heads. One hundred dollars for a sonnet. So we are all right in the new regime – hot stuff.

Did I tell you in the last letter that I saw Midsummer Night's Dream with Willie and Annie Dalton. OK, yes I did. If that comes to Toronto we must see it. We must get out quite a bit. I am slipping a dollar note for Cayke.

Lots of love
Ned

TO EUGENIE PERRY[183]

Sept. 2, 1936

Dear Miss Perry:

Your bright newsy letter came this morning. The thing I liked so much about all of you in Victoria was your delicious sense of humour and your capacity to accept criticisms, *of course affectionately given*.

The Viceregal party must have been a stunner[184] though I regret this high-hatting business, with its sickening affectations, this 'repel boarders' attitude

183 Martha Eugenie Perry (1898–1958) was born in Ontario, but lived most of her life in Victoria, BC. She wrote for journals on both sides of the Atlantic, published a book on the deaf, a book of fiction, and four collections of verse.

184 In a long letter to Pratt (24 August), Perry had described a short interview with Lady Tweedsmuir, wife of the new governor general (John Buchan, 1875–1940), in which Perry

to use your own flashing description. I wonder what some of you girls in that group will write when you fall in love – may God speed the day! You are such darlings and when you do fall, the plunge will make the Colorado Canyon seem just like the step from a spring-board in a YWCA. swimming pool.

I am sending a copy of my own CPM[185] as the issue is about exhausted.

Best of luck to you & the rest.
E.J. Pratt

TO HUGH S. EAYRS

Nov. 18, 1936

Dear Hughie, my own pal:

Thanks for your kind and characteristic note. It was a pleasure to do anything in which you were involved and I am glad the speech got across and that it made a contribution to the Fair.[186]

Robson[187] told me of the princely efforts you made to insure the success of the 'meet.' You and Reg Saunders next were the inspiration. Bill Deacon also was loud in your praises. He is almost as much a Macmillan man as myself, and of course a Macmillan man means an Eayrs man.

I am having an anxious time this week. Claire went into the Hospital (Wellesley) yesterday for her important foot operation. She is to remain there for a week or ten days with day and night nurses. She came out of the operation all right and so far is getting along fairly well though under strong sedatives. The doctor says if there is no temperature to speak of by Saturday she ought to come along well. That make this week a hectic one for me and Vi.

Thanks again old Hughie.
Neddie

---

had attempted to interest Her Excellency – and through her, the governor general – in the *CPM*. Because Lady Tweedsmuir was interested in the poetry of Audrey Brown, Perry and her friends had taken Brown with them, despite (to quote Perry's letter) 'the way the "Nanaimo poet" has more or less high-hatted us … I imagine it is just her natural inclination to "repel boarders."' Perry's meeting with Lady Tweedsmuir had some significant results. (See Pratt's letter to Lorne Pierce, 16 April 1937 [p. 155].)

185 Perry had given her own copy to Lady Tweedsmuir.

186 The first National Book Fair was held at the King Edward Hotel in Toronto, 9–14 November.

187 Albert H. Robson, business manager for *CPM*, was an art director with the firm Rous & Mann, and an associate of Tom Thomson and the Group of Seven.

TO EUGENIE PERRY

Dec. 1, 1936

Dear Miss Perry:

This is just a note to acknowledge your letter and enclosures.

I appreciate your kind sentiments so much and the warmth of your estimates and appraisals in your paper to the Book-Week meeting. I am passing on some of the comments to my colleague Pelham Edgar who is still bubbling with enthusiasm over the Victoria group.[188] We talk about you a great deal.

Congratulations on your 'The United Empire' article.[189] More power to you!

Victoria is fully represented in the forth-coming issue of the Magazine. I have put in your 'Lumber Camp' so am returning those enclosed with your letter. I like the accuracy of your observation.

Yes, we are going ahead with the mag. Drum up all the subscriptions you can. We may have to defer payments to contributors for a while but we shall continue to publish.

Most cordially
E.J. Pratt

TO E.K. BROWN

1937 FEB 3

TORONTO ONT 3
PROFESSOR E K BROWN
DEPT OF ENGLISH UNIVERSITY OF MANITOBA WINNIPEG

DEAR EDDIE TWO CHAIRS WILL BE TILTED AT DINNER TABLE SATURDAY EVENING IN HONOUR OF YOU AND PHELPS.[190] THIS CONSTITUTES INVITATION TO MY ANNUAL STAG PARTY OF TEN. WE WILL TOAST YOU BOTH IN SAMIAN THE FIGHTING MANS

188 The Victoria-based 'Poetry Group' which Pratt and other participants in the CAA conference at Vancouver had visited in August. (See the letter to Viola Pratt, 27 July 1936 [p. 149].)

189 The journal of the Royal Empire Society; Perry's article, 'British Columbia's Garden Isle,' was published in the November 1936 issue.

190 Brown was head of the Department of English Literature at the University of Manitoba. Arthur Phelps was still in the Department of English at Wesley College, Winnipeg. The invitation was to celebrate Pratt's fifty-fifth birthday on 4 February.

FLUID.[191] YOUR SWINBURNE ARTICLE[192] IMMENSE AM REFERRING MY STUDENTS TO IT.

NED

TO LORNE PIERCE

Victoria College
Toronto

April 16, 1937

My dear Lorne:

At a meeting of the business management of the C.P.M. last week it was decided that the magazine should have some prose discussion in addition to the main body of verse content. Five or six leading prose stylists were picked out to come to our rescue as we want a bang-up number for June in view of His Excellency's promised cooperation.[193] You and Pelham are being asked for a short article or letter each. I know it's a kind of imposition but the demand is growing for auxiliary critical contributions. Would you be so kind as to let me have say any thing between 1000 and 1500 words (about four pages of our issue) about our need for just this sort of a medium in Canadian life, the relation of poetry to contemporary life, its awareness of the zeitgeist, etc. etc. I know you are heavily overhauled but you are a necessity to us old chap.[194]

You could revamp some earlier essay if you like.

The other thing I wish to do is to hand on to you a new poem just completed – The Fable of the Goats.[195] I would like to read it before the R.S.[196] in late May, but it seems that I shall have to go South with Claire on a health trip – suggested by the family physician.[197] I leave on May 24 returning June 20, so I miss the R.S.

If you will do the article or letter, could you let us have it by May 10th?

Affectionately
Ned Pratt

---

191 An allusion to Byron's *Don Juan*: 'In vain – in vain: strike other chords; / Fill high the cup of Samian wine!" (canto 3, section 86, stanza 9).

192 'Swinburne: A Centenary Estimate,' *UTQ* (January 1937): 215–35.

193 As a result of the efforts of Eugenie Perry and other overtures, Lord Tweedsmuir had agreed to address a public gathering in the autumn on behalf of the magazine. (See the letter to Perry, 2 September 1936 [pp. 152–3].)

194 Pierce contributed an essay, 'The Interpreter's House,' published in the June 1937 issue.

195 *EJP: CP* 2.12.

196 Royal Society of Canada.

197 The Pratts's cruise on the *Lady Somers* took them into the Caribbean as far as Kingston, Jamaica, where they spent several days. Returning, they visited Nassau in the Bahamas and Hamilton, Bermuda.

TO GEORGE HERBERT CLARKE

May 15 [1937].

My dear Herbert:

Thanks for your ode.[198] It is a noble one and I would like to publish it but recommendations are coming in from subscribers & contributors that we confine ourselves to previously unpublished stuff. This may come to be our policy with a reservation that any poem printed about the time of the mag. issue might be included.

But I want to whisper a little secret to you which will not be out publicly for ten days. We are giving the prize of the year – the annual 'Seranus Memorial Prize'[199] to your 'Hymn' as the best poem of the four issues. You will therefore be receiving a cheque for $25.00 and the official listing as prize-winner in the forthcoming issue (June).

There are two or three little matters I want to mention to you. Although our magazine is definitely established now yet our finances are quite low, and we have had to postpone payments to contributors which of course are small individually but make up an important sum in the aggregate for the magazine. The Committee decided to make the little individual payments to young and comparatively unknown poets for encouragement, and appeal to the others to relinquish their 'honoraria' until the magazine got well on its feet.

Ten of us put up four hundred dollars with the bank to keep the quarterly going for two years. We don't expect to get it back: so it's a gift. And when a contributor received two prizes, he would get the *larger* one which would supplant the lesser. Is that satisfactory to you? You get the *Seranus* definitely but the treasury can't stand the drain of other payments now. Perhaps in future years we may be able to pay bigger page rates. At present the pay is a gesture.

Congratulations, old boy.

198 'Ode on the Burial of King George the Fifth.' George V had died on 20 January 1936.

199 The prize for the best poem in volume 1 of *CPM* was donated by Margaret Howard, a past president of the Toronto branch of the CAA, in memory of the minor poet and fiction writer Susan Frances Harrison (1859–1935), who wrote under the nom de plume 'Seranus.' Mrs Howard died shortly before the prize was presented, for the first and only time, in the autumn of 1937 to Clarke.

I am sorry that I will not be at the R.S.[200] The doctor says I must take Claire on a sea trip. So Vi & Claire & I go to the Bermudas on May 25 for three weeks. Insurance loans doing it.

Affectionately
Ned

TO PELHAM EDGAR

July 13, 1937

My good old Pelham:

This stationery may be that of the *Canadian Poetry Magazine* and suggestive of Toronto and dusty meetings of the Executive Committee, but this scene right before me is Vancouver harbour with a glacier and a sunset in the background.[201] The same old spot in Union College. I haven't been over to see Mrs Lefevre yet but I am going to give her a ring in a short while. I would like a joint of roast beef and a sample from that Roman decanter.

My golf is very spotty, two successive cards showing 84 and 105: still I persist at it, playing a game almost every day. My partners vary. One day Robertson (Classics),[202] another day Gordon of Edmonton,[203] and the next, Soward in History.[204] My classes are larger than last year – some forty, some twenty, the hours from eight to ten am.

I had an enjoyable afternoon the day before yesterday. Birnie[205] who is now married in a most[?] legal fashion, to Esther invited me to their apartment close to the University gates. Sedgewick,[206] Harrison,[207] Miss Hamilton[208] were with

---

200 Royal Society meetings.

201 Pratt was again teaching in the summer school at the University of British Columbia.

202 John Charles Robertson (1864–1956) had been professor of classics and dean of arts at Victoria College until his retirement in 1932.

203 Robert K. Gordon (1887–1973), a graduate of Toronto and Oxford universities and a member of the Department of English, University of Alberta, is best remembered for his *Anglo-Saxon Poetry* (in translation) (London: Dent, 1926).

204 Frederic H. Soward, a graduate of the universities of Toronto, Edinburgh, and Oxford, was professor and later head of the Department of History at the University of British Columbia.

205 Earle Birney.

206 Garnet G. Sedgewick (1882–1949) had become the first head of the Department of English Literature at University of British Columbia in 1920. A specialist in Chaucer and Shakespeare, he had delivered the Alexander Lectures at the University of Toronto in 1934.

207 Unidentified.

208 A graduate student working as a teaching assistant in the English Department at the summer school. Later in this letter Pratt refers to her application to replace Sally Creighton as a teaching assistant in English at Victoria College, Toronto.

us for cocktails. Sedgewick told us the news for the first time that Jack & Sally[209] had definitely secured their appointments, at which there was general rejoicing. Sedgewick would recommend Miss H. for Sally. She is going to write you applying for a readership. She could do the essay work and the seminar discussion well. You remember her work with you.

Garnet is flourishing as usual, full of his old tricks and quips. I am putting on a dinner for eight of them at the Quadra Club some Saturday in early August to repay some of their hospitality. I am being made a temporary member for that purpose. I supply the meal and Garnet[210] the refreshments other than coffee.

How are you getting along in the Laurentians? The scenery and climate must be perfect there. I hope your cottage is satisfactory. Give my best regards to Dona & Janie.[211] And my love to your grand self. How I wish you were here for a week or two. I feel lonely for my friends always.

Ned

TO EUGENIE PERRY

Summer School
University of BC.

July 21, 1937.

Dear Miss Perry:

Yes I am back again at this Summer School and hard at work on the preparation of lectures, etc. My schedule is a bit more exacting than last year's and my morning lectures beginning at eight o'clock make it impossible for me to stay over any week-end at Victoria. I should like so much to meet my old friends again but the only practicable date I have is Saturday August 14th. I could get away Friday evening by boat, getting into your city Saturday morning leaving again Saturday evening. I have to be here Sunday. Would that be convenient for you? I should like to have something the same as last year – just an informal foregathering with nothing set or too much organized. Just chat. Will you let me know.

That two dollar cheque was for the contribution.[212] It is small but it is meant only for a gesture of policy on the part of the magazine that if it had the funds it would pay more.

---

209 John H. and Sally Creighton were husband and wife.

210 Garnet Sedgewick.

211 Edgar's second wife, the former Dona Waller, whom he had married in 1935, his first wife having died in 1933. Their daughter was born in 1937.

212 Her poem 'Crimson' had appeared in *CPM* 1 (July 1936): 18.

All matters of finance are in the hands of the Business Manager N.A. Benson[213] 116 Glencairn Avenue Toronto. He would deal with that rebate point for you if you wrote him.

Hoping to see you and the rest,

Sincerely
E.J. Pratt

TO CLAIRE PRATT

July 29, 1937

My dear Cayke:

Your letter came yesterday. I am sending a few coronation threes, one King Edward and one unused Newfoundland. A contributor to the Poetry Magazine sent the stamp for return of the manuscript which of course is not current as postage in this country. So I put a Canadian three on and saved the Nfld for you. When you said the values of the Coronation Stamps[214] are going rapidly up did you mean the enclosed? I cannot see how stamps which are out by the millions I suppose could so appreciate. But perhaps they are more limited than we think.

Let me know what stamps to send you from here and I'll only be too glad to secure them for you.

I am slipping in a dollar for pocket money. I will send little Muds otherwise known as big duck a note in a day or two when my first cheque comes in here.

I am having another dinner down town tomorrow night. The English Department here – the visiting professors – are giving Professor Sedgewick a dinner (stag) in return for his stag last week. I have been chosen as Chairman at the dinner, to preside at the head of the table and select the menu. It is to be held at the Georgia Hotel and already I have seen the head Chef and instructed him as to the courses:

(1) Jellied cold consomme
(2) Roast rolled prime rib of beef to be brought in whole as a roast so I can do the carving. (You see it is a family reunion)
(3) Peas

---

213 Nathaniel A. Benson (1903–66) was born and educated in Toronto. He was at various times a journalist, teacher, and advertising executive. He wrote and published verse for many years, including several small books. He also edited the anthology *Modern Canadian Poetry* (Ottawa: Graphic Publishers, 1930).

214 Postage stamps for her collection. The 'Coronation stamps' were a special issue to mark the coronation in May of King George VI and Queen Elizabeth.

(4) Potatoes
(5) Yorkshire Pudding
(6) Raspberries & Cream
(7) Coffee
(8) Cheese
(9) Biscuits
(10) Conversation till midnight.

I wish Mother could get a line-in on the proceedings.

Much love my dear and to Muds.
Daddy.

TO CLAIRE PRATT

August 7th [1937]

Darling Cayke:

[ ] and now a word to dear Cayke. The time is short now, for on Sunday week the 22nd I start off on the midnight train.

I suppose this week you are up at Hazel's.[215] I have been wondering how you got on during the long trip. I felt a bit anxious considering the car. I will feel relieved when I get your letter that you are back in the cottage.

So you have been experiencing cooler weather. That's good though it is not so comfortable up at Atherley[216] as in Toronto under such conditions.

I am going to Victoria next week end just for one day to speak to the Poetry groups. I get rid of having to speak at the Summer Banquet of the School by going to the Island. I was put down on the Programme without my knowing, so I got them to take it off.

I spent an evening with the Daltons[217] last week. For two hours I sat on the couch with the dear old lady and scribbled notes to her. She read them over my shoulder and answered in speech. She is as deaf as a post, of course, and it was a bit funny to see me racing off the messages while Willie Dalton, the husband, beamed on the correspondence. I tried first yelling into her ear, but my loudest screams didn't register so I had to resort to the pencil. Mr Dalton could make her hear by cupping his hands and thundering into one ear. Occasionally

---

215 Hazel Joliffe, whose cottage in Algonquin Park Claire was visiting.

216 Viola Pratt's birthplace; a village near Orillia, about 85 kilometres north of Toronto.

217 See the letter to Viola Pratt, 16 July 1936 (pp. 145–6).

he himself failed and had to repeat it a few times. She is 76 and getting feeble physically though mentally very alert.

I suppose you and Nina[218] got my two letters with the notes.

Much love to you both
Daddy Ned

TO LORNE PIERCE

Sept. 13 [1937]

Good old Lorne:

Your note was on my desk when I arrived at the burg.[219]

I have to thank you for Mrs Dalton's 'Wheat' poem.[220] It is splendid and I am featuring it in the Christmas issue. I would like to see her get the Tweedsmuir Award[221] for that poem. I am also publishing 'Hathor'[222] in the September issue. Isn't it a gem?

Dear old boy, the 'folks' at Vancouver think a great deal of you. They love you. I had many a chat about your fine 'innerds'!

Ned

TO GEORGE HERBERT CLARKE

Oct. 18, 1937

My dear George:

The big meeting for the Canadian Poetry Magazine[223] is being held in Convocation Hall on Wednesday Evening Nov. 24th. The programme is now made up. Tweedsmuir gives the address and a half-dozen poets give readings of

---

218 The Pratts' housemaid.

219 Pratt had returned to Toronto, after spending the final weeks of the summer at the cottage in Bobcaygeon.

220 'Wheat and Barley' by Annie Charlotte Dalton was published in *CPM* 2 (December 1937): 24–30.

221 Dalton was awarded the Tweedsmuir Medal posthumously. She died in the winter of 1938.

222 'To Hathor: The Mistress of Turquoise,' also by Dalton, was published in *CPM* 2 (October 1937): 20.

223 See the letter to Lorne Pierce, 16 April 1937 (p. 155).

not more than five minutes per person.[224] We want you to come and read selections from your Ode[225] and particularly to receive the Seranus award of $25.00 in the presence of his Excellency.[226] Do not fail us George. Write immediately so I can hand on the information to the Committee in charge of programme.

Affectionately
Ned

TO F.R. SCOTT

Nov. 3, 1937

My dear Frank:

Thanks old chap for the $11.16.[227] I shall send on the $5.58 to Finch pronto.

I scarcely expected to purchase my Toronto villa on the strength of the sales, so I am not weeping over the results. It is too bad that you had to stand the brunt of the expense and the labour of accounting etc., but your begotten down the line towards the fifth or sixth generation will receive your reward in Utopia.

Perhaps the Book Fair[228] will stimulate movement but I have grave doubts. Poetry doesn't go over in this country – it simply doesn't.

Sincerely
Ned Pratt

224 The poets who read were Pratt, Charles G.D. Roberts, Wilson MacDonald, Katherine Hale, Nathaniel Benson, and George Herbert Clarke.

225 'Ode on the Burial of King George the Fifth.'

226 See the letter to Clarke, 15 May 1937 [p. 156].

227 Royalties from the sale of *New Provinces*, finally published by Macmillan in the spring of 1936. The amount was to be shared with Robert Finch, the other Toronto contributor.

228 An annual event sponsored by the CAA and designed to stimulate interest in Canadian books.

TO GEORGE HERBERT CLARKE

Jan. 12, 193[8]

Dear Herbert:

Thanks, old boy, for your suggestion regarding Queen's.[229] I should like to go very much. As I spent two years in B.C. my chances there are over. I am sorry about that, as I should dearly love to be with you in such a setting.[230]

My Summer courses in B.C. and Dalhousie[231] consisted of (1) Shakespeare and (2) Modern Poetry and Drama. Those are my specialties in Honours and Pass. I lecture also in Toronto on 19th Century poetry including the period of English 20,[232] so I could take it on with a lot of work on the prose side.

When does your Committee finally decide on appointments?

affec.
Ned Pratt

TO GEORGE HERBERT CLARKE

Jan. 28/38

Dear Herbert:

That 7.00 weekly room looks good to me.[233] Would you kindly engage it for me. I will take all my meals at the 'Cafe round the corner.' Regarding the 'Fable' it is true I did see the story in a small collection of Aesop,[234] but on a later

229 Clarke had proposed that Pratt be offered an appointment to teach at the Queen's University summer school in Kingston.

230 Clarke was to teach at the University of British Columbia summer school in 1938.

231 The Nova Scotia Teachers' Summer School held some of its classes on the Dalhousie University campus.

232 A course in Victorian literature.

233 A bed-sitting room in a house owned by a retired doctor, Richard Cartwright, and his wife. As the house was convenient to the campus, Pratt stayed there during all the summers he taught in Kingston.

234 Clarke had queried the source of Pratt's poem 'The Fable of the Goats.' Pratt recalled the fable from a school reader he had used long ago in Newfoundland but was mistaken in thinking he had seen it in a collection of Aesop's fables. Clarke correctly identified the tale as 'Les deux chèvres' from *Fables choisies mises en vers* by the French poet Jean de La Fontaine (1621–95). (See the letter to Clarke, 18 March 1938 [*EJP: Web*].)

examination of a larger and more authentic edition I couldn't find it. There was obviously some confusion between Aesop and Lafontaine. Sedgewick told me that he thought he saw it in an Aesop collection, but I doubt it was genuine.

Hoping to have a good time with
you at the Royal Society meetings,
Ned

TO J.R.M. BUTLER

Feb. 18, 1938

J.R.M. Butler
Tutor
Trinity College
Cambridge, England.

Dear Sir:

W.C.D. Pacey[235] of Victoria College in the University of Toronto is making application for a Research Studentship at the University of Cambridge, and I should like to support his appeal.

He is one of the most brilliant students the University of Toronto has had in recent years and one of the most deserving. He has led his year in Philosophy, English and History right up to the present and has shown a capacity for research in the necessarily limited fields of an under-graduate course. He has an energetic, original mind and thorough in the pursuit of any assigned subject.

He was 'proxime accessit' for the Rhodes, beating his rival in scholarly qualifications but falling somewhat below in respect to social and artistic attainments. The general margin was very slight.

He has since won the Massey Scholarship which, though considerable, is scarcely sufficient to cover his expenses abroad. He has no private means whatsoever.

---

235 William Cyril Desmond Pacey (1917–75), was born in New Zealand and educated in England and in Canada. He taught English at Brandon College in Manitoba (1940–4) and in 1944 moved to the University of New Brunswick, remaining there in several academic and administrative posts until his death. He is best remembered for championing Canadian literature in *Creative Writing in Canada: A Short History of English-Canadian Literature* (Toronto: Ryerson, 1952), *Ten Canadian Poets: A Group of Biographical and Critical Essays* (Toronto: Ryerson, 1958), his books on Frederick Philip Grove, and many scholarly articles.

He has put himself through his college career by prizes and scholarships and by working as a farm-hand during the summer vacations.[236]

All of the teaching staff who know him believe that he will fulfil his promises.

Yours sincerely

E.J. Pratt
Professor of English
Victoria College
University of Toronto

TO CHARLES G.D. ROBERTS

April 5/38

Dearest Charlie:

Thanks for your letter and batch of poems. I like them a great deal and should like to publish them or some of them in the *C.P.M.*

I have picked out three which are exceptionally fine – Bread for Wings, Cape Breton Hills, Untaught. I will put them in the next number, *June.*[237]

I am sending the rest back to you and I am communicating with Mrs. Eileen Cameron Henry.[238]

Here's to your Chicago trip.

Affectionately
Ned.

---

236 In a letter to David G. Pitt (29 March 1967), Pacey wrote: 'When I was a student [Pratt] somehow got the idea that I was a poor English lad who had come out to Canada to work on a farm and that I was working my way through college. Each September when I returned to Victoria he would … say "Well, Des, you're looking wonderful. That work on the farm agrees with you!" And if anyone else was around, he'd say: "Look at Des Pacey! He slaves away on that farm all summer but he thrives on it!" All this was a bit embarrassing, for I had come to Canada with my widowed mother who married a quite well-to-do Ontario farmer – and my summer farm-work was arduous but quite voluntary.'

237 'Bread for Wings' did not appear; the other two poems were published in *CPM* 3 (June 1938): 24–5.

238 A minor poet; she published *Sea-Woman*, a Ryerson chapbook, in 1945.

TO LEO COX

April 10, 1938

Dear Leo:

Thanks for sending me *River*[239] and my apologies for not writing you before, but I have been abominably busy. It is a fine book and I wish I had the time to review it. I asked Charlie[240] to do the job along with a couple of other *lesser* books. I'll keep watch on what he writes.

With best wishes
Ned Pratt

TO INA MCCAULEY

May 2, 1938

My dear Ina:

It was so sweet of you to write me that lovely letter with the appreciation of your students and yourself. That kind of appreciation is worth more to me than any financial rewards however big. The commercial returns from poetry are generally negligible anyway, but to get letters of enthusiasm from lovers of poetry and literature is the best type of compensation. I was greatly bucked up by the *University of Toronto Quarterly*, which has just appeared. In it there was published a review of Canadian letters for the year 1937 and my latest book[241] came in for warm and kindly consideration. I hope you will see it.

You mentioned some of my own favourites. Apart from the long satire,[242] the three which I like best are Silences, the Prize Cat (an allegorical treatment of Mussolini's snatch of Ethopia)[243] and 'The Empty Room.' I had written a poem

239 *River without End* by Cox was published as a Ryerson chapbook (1937).

240 Possibly Charles G.D. Roberts or Charles Clay. An unsigned review of Cox's book, Helena Coleman's Songs, and C.F. Boyle's *Star before the Wind* was published in *CPM* (June 1938): 54.

241 In the poetry section of *UTQ*'s annual survey of 'Canadian Letters' for 1937 (published April 1938), E.K. Brown had given Pratt's *FG* a brief but enthusiastic review.

242 'The Fable of the Goats.'

243 In fact, 'The Prize Cat' (also known as 'The Prize-Winner') was written at least two years before Italy invaded Ethopia in October 1935 and could not have been an 'allegorical treatment' of that event. (See the letter to F.R. Scott, 9 January 1934 [p. 118].)

on my mother's passing in The Iron Door to get some relief to my bewilderment, which I received because I have an ineradicable belief that we never die except only in the sense of physical dissolution. That belief has grown every year for it is unthinkable to me that Christ had his end on the Cross.

Of course you know that a few years ago we nearly lost Claire through Septicemia. I am always re-living those days and the 'Empty Room'[244] is a poem written in retrospect with the idea that had she passed, the partition between life and death would be very thin. I can scarcely read it to an audience for the catch in my throat; so I steer away from it. Your own mother whom I loved in Belleville, is very very near to you, not symbolically merely, but actually.[245] Nothing can deprive me of such facts as these.

I hear such glowing references to your good self and your work in London. They all love you. To get the affection of students is a real prize – to get the affection of a dog is a spot of sun in the gloom. Those dogs are human, aren't they?

We are getting along at Victoria in the same old way. We entertained at Burwash Hall the other evening all the Vic graduate teachers – some sixty of them. It was too bad you couldn't be present.

In addition to my work here I have been appointed as Editor of the *Canadian Poetry Magazine*, a little quarterly which is trying to get hold of young talent mainly. We have discovered a number of very promising poets throughout Canada. It is the only magazine in the country exclusively devoted to verse. So I am kept pretty busy but I like my work.

If ever we take a trip westward and pass through London, we shall certainly call on you. I remember my lecture trip a few years ago[246] and how much I enjoyed meeting the Vic gang.

Thanks again, dear Ina, for your letter and kind words. It did me good. I shall always be glad to hear from you.

Most cordially
Ned Pratt.

No doctoring or professoring me, *please*.

---

244 (*EJP: CP* 1.291). First published in *The Canadian Magazine* 79 (June 1933): 8

245 McCauley's mother had recently died. Pratt had known her when, as a student minister in the summer of 1909, he had been a supply preacher at the church she attended in Belleville, Ontario.

246 He had made a lecture trip to London, Ontario in May 1925. (See the letter to W.A. Deacon, 4 May 1925 [pp. 58–9].)

TO WILLIAM ARTHUR DEACON

[Spring 1938]

Dear Bill:

I am profoundly thankful that it was not the 'noose' anyway.[247] The correspondence in the names has added greatly to the gaiety of nations. Everybody has been twitting me upon it, and asking how much fucking had been done before the operations started. I'm through now in any case. Whatever opportunities come in through the future must be through the wardens. Let this be a warning to all: –

'He was a man who done a wrong.'

Ned

'The old Bezer, like the dog, must have its day,' a proverb which reminds me of the old Spanish saying –

'With patience and saliva the elephant screwed the ant.'

TO E.K. BROWN

May 31, 1938

My dear Eddie:

I will have that article in your hands by September 1.[248] I am going to the Queen's Summer School from July 5 to August 20. After that I shall be in Toronto and will look you up.

Your splendid review of Canadian letters[249] rejoiced me naturally; not only because of its cordiality but because of the attention which the Quarterly is giving to the Canadian scene. Scores of people have commended it to me personally.

247 Though not explicit, the subject is apparently Pratt's extramarital liaison with a young female graduate student for some months in 1937–8. They had met at the University of British Columbia in the summer of 1937, and she had subsequently transferred to Victoria College (*EJP: MY*, 217). (See the letter to Pelham Edgar, 13 June 1937 [pp. 157–8].)

248 As an editor of *UTQ*, Brown had asked Pratt for an article on Canadian poetry. His 'Canadian Poetry – Past and Present' (*EJP*: PAA, 69–80) was published in the October 1938 issue (1–10).

249 Brown's review appeared in *UTQ* 7 (April 1938): 340–1. In it, he declared that *FG* was 'the most important book of poetry by a Canadian in 1937' and commended Pratt's 'daring experimentation in techniques and … keen awareness of the structure and diseases of contemporary society.'

You would have had your ears burning if you had attended a luncheon in Hart House last month given to the Maritimers in honour of Premier MacDonald.[250] In the informal discussion afterwards three men spoke of you – Sir Robert Falconer[251] who greatly liked your review for its spirit and style; Mr MacLeod President of the Bank of Nova Scotia and a former friend of my father in Newfoundland.[252] He was interested in Maritime writers and said he was proud of the 'references'; and particularly Professor Alexander who said to a group that E.K.B. was the most able mind his class-room had revealed in a teaching experience of over forty years. That was something for Alexander who is usually reticent in praise. I look on you and Bush[253] as our top notchers. You have a tremendous horizon ahead of you, old boy.

My love
Ned

TO EARLE BIRNEY

Wed. p.m. [early 1939]

Dear Earle:

That second stanza of yours is a knock-out; it is as virile a bit of condensed expression as I've seen. So the 'Partisan R'[254] has taken it.

I can't find Potts's verse at hand.[255] It was a very short bit – about 12 lines and without a title. Not much good, but just over the border.

I should like to have 'The World Kitchen'[256] as suiting our C.P.M. The 'Requiem'[257] is powerful stuff. I prefer it personally to the others (excepting of

---

250 Angus L. Macdonald (1890–1954), a former professor at Dalhousie University Law School, was premier of Nova Scotia from 1933 to 1954, except for 1940–5, when he served in the wartime cabinet of Mackenzie King as minister of defence for naval services.

251 Knighted in 1927, Falconer (1867–1943), a former Presbyterian clergyman and professor of Greek at Pine Hill College, Halifax, was president of the University of Toronto from 1907 to 1932. Besides academic administration, he was celebrated for his public oratory and scholarly writing.

252 John Andrew McLeod, a native of Prince Edward Island, had been bank manager in Harbour Grace (1895–7) and in St John's (1898–1900).

253 Douglas Bush.

254 *Partisan Review*.

255 A west coast poet whom Birney found particularly irritating. Pratt published Potts's poem in the October 1939 issue of *CPM* (44).

256 By True Davidson; it was published in the April 1939 issue of *CPM* (20–1).

257 A sub-section of Davidson's 'World Kitchen.'

course your own). The March or late Feb CPM.[258] is made up and God knows whether the following issue will ever come out.

Ned

TO ARTHUR PHELPS

Thursday [1939]

Dear Art.

Your stuff was fine last night[259] – the high note sustained! I had the gang in to my place a little while ago – Dillworth,[260] Jennings,[261] Adaskin,[262] Healy Willan,[263] Hugh Morrison[264] – and we were talking of you. Gladstone Murray[265] claimed that your voice was a 'discovery' in the west. It came over beautifully with all the undulation. I wonder what old Hube[266] would think of your success now seeing that he used to damn the both of us years ago. He had reason to damn mine but certainly not yours.

Ned.

There were five listening in at our radio last night.

---

258 *CPM* 3, no. 4 came out in April 1939.

259 Phelps frequently commented on Canadian poetry in his broadcasts, but given Pratt's references to Phelps's voice and elocution teacher Hubert Greaves, the specific program referred to may be 'How Should Poetry Be Read?' a 1939 *CBC Essay*.

260 [*sic*]. Ira Dilworth was professor of English at the University of British Columbia until 1938, when he became manager of a radio station in Vancouver and regional representative of the CBC. In 1947, he was appointed supervisor of the CBC International Service in Montreal, and in 1950, national director of programming, based in Toronto. His anthology *Twentieth Century Verse* (Toronto: Clarke, Irwin 1945) 'broke new ground … by placing Canadian poets without much fanfare in the company of contemporary British and American poets' (Robert L. McDougall, *The Poet and the Critic*, 218).

261 Charles Jennings, director of programming at the CBC.

262 Murray Adaskin (1906–2002) was a Toronto-born musician and conductor. A violinist with the Toronto Symphony Orchestra from 1923 to 1936, he went on to become the head of the Department of Music at the University of Saskatchewan (1952–66).

263 Composer Healey Willan (1880–1968), born in England, taught music at the Toronto Conservatory, and was organist and choirmaster at the Church of St Mary Magdalene (1921–68).

264 Hugh W. Morrison was director of talks and public affairs broadcasts for the CBC (1938–42). (See the note to 'Morrison' in the letter to John M. Gray, 28 January 1947 [p. 394].)

265 William Ewart Gladstone Murray (1893–1970), formerly with the BBC, was general manager of the CBC (1936–42).

266 Their old friend Hubert Greaves had taught elocution. See the note to 'Hube' in the letter to Arthur Phelps, 9 August 1918 (p. 11).

TO GEORGE HERBERT CLARKE

Feb. 7, 1939.

My dear Herbert:

I should be very happy with English 22.[267] As far as the poetry is concerned, I have for five years given an Honour Course on the period from 1890 to the present (The Wilde-Dowson-Johnson company[268] to our contemporaries). I have also a graduate class in Hardy, one M.A. student in Gerard Manley Hopkins and one in Yeats.

My third year Pass Course runs from Wordsworth to Swinburne, and until three years ago I taught 19th Century thought – Carlyle, Ruskin, Newman, Mill, Arnold, Huxley, Morley and others. I could easily brush up this course. Edgar and I divided the work between us.

Unfortunately, I have never lectured on Chaucer. I do not want you to make any arrangements which would make it difficult for Vincent,[269] and if you get hold of an applicant who can handle Chaucer and part of English 10, feel perfectly free to secure him. I wouldn't mind it in the least as I realize the Summer School interests must be paramount to those of the staff. Herbert, make your decision apart from your esteemed affection for me as your friend. I understand.

If 22 suits you it suits me, but I couldn't do justice to Chaucer.

Affectionately
Ned.

267 This letter continues negotiations for a teaching appointment at Queen's University summer school. See Pratt's letter to Clarke, 27 January (*EJP: Web*).

268 Oscar Wilde, Ernest Dowson, and Lionel Johnson.

269 C.J. Vincent (1906–68), educated at the universities of Western Ontario and Harvard, taught English at Queen's University from 1937 to 1962.

270 Madge Hamilton Lyons Macbeth (1878–1965), an American by birth, lived most of her life in Ottawa, publishing several novels under the pseudonym 'Gilbert Knox,' including *The Land of the Afternoon* (Ottawa: Graphic Publishers, 1924), a satire on political and social life in Ottawa. Active in the Ottawa branch of the CAA, she was national president from 1939 to 1942.

TO MADGE MACBETH[270]

May 16, 1939

Dear Mrs Madge:

I have been actually sunk for two or three days thinking of what happened to you last Saturday night.[271] You came all the way from Ottawa to speak to us and then had to scurry off to catch your train without giving us a sentence of your speech. When you wrote me that little note at the table I didn't know that you had to rush for the train. I thought you meant that the attention of the audience was so draggy that you wouldn't get any response.

I really didn't know how to handle the old gentleman.[272] I wanted to pull him by the coat-tails but I thought he would be offended if I did, and as he indicated four or five times that he intended to conclude I just waited hoping he would do so.

If only you had been on before him! I understood that you would come first, till the last minute arrangements.

What will you think of our outfit anyway – a scurvy business! On my way home I exhausted all the vocabulary of oaths and nautical terms, on myself, the T.B. of the CAA,[273] and the Universe. Will you ever forgive us Madge?

Yours in pain
Ned Pratt

271 The incident referred to occurred at the annual dinner meeting of the Toronto branch of the CAA on 13 May, when, after being installed as branch president, Pratt chaired the subsequent proceedings.

272 Sir Charles G.D. Roberts, then in his eightieth year.

273 The Toronto branch of the CAA.

IV Historical Fact and Epic Construction, 1939–1944

... to show the relationship between fact and poetry ... historical and epic construction.
– E.J. Pratt to E.K. Brown, 20 April 1942

TO CLAIRE PRATT

[Kingston, Ontario]

Thursday pm.

[13 July 1939]

Dearest Cayke:

I have just written mother and now I am sending a little note to you. She sent me your letter written airmail. It came on the following day – so much faster than surface mail isn't it. By now I suppose you are at Red Deer and I am wondering how you are getting along.

I am liking my work here very much. I lecture from eight to ten, the same as last year. Then I come back to my house after a late breakfast and work at the Jesuit Relations[1] till four when I am whisked off to the golf course. Following eighteen holes I have dinner at the Club House, then whisked back again to the house. And so to bed.

Dr Cartwright is an old man about 76, and Mrs Cartwright takes such care of him. Every now and again I hear her saying to herself, 'Oh, here's Dicky,' and she bounces to the door to let him in. And '*D*icky *d*ear, *d*inner (alliteration)

1 *Jesuit Relations and Allied Documents*, ed. R.G. Thwarts, 73 vols. (Cleveland: Burrows Brothers, 1896–1901).

is re*ady*.' Again, 'Time to get up Dicky' 'Did you take your pills Dicky' 'Don't take the stairs too fast Dicky.' It's *Dicky, Dicky, Dicky* while his name is Richard Cobden Cartwright, M.D. In fact yesterday morning I called him Mr Dick just by mistake and then corrected it. They are two dear souls but I must say she is a little on the sentimental side when the dear Dick is in the house.

Now mind that you write me, now a letter, now a card, and let me know when you want a few nickels – I had almost said 'Dickels' – So strong is habit.

Lovingly
Daddy.

TO CLAIRE PRATT

[Kingston, Ontario]

Thursday [20 July 1939]

My dear Cayke:

It was good to hear from you at Sylvan Lake[2] and that you were enjoying your trip.

Mother and Phoebe[3] are going to visit Kingston tomorrow-night spending the week-end with me. I am making arrangements with a friend, Professor Neish,[4] to take us all out on a bass-fishing expedition Saturday afternoon. If we get any bass we shall cook them on the shore. I will make a fire on a stone fire-place and will cook the delicious morsels in bacon drip which Neish will bring along with him. Mother is motoring down staying over in a few places on the way and will return Sunday afternoon.

I am enclosing a clipping from the Globe and Mail about the inauguration of the trans-Atlantic air service. Will you get the Post officer of Red Deer to tell you how you should send covers.[5] I shall make inquiries here and send some. Perhaps the best thing would be to send them all to Uncle Art[6] & get him to return them to us later. If I get any further information I'll slip it along to you.

---

2 A small town on a lake just west of Red Deer.

3 A friend of the family.

4 Professor Arthur Neish, a biologist at Queen's University. He later joined the National Research Council, where he made a name for himself as a pioneer in plant biotechnology.

5 A philatelists' term for an envelope bearing a newly issued postage stamp and the postmark date. Claire was an avid stamp collector.

6 Pratt's brother Arthur lived in Liverpool, England.

I am working away at Jean de Brébeuf – (Breeboof) and making fair progress. I have at hand forty volumes of the Jesuit Relations and it takes quite a bit of ploughing to get through the thousands of pages and find out just what material is suitable. I am not going to hurry it too fast as the Anniversary is this Summer not the next as I first thought. 1939 is the tercentenary of the founding of the Jesuit mission 1639. So I am out one year. But that gives me more leisure though I have lost the opportunity of getting on with the book on the *big* pilgrimage to the Shrine.[7] Still there are others to come.

Love Daddy.

TO CLAIRE PRATT

[Kingston, Ontario]

July 28, 1939

Darling Cayke:

Thanks for your letter and for mother's which she sent on. I am so glad that you have had a good time so far and I am sure you will enjoy it right through. I am sending seven dollars to you and I would like if you would distribute fifty cents each to the children[8] from me keeping the balance for yourself. I do not remember how many there are.

I am playing in the Cataraqui Golf Tournament sponsored by the Summer School. I took part in the qualifying round yesterday and posted an 88, though one fellow from Alberta had a 78. The semi-finals come next week finishing up with the finals. I may get a lamp-shade or a tea-pot or vase or probably golf-balls. If I have any choice I shall select something for the house.

Next Sunday week I have to give a recital in the Grant Hall to the Summer students. I am giving the 'Titanic.' The audience is a large one – about 700 – something like the Halifax recitals though I don't get any pay here. I haven't heard anything yet from the Association of Canadian Clubs about that projected tour next Spring to the West.[9] I hope they don't pass it up, as the trip will be grand for me to get in touch with the Clubs through the country.

---

7 The Martyrs' Shrine at Midland, Ontario, near Georgian Bay.

8 Her cousins, Ralph Whitney's children.

9 The Association, which had sponsored his recital tours in 1927–8, had proposed a tour for the spring of 1940. The outbreak of the Second World War in September 1939 caused a postponement and eventual cancellation.

The Cartwrights[10] have recently got a small dog and do you know what Mrs Cartwright has called it? 'Dicky'! Now when I hear the name called out there are always two responses (1) the slow steps of the doctor coming down stairs to dinner and (2) the scamper and bark of the terrier. Imagine it – 'Dicky' again. When I see the dog I name it always 'Ticonderoga'[11] ironically, long for 'Tic.'

Well, darling, write when you get a chance and my best to the whole family especially to Ralph and Ernestine[12] – Felicitations.

lovingly
Dad.

TO CLAIRE PRATT

[Kingston, Ontario]

Aug. 1 [1939].

Dearest Cakes:

Your early letter came last night and I am breathless at the way you write. Your description of the lake and the clouds was a prose poem. You really do not know how beautifully you can write. It is either modesty or an inferiority complex which denies the ability. Now cultivate it because it is an immense joy when it is pursued.

I am sending this note to Sylvan Lake as you will get it sooner. Last week I sent seven dollars to you. I suppose you have it by this time.

I am in the midst of my tournament throes.[13] I won the first competition beating my partner by four up and three to go – a sound hiding. That is, there were sixteen players – eight pairs. If I win in the next, then I go on to the third competition, two pairs against two pairs, and if I win then I am in the final. It will be a battle royal and I may go down with my flags flying – a noble defeat. I shall transmit the news.

---

10 See the third paragraph of the letter to Claire Pratt, 13 July (pp. 173–4).

11 An Iroquois place name meaning 'between two waters.' Pratt seems to have had the notion that it was a personal name. See the discussion of Indian names in his letter to Viola and Claire Pratt, 23 July 1940 (p. 189).

12 Ralph Whitney had just married his second wife.

13 The summer session golf tournament at the Cataraqui Golf Club.

It seems that there will be no reading lamp or punch bowl this time, but another cup to the victor. That will mean one at each end of the mantelpiece in the living room for you and mother to gloat over with your optical lamps.

If the Midland celebrations[14] last into August I may run up to the Shrine after my lectures. Would you like to come with mother and me to see the burning of St. Marie and the martyrdoms with real Iroquois Indians making the grand assault on the Hurons and the missionaries? Perhaps Mary Ellen[15] too would like to learn a little of Canadian history written in blood and fire! Derry[16] might like to come back with you to witness the event. Tell him he is invited and any of the others who might be able to stand red-blooded history. Your Pentecostal camp-meeting would be a tame thing in comparison. Even a wrestling bout would be an affair of two love-birds alongside of it.

Lovingly
Dad

TO GEORGE HERBERT CLARKE

Tuesday am.

[Aug. 1939]

Dear Herbert:

Your letter and the Eagle poem[17] just came. Thanks for the emendations: they are all needed and I am returning the poem for possible inclusion in the number after next. If the Committee find it too long, please return it. I am only sorry that I have no short pieces to submit.

---

14 Celebrations of the tercentenary of the founding of Fort Ste Marie, including a dramatic pageant depicting some of the historical events.

15 A school friend of Claire.

16 Unidentified.

17 Pratt's 'The Old Eagle' (*EJP: CP* 2.38) was published in *QQ* 46 (Winter 1939): 428–30. It appeared in *SL* and *CP1* and *CP2* as 'The Dying Eagle.'

I have been making further inquiries about MacKinnon[18] and all the recommendations are of the highest praise. Malcolm Wallace[19] and Knox[20] think highly of him. His M.A. was of the first class Honours rank and easily the best of the English School last Spring. I feel sure that he would make an excellent teacher and a loyal colleague. He comes from a good family and has been brought-up in an atmosphere of culture & refinement.

Although he took a Second Class once in E & H,[21] yet his English part was first. His extra-curricular activities were manifold and I am confident that his future work, granted concentration, will be admirable.

affectionately
Ned Pratt

P.S. I may say that MacKinnon was our own Department's suggestion for Fellow at Victoria 1939-40, but our funds are inadequate

---

TO MEMBERS OF THE CANADIAN AUTHORS ASSOCIATION

21 Cortleigh Blvd., Toronto, Sep. 30, 1939

Dear Sir:

This is to direct your attention to a 15-minute radio program originating in Toronto over the coast-to-coast hook-up of the CBC. This program is a review of war books by William Arthur Deacon.[22]

Our interest arises from the fact that we understand that it is likely to be the only broadcast of a literary nature for the duration of the war, with the exception of a possible second broadcast in connection with Canadian Book Week. There is, however, the possibility that book reviews can be reinstated if there is

18 M.M.H. ('Murdo') MacKinnon (b. 1917) was educated at the University of Toronto. He taught English at the University of Western Ontario (1946–64) and was for some years head of department there before becoming dean of arts and professor of English (1975-82) at the University of Guelph (1964–70).

19 Malcolm Wallace (1873–1960) was born in Essex County, Ontario, and was a graduate of the universities of Toronto and Chicago. He was professor of English at University College, Toronto, and head of department (1926–44). He is chiefly remembered for his *Life of Sir Philip Sidney* (Cambridge: Cambridge University Press, 1915). He and Pratt were golf and stag-party cronies for more than thirty years.

20 R.S. Knox.

21 English and history.

22 The Second World War began on 1 September with Germany's invasion of Poland. Canada entered the war on 10 September.

sufficient interest shown in this first – and, so far, only – scheduled Canadian book review on the air.

It is our suggestion that all branches of the Canadian Authors Association interest their members in this event. If they desire, as we think they will, that such broadcasts be continued, we urge that they write the station from which they have heard the broadcast. They should state their appreciation and express the hope that book reviews be again a regular feature.

We may say that members of the Toronto Branch, with whom we have talked, feel that a general effort on the part of those interested in literature should be made at this time to increase the percentage of CBC time devoted to books. We assume that you and the members of your Branch are as concerned as we are that steps will be taken to impress the CBC with the fact that we, as individuals, are anxious to have these broadcasts included as regular network programs.

The way to do this, as you know, is to have letters reach the stations through which the broadcast has been heard. The present policy of the CBC would appear to be a trend toward commercial programs and war news. Whatever the merit of these, we feel that it should not be done at the cost of eliminating book reviews. May we have your views on this whole situation?

Yours truly, E.J. Pratt, President

7:45 E.S.T. Oct., 6th.

TO MADGE MACBETH

TORONTO ONT FEB 15 [1940]

MRS MADGE MACBETH
324 CHAPEL ST OTTAWA ONT

RESOLVED THAT THE EXECUTIVE OF THE TORONTO BRANCH AFTER CAREFULLY CONSIDERING THE PROPOSAL TO TAKE OVER THE CANADIAN BOOKMAN[23] AND RENAME THE ORGAN OF THE ASSOCIATION THE CANADIAN AUTHOR AND BOOKMAN ARE UNANIMOUSLY AND UNALTERABLY OPPOSED TO THUS

23 *CB* had been the official organ of the now-defunct Association of Canadian Bookmen, an organization mainly of booksellers and publishers. *The Canadian Author* was the official organ of the CAA. This proposal to amalgamate the two under the auspices of the CAA was approved despite the objections of the Toronto branch. The first issue of *The Canadian Author and Bookman* appeared in April 1940.

SUBORDINATING THE NAME CANADIAN BOOKMAN FOR AN ASSOCIATION SUCH AS OURS IT IS MORE IMPORTANT TO HAVE A NAME WHICH INDICATES AND INCLUDES ALL THOSE WHO LOVE GOOD BOOKS AND READ THEM AS WELL AS THOSE WHO WRITE THEM THIS BRANCH STANDS PAT ON THIS RECOMMENDATION AND WILL OPPOSE ANY DIFFERING DECISION

THE EXECUTIVE
COMMITTEE OF TORONTO
BRANCH, E.J. PRATT
PRESIDENT.

TO LEO COX

March 27/40

Dear Leo:

Thanks for your kind letter and for the consent of Lady Roddick to the appearance of her name.[24] It involves no liability of course.

Could you let me have a few poems from the Montrealers. A representation might soften criticism though, of course the Barry-Henderson-Sproule outfit[25] do not count.

I have just refused a long poem of LeClaire[26] – sent it back with a rejection slip. It may make him mad but I simply couldn't take it. Have you two or three more of your own? I need that stiffening. And, if you could let me have three or four Montreal pieces, it would help to counteract the Toronto flavour of that recent competition.[27]

Sincerely
Ned.

---

24 Born Amy Redpath (ca 1880), widow of Montreal surgeon, medical professor, and dean of medicine at McGill, Sir Thomas Roddick (1846–1923). By 1940 she had published a dozen or more books of verse. She had agreed to let her name appear on the masthead of the *CPM* as a member of the Advisory Council on Awards.

25 Lily Barry, Christine Henderson, and Dorothy Sproule: active members of the Poetry Group of the Montreal branch of the CAA.

26 Gordon LeClaire (b. 1905), a high school teacher of English in Montreal, who sometimes travelled as a lecturer and recitalist. He published his verse in journals, as well as a half-dozen slim collections.

27 The competition for 'best poem of the year' published in the *CPM*.

TO LORNE PIERCE

June 7, 1940

My very dear Lorne:

Your letter and kind words of appreciation and stimulus duly received. My lord, I am glad to have the gold[28] and particularly your illustrious name which will remain in the vault of Victoria College for safety. The medal will be taken out from time to time to be shown my intimate friends.

I am bringing out Brébeuf in a few weeks. I think it is the best work I have ever done in my life, but the war market is not hospitable to poetry I am afraid.

As ever
Ned.

TO ELLEN ELLIOTT[29]

Victoria College
Toronto

June 7, 1940

Dear Miss Elliott:

The enclosed type script might do for the jacket.[30] I have taken it largely from a previous blurb and added the recent news. I don't want to 'put on the dog' too much.

I think that the quotations might be appended, and one of the lecture bulletins could be forwarded to Southam.[31]

I want to thank you personally for your interest in the coming volume. You can count on me for any cooperation with Macmillans of course, as always. My memories are sweet, and the staff are my best of friends. Just let me know when I can be of any service whatsoever.

28 Pratt had just been awarded the 1940 Lorne Pierce Gold Medal for 'achievement in imaginative and creative literature.'

29 Ellen Elliott, born (1900) in England, joined Macmillan of Canada as a secretary in 1920. From 1925 to 1937 she was secretary to the company's president, Hugh Eayrs. Appointed secretary of the company in 1937 and managing director in 1939, she became company director in 1942.

30 Of *BB* (*EJP: CP* 2.46).

31 A major Canadian news agency.

You will not forget the sliding scale when you come to make out the terms.

Yours very sincerely
Ned Pratt

TO GEORGE HERBERT CLARKE

June 21, 1940

My dear Herbert:

I have been reading your 'Catastrophe in King Lear'[32] and finding it informative and stimulating. I wish you would gather your monographs together in a collected volume.

What about your Hamlet?[33] Are you having it published in the Transactions? Might I have a copy of it? It is both comprehensive and succinct.

Earle Birney has submitted some poems to me for consideration by the Canadian Poetry Magazine. As the poor old magazine may not bring out another issue on account of the Blitzkrieg,[34] I am passing the best of his verses on to you.[35] I asked Birney to submit them officially which he has done. I think some of his verse has quality such as the *Monody* and *1940* though I think '*Lament*' is a little stiff.[36]

If you find them unacceptable you might return them in his enclosed envelope. Birney is quite a brilliant fellow and will go far.

I hope to see you before you go south.[37]

Affectionately,
Ned.

---

32 Clarke's paper had been published in *QQ*, 41, no. 3 (Autumn 1934): 368–82.

33 'Hamlet in the Twentieth Century,' a paper Clarke had delivered at the recent meetings of the Royal Society of Canada, was published in *Royal Society Transactions*, 3rd series, 34 – section 2 (1940): 1–13.

34 Pratt was writing as France fell to Hitler's forces. The Battle of Britain was about to begin.

35 To Clarke as editor of *QQ*.

36 'Monody on a Century' was published in *CPM* 5 (September 1940): 25.

37 Clarke was leaving to teach summer school in Tennessee.

TO VIOLA PRATT

[Kingston, Ontario]

Thursday morning [4 July 1940]

Dearest Vi:

I got Claire's card this morning and I shall write her soon. I suppose Bolton Camp, Bolton, is enough.[38]

I am very comfortably situated here, same room, same lecture hours, same friends. As soon as I rounded the corner of University Avenue and Union, there was the old lady, the nurse of John Austin,[39] 94, sitting on the verandah, rocking her chair, watching all the automobiles as they passed. The two dogs were at her feet in exactly the same position as when I saw them last. I called on Austin last night and spent a couple of hours with him. He has grown fatter I think, but he is the same cheery genial old self.

I saw Pete McQueen[40] today. He is teaching Economics. I expect to play the odd game with him. The Steaceys[41] were out at the golf Club sitting in the same arm chairs talking over their scores. Bill Robertson was a little balder, and the golfing Professional Bill Greene wore exactly the same clothes and cap and tie as last August.

Mrs Cartwright has just come up to put a dish of strawberries on my desk. She has two boarders a Dr Taylor, professor of Chemistry, and his wife who occupy the up-stairs rooms.

I had my first lecture, to a class nearly twice the size of last year – the room was full with approximately 60. About a dozen of them were old students.

I had my breakfast at ten over at the Coffee shop. Same management, and same diet – bacon and two eggs, toast and coffee. Then from 11 to 4 I am here in this room working up some Shakespeare lectures. I am going to write them out in simple detail so I can pass them on to Claire. They will simplify the business when she starts to study.[42]

38 A children's summer camp 20 kilometres northwest of Toronto where nineteen-year-old Claire was working as a counsellor.

39 Dr L.J. Austin, a neighbour of the Cartwrights, had been professor of surgery at Queen's University.

40 Robert ('Pete') McQueen (1896–1941) was professor of economics and head of the department at the University of Manitoba, and a director of the Bank of Canada. He died in a plane crash in February 1941.

41 Walter Steacey was a Kingston businessman with whom Pratt played golf.

42 Claire was to begin university studies at Victoria College in September.

The war news is fearful. Mrs Cartwright's nephew John MacIntyre – her sister's son – enlisted as a wireless operator on a transport. The ship was torpedoed off the coast of Ireland last week and many were lost. John was saved – so the report came yesterday. I listened in today to the account of the English-French fight off the coast of Africa.[43] The good part of it is that now the French remaining squadrons are with the English in the struggle.

I wonder how you got on the last two nights. Last night you were by yourself. I wish someone would stay in the house with you. Make sure all the doors are locked and that you telephone Alice in the morning at a precise hour.

What books are you reading? And tell me just what you are doing all through the day. Spending much of the time at the Wesley Buildings[44] I suppose!

In a few days Brébeuf will be out and I will send you the first author's copy forwarded to me. It is quite exciting particularly when the pilgrimages will soon be on the way. I think we ought to take a trip up there on one week-end in August before the end of the sessions – Saturday morning early getting back at night possibly.

I hope Claire will be comfortable at Bolton. Did she take a fly-tox container with her. It is likely that with so much rain, there will be a lot of mosquitoes. She evidently was looking forward to the experience and undoubtedly it will be good for her. Is there telephone connection with the camp direct?

My, but this writing table is wobbly and I can't get my knees underneath: so I am writing sideways.

Write me very soon my darling Vi,

With every love
Ned.

TO PELHAM EDGAR

152 University Ave
Kingston, Ont.

July 19, 1940

Dearest Pelham, Dona and Jane:

Here I am at the same place as last year teaching a class, playing golf and taking whatever solids and fluids are available in a dry and lean Presbyterian

---

43 On 3 July a British naval task force attacked French naval units at Oran, Algeria, to prevent their falling into German hands.

44 Location of the head offices of the United Church, Ryerson Press, and the United Church Publishing House for which Viola worked.

community. 'Brébeuf' has at last come out and it looks fine in format and type. I am giving a lecture on it at Grant Hall Sunday evening, July 28, to about four hundred students and visitors and the manager of the Book Department of Queen's is putting some copies on display at his store. I trust at least one per cent of the auditors will take a look at the cover in any case.

Miss Elliott says that she sent a copy direct to you from the store. I hope you got it.

Pelham you have been a peach right through the whole operation and I love you for it. I hope the final set-up appeals to you. Deacon is reviewing it in the Aug. 3 Globe & Mail[45] and I know Morgan-Powell will give it space.

Are you having any golf on the old course at the University? My golf is spotty running from 85 to 102 on two successive days. There is a tournament on next week sponsored by the Extension Dept of the Summer School. I won the cup two years ago; lost it last year to a dub (on handicap) and I am trying the chances again. What are you doing old dear this summer? Isn't it too bad we can't have a day or two together when the holidays are on? We must do our damnedest to see a lot of each other in the early fall. I feel I depend more and more on my friends as time goes on. It is a deep-seated instinct.

A chap here named Steacey in the dry goods business promises to send me a dozen partridge in October. What a feast if he does! I hope Bert[46] joins our company again. We have lost sight of him practically during the last six months. Hincks[47] told me that it is one of his ambitions to regain the lapsed evenings. It alone is life and life abounding. Damn Hitler! He has put the crimp in everything even in our festal birthrights.

Do write me darling boy.

Enclosed for my little niece[48] from her god-uncle, for her savings bank the sum of one hundred cents.

Ever affectionately
Ned

---

45 W.A. Deacon's extremely positive review was published at the end of July: 'A Peak of Canadian Heroism,' *Globe and Mail*, 27 July 1940, 20.

46 Albert ('Bert') H. Proctor (b. 1878), president of Jones, Proctor Bros. Ltd, Toronto insurance brokers.

47 Clare Hincks.

48 Edgar's daughter Jane.

TO CLAIRE PRATT

152 University Ave
Kingston

July 19 [1940].

Friday

Dearest Cáyke:

So you are back again – this time I am sorry to learn with a cold. I remember that you had one last year after you returned from camp. It is too bad, but still remain in bed until it has cleared up.

I didn't manage to get you that history of Philosophy by Durant[49] before I left. But I shall certainly get it when I come to Toronto and we shall have readings from it regularly so you will be acquainted with the main problems before you start the course. It will be an immense value to know what it is all about when the professor starts lecturing. I know when I began studying in the first year I was months before I got a grip on the essentials and then it was easy. It won't be hard with a bit of explanation beforehand, because one problem follows another just as any proposition in geometry depends on the one preceding it.

If you read Hamlet through now to see the story and the plot and you clear up the hard passages by means of the notes you will find it easy going to understand the critical questions. It will be just pie to you.

I am preparing a lecture now on Brébeuf for Sunday evening after this one. I have to shorten up the poem by two-thirds so as to have it all over in a half-hour.

The Book Department of Queen's is going to take fifteen copies[50] and have them on display in time for the lecture. It will be interesting to see how many students buy it. There will be four hundred in the audience and I suppose a percentage will be interested in getting the book afterwards.

I am slipping a fiver inside just on account. I will reckon up arrears when I return.

Love to mother and to yourself.

Dad

49 William J. Durant, *The Story of Philosophy*, 2nd edition (New York: Simon and Schuster, 1933).
50 *BB* had been published by Macmillan on 15 July 1940.

TO VIOLA PRATT

152 University Ave
Kingston Ont.

Monday am. [22 July 1940]

Dearest Vi:

Your Sunday letter just came, but I am wondering if my last letter reached you. It should have been there Saturday. You will doubtless get it today.

I am sorry Claire has such a cold. That ear ache must have alarmed you, but I suppose if it didn't return by Sunday morning when you wrote then it must have yielded to the treatment. Just to think that she could catch such a cold in the middle of the Summer! – damp weather and the coolness probably did it.

I am worried about the conclusion to Brébeuf.[51] I wonder if it reads like a publicity passage for the Shrine. I don't want to have that effect. It is too short for an epilogue, I fear, though I tried to get the appearance of an epilogue by having asterisks separate the story from it. Claire's impression is exactly what Winnie Eayrs thought. I think the style is all right but too brief in lines. It looks like an afterthought. How did Deacon like the poem as a whole I wonder.[52] I didn't see the *Star*.[53] Too bad it was disappointing. Will you send me the clipping.

About the Macmillans, I don't think much damage will be done by postponing the publicity till the early fall. The Summer is a terrible time to get the book on the market. The Macmillan crowd thought so, but urged bringing it out for the pilgrims at the Shrine. The autographing party would be useless in August. It would count in October or November, so I don't expect much action in sales for a month or two except possibly from Midland. Clee[54] will do his best I am sure but it would be a big mistake to force premature action.

My chief concern is the response to the conclusion. I might leave it out altogether in another Edition. It would be too bad to have the total effect spoiled

51 The final section of the poem entitled 'The Martyrs' Shrine' (ll. 2115–37; *EJP: CP* 2.109–10)

52 See the note to 'Deacon is reviewing it' in the letter to Pelham Edgar, 19 July (p. 185).

53 The poem was reviewed, under the heading 'Poem Enshrines Martyrs with Halo of New Beauty.' See Pratt's comments in the letter to Viola and Claire Pratt, 23 July (p. 188).

54 Unidentified.

by a few lines at the end. Frank[55] thought that a conclusion of some bright character would be very desirable in which some reference might be made to the return of the black-robes etc. However, I had better wait until I see some of the critical reactions. I shall not worry about the stagnation in the market just at this time of the year.

I intended going to Toronto next week-end but I am to give the address in Grant Hall next Sunday evening. I mentioned it in my last letter that I was speaking on Brébeuf. It might help to stimulate sales here among the students. The Book Store is getting fifteen copies for display and availability. It will be in a way a test case of selling quality. With the books here at hand and open for inspection, if an address before three or four hundred people will not sell fifteen copies then there must be some fault either in the book or myself or both.

Well my love to both of you. I hope Claire is much better.

Lovingly
Ned.

TO VIOLA AND CLAIRE PRATT

[Kingston, Ontario]

Tuesday pm. [23 July 1940]

My darlings both:

I am writing again so you will be under no apprehension[56] about letters. If Claire didn't get her letter written I think last Friday then it is lost with a five dollar bill in it. I wondered first if I should reserve her allowance till I got back and then decided that I would send a fiver in the interval. Too bad but I fear it is gone.

I got one copy of the Star yesterday and wasn't too much disappointed in the review.[57] While it was short it was cordial at any rate, and the tone of it would stimulate sales among the priests and Catholics generally.

I have a letter from Macmillans today that they sent thirty copies to Lally[58] and his shrine at Lally's request. They also sent up an attractive poster. I think

---

55 Frank Upjohn (b. 1908), editor-administrator at Macmillan, joined the firm in 1931 as assistant manager (Educational Department); he was later manager of the general books and assistant manager of the company.

56 An error for '*mis*apprehension.'

57 'Poem Enshrines Martyrs with Halo of New Beauty,' *Toronto Daily Star*, 20 July 1940, 9.

58 Father Thomas Lally, S.J. (1889–1953), custodian of the Martyrs' Shrine at Midland from 1927 to 1953.

they are doing their best for the season. They said that they would put the pressure on later in the fall, make it in fact a fall book, which I want.

I am busy now preparing 'talks' on it, first for this Sunday evening and then amplified accounts later on when I may be called upon to speak. I was conscious of the dilemma as was Huckvale:[59] Bring out the book now when general interest was slack but appeal to the pilgrims, or ignore the shrine value and have it 'hot' for the fall. I think they have done the wisest thing.

I sent off a card this morning, Vi, asking for any names you can get out of Canadian history that appeal to the ear. I am making a point of good mouth-fillers. Brébeuf is central & good, but there are so many Indian names of persons and places. Ihonatiria,[60] Tsiouendaentaha,[61] *Manitoulin*,[62] etc. I like Ticonderoga[63] best of all for sound though it doesn't come in here. I will use the name, however, for illustration. Who were the other chiefs? Wacousta?[64] (Brant[65] is no good as a name.)

I hope Cayke is getting over her cold. I think I shall run in a week from Friday to break the spell, then I shall have only eight days or so after that.

We must take the Midland trip in late August.

Much love
Dad.

TO VIOLA PRATT

[Kingston, Ontario]

Monday morning. [29 July 1940]

Dearest:

I have just come back from the Restaurant after my late breakfast.

---

59 Acting president of Macmillan Canada.

60 The area near the Bay of Penetanguishene where Brébeuf ministered early in his mission to the Huron Indians.

61 A personal Huron name; see *BB*, l. 922 (*EJP: CP* 2.73).

62 The name (derived from the Algonquian word for 'mysterious being' or 'spirit') of a large island at the northern end of Lake Huron.

63 See the note to 'Ticonderoga' in the letter to Claire Pratt, 28 July 1939 (p. 176).

64 The title of John Richardson's early nineteenth-century semi-historical novel about the Indian wars, as well as the name of a fictitious character in the novel.

65 Joseph Brant (1742–1807), Mohawk Indian chief, missionary, and head of the Six Nations Indians.

How did you get on over the week-end with Claire absent? The heat still persists, worse I suppose in Toronto than it is here. Are you using the den downstairs? And are the printers still ringing up about the punctuation marks?

When will you know about Claire's return? Subject to how she likes the place and the weather, etc?

I had my evening with the book at Grant Hall. Nearly the whole Session of students turned out including the younger Education group who look like High School youngsters. The audience probably ran to 350. It went off pretty well. I followed my usual method of reading with descriptive bits and explanation. I used your Indian names which made quite a hit. One funny thing occurred. All the time I was speaking a huge bat was flying about the lighted hall, often sweeping past my face making me instinctively draw back to the amusement of the crowd. It impaired the effect somewhat. But at the very moment when I was giving your Monongahela (the Indian name for rabbit) there was a vicious sweep of the bat wings. I had just got to this part of my sentence – '*There is little four-footed animal*' known to the Canadian bush called a rabbit. The Indian for rabbit is 'Monongahela.' I had just said the underlined when the audience laughed outright. They thought I was going to say 'called a bat,' and that I was referring to the nuisance when I switched on to the rest. It was such an abrupt transition that it heightened the comedy. However, I got through the half hour all right. Really not long enough to do justice to the subject but quite long enough for the heat and the attention of the audience. It gave me some idea of what passages to read and what to explain in prose.

The Registrar and Dean were present and the Extension Director, and a number of clergymen. It must have pleased quite a few because this morning the first order of books (15) had sold and now they are on the second instalment.

On Thursday I have to talk to the Education students on the Ice Floes & Carlo[66] though I am about fed up with that subject. MacMillan the Director[67] says the audience will be different so that makes it easier.

If the original plan about Claire still holds and we have her back on Friday, come as soon as you like. If the heat wave persists don't travel alone, for I will leave on the mid-day Friday train getting back as last time and it will be grand to see your sweet face again. The odd run up breaks the long spell and then it will be only a matter of ten days after that when I shall be back finally. It does

66 Poems published in *NV*.

67 Pratt is mistaken. The director of summer school was John Matheson.

get a bit monotonous here. Austen[68] is out of town a lot so I miss him. I guess I shall be getting a line from you in the afternoon's mail.

Very lovingly
Ned

TO EARLE BIRNEY

152 University Avenue
Kingston, Ont

August 7, 1940

Dear Earle:

Your letter[69] just came and I am answering it immediately to catch you before Aug. 15.

Thanks for your kind comments on *Brébeuf*. Edgar, and Roberts and Deacon and many others have written me in terms of enthusiasm. Edgar is writing reviews both for the Toronto Saturday Night and the Ottawa Journal.[70] Pelham is the dearest fellow imaginable and his letters buck me up no-end. He read the whole book through to Duncan McArthur, the Deputy Minister of Education, whose summer cottage is close to Edgar's on Lake Huron. What a friend he is! McArthur has a great deal to say about School Library Selections and the Sales may be thus increased.

Yes I sent your poems to Clarke of the Queen's Quarterly the day after you got them to me in June.[71] When I got to Queens I discovered that Clarke had left early for his old university in Tennessee where he had lectured for many years. They had invited him down for Summer Sessioning. I received no word from him at all. I wonder if my letter reached him. I asked Vincent,[72] his colleague here, and he told me that Clarke was a terrible correspondent. But I wasn't satisfied, so I went to his office in the College to see if his mail might yet be on the table. No letters were there though there was a pyramid of second class matter.

---

68 [*sic*]. Dr L.J. Austin.

69 Of 3 August.

70 Edgar reviewed the poem in three publications: *Ottawa Journal*, 10 August 1940, *Saturday Night*, 17 August 1940, and *Poetry* (Chicago) (April 1941).

71 See letter to G.H. Clarke, 21 June 1940 (p. 182).

72 C.J. Vincent.

As he may be back in a short while I shall wait before I renew inquiries. If the Queen's[73] doesn't accept, I should like to give space in the C.P.M. I am putting in the two mentioned in any case and also this gorgeous thing on Dusk. Earle, I am not flattering you – I am sincere in saying that you write in the most richly imaginative manner. This Dusk[74] is a pippin: it is totally free of clichés: it abounds in original concentrated metaphors and similes – 'whitening ribs of the raft divers,' unsexed by distance, chartreuse heavens, copper sulphate and your Joshua simile are new, brand new and arrestingly apt.

What I want to do is this: Let me put in three or four (to make a little collection) in the issue of September 1st. subject to Clarke's decision. Will you send me new copies as I like to have duplicates. As Roberts[75] has sent me two poems I may have, in accordance with the Board's wish for publicity to let him lead off. Then you will follow. Roberts' name it is thought is important now to stimulate sales of the magazine, but your stuff is immeasurably better than anything I have for this coming issue. We do not pay for contributions as we haven't any money, but there is the possibility of a $15.00 prize (the first prize) which is paid, sad to say, about 3 months after publication. The prize is fixed by a vote of the judges but as I count considerably in the award it will certainly go to you for I am sure Edgar will agree with me on the merit particularly of Dusk and your short lyric – *rose, blood, bloom, etc.*[76]

If we can get the Queen's[77] publication (though Clarke is from Missouri as well as Tennessee) then there ought to be a double payment in time.

Go ahead and write, old dear, you have it in you – more than you think.

Incidentally, when you write your article,[78] don't be backward in any criticism you make of my work, especially my early work which I know has lots of flaws. I like criticism especially when the underlying note is appreciation.

Ned

---

73 *Queen's Quarterly*.

74 'Dusk on English Bay,' *CPM* 5 (September 1940): 25.

75 Charles G.D. Roberts.

76 Possibly 'Monody for a Century,' *CPM* 5 (September 1940): 26.

77 *Queen's Quarterly*.

78 Birney's review of *BB* appeared in *CF* (September 1940): 180–1.

TO VIOLA PRATT

152 University Ave
Kingston, Ont

Wednesday morning. [7 Aug. 1940]

Dear one:

Your card just came with the news that Cayke was back, brown and looking well. I wondered if she got my letter written Sunday.

The days here are getting a bit crowded with meetings, teas (silly most of them in the hot afternoons) and examination consultations.

I made a faux pas last week. When the Knoxes[79] were leaving here three weeks ago, Mrs Melvin who drove them to the train asked me to come and have dinner with them sometime. I said 'Certainly,' but thought I should wait to get the second notice with the specified date. She had mentioned the day but I didn't hear it: so when 7:30 arrived she telephoned the house to see what delayed me. Pete McQueen was there and two or three others but not *humble me.* I wrote her a letter of apology and explanation the next day. She then invited me for tonight. They are very nice, resembling the Knoxes – both man & woman.

Sunday afternoon I go to Mrs Lovel's. Her husband was Judge Lovel. She telephoned me to say that you were a brilliant editor and writer, how she enjoyed your W.F.[80] every time. She was always singing your praises and found that the contributors and sponsors or the magazine were of the same opinion. She didn't know me and I didn't know her personally, but since I was your hubby I must be on exhibition. I felt flattered. You must gather together your stories and plays sometime & get Ryerson Press to publish them.[81] I am sure they would go like hot cakes amd with such a constituency as the Un. Church[82] could create the sale would be great. Next year when you have more time it would be fun to collect them, wouldn't it?

79 R.S. Knox and his wife.
80 *World Friends.*
81 This collection, *Journeying with the Year*, was published in 1957.
82 The United Church of Canada.

Winters the Extension Director[83] and McNeill the Vice President[84] are having me at their places before I leave, so it looks as if every evening will be filled up.

I had a letter from Pelham[85] yesterday. He is most enthusiastic about Brébeuf. He spent an evening with Duncan McArthur (the Deputy Minister of Education)[86] who summers at London, and read nearly the whole poem. Duncan was 'bowled over' said Pelham. Isn't Pelham a wonderful friend? Doing more for me than he would do for himself. Not many colleagues would do that. He is also writing reviews of Brébeuf, one for the Saturday Night – perhaps this week's issue and one for the Ottawa Journal this Saturday.[87] Darling Vi, will you ring up the Montreal Star office on Bay St & see if they have a copy of last Saturday's issue, or if you are down at the bookstore corner of Yonge & Bloor two doors west, see if they have a copy. I do not know if the review has appeared yet but I must follow the Sat. editions to make sure. It may be in this coming Sat. Keep tab on it. And I would like a couple of copies each of the Sat. Night & the Ottawa Journal.

My love to you sweetheart & to
Cayke,
Ned

TO PELHAM EDGAR

[Kingston, Ontario]

Aug. 15, 1940

Dearest Pelham:

The 'Journal' just came in.[88] It was sent to me by a friend. The warmth, cordiality, affection, love of it all just about brought tears to my eyes. Were ever two such University colleagues two such friends? In our twenty years of partnership not one recriminating word between us. Day and night you have encouraged

---

83 Ross M. Winter (1903–68) was director of extension from 1934 to 1945.

84 William E. MacNeill (1876–1959), born in Prince Edward Island and educated at Acadia and Harvard, was for many years registrar and treasurer at Queen's University, and vice-principal from 1930 to 1947.

85 Pelham Edgar.

86 McArthur (1885–1943), a graduate of Queen's University, was head of the Department of History there (1922–34), deputy minister of education (1934–40), and minister (1940–3). See also the second paragraph of the letter to Earle Birney, 7 August (p. 191).

87 See the note to 'Edgar … Saturday Night and the Ottawa Journal' in the letter to Earle Birney, 7 August 1940 (p. 191).

88 Edgar had published a long review article on Pratt and *Brébeuf* in the *Ottawa Journal*, 10 August 1940, 21: 'A Vivid Poetic Impression of the Canada of 300 Years Ago.'

me, stimulated me and vastly helped me, and I have coveted success and accomplishment for you as you have for me. Your success has been mine and mine yours. When I think of so many of the stinking rivalries and animosities in other Departments, French, Physics, Psychology, etc., how fortunate our Relationship and our Department and I know that my love for you is deeper now *even* than it has ever been. If I should get a windfall on this *Brébeuf*, Jane[89] is going to get her education out of it. It is a big *if* because while all my former editions have taken care of themselves under the Macmillan sponsorship there has been no 'Jalna' break.[90] I suppose one shouldn't expect verse to work a market miracle, but, even if it doesn't, Jane is nevertheless going to get her porridge.

Bowles[91] should get a copy of the Journal. He would love it. He used to say to me that the English Dept. never gave him any trouble. With Potter[92] and Ford,[93] Lang[94] & Robertson[95] spitting on the carpet of his office every Monday morning, it was a relief when we went in to see him. We never brought sulphur into the sanctum. His esteem for you was an awe. Sometimes he was frightened of your ability. He said so once. And Burwash[96] thought the same of you. And Brown[97] recently remarked that Victoria had won two Royal Society Medals.[98] My admission into the R.S.C.[99] was largely a matter of your recommendation, and bless you, sweetheart, wasn't my 'Tweedsmuir'[100] the result of your choice?

We must try to get our old gang together this fall and renew our golf, our stags and our poker. I feel more and more the need of my old friends as I know

89 Edgar's three-year-old daughter.

90 Mazo de la Roche's 1927 novel *Jalna* had won the *Atlantic Monthly*'s $10,000 prize for fiction.

91 See the note to 'the Chancellor' in the letter to Arthur L. Phelps, 26 October 1922 (p. 16).

92 William A. Potter, a member of the Department of Oriental Studies, professor from 1925. He had died while on research leave in 1931.

93 Harry E. Ford, born in Ontario and a graduate of Victoria College, was professor of French there from 1915 to 1940.

94 Augustus E. Lang (1862–1945), a graduate of Victoria College, taught German there for many years and was librarian from 1907 to 1924.

95 J.C. Robertson.

96 Reverend Nathanael Burwash (1839–1918), president and chancellor of Victoria University, 1887–1913.

97 Walter T. Brown (1883–1954), a graduate of Victoria College, taught philosophy there 1912–28 and at Yale 1928–32. He returned as principal in 1932, becoming president and chancellor in 1941.

98 A.L. Burt, a graduate of Victoria College, had been awarded the Society's Tyrell Medal for History, and Pratt the Lorne Pierce Medal for Literature.

99 Royal Society of Canada.

100 He is referring to the Governor General's Medal he had won for *FG* in 1937. The 'Tweedsmuir' was awarded for the best poem in the first volume of the *CPM*. See the letter to G.H. Clarke, 23 June 1937 (*EJP: Web*).

you do. We must re-harness Bert,[101] Bernard,[102] Clare[103] and meet periodically. Clare has always been one of my very closest, dearest friends, and the last time I met him he stated his desire for the old-time reunions. We must all stand together in the misty days of the future. I should like to include Duncan[104] in the fraternity. You know him best. And also Vernon Mc.[105]

I am leaving for Toronto to-night. And I shall be there most of the time till College opens, so golf will be frequent. I won the silver cup again at the Summer School tournament with an 86 – the best score this Summer.

Since Jane has probably worn out her swimming suit might the little amount enclosed take care of her patches?

Love to her and Dona.

Most affectionately
Ned

TO E.K. BROWN

Oct. 9 [1940]

Dear Eddie:

It looks like a good list[106] though I am not so sure of Bourinot,[107] Ross[108] & Bowman.[109] Ross hasn't much sap though he has appeared a couple of times in

---

101 Bert Proctor.

102 B.K. (Bernard Kebel) Sandwell (1876–1954), born in England, was editor of *Saturday Night* (1932–52). He later served as rector of Queen's University, a governor of the CBC (1944–7), and honorary president of the CAA.

103 Clare Hincks.

104 Duncan McArthur.

105 J. Vernon McKenzie, born (1887) in New York and educated in Toronto, was editor of *Maclean's* magazine from 1920 to 1926, and later taught journalism at the universities of Toronto and Washington (in Seattle).

106 Brown had been asked to edit a special Canadian number of *Poetry* (Chicago), and had sent Pratt the list of Canadian poets he had chosen for possible inclusion, inviting his advice.

107 Arthur S. Bourinot (1893–1969), born in Ottawa and educated at Osgoode Hall, was a lawyer, poet, editor, and critic. He published numerous books including *Under the Sun and Other Poems*, which won the Governor General's Medal for poetry in 1939, and studies of Duncan Campbell Scott, Archibald Lampman, and other Canadian poets. He edited *CPM* (1948–54) and was associate editor of *Canadian Author and Bookman* (1953–60).

108 W.W. Eustace Ross (1894–1966), for many years a geophysicist at an observatory near Toronto, published several books of verse.

109 Louise Morey Bowman (1882–1944) spent most of her life in Montreal. She published three books of verse, including *Dream Tapestries* (1924), which won the Quebec government's David Prize, and *Characters in Cadence* (1938), notable for its imagistic qualities.

Chicago.[110] Bourinot occasionally comes across and Bowman used to do it but now she is sick and retired I hear. As for C.G.D. and D.C. S.,[111] yes! though there is the difficulty of rejection. The old boys, particularly C.G.D. are touchy, the latter sitting in the highest self-declared castle this mighty domain has known.

There are other writers I know – Mary Colman of Vancouver,[112] Margaret Avison[113] and what about a try at Birney. He has been writing lately. I know Kennedy,[114] Leslie,[115] MacKay,[116] Klein would measure up.

Will you let me see those four copies of 'Poetry' soon. Have them in your office will you, so I may get them when I drop in.

By all means we must get away from the products of the 'Maple Leaf' Milling Co., mustn't we?

When I have collected a few poems I shall submit them to you.[117] I think it is a grand piece of good luck to have you in charge of this affair. There is no one better in Canada.

Saturday Nov.19[118] at 7 is all serene. Whole crowd coming enthusiastically.

Always
Ned

---

110 *Poetry* (Chicago).

111 Charles G.D. Roberts and Duncan Campbell Scott.

112 Mary Elizabeth Colman (b. 1895) was a librarian who wrote verse and prose for magazines and had published several small books of poems.

113 Avison (1918-2007) was educated at Victoria College. Her first book of poems, *Winter Sun* (Toronto: University of Toronto Press, 1960), won the Governor General's Award. In 2003 Avison won the Griffin Poetry Prize for *Concrete and Wild Carrot* (London, ON: Brick Books, 2002).

114 Leo Kennedy.

115 Kenneth Leslie (1892–1974) was born in Pictou, Nova Scotia, and educated at Dalhousie University, the University of Nebraska, and Harvard. He published several collections of poetry in which he attempted to reconcile his Christian faith and socialist activism. His third book, *By Stubborn Stars* (Toronto: Ryerson, 1938), won the Governor General's Award. He was for some years editor of leftist magazines in New York and Boston, including the *Protestant Digest* and the anti-fascist comic book, *The Challenger*.

116 L.A. (Louis Alexander) MacKay (1901–82) was born in Hensall, Ontario, and educated at the University of Toronto and Oxford. He taught Latin in the Classics Department at Victoria College before moving to the University of British Columbia in 1941 and the University of California at Berkeley in 1948. He published two books of poetry: *Viper's Bugloss* (Toronto: Ryerson, 1938) and *The Ill-Tempered Lover and Other Poems* (Toronto: Macmillan, 1948).

117 See the letter to E.K. Brown, 17 January 1941 (*EJP: Web*).

118 An error for Saturday, 16 November.

TO ELLEN ELLIOTT

Oct. 28, 1940

My dear Ellen:

Thanks for the Cox cheque.[119] You are a darling to get things done promptly. I see four charcoal-broiled steaks in that little slip of paper, and you are to have one of them when the immediate rush is over.

I am glad that the special edition[120] is coming out soon. I am checking up on the emendations.

Last week Healey Willan and Campbell-MacInnes[121] telephoned me to come to a meeting for the purpose of discussing a Canadian Passion Play or Oratorio.[122] Lally at the Shrine and several of the Fathers are keen to have something which might be performed in the open air at Midland and, in a modified form, in the Churches. They want to base the play on 'Brebeuf and His Brethren' with the cooperation of Macmillans. Healey Willan will adapt the Gregorian chants and compose new music. MacInnes would sing and read passages from the poem. Lally says that in that amphitheatre up there they can accommodate 25000 people and the prospect of sale for the book is practically unlimited. Father Dorian and Father Phelan (of St Michael's College) are strong for it.

Now the following point is a somewhat delicate one. I do not know yet if the McGuigan[123] tea is on, but if it is, could MacInnes, Willan and Dorion come to it? They want to talk to the Archbishop about the scheme. If the blessings of the Mother of Churches goes with the project all is well and certainly the individuals have expressed themselves emphatically in favour. The C.N.R. would be strong for it in publicity. Cranston of the Midland 'Enterprise' has written me to go up and address their Historical Club and I can be sure of backing. That then is the 'tea-point' and I know you will understand.

---

119 For copies of *BB* that Leo Cox had sold at a book fair held by the Montreal branch of the CAA.

120 A cloth-covered, limited, signed edition of *BB*.

121 James Campbell McInnes, a celebrated baritone.

122 The musical and dramatic version of *Brébeuf* composed by Healey Willan was first performed at the CBC studios on 26 September 1943, with Ettore Mazzoleni conducting the orchestra and James Finlay producing the broadcast. The first public performance – by the Mendelssohn Choir and the Toronto Symphony directed by Sir Ernest MacMillan – was on 18 January 1944 at Massey Hall. In 1947, Willan adapted the script for performance by choir and organ, a version performed under his direction at the Timothy Eaton Memorial Church in 1967. The grand plans for regular performances at the Martyrs' Shrine in Midland did not materialize.

123 James Charles McGuigan (1894–1974) was appointed Roman Catholic Archbishop of Toronto in 1935. He was elevated to Cardinal in 1945.

I have received letters from Premier King[124] and Brockington[125] about Brébeuf – most cordial.

Many thanks.
Ned Pratt.

TO F.R. SCOTT

Dec. 4, 1940

My dear Frank:

I rang up Macmillans and found that[?] they bound about 500 copies, presented quite liberally to Reviewers and friends and sold something more than 100.[126] There was really no market in the public sense. I am quite agreed to let them go down the drain pipe. We got something off our chest anyway.

They wonder if the books would remainder at a dime. I still have a half-dozen copies out of the lot I bought.

I am knocking off the odd poem. The last one on the Jesuit Martyrs is historical though there are a few doctrinal errors or 'ambiguities' from the ecclesiastical point of view. When I bring Cardinal Villeneuve[127] and the Grand Master of the Orange Lodge of British North America[128] together arguing points I think I have achieved something in comedy.

The best of good luck, Frank.

Sincerely
Ned.

---

124 Prime Minister William Lyon Mackenzie King

125 Leonard W. Brockington (1888–1966) served as the first chairman of the CBC (1936–9) and special assistant to Prime Minister King (1939–42). He was later president of Odeon Theatres (Canada) and rector of Queen's University. A gifted public speaker, he won a coveted reputation as orator and broadcaster.

126 Of *New Provinces* (1936). Pratt exaggerates when he writes 'something more than 100' copies were sold. The number was closer to eighty.

127 Jean-Marie-Rodrigue Villeneuve (1883–1947) was the Roman Catholic archbishop of Quebec. He was elevated to cardinal in 1933.

128 A fraternal order founded in the seventeenth century to bolster the Protestant succession to the British throne. It came to Canada in 1830.

TO RALPH GUSTAFSON

January 16, 1941.

Dear Mr Gustafson:

I am honoured indeed by your invitation to contribute to the 'Pelican Series'[129] and I should be delighted to be included.

But as Macmillans of Canada (70 Bond St. Toronto) hold the copyright to all my books I fear I have no power to grant permission.

The Macmillans have always dealt directly with the publishers of anthologies in which my verses have appeared and they have been very reasonable. I am sending your letter to Miss Ellen Elliott, the editor in charge of copyright, and you will receive an answer at once.

May I say how much I have admired your stuff in the Canadian Forum and the S.N.[130] It has great strength and drive.

Yours sincerely
E.J. Pratt

May I say also that 'Still Life,'[131] not having been published in Book form, is in my own possession and accordingly you are welcome to it.

E.J.P.

TO RALPH GUSTAFSON

Jan. 31, 1941

Dear Mr Gustafson:

I am sending to you a poem published by the Canadian Forum, 'The Radio in the Ivory Tower,'[132] which I gladly give to you if you do not think it too long. It

129 Gustafson was editing the *Anthology of Canadian Poetry (English)* for Penguin Books.
130 *Saturday Night.*
131 A twelve-line lyric published in *Saturday Night*, 28 October 1939, 3. Pratt later revised the poem, added several more stanzas, and published it as the title poem in *SL* (1–2; *EJP: CP* 2.136). Gustafson included the original, short version in his anthology.
132 *CF* 19 (December 1939): 276–7 (*EJP: CP* 2.41).

has not been published in book form. I do not know how good it is or how bad it is – but the 'younger element' of the gang here like it.

You are also welcome to the 'Impatient Earth' from the *Queen's Quarterly*[133] though I prefer 'The Old Eagle' which was published by the same Journal in January 1939.[134] As I haven't a copy, you might take a glance at it if the issue is available in New York.

Out of these three and 'Still Life' you might make up the quota, though naturally I hope you may come to terms with Macmillans as you undoubtedly would prefer the selections from the 'Cachalot' and 'Titanic.' I should my self.

I think it is a grand work you are doing and my only feeling is one of gratitude to you. I believe strongly in you and your stuff.

With every kind wish
Ned Pratt

TO RALPH GUSTAFSON

Feb. 5, 1941

My dear Mr. Gustafson:

It was a great joy to receive your sheaf of poems. I had, of course, read them before and admired your gift of saying and suggesting so much with the finest economy of words.

The poetic cause up here is not receiving the support it should get. The little magazine some of us started[135] is petering out through financial deficits and the paucity of poetic contributions.

I noted what you said about copyright. I suggested to my publishers the advisability of the most reasonable terms. But I could not push the point for a number of reasons. First: the Macmillans held the copyright – had complete legal ownership of all my work up to the most recent compositions. Second: They have always been very decent to me. They took all risks at the start, and have fulfilled their part of the agreements.

---

133 *QQ* 45 (November 1938): 542 (*EJP: CP* 2.29).
134 *QQ* 46 (Winter 1939): 428–30 ('The Dying Eagle,' *EJP: CP* 2.38).
135 *Canadian Poetry Magazine.*

Third: although, by law, they could appropriate all the profits from the individual sales of poems to anthologies, they actually hand over to me the revenue slight though it may be – that is, the odd ten or twenty dollars – a practice not altogether characteristic of publishers. Hence, I have a feeling of loyalty to a firm which has so generously treated me. Other writers may not have the same relationship and the same feeling but that's their business.

I do hope that the negotiations will be satisfactory to both of you. It is a fine work you are doing. I have received a number of letters from 'the boys' who feel enthusiastic about your scholarship. And all of us hope that, in your capacity as Editor, you will not stint your own contributions for you are so definitely in the stream with a fine record behind you.

If you should run up this way later, will you let me know in advance. I should love to 'throw a little party' for you.

With every good wish

Sincerely
Ned Pratt

TO WATSON KIRKCONNELL

March 19, 1941

My dear Kirk:

When your note came in, I was just on the point of writing you about Friday evening of the 28th.[136] Vi and I would very much like to have you and your wife to dinner with us that evening and also have the two of you stay over night. Claire is staying at the Residence this year, which gives us plenty of room.

I do hope you can come to the recital and give us the bull or the frog.[137] It would put beef (or frog's legs) on the menu.

I hear great reports about your lecturing everywhere! Congratulations!

My father John Pratt came from Yorkshire, England, to Nfld as a young minister. My mother was the daughter of Captain Wm Knight whose ancestry went back for several generations of Newfoundland sailors to (I think) Devonshire.

136 The annual 'Canadian Poetry Night' recital sponsored by the Toronto branch of the CAA. Held on 28 March, it featured readings by Canadian poets.

137 Kirkconnell had recently published *The Flying Bull and Other Tales* (London: Oxford University Press 1940), which included 'The Clerk's Tale of Usquedunk, the Frog-King.'

But as hazy origins smoke up nationalities I can only say or suggest Devonshire, certainly English not Welsh or Scotch or Assyrian.[138]

Ned

TO A.J.M. SMITH

March 29, 1941

Dear Professor Smith:

Many congratulations on your Fellowship.[139] E.K. Brown and I rejoice in it knowing how well the honour will be vindicated. If you ever come to this city will you let me or E.K. know, so we can get the gang together in celebration.

Most sincerely
E.J. Pratt

TO A.J.M. SMITH

April 8, 1941

Dear Dr Smith:

Delighted to hear that you will be coming here for a time next Fall. That will be perfect for the assembling of the boys. I shall get Collin[140] up from London. But do not fail to let me know the exact date in August when you will be passing through. It is just possible that E.K.[141] and I will be in the city.

---

138 Pratt provided data on his family history in response to a request by Kirkconnell, who was to 'introduce' him at the recital.

139 Smith had been awarded a Guggenheim Fellowship to compile a comprehensive anthology of Canadian poetry. (Guggenheim Fellowships are awarded by the John Simon Guggenheim Memorial Foundation of New York to support scholarly research and artistic creativity.)

140 W.E. (William Edwin) Collin (1893–1984), born in England and educated at the universities of Toulouse and Western Ontario, was professor of Romance languages at the University of Western Ontario (1923–60). He published *Monserrat and Other Poems* (Toronto: Ryerson, 1930), but is chiefly known for *The White Savannahs* (Toronto: Macmillan, 1936), a pioneering study of major Canadian poets, including Pratt. See the letter to Scott, 19 September 1934 (p. 126).

141 E.K. Brown.

Your Ode[142] is very fine and characteristic of your stuff as I know it. I will be honoured to have it for the next number (July, I hope, if finances warrant). I rather suspect that the magazine[143] will go out by attrition. It is a thankless task.

Sincerely
E.J. Pratt

TO RALPH GUSTAFSON

May 15, 1941

Dear Mr. Gustafson:

May I offer you my congratulations on your 'For We Are Free' which won the first prize in the December number of the C.P.M. It was certainly the finest thing in the issue, and good poetry is damned hard to pick up nowadays. The prize is fifteen dollars but as our treasury is very slim the payment may be a bit delayed.[144] I shall ask the Executive to hurry up the prize payments as fast as possible.

With every good wish
E.J. Pratt

TO FATHER STANLEY MURPHY[145]

July 14, 1941

Dear Father Murphy:

I feel very much honoured with your invitation to give a lecture in the 'Canadian Culture Series.' The best audiences I have ever been privileged to address have been composed of men of your faith and culture.

---

142 'Ode: On the Death of William Butler Yeats.' Yeats had died in January 1939.

143 *CPM.*

144 Gustafson took the hint and waived the prize money. See the letter to Gustafson, 19 May 1940 (*EJP: Web*).

145 Head of Assumption College (later the University of Windsor), and a member of the Basilian Order, Murphy established the still-running Christian Culture Series – which Pratt misnames in this letter – during the Depression.

My interest in Brébeuf is more than literary. In a sense it is missionary. Though I am a Protestant, I may claim Brébeuf to be my favourite saint and hero. I want to make him known to the world.

I shall be delighted to visit both Windsor and Marygrove[146] if the latter place find it convenient. Any of your dates will suit me provided I know in time to arrange my fall and winter schedule. The earliest date common to both Colleges would be preferable.

I go by train rather than by car.

My personal affection to Father McCorkell[147] if you happen to see him. He is one of my choicest friends.

Yours sincerely
E.J. Pratt

TO GEORGE DILLON[148]

Aug. 5, 1941.

Dear Mr. Dillon:

I am deeply honoured by your request to submit some new poems for consideration in your magazine. I fished out three or four comparatively new ones from my desk but I didn't like them myself and I imagine their ultimate resting place will be the garbage can.

I am, however, working honestly, at a poem on Dunkirk[149] which should be completed within two weeks and if it isn't too long and too bad, I shall be delighted to send it along. If theme or treatment or space or any of the countless editorial angles should find the poem inadmissible, return it without the least

---

146 Marygrove College in Detroit, Michigan, was run by the Sisters of the Immaculate Heart of Mary.

147 A former professor of English at St Michael's College (Toronto) and principal of St Thomas More College, Saskatoon, Father Edmund McCorkell was superior general of the Order of Basilian Fathers.

148 Pulitzer Prize–winning American poet (1906–68) who assumed the editorship of *Poetry: A Magazine of Verse* upon the death of its founder and long-time editor, Harriet Monroe, in 1936.

149 Between 26 May and 4 June 1940, British, French, and Belgian troops had been driven to the French coast at Dunkirk by German forces; 333,226 soldiers were evacuated by over 800 boats, many private fishing vessels, leaving their equipment behind. The very real possibility of a German victory at this point in the Second World War was acknowledged by Winston Churchill on 4 June in one of his most famous speeches, "We shall fight on the beaches."

compunction. I have been an Editor myself and have some understanding of that side of the case.

May I say here how much I love your Magazine. With the exception of a few lean years of oatmeal fare, I have been a subscriber since 1916, and have been an unofficial publicity agent for Poetry in Canada. I used to get the odd letter from 'Harriet'[150] and the not-so-odd rejection slip with its little P.S. – 'I liked your "Erosion" or your "Magnolia Blossoms," but we are dreadfully overcrowded. It *nearly* got in.'[151] I owe Harriet an immense debt if for no other reason than she taught me how to palliate blows at unfortunate contributors, during my own editorial term of office.

Those were great days – Sandburg, Lindsay,[152] Frost, Yeats falling into my lap every month or so. They did so much for me in my callow twenties.[153] And I am sure that you have brought back the old glories. Jeffers, MacLeish, Fearing, Rukeyser[154] lay hold upon my soul. I liked 'Quiz' of Ruth Lechlitner.[155] I should like to meet Babette Deutsch.[156] She's a honey! If you should manage to come up to Toronto, Brown and I will put on a partridge dinner for you. He was most enthusiastic about you.

Floreat 'Poetry.'

With the best wishes,

Sincerely
E.J. Pratt

---

150 Harriet Monroe.

151 See the letter to Harriet Monroe, 6 February 1928 (p. 79).

152 The poetry of Vachel Lindsay (1879–1931) was championed by Harriet Monroe. Known as the 'Prairie Troubadour,' Lindsay was a mystic and activist known for performances of poetry which was written to be sung or chanted. His most famous book was *General William Booth Enters into Heaven, and Other Poems* (New York: Macmillan, 1916).

153 Pratt was actually thirty-four in 1916 when he first subscribed to *Poetry*.

154 Robinson Jeffers, Archibald MacLeish, Kenneth Fearing, Muriel Rukeyser.

155 Lechlitner (1901–88) published her first book of poems, *Tomorrow's Phoenix*, in 1937. Two other books followed.

156 A New York poet and critic, Deutsch (1895–1982) published many books of verse, several works of 'modern' criticism, and a biography of Whitman (1941).

TO PELHAM EDGAR

Aug. 8, 1941

Dear Pelham:

The Roberts review is perfect.[157] And it came in time! I wish you were here for to-morrow's final at Lambton.[158] The big shots have turned up. A doctor named Shell and I are spending the afternoon following them around. I have no doubt that my own score thereafter will go from 92 to 104. I shall pattern my trajectories upon Snead's.[159]

I haven't heard any more from Pascal,[160] since the letter he wrote immediately before his bomber departure for England. He was confident then that the show would go on. He returns about the middle of August when I hope I shall have some news.

This last week I have worked furiously at Dunkirk[161] which is just about finished. The Macmillans want it as a fall book though it is too late for the fall list. However, Huckvale and Upjohn said they will turn on special steam if I can get it in their hands by the first of October, which I can do. It is shaping out into four or five hundred lines mainly descriptive of the Regatta – composition of ships and crews and the great lifting operation.

The volume will have Dunkirk as a leader, followed by the shorter poems turned out during the last three years. The interest in Dunkirk as a topic is simply enormous in the States, some seven or eight novels coming out with the rescue as the core – no poem that I can discover in the announcements.

---

157 Edgar had reviewed Charles G.D. Roberts's *Canada Speaks of Britain, and Other Poems of the War* (Toronto: Ryerson, 1941) for the August issue of *CPM*.

158 The Toronto course where the Canadian Open Golf Tournament was being held.

159 Sam Snead, the celebrated American golfer. Snead won the Canadian Open in 1938 and 1940, and was the winner again in 1941.

160 Hungarian-born film producer (e.g., *Pygmalion*, *Major Barbara*, *Caesar and Cleopatra*), Gabriel Pascal was planning to film Paul Gallico's Dunkirk novelette, *The Snow Goose* (New York: Knopf, 1940). He had come to Canada to film snow geese at Jack Miner's bird sanctuary at Kingsville, Ontario. Learning that Pratt was writing a poem on Dunkirk, he asked him to supply verse to be used in the movie, promising a substantial payment. The film was never made, and Pratt was never paid. The verse written for the film vanished, though abortive lines on the snow goose theme appear in the manuscript of 'Dunkirk' in the Pratt Collection at Victoria College Library. Pratt's account of the affair in the letter to George Dillon dated 5 August is quite misleading. (See also the letter to Ellen Elliott, 7 October 1941 [p. 212].)

I am using a 'free' line like that of the 'Radio in the Ivory Tower.' I am having some fun out of it. Dillon, the editor of Poetry (Chicago) has asked me to send some stuff for an early issue. I may send him this – abridged. He says his readers 'are particularly keen to see some more of your work.' I hope he means what he says.

I saw Fennell the other day and he said that the Pageant[162] is sure to be a success but as a peace-time project. No one is committing himself just now. Willan wrote Flavelle[163] but got no response. Fennell was sure that a completed job on script and music would compel the music patrons to back it. There it stands.

We are having no out-of-town holidays. This is my first summer in years spent in Toronto with its 90s. The cellar is the only spot cool enough for a shirt. Claire is finding the heat very trying, poor little dear. She goes for her treatments twice a week to Friede.[164] I trust that he is helpful.

Do go on with your genius analysis.[165] There is room for a book with your galois style and sweep. That is one of my great newspaper experiences. And what *you* could make of Keats! Genius working against time and the tubercles!

I am looking forward to our gathering together in September and on – golf and stags and the swapping of jokes.

My love to Dona & Jane.

affectionately
Ned

161 Pratt had planned to bring out a volume to be called *Dunkirk, and Other Poems*, but his publishers decided to publish the poem alone. (See the letter to Ellen Elliott, 7 October 1941 [p. 212].)

162 A committee had been formed to devise a musical pageant based on *BB* to be performed at the site of the Martyrs' Shrine. (See the letter to Ellen Elliott, 28 October 1940 [p. 198].)

163 Sir Ellsworth Flavelle (1892–1977), born in Toronto, succeeded to the baronetcy of his father, Sir Joseph Flavelle, in 1939. A member of the governing body of many institutions and organizations, he was a prime mover of the *Brébeuf* pageant committee. He and Pratt were close personal friends for many years.

164 A Viennese doctor practising in Toronto.

165 Edgar had recently published a series of brief essays on 'writers of genius' in the *Globe and Mail* (e.g., Mann, Hardy, Yeats).

TO GEORGE DILLON

Aug. 26, 1941.

Dear Mr. Dillon:

I have just completed my job on Dunkirk and I am submitting two abridgements for your consideration.[166] The poem in its expanded form will be published as a volume by Macmillans towards the end of this year, probably late November. And Gabriel Pascal, the film producer, is negotiating with me for the screen rights of the poem as the Dunkirk setting of his play *The Snow Goose* which will appear next April. This appearance would not conflict with *Poetry* but the Macmillan publication might, as it cramps your time.

I am afraid that the poem is too long for your Magazine, but I should be very happy if you considered some part of it acceptable. I have arranged two sequences, the shorter one being less than two hundred lines which is long enough God knows. A third possibility would be an *extract* ending with the description of the crew which I think is the best part of the piece. Whatever you decide to do will be satisfactory to me. I have no short poems on hand, and, as the University term opens in two weeks, it may not be till next April or May that I shall again begin to seduce the Muses.

I should be delighted, as you suggested, to arrange a barter between *Poetry* and the Canadian Poetry Magazine, but the War has dealt such a heavy blow to our circulation that it is quite possible that we shall suspend publication till conditions improve. We have been running for five years on a shoestring.

With every good wish,

Yours sincerely,
E.J. Pratt

166 See Pratt's previous letter to Dillon, 5 August (pp. 205–6).

TO A.J.M. SMITH

September 17, 1941

Dear Mr Smith:

It will be a pleasure to see you and take you in charge when you are in this city. It is too bad we have lost E.K. Brown to Cornell,[167] but I shall gather the faithful remnant. I shall ask Collins[168] to come up for a week-end. Every facility will be given to you as far as I am concerned. The more progressive element of the University will be behind you, I know. I think it is a great national blessing that the Foundation[169] recognized you as the man for the job. The Garvin tradition[170] is alive only in the drawing-rooms and the cross-road churches.

Very sincerely
E.J. Pratt

My love to Frank Scott if you see him.[171]

TO MISS UDELL[172]

Sept. 19, 1941

Dear Miss Udell:

I do trust it was excitement on the part of the printer which occasioned the slips.[173] As the section beginning –
'Space, time, water, etc.'
stood at the top of the page on my m.s. there was nothing to indicate the paragraph. I have marked it.

---

167 Brown had accepted appointment to the headship of the English Department at Cornell University in Ithaca, New York.

168 An error for 'Collin': W.E. Collin, who was teaching at the University of Western Ontario.

169 The Guggenheim Foundation. See note to 'your Fellowship' in the letter to Smith, 29 March 1941 (p. 203).

170 The poetic tradition represented by John William Garvin's *Canadian Poets* (Toronto: McClelland, Goodchild & Stewart, 1916).

171 Smith was visiting Montreal, where Scott lived.

172 Secretary and assistant to George Dillon as editor of *Poetry*.

173 Pratt was returning page proofs of the extracts from *Dunkirk* that Dillon was publishing in *Poetry*.

Children of '*oats*.'[174] The error has probably more truth in the sentiment expressed than the original. It is lovely. Thanks to the printer for the suggestion. It has started me on a new train of poetic revery.

Will you let me have an extra half-dozen copies and charge it up to my account. Please renew my subscription as well. I think it has expired. Mr Dillon offered to exchange Poetry for the Canadian Poetry Magazine but as we may suspend soon I couldn't accept. Charge me with the 'sub' and the 6 copies.

Best wishes
E.J. Pratt

P.S. Would Mr Dillon kindly refer to the fact that the Macmillan Co. of Canada will publish 'Dunkirk' as a book this fall.

TO MARGARET FURNESS MACLEOD[175]

Sept. 22, 1941

Dear Mrs MacLeod:

I have just been thinking about my subject for the Montreal address.[176] You mentioned to me that some of the members suggested a poetry-recital of my own work. I should be perfectly satisfied to do that if it were desired. I find it difficult to mix the two – an analysis of contemporary poetry and my own contributions. If you have not printed the programme yet, how would the following title suit?

The Relation of subject-matter to poetic form
or
The place of research in verse composition
or
A Poetry Recital.

Any one of the three would be all right with me. A Poetry-Recital has this advantage. It allows me to enter into a discussion of verse techniques.

---

174 Pratt's line in the poem actually read 'Children of oaths and madrigals.'

175 A resident of Montreal, Mrs MacLeod (b. 1873) wrote verse for magazines and published several small collections. She served for several terms as president of the Montreal branch of the CAA; she and Pratt later became good friends and occasional correspondents.

176 Pratt was to address the Maritime Women's Club of Montreal. (See *EJP: Web* for summaries of the letters to MacLeod, 26 June and 2 July 1941.)

Will you let me know what you think of it?

Yours sincerely,
E.J. Pratt

TO ELLEN ELLIOTT

Oct. 7, 1941

Dear Ellen:

I hear the manufacturing costs are mounting so fast that it will be impossible to bring out the bigger edition except at a prohibitive price. As I do not think a price between 1.50 and 2.00 would sell the book, it would be better to go ahead just with the Dunkirk by itself in soft cover,[177] and wait for better times for any further production. Perhaps the balance might be included in a 'Collected' in a year or two.

There's another point. As I did some of the Dunkirk passages for Pascal last spring,[178] I want exempted from the contract the right to use any passages in film and radio production. Brockington is looking after the radio part. Could you put in a clause exempting radio and film? I am very keen about that. It may not come off for a year as the 'Snow Goose' is held up on account of the difficulty in sending English technicians over. Everything else could be 'as has been.'

Sincerely
Ned Pratt

TO A.J.M. SMITH

Oct. 8, 1941

Dear Arthur:

Your letter just came.

It was a delightful experience to have you with us for a week or two. Personally and artistically you made a home run, in fact, a number of them. You were a

177 The volume was originally to be called *Dunkirk, and Other Poems*. See the letter to Pelham Edgar, 8 August 1941 (p. 207).

178 See the note to 'Pascal' in the letter to Pelham Edgar, 8 April 1941 (p. 207).

blessing in the house. I could almost kick your ass for alienating the affection of my family. You certainly were their 'cup of tea' and whenever you return, believe me, you will be welcome. Wild duck next time or charcoal broiled steak!

You are doing for the first time in our Canadian literature a first class piece of critical work done not only by a critic but by a first class Canadian poet,[179] and the combination is rare, – but necessary from my point of view. I shall keep after Macmillans. I think they ought to give you a definite undertaking that they will bring it out. It looks as if they will from our conversations but every publisher needs prodding. The price of manufacture is rising so rapidly that they have decided not to bring out my edition of 'Dunkirk *and other poems*.' They said it would cost $2.00 which is absurd – that is, to do it properly with adequate binding. Accordingly they are producing just the 'Dunkirk' in soft cover next week.

Yes – I saw that brief account of the April number in the Saturday Night.[180] I do not know who the critic is – Owen – somebody, but it is a type of what appears when critical reviewing is farmed out to nondescripts. There is no more 'individual' poet writing today than yourself, but all the new ones are thrown unreflectingly into the Eliot pot.[181] And what the hell has Marriott to do with him either![182] The most asinine attitude to take over here is a negativism towards Canadian production particularly on the part of the younger writers who do the reviewing. And Garvin started it though it wasn't his intention – quite the reverse. That's the reason why your Anthology should come out and show the American public what we are doing. I think more of your own stuff ought to be included. Don't be shy about it. That pungent concentration of metaphor is one of your strongest points.

Let me hear from you occasionally. Pelham also would like the odd line. He thinks you are the berries.

The very best
Ned.

179 Smith was working on his anthology *The Book of Canadian Poetry*.

180 A review of the special 'Canadian' issue of *Poetry* (April 1941) edited by E.K. Brown: 'Canada Expects' by Owen Maclean, *Saturday Night*, 4 October 1941, 21.

181 The reviewer maintained that most of the newer Canadian poets were imitators of T.S. Eliot. Pratt was a rare exception, and, though 'an inferior poet to T.S. Eliot,' a better model for young Canadian poets.

182 Anne Marriott's 'Traffic Light' was called 'a poor imitation of Eliot.' Marriott (1913–97) published several books of verse in the 1930s and '40s, including the long poem *The Wind Our Enemy* (Toronto: Ryerson, 1939) and the collection *Calling Adventurers* (Toronto: Ryerson, 1941), which won a Governor General's Award, and, after a long period of silence, four more poetry collections in the 1980s and '90s.

TO LEO COX

Nov. 3, 1941

Good old Leo:

I am all set for the 12th. I am leaving here on the midnight train & will go to the Mount Royal. As I have to husband my throat quite a bit I should prefer to make no speeches at the lunch and dinner. The evening address will tax the old larynx enough. I should love nothing better than to eat, with you and Joan in easy conversation without other formalities. If the P.E.N.[183] wanted 'a few remarks,' I could tell them a little about 'Dunkirk' and perhaps read a small selection. But as I am closing my evening address with Dunkirk, and some of the P.E.N. might be at this reading, even *that* might not be necessary. My main pleasure will be seeing Miss Sime,[184] Mrs MacLeod and your grand old self.

affectionately,
Ned

TO E.K. BROWN

Nov. 4, 1941

My dear Eddie:

Ruth Jenking[185] has just come into my office with the magazine 'Think' containing your grand article.[186]

183 International PEN ('Poets, Essayists and Novelists') had its Canadian centre in Montreal. See letter to Arthur Phelps, 9 November 1926 (69–70).

184 Probably J.G. (Jessie Georgina) Sime (1868–1958), Montreal-based author of *Sister Woman* (London: 1919), a collection of stories about working-class immigrants, and *Our Little Life: A Novel of Today* (New York: Frederick A. Stokes, 1921).

185 A graduate of Victoria College and a Shakespeare scholar who taught there for many years, she was a close friend of the Pratt family.

186 'Canadian Nature Poetry,' *Think* 7 (September 1941): 54, 93.

Woodhouse[187] tells me you are maintaining your connection with the Quarterly. That is good news. We miss you terribly here – the greatest personal loss I have ever had in the University circle. I felt we couldn't keep you here forever as your career is only bounded by the sky itself. But I know your heart will be with us.

I am sending you a copy of 'Dunkirk' which is having a bigger sale than anything yet. It has been out not quite two weeks, and a thousand copies have been sold in the stores. I may get a real break. One advantage is that it is selling for 50 cents.

Brockington's reading is over the national hook-up on Armistice Day. That will help.

Do let us hear from you once in a while, and whenever you return on a trip, give us a word in advance so I can get the gang together. I will never never forget what you have done for us all. I have A.J.M. Smith with me for two weeks. He is a grand fellow and a wonderful admirer of yours. He's the Guggenheim chap this year.

Love to Peggy.
Ned Pratt

TO LEO COX

[late Nov. 1941]

Dear Leo:

Your Sonnet is really fine and I'll put it in the next issue. I may be able to jam it in the November one though I may have to force some adjustments.

I saw Ellen Elliott yesterday about your prospects for the G.G.A.[188] She said she would be delighted to see you get it. As far as I have canvassed the field, you have no competitor. She will send the books to the judges early in this winter for the spring announcement.

---

187 A.S.P. (Arthur Sutherland Pigott) Woodhouse (1895–1964), born in Ontario and educated at the University of Toronto and Harvard University, was professor of English and head of department at University College (1944–64). As a scholar and teacher specializing in Milton and the history of ideas, he profoundly influenced a generation of students at the University of Toronto. He and E.K. Brown had been editors of *UTQ* since 1932.

188 Pratt was campaigning Cox to receive the Governor General's Award for Poetry for his collection *North Star* (Toronto: Macmillan, 1941). He first mentions this in the letter to Cox, 13 November (*EJP: Web*).

Of course, the judges may be old fogies, and the unexpected may happen. Let me know when you come this way. Had a wonderful time at Montreal.

Ned

TO ELLEN ELLIOTT

Dec. 2, 1941

Dear Ellen:

Several people have brought to my attention the considerable number of commas which are scarcely distinguishable from full stops in Dunkirk.[189] They say it makes the poem hard to read, especially aloud. It is a fault of the printing. Compare, for instance, the definitely marked comma after 'escarpments,' line 18 page 1 with the others. I have to look the second time to identify them as commas.

Could this point be passed on to the printers should another edition appear?

Have you had any further word from the U.S.A.? Isn't it too bad that no one is handling Dunkirk at all when there should be a reasonable market. No reviews in the U.S.A. Several orders have come in to me from American individuals, mainly I suppose because Poetry of Chicago took note of the poem. For the reciprocity of the publishing trade can any pressure be put on those sons o' guns across the line, simply to stock a few and hand press copies around. We certainly sell their books. Why shouldn't they sell some of ours or at least have them in stock. They sold many hundreds of the Roosevelt and Antinoe, but nothing since.

yours as ever
Ned P.

---

189 On December 5, Elliott replied that the problem was owing to the Goudy type, 'but we will lift out the pesky Goudy commas and in something which looks a little more definite in our next printing.'

TO A.M. KLEIN

Dec. 23, 1941

Dear Mr Klein:

Your warm and cordial article in the 'Chronicle'[190] sent the blood through my arteries very fast. I appreciate your judgment intensely because I have always had the highest admiration for your poetry. E.K. Brown, Leo Kennedy, A.J.M. Smith and I are united in our praises of you. Certainly, you have given to this country so absolutely original a product that you have become a national discovery. Your stock is very high here in Toronto academic circles.

If you should visit this city will you let me know in advance, so I can get the gang to meet you personally.

Yours very sincerely
E.J. Pratt

TO CÉCILE DE BANKE[191]

Dec. 24, 1941

Dear Miss de Banke:

A merry Christmas to you, a happy new year and many many happy years ahead.

You were a blessing to this city and a real darling to your friends. I hear echoes of that recital[192] every day. That conclusion of 'Dunkirk' was read with such power and triumph that the lump is in my throat yet. You were simply magnificent throughout.

190 A review of *DK*: 'The Decencies Had Perished with the Stukas,' *Canadian Jewish Chronicle* 19 (December 1941): 3.

191 British-born and living in the United States, Cécile de Banke taught elocution at Wellesley College, a women's college in Massachusetts. An actress, elocutionist, and world traveller, she made several public appearances in Canada during the 1940s.

192 The event was sponsored by the Association of Teachers of Speech, of which Pratt was a patron, and was held on 24 November at the Harbord Collegiate auditorium.

Vi said it will be one of her great memories. With such a gift as you possess you should do more of that platform work. When you return to Toronto, we certainly want to see a good deal of you because we love you.

You will be glad to know that at an autographing party given by Simpson's Book Department last week, I signed 1100 copies. The book has now entered its 4th edition – within two months!

With affectionate regards
Ned Pratt

TO RALPH GUSTAFSON

March 17, 1942

Dear Mr Gustafson:

I am glad to see that you are engaged on another Canadian work.[193] I saw Frank Appleton[194] a little time ago and he said that your anthology would be out soon. Frank is quite enthusiastic, as we all are about you and your plans.

There are two men in this country who ought to be able to put you on to the best prose. One is Professor Pelham Edgar who is examining the Canadian fiction of this year for the annual awards. His address is 286 St George St. Toronto. He is excited over a novel on Halifax called 'Barometer Rising' by a friend of mine – Hugh MacLennan.[195] You may have heard of him. His address is Lower Canada College, Montreal – where he is teaching.

The other is E.K. Brown now assistant to the Prime Minister.[196] You probably know him. His address is Office of Prime Minister, Ottawa. He is compiling the

193 He was compiling an anthology of prose for Penguin Books. Entitled *Canadian Accent*, its publication was delayed by the war until 1944. He had also been asked to edit a collection for New Directions Press, *A Little Anthology of Canadian Poets* (1943).

194 Appleton's company, Appleton-Century, represented Penguin Books in Canada. The anthology of which he was speaking was *Anthology of Canadian Poetry (English)* (Harmondsworth, England: Penguin, 1942), also edited by Gustafson.

195 Born (1907) in Nova Scotia, educated at Dalhousie, Oxford, and Princeton universities, MacLennan published eight novels between 1941 and 1980. *Barometer Rising* (Toronto: Collins, 1941), his first, won him wide acclaim, and later novels won him three Governor General's Awards. Pratt first met him in Halifax during the summer of 1933.

196 Brown had been given a leave of absence by Cornell University to succeed Leonard Brockington as special assistant to Mackenzie King (February to September 1941).

April (Canadian) issue of the University of Toronto Quarterly,[197] and has the latest stuff at his finger tips. The best verse in these parts is being written by Abraham Klein of Montreal, Charles Bruce (Canadian Press Toronto), Leo Kennedy and A.J.M. Smith.

As regards my own position I may say that the Macmillan Copyright governs all disposal of my published stuff including the latest – 'Dunkirk.'

When I brought out 'Dunkirk' I had intended incorporating ten shorter poems into the volume but on later consideration decided against it. I may bring them out in a year or so, and if you want one of them now you are welcome to it as it is absolutely in my own possession. I am sending the following:

The Invaded Field
Come Away Death
Still Life
Dunkirk (a sonnet)

I think I sent you a year ago 'The Impatient Earth' and the 'Old Eagle.' If you still have them, of course you may use either, as they belong to the ten mentioned.

Personally I like the two printed in *Poetry* best,[198] as I fear now upon re-reading that the Dunkirk sonnet sounds a little facile in the middle.

However, if any one is acceptable to you it is yours without any fee whatsoever and I hereby give official permission for publication.

If you ever come up this way do let me know in time. It will be an honour to introduce you to fellows of your own gang – a grand group of men.

With every good wish
E.J. Pratt

197 The spring issue of the *UTQ* featured 'Letters in Canada,' a comprehensive critical survey of Canadian works published in the preceding year. Brown had been responsible for the poetry section of the survey since its inception in 1936.

198 'Come Away, Death' and 'The Invaded Field' appeared in the special Canadian issue edited by E.K. Brown: *Poetry* 58 (April 1941): 1–4.

TO RALPH GUSTAFSON

April 13, 1942

Dear Mr Gustafson:

Thanks for your letter. I am looking forward to your (Appleton) anthology.[199]

As 'Come Away, Death' was published by Dillon of 'Poetry,' his permission should be asked for just as a matter of course. Poetry wants only acknowledgement. Everything is clear at this end.

It is a grand sight to see you and Arthur Smith working together. It is an object lesson for so many of our Sectionalistic artists over here. We took a great fancy to Smith last fall. He captured the whole University group. Birney is our 'comer' in these parts. He has exceptional ability. I think his 'David'[200] is about as good a bit of work as has been exhibited here in years.

I should like to see Edel[201] getting the recognition he deserves.

Brown is in Ottawa now. I had lunch with him last week at the Chateau.[202] You can count upon him for the future as his heart and mind are with the Canadian scene.

The very best of luck.

Sincerely
E.J. Pratt

If you see Smith, tell him that the boys are still reminiscing about him.

199 See note to 'Frank Appleton … your anthology' in the letter to Gustafson, 17 March 1942 (p. 218).

200 A long narrative poem first published in *CF* (December 1941): 274–6. It was the title poem of Birney's first book of verse published by Ryerson later in 1942.

201 Leon Edel (1907–97), a member of the 'Montreal Group' of poets and critics in the mid-1920s. Moving to the United States, he taught at New York University and later at the University of Hawaii. His major work is a five-volume biography of Henry James.

202 Château Laurier.

TO E.K. BROWN

April 20, 1942

Dear Eddie:

Your letter and request made me proud and grateful.[203] I feel the same towards you as I do towards Pelham – a feeling of eternal thanks and obligation. You are of the blood royal in the highest sense of intellectual aristocracy and warm human friendship. This Penguin venture will have an incalculable effect if it can be pulled off commercially. It is an amazing opportunity. I hope Gustafson can see it through. I had a letter from him yesterday asking for permission to publish 'Come Away Death' in his new composite anthology.

It was too bad I didn't see you during your last trip. I telephoned the 'Alexandra'[204] twice but you were out.

I am sending to you, in addition to the formal answers to the queries, a paper which I read, at Woodhouse's request, to the English Graduate Club last winter.[205] Woodhouse wants me to put it in the form of an article for the Quarterly but I haven't yet decided. It is an attempt to show the relationship between fact and poetry in historical and epic construction. You may find certain things you need and when you have finished, will you send it back as I haven't a duplicate.

I shall make my answers on a separate sheet.

Vi sends her love to you & Peggy.

Ever your friend
Ned Pratt

1. 'Newfoundland Verse' was published by Ryerson's in 1923. It consisted of a collection of poems most of which were published individually in Canadian periodicals. The Ice-Floes, Carlo, The Shark, History of John Jones, In Lantern Light, 'Overheard by a Stream,' appeared in the Canadian Forum and two or three short pieces in Acta Victoriana – between 1919 and 1923.

---

203 Gustafson had asked Brown to write an essay for the new Penguin anthology. (See the letter of 17 March 1942 [pp. 218–19]). Brown decided to write on Pratt and had sent him a set of questions about himself and his work.

204 The Alexandra Palace Hotel.

205 The paper (delivered 6 November 1941) was not published in *UTQ*. Parts of it had been used in other 'talks' and would be used again in other public performances.

But before N.V. I had two '*experiences*' in verse to which I rarely refer because I am ashamed of them.

(a) If you have a copy of N.V. you will notice two fragments beginning page 115.

I had written a narrative poem in 1917 called Rachel, a story of Newfoundland sea life[206] – 600 lines long. Some of my friends out of their unwarranted enthusiasm cajoled me into publishing or rather printing it. It was a private printing limited to 500 copies[207] and done in New York. It was a tedious bit of writing full of conventional phrases like Neptune's sea horses racing along the brine or down the main (I forget which). In 1923 when I was making my collection I thought I would put in the conclusion mainly out of my love for an old friend Robert Ledrew who died about that time and to whom the poem was dedicated.[208] I do not list it now among my publications as it is poor stuff.

(b) 'Clay' was a philosophical poem – a lyrical drama so-called done in 1918.[209] I had high hopes of this at the time but on looking at it soberly later I concluded that it was exceedingly dull and verbose (Pelham thought so too and very definitely). I salvaged a small section of it – the conclusion – and there it is. Vi kept a copy of the original more as a souvenir. When any of 'my antiquarian' friends wish to see it now out of curiosity, I never show it until at least two hours after a meal – it upsets digestion so badly. To have published that would have been a misuse of paper pulp.

More than half of N.V. I would reject if I ever brought out a 'Collection.' I might retain only The Toll of the Bells, The Ground Swell, The Shark, The Ice-Floes and a few short lyrics like In Lantern Light, Come Not the Seasons, Before an Altar.

2. I left the department of Psychology in 1919 and immediately entered English at Victoria that same fall.[210] I took the job with a mixture of enthusiasm and timidity as I could not lay claim to any highly specialized knowledge of English – that subject being rather a hobby than an

206 *Rachel* was first formally published in *HTF* (41–58) in 1962.

207 Lila Laakso notes, 'Mrs Pratt claimed only 100 copies were printed and considering the scarcity of the poem, this figure seems correct' (*EJP: CP* 2.378).

208 See the note to 'Poor old Bob' in the letter to Phelps, 18 September 1918 [p. 13].

209 *Clay* was actually written off and on between 1917 and 1920.

210 In fact, Pratt was appointed to a part-time probationary position in the English Department in 1920.

academic pursuit. I had, in other words, 'to get it up.' Pelham was a Prince in every sense and had one blind eye for my limitations. He gave me the Elizabethan period, Sidney, Hakluyt & the crowd, and Shakespeare and a lot of generalized survey work. I owe so much to him – friend and critic.

3. The Witches Brew in 1924.[211] I was in England with Knox and Davis who introduced me and the Brew to George Gordon of Oxford. Squire of the London Mercury wanted it for his magazine but Selwyn and Blount couldn't wait long enough and they published it in England – 500 copies.

4. The Cachalot appeared in the Forum in 1925. I had not read Moby Dick at the time but I had read Bullen. I had spent the summer of 1925 in Newfoundland and visited the whaling stations.[212] Years before I had taught school in a little village called Moreton's Harbour (1903-05)[213] and there the whaling steamers would tow the whales into the harbour, moor them belly up until they were taken to the factories. I used to row around the whales some of which were 70 and 80 feet long. I got a good deal of the information first hand – the way they were killed by harpoons fired from a gun on the ship. I read Moby Dick in retrospect and very admiringly.[214] Macmillan's published this in 1926 together with the 'Great Feud.' The Cachalot was the first long poem that I really liked myself: – it was my first attempt to combine the serious and the comic in one production. It gave me the cue for the 'great Feud' as a technique which was followed to some extent in the Fable of the Goats and Dunkirk. It allowed me to bring in (with the more severe elemental and heroic qualities) the human idiosyncrasies which were absent in the Titanic and Brébeuf on account of the very nature of these subjects.

5. Teaching of the Elizabethan stuff perhaps unconsciously strengthened my impulse towards tragi-comedy. I could see life that way better than any other. 'Dunkirk' was from that angle of course. Pelham was strong for this direction – this blend of the lyric and epic, etc. I started to subscribe to the Chicago 'Poetry' in 1916 and have been a continuous student of

211 [*sic*]. It was written in 1923 and published in 1925.

212 He had spent some weeks in June 1925 in Newfoundland and had briefly visited a whaling station on the Burin Peninsula. But 'The Cachalot' had been all but finished before he made the trip.

213 Actually 1902–4.

214 There is strong evidence to indicate that, before writing 'The Cachalot,' he had read *Moby Dick* as well as Frank T. Bullen's *Cruise of the Cachalot* (London: Smith, Elder, 1898) and *Idylls of the Sea* (Toronto: Toronto News, 1899).

the new schools. It made for resiliency. Mere descriptive poetry – nature poetry, just for itself, never appealed to me. It was the backdrop only.

6. My interest in Brébeuf was mainly the appeal of the heroic in Canadian History. Why should such an event have been neglected – when writers would go mad over the way a grasshopper cocks his legs while jumping on a cabbage leaf?

7. No: I have never read O'Dowd[215] but should like to.

8. I always liked Masefield especially his grip on the vernacular in the telling of a story. This applies mainly to his early work like the Everlasting Mercy & Dauber[216] – not to his later verse. He lacks humour – his chief defect though the E.M. possesses a few unconscious veins. He would have been better for some fantastic exuberance, and he has no satire to speak of.

9. I had almost forgot it.

In the Department of Psychology, my time was taken up with the composition of a thesis on Saint Paul.[217] In an unguarded moment I consented with the publisher, Ryerson, against the victim.

I never mention this publication because the composition was done to a formula – and not a naked expression of the spontaneous poetic spirit.

E.J.P.
(In haste)

TO E.K. BROWN

Victoria College
Toronto 5, Canada

April [21],[218] 1942

Dear Eddie:

I forgot to answer the question about Midland in my haste to get the letter off.

---

215 Presumably the Australian poet Patrick O'Dowd (1866–1953). His *Collected Poems* (Melbourne: 1941) have a strong socialist bent.

216 *Everlasting Mercy* (London: Sidgwick and Jackson, 1913); 'Dauber,' in *The Collected Poems of John Masefield* (London: W. Heinemann, 1923).

217 His doctoral thesis, *Studies in Pauline Eschatology*, was published in 1917 by William Briggs, the precursor of Ryerson Press.

218 Pratt dated the letter 19 April, an obvious error as it is an afterthought to his reply to Brown on 20 April (pp. 221–4).

Yes I went over the sites the spring preceding my summer's attack on the subject. Father Lally conducted me over every square foot of the ground. I found out all the possible flora and fauna of that region, the edible plants, etc. in famine emergencies. The Relations[219] contained a lot of this information but there were inevitable inferences derived from a contemporary investigation of the country.

One other point.

I nearly always start a poem with the conclusion, working back to the beginning.

The Roosevelt's homecoming was done first: so the picture of the iceberg at the end of the Titanic. Then in the B. and his B. I was working over a simile for the Cross which would express alike shame and glory, something strongly vernacular set over against cultivated imagery and language.

Two slabs of board – nails – Jewish hill and so forth contrasted with trumpets, lilies, robes and so forth. That was the start as well as the dramatic conclusion.

NED

TO E.K. BROWN

[22 April 1942]

Dear EK:

Still another point[220]

The Martyrs' Shrine near Midland is built on the grounds of the Jesuit Fort and Residence at Sainte Marie.

The archaeologists are now digging up the soil and finding many relics of the 1640's. The granite bastions are there.

I may say that three poems of mine appeared in the London Mercury away back.

1) The Decision (1928). (2) Sea-Gulls (1932). (3) The Way of Cape Race (1932). (2 & 3 in the same issue).[221]

Ned.

---

219 *Jesuit Relations and Allied Documents*, Pratt's chief source for *BB*.

220 A second follow-up with additional information to Pratt's initial response to Brown's inquiries. See the letters to Brown, 20 and 21 April (pp. 221–5).

221 'The Decision,' *LM* 17 (January 1928): 244; 'Sea-Gulls' and 'The Way of Cape Race,' *LM* 27 (December 1932): 109

TO E.K. BROWN

May 2, 1942

Dear Eddie:

Yes, the conclusion of Clay[222] did represent my viewpoint and does yet – *more or less*. I can never see Nihilism behind any struggle. You may have the article as long as you need it.

I came to the University late as I had to earn my living and try to save a few dollars. My father – a Methodist clergyman – died when I was in my late teens.[223] I went to work in a draper's store at 15 in St John's Newfoundland, was cash boy and dry goods salesman till I was 18. Then I went back to school, took my Matriculation at the College in St John's, taught school for two years in a northern settlement, Moreton's Harbour, then preached for three years, till I was 24.

I don't know if these extra details are of value but my three years at the draper's store were taken up in receiving and exchanging cash, and in selling corsets and brown sugar. I learned a little finesse in suggesting bust measurements – and established a reputation for conservative estimates.

Ned.

TO RALPH GUSTAFSON

May 2, 1942

Dear Mr Gustafson:

I saw Earle Birney today and he says that he is busy gathering material for you. We hope that, in your presentation of the Canadian scene, you are not neglecting your own fine contributions. I am eagerly anticipating the Penguin Anthology (Toronto Edition). I trust Klein of Montreal is represented in your general collections. I hear that A.J.M.[224] is going to be in Toronto sometime soon. It would be grand if the two of you could be here together.

---

222 Only the concluding section of *Clay*, entitled 'A Fragment from a Story,' was published in Pratt's lifetime: in *NV*. (See item 1 (b) in the letter to Brown, 20 April 1942 [p. 222].)

223 Pratt was twenty-two when his father died in March 1904. He was twenty-five when he completed his probationary preaching and went to Toronto to attend Victoria College.

224 A.J.M. Smith.

You are, of course, welcome to the Prize Cat and Come Away Death. I will assume responsibility for the former: so go ahead.

As ever,
E.J. Pratt

TO WATSON KIRKCONNELL

May 6, 1942

Dear Kirk:

Can you do something immediately for me? First let me congratulate you on the Medal.[225] When I was at Ottawa last month I put up your name and it was accepted. Now the President[226] has asked me to read your *Citation* and present you, which I am delighted to do.

Will you let me have at once a little biographical sketch with your honours, positions, changes of work, and whatever publications you would like me to mention. The citation is relatively short, so I must touch the high spots. I submitted your list of 'pubs' to the society but they retained the copy.

It will be a grand pleasure to see you. Bring along your clubs if you want a game.

Ned.

TO E.K. BROWN

[May 1942]

Dear Eddie:

You are right about the 'Roosevelt.' I had a very hard time with it. If it hadn't been for Pelham's generosity and his friends' I might never have finished it.[227]

---

225 Kirkconnell was to be awarded the Lorne Pierce Medal for 1942. Pratt's citation was published in the *Transactions of the Royal Society* for 1942.

226 Of the Royal Society of Canada.

227 Edgar had canvassed some of his well-to-do friends for funds, which enabled Pratt to visit the *Roosevelt* in New York in December 1928 and interview some of its crew. See the letter to Pelham Edgar, 2 August 1945 (pp. 361–2).

I had a great deal of data about the event, but it seemed to resist all my efforts to shape it into a poem. No matter how I tried to imagine and feel the human drama of it, it wouldn't come to life. I felt I was just fumbling with bricks and stones, inert materials so to speak, that I couldn't seem to get 'transmogrified' (your word, but a good one that) into a reality. I began to realize that unless I could stand on the very spot, talk with those who had lived through it all, and get a *physical feeling* of the whole thing for myself I might as well give up. I'd never had that experience before as I recall. Finally good old Pelham came to my rescue and I went down to N.Y. and got it all first hand.

Hope this finally concludes your queries, but ask me more if you have to. My appreciation of what you are doing is overwhelming.

As ever
Ned

TO GEORGE DILLON

May 30, 1942

Dear Mr Dillon:

Some of your Toronto well-wishers were distressed over the announcement of the 'Poetry' condition.[228] We feel that to fold up after a generation of full-blooded life is a literary tragedy of national significance. A.J.M. Smith and I were discussing your magazine last night and hoping that the response to your appeal would be life-saving. How have people reacted to your call?

E.K. Brown wrote us from Ottawa to say that George Ferguson, Editor of the Manitoba Free Press, and a member of the Rockefeller Foundation, was present during a session of the Committee when the 'Poetry' appeal was made. Ferguson, who considered the Canadian April number magnificent, strongly supported 'Poetry.' I trust the other members feel likewise.

We appreciate your difficulties here as our own Canadian Poetry Magazine may have to be suspended through the 'Duration.' I hope you weather the gale.

Yours sincerely,
E.J. Pratt

I like the work of that youngster Shapiro.[229]

228 *Poetry* (Chicago) was in severe financial straits and had appealed for donations.

229 Karl Shapiro (1913–2000) published his first book of verse, *Poems*, in 1935. His *V-Letter*, a collection of army poems, won a Pulitzer Prize in 1945. From 1950 to 1956 he was editor of *Poetry*.

TO CLAIRE PRATT

21 Cortleigh Blvd.
Toronto

Wednesday Evening
[early June 1942]

Dearest Cayke:

I have just come away from the tabulation of the second year with Brett and Anderson.[230]

There were three students in P & E who received First Class Honours and you were one.[231] Andy[232] knew your term mark and pointed your results out to me. He was delighted and said that your final on his paper was excellent. You got a 75. A St Michael's student got a 77 and a Trinity chap got a 76 and you came third with a 75. You had the highest marks in 2e.[233] And your aggregate *Phil*[234] mark was 303 out of 400.

The totals for the course ran

(1) 535
(2) 530
(3) 523 yours.

You made 150 out of 200 in 2e English and 107 out of 150 in 2h.

Anderson was most pleased: so was Goudge.[235]

The student just below you had a 69% so the difference was considerable.

I don't know when the lists will be published – probably Saturday. I shall keep a copy for you in case you don't get one.

230 They were reviewing university examination results. George S. Brett (1879–1944) was head of the department and Fulton H. Anderson (1895–1968) was a professor of philosophy in the University of Toronto. (While certain academic disciplines such as English were affiliated with the institutions that made up the university, others such as philosophy were solely 'university' disciplines.)

231 Claire had just completed the second year of Honours Arts in Philosophy and English ('P & E').

232 Fulton H. Anderson.

233 English.

234 Philosophy.

235 Thomas A. Goudge was another professor of philosophy who had taught Claire. He was author of several scholarly works, including *The Thought of C.S. Pierce* (Toronto: University of Toronto Press, 1950).

Mother and I are delighted. I couldn't find out anything about the history or the Fine Arts marks. They were not on the Honours list but I guess you are all right there.

Well we are looking forward to your coming back. We shall leave for Port Hope[236] on the Tuesday. All well.

Much love
Daddy

Don't give details of this letter to anyone.

TO LORNE PIERCE

June 9, 1942

Dear Lorne:

I hear that you are bringing out a small volume of Birney's poems.[237] I hope you succeed for Birney deserves a success. He has a note all his own. I have published a good deal of his stuff in the Canadian Poetry Magazine.

You can make use of the following statement, or any part of it, for your publicity if you so wish.

'Earle Birney's poems are original in their daring use of phrase and imagery. He has the gift of vitalizing language by infusing fresh meanings into words while preserving their basic connotation. Ideas are packed into his lines. What he says is worth saying and it is said well. 'David' is a superb story, dynamic in its feeling, musical in its elaborated metrics – and intense human drama placed against a brilliantly executed backdrop of the mountains.'

It was good to see you the other night at the R.S.C.[238]

Yours Sincerely
Ned Pratt

236 Claire was visiting friends there.

237 Earle Birney's *David and Other Poems* was published by Ryerson Press in the fall of 1942. Pratt reviewed it in *CPM* 6 (March 1943): 34–5.

238 Royal Society of Canada.

TO LORNE PIERCE

June 20, 1942

Dear Lorne:

Thanks for your beautiful brochure on T.M.[239] I wish I could see more of you.

The Pelican looks like a good anthology,[240] though I feel convinced that the new substantial work which is being compiled by A.J.M. Smith will be the definitive job for the next ten or fifteen years. It is time for something to succeed Garvin's. I am backing Smith and trust he will receive support generally.

Many thanks and greetings
Ned Pratt

TO LEO COX

June 28, 1942

Dear Leo:

Your letter warmed the cockles of my heart. And your article on C.P.[241] was a honey. I feel very much indebted to you for so many kindnesses in the past, and I am honoured by your suggestion of an article upon my work. I enjoyed your poems in the issue,[242] but I should very much like to know why your North Star didn't get the G.G. Award.[243] That little chapbook of 8 pages by Anne Marriott[244] is not in the same class. Pelham Edgar, Bill Deacon and I are incensed over the way that damned Ottawa National Executive are acting. It is an infernal combination

239 *Thoreau MacDonald: Being a Talk on the Artist Given in Hart House, University of Toronto* (Toronto: Ryerson, 1942).

240 See the letter to Ralph Gustafson, 15 June 1942 (*EJP: Web*).

241 An article on *CPM* that Cox had published in the Montreal.

242 The Spring issue of *CPM*.

243 See the letter to Cox, late November 1941 (pp. 215–16).

244 *Calling Adventurers!* See the note to 'Marriott,' letter to A.J.M. Smith, 8 October 1941 (p. 213).

(Macbeth-Gaskell).[245] They evidently run the C.A.A., appoint judges on awards, set the pace for Canadian literary activity. I don't know who the three judges were,[246] but I am sure Gaskell had the say. He has been at cross-purposes with us all except his own gang. He has hit the Canadian Poetry Magazine a number of dirty underhand 'blows,' and he makes use of his cross-country drives to enhance his own personal prestige & power. Dorothy Herriman here works hand in glove with him. She entertained Anne Marriott last year and I'll bet you dollars to doughnuts there's collusion all along the line. I had assumed your volume would get the award. I couldn't see a competitor at all in sight. There wasn't one. But eight pages of journalistic hackwork![247] Ye gods!

Well, old chap, when you come this way let us know. Vi sends her love to you. My best to you and Leslie[248] et al.

Ned Pratt

TO EUGENIE PERRY

July 2, 1942

Dear Miss Perry:

Thanks for the *Swinging Gate*. I shall include it next time.

I don't think Dr Edgar would take that job.[249] Personally I should like to see him get it as there is growing dissatisfaction with the Gaskell-Macbeth

---

245 In the letter to Lorne Pierce, 28 June, Pratt calls them 'that totalitarian outfit down there in Ottawa' (*EJP: Web*), referring to Madge Macbeth, three-term national president of the Canadian Authors Association, and Eric Gaskell, the national secretary. The executive had become a source of irritation to many members of the CAA. Pratt as editor of *CPM* was encountering significant interference. (See the letter to Eugenie Perry, 2 July [pp. 232–3].)

246 Judges' names were not made public until 1943. However, notes in the files of W.A. Deacon, chairman of the awards committee, indicate that the judges for the poetry competition were Duncan Campbell Scott, Ian Dilworth, and A.M. (Alexander Maitland) Stephen.

247 The poems of *Calling Adventurers!* had been written as choruses for *Payload*, a CBC documentary about bush pilots in northern Canada.

248 Leslie Gordon Barnard (1895–1961) was a Montreal writer mostly of fiction: short stories in *One Generation Away* (New York: Holborn House, 1931) and *So Near Is Grandeur* (Toronto: Macmillan, 1945), and novels *Jancis* (Toronto: Macmillan, 1935) and *Winter Road* (serialized in *Canadian Home Journal*, 1939). A long-time member of the CAA, he had been national president from 1937 to 1939.

249 National president of the CAA. Edgar had held the post in 1935–7.

management.[250] They are ruining the C.A.A. by their autocratic methods. Gaskell takes on the functions of a President or a Dictator. We are thoroughly disgusted here. We should like to see Kirkconnell get the Presidency.[251]

With best regards
E.J. Pratt

TO A.J.M. SMITH

July 15, 1942

Dear Art:

That was a grand letter. The 'notes' are wonderful.[252] They are so cordial, so generous that they create in me a deep sense of obligation. I feel that you are the leader of the younger generation of Canadian poets and you have a great horizon of years and reputation ahead of you. You inspire both admiration and affection everywhere you go.

I hope this anthology will start off from a real springboard.

I think Klein is unique. He seems to have the whole racial territory to himself in this country. Will you let me know Moe's address.[253] I shall write him immediately, strongly endorsing Klein. I have a high respect for his courage and intellectual power. The quicker we can get to work on Moe the better.

I have looked up Hermia Harris Fraser's address.[254] It is 1245 Seaview Avenue, Victoria, B.C. Those Haida songs are good. Of course, you have permission to publish them.

My best to the Montreal boys.

Cordially,
Ned Pratt.

---

250 See the note to 'an infernal combination (Macbeth-Gaskell)' in the letter to Leo Cox, 28 June (pp. 231–2).

251 Watson Kirkconnell was elected president in September 1942.

252 He had sent Pratt a draft of notes he had written on Pratt's poems to be included in the anthology *The Book of Canadian Poetry*.

253 Henry Allen Moe, director of the Guggenheim Foundation in New York. Smith was urging Klein to apply for a Guggenheim Fellowship.

254 Born in New Brunswick in 1902, Fraser was raised and educated in Yukon and British Columbia, where she developed an interest in the Haida Indians, writing poems on Haida themes which were published in *Songs of the Western Islands* (Toronto: Ryerson, 1945).

TO GEORGE DILLON

Aug. 26, 1942

Dear Mr Dillon:

You asked me last winter to send along some more verse whenever production got under way. I did not have anything worthwhile at the time, but since the University year closed I have had leisure to work out a few pet themes. I am sending to you the main effort for your consideration. If it is too lengthy or unacceptable on any other ground do not hesitate to return it.

'The Truant'[255] is the working out of the 'rebel theme' with a contemporary twist. I finished it last week.

I hope the New York Herald acknowledged 'Poetry' in publishing your 'Dunkirk' segment last fall.[256] They put in practically the whole thing on their book page. I didn't see it but a friend of mine from Harvard[257] wrote me that the paper featured it. That certainly was good publicity for the poem. Since then it was read in its entirety by the B.B.C. and by the C.B.C. The sale of the book reached its 4th edition (a thousand each).[258]

Brébeuf also has had a good run – 7000 copies. An American order came in last month for 3000 – taken by the Basilian Press of Detroit.[259]

It was a joy to us all to find how enthusiastic was the response to your appeal for a sustaining fund. We were less fortunate in Canada for our own magazine, which will probably go into suspension till after the War.[260] The restricted character of our constituency together with our appalling taxes is responsible.[261] For the interim I am confident that Chicago 'Poetry' will get a number of our subscribers. I shall do my best to enhance your circulation. Shapiro's work is the most interesting thing I have seen in many moons.

There are a few Canadian developments you may like to know. Gustafson's Anthology (Penguin) is meeting with wide acceptance. A.J.M. Smith is completing

---

255 Pratt wrote 'The Truant' during the summer of 1942. It never appeared in *Poetry*, but was published in *CF* 22 (December 1942): 264–5.

256 'Dunkirk' had appeared in *Poetry* 59 (October 1941).

257 Douglas Bush.

258 This was the fourth 'printing' of the first edition.

259 Macmillan produced an edition specially for the Basilian Press. See letter to Father Murphy, 17 March 1942 (*EJP: Web*).

260 *CPM* often appeared irregularly, but it did not suspend publication during the war.

261 In the left margin, Pratt has marked this section of text as 'Confidential.'

his – a very substantial historical anthology which I am sure will be a Canadian classic. It is a 'Guggenheim' venture, and will have an American appeal especially for School and College Libraries. We have also an enterprising group of youngsters who will be heard from in the near future. They have marrow in their bones. A Renaissance is getting into existence.

Coming back to 'Poetry' I would suggest that contributors (if they can afford it) throw back their cheques into your treasury for a critical year or two and be given subscription credits. The returned payments would not be much of a sacrifice for individuals whereas the aggregate would be a considerable help to the magazine. This certainly applies to the enclosed 'Truant' which, should he wander back to the author through unavailability, may be replaced later on by two or three shorter and more domesticated poems.

With every good wish,

Yours sincerely,
E.J. Pratt

TO PELHAM EDGAR

Sept. 1, 1942

My dear Pelham:

Your description of the place[262] reminded me of the happy days long ago at Bobcaygeon when Claire used to yell with delight at plunging into the lake. The memories are very wistful now because her swimming and leaping days are over. The problem is getting more and more sombre every year: it is affecting Vi deeply.

We have remained in the city all the summer. Fortunately the heat has been tolerable. I have done a few things – some half-dozen poems, short and semi-long. I think two of them have come off. The 'rebel' one[263] is the best because there is an idea behind it to sustain the mood.

262 Edgar and family were holidaying in the Gatineau Hills before moving to Ottawa, where he was to be a censor in the Post Office Department.

263 'The Truant' (*EJP: CP* 2.125).

You mentioned the 'Oratorio'[264] and the Ottawa mix-up. Pelham you and I have a jinx or some ironic spirit presiding at the Cash desk. The Pageant certainly looked as if it would 'break' with all those dinners and ceremonies and black ties,[265] to say nothing of baronets and Presidents of Chambers of Commerce. That's off I suppose till well after the War. Then Pascal had a row with Shaw over 'Saint Joan' – Brockington told me. It seems that G.B.S. held on to the money bag. That squelches the Snow Goose[266] – till *when*?

Now Healey Willan tells me that he has given up hope of anything this fall on the Oratorio. Bushnell[267] is skeptical of the 'popular' appeal. Healey says Bushnell's ideal of music is 'When the roses bloom in June I'll come to you.' And there's the heck of an amount of jealousy within the grades of the hierarchy where each official resents any appeal made over his head to a higher authority. I wrote Jennings[268] more than a month ago but received no answer. Healey claims that Jennings can do very little now that the C.B.C. is on the spot. It is true that they have made some kind of settlement but still controversy is in the air, and people are wondering if Murray[269] has come out of his jag long enough to inquire what it is all about.

Within three weeks we shall be reflecting on a much curtailed enrolment in the College.

However – enough of this gloom – there's golf and the odd drink! People are much worse off in Poland and the Caucasus. And, granted our health, what the Hell!

It will be good to see you again. Damn King and the Ottawa population.[270]

Love to Dora, Jane & yourself
Ned.

264 A radio version of the musical score by Healey Willan for the proposed *Brébeuf* pageant.

265 A series of fund-raising dinners and other social functions mounted by the pageant committee had seemed to ensure the pageant's success. The 'baronet' is Sir Ellsworth Flavelle, chairman of the committee.

266 See the note to 'Pascal' in the letter to Edgar, 8 August 1941 (p. 207).

267 Ernest L. Bushnell (1900–87), later vice-president of the CBC, then a member of its programming division. The corporation had earlier expressed an interest in the *Brébeuf* 'oratorio' and made tentative plans to produce it on the national network.

268 Charles Jennings, director of programming at the CBC.

269 W.E.G. Murray (b. 1892), general manager of the CBC from 1936 to 1942.

270 For taking Edgar to Ottawa for 'the duration' as a postal censor.

TO A.J.M. SMITH

Victoria College,
Toronto, Ont.

October 2nd. [1942]

Dear Arthur:

I was glad to get your letter today with its news about the Anthology. I had been wondering just what progress it was making. My interest in the venture is so keen that I decided to go over and have a long and intimate talk with Malcolm Wallace (the U.C.[271] Principal) about you and your work. And here is the summary of our conversations.

First of all, he expressed the heartiest appreciation of your article in the Quarterly.[272] He thought it the finest bit of Canadian criticism he had seen in content and in pungency of style. He was most enthusiastic.

I then went over your difficulties in the preparation of the Anthology and in the securing of a publisher to take the risks of the publication. I said that the permissions would probably run into four figures or close to it, and that since you are doing a magnificent job for Canada and its literature, it was unfortunate and unfair that you should have to shoulder so heavy a burden.

Wallace suggested that you should communicate to him a statement of the whole circumstances of the undertaking: – the approximate size of the volume, the number of pages, the rough assessment of permission costs, the presence or absence of illustrations (I told him I thought there weren't any), and a guess at the probable market. He said that as Chairman of the University Press he could prevail upon the President and the other directors to undertake the publication of the book at the University expense with the exception of the permission costs. But if you or the Foundation[273] could guarantee those costs, repayment of such costs to you would be a first charge on the profits. He did not think the Board could be persuaded to take the initial risk of the copyright expense, though he felt sure they would obligate themselves for the rest. He would point

271 University College.

272 'Canadian Anthologies, New and Old,' *UTQ* 11 (July 1942): 457–74.

273 The Guggenheim Memorial Foundation had awarded Smith the fellowship that enabled him to compile the anthology.

out to Cody[274] that it would be a disgrace to let a book like that go begging for print especially among American publishers and it is possible that the University might extend its concessions.

I mentioned the negotiations with the Chicago Press. Of course, if that Press would publish the book at cost, it would be hunky-dory, but supposing they refused, then the Toronto Press would do it and negotiate with Chicago for the handling of the American sales.

You can depend on Malcolm to do his damnedest. He loathes the Garvin outfit[275] and thinks that it is time to have the 'real thing' represented in this country. He wanted to know what the price of the book would be and I said that it would be about $3.00.

This proposition looks good, Arthur. I don't think that the division into (a) 1850-1890 and (b) recent, would be advisable. It would dissipate interest. An historical anthology is absolutely necessary.

I shall be delighted to write Jordan[276] a long emphatic letter, but before doing so I should like to get your reaction to this present proposition. If you agree with it and you get back from Wallace and the Board a contract satisfactory to you, then I could impress upon Jordan the necessity of pushing the American edition.

I think that the size of the volume might be to some extent reduced by the curtailment of the 1850-1890 period. All the 'boys' feel that the early production is too tenuous to stimulate much interest and that some degree of distaste might be generated, by prospective readers through large doses of Sangster, Mair, Cameron[277] and others. It is so remote. However, you will know best what to do. Some saving of expense might be achieved with Macmillans. I will work on Ellen.[278] Instead of Dunkirk or sections of it, the Truant of mine could be used. It is less than half the size of Dunkirk: it would be preferable in its entirety, than Dunkirk in sections, and it would cost you no expense as now I control it. Pelham is very enthusiastic about it, and it is the only good thing that I have done this last summer. The other poems need a lot of further revision, and some of them are flops. You are naturally welcome to anything of mine not yet published in book form.

And again, just suppose, as a matter of hypothesis, that the permissions pile up through McClelland and Stewart, Collins, Ryerson, et al, and you find it hard to

---

274 Henry John Cody (1868–1951), a clergyman of the Church of England long involved in university administration, was president of the University of Toronto (1932–44) and Chancellor (1944–7).

275 J.W. Garvin's anthology, *Canadian Poets* (Toronto: McClelland & Stewart, 1916, 1923).

276 Manager, University of Chicago Press.

277 Minor nineteenth-century poets: Charles Sangster (1822–93), Charles Mair (1838–1927), George Frederick Cameron (1854–85).

278 Ellen Elliott.

raise the wind. I shall underwrite the job to the extent of $200.00 at my Bank. I could borrow that amount from the Royal Bank of Canada, taking a chance on the royalties, and if you happened to kick off through flu or cabaret involvements, I would honour the debt myself rather than make it go through your rickety estate. But I do not anticipate such a contingency. I have too much faith in your virility, your literary judgment and the book itself. But do get that letter off to Malcolm Wallace. He is hot for it and holds the University Press in the hollow of his capacious palm. A saw-off with the Chicago Press is certain with such a backing. That is, of course, if the University of Chicago is cold or tepid on the subject.

By the way, Professor Clarke of Queen's University is retiring next year. President Wallace came down to Toronto last month to see me about a successor as Head of the Department, and I put in a strong recommendation of your worthy self. I don't know what will come of it, but I feel sure that your destiny is in Canada. The Anthology will be of great significance if it can be pulled across.

With all my stag enthusiasm
and affection,
Ned Pratt.

Forgive type errors. I thump the typewriter with one finger.

N.

TO A.J.M.SMITH

Nov. 15, 1942

Dear Arthur:

I have just written letters to Ellen Elliott and Lorne Pierce suggesting moderation regarding permission costs. As Lorne is deaf and Ellen is out of the city for two or three days I thought the written message would be more effective. I emphasized the fact that you were doing a noble work for Canadian literature and that a good deal could be written off by them by way of publicity. I hope and believe they will be reasonable.

I think that the 'In the Skies' extract[279] is a wise choice. 'Dunkirk' has completed four editions[280] of one thousand each and is still selling, so there ought to be a wide appeal. Your selection of my stuff is most generous and I am deeply and affectionately grateful. I shall act as a kind of Canadian agent for you.

---

279 From *DK*, ll. 270–365 (*EJP: CP* 2.121–4).
280 This should read 'printings.'

Whatever substitutions you finally decide to make in favour of my recent verse will, of course, have no copyright fee. All that I have written in the last eighteen months is under my own control and if the U of C.[281] Press needs my covering signature it is welcome to it.

I came across our mutual friend Carol Cassidy[282] the other day. She wishes to be remembered to you. She has written some excellent stuff. I hope she is represented.

The best of good luck to you,
and more power to your pen.
Ned Pratt

TO RALPH GUSTAFSON

Nov. 18, 1942

Dear Ralph Gustafson:

I deeply appreciate your request to include some of my verse in your issue of 'Voices.'[283] You are perfectly welcome to print anything which may appeal to you, and wherever I have copyright possession there will be no expense involved. Pieces like 'Still Life,' 'Come Away Death,' and the enclosed[284] are my own. The earlier stuff is Macmillan's. Arthur Smith wants the 'Truant' for his Anthology which will probably appear after your Spring number.[285] The Canadian Forum is publishing it in the Christmas issue. If you like it, it is yours. You are free to accept or reject anything. Will you return what you do not need?

---

281 University of Chicago.

282 Alice Carol Coates Cassidy (1906–94) was raised in Japan, and after graduating from the University of British Columbia, returned there until the outbreak of war. She engaged in educational work for several years in Canada, the United States, and Britain, and published several books of poetry as 'Carol Coates,' including *Fancy Free* (Toronto: Ryerson 1939), *The Return and Selected Poems* (Toronto: Caronell Press 1941), and *Invitation to Mood* (Toronto: Ryerson 1949).

283 Gustafson had been engaged by the American journal *Voices* to edit a special Canadian number for Spring 1943.

284 A typescript of the poem 'Autopsy on a Sadist' (*EJP: CP* 2.133).

285 Smith did not use 'The Truant' in his anthology; Gustafson used it and 'Autopsy on a Sadist' in his special issue of *Voices*.

Your 'Lyrics Unromantic'[286] is a delight inside and out. I have been showing it around to my friends who say they have never seen a better bit of workmanship. The verses are pure sculpture and the ensemble type, paper, design, cover – exquisite. I am proud to have it on my mantelpiece.

Thanks and again thanks.
Ned Pratt

TO CÉCILE DE BANKE

Nov. 21, 1942

My dear Miss de Banke:

Your card just came and I am naturally thrilled to find that 'Dunkirk' is going on the air December lst.[287] Indeed I shall be listening in if the C.B.C. will make the connection. A little group of University people will be turning the dial at my house. We would love to hear your wonderful voice again though possibly you may be only directing the choir. 'Dunkirk' has gone through four editions[288] this year and is still selling.

Your visit to Toronto is a fragrant memory. Do you bowl them all over everywhere you go? I can readily understand it, though such a combination of charm and dynamic is most rare.

With every cordial feeling

Yours Sincerely
Ned Pratt

---

286 A collection of Gustafson's verse recently published in New York 'for a private occasion' (Gustafson to Pratt, 8 November 1942).

287 A choral reading by de Banke's choir at Wellesley College broadcast by a local American station.

288 This should read 'printings.'

TO A.J.M. SMITH

Nov. 30, 1942

Dear Art:

It is good news that the Publications committee of the U of C.[289] Press have accepted the Anthology. I trust that the Trade[290] soundly confirms the decision. I hope also that the permission costs do not frighten them off. Mrs Bowman could let you have something new though I think she has declined a lot in her output both in quality & quantity. A.A. Brown might release some stuff not published in book form. She is, of course, more important than Mrs Bowman, though a little modesty would help a good deal in assessing financial values of the wares. The two of them have shown very little development either in ideas or expression.

I wrote Miss Elliott and her letter contained two points of interest.

(1) The rival publishers demanded what she thought exorbitant rates when she approached them about permissions. That was the time when Macmillans were awaiting the reaction of the American firm before committing themselves. She then claimed, after the American refusal, that she could scarcely charge less for the Canadian Macmillan imprint. But she suggested that the costs might be diminished if the Chicago Press would give the Macmillans the Canadian agency.

(2) She mentioned $150.00 as the Macmillans cost but I did not know until I received your letter this morning that such a sum referred to my verse exclusively. That looks to me a very large sum, but I am between the devil and the deep sea in any negotiation on the point. They have always split commissions with me for fifteen years which is sheer generosity on their part inasmuch as the contracts make them absolute owners after my 10% royalty has been paid. Hence there is a point of punctilio. If this money happens to come out of your own pocket some of it will be refunded to you.

I think that her suggestion about Macmillans serving as representatives of U of C. deserves attention. Compare Gage's order[291] with that of Macs.

289 University of Chicago.

290 Trade committee.

291 Gage and Company, Toronto publishers, mainly of textbooks.

I gave a farewell dinner to Sirluck[292] and Bissell[293] two weeks ago. We drank your health.

Cordially
Ned

TO A.J.M. SMITH

Dec. 7, 1942

Dear Art:

I am glad to report progress on the Canadian side of the Anthology. As luck had it Mrs McCool[294] rang me asking if I would act as one of the two Canadian readers. She said that Chicago would probably act upon a favourable verdict from myself and Daniells.[295]

I spent the week-end drafting a letter of the strongest recommendation claiming that it is an anthology for a decade or longer; that it is the only thing extant with a searching and comprehensive introduction, that the University of Toronto was behind it as a unit, and that, as far as I knew, English professors in other Universities had pronounced well upon it. I told them what Malcolm

292 Distinguished Milton scholar Ernest Sirluck (1918–2013), a graduate of the University of Manitoba (1940), was then a graduate student and teaching fellow at the University of Toronto. He later taught English at the University of Chicago, returning to Toronto in 1962 to serve as dean of graduate studies and later vice-president. He went on to become president of the University of Manitoba (1970–6).

293 Claude Bissell (1916–2000), with degrees from Toronto and Cornell, was then a lecturer in English at University College, Toronto. Later he was professor of English and dean of residence at University College, and president of the University of Toronto (1958–71). He is the author of many scholarly publications, most notably a two-volume biography of Vincent Massey (1983, 1986).

294 Katherine McCool was textbook editor, subsequently editor-in-chief, at Gage and Company, which was considering acting as Canadian agent for Smith's anthology.

295 Roy Daniells (1902–1979) was born in England and educated at the universities of British Columbia and Toronto. He taught English at Victoria College in the 1930s, and later at the universities of Manitoba and British Columbia, where he established a program in creative writing and championed the study of Canadian literature. In addition to scholarly work on Milton and seventeenth-century literature, he published two books of poetry, *Deeper into the Forest* (1948) and *The Chequered Shade* (1963), both with Macmillan. For his services to Canadian literature, he received the Lorne Pierce Medal in 1970 and was made a Companion of the Order of Canada in 1971.

Wallace said about your 'Quarterly' article,[296] – and he has taught students for forty years. Finally I said that I would put my total weight behind the promotion of the sales.

I had just before writing my letter seen Lorne Pierce. He is enthusiastic over you and wanted the Ryerson's to represent the Anthology here. He knew Gage was after it – but thought Gage was rather a jobber and text-book firm, not a publisher in the strict sense. He said Ryerson's would probably start off with a 500 order but I told him that Gage would hit 1000.

It would be fine if Chicago had two bidders and I advised Pierce to get in touch with Chicago. The important thing, however, is to get the book published. My only criticism was that you were not adequately represented quantitatively. As the leader of the younger group you ought to have given yourself more spread of wing – another half-dozen. Do that.

I did not introduce the problem of the 'strong meat'[297] to Mrs McCool. She mentioned it to me in my office. I told her that your Ballade[298] was a clever poem impeccable on artistic grounds like MacInnes' 'Zalinka.'[299] Whatever objections might be urged against its inclusion would be strictly commercial – those of a salesman approaching a Board or a teacher in an Ontario High School. She wondered if two editions might be brought out – one for the general public, and one perhaps half the size and selling at a cheaper rate, well within the pocket range of the average student. Public Schools and particularly Catholic Separate Schools form a large part of the publisher's constituency, and as we all know mothers and thwarted aunts often raise a stink of the special Puritan variety. This is exclusively a publisher's approach in respect to schools.

Before you decide on anything get Daniells' reaction. Toronto put Morley Callaghan's books on the upper shelves[300] and I got into trouble myself for referring, indirectly but obviously, to farts in a gastronomic poem.[301]

---

296 'Canadian Anthologies, New and Old,' *UTQ* (July 1942).

297 Poems that might offend 'community standards' of morality and religion.

298 'Ballade un peu banale,' a satire on religiosity that might easily be mistaken for an attack on religion.

299 A poem by Tom MacInnes. Mildly and fancifully erotic, it begins: 'Last night in a land of triangles, / I lay in a cubicle, where / A girl in pyjamas and bangles / Slept with her hands in my hair.'

300 Callaghan (1903–90) was author of numerous short stories and novels, notably *Such Is My Beloved* (Toronto: McClelland & Stewart, 1934), *More Joy in Heaven* (Toronto: McClelland & Stewart, 1937), *The Loved and the Lost* (Toronto: Macmillan, 1951), which won a Governor General's Medal, *The Many Coloured Coat* (Toronto: Macmillan, 1960), and *A Fine and Private Place* (Toronto: Macmillan, 1975).

301 A reference to lines in *The Depression Ends*: 'Nor heard his stomach like a flue / Roaring with wind instead of fuel.' When the poem was first published in *CF* (October 1932), Pratt had used the word 'belly' instead of 'stomach.' Because of readers' complaints, his publisher requested the change when the poem was published in *MM*.

With regard to W MacDonald[302] and Audrey Brown they should be included, if possible. I hate MacDonald's guts but he is immensely popular in the schools. He gives addresses every month to literally thousands of students and he has a wide following amongst newspaper critics. He could do a hell of an amount of damage because he is like a copperhead in attack. The omission of Brown would be unwise, and perhaps one of Benson[303] like his Elegy in Spring might be found. At their best they are presentable enough if they are not too snooty about prices. The first consideration is obviously merit and though there is a lot of romantic junk about them yet if merit and public approval can be combined, it would help the anthology.

I am concerned about the size of the permission fees. I hope the U.C.P.[304] won't finally balk at the amount. I know that if I were just starting out as a poet I would regard inclusion in such an anthology as yours, of far greater value than compensation in dollars, no matter how poor I was financially. It is an honour for these youngsters and they should so consider it.

I am glad that Pierce has moderated the fees. I wrote Ellen,[305] as I stated before, but Pierce may use a bit of influence himself with the firm. I would suggest the elimination of Brébeuf which might cut out nearly one third of the costs. Your list appeals to me: (l) The Cachalot I & II; (2) Silences; (3) The Dying Eagle; (4) In the Skies;[306] (5) Come Away Death. You are welcome to any such short pieces as (3) & (4) or 'Still Life' which I think you have as I own these, though I should like the 'Prize Cat' if Ellen would throw it in. However, you do what you think best. I feel I am most generously represented. Pierce said he would like a section from the Iron Door. I am against it as my interest in that poem (which was a very personal expression) grows less and less. As it was written on the occasion of my mother's death it is scarcely a thing which should be too much publicized. And besides the *three* long pieces are *extracts*, and this would make a *fourth.*

By all means bring out a volume with Pierce.[307] He spoke admiringly of you, and your note is so individual that it speaks for the 'new guard' who will impressively come into the ranks as the years pass. I used that argument with Hugh Eayrs when 'New Provinces' was issued and the book awakened a critical audience to a sense of progression in the poetic art of this country.

One point about the Preface. To avoid creating the impression of too centralized a sponsorship, I think my own name might be omitted. Victoria College is

302 Wilson MacDonald.

303 Nathaniel A. Benson.

304 University of Chicago Press.

305 Ellen Elliot.

306 An excerpt from 'Dunkirk.'

307 Smith would publish his *News of the Phoenix and Other Poems* with Ryerson in 1943.

already represented by Pelham and Norrie,[308] and since I have been selected as reader by Gage, and so fully represented in content, it would be very advisable to remain behind the scenes. I can work far more effectively for the sales of the anthology and speak more frankly in an unobtrusive way. That gives me more elbow-room.

Keep me apprised of everything, old chap, and indicate what other methods can be used. This anthology is a project for years.

Cordially,
Ned

TO GEORGE HERBERT CLARKE

Jan.12, 1943

Dear Herbert:

Collip[309] has written me asking for a nomination for the Lorne Pierce Medal. I am nominating you.[310] Would you send me as soon as possible a complete list of your publications so I can forward them on. It may be that the French Committee may decide to nominate a Frenchman this year – I don't know.

Yours as ever
Ned

TO LEO COX

Jan.12, 1943

Dear Leo:

Thanks very much for 'Night Wind.' It is superbly rhythmical and suggestive. I shall put it in the forthcoming issue late Feb. or March.[311]

---

308 Pelham Edgar and Northrop ('Norrie') Frye had been thanked for assistance in Smith's preface.

309 James Bertram Collip, professor of biochemistry at McGill University, later dean of medicine at the University of Western Ontario, was president of the Royal Society of Canada in 1942–3.

310 Clarke was awarded the medal for 1943.

311 Cox's poem appeared in *CPM* 6 (March 1943): 18.

Could you do something for me? Ask P.K. Page[312] for a poem, say within 30 or 40 lines. I haven't her present address. I think she is a honey and greatly enjoy her stuff in the *First Statement*,[313] both prose & verse.

Will you let me know when you are going to be in Toronto. If it isn't Friday I would like you to have lunch with me at Hart House.

Vi joins with me in sending love.

Ned.

TO PELHAM EDGAR

Jan. 16, 1943

My dear Pelham:

I was greatly surprised to see from your letter yesterday that you had not received my long epistle written jointly to you and Harry.[314] Over a month ago I took an evening off to concoct what was really a love letter to you both and addressed it to you c/o Harry 222 Daly Avenue. I am sorry that it was lost in the mails because it contained virtually the history of the University of Toronto for the period since your departure. It was intimate and revealing. I do hope it turns up as messages were whispered into your ears in true Masonic fashion. And I told Harry what I thought of him as a loyal son of the Church and of the Order of Good Cheer. The last poker party held at the Royal York was analyzed and synthesized, with a little thumb-nail sketch of the faces of winners and

312 Patricia Kathleen Page (1916–2010) was born in England, raised and educated in Alberta. She first published poems in various magazines and in *Unit of Five* (Toronto: Ryerson, 1944), a collection of verse by five young poets. In 1954, she won the Governor General's Award for Poetry for *The Metal and the Flower* (Toronto: McClelland & Stewart); in 2010, she was nominated for the Griffin Prize for Canadian poetry. She was also a painter under the name P.K. Irwin. At the time of this letter, she had been published several times in *CPM*, most recently in April 1942 ('Remember the Wood,' *CPM* 6 [April 1942]: 16). She responded to Pratt's request, and 'Isolationist' appeared in *CPM* 6 (March 1943): 17, and 'The Clock of Your Pulse' in *CPM* 7 (August 1943): 12.

313 A 'little magazine' founded in 1942 in Montreal by a group of young poets under the editorship of John Sutherland. (See the letter to Sutherland, 5 January 1944 [pp. 272–3].)

314 Colonel Henry Osborne (1874–1949) was a career soldier who had served in the First World War. He was secretary general for Canada of the Imperial War Graves Commission and a founder of the Dominion Drama Festival. Pratt had known him when he lived in Toronto before moving to Ottawa.

losers – Malcolm,[315] J.S. MacLean,[316] Meech,[317] Arthur, Andy, Bert[?],[318] Ned. We even measured the angle at which your glass was tilted in loving memory and you were included as a beneficiary in the grace before the meal.

We have had two poker parties in this long interval. At the first I was blasted with ecstacy at winning the astronomical sum of $8.25. At the second I was neutralized by a loss of $9.75 at Frank Hay's.[319]

Then followed a bout with the flu[320] which lasted for nearly three weeks temperature at 102. I haven't regained my taste or smell yet. I rang up Dora yesterday to explain that I had written to you, I grieve to think that you have been under the weather. I hope you have fully recovered. I trust that Harry gets through this dismal winter without infection. I would love to get to Ottawa but can see no chance till late April, if even then. Every day holds lectures even Saturday and we are very short-handed.

Just before I got your letter I was on the point of asking you to do a 250 word review of Birney's David.[321] He especially wanted a review from you for the C.P.M. If, however, you are too much fatigued by your work, I'll try to make another arrangement.

The other little matter is this. The next time you have a dinner of a special character will you buy for Harry a liqueur[?] and have him open it with my blessing just after the stag grace which may be slightly altered to suit the post-lude. It would do me a lot of good to know the exact hour of the meal and the ceremony so that my telepathic vision may be opened and the vibrations properly keyed.

My richest love to Harry and Brock.[322]

Affectionately
Ned.

315 Possibly Malcolm Wallace.

316 An American-born professor of English at Victoria College, J.S. MacLean was author of many scholarly articles and several books, notably *John Locke and English Literature of the Eighteenth Century* (New Haven, CT: Yale University Press, 1936) and *Agrarian Age: A Background for Wordsworth* (Yale Studies in English, 1950).

317 Born in Toronto in 1893, a lawyer by profession, Richard Meech was vice-president of Loblaw Groceterias Ltd. and a director of the Great Lakes Paper Company. He and Pratt were friends for many years.

318 Arthur and Andy are unidentified; Bert may be A.H. ('Bert') Proctor.

319 Unidentified.

320 Pratt is understating his medical problems. That autumn, he had been on medical leave from Victoria College during November and December (*EJP: MY*, 300-1). See the letter to Lorne Pierce, 15 November 1942 (*EJP: Web*).

321 Pratt wrote the review himself. It appeared in *CPM* 6 (March 1943): 33–4.

322 Leonard W. Brockington.

TO M.M.H. MACKINNON

Jan.26, 1943

Dear Murdo:

Thanks for your letter. I heard about that wonderful migration of the Highland families to New Zealand.[323] Dr Henry Munro, Superintendent of Education for N. S. at Halifax told me the story several years ago when I was lecturing at the Summer School. It is an amazing tale and might start the processes going some time.[324]

No, I don't think I will take the Queen's job.[325] I told Wallace that if it were ten years ago it might be different. It is hard to pull up stakes especially when most of my life is wrapped up in my friends and associations.

Clarke gets out next spring and his successor is not yet determined.

The best of good luck to yourself and Elizabeth.

Cordially
Ned Pratt

TO A.J.M. SMITH

Feb. 16, 1943

Dear Art:

I am delighted that the anthology is rolling along. I think your additions are excellent notably Birney and Wreford.[326] I had a letter from Wreford (whose actual name by the way is James Wreford Watson). He is a Professor at McMaster

323 MacKinnon, in the RCAF at Sydney, NS, had told Pratt about a shipload of Cape Breton Scots who had gone to New Zealand in the 1870s.

324 He sees a possible poem in the story.

325 R.C. Wallace, principal of Queen's, had offered Pratt the headship of the Department of English in succession to G.H. Clarke, soon to retire.

326 James Wreford Watson (1915–90) wrote as 'Wreford.' He was professor of geography at McMaster University, and later joined the Federal Geographical Bureau, serving as Canada's chief geographer. His poems appeared in *Unit of Five* (together with verse poetry by Louis Dudek, Ronald Hambleton, P.K. Page, and Raymond Souster), and he won a Governor General's Award for Poetry for *Of Time and the Lover* (Toronto: McClelland & Stewart, 1950).

University and I am nursing him along in the Canadian Poetry Magazine. I believe in him. He and Kirkconnell ought to do something for the book at McMaster. McLaren[327] & Daniells are good too. I hope Daniells is really enthusiastic. He criticized Gustafson's 'A'[328] quite heavily I hear. Phelps[329] will be of help. I have a letter on my desk now from him saying he is speaking on Can Poetry tomorrow night over the network and he is going to devote some time to me, he says. I am counting on him to give a boost in his classes.

Regarding the great Dean Sir Charles God Damn R.[330] as he is called, we must remember he is 83 and getting set. I hope to God, Art, when we get old, if we ever do, we won't be trying to unseat the flaming Jove from his throne with our hubris and bloody conceit. I hope the Doyen allows a few of his poems to pass through your sieve without putting on his pince-nez and croaking arias about prices above what Shaw[331] would ask for the misuse of the English language!

I hope you get something from the goddamnedest ass in Can history, W.M.[332] just for the purpose of satisfying the female adolescents in the High Schools who really do read & buy his books and who would lick his ass in the bargain. One must be a realist in the publishing business. I think Lorne[333] will be all right. He was sorry about Gage but not in the least resentful. He likes and admires you and your work.

I had dinner with E.K.B.[334] a little while ago. We can count on him. Drop him the odd line. I had a long letter from Herbert Davis President of Smith College Northampton Mass. He is an old and tried friend. I will get in touch with him later.

I don't know how long I shall continue editing the C.P.M. I am getting about sick of it. Who would think that some of the females who in real life are so cold that they would piss icicles would get Vesuvian with the rejection of their poems or even with the delay of publication. And what poems, ye gods! They're talking about their cunts all the time in verse in lieu of their actual existence.

---

327 Floris Clarke McLaren, a British Columbia writer, born (1904) in Alaska. Her verse focused on the western landscape and Pacific seascape and was published in magazines and one book, *Frozen Fire* (Toronto: Macmillan 1937).

328 *Anthology of Canadian Poetry* (Harmondsworth, England: Penguin, 1942).

329 Arthur L. Phelps.

330 Roberts.

331 Neufville Shaw, a Montreal writer whose modernistic verse Pratt particularly disliked. (See the note to 'the Preview editor Shaw' in the letter to Smith, 28 January 1944 [p. 276].)

332 Wilson MacDonald.

333 Lorne Pierce.

334 E.K. Brown.

Here's to you old faithful. I am giving a lunch tomorrow to Sirluck & Bissell who are in Toronto on a week's last furlough. We shall toast you.

Ned.

TO A.J.M. SMITH

Feb. 24, 1943

Dear Art:

I conveyed your good wishes to Sirluck, Lorne, Earle, Carol[335] and a few others. Last night I met Mrs McCool[336] at a dinner and she said that the U of Chicago people were enthusiastic over you and the Anthology. I knew Sir C.G.D.[337] would be quite amenable to the Anthology and its plans. He gave an address on Monday night at the Conservatory of Music on behalf of the Russian fund.[338] It was a recital rather, and he raised about $100.00, not bad for an old chap of 83.

MacDonald's[339] reaction to your letter was typical. I remember his 'Song of the Ultimate' – one of those vague Whitmanesque imitations. He tried to ape Whitman by vaporizing about the Universe. He claimed he (MacD.) was greater than Whitman and even greater than Plato. We are used to that kind of bilge here. If he refuses anything then there is nothing to do but make it appear as a copyright difficulty. I would suggest that he be asked to submit a few including 'Exit' leaving it up to you to select any you like at 25.00 per throw. That would let you get out with Exit only. He is such a shit that I would even pity his own poems if they were stuck up his ass. He was meant to follow Clydesdale's horses all his life and close under their tails.

Sirluck & Bissell had lunch with me and the gang last week. They are off to Camp Borden[340] for some more training before going over seas.

The best,
Ned.

---

335 Ernest Sirluck, Lorne Pierce, Earle Birney, Carol Cassidy.

336 See the letter to Smith, 7 December 1942 (p. 243).

337 Charles G.D. Roberts.

338 The Aid to Russia Fund. When Germany invaded the USSR in 1941, it became an ally of the West. A number of funds to aid that country were set up in Canada.

339 Wilson MacDonald.

340 A military training base 80 kilometres northwest of Toronto.

TO MERRILL DENISON

April 5, 1943

Merrill, old dear,

I have just finished *Klondike Mike*[341] and think it immense. It has just reincarnated Jack London[342] of whom I have always been a great admirer. I can feel yet the hand-holds of Burning Daylight[343] and the last great scene when in his mind he flings the eucalyptus stuff over the gold dust as he listens to the cluck cluck cluck of his wife.

Merrill, I read K.M. in two successive nights and never missed a word of it. I ate his beans and bacon and drank his tea-lye. I petted Scotty,[344] made up a toast to Rosie & Emmeline expatiating on the fleshly beams of their prototypes[345] – a gorgeous bit of writing on your part. I sold the 150 pounds of feminine warmth 'on the hoof.' I roared over that. It was in your best vein. And my God, that piano! I can see the bugger going over the Chilkoot with its 45°.[346] And that fight in Soapy's pub? What a fight! Jack London didn't do it any better. I have always lamented the fact that this country lost you to New York – our only dramatist. I hope your books will sell by the hundreds of thousands and that it will get you leisure to write and dramatize. Those 'Sunny Sisters'[347] – what a sextette. I grinned my neck off in certain chapters. No wonder Chris Morley[348] was enthusiastic. Remember me to him. I met him in Toronto several years ago.

Love to Muriel and hugs & kisses
to yourself.
'Neddie'

341 *Klondike Mike: An Alaskan Odyssey* (New York: Harper & Brothers, 1943) was Denison's semi-fictional biography of Michael Ambrose Mahoney, an Alaskan prospector of the 1897–8 gold rush days.

342 American author (1876–1916) of such tales of action, adventure, and rugged characters as *The Call of the Wild* (1903), *The Sea Wolf* (1904), and *White Fang* (1906), all published by Macmillan.

343 A short story by Jack London.

344 The 'lead dog' in the team

345 Two boats used on the river. In the book Denison wrote: 'The names were dubious compliments to two unidentified ladies whose well-remembered beams inspired the McMillan boys to take time out for a brief ribald ceremony' (Forum Books edition, 1945, 101).

346 The tramways on the Chilkoot Trail moved people and supplies towards Dawson City during the Klondike gold rush.

347 The Sunny Samson Sisters Sextette: 'their reputed names were Essie, Bessie, Tessie, Ethel, Maude, and Nellie' (Forum Books edition, 1945, 175).

348 Christopher Morley (1890–1957), American novelist, essayist, literary columnist, and sometime contributing editor of *Saturday Night Review*.

TO LORNE PIERCE

April 29, 1943

My dear Lorne:

It was good to see you at the Exhibit two weeks ago and to hear your finely polished paper – the best of the three.[349]

I am enclosing a few words for Dorothy's book.[350] If you make use of me, just state the name E.J. Pratt without any frills of Professor or Doctor. And remember that I am not 'official' Head of the Dept. That is J.D. Robins, a purely administrative capacity. My position is known as 'Senior Professor of the Dept.'[351] but I do not like official references.

Affectionately
Ned.

TO E.K. BROWN

May 11, 1943

My dear Eddie:

May I say first that Vi and I want to put on a dinner at the York Club for you and Peggy on your visit to Toronto. We'll have the Norwoods and others and after dinner we can chin the roof off. We must decide on a date convenient for all.

The reports of my sickness were exaggerated.[352] Deacon said in his Fly-Leaf[353] that I was in the doctor's hands, and had to spend most of my time in bed. I have got about one hundred letters of commiseration, and even Sir Robert Falconer[354] at a reception last week asked me how my 'coronary' was getting along. How things multiply.

349 The exhibit of papers and mementos of Marjorie Pickthall (1883–1922) on the sixtieth anniversary of her birth. Pierce was custodian of her papers. His address was published by Ryerson Press as *Marjorie Pickthall: a Memorial Address* (1943).

350 Dorothy Livesay's third collection, *Day and Night*, published by Ryerson Press in 1944.

351 Upon Edgar's retirement in 1938 as head of English at Victoria, J.D. Robins was chosen to succeed him. Having been passed over, Pratt, two years Robins's senior, was named 'senior professor' as compensation.

352 See the letter to Pierce, 15 November 1942 (*EJP: Web*).

353 Deacon's weekly column of 'information and literary gossip' in the *Globe and Mail*.

354 See the note to 'Sir Robert Falconer' in the letter to Brown, 31 May 1938 (p. 169).

The long and the short of it is that I have a high blood pressure which, while not critical, demands a certain amount of care and easing off of work. I have attempted so many things aside from the academic routine, but I am quitting the non-essentials like the Canadian Poetry Magazine and, thank God, any involvements with the C.A.A. and their eternal disputes on small points.

Any lecturing extra-mural which I shall do will be recitals, which do not bother me at all, as I am on familiar ground.

I do not think that I should do the W.I.B. tour[355] if that means exposition of Canadian aims in the War etc., etc. as I feel I am not qualified to do it, and the preparation would imply a great deal of research. I suppose the lecturer must be prepared to answer questions about Canada after the lecture. If it meant only lecturing and readings on Poetry that would be different.

I should think that you are the best man for that job in the Dominion, and I shall certainly say so to the W.I.B. if they approach me. But I suppose you are full up to the gills with activities as you have always been. Still, you would be preeminently qualified to do it.

I like recitals and hope to make them the one additional chore.

I am so glad that Pierce has accepted your book[356] and I hope it issues in a contract soon. Knox was enthusiastic about your article.[357] He mentioned it to me last winter. I have a strong desire to see you keep in close contact with all that goes on in the literary life of this country.

Brébeuf is going well in the states. The Basilian Press has notified me that it is getting fine reviews. It takes eight months to start it on its way.

It will be a joy to see you next month. Best to Peggy.

Yours
Ned Pratt

355 The CAA had set up a Writers' War Committee to work in conjunction with the Wartime Information Board (WIB), a federal agency, to 'channel more effectively contributions of Canadian writers toward the War effort at home and abroad.' Pratt was a member of the committee.

356 *On Canadian Poetry*, a study focusing mainly on a few major poets, including Pratt, published by Ryerson Press later that year.

357 'Mackenzie King of Canada,' *Harper's Magazine*, January 1943, 192–200.

TO A.J.M. SMITH

May 13, 1943

Dear Art:

I am very excited over the possibility of your return to Canada via Queen's.[358] I was on the point of dropping you a letter when yours came this morning.

Principal Wallace came up to see me about the English appointment. We had lunch together at Burwash Hall and talked for an hour. He told me that you had been to see him and he was very favourably impressed. There were three possibilities he was considering:

(1) Woodhouse, who could scarcely better his position by leaving Toronto. In fact, W. is definitely out.
(2) G.B. Harrison[359] the English Shakespearean scholar. Wallace had been in touch with Vincent Massey who had made inquiries and found that G.B.H. would come as the Head of the Dept. if he received the offer.
(3) Your good self. He discussed all the points:
    (a) age, and Headship over older men
    (b) your teaching ability
    (c) your promise.

He had made investigations at Michigan State C. and found that you had an excellent reputation as a teacher. As regards promise, I told him that no one in Canada had a more brilliant future as critic and writer (prose and poetry). I instanced your articles in the Quarterly and quoted what Malcolm Wallace had said about them. And then you were undoubtedly the leader of the younger Canadians of the vital and progressive variety and that it would be absurd to import an Englishman when the homebrew was just as potent or more so. G.B.H. might possibly have a thin piping voice which, for all its scholastic timbre, might remind medical students of capons and drawn cats.

358 George Herbert Clark had retired, leaving the headship of the Department of English at Queen's University vacant. (See the last paragraph of the letter to Smith, 2 October 1942 [p. 239].)

359 A graduate of Cambridge University, Harrison taught English for many years at the University of London. He was head of English at Queen's University (1943–9), before leaving for the University of Michigan. Author of many scholarly works, he is best known for his *Introducing Shakespeare* (Penguin, 1939).

Regarding age, he said that perhaps a rotating chairmanship might be created which would soften chronological discrepancies, and that though the Headship might not be on the market, a high middle rank with substantial promotion in reasonable sight could be given.

He seemed quite disposed towards you. G.B.H. is the only rival. I do not know him but my experience of Englishmen has taught me to steer clear of those linguistic breakers.

I do hope you get the job. I am glad Lorne Pierce has written Wallace. Let me know if you get any news.

Ned

TO A.M. KLEIN

June 9, 1943

My dear Mr Klein:

Your poem[360] is grand. I think it is the most incisive satire I have come across in many moons. It is written in your best and most original vein. I have always been a keen admirer of your work and have hoped that enough leisure would be granted you to exercise to their full measure your abundant gifts.

After reading the poem I immediately forwarded it to Macmillans with the strongest recommendations.[361] Still I may not have as much influence as you think. I made the same recommendations for Birney's 'David' and A.J.M. Smith's Anthology but they had to go elsewhere. I haven't had any word from Macmillan yet but as soon as I hear I'll let you know.

Sincerely yours
E.J. Pratt

---

360 'The Hitleriad.'

361 In spite of Pratt's recommendation, Macmillan did not publish the book. It was published in 1944 by the American firm New Directions Press. Pratt reviewed the book favourably in *CF* (October 1944).

TO MALCOLM ROSS[362]

Toronto

July 22, 1943

Dear Malcolm Ross:

I have to thank you for your kind suggestion made to Charlie Clay that I should be included in *Norte*.[363] He asked me to submit material and a glossy print which I am now doing. The material, he said, should be an account of myself running into about 500 words. I couldn't very well write an article about myself, so I am sending just a *factual* statement which might leave an editor free to make his own appraisals and criticisms. E.K. Brown has just completed an article,[364] and so has Pelham Edgar for the Quebec Protestant Schools.[365] I haven't seen either but I wonder if *Norte* would be interested in an abbreviated version. Professor Edgar is in Ottawa with the Board of Censors.

I am deeply grateful for what you are doing. You are making marvellous contacts for us and we owe you a debt. I do hope I shall be able to see more of you in the days to come. I hear quite often of your fine work.

Yours sincerely
Ned Pratt

TO ELLEN ELLIOTT

Victoria College

Tuesday, 17 [Aug. 1943].

Dear Ellen:

I have just finished typing and gathering together the poems which I should like to have published.[366] Most of them have been printed in magazines. The

362 Malcolm Ross (1911–2002) was born in Fredericton, NB, and educated at the universities of New Brunswick, Toronto, and Cornell. Later professor of English at Manitoba, Queen's, and Dalhousie, he served as editor of QQ (1953–6) and general editor of McClelland & Stewart's New Canadian Library (1958–78).

363 A Spanish-language journal published in Cuba, devoted to cultural affairs and international relations. Ross was consultant for a special Canadian issue of the magazine.

364 'The Originality of E.J. Pratt,' *Canadian Accent* (1944): 32–44.

365 'E.J. Pratt,' *Educational Record* (July-September 1943): 178–80.

366 In a new collection which he entitled *Still Life and Other Poems*.

very latest – 'Still Life' – has not appeared.[367] It is the poem I have put most time on, and most revision, and as it sounds a key note to the general style and content, I should like to make it the title poem.

I hope you will like them. You may feel like rearranging the order of contents a bit. Do so, If you feel it is desirable.

The 14 poems count up to exactly 1050 lines which ought to make a book of between 30 and 35 pages.

It is very good of you to work this matter into your heavy schedule and worries etc. of this year.

In a couple of years or so I may approach you with a *Collected*[368]; but I think I ought to be before my 'constituency' now since it is two years since Dunkirk appeared.

With my very best,
Ned Pratt

TO WATSON KIRKCONNELL

21 Cortleigh Blvd.,

Sept.8, 1943

Dear Dr. Kirkconnell:

On account of increased pressure of work I feel obliged to relinquish my position as Editor of *The Canadian Poetry Magazine*.[369]

During the last seven years it has been a pleasure to watch the rise and growth of *The Magazine* as the medium for poetic expression throughout the Dominion. Many of the best contemporary Canadian poems have been first printed in its pages, and we look back in pride upon the vitality which has given *The Magazine* a continuous existence, when so many periodicals devoted exclusively to poetry have ceased publication.

It has been a privilege to be associated with a very capable executive who have sustained the literary venture with their energies and enthusiasms – notably,

---

367 The original short version of the poem *had* been published in *Saturday Night*, 28 October 1939, and in Gustafson's *Anthology of Canadian Poetry* (Penguin, 1942).

368 He did so later that year. (See the letter to Ellen Elliott, 1 November 1943 [pp. 265–6].)

369 Pratt addressed his resignation to Kirkconnell as national president of the CAA.

Dr. Jacob Markowitz, the former Business Manager[370]; Prof. Pelham Edgar; Mrs. Emma Benson, the Secretary[371]; and Mr Nathaniel Benson, the Managing Editor who, as the choice of the Executive, now becomes Editor-in-Chief.[372] I bespeak for the new Editor the loyal cooperation of all the subscribers, contributors and donors who have so faithfully stood by the enterprise in the past.

Yours sincerely,
E.J. Pratt

TO WILLIAM ROSE BENÉT[373]

September 9th, 1943

Mr. William Rose Benét,
Pigeon Cove
Cape Ann, Massachusetts,
U.S.A.

Dear Mr Benét:

The Macmillans have just forwarded me a copy of your most cordial letter. It came as a wonderful thrill, for my admiration of the Benét brothers[374]

370 Markowitz (1901–69), a graduate of the universities of Toronto and Glasgow, professor of research in experimental surgery at the University of Toronto, and occasional medical author, was a staunch supporter of the *CPM*. With the Royal Army Medical Corps, he was taken prisoner at the fall of Singapore in February 1942 and spent several years as a Japanese prisoner of war. He and Pratt were close friends.

371 The wife of Nathaniel Benson, herself an active member of the CAA.

372 Benson, though appointed editor, never served, as his advertising firm moved him to New York in October 1943. Sir C.G.D. Roberts assumed the post but died in November, before his first number was published. Anabel King (a member of the Toronto branch of the CAA) accepted an interim appointment until June 1944, when Kirkconnell took the post and served until 1946.

373 American poet, novelist, essayist, and editor, William Rose Benét (1886–1950) was best known for his columns and reviews in the *SRL*. In 1941, his *The Dust Which Is God* (New York: Dodd, Mead, 1941) won the Pulitzer Prize for Poetry. Other publications include *The First Person Singular* (New York: G.H. Doran, 1922) and *The Flying King of Kurio* (New York: George H. Doran, 1926).

374 William Rose Benét's younger brother was poet and novelist Stephen Vincent Benét (1898–1943), best known for his long narrative poems *John Brown's Body* (New York: Doubleday, Doran, 1928) and *Western Star* (New York: Farrar & Rinehart, 1943), both of which won the Pulitzer Prize.

has been genuine and deep for many years. I shall prize this tribute as long as I live, ranking it with letters I have received from the late C.P. Scott of the *Manchester Guardian*, and Edwin Arlington Robinson[375] on the appearance of 'The Roosevelt and the Antinoe,' from J.C. Squire on the 'Cachalot,'[376] and from Laurence Binyon and Masefield on the 'Titanic.'[377] As those letters, like your own note to Macmillans, were completely unsolicited, the experience is all the more gratifying.

As part of my work here in Victoria College is to lecture on contemporary poetry, I have often presented your work and that of your brother to classroom audiences. I think I am temperamentally constituted to enjoy such work because it perfectly conforms to my thesis that poetry ought to be, at least in part, the expression of a grand binge, making for healthy physiological releases where the world for a time is seen backside-up and the poet becomes gloriously emancipated from the thralldoms of day-by-day routine. I think your 'Merchants,' the 'Whale,' and 'Jesse James' illustrate my point.

I am still left breathless after reading 'John Brown's Body.' I had never corresponded with your brother. I wish now I had, just to tell him that the students here used to call it 'Pratt's Bible,' so frequently did I bring it into the classrooms and on the public lecture platforms. I feel yet that it is the greatest poem produced on the North American continent. Last year I piloted an M.A. thesis on your brother's work through the University of Toronto. It was written by a Miss Lois Darroch and she showed me with pride two letters she received from him, answering some critical and biographical points. She wants now to get a publisher for it. His death came like a personal shock to me and to her. What a pity there is not more fraternization between the Canadian and American writers. We scarcely ever get to know one another personally. It was my good fortune to meet Christopher Morley at the home of my great friend, Hugh Eayrs, President of Macmillans in Toronto. 'Chris' made a grand impression on the boys here. I wish there was more of that kind of exchange.

Miss Elliott tells me she sent you a few copies of my verse. She would have sent the rest but they are out of print. I have, however, a copy each of two earlier books which I am mailing to you. The 'Witches' Brew' is an extravaganza

---

375 It does not appear that Robinson ever wrote Pratt directly about *RA*. He is probably thinking of Robinson's reader's report on the poem for Macmillan (New York). (See the letter to Pelham Edgar, 6 August 1929 [p. 85].)

376 There is no evidence that Squire ever wrote Pratt about 'The Cachalot.'

377 Binyon did write Pratt about 'The Great Feud,' and Masefield wrote him about 'The Cachalot' and *RA*, but no evidence has been found to suggest that either wrote him about *Titanic*.

written in celebration of my fifth wedding anniversary and dedicated to my wife. I had no intention of having it published as I thought it too inconsequential. It was intended merely as a reading following a dinner at which some of my writing friends were invited. One of the guests suggested that it be sent to Squire, who submitted it to Selwyn and Blount, who to my amazement published it.[378] No wonder the firm went out of business a little later! I never made any claims for the poem if such it might be called. It was a straight 'let her go Gallagher' for a wedding feast. I was greatly amused by some of the English reviews – the Edinburgh *Scotsman* labouriously trying to extract a 'meaning' out of it, and another Scotch paper coming to the conclusion that it was a liquor advertisement, and still another claiming that it was a libel on the brands.

The 'Titans' contains two poems – the Cachalot and the Great Feud. I notice that you saw the first two parts of the Cachalot in a recent Canadian anthology. Would that be A.J.M. Smith's anthology just published under the Guggenheim Foundation? The third part was omitted as being too long. This poem was written when I was visiting my home country, Newfoundland, a few years ago.[379] I spent some time at a whaling factory after a steamer towed in a whale, and I was impressed by the size of a huge fellow that was moored belly up in the harbour. *The Great Feud* ran away with itself, I fear, unable to stand the compromise between high seriousness and high spirits.

May I thank you again for your interest. It has lifted me into the clouds. If ever you feel like coming to Toronto, will you let me know in plenty of time. I shall prepare a dinner for you at which I hope there will be roast grouse basted with Madeira.

In all sincerity of feeling,

yours,
E.J. Pratt

---

378 This account of how *WB* was published is quite misleading. He worked hard to get the poem published and was greatly relieved when Selwyn and Blount after some persuasion agreed to take the poem. (See the letter to Lorne Pierce, 24 September 1924 [pp. 55–6].)

379 See the note to "summer of 1925 … visited the whaling stations" in the letter to E.K. Brown, 20 April 1942 [p. 223].

TO E.K. BROWN

Sept. 14, 1943

My dear Ed.

Knox writes me that you have been at your kind work again.[380] Davis is working out a scheme of lectures with *Smith* as a centre.[381] Ross of the W.I.B. is communicating with Newton of New York.[382]

If Davis could connect his dates with November 22 and 23 for Cornell it would be very convenient. The W.I.B. want Brébeuf presented as it gives a national colouring to my trip. That suits me. I prefer a regular lecture to discussion. I am bringing out a new book called 'Still Life' through Macmillans this fall. I might do a bit of reading from that, if advisable. I hope this tour is not giving my friends any worry.

How is your Ryerson publication[383] coming along? A.J.M. Smith's anthology is out and it looks fine.

Will you let me know at your convenience what you think I should do at Cornell and I'll prepare the material but the main thing is seeing you and Peggy.

Affectionately
Ned Pratt

TO E.K. BROWN

Sept. 20, 1943

Dear Eddie:

Thanks for your cordial letter.

380 Pratt had agreed to make a short American tour under the auspices of the WIB (see the letter to Brown, 11 May [p. 254]). Brown was trying to ensure that Pratt visited Cornell University, where Brown was head of English. (See letter to Malcolm Ross, 14 September [*EJP: Web*].)

381 Herbert Davis was then president of Smith College in Northampton, MA.

382 Probably Ted Newton, an associate professor at McGill University, then attached to the WIB and stationed in New York.

383 See the note to 'Pierce has accepted your book' in the letter to Brown, 11 May (p. 254).

Of the subjects listed for the fall term I should like to try my hand at Wordsworth for the Romantic course.[384] I am more familiar with him than with Spenser or any of the others for that matter. I could relate him or rather 'un-relate' him to contemporary thought if you know what I mean. The second lecture might be Brébeuf as it happens to be highly specialized in my own knowledge and investigation, though I should give practically what I gave at Vic and later at the Graduate Club here when Sirluck was President. Each lecture takes 50 minutes. I read it from a reading desk.

By the way, the C.B.C. is giving an hour radio symphony of Brébeuf over the national network next Sunday night.[385] Thirty-five voices & thirty orchestral pieces, with Lyndon Smith[386] as narrator and E.A. Dale as Brébeuf. It starts at 10:15. I hope you can tune in to it. Healey Willan has composed the prologue and epilogue.

Thanks old dear for all your multitudinous kindnesses to me. Later I shall write a longer letter giving all the local chatter. We shall keep in touch with each other.

Ned P.

TO ELLEN ELLIOTT

Oct. 27, 1943

Dear Ellen:

I called in yesterday to see your adorable smile but you were out, but I was compensated by the sweet face of Ibbie[387] who took ten minutes off to talk to me.

Just this minute the enclosed letter[388] was dropped in my box, and before answering I am sending it on to you for advice.

---

384 Brown had asked Pratt to give a lecture or two to his students.

385 On 26 September. See the note to 'the Oratorio' in the letter to Pelham Edgar, 1 September 1942 (p. 236).

386 A member of the faculty of Trinity College, Toronto.

387 Isobel Syme, Ellen Elliott's secretary and assistant.

388 Dated 25 October 1943 from Milton Rugoff, an associate of Alfred A. Knopf. Rugoff wrote that, as the publishers 'of many excellent American and British poets,' the American publishing house had been 'hoping for some time to add a Canadian writer to that list,' and asked that Pratt send some of his work for consideration.

I think the Sat. R of L. with Benét's influence must have been partly responsible for the interest. Don't you think this is a good chance to make a contact, as I never had much enthusiasm for Brett[389]?

I understand Knopf is one of the most enterprising of the American publishers. Have you any connection with him? I think Hughie[390] knew him and admired him.

Would Knopf take Still Life and might he be prepared to take the 'Collected'[391] next fall? You would know what best is to be done. As soon as I hear from you I shall write Knopf telling him I am leaving the matter in your hands.

Bless you
Neddo

Please return letter

TO A.J.M. SMITH

October 30, 1943

Dear Art:

Deacon came across at last and I am sending you the review.[392] Two weeks ago the Toronto Daily Star had a notice rather than a review, but the notice was very favourable.

I was apprehensive at first about W.A.D's[393] proposed review because of certain omissions. I had heard him say that he feared the schools which adopted it might get a false perspective. So I took it in mind to go down to see him just to explain a few facts. I told him that I was not going to object to any criticism made of the book on artistic grounds provided he did it in the light of correct information. I said that from my own standpoint I hailed the prominence A.J.M.S. gave to the newcomers. The old fellows had their share of attention and while it was a gamble to speculate on the new at least it was courageous as well as hospitable.

---

389 George Platt Brett, Sr (1859–1936), publisher of the American division of Macmillan Publishing.

390 Hugh Eayrs.

391 The volume Macmillan of Canada planned to bring out in the fall of 1944.

392 A review of Smith's anthology, *The Book of Canadian Poetry*, published in mid-September, appeared in the *Globe and Mail* on 30 October.

393 William Arthur Deacon.

But the chief thing I feared was the MacDonald exclusion. Deacon at first was very pronounced about it until I gave him the low-down on M's attitude toward the anthology. He put certain intolerable conditions on the anthologist which no self-respecting editor could accept. I told D I saw the letter M wrote about his space, and to my surprise D said that he had twice put those conditions to preceding anthologists and they had fallen for it, but now it seems a third had called his bluff – yourself. D then told me he did not intend referring to the omission. Benson & Kirkconnell didn't bother him in any way, and in the case of MacDonald it was his own damn fault – his arrogance. So here is the review – the longest in the issue. He differs from you in spots but the chief thing which I greatly appreciated was his commendation of it for the schools. On the whole the review was far better than I expected.

I hear good individual reports, one person saying last night that the book would be selling for twenty years, slowly indeed but surely. I notice by the same paper that your News of the P[394] is out. I am keen to see it. I shall buy it for my Christmas presents.

affectionately
Ned.

I am glad that Deacon so worded his commendation as to make it quotable.

TO ELLEN ELLIOTT

Nov. 1, 1943

Dear Ellen:

Your secretary gave me the gist of your letter[395] on Saturday morning and to save time of correspondence I asked her if you would get in touch with Knopf. Your suggestions are just what I want. I prefer Knopf as he is enterprising and Brett[396] is certainly not. But I understand your official connection and you have the right solution.

---

394 Smith's *News of the Phoenix*. See the letter to Lorne Pierce, 3 September 1943 (*EJP: Web*).

395 Although she considered it 'slightly unethical,' Elliott's proposal was that Knopf be sent the page proofs of *SL*. If he rejected the book, she could then offer it to Macmillan in New York. She feared that if Knopf brought out a larger selection of Pratt's poems, which he seems to have had in mind, it might interfere with the Canadian market for the proposed *Collected Poems*. (See the letter to Elliott, 27 October 1943 [pp. 263–4].)

396 George Platt Brett, Jr. (1893–1984) who became president of the Macmillan Company in New York in 1936.

What I am concerned about is the 'Collected' next summer or fall. That is the important thing for me, and for either Knopf or Macmillan to take it for the U.S.A. would be excellent. I have a hunch that the larger volume will sell in a substantial way especially when so many of the individual books are out of print. I have had scores of letters asking where the *Titanic* might be procured.

Benét is reviewing *Brébeuf* soon. That will help the Basilian Press to get rid of their stock.

Best of luck
Ned.

TO E.K. BROWN

Nov. 3, 1943

Dear Eddie:

Your book on Canadian Poetry just came to me an hour ago and I have given it a first rapid reading. It is magnificent – the best bit of critical prose we have yet had. I am thankful that it is critical: it is the sort of thing I like – a warm *appreciation* tempered with a detached discernment. I laughed over your good-natured sallies at some of my earlier work, and I deeply appreciate your generous estimate. I am sending a copy to William Rose Benét who has been corresponding with me and who wrote cordially in the fall number of the S.R.L. Oct. 16. He will love your references to the Cachalot. Benét is a man you ought to know. I shall see him when I get to New York after leaving Cornell. I shall tell him about you.

I think Ryerson's ought to send him a review copy as well. There is an interest developing regarding Canadian letters and you and Smith are responsible. Knopf and the N.Y. Macmillans have on their own initiative written Toronto Macmillans to publish a 'Collected' of mine.[397] I am bringing out a slim volume 'Still Life' next month, and certainly a Collected next year.

I am giving your C.P.[398] as my Christmas presents and shall buy them at the book stores to stimulate as much interest as possible. Congratulations and thanks.

Ned

---

397 This was not strictly true. See the letters to Ellen Elliott, 27 October and 1 November 1943 (pp. 263–4 and 265–6).

398 *On Canadian Poetry*.

TO A.J.M. SMITH

Nov. 8, 1943

Dear Arthur:

Just a line to acknowledge your letter today. You do not need to worry about the Globe & Mail.[399] That comparison between Scott & Klein[400] is without the remotest sense and really without the remotest significance. I told him (W.A.D.) that you were a tremendous admirer of Scott and the anthology proves it. I happen to admire both Scott & Klein as you do. Really, Art, it does not make much difference to the final estimate of your anthology. Ross's article in the Ottawa Journal was something like Deacon's though it had more praise.

We are going to use it in the University. Frye, MacLean[401] & I are advocating the substitution of yours for the Broadus[402] which is out-of-date.

Frye has written, not a review, but an article, for the Canadian Forum which has more influence with teachers than any newspaper. I have heard the finest praise of the anthology from many discerning critics. It will have a steady sale. I hope it will go across in the States.

Yes, the radio was very successful, and the CBC. are repeating it as the last of a series on Canadian composers.[403] Sir Ernest MacMillan[404] is putting it on in Massey Hall on January 18 with the Mendelsohn Choir. So it is going.

I am looking forward to your News of the Phoenix. It ought to be out soon.

Always
Ned

---

399 W.A. Deacon's review. See the letter to Smith, 30 October 1943 (pp. 263–4).

400 Duncan Campbell Scott and A.M. Klein.

401 See the note to 'J.S. MacLean' in the letter to Pelham Edgar, 16 January 1943 (p. 248).

402 An anthology used in English survey courses. See the letter to Hugh Eayrs, 27 March 1934 (pp. 123–5).

403 The *Brébeuf* oratorio. See the note to 'the Oratorio' in the letter to Pelham Edgar, 1 September 1942 (p. 236).

404 Ernest MacMillan (1893–1973) was born in Toronto and educated in music at Edinburgh and Oxford universities. He was principal of Toronto's Royal Conservatory of Music (1926–42), dean of music at the university (1927–52), conductor of the Toronto Symphony (1931–56), and director of the Mendelssohn Choir (1942–56). Widely renowned also as a teacher and composer, he was knighted in 1935.

TO ELLEN ELLIOTT

Nov. 11, 1943

Dear Ellen:

Maybe Knopf's decision[405] is the best after all. Since Benét's review or article[406] concerned what has been published in book form, it would be wise to concentrate on the 'Collected' which could be got ready for early fall next year. This would be my preference in any case. Then we would have both Knopf and Macmillan considering the proposition with lots of time comparatively. It is too late in 1943 to bring out an American edition. Let the matter drop for the time being and have 'Still Life' simply as a Canadian presentation. Knopf's letter is quite reasonable and favourable, I think, considering the circumstances.

Yours,
Ned

TO A.J.M. SMITH

Dec. 5, 1943

Dear Arthur:

I have just returned from Cornell, New York and Smith College to find your beautiful News of the Phoenix awaiting me. It is a gorgeous book in format, paper, type and general content.

Did you see Frye's long article on your anthology in the Canadian Forum of this month?[407] I am sending you Sandwell's editorial on it. Sandwell thought highly of your anthology and Lorne's exhaustive treatment[408] ought to take hold of a wider public than read the Forum.

405 See the note to 'your letter' in the letter to Elliott, 1 November (p. 265). Knopf decided not to publish an American edition of *Still Life*, preferring to publish a more comprehensive collection of Pratt's work.

406 *SRL* (16 October 1943): 24.

407 'Canada and Its Poetry,' *CF* 23 (December 1943): 207–10.

408 Lorne Pierce had reviewed the anthology in *The United Church Observer* (November 1943).

I went into Brentano's and Scribner's at New York[409] and found several copies at the latter store but none at B's. I told the clerk that he should have a number on display. I hope it is getting a sale.

Are you coming up this way for Christmas? E.K. Brown will be here for several days. Let us all make contacts.

My 'Still Life' will be out in a week, I hope. I shall send you a copy.

As ever
Ned.

TO E.K. BROWN

Dec. 6, 1943

Dear Eddie:

I intended writing before this to thank you and Peggy for all your wonderful hospitality,[410] but I was waiting for the appearance of my latest volume which should have been out by now.

I had a grand time with you and I loved all the boys. Give them my best, will you?

I wrote Pierce this morning asking him to write Tinker personally for a review in the 'Yale.' I was thrilled by Tinker's remark.[411] I owe all this to you old chap.

On my desk now is another letter from Alfred Knopf asking for the American rights to my Collected next summer. I think it is much better to appear that way in the USA. than by Still Life which is too slim a volume.

Benét was more than kind and enthusiastic in New York. He said he received your book and intended to review it though he spoke of a mountain of books on his desk.

I had Thanksgiving Dinner with MacIver and dinner next night with Bart Brebner. He said you gave a grand talk to the graduates of Columbia some time

---

409 Bookstores.

410 During his November visit with the Browns in Ithaca, NY.

411 In a letter to Pratt (3 December), Brown wrote that he had sent Chauncey B. Tinker a copy of *On Canadian Poetry*, and that Tinker had replied: 'Of all the people in your pleasant book, I'd most like to know Pratt. What a man! And to think of him in a university setting! That passage about the silences of the sea. He seems like a man who should be visited in pilgrimage. He seems free of the sad incompleteness of Lampman.'

ago. It is you who ought to be the ambassador. You make a great impression wherever you go.

I am going to place your C.P.[412] wherever I think it ought to attract attention. I think Auden[413] and Jeffers[414] ought to get a copy. Would you have their addresses by any chance? Those are the fellows one should reach and Sandburgh[415] too.

I had a glorious time at Davis's.[416]

We are looking forward to seeing you and the loved one and baby Xmas time.[417]

Ned

TO WILLIAM ROSE BENÉT

Dec. 15, 1943

My dear Bill:

My desire to return to New York is like a nostalgia. Only the family strings prevent me at this very minute from renewing the trip. That evening I had with you and your lovely wife at the Prince George I count as one of the choicest experiences of my life. I wonder if you realize how much you have meant to me and how deep is my gratitude for all you have done out of the kindness of your heart. I shall never forget you and some day I may be able to reply in kind. All the papers of Toronto and some outside have referred to you and your Phoenix Column[418] and I have found that everywhere your name is editorial and poetic gold.

Knopf wrote me last week asking for an examination of my forth coming Collected. He seemed much interested, referring to our 'mutual friend Bill Benét.' It would be a triumph for me if he takes it for the U.S.A. The Macmillans are getting me to start at once on preparing the volume so that early in the New

---

412 *On Canadian Poetry.*

413 W.H. Auden (1907–1973), British poet but an American citizen and living in the United States.

414 Robinson Jeffers (1887–1962), American poet.

415 [*sic*]. Carl Sandburg (1878–1967), American poet.

416 Herbert Davis, president of Smith College.

417 The Browns were expecting their first child near Christmas and were coming to Toronto for the event. They had taken an apartment where Peggy (Mrs Brown) and the baby would remain all winter, though he had to return to his duties at Cornell. A son named David Deaver, the latter being his mother's maiden surname, was born on 30 December 1943.

418 His review of Smith's *News of the* Phoenix in *SRL.*

Year they may make plans for the fall of 1944. They are writing Knopf to see what plans are most practicable.

I am sending you a copy of 'Still Life' which is just off the press. The edition is 1000 and 500 have already been sold by advance orders. It is a slim production but I think you might like the Truant which is the poem best appreciated here in the University. It will be incorporated in the Collected. Since quite a few of the books like the Titanic and Many Moods are out of print, yet still in demand here, it would look like an auspicious time to get the large volume underway.

I have read your wonderful Dust Which Is God and now my wife is reading it. I am sending the other copy to my brother in Newfoundland who is very fond of a type of literature which is autobiographical and also world commentary. I shall treasure mine, and it shall repose on my mantelpiece in the central position for my friends to see. God bless you again. Give my warmest affection to Mrs Benét. I know my wife would love her. By and by if the U.S.A. should become smashed by either the extreme Right wing or the Left and Canada should have a lag of a few years before catastrophe overtake her, there will be a domicile for both of you.

Affectionately.
Ned Pratt

TO CÉCILE DE BANKE

Dec. 15, 1943

My dear Cecile:

It was a great pleasure to hear from you again.

Your 'Silent Laughter'[419] is a honey. I was keyed up to the high pitch all the way through and was tremendously impressed by the original and dramatic conclusion. The callousness and pride of the local female magnate, the resentment of her victims, the ostracism, the crash and her revenge on the inhabitants of Herring Cove by humiliating their civic sense by a most unexpected role, and then the crowning irony of that regal laying out! It looks to me like

419 De Banke had sent Pratt a typescript of one of her short stories.

an O'Brien[420] star. Why don't you try it out in the Atlantic or Scribner's[421]? It is too good for the popular periodicals. If I were you I should certainly make out a number of copies and circulate them to the more exclusive magazines. The best magazines here are the Saturday Night of Toronto, the Queen's Quarterly of Kingston, Ont. They do not pay much, nothing like the American remuneration. I doubt that there has been a better climax in any recent short story than yours. That motif of subtle revenge is crashing. I took the story home with me and Vi read it aloud last night. She was impressed by the style and the sense of dramatic values. You ought to know something of such values in your line of teaching and you decidedly do.

It will be a wonderful pleasure to see you in April. We hope you will be staying some time so that Toronto can renew its acquaintance.

As for myself – Still Life just came off the press this week and I am sending you a copy. I expect to bring out a 'Collected' next fall.

With every good wish,
Ned Pratt

TO JOHN SUTHERLAND[422]

Of *First Statement*

Jan. 5, 1944

Dear Mr Sutherland:

Thank you very much for your letter of appreciation.

I wondered why my December issue[423] had not reached me and several of my friends at the University missed their copies.

---

420 An obscure reference, possibly reflecting the influence of Flann O'Brien, the pen name of Irish writer Brian O'Nolan (1911–66) whose novels include *At Swim-Two-Birds* (London: Longman's, 1939).

421 *Atlantic Monthly* or *Scribner's Magazine.*

422 John Sutherland (1919–56) was born in Nova Scotia and attended Queen's and McGill universities. In Montreal in 1942 he founded *First Statement*, a 'little magazine' of literary criticism and the work of new writers. After three years it merged with *Preview*, a similar journal, to form *Northern Review* (1946–56) with Sutherland as editor. Despite persistent illness, he was a prolific, often acerbic literary critic, best known for his *The Poetry of E.J. Pratt: A New Interpretation* (Toronto: Ryerson, 1956).

423 Of *First Statement.*

I have just sent off a letter to W.A. Deacon expressing in emphatic terms my own esteem of First Statement and urging him to assist its struggle for existence.

I had lunch with Collin and Adeney[424] the other day and we feel that of all the recent magazines devoted to Canadian Prose and Poetry, First Statement has the most promise for the future. It has the best younger writers.

I would suggest that you circularize your subscribers, active and prospective asking them to contribute towards a sustaining Fund. It is hard to keep a magazine going on subscriptions only. I noticed your ad in the Canadian Forum of this issue. I hope you get results.

I have been more than pleased than I can say with much of your verse. All that you need is a feeling of stability – at least a bread-and-butter groundwork that will relieve you of anxiety every time you go to Press.

I feel certain that a circular appeal would get a response.

Wishing you every success,
Yours sincerely,
E.J. Pratt

TO RALPH GUSTAFSON

Jan. 6, 1944

Dear Ralph:

Thanks for your note and cheque.[425] You did not need to send me anything for my verses as the recognition you and A.J.M. have secured in the United States for Canadian writers is many times more valuable than any financial reimbursement. You have done a grand job for us all. I am sending you with my compliments a copy of '*Still Life*' which just appeared (Macmillans).

With every good wish, and if you should be passing through this city will you let me know.

Yours sincerely
Ned Pratt

---

424 Marcus Adeney (1900–98), a member of the Faculty of Music at the University of Toronto, was born in England. He was a cellist with the Toronto Symphony Orchestra (1928–44), a member of the Solway String Quartet (1948–58) and the CBC Symphony Orchestra (1952–63). He published verse, reviews, articles on music and literature, and one book, *Tomorrow's Cellist: Exploring the Basis of Artistry* (Toronto: McClelland & Stewart, 1973).

425 For $4.00 for 'The Prize Cat' and 'Come Away, Death,' included in Gustafson's *A Little Anthology of Canadian Poets* (Norfolk, CT: New Directions, 1943).

V Steering between Extremes, 1944–1948

I have always tried to steer between two extremes … prepared to take the adverse … with the favourable.

– E.J. Pratt to Margaret Furness MacLeod, 25 January 1944

TO MARGARET FURNESS MACLEOD

January 25, 1944

Dear Mrs MacLeod:

Thanks for your kind and characteristic letter. I had not read the review in the Gazette and I do not know who Phyllis Campbell[1] is. She is of course entitled to her own judgment and has the right to pick out poems she does not like and criticize them. But I have always tried to steer between two extremes – sentimental obviousness on the one hand and extreme unintelligibility on the other. The Reviewer obviously has in mind the 'Truant' which is an indictment of sheer mechanical power, say Hitler's God or the Teutonic Creation, by man who has developed a moral sense and a will. However, I am prepared to take the adverse reviews with the favourable, so it doesn't bother me.

I am glad that you are bringing out a book. I shall be glad to see the contents and give my judgment. I have seen quite a lot of your work in the past and enjoyed it. I do not think, however, that I could write the 'foreword' as I have been asked by six of my writing friends in the last two months to write prefaces and

1 An error for Phyllis Williams, editor of the Montreal *Gazette*. See the letter to A.J.M. Smith, 28 January 1944 (p. 276).

have refused as I gave it up several years ago. A book of poems does not need a preface. It rather prejudices the author. That is the general opinion and I think a fairly sound one.

Send the ms. to Macmillans or Ryerson's and let them decide on it.

I shall look on its appearance with great interest.

Best regards
E. J. Pratt

TO A.J.M. SMITH

January 28, 1944

Dear Arthur:

It was lovely to get your letter this morning. Sorry to find you had the flu. I have also had it, in fact just out with a big cold sore on my upper lip. Take care of yourself.

I wrote a strong letter to Moe of the Guggenheim for Klein.[2] I gave him preference over Kirkconnell[3] who is also applying. Klein is younger and on the make and possesses much more creative genius. I hope he gets it.

Pierce tells me that the Phoenix[4] is selling. I am enclosing a review of the book by a Mrs Dorey[5] a friend of my wife's. She is the wife of a missionary, has written a book of rather sweetish verse but I am glad to see she had the good sense to say a few just things about your book. The Observer has about 40 000 of a circulation and it ought to help sales. I notice also that Sanderson of the General Public Library[6] listed your Anthology in his bulletin of 150 books for 1941-1943. He states that it is a fine comprehensive valuable anthology. In fact it is the only volume of Canadian verse listed in the whole collection. I am

---

2 In October, A.M. Klein had applied for a Guggenhiem Fellowship, listing Pratt among his referees. Henry Allen Moe was trustee of the John Simon Guggenheim Memorial Foundation (1945–66).

3 Watson Kirkconnell.

4 A.J.M. Smith's *News of the Phoenix*.

5 Alice Ann Dorey, wife of Reverend George Dorey, a United Church overseas missionary who was moderator of the church in 1954–6. Dorey's review had been published in the *United Church Observer*.

6 Charles R. Sanderson (1887–1956), head librarian, Toronto Public Library since 1937.

pushing it among my teacher friends claiming that is is the only anthology yet published that had an '*intellect*' behind the compilation, and I think both the anthology and the Phoenix will mutually help the circulation.

The Still Life volume divided the critics (newspaper critics) very sharply. I suppose like your anthology that will always be the way with anything of an experimental character. The Sat. Night & the Globe featured it. The Montreal Gazette damned it for its obscurity. The Gazette editor is a woman named Phyllis Williams.[7] She had not a good word to say about it. The Hamilton Spectator was greatly puzzled over the Truant. I thought it was clear enough that I was making an indictment of Power by humanity. Still I am prepared to take everything, though I must say that the Preview editor Shaw acted like a shit on your anthology.[8] I didn't mind the criticisms so much as the prejudice. It was so blatantly obvious that the whole article was a build up for the Preview editorial coterie. After damning all Canadian literature up to the present, there came in the last paragraph a eulogy of the Anderson Scott Page Ruddick gang.[9] The new Light had arisen now and Poetry had just been stalling for those bastards to rise in their effulgence. I don't know Shaw but he gave his case away by that last paragraph. Only a god-damn imbecile could have been guilty of such patent self-infatuation. All of the great ones listed were Preview Editors except Watson.[10] The only notable omission was Preview – Ruddick.

I wonder that Frank[11] doesn't put some of those drips in a sack and drop them in a sewer. The First Statement[12] – a rival of Preview – may give you a better showing. They at least have Klein among them – 'sed unun leonem.'[13] All we want is a discriminating criticism, severe at times as it may be, – not a self-interested extermination. They ought to have been thankful that an anthology had come out

7 In the letter to Margaret Furness MacLeod, 25 January 1944 (p. 274), he calls her Phyllis Campbell.

8 Neufville Shaw (b. 1915), editor of *Preview*, had attacked Smith's *Book of Canadian Poetry* in a review-article entitled 'The Maple Leaf Is Dying' (*Preview* 17 [December 1943]: 1–3).

9 The Montreal poets and critics who produced and published in *Preview*. Besides Shaw, they included Patrick Anderson (1915–79), author of several small books of verse; F.R. Scott, the 'old man' of the group and only briefly a member; Bruce Ruddick (1915–77), a psychoanalyst who had published verse in several magazines; and P.K. Page. The group broke up in 1946.

10 James Wreford Watson.

11 F.R. Scott.

12 See the note to 'John Sutherland' in the letter to Sutherland, 5 January 1944 (p. 272).

13 [*sic*]. The Latin phrase is '*unum sed leonem*' (one, but a lion'). In a fable by Aesop, a number of foxes were reproaching a lioness because she bore only one cub. She is said to have responded as follows: 'one, but a lion.' The moral is that quality should be valued over quantity.

which was catholic enough to admit the old and the new, the traditional and the experimental. Shaw & Ruddick were mad they weren't included.

Frye and the boys here think the Preview stank in that estimate.

Well enough of that. When are you coming this way? We had hoped to have you here Xmas time. E.K. was here. Did you know Peggy has a son. E.K. may go to Chicago.[14] A secret yet, but quite a possibility. Would you like to start something towards Cornell yourself? E.K. will be up here in March for a week or two.

We ought to contrive to get together oftener. If only the finances permitted. I was greatly cheered to see the fine references to you in so many papers – some of them American – 'the leader of the new generation of poets.' If I could only get you a decent job with leisure to write. Essays are buggerish in the way they plug the intellectual outlets.

Well God bless you. Let us keep up a correspondence. I hold you in perpetual gratitude for – one thing among others – your anthology got the ear of Benét who introduced me to Knopf who has written me asking for the American rights of my 'Collected' next fall. Ellen Elliott is in New York now negotiating with Alfred. I hope nothing throws sand in the gears.

affectionately
Ned

Vi & Claire send their best.

They like you very much.

TO WILLIAM ROSE BENÉT

Feb. 10, 1944

Dear Bill:

Your letter was lovely. Vi (Viola) and I talk about you and Marjorie very very often. Marjorie resembles Vi a great deal. That is one reason why I liked her so much though I only met her for an evening.

My daughter Claire is trying to enter Columbia University next fall for graduate work if her health holds out. The three of us will probably make a visit to

14 E.K. Brown had accepted a professorship at the University of Chicago.

New York in September and spend a week or two. It will be such a joy to see you and Marjorie again.

I have made quite a few friends in New York. I had a grand letter from Mark Van Doren[15] yesterday in appreciation of Brébeuf. I have never met Van D. though of course I have read much of what he has written.

Thanks for sending 'Men of War.'[16] I like the tragic note in words like 'thereafter' and 'Victory earned that was not to be.' That courage beyond physical death. Do you know I was so struck with your 'Chapelle' in the January 15 issue of the S.R.L.[17] that I showed it around, and wrote the Editor about it, hoping we get more of that affirmation of life in contemporary verse. A great many of our newer writers are losing all sense of values, aesthetic and moral. They have nothing to say and have abjured the imagination.

I am delighted you are bringing out a volume next Fall.[18] I want to give readings and lectures on you up this way, and your volume will be a valuable repository.

Miss Elliott of Toronto Macmillans has just returned from New York where she was in negotiation with Knopf over my volume. She was delighted at the proposal of a publication next fall in the U.S.A. I submitted my stuff to her last month having eliminated a lot of what I thought was undesirable. It may still need some pruning but as long as I have some metal that rings when it hits the oak I shall be pleased. I find it exhilarating to have the same imprint as your good self and I realize with love and gratitude what you have done for me. Never shall I forget it.

Well, here's to next September and to many an hour with thick speech trying to articulate the inexpressible.

Love from Vi, Claire and myself
to you and Marjorie.
Ned.

15 American poet (1894–1972), critic, and anthologist, and a professor at Columbia University.

16 A poem by Benét.

17 *Saturday Review of Literature.*

18 *Day of Deliverance: A Book of Poems in Wartime* (New York: Knopf, 1944).

TO WILLIAM ROSE BENÉT

May 18, 1944

Dear Bill:

The Macmillans have just telephoned me the decision of Knopf to publish the book himself, which has caused me very great delight. Once again, my loved friend, I owe to you a tremendous debt. You started all this last summer and I think you realize how deep you are in my heart.

I am happy too that Knopf is taking so much of the Macmillan content. The extravangazas at the end of the collection have always been controversial and though the Canadian firm will publish them, I think it is sound judgment to omit them in a first appearance in the States.[19]

Knopf has asked for a photograph. As a matter of fact, it is fortunate for me that Kenneth Forbes[20] has just finished an oil portrait which is being photographed. I have had thirty sittings and it ought to look a little like me. My usual photos are lousy in the extreme, perhaps too close to the original. This, however, is [....] better.

Miss de Banke of Wellesley spent an evening at my home last month, and rhapsodized about your presence at the Speech Festival[21] – how honoured she was at having you read your stuff.

If my daughter Claire is well enough to go to Columbia next September, Vi and I will spend a week or two in New York with her. We shall certainly get in touch with you and Marjorie. It will be such a joy to see you both again.

I was delighted to find Western Star won the Pulitzer. To have two brothers winning that honour shows how blood counts.[22] Western Star and The Dust Which Is God both stand on my mantelpiece *centrally*.

---

19 In the American edition only 'The Great Feud' and 'The Fable of the Goats' were excluded from the sub-section headed 'Extravaganzas'; 'The Witches' Brew,' 'The Depression Ends,' and 'The Truant' were retained.

20 The portrait by Toronto-born Kenneth Forbes (1892–1980) hangs in the E.J. Pratt Library at Victoria University.

21 See the letter to Cécile de Banke, 12 January 1944 (*EJP: Web*). Poets invited to the 'Festival of Spoken Poetry' at Wellesley College included American writers Leonard Bacon (1887–1954), Muriel Rukeyser (1913–80), Benét, Theodore Spencer (1902–49) and Winfield Townley Scott (1910–68).

22 William Rose Benét had won a Pulitzer Prize for *The Dust Which Is God* in 1941.

My richest love to you both.
Ned P.

What a grand issue that of the 29th of April was![23]

TO ELLEN ELLIOTT

June 7, 1944

Dear Ellen:

I think those terms of Knopf are excellent.[24] I hope he can bring the book out by September as I expect to be down in New York for a week or two if Claire goes to Columbia University. I should like to have it out when I am there.

If he cannot get Benét to give that introduction,[25] he can make use of much that Benét has written in favour of the stuff already. Benét may prefer to do his work editorially which would be just as effective as a direct sponsorship. However, we shall see. Thanks so much old dear for such prompt action. I hope Knopf will not delay.

Ned Pratt

TO ALAN CRAWLEY[26]

June 26, 1944

Dear Mr Crawley:

Let me congratulate you on your two issues of Contemporary Verse. It is a great credit to your selective insight that you should bring out such fine stuff. The first

---

23 Brown's essay "To the North: A Wall against Canadian Poetry" (pp. 9–11) and a review of *SL* by Benét in "Seven Good Poets" (pp. 23–4) both appeared in *SRL* on 29 April 1944.

24 Terms of a contract to publish an American edition of Pratt's *Collected Poems*.

25 Knopf had asked Benét to write a brief introduction to the volume.

26 Editor of the small magazine *Contemporary Verse*, co-founded in 1941 by poets Dorothy Livesay, Floris McLaren, Doris Ferne, and Anne Marriott. Publishing a high quality of innovative modern verse, it continued to publish until 1952. Crawley's detailed critiques – even when poems were rejected – inspired many Canadian poets.

poems are real 'leaders' – *Paschal Lamb*[27] and *West Coast*.[28] Knowing Earle Birney so well I could catch particularly the dramatic spell of Dorothy Livesay's tribute.[29]

May long life attend ye.

Yours sincerely
E.J. Pratt

TO VIOLA PRATT

[Kingston, Ontario][30]

July 18, 1944

Dearest Vi:

Your letter just came. I hope you have kept the picture of the cow. I want to see it.

On Friday evening I get in. The train (C.N.R.) leaves here after six, and it is about 3 hours run, a little more I think.

I shall be glad to see the scarlet runners even if they are nipped off at the top.

I had a letter from Birney last week telling me about his experiences. He is now a major and getting a whole grist of knowledge about personnel which he hopes to put into a novel or something by and by.[31]

Professor Alford of Fine Arts[32] is here teaching in the Summer School. I had lunch with him today.

I have been asked to speak this coming Sunday in Grant Hall on Newfoundland – Sea Verse and the rest of it. I tried to get out of it first by telling them that I was

---

27 A poem by Vancouver writer Doris Ferne. (See the letter to Viola Pratt dated 27 July 1936 [p. 149].)

28 A long poem by Dorothy Livesay.

29 The poem 'West Coast' is about commitment to the war effort – specifically, to the building of ships. Since the shipbuilders include at least one who, like both Livesay and Earle Birney, was a peacetime pacifist and leftist revolutionary, Birney's enlistment in the army and commitment to the war was a fairly obvious subtext of the poem.

30 Pratt was teaching in the Queen's summer session. (See the letter to Viola and Claire Pratt, 18 July [*EJP: Web*].)

31 Birney used these experiences in his novel *Turvey: A Military Picaresque* (1949). See the letter to Birney, 2 November 1954 (p. 590).

32 E.J.G. Alford, born (1890) in England, professor of fine arts at the University of Toronto 1934–45. In 1945 he joined the Rhode Island School of Design.

going to Toronto but they countered by saying that my train arrives at Kingston at 7 p.m. and the meeting doesn't begin till 8:30. So there I am. It won't be much of a task anyway, as it is mainly reading.

I haven't received Irwin's letter[33] yet so I wrote him today. I hope the cheque wasn't picked up and forged. Probably it wasn't sent.

Lovingly
Ned

TO VIOLA PRATT

152 University Ave.
Kingston, Ont.

Thursday [27 July 1944]

Vi darlin':

That was not Tarzan at all you sent, but Mandrake.[34] Tarzan went out of business about six years ago and now Mandrake holds the stage. But as I have grown a bit tired of the magician in his new role, though he wears the same cloak, do not send the clippings any more. Besides, my silver gown[35] takes his place when I want something to gaze at and meditate thereon.

So Irwin's letter didn't have the cheque. As soon as I get the letter I shall notify him.

Just now when I went over to the coffee shop for my four o'clocker I saw Gwen Norman[36] to my astonishment as I had no idea she was here at work. She is in the General Hospital not as a nurse but as a laboratory assistant taking blood counts. When she was in the shop in came a fellow also employed in the Hospital just as broad as he was long. She introduced me to him as 'This is Mell' – that's all I know. He is about four feet two in height and four feet six in

33 William Arthur Irwin (1898–1999) was associate editor (1925–43) and then managing editor (1943–5) of *Maclean's*, and was appointed editor in 1945. He was later commissioner of the National Film Board (1950–3) and, after diplomatic service in Australia, Brazil, and Mexico, became publisher of the Victoria *Daily Times* (1964–71). He had asked Pratt to write a poem on the return of the troops from overseas. Pratt accepted the invitation and a $50.00 retainer fee. This is the cheque referred to in this letter. (See the letter to Edgar, 7 August 1944 [p. 285].)

34 Popular newspaper comic strips.

35 His favourite white dressing gown with coloured stripes.

36 Daughter of Dr James Norman, the Pratts' family physician.

width. A nice happy-looking chap but with lots of beef in the lateral dimensions – something like Mr Fenwick[37] but shorter.

I am working hard at 'They Are Returning'[38] but it is too early to say if it is going to suit or it is good. I think it will turn out all right. Maclean's mean business evidently so I shall have to mean the same. I am now in front of the window, feeling a little bit unnatural as I had to take off both my silver gown and outside shirt because of the heat.

It was warming (or should I say refreshingly cooling) to get your letter. My deep love to you & Rosie[39] and Possie.[40]

Ned

TO PELHAM EDGAR

152 University Avenue
Kingston, Ont.

Aug. 7, 1944

Dear Pelham:

I heard from Vi that you rang up on your way to the north. Sorry I couldn't connect with you but I had only one week-end with my family.

In another week I shall be through the Queen's Summer Session and be glad to return.

I have two courses, one in modern poetry and drama which is up my alley and one covering everything written by everybody since Spenser down to one Alfred Lord Tennyson. The fellows here are quite congenial; Alexander,[41]

---

37 Reverend Mark Fenwick (1858–1946), British-born Methodist (later United Church) clergyman who served in Newfoundland for many years. Known for his rotundity, he was guardian of the Methodist College Home in St John's when Pratt was in residence there as a student in 1901–2.

38 The poem Pratt had been commissioned by Arthur Irwin to write for *Maclean's*. (See the note to 'Irwin's letter' in the letter to Viola Pratt, 18 July [p. 282].)

39 A new pet name for Claire, prompted by her recent interest in the Rosicrucian Order, a secret society founded in the seventeenth century and having as its chief symbol a cross with a red rose at the centre.

40 A family pet name for Pratt's sister Florence (Floss), who then lived in Toronto.

41 Henry Alexander, born (1892) in England, educated at Liverpool and Oxford universities, joined the English Department at Queen's in 1922, becoming head of department in 1949. A specialist in linguistics, he published *The Story of Our Language* (1940), several translations from other languages, and contributed to *The Canadian Dictionary: French-English, English-French* (Toronto: McClelland & Stewart, 1962).

Vincent,[42] Roy[43] (when out of his cups and even then), Jewett of Dalhousie,[44] and Alford of Fine Arts, Toronto. I have a game of golf nearly every day, 9 or 12 or occasionally 18, playing about 90. Had a fine party the other night with Dr Miller[45] and his wife, & Roy and his lady. Taught all of them poker with beans for chips, *white* for 5, *brown* for 10, *black* for 25. I regaled them with stories of you and your royal flushes, two cards wild, etc. How much I should like the return of the old days with Bert,[46] Alan,[47] Dick,[48] and your good self! Will you be coming back?

The Collected edition will be out in September. Macmillan here, and Knopf in New York, but in March. Knopf made out a very attractive contract. He wanted to do all the manufacturing from print and paper up, so it is an independent affair, the copyright being entirely in my own hands. He thinks he can do something with it in the U.S. and is assuming all costs. In a way, I am glad it is next spring as it gives the Basilian Press a chance of disposing of more of the 3000 copies of Brébeuf bought from Macmillans. Brébeuf is selling well yet here and in America, five editions all combined. It will be in both the Collected and the Selected. The latter omits the Great Feud and perhaps the Witches' Brew, to save paper – about forty pages I think.

I am told by Frank MacDowell[49] that interest in the pageant is growing in the northern towns and that Drew[50] is very sympathetic. I trust the thing will be resumed after the war. The excavations have helped the idea substantially, Currelly[51] says.

---

42 C.J. Vincent. See the note to 'Vincent' in the letter to G.H. Clarke, 7 February 1939 (p. 171).

43 James A. Roy, born (1884) in Scotland, educated at the University of Edinburgh, taught English at Queen's from 1920 until his retirement in 1950.

44 Arthur R. Jewett, born (1904) in England, was associate professor of English at Dalhousie, and later principal of Bishop's University.

45 Norman Miller, born (1889) in Ontario, educated at Queen's and Harvard universities, was professor of mathematics at Queen's 1919–56.

46 A.H. ('Bert') Proctor.

47 Probably Robert Allan (Alan [*sic*]) Barr (1890–1959). Born in Chiswick, England, Barr was a Toronto artist, best known for his portraits, still lifes, and landscapes. Pelham Edgar was one of his subjects. In 1943–4, he taught at the Ontario College of Art.

48 Richard George Meech. See the note to 'Meech' in the letter to Edgar, 16 January 1939 (p. 248).

49 Franklin McDowell (1888–1965) worked in public relations for the CNR. He was editor of the *CNR Magazine*, and a freelance journalist. In 1939 he won a Governor General's Medal for his novel *The Champlain Road*, which dealt with some of the same historical material as Pratt's *Brébeuf*.

50 George Drew (1894–1973) was premier of Ontario and minister of education from 1943 to 1948, when he became leader of the federal Conservative Party. He resigned in 1956 after losing two elections.

51 See the note to 'Currelly' in the letter to W.A. Deacon, 11 July 1931 (p. 92).

Claire goes to Columbia in mid-September. Vi and I are going down with her and will spend a few days in New York getting her installed. I hope we are doing the right thing in letting her go. We shall be terribly lonely without her, but if her health holds, it may be wise. She has been feeling better during the last two or three months.

I haven't been doing much writing this summer as some of my time has been taken up with getting out the edition. I am, however, writing one thing called 'They Are Returning' asked for specially by Maclean's to celebrate the coming back of the boys. I have it almost finished – about 200 lines. Maclean's will publish it immediately the European war ends, and they have contracted to pay me $200.00 for it – the biggest sum by far I have ever received for a single poem. They gave me $50.00 as a retainer. It is something in the Dunkirk manner. I hope it satisfies them. The fee will be placed to Claire's account.

Give my love to Harry,[52] Brock,[53] O'Leary,[54] Angus MacDonald[55] if you see them, and particularly to Dona and Jane.

Affectionately
Ned

TO EARLE BIRNEY

Aug. 8, 1944

My dear Earle:

It was grand to get a letter from you and so full of news. I am glad you got the chocolates. I am sending another box just as soon as I get back to Toronto. At present I am at Queen's teaching in the Summer Session. The job ends on the 17th and not too soon for me. I want to get back to Vi and Claire at 21 Cortleigh.

Claire is going to Columbia in mid-September to take a course in 'International Reconstruction,' brave little soul so full of youthful idealism and

---

52 Colonel Henry Osborne. See the note to 'Harry' in the letter to Edgar, 16 January 1939 (p. 247).

53 Leonard W. Brockington.

54 Michael Grattan O'Leary (1889–1976) was born in Percé in the Gaspé, Quebec. He was a leading journalist at the *Ottawa Journal* and a member of the parliamentary press gallery, eventually becoming editor. A staunch member of the Conservative Party, he was appointed to the Senate by Prime Minister John Diefenbaker in 1962.

55 Angus L. MacDonald (1890–1954). A former professor at Dalhousie University Law School, MacDonald was premier of Nova Scotia from 1933 to 1954, except for the period 1940–5, when he was minister of defence for naval services in the wartime cabinet of Mackenzie King.

ambitions far beyond her physical capacities. At any rate we are letting her do whatever she desires to do consistent with her health. Vi and I are going down with her for a few days to see her installed.

How I long to see you back with the grand lads Ernie and Claude.[56] I miss you tremendously. The past winter was pretty bleak socially, and my room at 21 clamoured for the oldtime cigars and spitoons to say nothing of the roof-shattering laughter.

I believe that we shall have a good time writing when we all get together in mutual stimulation.

I am very much like yourself, in being fed up with that bunch of conceited asses and decadents in Montreal – the Anderson, Shaw, Ruddick coterie.[57] They think that there was no Canadian writing before they appeared. Anderson comes out here from Oxford — a self-advertised President of the Union – and immediately puts up his shingle metaphorically as the one and only specialist in poetry worth recognition. He takes a look at the landscape in a Canadian train and at once becomes the 'inside interpreter.' They are now starting an association called the 'Federation of Canadian Writers' with themselves as the 'Provisionary Committee.' You should see the bloody naivities they put into print – there isn't one live thought or emotion. They want to get out a Canadian magazine subsidized by Government Funds. I agree with you that the whole crowd – Auden, Spender, Thomas and particularly Barker[58] are most obnoxious and doing a lot of harm to the youngsters with ability who take them at their face evaluation and copy them.

You know Earle I think your Joe Harris[59] a real pippin. I had dinner with B.K.S.[60] and a group just before coming to Kingston, and B.K. said he was proud of that poem. I told Esther it was about as fine a piece of vivid writing as I have seen in a dog's age – masterly. I think you should give us a Canadian 'Grapes of Wrath' out of your experiences in England and I am delighted you are systematically taking notes. I am sure you have the first great Canadian novel in your fist. Great days are ahead of us if we survive. Besides we want some real criticism informed and penetrating. It will come.

---

56 Ernest Sirluck and Claude Bissell.

57 See the note to 'the Anderson Scott Page Ruddick gang' in the letter to A.J.M. Smith, 28 January 1944 (p. 276).

58 W.H. Auden (1907–73), Stephen Spender (1909–95), Dylan Thomas (1914–53), and George Barker (1913–91) were among the most successful and influential poets then writing in the modern idiom and using the new techniques.

59 'Joe Harris 1913–1942,' an elegy for a Canadian soldier written in an experimental 'prose-poetry' form.

60 B.K. Sandwell.

Macmillans are bringing out my 'Collected Poems' next month. They have gone to town upon the construction of it despite paper shortages, etc. The whole 12 books are to be in one volume of 350 pages. I am a bit excited though I feel it is a gamble in this country. I said the 12 books. I meant the best selection – many of the earlier verses I don't like now are excluded.

The best news, however, is that Knopf made me a very attractive offer. He wanted to bring out an independent edition, making the book his own from the print up. I signed the contract with him last month. His won't be ready till March but he told me that he had a most enthusiastic verdict from his three judges. I may 'break through' with the american edition, though again I have my fingers crossed. If it really goes across I shall stand the 'boys' a stag a week till the royalties play out.

The academic news I suppose you know. Wallace is out of U.C. and Woodhouse is Head of the Department. Much burning and many headaches as a result, though Wallace and Alexander approved. Wallace would have preferred Knox but thinks Woodhouse will hold up the scholarly end. J.F. Macdonald[61] blew a fit when he got the news and spoke only in Scots for a week afterwards. Priestley[62] has been appointed Assistant Professor, and Robbins[63] takes his place at BC.

I wish the bloody war were over and the lads were on their return on the peaceful Atlantic.

I think your 'Letter Home' could find a place anywhere. I am out of the C.P.M. now. Resigned 2 years ago, and have no say about the contents. Was fed up with the business.

I am keen to see your Conrad Kain[64] ballad. Do you know that I climbed Mount Cathedral with him in August 1913 when I joined the Alpine Club.[65]

---

61 John F. MacDonald was born (1878) in Huntington, Quebec, and was a graduate of Queen's and Chicago universities. MacDonald was professor of English at Queen's (1908–25) and at University College, Toronto (1925–48). He was one of several editors who worked with Pratt on the Macmillan Shakespeare.

62 Francis E.L. Priestley (1905–1990), born in England, educated at the universities of Alberta and Toronto, was professor at Alberta (1931–6) and British Columbia (1940–4) before joining the Department of English at University College, Toronto, where he remained until retirement.

63 William Robbins (1909–95) was born in Cranbrook, BC, and educated at the universities of British Columbia and Toronto. He was professor of English at the University of British Columbia until his retirement in 1977.

64 Austrian Conrad Kain (1883–1934) was a celebrated mountaineer and guide who lived for many years at Invermere, BC, having moved to Canada in 1909 to lead climbs at the Alpine Club of Canada's Lake O'Hara camp. In July 1913 he reportedly was the first to climb Mount Robson, the highest peak in the Rockies. Birney's poem about him was first published in *National Home Monthly* (December 1949).

65 Pratt had joined C.B. ('Charlie') Sissons of Victoria College in an expedition to the area near Banff, where he did indeed qualify himself for membership in the Alpine Club. But the date was 21 July 1913, not August. (See *EJP: TY*, 124–5.)

Mount Cathedral was easy of course, but I received my graduation pin from a fellow named Wheeler[66] who was director of the Club at the time. We called the climber Conrad without the Kain. He did Robson by himself didn't he?

Well Earle, old dear, let me hear from you again. My love to you.

Ned.

TO WILLIAM ROSE BENÉT

[Kingston, Ontario]

Aug. 13, 1944

Dear Bill:

Your letter had the refreshing smell of kelp from Pigeon Cove.[67] I can picture you looking out from that stable-study window, occasionally spattered, I bet, with foam on the rough days. What a place to spend a summer! It made me long to get back to Turk's Gut or Seldom-Come-By in Newfoundland.[68] At present I am in Kingston, Ontario, lecturing to classes in the Queen's University Summer School. I am by myself as I found it impossible to get any kind of decent quarters for Vi and Claire. By next Thursday I shall be back in Toronto and making ready to go down with them to New York. Claire is going to spend a year at Columbia taking a new course in International Reconstruction. She has been somewhat better in recent months and I trust she will be able to face the year's work without too much disability. The three of us will leave about the middle of September, spend a week (Vi & I) in New York getting Claire installed. I shall give you a ring if you are back from Cape Ann. I should love to see the two of you again and spill the odd yarn and a little whisky if the latter is available as it certainly is not here in Toronto.

---

66 Arthur Oliver Wheeler (1850–1945), surveyor and mountaineer. He co-founded the Alpine Club of Canada in 1906 with journalist Elizabeth Parker (1856–1944), and served as its first president.

67 A seaport village in Massachusetts near Cape Ann and Gloucester where the Benéts had a summer residence.

68 Turk's Gut is a tiny hamlet in Conception Bay, and Seldom-Come-By a fishing community on Fogo Island, Notre Dame Bay. It is most unlikely Pratt had ever visited either place, but the names appealed to him.

It must have been nice to have your son and family with you at the Cove. So he covered the Convention for Tass.[69] I have some little connection with Tikhonov, the Russian poet.[70] He wrote me a letter last March suggesting a change of books of verse. I like his stuff immensely though, of course, I know it only in translation. I have an idea that there will be a growing traffic in Russian and American literature after the war. The Russian fellows at the Ottawa Legation are grand chaps. I have met them several times at Conventions.[71] I hope the new administration in the U.S.A. will be pro-Russian as Roosevelt's is. Our household, like your own, is 100% Roosevelt as it is Churchillian. We think he is the greatest since Lincoln. He is welcome to a fourth or a fifth as far as we are concerned.

I think I told you in a previous letter that I presented my nephew Ewart Pratt[72] with a copy of your Dust Which Is God and he enjoyed it as he would a fine historical pageant. He is a Lt. Commander in the Navy though only 25. I trust your new book will sweep the country.

I am awfully pleased over the Knopf contract. It was signed two months ago and with very favourable clauses for me. I am deeply conscious of what you have meant in the negotiations. It was you who brought the stuff to Knopf's attention in the first place and sustained the interest.

The Macmillans are bringing out the Canadian Edition next month and are making big promotional arrangements – 'going to town on it' they say. I shall send a copy immediately it is off the press or perhaps the unbound sheets, if you would like to glance through them. I am so happy that you are writing the introduction to the 'American.' It is really more than I could ever expect as an entree to the American public.

The Canadian Edition is not much less in size than the other[73] – only two or three of the Extravaganzas being omitted according to Knopf. I am really glad

69 TASS (Telegraph Agency of the Soviet Union) was the official news agency of the USSR. The 'Convention' is the Democratic Party's nominating convention in Chicago which on 21 July 1944 chose Franklin Roosevelt to run for an unprecedented fourth term as president.

70 The earliest books of Nikolay Semyonovich Tikhonov (1896–1979) celebrated the 'revolutionary romanticism' of the civil war of 1917–19. During the Second World War, he published many patriotic poems and essays including *Leningrad Tales* (1943), describing the siege of Leningrad. He won three Stalin Prizes.

71 See *EJP: MY* for a summary of Pratt's Russian connections and involvement with the Canadian-Soviet Friendship Council (305–7, 332, 353). One of these conferences is described in his letter to Claire Pratt, 13 November 1944 (pp. 303–4).

72 His brother Calvert's elder son.

73 An obvious error: the proposed American edition of *Collected Poems* was the smaller of the two.

the *Great Feud* is out, at any rate. The Macmillan readers wanted it in as 'Titans,' which included it, has been out of print for some years and there has been a bit of a demand for it in the stores.

Do you see the Toronto Saturday Night regularly? Sandwell, the editor, is a great admirer of yours and constantly refers to your interest in Canadian letters. Your 'Dust' is the main feature for us all.

Since I wrote you last, I have received a number of welcome letters about *Brébeuf* and *Dunkirk*, chiefly from Tinker of Yale, Mark Van Doren and Theodore Spencer. Brébeuf will be included in both editions. It is still selling as a single volume (fifth edition).

You asked me Bill about the dates of the books.[74] Here they are.

(1) Newfoundland Verse, 1923
(2) The Witches' Brew, 1925
(3) Titans (Cachalot & The Great Feud) 1926
(4) The Iron Door, 1928
(5) The Roosevelt and the Antinoe, 1930
(6) Verses of the Sea, 1930
(7) Many Moods 1932
(8) The Titanic 1934
(9) The Fable of the Goats 1936 (Governor General's Medal)
(10) Brébeuf and His Brethren 1939 (ditto)
(11) Dunkirk 1941
(12) Still Life and Other Poems 1943

I have asked Macmillans that no copy of the Canadian Edition be sent to the American columns for review as it might stale the Knopf publication. They agree.

I am sending to you a copy of Brown's book On Canadian Poetry which gives [.....] full biographical data. The skeleton is this. Born at Western Bay, Newfoundland, 1883,[75] son of a Methodist clergyman, taught school in a fishing village (Moreton's Harbour) for two years, came to Victoria College, University

74 Some dates of publication given here are incorrect: *ID* was published in 1927, not 1928; *Titantic* was published in 1935, not 1934; *FG* was published in 1936, not 1937; and *BB* was published in 1940, not 1939.

75 He was actually born in 1882, and his appointments to the staff at Victoria College were as follows: joint-lecturer in English and social work, 1920–3; lecturer in English, 1923–5; assistant professor, 1925–30; professor, 1930–8; senior professor 1938–53.

of Toronto 1907, graduated in Philosophy 1911, appointed Professor at Victoria College, Assistant Professor 1920, Professor 1929(?) (I have forgotten exact year).

This looks a bit rambunkshous[76] but what's that among friends.

My love to you and Marjorie
Ned

TO MRS STAGG[77]

August 31, 1944

Dear Mrs Stagg:

I might mention a few more facts about 'Brébeuf and His Brethren' which would possibly be of some interest. I forgot to state them on the forms you sent me.

The book is making a big appeal to the Roman Catholic constituency of Canada as well as to those who have a non-sectarian historical interest. Several hundreds have sold at the Martyrs' Shrine near Midland, Ontario, and some five thousand have sold throughout Canada generally. I hope that the inclusion of the poem in the *Selected Poems*[78] might stimulate an American-Catholic appetite which might be indifferent to the rest of the menu.

Last year Dr. Healey Willan of the Toronto Conservatory of Music built an oratorio around the poem for the Canadian Broadcasting Corporation and it was presented over the national network in a one-hour performance in September. There was a demand for a repeat performance and it was given in April of this year (orchestra and choir). Last January it was performed in Massey Hall, Toronto, by the Toronto Symphony Orchestra and the Mendelssohn Choir under the direction of Sir Ernest MacMillan before four thousand people. When I was in New York Last December two of my friends, Professor R.M. MacIver[79]

76 A humorous variation on 'rambunctious.'

77 An editor at Alfred A. Knopf, Inc., publishers of the forthcoming American edition of Pratt's *Collected Poems*.

78 The tentative title of the proposed volume.

79 Robert Morrison MacIver (1882–1970), a pioneer of the study of sociology. Educated at the universities of Edinburgh, Oxford, Columbia, and Harvard, he was professor of political science and later head of department at the University of Toronto (1922–7) and professor of social science at Columbia University (1929–50). He was president (1963–5) and then chancellor of the New School for Social Research (1963–6).

and Bart Brebner[80] suggested that I get in touch with the N.B.C.[81] to explore the possibilities of an American broadcast. I did not do so at the time but I wonder if you would consider it advisable to make the contact at some later date when the book (Selected Poems) gets a start. I shall leave that to your judgment. The broadcasts here certainly stimulated the sales. We can talk that over by and by. I am going to New York on September 15th for a few days to see my daughter installed at Columbia University, and I shall give you a ring if you have a few moments spare time.

Enclosed is a description of the MacMillan performance.

Gratefully yours,
E.J. Pratt

TO WILLIAM ROSE BENÉT

[New York, N.Y.]

Sept. 15, 1944

Dear Bill:

It is my bad luck this time that practically all of my New York friends happen to be out of town – Ted Newton,[82] Bart Brebner, John MacDonnell,[83] Merrill Denison, yourself and the good wife.

Vi and Claire and my sister (the nurse) are here in my room talking about you and sending you and Marjorie their good wishes.

I have just returned from Knopf's where I had a short though delightful chat with Mrs Stagg, and a couple of girls on the 9th floor who were your great admirers. I purchased a copy of your Day of Deliverance[84] and I am jotting down a few of my impressions. It is a grand book, Bill. The themes and their treatment strike a very responsive note in my heart. Having read a recent issue of the Partisan[85] where not a damn line was intelligible, and not one human emotion

---

80 John Bartlet ('Bart') Brebner (1895–1957) was born in Toronto, educated at Toronto, Oxford, and Columbia universities. Brebner taught briefly at the University of Toronto, moving in 1925 to Columbia University in New York, where he taught history for the rest of his life. He published a number of scholarly, historical works.

81 National Broadcasting Corporation.

82 See the note to 'Newton of New York' in the letter to E.K. Brown, 14 September 1943 (p. 262).

83 A member of the Canadian Legation in New York.

84 A miscellaneous collection of verse by Benét published that year.

85 *Partisan Review.*

was evoked, it was a treat to come upon great subjects nobly handled with the salt of surf and the smell of the loam in the lines. Your Day of Deliverance has the swing of Handel's Dead March with the burial notes struck in succession – Belgium, Norway, Czechoslovakia, Denmark, Holland, Greece, and so forth, ending up, as the March itself does, with the triumphant chords – the stars in the hand of the giant on the mountains!!

Regarding Laval with his 'rat-squeak,'[86] I may say that Lester Pearson,[87] who is Chairman of the Food Commission at Washington (and a Victoria College mate of mine) told me that he sat opposite to him at Geneva and had every opportunity to study the rat's face. He never saw a face for which he had a greater revulsion.

I felt keenly the pathos of your 'Burning Orphanage.'

The Middle Watch is very strong. The Stones Speak is one of the finest things in the collection. It is stark and eerie. You link up the past and present in Drake and Franklin. And often the humanitarian, racial note is struck as in the Swimmer 'inching the raft ashore.' What a story for a ballad – and you have done it!

Chappelle, of course, I had seen last winter. Some day, too, I shall see your *Cape Ann.*

I am going to make the Day of Deliverance my Christmas presents this year. I shall order them from Ryersons who are Knopf's agents in Toronto.

We are leaving here on Tuesday but I hope to be in New York again next Spring when my Knopf book appears.

Good luck my friend.
Ned Pratt

---

86 Pierre Laval (1883–1945), French politician, premier of France in the 1930s. He collaborated with the Germans after the collapse and occupation of France in 1940, becoming Hitler's chief 'French henchman' from 1940 until the German retreat in 1944. He was executed for treason in 1945.

87 Lester B. Pearson (1897–1972) was born in Ontario and educated at Victoria College and Oxford University. He taught history at Victoria College in the 1920s, then joined the Department of External Affairs. From 1935 to 1948, he held several high government offices at home and abroad before serving as minister of external affairs, leader of the Liberal Party of Canada, and then prime minister (1963–8). He was awarded the Nobel Peace Prize for his efforts to bring peace to the Middle East in 1956.

TO JENNY PINCOCK[88]

Sept. 30, 1944

Jenny dear girl:

I am terribly ashamed that I have not answered your letter before this. When your second came today I said to Vi that we owed a deep apology to Jennie, but here are the circumstances. We were away to New York just after you wrote, to get Claire installed at Columbia University. I returned before Vi, as Claire was not feeling so well and needed her mother for some time. There was a recurrence of the old trouble which has since occasioned long-distance telephoning between N. Y. and Toronto. When I got back, however, I do not know where Vi had placed your letter. We just discovered it today or, at least, Vi took it out of the drawer of the bureau and said – 'Write Jennie at once.' That is the reason for the delay plus our worry over Claire, day-by-day reporting.

I have read 'Hidden Springs'[89] and feel that the subject is treated with pathos and tenderness. The natural scenery is worked in harmoniously forming a background for the human story. The Mary-James love motif is worked out beautifully and that section on the 'Herodian zeal' is powerful. What a year 1692 must have been in America.

We often wonder how you have been getting along – always in your fine courageous way, we are sure. We have a lot ourselves to test our faith and courage.

My book – 'Collected Poems' is not out yet, though it was promised for September. I shall send you a copy immediately it appears, perhaps about the middle of October. Publication is the most difficult thing today in Canada. I had to urge every argument to get my book out. The ms. has been in the hands of Macmillans since last winter.

Very affectionately
Ned

88 Jenny O'Hara Pincock (1890–1948) was the wife of Pratt's childhood friend Newton Pincock. She was an ardent spiritualist as well as an accomplished musician and amateur poet. Her *The Trails of Truth* (Los Angeles: Austin, 1930) includes an "Account of this Seance under Mrs. X's pen" (76–80). Claire Pratt identified 'Mrs X' as her mother.

89 A long 'historical' poem reflecting her interest in spiritualism. Pratt wrote a foreword when it was published in 1950 as *Hidden Springs: A Narrative Poem of Old Upper Canada and Other Poems* (privately printed).

TO CLAIRE PRATT

Oct. 2, 1944

Dearest Cayke:

Your two letters came this morning just when I was on the point of rushing to catch the 10 a.m. bus. I read one while mother read the other and that one I took with me on the bus and managed to decipher, through the bumps such euphonic words like Philharmonic, Ida Rose Luke[?], Madame Kung, Vitone, Qam link, Cara, Slara[90] – So you see I actually read it to the best of my ability. When I get home tonight I shall diligently scan the golden syllables again.

We went to see Yanka yesterday, to wish her good bye, and to give her some letters and things. I told Stefan[91] of the thrill I had at Othello and the greater thrill when I had lunch with Robeson[92] and Ferrer (Iago)[93] the following day. Robeson is one of the finest specimens of humanity God ever made. He is so courteous and humane and highly educated and intelligent. I never saw a better Iago than Ferrer.

Mother and I yesterday went out to the Toronto golf links and tea with Mrs MacKay and her daughter of the Women's Press Club.

And now my love I must get
ready for my first lecture in 4(g).
Dad

---

90 A playful list of words and phrases from Claire's last letter, reflecting her studies in international affairs at Columbia, her social life, and recent purchases. The allusions are (in sequence) to the New York Phiharmonic, a new friend named Ida Rose (see the letter to Claire Pratt, 27 March 1944 [p. 325]), the sister of Madame Chaing Kai-Shek (Madame Kung), the active ingredient heralded in advertisements for Jergen's Face Cream (Vitone), a form of modulation used in radio communications (Qam link), a new friend named Cara, and Soviet long-range aviation (SLARA). The logic of the sequence is – as Pratt says in his letter – purely 'euphonic.'

91 Yanka's brother.

92 Paul Robeson (1898–1976), black American actor, singer, and activist. This ground-breaking inter-racial production of *Othello*, with Robeson in the lead role, opened on Broadway in fall 1943 and, in September 1944, began a seven-month tour of forty-five cities.

93 José Ferrer (1912–92), Puerto Rican-born theatre and film actor and director.

TO CLAIRE PRATT

21 Cortleigh Blvd.
Toronto

October 13, 1944

Dearest pumpkins:

I am off tomorrow to Montreal for three days. I have to give a lecture on *Brébeuf* to Loyola College which consists of some two hundred priests and three hundred nuns (charming penguins) and another lecture to the Montreal Branch of the Canadian Authors' Association (angry penguins).[94]

Then the following week I go to Kitchener.

The Collected Poems came off the press today and I was presented with six complimentary copies. The first one I gave to mother, and the second I am herewith forwarding to you. Macmillans are putting out a large edition of three thousand bound copies. They will be on the bookshelves next week. It will be interesting to see how the public take them up. Knopf will have the American edition next spring. It will be independent of Macmillans altogether. Some day I should like you to take a run into Mark Van Doren's office and announce yourself. He wrote me a beautiful personal letter on Brébeuf. Is Bart Brebner at Columbia this year? I was under the impression that he had leave of absence.

Now don't work too hard. Get yourself any little comforts over and above the necessities. Are you finding my flashlight of any use? I am glad that Bee[95] is at Columbia. I played nine holes with her father yesterday and knocked the stuffings out of him. It was sweet revenge because two weeks ago he trimmed me. I came home in the deepest gloom, so deep that I could not find any consolation even in my silver gown. I flung it in a rage into the corner. Mother had to fix me up with an extra steak. I feel better today. I suppose it was the appearance of the book. Dorothy and Amy[96] are doing their best to compensate for your absence. They are very nice girls.

With much love,
Father (Lord help me).

---

94 An allusion to the Australian avant-garde journal *Angry Penguins*.

95 Beatrice Wallace, daughter of Pratt's friend, Malcolm Wallace.

96 College friends of Claire; Amy lived with the Pratts until Christmas that year.

TO CLAIRE PRATT

The well-known
21 Cortleigh Blvd.
A very peaceful Sunday,
Mother knitting,
Father typing,
Dorothy studying,
Amy over-sleeping.

10 a.m. E.S.T. [22 Oct. 1944]

Dearest internationalist:

I had an interesting experience the evening before last when I addressed a large group of nurses in the auditorium of the Sick Children's Hospital. The president is Margaret McLaughlin the daughter of Hugh McLaughlin who is the brother of my friend Billy McLaughlin[97] who is the father of Barbara McLaughlin, your classmate at St. Clement's.[98] They asked me to talk about the Collected Poems and to read a few of them. I chose the dog poem The Reverie on a Dog, and I told a story which had them all laughing, especially one person who giggled all the way through. I kept looking over at that individual and who should it be but Dilly,[99] looking very skeptical and unconvinced but very, even hilariously, amused. The story is the same one I told the Victoria Women's Association some time ago when Mrs Sissons[100] went home and told her husband that I was the biggest liar in Canada. You remember Cluny Macpherson[101] who owned a lot of Newfoundland dogs. There was one which was his favourite called Jack (as unlike Jack Myles[102] as one can imagine). He used to take this dog with him on his medical rounds and show him to his patients to bolster up their morale

97 The brothers, Hugh McLaughlin (b. 1892) and William McLaughlin (b. 1894), were partners in the Toronto law firm McLaughlin, Johnston, Moorhead and MacAulay, legal consultants toMacmillan of Canada.

98 The Toronto school which Claire attended in the 1930s.

99 The nickname of Claire's friend Adele.

100 Wife of C.B. Sissons, with whom Pratt climbed Mount Cathedral in 1913.

101 Cluny Macpherson (1879–1966) was Pratt's second cousin (their mothers were first cousins). A graduate in medicine from McGill in 1901, he spent his entire career, apart from war service, in Newfoundland. He and his brother Harold bred Newfoundland dogs.

102 The neighbour's dog.

as the dog was most intelligent and affectionate. Cluny taught him many words like come, go, fetch it, go and find Harold, go to the store and stay there until I come for you, good night and good morning, and the dog would reply with barks, each bark representing a word and varying pauses between the barks also indicating ideas. One loud bark meant *Jack*, two meant *immediately*, three fast barks *coming*, and so on. Well, one day Cluny left the dog at Harold's store in the morning telling him to sit there under the table of the office until he picked him up on his return to the house which was about two miles from the store. Cluny, however, was very busy that day and drove back to his house about six o'clock, when a message came from the store from the manager – 'Say, Doctor, it's time to close up, but we cannot get this darn dog out of the office. Two of us have been pulling at him but he braces his legs against the table refusing to budge. What are we going to do?' Cluny replied, 'Is there a telephone near?' 'Yes.' 'Put the receiver to his ear,' which the man did. Cluny said – 'Come home Jack.' The dog barked back – One loud bark, then three fast ones, then two, – 'Jack coming immediately.' Jack was home in two minutes. By this time, Dilly became almost uproarious and I had to close the lecture. A good time was had by all (I hope).

Next Thursday I go to Kitchener to speak to the Canadian Women's Club. I shall tell that story.

I hope you will soon be better dear,

Father.

TO CLAIRE PRATT

Wednesday [25 Oct. 1944]

Dearest pumpkins:

It was such a joy to get your long distance message Monday evening. Do ring us up often between six and seven p.m. if for no other reason than to give us the sound of your voice. It is a tonic. Sometimes it is like a whiff of the Atlantic, and sometimes like a warm breeze blown in from the Caribbean. Even if it is not like either, at least telephone.

I have just come in from Kitchener. I left yesterday at 2 p.m. but made an absurd misconnection. I was told to purchase my ticket first to Hamilton, as the bus stopped there and a new bus took up the journey. Well and good, I did. It arrived at Hamilton at 4. I got off and bought a new ticket for Kitchener and was told to go to platform 4 and take a bus marked Guelph, Kitchener, etc. It was to leave at 4.15. In came the Guelph bus at platform 4. I got on with my ticket for Kitchener. 4.15 came but no sign of a departure. I thought that there was some delay, that was all. At 4.30 the conductor boarded the bus and asked for our tickets. I told him that I was going to Kitchener and he replied – 'This bus only goes to Guelph, the Kitchener bus left a quarter of an hour ago.' I said what do I do now? He said – 'Rush into the station and buy your ticket to Guelph and it may be that you will get there in time to catch another which goes to K.' I got my ticket and got into Guelph at 6 p.m. the time that I was expected at K. I had to telephone Mrs. Smith, the President of the Canadian Club of K, and just when the last nickel sounded in the slot the bus arrived and the conductor was shouting 'all aboard for Kitchener.' I had to howl at Mrs. Smith – 'I'm now leaving Guelph by mistake.' I rang off and literally jumped on to the bus, and got in an hour late. I was met at the station by a Mr. Pollock, a manufacturer of radios who brought me to his home and gave me a gorgeous dinner of fried rabbit (I can see you gag), a gorgeous repast. His wife had it all prepared for me because she was told by a friend that fried rabbit was the Newfoundland national dish, which, of course, I said it was. After that I went to the Town Hall and delivered an hour's lecture on seals, dogs, sharks and whales, ending up with one on nurses which I thought fitted in well with the general classification, excluding dear Aunt Nell naturally. Here I am now in the house alone. Mother has gone to Phoebe's.[103] Amy and Dorothy have slipped off to a show, and when I have penned this epistle I'll go to bed as I did not get my quota of sleep at the Kitchener Hotel. You know my tricks.

[ ]

Mr Pollock said he would give me a beautiful radio worth $400.00 retail for the wholesale rate of $150.00 by and by if I wanted it. That radio will be yours when you finally come back. He had one in his house and a symphony came in just as if it were in Massey Hall with marvellous tone. You will be thrilled with it.

Give our love to dear Bee. She is a princess in the midst of the world's Maharahnees. Was there ever a more wonderful family than the Wallaces? Her father is my greatest friend in the world. And her mother is just inexpressible, that's all about it, and as for yourself you are the most super-duper stylist in the art of letter writing since the days of gentle Charles Lamb. Lord bless you all.

Lovingly,
Crazy Pop.

---

103 A long-time friend of the family. See the letter to Claire Pratt, 20 July 1939 (p. 174).

TO CLAIRE PRATT

Oct. 30, 1944

Dearest Cayke:

Your two letters came this morning right from the Hospital for S.S.[104] We think you did the right thing in taking hold of it at the start, instead of allowing the temperature and discharge to go on for months.[105] They are doing what Dr Norman suggested last May – intra-muscular treatment which according to Norman is much more effective than intravenous.

We hope that you will be out of the hospital in a few days and much improved. Rest all you can and don't get involved in too many social engagements in the city.

I am rushing this note off in the office between lectures, and will write more fully later.

Much love,
Father.

TO 'WILLIAM NOBLE' (HAROLD HORWOOD)[106]

November 2nd, 1944

Dear Mr Noble:

It is a great satisfaction to learn that a group of Newfoundland writers have undertaken to start a journal in the interests of Letters.[107] There can be no question that talent is lying about merely waiting for an adequate medium of expression. You may be surprised at the rich ore you will discover when you open up the veins.

104 The Hospital for Special Surgery in New York specializes in orthopaedic procedures.

105 Claire had had a flare-up of the chronic osteomyelitis that had affected her off and on for more than a decade.

106 'William Noble' was a nom de plume used by Newfoundland-born (1923) writer, politician, and activist Harold Horwood (1923–2003).

107 The short-lived journal *Protocol* (two issues) was initiated by the members of a small literary club of young St John's writers who in 1943–4 included (among others) Harold Horwood, his brother Charles, Irving Fogwill ('John Avalon'), and David G. Pitt.

As editor for several years of a poetry magazine, I have become more and more convinced of the importance of an audience to stimulate and sustain creative effort. A magazine is the chief means of securing that audience. The Renaissance in England and America during the first years of this century owed much of its spirit and direction to small but influential periodicals devoted to literary production and criticism.

I wish every success to your venture. I hope you will be pulling Newfoundland Wordsworths and Byrons out of the coves in the coming years. Good stuff is there. To find it, and encourage it, is one of the chief functions of the proposed journal.

Yours loyally,
E.J. Pratt

TO JENNY PINCOCK

November 2, 1944

Dear Jenny:

I think you could work a really good thing out of the Mary-James series.[108] I had no criticism to offer because I knew it came right from your own 'Hidden Springs' and that sort of source is sacred. Technically, the work is sound, but I doubt the market possibilities. I was in at Macmillans recently and the Editor told me that literally hundreds of manuscripts were in arrears and no new ones being taken on.

But still, I remember the saying of Hugh Eayrs, the late President of the Canadian Macmillans and a great friend of mine, that people search for religious truth always after a war or a great catastrophe. It was so after the last war. People were buying up Lodge & Crooks[109] and the rest. It will be so in two or three years time. Why not go ahead very slowly & carefully and work out your stories. Then submit them when paper and labour are more abundant than at present.

As for the medium, there is no doubt that prose is more easily disposed of than verse – plain direct prose which is beautiful in its very simplicity. As a rule

---

108 Characters in her poem 'Hidden Springs.' See the letter to Jenny Pincock, 30 September 1944 (p. 294).

109 Sir Oliver Lodge (1851–1940) and Sir William Crookes (1832–1919) were British scientists active in 'psychical research' and authors of books and articles on the subject.

persons take a look at a book of verse and pass on. That's a fact, until one has established himself or herself.

Thanks for that invitation, but the academic duties here include lecturing every Saturday and a complete rush.

Blessings on you
Ned.

TO CLAIRE PRATT

21 Cortleigh Boulevard,

(noteworthy as the place where Claire Pratt resided for twelve years before she took up her abode in Columbia University)

Time – Saturday night just after a show at the Uptown where Poss, Mother, and I saw

'This Merry Breed'[110] by Noel Coward. [4 Nov. 1944]

Dear:

Last night we had a dinner at the house, a regular old-fashioned dinner party. Guests were Principal Sidney Smith,[111] Sir Ellsworth and Lady Flavelle, Clark and Nora Locke,[112] Amy and Dorothy. I had ordered a roast from Loblaw's and since there were ten people at the table I had to carve at a side table, a job which I performed to the king's taste, even if I do say it myself and call down on myself from you the charge of meek humility and holy boldness. We had as vegetables potatoes, onions and squash. The dessert was french pastry. Coffee was served in the living room before a fire made from charcoal and briquettes.

---

110 An error for *This Happy Breed*, Coward's 1943 play, filmed in 1944.

111 Sidney Earle Smith (1897–1959), born in Nova Scotia and educated as a lawyer, was a professor of law at Dalhousie University and Osgoode Hall before serving as president of the University of Manitoba 1934–4. He was president of the University of Toronto from 1945 to 1957, when he was appointed minister of external affairs.

112 Clark Locke (b. 1890), president of Clark E. Locke Ltd., a Toronto advertising firm, was a long-time friend of Pratt's. His wife Norah was a daughter of Honourable George S. Henry, premier of Ontario 1930–4.

The conversation afterwards centered upon Gabriel Pascal and my trips to Windsor and Bigwin Inn and on the speculation as to whether Gabe would ever pay me the one thousand dollars which he told Brockington he would pay me on account, meaning that much more was to come later when the Snow Goose was on the films.[113] Brock had seen the archangel in London last summer and the latter said – 'Remember me to your friend and tell him I haven't forgotten him.' There it ends at present.

Tomorrow, we plan to go to Church, probably in the evening as we get a better chance of being seen by Dr Brewing.[114]

It is now ten o'clock and bedtime,

With paternal solicitations,
Father Furious.

TO CLAIRE PRATT

Monday p.m. [13 Nov. 1944]

Dear Cayke:

We were so delighted to get your letter this morning. It does my heart good to find that you are having a jolly time of it, going out to lunches and dinners, and not doing too much work on your course. You are in New York mainly for the experience of travel and making new acquaintances, and to put your head in a study bag would only neutralize all our expectations. The chief worry I had was over that law and government subject. I am told it is a very severe course in our University, especially hard for a student who had not received instruction on it before. You were wise in postponing it and intensifying on the language and social work. Besides, it is not essential to any employment you will have here on your return, though perhaps helpful.

This week is a big time in Toronto. The Congress on Canadian-Soviet Friendship[115] is having its sessions on Friday, Saturday and Sunday. I have to

113 See the note to 'Pascal' in the letter to Pelham Edgar, 8 August 1941 (p. 207).
114 Reverend Willard Brewing (b. 1881) was minister from 1938 to 1954 of St George United Church, Toronto (of which Pratt was a member) and moderator of the United Church in 1948–50.
115 See the letter to William Rose Benét, 13 August 1944 (p. 289).

spout on Saturday morning for fifteen minutes. Professor Simmons of Cornell[116] makes the main speech.

I ran into Macmillans today and found that they had sold already one thousand copies of the Collected, and that is before the Christmas season, long before. Morgan-Powell of the Montreal Star wrote a grand review. The firm is sending out 11000 circulars through the country which ought to yield some results.

I shall write again in a couple of days.

Lovingly,
Father promising.

Vitone[117] is just as good cold. Take care.

TO E.K. BROWN

Nov. 15, 1944

Dear Ed:

The book is going well. One thousand copies sold in two weeks, Macmillans are expecting to dispose of most of the edition (3000) by Christmas. The reviews are most heartening all over Canada. Most of them, incidentally, refer to your 'On Canadian Poetry' as authority. So it helps both books. You have been a wonderful help and inspiration from the very beginning. It is a debt I shall owe all through my life. We discussed you and your work again last week. We had 'another' dinner in honour of Sidney Smith, this time at our house. The Flavelles & Lockes & Smiths. Sid's wife is charming too. After the dinner we '*repaired*' (double connotation) to the living room and there *before* a charcoal fire, and *outside* of old rye (Seagram's) we swapped yarns till midnight. Smith said he left in a mood of extreme exhilaration. He loves the Browns. I think we have a *winnah* in him.

Next week G.B. Harrison is coming to a dinner with the Woodhouses.[118] I am exchanging with him at Queen's next spring, and this time the party is on me.

---

116 Ernest J. Simmons (1903–72), author of *English Literature and Culture in Russia, 1553–1840* (1935), was a pioneer in the academic study of Russian literature and culture in North America.

117 See the letter to Claire Pratt, 2 October 1944 (p. 295). Vitone was advertised as the main ingredient in Jergens Face Cream.

118 A.S.P. Woodhouse and his mother.

I wouldn't, if I were you, go to any trouble about the Quarterly review.[119] I should much [prefer] something short – perhaps more in the form of a notice, as all the content has been reviewed from time to time in the pages. It's the American public I am interested in, and Knopf would be better pleased to have the publicity fresh. The S.R.L.,[120] the N.Y. papers and magazines like Poetry are the important media.

A.J.M. Smith has written most cordially about the publication: so has Klein. I don't expect anything but scorn or indifference from the other Preview crowd, but they don't count half as much as they imagine in this country.

It will be grand to see you Xmas or New Year if you can make it.

Love to Peggy and the kid.

Always
Ned.

TO A.J.M. SMITH

Nov. 15, 1944

Dear Arthur:

Thanks for your warm words. You always made my heart leap with Wordsworthian joy. Klein's letter came in the same mail. I have got to admire and like Klein more & more. I spent a week-end in Montreal a little while ago speaking to the Loyola College and I called on Abe. It was my first contact face to face and my earlier impressions of respect were deeply reinforced. We talked and smoked for two hours and then took a taxi trip around the city. I told him that I wrote the strongest endorsement of his Guggenheim application[121] last year but they gave the award to a history professor. I said that the two men of Montreal and the only two that at present showed promise of literary immortality were the two of you. He has unbounded admiration for you. It was a delight to read his review of your book in the Canadian Forum.[122] It was written out of his heart and mind both.

---

119 Brown reviewed Pratt's *CP1* at length in *UTQ* (January 1945): 211–13.

120 *Saturday Review of Literature.*

121 See the letters to A.J.M. Smith, 15 July 1942 (p. 233) and 28 January 1944 (p. 275). Smith and Pratt had been encouraging Klein to apply for a Guggenheim for some time.

122 'The Poetry of A.J.M. Smith' [Review of *News of the Phoenix*], *CF* 23 (February 1944): 257–8.

He has his troubles with Preview particularly with Anderson[123] whom he described as an objectionable egoist with a constant sneer at all human effort but his own. The editorial board is ridden with internal jealousies. They were jealous of his Hitleriad[124] and of Klein's article on you. They are jealous of any success another receives. It was refreshing to know a man like Klein with his broad humanity & tolerance. He has your own catholicity and also your critical intelligence. You certainly combined both in your anthology.

I asked Klein to let me know when he planned to come to Toronto. What an evening we would have together with the handpicked boys! I hope you will stay a long time with the gang when you come.

I have been asked to exchange with G.B. Harrison for a week or two next early spring. He takes my lectures & I his. He is a fine fellow though at first a little stiff, but there's nothing like rye to soften the harsh lines.

Claire is in New York at Columbia University taking 'International Studies.' She will spend her Christmas vacation with us. We have two of her friends living with us now – her school mates. Vi would love to see you again. She thinks you're a pippin.

As ever,
Ned

TO CLAIRE PRATT

21 Cortleigh Blvd.

Tuesday evening [21 Nov. 1944]

Dearest Cakes:

Both your letters came yesterday morning. I was interested in Margaret Avison's letter. Both Dr. Wallace and Margaret would like you to be associated with the Institute[125] when you are through your work at Columbia. There is no hurry of course. They know that you are contemplating a two-year course, and the Institute is a growing affair with a long-term plan. You will know best how to

---

123 See the note to 'the Anderson Scott Page Ruddick gang' in the letter to A.J.M. Smith, 28 January 1944 (p. 276).

124 Klein's verse satire of the Nazi regime, published by New Directions Press in 1944. Pratt had reviewed the book in *CF* (October 1944) (rpt *EJP: PAA*, 164–6).

125 Malcolm Wallace was head of the newly organized Institute of International Affairs in Toronto. Margaret Avison was his assistant.

answer Margaret's letter about that French appointment, but it looks good to us because the language is something you can go on studying indefinitely after you get back. You could take an occasional course here in Victoria in spare hours and master the subject. We would suggest that you put the case to both of them and let them see what the prospects are. I shall not say anything myself to them unless you give me the word. I feel sure that the demand for helpers will be considerable after the war, so you do not need to worry about the immediate situation. The setting is most desirable, isn't it?

As for the $80.00 a month, the amount will be paid regularly, because it is there on the books. $1200.00 was earmarked. There are five more payments and if it is more than you need for this year, the surplus will be available for next year, if the government should feel fit to lower the grant, or if you did not get the fellowships repeated. You could leave ten dollars a month aside provided our own allowances were scanty next year. It is a bit inconvenient for you to have the draft cashed by aunt Nellie but I guess that is unavoidable. We should like too for Nellie to get the odd ten dollars as a little gift. Mother is going to send her something for Christmas. We shall not send the draft for Christmas to you, but rather give it to you in American notes when you return at the New Year.

Mother, Dorothy, and Amy are down at the Royal Alexandra seeing a show tonight, and here am I at the typewriter writing you and keeping house.

Love,
Father.

Claire, come to Cortleigh, twenty-one,
It's the highest of my wishes,
For certainly it is no fun –
My doing all those dishes.

That you'll come soon – it is my hope
For my Columbia daughter;
I'm sick of flakes of ivory soap,
Ammonia and hot water.

I know that Mother does her best,
But she will not obey me,
Nor do I get a moment's rest
With Dorothy and Amy.

From Father Forlorn
(in a doggerel mood)

TO LOUIS MACKAY

December 7, 1944

My dear Louis:

My wife and I have just finished reading your review of the 'Collected'[126] and we felt warm Caribbean waves rolling over us. It was a wonderful piece of work, really an article rather than a review. I was thankful for the criticisms and discriminations and thankful for your most kindly commendations. It was love of you, my good old friend, as well as appreciation of your work which prompted me to make this acknowledgement. I never had such a paragraph written about me like that last one in your review. It had the tones of I Corinthians. Vi and I were silent for five minutes after reading it.

What are you doing yourself? I told Hector[127] how much I enjoyed your little squib in the Canadian Forum a few issues ago about Margaret Avison's review of Dorothy Livesay, the one referring to the size of the mountains, etc. Wit like that should be turned on subjects generally. You have a Horatian volume in you and more besides if you could find the time. I do hope you are keeping up the Hylas[128] touch too. Remember I gave you your introduction through the C.P.M. which now I have abandoned. A.J.M. Smith is a very great admirer of yours. We think that Nunc Scio[129] is a marvellous bit of concentration, as fine as anything in the whole collection.

When are you coming this way? Some day soon, I hope, to gladden our hearts. Our love to Constance.

Yours as ever
Ned

126 *CF* (December 1944): 208–9.

127 See the note to 'Hector Charleworth' in the letter to Lorne Pierce, 15 July 1927 (p. 72).

128 'Hylas' is the title of a poem from MacKay's *Viper's Bugloss* (Toronto: Ryerson, 1938) that had been anthologized in Smith's *The Book of Canadian Poetry*.

129 '*Nunc Scio*' was another poem in the collection, echoing '*Nunc scio quid sit amor*' ('now I know what love is') from Virgil, *Eclogues* VIII.

TO CLAIRE PRATT

Dec. 11, 1944

Dearest Cayke:

In a little more than a week you will be home with us.

You would have enjoyed last night if you had been at Boris Berlin's.[130] We had dinner first with him and his wife and the Russian Secretary – Mr Koudriavtsev.[131] Later on about twenty people came, nearly all musicians (a few of them were painters like A.Y. Jackson[132]). Reginald Godden[133] played a concerto (Russian) on the piano. Do you remember Godden? He has just come back from the Reginald Stewart orchestra[134] where he was first solist. This was the 39th time he had played it and it was marvellous – all the more considering that he has severe arthritis in his fingers. He has had it for five years yet somehow he played in spite of it.

We spent the afternoon at the Falters,[135] our old Jugoslavian friends. Mother will tell you what Mrs Falter is doing for a living.

I am doing some editorial work for Bill Clarke (Oxford)[136] and it is taking my spare time.

Much love
Father

130 (1907–2001). A Russian-born musician and composer who taught at the Toronto Conservatory of Music.

131 Sergei Koudriavtsev, first secretary of the Russian legation in Ottawa.

132 Probably the most celebrated of the Group of Seven painters.

133 A graduate of the Toronto Conservatory of Music, Godden (1905–87) was a concert pianist, and later principal of the Hamilton Conservatory of Music. He premiered a number of works by Prokofiev (including Seventh Piano Sonata, 1944; Third Piano Concerto, with the TSO, 1945), Shostakovich, and Copland to Canadian audiences.

134 From 1942 to 1953, Reginald Stewart (1900–84) was conductor of the Baltimore Symphony Orchestra. It is not clear whether Pratt is referring to this orchestra.

135 Recent immigrants whom the Pratts had met through Malcolm Wallace.

136 W.H. Clarke (b. 1902) had been with the Educational Division of Macmillan of Canada (1925-30), but left to form the publishing firm of Clarke-Irwin in partnership with J.C.W. Irwin. From 1936 to 1949, he was manager of the Canadian branch of Oxford University Press.

TO CLAIRE PRATT

Wednesday [13 Dec. 1944]

Dearest Cayke:

This is just a little note as both of us are writing longer tomorrow. Mother told me to send a card this morning but I didn't have one so I postponed it till now.

Philip Grove[137] and his son Leonard spent last night with us. He is just able to walk with a stick and helped by his son. Poor old fellow. His book had only 100 advance sales but Macmillan is publishing it by the first of the New Year. He looked so pathetic and the wee boy, though he is 14 years, looks like 10.

Grove repeated his tale of woe and again today at the College he told it to Currelly. He has it off by heart even the accented words and the breath pauses.

Tonight we are going to the Museum where President Cody is giving a reception to Sidney Smith the new Principal. Leslie[138] is calling for us in his car.

Love
Dad

TO ALBERT G. HATCHER[139]

Jan. 3, 1945

Dear Bert:

Cal sent me a grand sonnet of yours[140] but it sent me off on the hunt for a word which kept me nosing dictionaries for two hours. I finally trailed 'suent' down to a dialect form Old French brought over to England, Lord knows how many

137 See the note to 'Grove' in the letter to Hugh Eayrs, 24 February 1934 (p. 122).

138 Reverend C.W. Leslie, a professor at Emmanuel, the theology college of Victoria University.

139 Hatcher (1886–1954) was born at Moreton's Harbour, Newfoundland, and had been a classmate of Pratt at the Methodist College in St John's in 1900–2. After studying at McGill, the University of Chicago, and Columbia University, he taught at the Royal Naval College of Canada in Halifax and at Bishop's University before being appointed president of Memorial College, St John's, in 1933. In 1949, he became the first president of Memorial University of Newfoundland.

140 Hatcher's sonnet 'To Calvert Pratt, on Receiving a Book of his Brother's Poems' – Pratt's *Collected Poems* – reads as follows:

centuries ago.[141] I felt that the word must have meant *smooth* and *flowing* by the mere feel of it. When Cal told me that you got it at Burin[142] and that it referred to the cleaving prow of a ship, then I knew there was a deep compliment conveyed in the later implications of the lines. For which much thanks. It was good to hear about you. My friends, like Robinson (Mathematics)[143] and Boyle,[144] talk about your McGill achievements with admiration.

The best of the New Year to you.

Sincerely,
Ned Pratt

As one slow sailing on an even keel
Down some safe harbour round a suent bight,
Eyes on the landwash, thoughts adrift, hand light
On tiller, foot on half-taut sheet, may feel
A sudden sharp breeze and the quick heel
Of startled craft, see the flash of white
Horses, hear the stearin* squeal, and know the might
And thrill great outer oceans can reveal
To inner sheltered seaways; so we know
By Pratt's strong-measured chanting of the might
Of puny men, of cataclysmic blow
Of berg and beast and the tumultuous roar
Of belly-filling laughter, then – alas! – the sight
Of slaughtered saints and – ah, the iron door.

*Local Newfoundland name for Arctic tern (*DNE*).

141 See line 2. The word (spelled 'suant' in the *OED* and derived from Old French) is 'of a tree or structure, straight, true; of a curve, esp in the hull of a vessel, smooth, graceful, with correct sheer; smooth, even; pliant' (*DNE*).

142 A fishing community on Newfoundland's south coast. Hatcher had lived there as a boy in 1897–8.

143 Possibly Gilbert de Beauregard Robinson (1906–92), an expert on symmetrical groups. He graduated from the University of Toronto in 1927 and completed his PhD at Cambridge in 1931, returning to join the faculty at Toronto until his retirement in 1971. During the war, he had been seconded to work on cyphers and codes, and was one of the founding members of Carleton University.

144 Robert William Boyle (1883–1955) was born in Newfoundland and educated at Methodist College in St John's (he and Pratt were classmates), and at McGill and Manchester universities. He taught physics at the University of Alberta and did anti-submarine research for the British Admiralty during the First World War, later serving as a director of the National Research Laboratories in Ottawa (1929-49). He is best known for his work on sonar.

TO CHARLES D. ABBOTT[145]

January 28, 1945

Charles D. Abbott, Esq.
The University of Buffalo
New York

Dear Mr Abbott:

I greatly appreciate your request to send some manuscripts of my verse to your library and I should be honoured to do so if I could get over some technical difficulties here at my own University. I have a tacit understanding with the President and Librarian of Victoria College to pass over the manuscripts to the Library some time in the future. As they laid stress particularly upon all the work sheets of *Brébeuf and His Brethren* and the *Titanic*, I shall have to reserve these for that purpose. I might be able to submit a few of the others to you and I shall go through them to see if they are decipherable. The Macmillans put the *Roosevelt and the Antinoe* ms. on exhibit last year during an 'Arts and Letters' tour of Athlone,[146] but some of my friends regarded the manuscript as that of the *Titanic*, so illegible was the pencilling. In writing a poem I never conceived the possibility that anyone would ever be interested in the original; hence the chaos. Any reader or student would at once infer that the author had creeping paralysis. And again, the composition is mixed up in the same book with drafts of speeches, letters and lectures. However, I shall take a look through them and see if anything is available. I shall have to consult the College in any case.

My love to Bill Benét when you see him. He is one of the grandest fellows America has produced.

Yours sincerely,
E.J. Pratt

145 A graduate of Oxford, where he had been a Rhodes Scholar, Abbott (1900-60) was professor of English and director of libraries at the University of Buffalo, where he established the Contemporary Manuscripts Collection of manuscripts and correspondence from hundreds of twentieth-century writers.

146 The Earl of Athlone (1874–1957), married to Princess Alice, a granddaughter of Queen Victoria, was currently governor general of Canada (1940–6).

TO A.M. KLEIN

Feb. 7, 1945

My Dear Abe:

I have just been reading your 'Poems'[147] with delight. I love those old and beautiful rhythms of the Old Testament and you have caught them admirably. I took Hebrew for three years in the University of Toronto and though I am ashamed to say I have forgotten much of it, yet enough remains to yield a fragrance which I can recognize when I read your verse. You have a grand lyrical gift and a depth of sincerity which is precious and rare today.

Yours sincerely
E.J. Pratt

TO CLAIRE PRATT

Feb. 7, 1945

Dearest Cuckoo:

The above appellation is the fruit of a lecture given to the class in IV Poetry and Drama last week. It caused the *one* laugh of the year. Somebody parodied Wordsworth's 'To the Cuckoo' which runs in the original:

> O blithe new-comer! I have heard,
> I hear thee and rejoice.
> O Cuckoo! Shall I call thee Bird
> Or but a wandering Voice?

147 Klein's newest collection (Jewish Publication Society 1944).

The parody was written by W.P. Ker[148] who imagined what Wordsworth would have done had he been asked to set a question on an examination paper about the poem – the 'Cuckoo':

> O Cuckoo! Shall I call thee Bird
> Or but a wandering Voice?
> State the alternative preferred
> Give reasons for your choice!

Now why the association here. I am busy at a verse on you:

> O blithe Late-goer! Will you not
> Return to us again!

That's all so far. Perhaps the balance will come after another stag party. By the way the party was a howling, laughing success. Malcolm Wallace led the conversation with Reid MacCallum[149] asking all the questions. Knox,[150] Underhill,[151] Edison,[152] MacGillivary,[153] Priestley[154] were the others. They left at midnight very quietly indeed.

Miss Riese[155] said that she went to a show with you the night before last. New York is getting nearer and nearer to Toronto. Your telephone message Saturday afternoon was just across the street.

---

148 William Paton Ker (1855–1923), Scottish-born medievalist, professor, successively, at Cardiff, London, and Oxford universities.

149 A professor of philosophy at University College, Toronto, especially interested in aesthetic theory. A volume of his essays, *Imitation and Design* (Toronto: University of Toronto Press, 1953), was edited by William Blissett after his death in 1949.

150 R.S. Knox.

151 Frank H. Underhill (1889–1971) had been Pratt's classmate at Victoria College. He studied at Oxford and taught at the University of Saskatchewan before being appointed professor of history at Toronto in 1927. One of the founders of the CCF party in 1933, he was an outspoken social and economic commentator, sometimes at odds with the university administration.

152 Probably John G. Edison (b. 1913), Toronto lawyer, graduate of the University of Toronto and Osgoode Hall, and a casual friend.

153 James R. MacGillivray (1902–92), a professor of English at University College, was best known for his *John Keats: A Bibliography and Reference Guide* (Toronto: University of Toronto Press, 1949).

154 Francis E.L. Priestly.

155 Laura Riese had been Claire's French teacher at Victoria College.

The more I read of Dr Wells' stuff the more I admire his style and sanity. He is a grand fellow and it will be a joy to see him and know him some day.

Write us often if it is but a card –

lovingly
Father
after the 'stag'

TO CHARLES D. ABBOTT

Feb. 19, 1945

Dear Mr Abbott:

I went through my old scrap books last week and I found the first draft of the 'Titanic.' I haven't looked at it for ten years as I thought I had done with it once it had been published. It is full of alterations. The 'Poker game' on board seems in legible condition.

You are welcome to it. I searched for my *Newfoundland Verse* originals but failed to find them. They must be somewhere in the dust bins. However, *The Titanic* meant more to me than anything else except *Brébeuf and His Brethren*.

With every good wish

Yours sincerely
E.J. Pratt

TO CLAIRE PRATT

Monday 8:43 p.m. [19 Feb. 1945]

Dearest Cakie:

Your letter came today with its wealth of information about the Tempest. Did I tell you that Professor Harrison of Queen's is going to lecture on that play to my First Year Honours and the Third Years Thursday and Friday? And we are going to Kingston for one week – March 3 to March 10.

A nice surprize came to me today. I had been doing some manuscript reading for Bill Clarke of the Oxford Press – a long ms. on the history of

Newfoundland.[156] All I had to do was to watch for mistakes – spelling, syntax, uncouthness, etc. He asked me to keep records of the hours spent – which came to thirty-five. I expected about fifty dollars. I couldn't believe my eyes when I opened his letter this morning and found a cheque for $150.00. (I am giving Mother a dress out of it and) I shall send you some when your stock gets low. You must inform me when.

Did I tell you, too, that Knopf has his date of publication fixed for April 9th? I think I did when I wrote last.

Next Friday I have lunch with Ellsworth Flavelle and Frank MacDowell to discuss the renewal of the Brébeuf pageant.[157] We had gone into the matter with President Cody and asked him to give Healey Willan a Sabbatical year so he could devote all his time to the music. Cody said he would approach the Board of Governors, and he thought there was a likelihood that Willan would get it, although the Sabbatic year had gone into disuse for a long time. Willan will be relieved of all academic teaching if the proposal goes through. Just imagine what a composition it will be if he devotes his whole year to it. He will make it the magnum opus of his career.

I am through now with stags for this term and am giving all my time to the preparation of lectures. The Fourth Year (Drama and Poetry) is a fine year although it is difficult lecturing on Somerset Maugham[158] with three nuns in the class. They gagged a bit at Shaw's Epilogue[159] where the soldier from Hell talks about the congenial company down there – emperors and popes and the rest of the gentlemen of fortune. I don't know what they will think of Green Pastures[160] with God smoking his aristocratic and 'expensive' ten cent cigars. I shall be skating on thin ice all right. I shall put some of the passages in pianissimo. Nuns are such sweet things anyway, with their gentle white faces framed in black. Lord love them I say.

Duckie, tell us all the news about the academic side – whom you meet, what lectures you like best, what reading you have in sight. Is there any synopsis I can make for you.

Always lovingly
Father

---

156 R.A. MacKay, ed., *Newfoundland Economic, Diplomatic, and Strategic Studies* (Toronto: Oxford University Press 1946).

157 See the note to 'the Pageant' in the letter to Pelham Edgar, 8 August 1941 (p. 208).

158 He was teaching *The Circle* (1921) by British novelist, short-story writer, and playwright Somerset Maugham (1874–1965) – a 'drawing-room comedy' on the theme of romantic love and mildly risqué in spots.

159 To *Saint Joan*.

160 The 1930 Pulitzer Prize–winning play by American playwright Marc Connelly portraying the story of Creation as told by a southern black preacher to a Sunday school class.

TO PELHAM EDGAR

Feb. 21, 1945

My dear Pelham:

Bert[161] and I planned a joint letter to you, to be concocted at his house just after dinner. You had asked for a *gossipy* letter, and we intended to make it such. But the dinner is still in the offing, waiting I suppose till the sixty inches of snow (our Toronto fall so far) gets down to at least fifty-nine. It is one polar winter here. I haven't been able to get my car out of the garage for 2 months – since the big snowfall. And I don't see any chance of doing it till the spring.

Claire came up for ten days and returned by air. She seems to be better in health after her last New York treatment with penicillin. With fingers crossed, we hope. She is doing well with her examinations.

The Knopf edition is slated for April 9, subject to priorities of course. Did I tell you that Tinker of Yale, Bush and Spencer of Harvard and Mark Van Doran of Columbia sent in enthusiastic statements to Knopf? It will have a good 'academic' start, but what will be the popular demand, who knows?

I don't see much chance of getting to Ottawa for some time.[162] How I should love a stag with you and Henry & Brock.[163] By the way Brock told me last month when he came to the York Club dinner that he heard you read recently and was thrilled by it – 'Wonderful,' he said. He ought to know certainly.

Next Tuesday we go to the Royal York to attend Cody's farewell. We had a sweep in Vic on the length of his valedictory. Twelve of us are in on it, with Moff Woodside[164] holding the bag. 25 cents a ticket. I bet on 80 minutes the highest of the 12. The one nearest cops the funds. My watch will be on the dinner table all the time to make sure no blighter puts a fast one over on me. Frye, MacLean,[165] and I meet at Kay Coburn's[166] apartment one hour before the dinner for a drink. I am bringing a mickey down! So is MacLean. Merely precaution

161 Bert Procter.

162 Edgar was still working in the Censor's Division of the post office, Ottawa.

163 Henry Osborne and Leonard W. Brockington.

164 Moffatt Woodside (1906–70), a graduate of Toronto and Oxford universities, was professor of ancient history at Victoria and its registrar from 1944 to 1952. He served as dean of arts for the university (1952–7) and in 1959 was appointed principal of University College.

165 Northrop Frye and Kenneth MacLean.

166 Kathleen Coburn (1905-91) was a colleague in the Department of English at Victoria College, appointed as instructor in 1932 and professor in 1953. A distinguished Coleridge scholar, she was general editor of the collected works of Samuel Taylor Coleridge

against extreme debilitation through the address. I am supplying myself with *two* Pandora Panetellas[167] as an extra.

My love to Dona & Jane. I am enclosing a St Patrick's Day present for Jane.

When Bert's dinner comes off, expect a bawdy hybrid of thought and expression.

Ned.

The best to Duncan, Harry, Brock, O'Leary[168] & Angus MacDonald (if you see him.)

TO CLAIRE PRATT

Sunday, p.m. [25 Feb. 1945]

My dear:

My silver gown has recently been causing me much embarrassment. Here I was sitting down on the couch in the living room, meditating in the night watches, doing no harm to any one and saying nothing. I wanted a quiet spell after a day's work lecturing on Green Pastures but who should come into the room but mother, Dorothy and Poss. They suddenly burst out into irreverent laughter. They said 'Turn around,' which I did very meekly. The gown had unravelled from the neck down to the end in a geometrically vertically direction and there was another rip right across the shoulders perfectly horizontal. The two ravels made a completely symmetrical cross embroidered with green and red and white threads. They made me take it off so I could see the new pattern. I considered it most ritualistic and beautiful, something that could grace a cardinal or archbishop performing altar functions. But the three of them made wide grimaces and ribald guffaws until I swore that I would not make another address on Brébeuf and His Brethren for a full month. Mother said – 'Isn't he cute?' Poss said – 'Doesn't brother look priestly and angelic?' and Dorothy had to chime in with – 'Wouldn't I like to see him give a lecture on Blake with that perfectly adorable apparel.' Cayke, you will have to write them and admonish them. I am in the completest confusion. I must wear that gown until it drops off. I have got in the habit of thinking and composing with it. Rhythm flows more evenly when I feel its priestly folds around me. I was so mad that I cut mother's allowance by three cents a week and I refused

167 Long, slender cigars.

168 Duncan Campbell Scott, Henry Osborne, Leonard Brockington, and Grattan O'Leary.

to say good-night to Poss when she left, and as for Dorothy, I just slap the prune soufflé on her plate when dessert comes around. They are deep in apology now and they go up stairs to giggle. But this Sunday was a heck of a day, and I thought I would get every thing off my chest by dropping you this letter.

Will you please ask Nellie for her suggestions. If I had you and Nellie with me, then there would be three of us against their three and I would call in Ruth Stouffer to act as referee. I did not go to Church today once and I feel in an unusually blasphemous mood. What are you going to do about it?

Father in Purgatorio.

TO HENRY W. WELLS[169]

Victoria College,
Toronto, Ont.

February 26, 1945

Dear Dr Wells:

Your ms. came today and I have had time only to give it a very light and sketchy reading. Later when I go through it intensively I shall write you at length and offer some comment. On first appraisal I am gratified with both substance and form. Your enthusiasm and tolerance affect me deeply and you have brought out into sharp focus certain points barely alluded to or omitted altogether in other reviews and articles.

If I were compiling the volume[170] again I think I would start with the *Titanic* because it is [a] more substantial piece of work than *Dunkirk* and because the theme has an enduring contemporaneity independent of the issues of war and peace.

I am amazed at the brilliance you exhibit in probing into past literatures for your analogues. Comparative study is the only valid type of critical investigation that is worth anything and you have a superb background in your own scholarship. I may repeat that I feel tremendously honoured by your interest and research.

---

169 Henry W. Wells (1895–1978) was an American critic who lectured in comparative literature at Columbia University. He and Canadian critic Carl Klinck were working on a book on Pratt which was published in 1947 as *Edwin J. Pratt: The Man and His Poetry*.

170 *CPA*.

Please call upon me for any and every kind of information. It will be a delight to work with you and Dr Klinck[171] in regard to personalia and technique. As for a publisher, we can keep our eyes open for the most effective approaches. Our Canadian Macmillans have been very good to me here. They have sold nearly 20,000 copies of my books since I started, including 3000 of this Collected, but their sales have been nearly all in Canada. Their weakness, however, is in making foreign connections. Ever since the death of Hugh Eayrs, the former President, the firm has been sluggish in establishing American and English contacts. The Knopf publication is completely independent of Macmillans, no representation having been made to Knopf by the Canadian firm. Knopf himself wrote me offering his imprint on the advice of his readers who came across my verse in an American anthology and in a review by Benét in the Saturday Review of Literature. Benét had not seen a line of my work till a year or so ago. Since then he has become a truly great friend. I would suggest that we wait till we see how the Knopf volume goes. If it is taken up well by the American public, he might like to back it up with your critical work as he could not but see how helpful it would be in getting extensive currency for the verse. After we hear from him we could decide. If he were backward, we could then put it up to Macmillans. I feel sure that Ryerson's here would be interested. Knopf tells me his publication date is April 9th which is close.

I should like to tell you and Dr Klinck something about the Brébeuf composition. Of all the poems, it typifies best the struggle to attain dramatic objectivity. I lived for a year practically with the Jesuits,[172] attended Mass, spent hours and days in the Cathedrals before the altars, became almost a Catholic to get inside Brébeuf. Then, when the poem was published, it was an effort to slide over from the Catholic authoritarianism back to my original Protestant individualism, for I was born and brought up a Methodist. In Newfoundland the fights were always on between the sects, as you can readily imagine. Later on, I should like to expand this at leisure.

May I now just add a word of gratitude for your interest in my beloved daughter Claire. She was thrilled by her visit to your home. The strongest thing about

171 Carl F. Klinck (1908–90) was a graduate of the University of Western Ontario and of Columbia (where he met Wells as a doctoral student in 1943). In 1945, he was appointed dean of Waterloo College (later University of Waterloo), and in 1947, head of the English Department at the University of Western Ontario. He published widely on Canadian literary subjects and was general editor of the *Literary History of Canada* (1965, 1976).

172 Not strictly true, though he did visit various Jesuit institutions in Guelph and Toronto, and conversed often with members of the Society.

her is her spirit. Her will is an amalgam of iron and manganese, a triumph of mind over matter.

Ever gratefully
E.J. Pratt

TO LORNE PIERCE

[3 Mar. 1945]

Dear Lorne:

Yes, Knopf seems to be going to town on the *Collected*. I do hope I get a break in America. I keep my fingers crossed, however. I am anxious to have that book sell in Canada too, if the technical difficulties can be overcome. I trust that you and Bob[173] can come to some rapprochment. I hear that men like Tinker of Yale, Bush and Spencer of Harvard, Mark van Doran and Henry W. Wells of Comparative literature in Columbia, have written most enthusiastic reports, to say nothing of Benét. The launching is propitious, but … but I still remember what happened to the Titanic in the physical sense.

My love to you Lorne in any case,

Affectionately,
Ned

TO CLAIRE PRATT

21 Cortleigh Blvd.
Toronto, Ont.
The Lord's Day,

In the Evening,
March 12, 1945

173 Robert Huckvale of Macmillan of Canada. Pierce's firm, Ryerson Press, was the Canadian agent for Alfred A. Knopf Inc., publishers of the American edition of Pratt's *Collected Poems*, but Macmillan did not want competition in Canada for its own edition.

Dearest Cayke:

We came back from Kingston Friday night, getting here before the Harrisons left. I suppose mother told you some of the doings down at Queen's and so if I happen to coincide a bit with hers please excuse me. Did she tell you all about the noises we heard in the Harrison house? You would never believe half of it. The radiators actually talked to us through the night. Sometimes it would be a loud knock as if they were signalling our attention, then two knocks to indicate (according to my deductions) that we were listening, and then they would go on for hours trying to make themselves understood in terrific blasts and rattles. In the reading room we heard some one snoring continually day and night. Really, Cayke, it was snoring and there was no discernible cause. It was just snoring, easy comfortable snoring (for the snorer) but diabolically realistic for us. Sometimes the noise would come from the roof, from the ceiling, *beckoning, beckoning, beckoning.*[174]

But that wasn't all. There were two girls staying in the house, two second year Medical students, who talked until midnight, then talked as they went down the stairs to get their midnight meal of eggs and toast, then talked as they came back to their room at 2 a.m., and then preceded to talk in their sleep till dawn. What do you think about that? They actually slid the drawers of the bureaus in and out, shifted chairs and the chesterfield, let fall their shoes from a height of five feet six. Well there's the end of the melancholy business. I *was* glad to get back to 21 even with Jack around.

On the whole, the trip was successful. I enjoyed the classes, and was glad to meet some of my old friends like Dr. Wallace,[175] Professor Melvin,[176] Conacher,[177] Prince,[178] Alexander,[179] Roy.[180] We were invited out practically every lunch and dinner. The big event was a dinner at Dr. Boucher's – chicken, potatoes, '*turnip*' salad, ice-cream and soufflés, mints and coffee, and then I had to go to the Biological Hall to give a lecture on the Titanic. I was so full that when I came to describing the dinner on the ship I nearly slid down from the desk from embarrassment because ten of the people at the recital were at the Boucher dinner.

---

174 Underscored by hand: (in sequence) single, double, and then triple lines.

175 R.C.Wallace, president of Queen's University.

176 G. Spencer Melvin in the Faculty of Medicine.

177 Possibly William M. Conacher (1877–1958), who taught in the French Department at Queen's University from 1915 to 1947. He had been editor of the *QQ*, and was a founding member of the Queen's Faculty Players.

178 Unidentified.

179 Henry Alexander.

180 James A. Roy.

Mother turned red, and I had to turn my face away from her several times and focus on the physiogamy of the President whose fine Calvinistic features served as a steadying antidote.

I lost my way many times coming home from the theatres and other places, though I had been at Kingston five times. We are a pair indeed. I cannot tell east from west and mother cannot tell her right hand from her left. So do come home soon.

I have just been reading Wells' books and monographs again. He is a master of literry style and has in addition a classical sense of balance. I shall look forward to seeing him in the future, though my going to New York in April is highly problematical.

Lovingly,
Father Ned.

TO CLAIRE PRATT

21 Cortleigh Blvd

March 14, 1945

Dearest Cayke:

First let me wish you many, oh so many, happy returns of the coming Sunday or whatever day the birthday happens to fall upon.[181] Mother and I and Dorothy have just been wondering how you are going to spend it. Make it a real day in any case, but not too fatiguing. If you were here we wouldn't let you get up till noon and then you could stay up till midnight and yes, by George, I'd stay up too for the occasion.

I have had a busy day – a rather hectic one. I had an appointment at the C.B.C. on Davenport Road at 10:30.[182] I decided that it would take three quarters of an hour to get there, so I had to get up at 9:15, dress by 9:30, breakfast by 9:45 and then catch the 10:00 bus. Mother had to leave early so Dorothy called out at 8:45 before she left. I looked at the watch and said – 'O just 8:45. I don't have to get up till 9:15.' So dozed off and jumped up to find it was 9:45. I was in the kitchen at 10, telephoned a taxi which couldn't get to the house till 10:30. Then phoned the C.B.C., explained the delay, & got there by 11. As it happened the

181 Claire's birthday was 18 March.
182 The CBC was dramatizing parts of *BB* for a school broadcast.

Brébeuf man[183] was himself late; so was the narrator who had to ask me questions while both questions and answers were recorded on the disc. Brébeuf had a fit of the sneezes, Champlain[184] had a cough while I had a hangover (please don't anticipate me) from a throat cold which made me hhkkk in several places. Miss Stevenson, the operator in charge, would call out after a sneeze, 'Record's off. Try again. Brébeuf's fault.' Then the conductor asked me a question – 'What do you teach, Dr Pratt?' I answered – 'English Literature in V-V-Vict - - - -.' Miss Stevenson called out, 'Second record on the burn – try again.' So we did and Lalemant[185] this time sneezed. So it was four records before we struck the accepted rendering. Earle Gray[186] is taking Brébeuf. The play with music is to go on in all the schools of Canada on April 13 at 10 a.m., that is, in all schools equipped with radio and most of them are today.

I shall send you $60.00 by the middle of April through the Royal Bank as a belated birthday present.

Mr Brockington telephoned today to say that he received a nice letter from John Masefield acknowledging receipt of the Collected Poems from L.W.B. He put in some very warm comments – one of which was 'Was Pratt actually on the Titanic? I cannot believe he was not.' That was encouraging, wasn't it? – I mean in one sense, of course. Brockington has proved himself such a true friend, hasn't he?

So you have to get to work on a thesis, eh? What will be the subject? Those five hours per day look pretty formidable to me. Are you getting down to the schedule idea? Can I work up some one point of the general idea to be of some assistance. I fear my ignorance of the subject may be colossal, but it is never too late to learn.

We are delighted that you find the life in New York congenial. If you could only get the proper vitamins! You must stock up when you return. All the people here send their kindest regards to you. Frye today and Ruth Jenking – Miss MacPherson[187] and Dr Brown[188] – Currelly and Surerus[189] – Why those pairs you ask? Just haphazard I reply.

Well, my bed-time has struck. It is now ten and Jack has emitted his last bark for the night.

With love forever
Father

183 The actor playing Brébeuf in the dramatization of the poem.
184 A character in the poem.
185 A character in the poem.
186 [*sic*]. Earl Grey Public School in Toronto.
187 Jessie MacPherson, dean of women and associate professor of philosophy at Victoria College.
188 Walter T. Brown.
189 John Alvin Surerus (1894–1976) was educated at the universities of Toronto (Victoria College, 1915) and Chicago. He taught in the German Department at Victoria College from 1925 to 1962, serving as head of the department from 1932 to 1962.

TO CLAIRE PRATT

Tuesday [27 Mar. 1945]

Dearest Cayke:

Where do you think I am now? In the upper room with the Fourth Year Mod. Poetry and Drama watching them write a test – the farewell event of the year. Jackie Doherty is directly in front of me. She came in a little late and I had to write out the question specially for her – the poor little thing. Mary Martin is over there on the left with her pen in her mouth and her eyes glued on the ceiling. Franz Zremen is on the opposite side near the window which is wide open as it is a perfect spring day. In five minutes the test is over. It is a nice class.

Last Friday evening was the Senior Dinner. Mother and I went instead to a Russian affair at the Eaton Auditorium. We went down to the Royal York and brought up Brockington to make the opening address.

Kay Coburn made the toast speech at the Dinner and got off a good one at my expense. She said she remembered her Senior dinner because I sat next to her at the head of the table. She remembered two things. (1) I came in with my rubbers on (I am sure I didn't). And (2) I drank her glass of water in addition to my own. I'm damned sure I didn't but the whole year was convulsed at the account.

What a lovely snap-shot you sent us of your self and Ida Rose. Ida has a beutiful sensitive face. There is a lot of refinement behind that face. And there was your own sweet phiz which is not to be sneezed at by any manner of chance. It was good to get the pictures. You look splendid.

I must close now as the time is up for the test – More anon.

Love
Father

TO CLAIRE PRATT

March 31, 1945

Dearest Cayke:

I feel very righteous today, exceptionally so. In fact, I have come to the conclusion after many premises that I am a highly important individual in this house. If you have any doubt lurking in the crevices of your mind, you just ask mother. I have finished not only washing but drying the dishes, all of them, and they were many. Mother gave me not only the breakfast dishes but the lunch ones and piled on top of them all the plates, saucers, cups, bowls, knives, jars, egg-cups which she had used in preparing for a 4 to 6 afternoon party this very day. I had nothing wherewith to relieve the monotony. I just washed and rubbed and glared at the rain which drenched the window in front of the sink. Had only the sun shone, or a robin sung, there would have been a little compensation. I came, however, to the conclusion that there was one other important 'thing' in the house and that was the rubber strainer that Aunt Agnes[190] gave Mother. It cooperated magnificently. But I cannot resist the conviction that Mother is inwardly laughing at me. Even now, when I am in the den writing you, she is whistling in the kitchen and you know what that signifies. I try to drown it out by *banging* ON THE KEYS.

We were delighted to get your letter and card this morning and also your letter from Denise. Mother will send her letter back to you. Isn't it great to be hearing all those concerts in the greatest musical centre in the world? These are things to remember forever, experiences which enrich life for good. I shall not be able to get to New York this spring because I have to lecture to the returned Service Men. The University has established a course for the First Year Pass which runs from April to the end of August. I have to take my turn in May and August with a slack period in the summer. That period gives me a chance to accept the offer of the Naval Department to take a trip on a destroyer to Newfoundland and elsewhere.[191] I do not know the exact time as naturally the details are a secret.

I finished my lecturing to the third and fourth Year Honours last week. I still have the first Honour and the third Pass which will run me till the middle of April, and then come the examinations and marking. Mother is getting a lot of supervising this year from Bert Laidlaw.[192] It is easy work apart from the monotony.

Dorothy is away today. She went up to Barrie to her sister's. She returns on Monday. This afternoon Ottylene,[193] Jean Ross,[194] and Peggy Ray[195] are coming to

---

190 Calvert Pratt's wife.

191 Commander Lorne Richardson – formerly a professor at the Royal Military College in Kingston, where Pratt had first met him, and in 1945 director of naval education, Department of National Defence – had arranged for Pratt to be invited to spend several weeks in Halifax as guest of the Navy to research a poem recounting the wartime exploits of the Canadian Navy.

192 As registrar at Victoria College, Laidlaw coordinated supervision of final examinations.

193 Ottylene Fife worked in the office at Victoria College.

194 A graduate of Victoria University who had studied painting in China. She and Claire sometimes went sketching together.

195 Margaret Ray was associate, later head, librarian at Victoria College.

help *me* prepare sandwiches. (Mother whistling again). As it is raining I have to pick them up at Yonge and Briar[196] in a few minutes. So, best love,

Father

TO CLAIRE PRATT

Sunday Noon [Apr. 1945]

Dearest Cayke:

It is a quiet, sunny, sleepy Sunday morning, and apparently I am the only one at work, for this is my fourth letter and there is not much sign of stir on the floor above me, nothing but the hum of Dorothy's[197] voice which I presume is concerned with advice to mother upon the matter of cooking turnips. I presume this, because there is a distinct smell of that most delectable vegetable pervading my den at this moment.

Emma Moffitt[198] spent the night here and I have just taken her out to Yonge and transported her to the street car. Also last night I had a flock of priests in the den. A lecturer named Nims[199] from Notre Dame University in the States came up to speak to the students at St. Mike's, and as he was a well-known poet I was asked to take a part in the entertainment. I therefore rounded up Father Shook,[200] Father Kelly,[201] Father Flahiff[202] and Norrie Frye, took them all over

196 Briar Hill Avenue.

197 Dorothy Sigmund.

198 A long-time friend of Viola Pratt. She taught English at the School for the Blind in Brantford, Ontario, and later at Brantford Collegiate.

199 American poet John Frederick Nims (1913–99) was educated at DePaul University, the University of Notre Dame, and the University of Chicago, where he received his PhD in 1945. He was a contributor to *Five Young American Poets* (1944) and published several books of poetry, including *The Iron Pastoral* (1947), *A Fountain in Kentucky* (1950), *Knowledge of the Evening* (1960), *The Kiss: A Jambalaya* (1982), *The Six-Cornered Snowflake and Other Poems* (1990), and *Zany in Denim* (1990), as well as textbooks and critical studies.

200 Father Laurence K. Shook was educated at Harvard and taught medieval English literature at the Pontifical Institute.

201 Father John M. Kelly of the Philosophy Department at St Michael's College. He was president of the University of St Michael's College from 1958 to 1978.

202 George Bernard Flahiff (1905–89) was educated at St Jerome's College and St Michael's College before joining the Basilian Order. He studied at the University of Strasbourg (1930–5) before returning to Canada, where he taught at the Pontifical Institute of Medieval Studies (1935–54) and in the Department of History at the University of Toronto (1940–54). He served as archbishop of Winnipeg (1961–89) and was appointed cardinal in 1969.

with Nims to Hart House for dinner, followed that with a tour through Hart House, and that again with an evening in my den. You may remember Father Flahiff. He is the one related to Mrs. Parsons. His brother married Mrs. Parsons' daughter. It was a grand time all round. The conversation was not in the least bit theological and could only be called religious by the most elastic definition of that term. We told stories, and when we ran out of them, I called on Frye to give an account of his Blake[203] which he has just finished for publication.

Friday afternoon Bart Brebner spent two hours with me in my office talking over old times. He said that you were loved by all in Columbia. Every time he sees Hyde (who is very deaf), Hyde says what a dear fine girl Miss Pratt is. Literally true. About next year, if you don't get a renewal of the scholarship there will be plenty of funds to see you through, so make the necessary plans if you feel like it. [ ]

I haven't seen the book yet though it is here in the Customs but it can't be cleared until I get a pro Forma from Knopf with a statement that the copies are presentational. Macmillans are not very keen to have the Knopf book in this country because they think it would cut into their own sales. It makes me vexed to think that they ran out of stock at Christmas, and now they won't cooperate with Knopf. I think, however, that we can straighten out the tangle in a few days. In the meantime if you or Nellie is down at Brentano's you might ask about it and get a couple of copies for me to be sent up or brought when you come.

With love
Father

TO WILLIAM ROSE BENÉT

[17] April, 1945

Dear Bill:

Only today did I get my presentational copies of the Collected Poems from Knopf. It was not the publisher's fault. The books had been at the Customs for more than a week, but I had a job getting the forms completed for the release of the parcel. Your introduction is simply glorious; There is no other work to describe it. All my love went out to you when I read it. My wife is reading it now

203 Frye's *Fearful Symmetry: A Study of Blake* (1947).

for the third time. She is laughing and calling out to some guests in the house – 'Come and see what Bill says about Ned.' There is one thing among many fine things about you Bill and that is your greathearted enthusiasm for a friend and his work. There is no one in America whose word counts for more in the literary world of the magazines, and you possess a quality I wish to God more of the academicians possessed – readability. If I did not know a fellow named Ned Pratt and stumbled across that introduction in a New York book store, I would most certainly buy the book. I hope the general reaction will be the same. Time will tell. The Knopf edition is grand. I am as pleased as Punch. I hope the sales won't let A.A.K.[204] down. He is a peach of a chap to work with.

It is nice to have your name twice mentioned in the list of the Borzoi books[205] opposite to Collected Poems. I am proud to be in your company and still prouder to be called your friend. Whenever I feel in the mood to pray, I thank the Heavenly Father for two things, to wit: that you stumbled across Smith's Canadian Anthology,[206] and that the Spirit stirred me to go to New York in November 1943 when I met you in physical presence and had holy communion with your spirit.

The Canadian edition is going well – on the way to 3000 copies, and still steadily going.

Some day we must celebrate, Bill. My very best to your wife. If you happen to see any of my old friends, Merrill and Muriel Denison, Ted[207] and his wife of the Canadian Legation, Hugh and Mrs. Scully, Canadian Commissioner,[208] John and Mrs. MacDonnell, Bart Brebner and his spouse, Henry Wells, and the rest, tell them they are remembered in my vespers (Brébeuf influence).

Yours as ever
Ned

204 Alfred A. Knopf (1892–1984), founder of Knopf publishing house.

205 The general trade name of Knopf's most prestigious books, represented by the image of the borzoi – the Russian wolfhound. Several of them were listed on the title page verso of *CPA*.

206 A.J.M. Smith's *The Book of Canadian Poetry*.

207 Edward Newton.

208 Hugh Day Scully, born (1893) and educated in Toronto, was commissioner of customs (1933–40) and Canadian consul-general in New York (1943–9).

TO CLAIRE PRATT

21 Cortleigh Blvd.

Wednesday eve. [18 Apr. 1945]

Dearest daughter:

I was sorry I wasn't home last night when you telephoned. I missed your golden syllables. As a matter of fact I stayed down at the office and had dinner with the Fryes[209] because I had to attend a meeting at the Conservatory of Music for the establishment of the Independent Association for the Liberty of Free Speech. It sounds pretentious. Margaret Gould of the Star[210] started it, and when I got down – a bit late I must confess – the meeting was called off. I came home after the wash-out and missed your message.

I suppose mother told you all about the Winnipeg trip.[211] It is exciting and mother and I are anticipating the journey quite eagerly. We are going to stay with the Grahams.[212] We shall be gone nearly a week including the transits. The honour is high, the D. Litt. being possessed by only three in the Toronto University, W.P.M. Kennedy of Law one of them. Roy Daniells presents me at the Convocation. The other two being honoured are Sidney Smith and the Lieutenant-Governor of Manitoba.[213] I do not have to make a speech at the Convocation fortunately, but I have to give an address at the Alumni banquet at the Fort Garry Hotel. There may be two or three other things later to be defined.

I had a lovely letter from Wells yesterday. He has become almost like a brother to me, his interest is so warm and enthusiastic. I met Klinck last week and took greatly to him. He does the biographical sketch and the general background. Tell Wells that if he ever comes to Toronto he will be given a royal welcome.

The Knopf book[214] came yesterday and we are all delighted with it. It omits the Great Feud and the Fable of the Goats, but I am fortunate in having Knopf bring out the book at all. We shall wait now for sales. If it goes well you will live

209 Northrop Frye and his wife Helen.

210 A journalist known for her crusade for civil liberties.

211 The University of Manitoba was to confer on him the degree of Doctor of Letters.

212 Reverend William C. Graham (b. 1887) was principal of United College (formerly Wesley College and later the University of Winnipeg) (1938–55). Pratt had known him since they were both students in Toronto.

213 Roland F. McWilliams, born (1874) and educated in Ontario, was lieutenant governor of Manitoba (1940–53).

214 The American edition of his *Collected Poems*.

in luxury next year at Columbia. In fact the Canadian sales will look after that side of it on their own account. Don't worry about the renewal of the scholarship. That may not come on account of the splitting of the course.

It looks as if the Ontario Schools are going to bring out a text of narrative poems for a year from now and the whole book is to consist of my work, namely, Brébeuf, The Titanic, The Cachalot, and two or three others.[215] The Committee met last week at the meeting of the O.E.A.[216] and passed the resolution unanimously. It has now to go to the department.[217] Macmillans will bring it out. I will let you know the terms for myself when the thing materializes.

Lovingly,
Father.

TO CHARLES D. ABBOTT

May 7, 1945.

Dear Mr Abbott:

I appreciate the honour of this invitation[218] very deeply, and the pleasure will be enhanced by meeting you personally after our correspondence. As to topics I should like to suggest any one of three:

(1) The 'Titanic' – a study in irony
(2) Source-material and verse
(3) The Jesuit Missionaries to Canada

(1) and (3) have a Canadian-American relationship whereas (2) is a personal investigation into the nature of research and poetry. Might I feel free to quote short extracts from my own verse to illustrate the subject? I have a slight preference for No (l) though if you thought (2) or (3) more appropriate it would be perfectly satisfactory to me.

---

215 The book, *Ten Selected Poems*, was not published until 1947.
216 Ontario Education Association.
217 Ontario Department of Education.
218 To address the Phi Beta Kappa Society at the University of Buffalo.

An address on any one of the topics would take three-quarters of an hour – certainly less than an hour. I should like to have a stand, lecture stand, or music stand, on which to place a manuscript, if that is available. I may be quoting from two or three books.

I shall be leaving Toronto on Monday getting in to Buffalo in the afternoon. I shall let you know exact hours and stations when I get my ticket.

It will be very kind of you if you can make arrangements for me to stay over night.

Yours very Sincerely
E.J. Pratt

TO CLAIRE PRATT

May 11, 1945

Dearest Cayke:

Your letter of the 9th came today. I stayed in and picked up the mail at 10 a.m. Mother went down early to preside at the examinations and I took the car and picked her up at noon because it began to rain. She read the letter in the car as we motored up to Poss's for lunch. I had to go back to the College and mother had to get a book at the Reference Library, so we started off in a real rainstorm and when we got to College and St. George whom should we meet but Dorothy (Kristen) and Margaret Avison, looking like drenched ducks at the door of the Library. I took them all home. Margaret is working part time at the office of the University Registrar and part time at the Institute. She looks still as pale and poorly as ever. I think she just keeps going on coffee and cigarettes.

We are preparing for Winnipeg. Telegrams and airgrams are arriving every day since the announcement in the Winnipeg papers offering us lodgings and hospitality but we are going to stay with the Grahams. George Ferguson, the executive editor of the Winnipeg Free Press,[219] wanted us to stay with him and his wife. So did Ernie Hunter.[220] The programme is as follows. Convocation at 9:30

---

219 George V. Ferguson (1897–1977), born in Scotland and Oxford-educated, joined the *Free Press* in 1924, serving as managing editor from 1934 to 1946, when he became editor of the Montreal *Star*.

220 Reverend Ernest Crosley Hunter (b. 1889) served United Church circuits in Toronto, Hamilton, and Winnipeg. He was minister of Knox United Church in Winnipeg and later of Trinity United, Toronto (1948–56).

Friday morning. Lunch for the Faculty and Alumni and Graduates at 1:00 where I am supposed to give 35 minutes of a speech. That same evening I am to give a lecture recital at Knox Church (Hunter's) with Sidney Smith, our new Toronto University President as my Chairman. We have become very fond of Sid and his wife. The next day the 'functionaries' Smith, Thorvaldsen[221] (who gets the degree of Doctor of Science), the Lieutenant-Governor of Manitoba[222] (who along with Sid gets an L.L.D.) and the present dish-washer of 21 Cortleigh, are lunched at the Manitoba Club by Mr. and Mrs. Armes (the President of the Un. of Man. and his wife). What comes after that is not known till we get out there. One good thing is mother has all her magazine work over for the month, so she has nothing to do but receive the hospitality of Winnipeg. How we wish you could be with us! That would make the trip complete indeed. To compensate for your absence we are going to give you a round of festivities the first week you return. You will not be allowed even to touch a dish except that from which you eat. I am seeing to that, at what cost no one but myself will know.

I did not enclose another name which I had in my mind when I wrote last but somehow I omitted it. When I was at the Arts and Letters Club yesterday Ettore Mazzoleni[223] asked me when his Knopf book would be coming. He wants one and paid me for it. There will be others later when you are through with exams. Would Janka[224] or Nellie order a copy from Brentano and get him to send it post to Mr. Ettore Mazzoleni, 104 Golfdale Road, Toronto. There is no hurry. In two weeks time or even later. Don't bother about going down yourself in the midst of your rush.

Much love,

I got your copy of the Saturday Review of Lit. and liked the article by Robert Hillyer.[225] I think it was quite appreciative coming from him, a very reserved critic.

---

221 Thorbergur Thorvaldson (1883–1965), born in Iceland and educated at the universities of Manitoba and Harvard, was head of chemistry at the University of Saskatchewan (1919–48) and dean of graduate studies (1946–9).

222 R.F. McWilliams.

223 Born (1905) in Switzerland, Mazzoleni was a musician, composer, and conductor. He was also a teacher at the Toronto (later the Royal) Conservatory of Music, and for some years its principal.

224 A college friend of Claire.

225 Robert Hillyer (1895–1961), Pulitzer Prize–winning American poet and critic, reviewed Pratt's *CPA* in *SRL* (28 April 1945): 11.

TO CHARLES D. ABBOTT

May 30, 1945

Dear Carolvs:[226]

I have been just telling my wife about you and your adorable Tressa or Teresa (I didn't get the name in print), and she, my wife, said – 'Aren't Americans like those the finest good-will ambassadors on this earth? No wonder Canadians and Americans are getting drawn closer and closer together every year when people like the Abbotts and the Benéts exist on the continent.' Well, these are my sentiments emphatically. I loved the two of you and the memory of my visit will remain with me green and fresh for years.

I recounted the outstanding incidents around the table at a dinner party tonight. Your meeting me at the station with that paragon of canine femininity, *Good*; the trip to the Library with the expenditure of rationed gas; my bewilderment in not finding my collar and cuff studs; the graciousness of your wife (may this world grant her fullness of days and health and the next, plenary felicity); the cocktail party at the Perrys' with Aunt Lavinia's foreboding that I might give an hour's lecture in Latin (God rest my pseudo-classical soul); the meeting again with the charming Perrys and Max, their bonhomie, and the flow of conversation over the home-bred ham and the strawberries; the Phi Beta Kappa installations, the warmth of the audience during the lecture which soothed my nervous heartbeats; the collation; the drive to the Mitchells and the restoration from the lecture with the cordial that never fails; the solicitude of the Dean of the Saturn Club over my late arrival; my rolling home at 1:30 a.m. to fall into a comfortable bed and sleep till 9.

But running all through these reminiscences is the Abbott thread. It is much more than worth the trip to have met you in the flesh after all our correspondence. I feel I have made a personal friend, not merely an academic acquaintance. And I take pride in the honour of the invitation to lecture before such a fraternity.

Very cordially,
Ned (EDVINVS) Pratt

I shall be off in ten days to take that summer trip on a destroyer. If the poem does not turn out to be a dud I should like to send you the ms.

---

226 The use of a 'v' in place of the 'u' in the latinized version of Charles Abbott's first name, is a nod to the letterhead of the Saturn Club, where Pratt had stayed during his visit: 'THE SATVRN CLVB.'

TO PELHAM EDGAR

May 31, 1945

Dear Pelham:

It was good to hear from you, laddie. Bert[227] and I had planned an evening at his house when we intended to concoct a letter jointly, but the event is still in the offing.

We have been exceptionally rushed. I never knew a spring so hectic. Claire will be coming home within a week and we are preparing for her. She is tolerably well.

Our Winnipeg trip was one of concentrated hospitality. It can only be described by word of mouth, in fact sotto voce. If I get to Ottawa on my trip East I shall certainly get in touch with you first thing.

The Dept. of Naval Education has suggested that I go to Halifax and get atmosphere and information on the Haida and her exploits in the war.[228] It may take a month or so, and it is quite possible I shall leave Toronto by the middle of June. I am not being paid anything for it, but it would be worth while to undertake it for the sake of the subject. It would mean a year's job in the spare time.

If I can get [to] manoeuvre a stay for a couple of days in Ottawa I shall certainly do so. The Director has suggested that I get hold of the information files. All access is opened to me. I hope I can justify the venture.

Talking about pensions, old boy, do you not realize that in four or five years I am also on the academic shelf. Just think of it. That is one thing I cannot adjust myself to – age. I don't feel it – but I guess that is what they all say. It seems only three or four years ago that I linked up with you on that second floor of Vic. Gad how time buffaloes a person's mind and orientation. Well, here's to our crowd dear pal! May we drink it later when Ontario flows a little more freely.

The blessing of God on ye and on your wife & bairn,

Sez
Ned

Will you return the Times account of the 'Collected'? I have only one left of the S.R.L. The reviews generally are very kind, but I haven't heard a word from Knopf of how the book goes.

227 Bert Proctor.

228 The *Haida*, a 'Tribal' class destroyer of the Royal Canadian Navy, had had an extraordinary record of daring and successful exploits against German submarines during 1943–5 and was an obvious subject for a naval 'epic.' But learning that William Sclater, a former commander of the ship, was writing a book, Pratt chose to concentrate on the exploits of convoy S.C.42 during the height of the Battle of the Atlantic in 1942.

TO WILLIAM ROSE BENÉT

June 8, 1945

Dear Bill:

My friends are devouring your wonderful Introduction.[229] Every substantial review has referred to its warmth and high spirits. I reply that the Introduction is just Bill Benét, my most loved American friend. The 'boys' chortle and chuckle over some of your paragraphs.

I am enclosing the last thing I have done.[230] It is appearing in MacLean's Magazine (Canadian) next week and will be recited over the air through the Canadian Broadcasting Corporation next Tuesday evening, June 12 at 10:15.

I was hoping first that I could submit it to an American publication, as MacLean's have *only* the Canadian rights, but I imagine that its prior appearance anywhere else would destroy its chance in an American magazine. I should like, however, to get the larger audience for it at least in sections. In any case, I shall be glad if you personally will like it.

In a week's time I am off to Halifax and expect to spend some time on a destroyer at the invitation of the Naval Department of Education. They have asked me to write a poem on the 'Haida' one of the Tribal Destroyers in the Canadian Navy. I shall be gone six weeks, and it might take me a year afterwards to do the job as it involves the study of the convoy system. This mission is a bit confidential as the war is still on with Japan and I cannot give names for publication. The stuff on its raw sides is hot.

I shall write you later when I get any dramatic information.

I spent last Tuesday night in Buffalo. The Phi Beta Kappa of the University of Buffalo invited me to give the address at the annual meeting – I spoke on 'The Titanic, a study in irony' and read excerpts from the poem. The Buffalowans are grand people. I love Americans anyway. You created my taste.

As ever,
Ned.

229 Benét had written the introduction to *CPA*.

230 'They Are Returning,' written by commission for *Maclean's*. See the note to 'Irwin's letter' in the letter to Viola Pratt, 18 July 1944 (p. 282).

TO ELLEN ELLIOTT

Victoria College
Toronto, Ont.

June 15, 1945

Dear Ellen:

There has been so much favourable reaction to *They Are Returning* since its appearance in MacLean's and on the C.B.C. last Tuesday night, and so many suggestions that it be published in a little chapbook or booklet, that I am enclosing a complete copy for your consideration. Do you think it would be advisable to bring it out say in soft cover next fall early so we may get all the value out of its timeliness? The MacLean's brought out an abridged form. The C.B.C. gave the whole thing which is some seventy lines longer.

One reason why I should like to have it produced is that I may not have another book for two or three years. This is the only poem I have written in two years, and the one now projected on the convoys and the R.C. N.[231] generally, will take me two years or more from now. The Naval Department is asking me to do a really big job and I can not afford to hurry it. The other reason is that the period of the return of the men will be mainly in the next six months, and the poem will have a special application for that period.

I am leaving town for Ottawa on Monday and I shall be staying at Colonel Henry Osborne's till Friday, June 22. If you have time to look into the matter early in the week, will you drop me a line c/o Henry, 222 Daly Avenue. After June 22, I shall be at Halifax, and my address will be The Halifax Club, Halifax, until August.

With best wishes,
Ned

231 Royal Canadian Navy.

TO VIOLA AND CLAIRE PRATT

CNR

Saturday 9.30 p.m. [23 June 1945]

Dears:

Here I am attempting a note on a rocky train within one hour of Halifax. The trip was a bit monotonous as I did not meet one person whom I knew, but it wasn't too bad.

Just before I left I had a dinner given me at the Rideau Club Ottawa by Harry and Pelham. Boyle,[232] Gratton O'Leary (of the Ottawa Journal), Alex Johnston,[233] and Senator Norman Lambert[234] were there. And Friday noon Billy Boyle gave a lunch with the same crowd, with Brockington[235] coming in afterwards.

Most important of all I got a letter from Chief of the Naval Staff Capt. Harry de Wolfe[236] to the Admiral of the North Atlantic Squadron giving me access to everything, ships, officers, ratings and the officers' mess at the Admiralty House in Halifax. I can get the use of the Admiralty Barge – the Moby Dick, for short runs around the Port. I may get a trip in a destroyer if one is available.

I shall have a week in Halifax before I start any lecturing and I am going to concentrate naval activities within that week if possible. There will, however, be week-ends, Friday afternoon till Sunday night, when I can get a lot of interviews.

Bill Strange[237] and Lorne Richardson loaded me with information and introduced me to a number of fine fellows who were marvellously cooperative. Did I tell you on the last card that Mazzoleni[238] came into Harry's place Wednesday evening and mingled with the boys. Oh this train!!

---

232 See the note to 'Boyle' in the letter to Albert G. Hatcher, 3 January 1945 (p. 311).

233 Unidentified.

234 Norman P. Lambert (b. 1885), educated at the University of Toronto, was for some years on the staff of the *Globe and Mail.* He was appointed to the Canadian Senate in 1938.

235 Leonard W. Brockington.

236 Harry George de Wolfe (b. 1903) joined the Navy at age fifteen. Given command of a destroyer in 1939, he saw naval service at sea until 1942, when he was posted to Naval Headquarters in Ottawa. He was chief of naval staff (1956–60). (Pratt is incorrect in describing him as chief of naval staff in 1945.)

237 William Strange (b. 1902) wrote for the *Toronto Daily Star* and *Canadian Comment* during the 1930s. He was appointed lieutenant commander of the RCNVR in 1942 and posted to Naval Service Headquarters in Ottawa. In 1945, he was director of naval information.

238 Ettore Mazzoleni. See the letter to Claire Pratt, 11 May 1945 (p. 333).

In an hour I shall go straight to Pine Hill Divinity Residence.[239] There will probably be some mail for me at the Halifax Club. I shall decide which place shall be my postal centre after Monday. I think however, it shall be Pine Hill. You can write there till I tell you otherwise.

Coming to Halifax will be strange after ten years.

My dearies good night now.

Ned.

TO ELLEN ELLIOTT

June 24, 1945

Dear Ellen:

Thanks for your telegram and letter. I just ran into the Halifax Club and the porter gave me the letter.

I spent an evening with the boys of the Rideau Club, Ottawa; when '*They Are Returning*' was read to the members including Harry Osborne, Pelham Edgar, Senator Norman Lambert, Sir Lyman Duff,[240] Angus MacDonald, Grattan O'Leary and a score of others. You see I got into 'Tory' company through Harry Lambert who is on the CBC. commission[. He] is asking Frigon[241] for a repeat performance soon. The response is far greater than I had expected or even hoped. The timeliness is helpful. I think a 60 cent book with a brochure appearance would do nicely. The C.B.C. readings would be good anticipatory advertisement while MacLean's would be the same inasmuch as their publication was only three fourths or less of the original poem.

As I mentioned in my letter I can hardly expect to bring out another volume within two or three years. I am getting every opportunity under Ottawa authority to visit destroyers and ships generally. I have a letter from the Naval Board to the Admiral of the North Atlantic suggesting trips here and there. I can see that an epic on the R.C.N. must take time, at least two years, to do it properly and I should like to make it the best thing of my life.

---

239 The student residence of Pine Hill Divinity Hall at Dalhousie University.

240 Lyman Poore Duff (1865–1955) practised law in British Columbia before being appointed in 1906 to the Supreme Court of Canada, where he served for nearly forty years. Knighted in 1934, he was chief justice from 1933 to 1943.

241 Augustin Frigon was general manager of the CBC (1944–51).

Did I tell you that Simpsons[242] is taking a page of advertisement for July 1 and using a small section of the They Are Returning? Miss Mary Dalley[243] told me that when the poem is published as a whole the firm will put 'weight' behind the publicity. I didn't charge anything for July 1, as the whole business is a patriotic gesture, but I readily acceded to the idea of the publicity later. Do you know Mary? She is a peach and I am sure she will do anything to support sales next fall.

While the book will not be hard cover, I think it should be more durable than Dunkirk which frayed easily, even if the price had to be 60 cents or so. You will understand this part of it better than I and I'll trust your judgment.

I shall be back by the 12th of August.

Yes, Wells is going to town. He says the book[244] is on your poor little pooh-pooh. Bart Brebner of the History Dept. of Columbia says it is a grand job he has done. Wells has Klinck do the biographical part and Wells himself has done the critical analysis. He sent me some chapters on the Titanic, Brébeuf, & the Roosevelt which are all any man could wish in point of enthusiasm. As the book will support Knopf's edition shouldn't Knopf do the job with a Canadian backing? If the 'Collected' has a steady sale the other would supplement it as Wells is the best authority on American poetry in the U.S. His two books *The Old and the New* and the *American Poets* are in their way classics and I feel greatly bucked up. His account of the 'Titanic' poem thrilled me more than the poem itself.

I shall be writing you again in a few days as I am going to dot the i's and cross the t's of the new poem & send it on. Would it be possible to have three copies of it and give me one, as I have to rely on my writing which is a bit illegible as you know.

Take care of yourself & have a holiday. My address will be the Halifax Club, Halifax, N.S.

Ned

242 Robert Simpson Ltd., a large Toronto department and mail order store.

243 A member of Simpson's staff, responsible for the book department.

244 The book on Pratt that Wells and Klinck were writing.

TO VIOLA PRATT

Sunday a.m. [24 June 1945]

Dearest Vi:

Here I am at the Halifax Club. I spent last night quite comfortably at the Pine Hill Divinity Residence. The Matron, Mrs Marion Grant gave me a room which after all is for myself alone, the other fellow not turning up for the Summer School. It's like all Residences – a little bed in the corner and long corridors outside, the dining room being downstairs, the menu being cornflakes, egg, bread, coffee, marmalade. All right. I left early this morning to scout around and get to know the streets and my way about, to make certain I distinguish between north and south and remember the names of the principal streets.

I found my way to the Club with the aid of 6 men and 1 woman taken separately, helped out by two street car conductors. Dr Henry Munro had made the arrangements for me, so here I am with all the privileges. I think you had better address all letters to this Club. It is central and I shall be here for lunch regularly except when I am out on the ships. I have yet to get in touch with Lt. Commander Slater.[245] I shall do so today and see what can be done about boarding the destroyers. Certainly I have not lacked Ottawa authority.

So the furnace man came. Your letter reached me on the afternoon I left Ottawa, just in time. I do hope the heat comes on uninterruptedly next fall. Did he mention the radiator system as partly responsible? He might have cleaned out that perhaps.

I am going over now to the CNR station and get my trunk – valise. I couldn't bring it up last night as the place was thronged. I may have to pay something for storage.

Let me know if the C.B.C. brings out 'Returning' soon. Senator Norman Lambert of Ottawa was going to suggest its reappearance to general manager Frigon. Macmillans will bring it out but I think it will be impossible to get a hard cover on account of the bindery business being such a bottleneck. They might do it a year from now but that's too late. If it is soft they can manage it in two or three months – 2500 copies.

245 [*sic*]. William Sclater was born (1907) in Scotland and, after military service in the Far East, came to Canada in 1931. He served with the Canadian Navy during the Second World War. His *Haida* won a Governor General's Award in 1947.

Ellen Elliott told me too that they were most interested in Wells' book. If Knopf & Macmillans together can bring that out for American & Canadian publication it will be a grand thing for a steady sale for the future. Ellen was in New York last week and Knopf told her that while the sales at present were not great, yet they were steady and he expected a steady sale for years, but certainly Wells' book would help and I am glad Macmillans would take a good slab of the issue.

Love
Ned.

TO VIOLA PRATT

Tuesday
June 26 [1945]

Vi dear:

Your letter written on Sunday p.m. just came. It took just the third day which is normal. I am installed quite comfortably – a good room and bed at Pine Hill Residence. I leave there after breakfast and come right down to the Halifax Club where I meet my old friends at lunch. I had lunch with Sir Joseph Chisholm and the American Consul yesterday. In the afternoon I was called for by Bill Sclater (Lt Commander) who took me for a trip on the Admiral's barge – the Moby Dick. We visited the Haida, and the minesweeper Kapuskasing, and I had tea & dinner with Lt Com. Sturdy[246] and his officers. Late in the evening an English minesweeper drew up and the officers boarded our ship for a lengthy chat.

Today Bill is taking me out on the Ad.[247] barge (outside the Harbour) to dip a salute to the Aquitania which is coming in with a load of troops. The barge is misnamed. It is a beautiful yacht red-painted used by the Admiral on his rounds from ship to ship. As it happens Admiral Jones[248] is away this week and

---

246 John Rhodes Sturdy joined the Royal Canadian Naval Volunteer Reserve in Montreal in 1941. He served on a number of naval ships including the minesweeper *Kapuskasing* of which he was first lieutenant. In 1942, he was liaison officer with Universal Pictures for the filming of *Corvette* with Randolph Scott.

247 Admiral's.

248 George C. Jones (1895–1946) joined the Navy in 1911 and served in the First World War. He commanded the North Atlantic Squadron of the Royal Canadian Navy (1940–2) and was chief of naval staff (1944–6).

Sclater is in command. The big event will be towards the end of the week when the new ship (destroyer) Micmac goes for her first speed and gunnery trials. I am invited so that will be an experience indeed.

It is certainly going to be a difficult job learning the ways of the ship and her instruments – bigger even than I anticipated and I'll take the necessary time.

They Are Returning will be published all right but I expect it will be a compromise on the cover. They can't get it out in hard cover this fall as the binding bottleneck is just as bad as last year. Ellen told me that they would make it nicer and more durable than Dunkirk.

Will you watch for July 1st papers & see if Simpson's ad features the poem & what part it selects. Simpson's will be quite a help next fall when the thing appears. I told Ellen that Clee[249] is no longer there but I am glad that it is the business side of the firm not simply the book section that is interested.

So the heat wave has struck you. I hope you don't suffer too much with it. Keep in or around the house and premises. Get under the shade of the scarlet ramblers.

I am writing this letter now in the reading room of the Halifax Club. The word *Silence* is written in big Capitals over the mantelpiece. It suits me splendidly. The room is quite dark and cool. Halifax, as you know, *swelters* in the 80's.

Well darlin' every good wish to you.

Love,
Ned

Did I tell you that I left my waterproof at Harry's and he had to send it on express?

TO CLAIRE PRATT

June 27, 1945

Sweetest Cayke:

I shall pen this little note to you. One might think I was a prince of the royal blood the way I am feted by the naval officers here. I go around in the Admiral's yacht, the Moby Dick, gangways are put down for me, the hands of officers and ratings assist me over rails and up ladders until I feel almost uncomfortable at the vice-regal attention.

---

249 Unidentified. See letter to Viola Pratt, 24 June 1940 (p. 187).

Yesterday I went out on the Moby Dick to meet the Aquitania beyond the gate of Halifax. She came in with 8000 soldiers and our little green and red yacht (barge) accompanied her in officially to the dock. On the other side of the big ship a fire boat was sending up huge streams of water from six fire hoses and sirens were blowing all over the harbour.

Today I was guest on the *Micmac* the last tribal destroyer to be built in the Halifax yards. She went out on her gunnery trial. I had my photograph taken with the Commander on the bridge. If they release it I shall send it on but I do not think you and mother would recognize me all buttoned up with the wind breaks and reefers looking strangely odd with my grey fedora on top of it all.

It was quite cold and blustery because we were on the fringe of the great hurricane which was sweeping north from Nantucket. But I wasn't in the least seasick, having remained on the bridge all day except for one hour for dinner. Nevertheless, as I am writing this, the walls of the Club room are heaving.

The officer (first Lieutenant) put wool in my ears and told me to keep my mouth open when the 4.7. (four-pound-sevens) opened fire. The shots were seen three miles away sending up geysers as the shells exploded when they hit the water.

So I have had my destroyer run. I am glad it came this week when I was free. The rest of the week I shall occupy in studying the ships.

The RCN car comes for me every morning at the Halifax Club and takes me to the Dockyard then brings me back. If it goes on much longer I shall put on the attire of an Indian Maharajah or the Prince or Duke of Plazalora.

Most of my buttons burst off my coat and vest today, so tomorrow I am going to Woolworth's to get a kit of needles, buttons, thread and a scissors. No longer shall I have occasion to wear my silver gown.[250] Tell Mother to donate it to the museum. I have travelled miles ahead of dull undergraduate apparel. It belongs now to the class of short pants and dickies. Away with it! It has no further spell over me – no power to inflate my spirit. Tell mother, I say, to put it out on the clothesline for a scarecrow, or to wave it in front of Jack the next time he barks.

With worlds of love to you
and mother,
Father- hub.

250 See the note to 'my silver gown' in the letter to Viola Pratt, 27 July 1944 (p. 282).

TO PELHAM EDGAR

June 29, 1945.

Dear Pelham:

I have had a week of almost bewildering activity on the sea. I spent days on the Haida, Kapuskasing and other tribals and minesweepers, on the bridge, in the wardrooms and down in the engine rooms and stokeholds.

The letter I got from the Chief of the Naval Staff worked wonders. Signals came from Ottawa to the Staff here and really it was a gala week. Yesterday I went out as the guest on the Micmac on her trial spin and gunnery practice. Today I had a fifty mile trip on a Fairmile[251] and the rest of the time I spent on the Moby Dick the Admirals 'barge' so that wherever I went sailors stood at attention on the ship. It was so damned funny, having the gangways put down for crossing from the dockyards to the ships, being helped over rails and simply drowned in Nelson's blood at the end of every voyage – a concoction of double-distilled rum which took the varnish out of the intestinal canals. I dined with the Captains of the Skeena & Iroquois. Foursomes are being arranged out at the Brightwood links and dinners at the Lord Nelson. What an orgy! I have put on six pounds the result of heavy and bloody carbohydrates every meal.

And now next week, I have to lecture to the NUNS at the Convent of the Sacred Heart. God bless the dears!

Right through the ten weeks I am here I am going to use the Admiralty pass and make good use of it.

In reciprocity I gave two dinners of broiled lobster to ten Captains & Commanders, and rolled home to my lodgings at the Pine Hill Divinity residence at 1 a.m.

'They Are Returning' is going on the air as a 'repeat' next Sunday as a special feature in the July 1 celebration. It evidently is taking hold. The Nova Scotia station is putting it on again on July 26, the reader being Ted Roberts,[252] a magnificent reader who once played Antony in Benson's[253] Julius Caesar twenty years ago.

---

251 A small naval craft, in size between a torpedo boat and a corvette.

252 A part-time actor affiliated with King's College, where he taught elocution and sometimes led the glee club choir.

253 Nathaniel A. Benson (1903–1967) was born and educated in Toronto. At various times a journalist, teacher, and advertising executive, he wrote and published several small books of verse and edited *Modern Canadian Poetry* (Ottawa: Graphic Publishers Ltd., 1930).

He is the most wonderful reader & declaimer I have met in a long time – a friend of Wilson Knight[254] by the way. Macmillan's is bringing out the poem early in the fall.

What a grand night we had with Boyle, Harry, O'Leary, Lambert. I took a great shine to Lambert. It was a peak of exhilaration.

My love to Dona, Jane & your dear self.

Your reading last week in that little circle was just sublime.

lovingly
Ned.

TO DOUGLAS BUSH

Halifax Club
Halifax N.S.

July 1, 1945

Dear Doug:

I was delighted to get your note this morning. It was forwarded to me from Toronto.

Thanks for your kind words about the 'Collected' edition and for passing the volume on to Bliss Perry[255] whose work I have long known and greatly admired. To have Perry even to read some of the contents is an achievement for me.

I trust the Knopf edition gets a view, for the sake of Knopf who took over all the risk of a Canadian publication in the U.S.A.

You may wonder – why this letterhead? Well, I had a break. The Admiralty Board at Ottawa offered me access to the ships of the Navy for the Summer for the purpose of getting a poem 'done' on the operations in the North Atlantic. The Board wants records in verse as well as in documentary prose. I've taken on a big job because, although I should know something of the sea and fore-and-afters, I know little about destroyers and corvettes. Hence I have spent the last two weeks

---

254 Shakespearean scholar, director, and actor G. Wilson Knight (1897–1985) had been professor of English at Trinity College, Toronto, during the 1930s. He and Pratt had become good friends.

255 Perry (1860–1954), American author and scholar, taught English literature at Princeton (1893–1939) and at Harvard (1899–1930). He was the author of many books, fiction and non-fiction. Bush had been his student in the 1920s.

out to sea in the Micmac, a tribal destroyer.[256] She had just been built and had to go through her gunnery and speed trials. I had exciting times on the bridge with Commander Hennessey listening to the 4.7s sending shells five miles out and to the Oerlikons 'ratatatating' a hundred yards from the ship at an imaginary sub. My ears are still buzzing though they were filled with wool during the shooting.

The dinners at night were hilarious in the wardroom. Double-distilled rum straight from Newfoundland and called 'Nelson's blood' fortified us for all the ordeals. I loved the boys and their hospitality. I got yarns that are simply incredible and my job I suppose is to make them credible.

I went out one day on the Admiral's barge – the '*Moby Dick*' – to accompany the Aquitania into the Halifax dock. The Coxswain was a commando on D-Day and given the cushy job because of exploits which were worthy of a V.C.

The Head of the whole business here is Vice-Admiral Jones. He is a grand fellow packed with a gorgeous brand of profanity. He gave me a Pass to any bloody spot in the circus.

During the next week I shall be in and out of Halifax. I am due to arrive in Toronto by the 10th of August.

With every good wish.
Ned Pratt

TO VIOLA PRATT

July 1, 1945

Dearest Vi:

I sent a telegram about the broadcast which takes place tonight at 8:45. I hope Gregory[257] is as good as Drainey[258] though the latter came in for a bit of criticism.

---

256 This is very misleading. Pratt had been in Halifax only one week and had spent one day on the *Micmac*.

257 Context suggests that this is to be the presenter of that evening's CBC broadcast of 'They Are Returning'; however, in the letter to Viola Pratt, 8 July 1945, Pratt compares the performances of 'Maynard' and John Drainie, who had narrated the original broadcast on 12 June. (See the letter to Ellen Elliott, 15 June 1945 [p. 337].)

258 [*sic*]. John Drainie (1916–66) joined the staff of the CBC in 1941 after several years as a radio announcer and actor, and a short stint in Hollywood. He later worked as a freelance announcer and actor. He is best known for playing Jake in the long-running radio series based on W.O. Mitchell's *Jake and the Kid*, and for the one-man stage show in which he played humorist Stephen Leacock. Pratt consistently misspells his name as 'Drainey.'

So Calvert[259] came and went. I had a funny experience last week. A message came from the Nova Scotia Hotel to the Halifax Club. 'Your nephew, sir, is telephoning you. Would you call to see him at room 610.' I immediately hiked over, went to the room, knocked, and was admitted. I apologized for entering the wrong room as I didn't know the occupant. As I was leaving he said, 'Why, it's Uncle Ned. I know you from Uncle Cal.' It was Jack[260] whom I had never seen or I might have seen him when he was a baby. He had intended going to Toronto but found that accommodation on the trains was impossible through the congestion of soldiers. Hence he is returning to St John's. Jack is a very handsome fellow – well-built and bears no resemblance whatsoever to any of the Pratt family, in my judgment. I couldn't detect one trace of similarity except perhaps to Will[261] and that was slight. He was exceedingly nice and affable, less constrained than Ewart,[262] less formal. I spent an hour with him and his friend, a chap named Dawe from Bay Roberts.[263]

I haven't seen Ewart yet but expect to soon. His address is the Sword and Anchor Apts Halifax.

Yesterday I was on the Moby Dick again, this time to escort the Pasteur, a liner of 40,000 tons, into dock. Six thousand soldiers were on board.

I do not have to take any more lengthy trips now, unless Admiral Jones invites me specially. He wrote the general invitation first. It is Lt. Cdr. Bill Sclater who is my guide. I am quite fond of him and he makes sure I see and hear everything. Next Wednesday I start lecturing – twice a day. I do not expect I shall be getting any golf or at least much golf this summer. I shall be too busy. All my spare time will be taken up in quizzing sailors. I shall not start writing till after I get back and I really do not know what kind of a thing it will turn out to be.

Sunday (today) is a lonely day. I am at the Halifax Club all day writing & reading, gets information into shape. I wish I could fly across to 21 Cortleigh to see dear you and Cayke. The first week, though it was full of excitement, did seem long. I am looking forward now to Aug.12 when I land in the presence of my beloved. Watch the beans.[264]

With an Atlantic of love,
Ned

---

259 Not his brother, who was invariably called Cal, but his brother's younger son.

260 John Kerr Pratt (1909–80), eldest son of Pratt's brother James. A St John's businessman, he was father of the painter Christopher Pratt.

261 William Knight Pratt (1878–1924), Pratt's eldest brother, who had left home as a young man and died 'under mysterious circumstances' in the United States.

262 Elder son of his brother Cal.

263 John K. Pratt had married Christine Dawe of Bay Roberts; this was probably a relative.

264 The scarlet runner beans he grew in the backyard at Cortleigh Blvd.

TO ELLEN ELLIOTT

July 7, 1945

Dear Ellen:

The cover design is good.[265]

I have been thinking over the sub-title – 'A Canadian Poem' and have come to the conclusion that it is not necessary in the Canadian publication. I had in mind only the possibility of an American magazine appearance following Maclean's, but that is now not feasible.

I do not think Knopf would want to publish anything else by me just now because the 'Collected' is only being started and it would conflict with the larger interest. It will take a good year before the big volume gets known properly in the States.

Perhaps Knopf might be interested later.

I know you are keeping in mind the English market for the Collected now that the European war is over. I imagine that a newer and more modern publisher might be interested over there rather than the English Macmillans. I have had considerable correspondence with English writers wondering why my books are not available in any of the stores. Vincent Massey wrote me sometime ago hoping that the 'Collected' might be procurable soon.[266] I suppose the paper situation must be easing up.

You will let me know, I am sure, whenever the chances improve.

In the meantime I think we could eliminate the sub-title in 'They Are Returning.'

The best
Ned P.

TO VIOLA PRATT

Sunday a.m. [8 July 1945]

Dearest Vi:

Your welcome letter written Friday afternoon was just brought in to me by the Secretary of the Club.

265 For the booklet *TAR*.
266 These letters have not been found.

I have just come down from Pine Hill to spend the day at the Club reading and working.

I am going to change my room at the Residence if it is possible. There are 100 girls in the place that keep up an infernal racket till long after midnight. They are Normal School teachers and though there is a notice posted up on every door to keep quiet at night, they pay no attention to it. Friday night I couldn't stand the tramping in the room overhead and the shrieking. I went outside and banged on the walls and called out in a most plaintive voice – 'Please keep quiet. Time 1:15 a.m.'

And then last night sharp at 12, all the buzzers started going at once and a gong just outside my door clanged for ten minutes at full blast. A girl kept hitting it with a stick while all the school got up and rushed down. I didn't know till this morning it was fire alarm drill. Boy, how they shrieked with delight at the mock alarm. I nearly shrieked with panic for I was just beginning to doze off.

Give me the destroyers and their four-point-sevens going off at fast time than those howling mad whirling dervishes of Nova Scotian Normal School teachers. So this morning I asked the matron if she could find a room somewhere in an attic or basement where I might get out of the range of chaos. She smiled & said she would look into the matter.

Other than that, the situation is good. Give me the cabbage-bean tempo you refer to or the destroyers – two extremes and I'll enjoy life.

So you preferred Drainey to Maynard on the broadcast.[267] So did I. Drainey caught an enthusiasm and a pulse which Maynard, though good, did not, in his otherwise fine & deliberate enunciation.

Tell Cayke I wrote Wells[268] yesterday and told him that she threatened me with the doom of the dinosaurs unless I acknowledge his pleiocene pamphlets.[269]

Best regards to Dorothy and Carol[270] and love to your sweet self and to Cakes. The weeks are slipping away. Halifax is an awful city to live in. Still I am saving on this trip. Henry Munro is making a special allowance for me to cover transportation. Cakes will have her thousand all right for next year besides what she has now in New York.

---

267 Drainie's name is consistently misspelled. Drainie had been the narrator of the original broadcast of 'They Are Returning' on 12 June; Maynard is unidentified, but context suggests that he narrated the second broadcast on 1 July.

268 Henry W. Wells.

269 Reference obscure.

270 Dorothy Sigmund and Carol Cassidy.

I am finding it hard to get started on the poem. Can't select the right form apparently. Guess it will come eventually.

Lovingly
Ned.

TO VIOLA PRATT

Halifax Club
Halifax N.S.

July 14, 1945

Darling Vi

Your letter of yesterday evening came this morning. What a transit for the air mail! I send mine surface and air alternately.

Yes I have a very quiet room now. Dr Stanley Walker, President of King's College,[271] offered me a very large room in his Residence with bath, many cupboards and a reception room. The whole suite was used by the Commanding Officer in the Navy and was known as the Quarter Deck. It is so quiet I can hear the squirrels scamper and the pigeons coo. No snoring, no fire alarms, no leap-frog at midnight. It is ideal now.

Bill Sclater is one of the best friends I have ever made. He was really assigned by Admiral Jones to look after me. The staff car and the Admiral's Barge are at my disposal though I don't intend to outwear my privileges. Bill is Public Relations Officer and has the rank of Commander. His wife, Gladys Jean, formerly of Glasgow is a charming little girl with the most delightful Scotch accent I have ever heard (apart from your own, of course, ha! ha!). They were married last October and were engaged four years ago, but they have seen each other only on the odd week-ends all that time. He has been in Malaya, Hong Kong, the Mediterranean, in fact all over the world, and hopes to write after the war. His wife you would like immensely I am sure. I hope they live in Toronto. He is a cousin of Dr Sclater[272] who married them. He is volunteering for the Pacific

---

271 Born (1890) and educated in England, he had been professor of history at King's College since 1923 and president since 1937.

272 Reverend J.R.P. Sclater, born (1876) and educated in England, had been minister of Old St Andrew's United Church in Toronto since 1924. He was moderator of the United Church (1942–4).

– just out of a sense of duty – as he certainly wants to settle down after living in a turmoil for six years. He's bringing out a book on the Haida for Bill Clarke.[273] That is the reason why I have enlarged my subject to the R.C.N. activities generally and will start with the Skeena – just as full of action as the Haida. In that case there will be no conflict between Macmillans & Oxford. It suits my plans just as well and it doesn't cut in on either Bill Sclater or Bill Clarke.

The job will take a long time and it will be difficult. But I have no need to be rushed. And '*They Are Returning*' will fill in the gap between the Collected and the RCN. (whenever the latter is published – say two or three years).

Ellen[274] says the paper shortage is terrible and the bindery business still worse. But she will bring out an edition of 2500 with better, more durable paper than 'Dunkirk.'

Poor Carol with that awful expense.[275] The sum is terrific, $330.00! How they soak the poor in heart in this world and I may add the poor in pocket.

I have to give two recitals this next week – the Summer School on Thursday night and Mount St. Vincent (where Sister Mauyra is if that is any enlightenment to you) on Friday. I am being paid $25.00 for the first and I have offered the second gratis for I couldn't gyp that flowery-bowery brood of wimple-covered Sisters of Mercy. They are sweet and their penguin costumes would greatly appeal to Cayke. I do not, however, intend to make any analogy on Friday night with the tumbling denizens of the Arctic as they roll down to the waters.

With everlasting love,
Ned.

TO HENRY W. WELLS

July 17, 1945.

Dear Henry Wells:

(I think it is about time that we quit this Doctoring and Professoring each other. Bart Brebner always referred to you as Henry and somehow I have got into the habit of talking about you to my friends in the same manner. What about it?)

Well to business. Your letter today was a delight. It was so helpful constructively, as I have always realized the soundness of your critical judgments.

273 W.H. Clarke of Oxford University Press.
274 Ellen Elliott of Macmillan.
275 Reference unknown.

In fact I have just sent an air letter to the Macmillan Editor asking her to change the word 'lofty' to 'stubborn' to avoid the *cliché*.[276] You are right there. I had some qualms myself when I put it in. I had thought first of putting it in italics as it is a repeated borrowing, Milton having cribbed it from Spenser in the first place.[277]

I spent the last two hours selecting a word out of about one hundred possibles. 'Stubborn' would be at least fresh in this context but, more than that, it conveys to me the suggestion of the terrifically intractable material out of which the new world must be built. It gives the sense of counterpoint necessary to the evolution of a theme. I may be overworking a simple matter but I think the change gets rid of a facile run and substitutes an architectonic point. I thank you for it.

I went over the proof two days ago and made two or three other changes. I changed the word *refine* to *congeal*. The former has been used often enough e.g. 'in wickedness refined' and so on. *Congeal* suggests that frozen indifference to anguish on the faces of the camp commandants. The photographs coming from Germany reflect it.

Again, I changed 'Prussian' (Maclean's) to 'regimental' – not a very important change perhaps but it avoids the hackneyed 'Prussian boot.' That was pointed out to me by an esteemed English colleague who heard the poem on the radio and felt the phrase was jarring.

The Maclean's presentation was a bit disturbing. Apart from the red saturation of the type on the first page which made it so hard to read, the editor exercised his editorial discretion to comply with space requirements. It simply *had* to go on *two* pages so the vignettes, units in themselves, were deleted. They always do these things, and since they paid me $150.00 for the poem they reckoned they had proprietory privileges. The radio version, however, kept in the passage – 'What made the change?' and the bit on the *plasma*.

I am interested in your new project on Emily.[278] I admire her work very much indeed; have always done so. What a lift from early obscurity that girl is deservedly getting today! And what I love about you and your work is your superb catholicity as against the dogmatism and pedantry of so many critics writing at this moment with their blindness to the great tradition and its values. I shall look forward to your book.

---

276 This section of the letter is closely paraphrased in *E.J. Pratt: The Man and His Poetry*: 'Pratt will devote any amount of time to avoid a cliché' (55).

277 Milton's lines 'Who would not sing for Lycidas? he knew/ Himself to sing, and build the lofty rhyme' ('Lycidas,' 10–11) echo Spenser's 'That little that I am shall all be spent / In setting your immortal prayses forth: / Whose lofty argument, uplifting me,/ Shall lift you up unto an high degree.' (*Amoretti* 82, 9–12).

278 Emily Dickinson (1830–86), American poet. Wells's study was published as *An Introduction to Emily Dickinson* (Chicago: Packard and Sons, 1947).

I am delighted at the interest both Macmillans and Knopf are taking in your manuscript.[279]

I am gathering material every day for my new task. As I said before it may be two years before I get it completed. I haven't decided on the form yet. Blank verse is playing about in my mind. I do not think the tetrameter suits it. As you say that form is a bit slight for the compass. A variation as in 'The Witches Brew' might do, as so many moods could be poured into it. I should dearly like if you could think over the question and offer your opinion later on when I make further progress. Any letters from you will be deeply appreciated. I enjoy this correspondence with you more than I can tell.

Most sincerely,
Ned Pratt

TO VIOLA PRATT

Thursday a.m. [19 July 1945]

Dearest Vi:

You may be hearing about the explosions at Halifax.[280] They started last night on the other side of the Harbour, and all through the night they kept going.

The ammunition depots caught fire and much glass was destroyed. The C.B.C. made it out to be worse than it was though the damage to property was considerable. There weren't many casualties. The site is about six miles from the University but the sounds were like heavy thunder claps.

This morning when I went down to the Convent I found all the nuns out in the grounds under the trees. The lecture was called off, and so was the 11 a.m. one. I don't think I shall be lecturing tonight nor tomorrow night as students' nerves are in a bit of a tatter.

I am just sending this off by airmail in a rush as telegrams are prohibited for most of this day. I did think of telegraphing you merely to allay fears which were created unnecessarily by exaggerated reports.

---

279 Of the book on Pratt which he and Carl Klinck were writing.

280 On 18 July 1945, Halifax was wracked by a series of severe explosions. They began in the late afternoon, when a carelessly thrown cigarette ignited straw in an ammunition barge near the Navy's main Bedford Basin Magazine. The fire spread to several sections of the magazine, causing a series of powerful blasts. Casualties, fortunately, were few, but there

I suppose by now Claire is back from Stauffers'[281] and at work in the Wesley Bld.[282]

Lovingly
Ned.

TO E.K. BROWN

Halifax, N.S.

July 27, 1945

Dear Ed:

Your letter was forwarded to me from Toronto. Here I am at Halifax between naval trips. Most of my time I spend on destroyers and frigates and on the Admiral's barge, the *Moby Dick*.[283] They gave me access to every thing, ships, logs, and files and I remain here until the 10th of August. Imagine an Admiralty Staff car placed at my disposal for nearly two months – to go any where I like. Last week-end Commander Sclater took me from Halifax to Liverpool (130 miles) where I stayed on board of the Port Colborne, a frigate, and got a lot of data about asdics.[284]

I do not expect to get this job done inside of a couple of years. It is a tremendous task and I haven't yet decided on the form it should take.

I have so much news to tell you when we meet that I can't put on paper. When you come to Toronto give me first chance to get at you for several dinners and evenings. I shall burst otherwise. It gives me joy to know you will be in Toronto for a fortnight. I shall be there all through September. I have the

---

was considerable damage in the city of Halifax, primarily 'windows and doors and plaster' (letter to Viola and Claire Pratt, 20 July [*EJP: Web*]).

281 Ruth Stauffer was one of Claire's classmates. Claire visited the Stauffer family farm from time to time.

282 The United Church Publishing House, where Claire worked for several summers, assisting in the production of the church's *Year Book*.

283 A considerable exaggeration.

284 A device using high-frequency sound waves to detect underwater objects. The name is derived from the scientific body in England responsible for its invention: Allied Submarine Detection Investigation Committee. It was changed to *sonar*, derived from '*so*und *na*vigation *r*anging.' Pratt's schoolmate Dr Robert William Boyle was one of the inventors.

dope on Stanley[285] right from the mouths of horses and asses. God it is funny, and serious. Stanley's defects are only temperamental. I always admired the fellow for courage but I still think Aristotle's golden mean is as good as anything Christianity has to offer in respect to that one important virtue.

And then there's H.L. Stewart, of Philosophy. I saw him yesterday. He is writing an article to Cultur (Quebec)[286] on the sad condition of Universities in this country saying that they have never been at a lower ebb. He roared all this out to me at the car intersection yesterday. He drowned the cars and you should know what Halifax cars are like. His particular animosities are Sid Smith and the new Pres. of U.N.B. When he discovered that I was a special friend of Sid's he moderated his voice. He had coined one clever phrase which he thinks will act like H.E.[287] when it is published. Referring to University Presidents he said they might know something about the government of people but they know nothing about the government of *prepositions*!! A direct slap at Sid & the other fellow. I told him that Sid was making good at the U of T, and that if he sometimes lost sight of the nominative case, well, it was a fault which we all committed occasionally. Stewart has become rabid on the point. That's only a fraction of the story.

I went through the Halifax explosion last week – got turned round in my bed at the now famous 4 a.m. detonation. More of that anon.

I didn't tell you that the poem I worked at last winter & spring was put over the C.B.C. twice this last month. It is called 'They Are Returning,' on the men coming back. It seems to have gone across. I can't tell yet what virtue it has but at least Edgar was enthusiastic and Ed. Corbett[288] – a fair balance of critical temperaments.

It is an occasional piece like Dunkirk, though not quite as long. Macmillans are printing three thousand edition next month. All I can say about it is that it may fill out the interval between the Collected and the next (more substantial) appearance which may be two or three years. I am not putting up any special claims for it beyond its timeliness. I hope you will like it however. I shall send you a copy when it comes out. It will appear unpretentiously, in the form of a brochure; soft-covered.

---

285 Carleton Stanley (see the note to 'Stanley' in the letter to Hugh Eayrs, 9 July 1932 [p. 98]) had just been relieved of the presidency of Dalhousie University.

286 One of the few bilingual scholarly journals in Canada.

287 High explosives.

288 Edward A. Corbett, born (1887) in Nova Scotia and educated at McGill University, was director of the Canadian Association for Adult Education. He was a founder of the Banff School of Fine Arts (1933) and developed several educational radio series, including *Farm Radio Forum* and *Citizens Forum.*

I shall be glad to see your article on Conrad.[289] Of course, I think he is worth a dozen Jameses. He always thrilled me while James often bored me. That intensity of life, as you say, and the sense of conflict mean so much.

You are well known here in Halifax. Judge Chisholm (now Sir Joseph) and Henry Munro (Superintendent of Education) knew your 'On Canadian Poetry' from beginning to end. So did Dan Harvey (archivist),[290] a real admirer of yours. He thinks, as Sandwell[291] does, that you are the one incisive critic we have.

The 'Collected' is having a good press in the States. Knopf reported to Mrs Elliott[292] that while the sales did not start off with a bang yet there was a steady stream of orders increasing, slowly but surely from month to month, and that he had a long-term view of the book. The New York Times had a good review – Rosenberger's[293] and then a warm reference to it this week in a more general article by J. Donald Adams.[294] Adams wrote to me specially a few days ago inviting me to see him in New York should I go down.

Thanks old chap for the word passed on to the Yale review. I have had four letters from Tinker.[295] He is a dear.

What conference is this at Banff?[296] How I wish I could be with you. In fact I miss you a lot, but there is always the hope of having you return to Toronto.

Remember, much of your time in Toronto in September belongs to me.

My love to Peggy & yourself. Vi loves the two of you as much as I do and that's saying sumpin.

Ned.

289 Brown's article, 'James and Conrad,' was published in the *Yale Review* (Winter 1945–6): 265–85.

290 Daniel C. Harvey (1886–1996), formerly professor of history at the universities of Manitoba and British Columbia, was chief archivist at the Public Archives of Nova Scotia in Halifax.

291 B.K. Sandwell.

292 Ellen Elliott of Macmillan.

293 Coleman Rosenberger was a New York journalist who wrote for several American papers. His review of Pratt's *CPA* appeared in the *N.Y. Times Book Review* 20 May 1945, 5.

294 See letter to Adams dated 14 June 1945 (*EJP: Web*). Adams's 'warm reference' to Pratt's *CPA* appeared in the *N.Y. Times Book Review*, 22 July 1945, 2.

295 Professor Chauncey B. Tinker of Yale University. See the letter to E.K. Brown, 6 December 1943 (p. 269).

296 The Banff School of Fine Arts was established by the University of Alberta on a grant from the Carnegie Corporation in 1933 to teach summer courses in theatre, music, and fine arts. In 1944, a special Writers' Conference had been held to encourage Alberta writers. In 1945, the school was to host a similar conference in cooperation with the American English Association, and Brown had been invited to speak.

TO VIOLA AND CLAIRE PRATT

Friday pm. [27 July 1945]

Darlings both:

Well it is now only two weeks tomorrow. I have my ticket and reservation. I leave here Saturday morning Aug. 10th[297] arriving on Sunday night about ten. Won't it be grand to be back?

I am not going to be so far away again. It is too lonesome.

I had a grand letter from E.K. Brown today. He is going to Banff with the U.S. English Association at the end of August to give an address on Historical material for poetry and he is taking Brébeuf as his main theme. What a friend E.K. is! He sends his love and Peggy's to you & Claire and says he will be in Toronto for two weeks in late September. – We must plan to be with them a bit.

Last night I gave a broadcast on Brébeuf & Silences etc. for a half-hour, through the Halifax local. The 'Chronicle' gave me the records afterwards. They are only able to repeat about a dozen times. I heard my voice today. I can-not tell it as mine. It sounds so much like Mackenzie King's that it is terrifying. And you should hear the whistling whenever an *S* sounds. It shrieks like a siren. I asked the operator if the audience heard it like that, and he said – 'Oh no, all that sibilance is removed by new technique. Thank God. At any rate we must have it when I get back. Put it on once just for entertainment. You will laugh even at Brébeuf.

In any case dear Claire there is $15.00 out of the broadcast for you which I shall send on next week.

I go down to Stewart's[298] a week from tomorrow.

Love & love.
Ned.

297 Saturday was actually 11 August.

298 H.L. Stewart. See the letter to E.K. Brown dated 27 July 1945 (p. 356).

TO VIOLA PRATT

Saturday am. [28 July 1945]

Dearest Vi:

Your letter regarding Birney, Donald Adams, Wyndham,[299] Carol, Floss, Ruth, Norrie, Dorothy[300] just came, and I am rushing off this note to catch the Saturday mail. Thanks for the N.Y. clipping. I just received it from the Sec'y of the Club. Judge Chisholm pointed it out. It all helps.

Do you know that you used a most graphic word to describe Toronto's entrance into the heat wave? 'We have *lurched* into a heat wave.' Excellent – how much more powerful and picturesque than 'entered.' It connotes stumbling, lassitude, inebriation, vertigo which come with the 90's. Keep it up, and tell Cayke that she often hits on those unusual and idiosyncratic expressions especially when she does it unconsciously.

I have just returned from the launching of the 'Cayuga,' a destroyer. The wife of the Commodore hit the plates three times with the bottle of champagne before it burst. Egad, she was nervous after the second dud, with five thousand people looking on and laughing.

I remarked to Chisholm, 'Third time is lucky,' but I hope she doesn't have to hit it the 4th time. She put her bag down for the third shot and used her whole body. She was as thin as a tooth pick. I thought she would crack in two and I wondered if it was her spine or the bottle that made the noise. 'Rule Britannia' was played as she swung her arms to the rhythms.

I shall keep the account given by the papers and the photographs & send them on to you.

I am getting ready now for my recital tonight to the sweet penguin-dressed sisters.

Ned.

---

299 Modernist painter, writer, and critic Percy Wyndham Lewis (1884–1957) was born in Amherst, Nova Scotia, to British and American parents, and lived most of his life in England, where he was educated at Rugby School and the Slade School of Art. One of the founders of vortism, an artistic movement influenced by the Bloomsbury Group, cubism, and futurism, he served as an artillary officer in the First World War before being appointed by both the British and Canadian governments as a war artist. When the Second World War broke out in 1939, he moved to Toronto, where he and Pratt were casual friends.

300 Carol Cassidy, Pratt's sister Florence (Floss), Ruth Stauffer, Northrop Frye. and Dorothy Sigmund.

TO CLAIRE PRATT

Wednesday noon [1 Aug.1945]

Dearest Cayke:

I am enclosing a cheque for $25.00. This morning I received my pay for the Summer School recital last Thursday night.[301] As there would be 50 cents discount on the cheque if I sent it to Toronto I deposited it in my bank here and am sending its equivalent drawn on the Royal Bank.

I hope you don't have to work much in this heat wave which I hear has invaded Toronto. Up to the present it has been fine but you are bound to get the waves sometime or other.

The weather here has been perfect, with the nights quite cool. Last evening I sat out on the lawn with Professor Burns Martin[302] and we swapped stories. He told me one of a couple of chaps at Harvard who decided to put over a fast one on the critical cults in poetic criticism.[303] They took a subject and worked out a poem each independently. They then exchanged and each cut out any line which contained an idea or was intelligible. Then they combined the two and submitted the product to an exclusive magazine which printed it with the comment that the poem opened up a new epoch in American poetry. The two authors then put it out in the form of a small book with brilliant format and fine printing and enclosed the comments of the press all favourable. At the bottom of the cover they told the public of the joke they perpetrated. To what depths has the school of obscurity sunk?

Well love to you both! Saturday week I leave here and won't it be good to get back?

Father

301 His recitals took place on Monday, 23 July, at Dalhousie and Saturday, 28 July, at Mount St Vincent – not on Thursday as indicated here.

302 Professor of English at Dalhousie. A frequent reviewer of books for the *DR*, he had treated Pratt's *SL* very harshly in 1943.

303 This anecdote is an Americanized variation on the famous 'Em Malley hoax' perpetrated in 1944 on the Australian avant-garde journal *Angry Penguins* by James McAuley and Harold Stewart. The two invented a fictional poet and wrote his masterwork, a collection of seventeen poems titled *The Darkening Ecliptic*, which was hailed by several major critics and writers as a brilliant piece of surrealist writing.

TO PELHAM EDGAR

Halifax, N.S.

Aug. 2, 1945.

Dear Pelham:

Your letter[304] came yesterday when I was having lunch with a couple of officers (naval) at the Halifax Club.

The 'Roosevelt' business[305] started in 1928. I think it was November when I remarked to you that I should like to spend a week on the steamer and get all the details from the officers and crew. I deplored my lack of funds for the enterprise and you, unknown to me, wrote Flavelle,[306] Stanley MacLean, R.Y. Eaton,[307] MacKelcan[308] and two or three others. The amounts were $50.00 from each I think, totalling $250.00. I was rich for the first time.

The President of the United Steamship Line wrote me offering the courtesy of the ship for as long as I liked. I went and stayed one week on board. I was interested specially in the funeral service held in the saloon of the R on the night of the storm when the two sailors Heitman and Wertanen were drowned. There was a Catholic service following the Protestant one. The service was conducted by a priest who went up on deck at 2 am. and presented the crucifix to the floating bodies. The second officer found out the stateroom occupied by the priest and together we went up the stairs to the boat deck where the priest holding on to a guy rope, flashed the crucifix to the sea.

304 Edgar was writing an essay on Pratt for a special issue of the Quebec journal *Les Gants du Ciel* devoted to English Canadian writing. He had asked Pratt to answer questions about certain of his poems.

305 A reference to Edgar's assistance in arranging financing for a trip to New York to do research on the *Roosevelt* and *Antinoe* story.

306 Not Sir Ellsworth Flavelle, but his father Sir Joseph Flavelle (1858–1939), a wealthy Toronto commercial magnate and financier. He was widely known for his philanthropy.

307 Robert Y. Eaton (1875–1956), a nephew of Timothy Eaton, was an executive of the T. Eaton Company (1904–42), and served as director of several other commercial and financial institutions.

308 Frederick R. MacKelcan (b. 1882) was a lawyer who held executive posts in several corporations and was for many years associated with a number of artistic and cultural institutions in Toronto.

I got the exact messages transmitted from the Antinoe to R and from R to A. A wireless officer described the sounds of the dots & dashes and I made up my own metaphors, etc.

The crew lowered the lifeboats and pulled them up, to show me the process.

The most intricate job was the manoeuvring of the Roosevelt for position. It was a marvel of seamanship and boatmanship.

Brébeuf

Father John Penfold of the Jesuit Seminary at Guelph gave me a lot of help on the matter of ritual. Also Father Lally, the priest in charge of the Shrine. He took me around the sites of the fort and over the general area.

I got the present flora of the Midland territory, assuming it was the same three hundred years ago.

The volumes of the Relations[309] dealing with the period from 1625 to 1650. (I forget the exact numbers.)

Parkman's two volumes on the Jesuits.[310] I used P. for the bird's eye view and went to the Relations for exact details.

When you come to Toronto I shall rake up the lecture I gave[311] – I haven't it with me here, but I think it is at the office. I get back on Aug. 13th. Can you spare a few hours? Let me know your date of arrival. Perhaps we could have a round of golf, too.

The present project is a bit hampered by the secrecy of much of the data. I can't tell everything, as anything I commit to writing must be passed by the censor, such as asdic and Radar techniques which are marvellously fascinating. Imagine a sound, an *echo* being a determinant in the life and death of a ship and crew. The 'Skeena' affair is wonderful.

I spent last week-end on board of the Port Colborne, a frigate, and many days on the Iroquois, Algonquin, Haida, getting first hand stories, and having explained to me gunnery, and speed, pressures, etc.

The Admiral (Jones) has given me top priority — everything practically at my disposal. I have passes for every place & every thing. In fact it is a bit embarrassing. It makes my own job ahead such a personal obligation.

309 *Jesuit Relations and Allied Documents*, ed. R.G. Thwaites, 73 vols (Cleveland: Barrows Brothers, 1896–1901).

310 Francis Parkman, *The Jesuits of North America in the Seventeenth Century*, 2 vols (1867).

311 Pratt had lectured on the poem on several occasions. (See the letters to Claire and Viola Pratt, 23 July 1940 [p. 188], Claire Pratt, 13 October 1944 [p. 296], and Charles D. Abbott, 28 January 1945 [p. 312].) For a compilation of Pratt's commentaries on *BB*, see *EJP: OHLP*, 11–26. A description of the scripts (six typescripts and two holographs) in the Pratt Collection is provided by Susan Gingell in *EJP: OHLP*, 192–6.

I haven't written a line yet, have nothing but data, data, data. The task of selection and elimination is tremendous. I may get at it in early fall.

I'll have a good old chat with you on our return.

Love to Dona & Jane,

affec.
Ned.

TO RALPH GUSTAFSON

Toronto 5, Canada

August 21, 1945.

My dear friend Ralph:

It was a joy to get your letter today together with your Penguin[312] and your Poetry and Canada.[313] I think you are doing a magnificent job for us all and the most pronounced feelings in my heart are those of indebtedness and gratitude. Where would Canadian writers be in England and the United States without sympathetic critics and craftsmen like you and Smith and Brown?[314] So far from contributors receiving royalties from you, they ought to be sending you Christmas presents. Hence I am returning the cheque. If I were hard up, it would be different. The royalty, as you say, may be small, as far as each contributor is concerned, but if all the royalties were turned in to the general cause, the transaction might alleviate the cost of the burden which I know must be considerable these days.

You ask me for a poem for CDN Accent II.[315] That, too, is very good of you. I wish I had a few for you from which to make a selection. As a matter of fact I have just returned from the East where for two months I have been the guest of the Royal Canadian Navy, gathering material at sea on the destroyers. I am sending *They Are Returning*. It is my initial instalment on general lines. If there is a selection which might fit your purpose, you are most cordially permitted to use it without cost. I have given permission to Margaret Fairley to use an

---

312 Gustafson's latest anthology (verse and prose): *Canadian Accent* (Penguin 1944), containing Pratt's 'Come Away, Death.'

313 *Poetry and Canada: A Guide to Reading* (Canadian Legion Educational Services, 1945).

314 A.J.M. Smith and E.K. Brown.

315 A second *Canadian Accent* did not materialize.

excerpt for her Anthology[316] which may not be out for a year. Macmillans have published it indeed, but it is just out and no contract is signed. If the Canadian Macmillans should query the appearance (which I am sure they won't), you can make use of the attached permission.[317] I can settle it with them. That is, of course, if you find anything in it acceptable. I am also enclosing a short poem, hitherto unpublished, *The Yeas*,[318] which you might consider as a substitute. Should neither suit, please exercise your discretion of refusal. I shall understand perfectly.

I am grateful for your two excellent books. I use your Flight into Darkness[319] in discussing poetry with students. I think that last stanza on Galileo simply superb. I get the Housman razor-and-beard thrill[320] every time I read it. Scientific history is wrapped up in the analogy and also the clerical dogmatism opposed to it. I read it to my wife tonight and she was thrilled by it.

Many thanks for your listing of the *Collected*.[321]

Yours sincerely,
E.J. Pratt

[Enclosure]

Dear Mr Gustafson:

I gladly give permission to use '*The Yeas and the Nays*' and/or any excerpt from *They Are Returning* for Canadian Accent II, should you find the verse acceptable. There is no cost.

Yours sincerely,
E.J. Pratt

Halifax, N.S.

---

316 Writer, educator, and political activist Margaret Adele Keling Fairley (1885–1968) was the wife of Barker Fairley (see the note to 'Fairley' in the letter to Lorne Pierce, 20 January 1927 [p. 71]). Her anthology, *Spirit of Canadian Democracy: A Collection of Canadian Writings from the Beginnings to the Present Day* was published later that year.

317 See the enclosure.

318 The poem 'The Yeas and the Nays' (*EJP: CP* 2.369) was not published in Pratt's lifetime.

319 A collection of Gustafson's verse published in 1944.

320 Poet A.E. Housman (1859–1936) wrote in *The Name and Nature of Poetry* (1933): 'Experience has taught me, when I am shaving of a morning, to keep watch over my thoughts, because, if a line of poetry strays into my memory, my skin bristles so that the razor ceases to act.'

321 In his critical work *Poetry and Canada*.

TO ELLEN ELLIOTT

[Nov. 1945]

Dear Ellen:

I think the idea is excellent.[322] Ryerson has been at work as you know for many years bringing out chapbooks in the hope that out of a large number of writers a few important ones might emerge. A few did and I suppose their future production will be under their imprint. I feel that the majority of them, like Colquhoun[323] and Woodrow,[324] never amounted to anything, but a few succeeded.

I always wanted the best of these young writers to be Macmillan's, but one of course can't prophesy with certainty. You remember when that Macmillan anthology 12 years ago,[325] which included Kennedy, Finch, Dorothy Livesay, Frank Scott & A.J.M. Smith, was being considered, I had a long conversation with Hughie about its advisability. He knew it wouldn't be very popular at the time though there was a good chance that two or three of the contributors might later receive recognition. Leo Kennedy came on well and Dorothy Livesay & Smith. Finch I understand is approaching Oxford for his collection[326] and Frank Scott has just been published by Ryerson.[327] I don't know how far Scott will go, not very far I think, and Finch will not be popular, but still nearly all of these names are considered significant today. There are new ones, too, like Anne Marriott & Birney & Cox,[328] whom [...] has sponsored, and these three are to be heard from in the future. Birney is a hard chap to get along with but he has a future, speaking quite objectively.

---

322 Elliott had written to ask his views of a proposal by Macmillan of Canada to publish more poetry by new, young writers in collections of some 'considerable size and substance,' rather than 'thin sheafs of the chapbook variety.' But few such volumes appeared during the next decade. She had also sent him several manuscripts recently received and requested his critical verdicts. See latter part of the letter.

323 Kate G. Colquhoun, whose *The Battle of St Julien and Other Poems* had been published as a Ryerson chapbook in 1928.

324 Constance Woodrow (1899–1937), whose *The Captive Gypsy* had been published as a Ryerson chapbook in 1926

325 Possibly a reference to Ethel Hume Bennett's anthology *New Harvesting*, published by Macmillan in 1938 – eight, not twelve, years earlier.

326 Finch's *Poems*, published by Oxford University Press (1946), won the Governor General's Medal for poetry for that year. (See the note to 'the onslaught on Finch' in the letter to Earle Birney, 30 September 1947 [p. 408].)

327 *Overture* (Toronto: Ryerson, 1945).

328 Leo Cox.

Personally I don't like chapbooks and I think with you that if a writer has any stuff in him he ought to wait till he can produce a substantial piece of work. The only virtue the chapbook has is that it gives some kind of unity to the selections. All the productions come out with a name which indicates a type of formal content, giving a probationary sign for the critics, 'This is the way he starts; see if he justifies the confidence.'

Nevertheless, I am aware of the objection on the part of young or old writers that they don't want such an introduction to the public. It too clearly indicates probation and it certainly puts them in a class which has proved with very few exceptions to be commonplace.

Writers will be coming along in greater numbers in the next few years and I think you have the right idea of bringing out solid collections of the best as far as one can humanly judge them. I have been watching them, as some come out of this University and they often talk over their problems with me. I have met a number whom I would not recommend to you under any conditions. There are others who are good but highly specialized from a commercial point of view. What we need are writers whose good stuff will have a renovative effect.

The most vocal group in this country are the Montreal writers. Some of them I detest heartily for their arrogance, but there are others of ability and humility like Smith, Klein, Kennedy and the foremost woman poet of the group, P.K. Page. I published some of her stuff in the C.P.M. and she gets into some of smaller & more eclectic American magazines. One thing about her which would favour her publisher-to-be is that she is very much appreciated by the new and 'modernistic' group. She is the 'best' of the Montrealers though she is now living in B.C. My criticism of some of her work is the general curtain of obscurity which has beset the whole gang but she is moving out of it and I think she will be as well known as DL[329] and as well accepted in the future. Of all the younger women poets (I think she is under 30) she has the most 'class' and I would endorse her publication.

I do not care so much for her leading poem, 'Personal Landscape,'[330] with its artificial diction. She might better spare 'Where Flowers line the Roads,' which has a cool beauty. 'The Stenographer' is good with its fresh imagery. So is 'Condemned' with its social emphasis. The whole collection is not going to

329 Dorothy Livesay.

330 Elliott had sent Pratt manuscripts of three books of verse, one of which was Page's *As Ten as Twenty*, on which he comments here. Despite Pratt's endorsement to Macmillan, the book was published by Ryerson Press in 1946.

be very popular but she has a following already which might absorb a modest edition in a reasonable time.

Paschal Lamb and Other Poems[331]

Some individual lines are unnecessarily harsh and unrhythmical

Like the 8th line in 'Apology for Munich':

'While whippets coursed, striplings ate idleness.'

Besides the title is ambiguous and there are a good *number of misspellings.* 'On Some Canadian Verse' is clear and strong.

'But One Tall Gable' has a de la Mare touch.

She has developed strength in such poems as 'Skeleton,' 'Scorched Earth,' 'Jew Baiting,' and tenderness in 'Waiting.'

Mystic symbolism in 'Victory.'

'Forest Music' was a good poem in the Canadian Forum and, if I mistake not, the 'Reindeer Saga.'

Doris has a large group of friends in Victoria and her personal leadership for years over the poetic sorority should mean a few sales there. Her artistic modesty is seen in the slim collection presented, for she has been writing good stuff for 20 Years.

Brief for Beauty – Reba Hudson[332]

Certain jarring lines should be smoothed over.

Here is no cognizance of verse. Very jarring.

Wild rosebushes in Autumn is exceedingly musical and picturesque.

I shall be happy to come down sometime when convenient and talk over the whole matter with you, if you would like me to do so. We are expecting a visit from Dr Edgar in a few days time which will tie me up for a while. I think your suggestion is a very good idea.

Sincerely,
Ned.

331 The title of the second manuscript Elliott had sent him. It was by Doris Ferne and was published by Macmillan in 1946.

332 The third manuscript, published by Macmillan in 1947.

TO CARL KLINCK

Nov. 21, 1945

Dear Carl:

This is a grand piece of work[333] and reads like an exciting novel. I am more pleased than I can say.

I have made only two or three corrections.

(1) The reference to Catholicism. I have to watch that so I deleted 'became almost a Catholic.'[334] I might be taken up on that literally. It is strong enough as it stands.
(2) I changed the phrase 'Pratt would have changed it' (Victoria College) to would not have gone to it, as the first wording would imply more power than I possessed.[335] Vic has always been very broad and catholic (small c).

The best,
Ned Pratt

TO E.K. BROWN

Dec. 19, 1945

Dear Ed:

Wells wrote me to say that you introduced him to the audience in as fine a couple of paragraphs of speech as he had ever listened to.[336] He thought you a 'prince of a fellow.' He has glowing admiration for you as man and writer.

All my friends liked him greatly. He will always be welcome to our Toronto circle.

333 The manuscript of *Edwin J. Pratt: The Man and His Poetry* by Klinck and Henry W. Wells.

334 Klinck had used these words referring to Pratt's preparation for the writing of *BB*. The finished version instead quotes from a different passage from Pratt's letter to Wells, 26 February 1945 (p. 320): 'Pratt says, "I lived for a year practically with the Jesuits"' (*Edwin J. Pratt*, 57).

335 Klinck had written that, had Victoria College been 'an academic brotherhood' of 'weary faces and conventional minds,' Pratt would have changed it.

336 Henry W. Wells had given a lecture at the University of Chicago. See the letter to Brown, 12 October (*EJP: Web*).

Yes, I contributed a short article, really a review of Dorothy Livesay's work.[337] I was too pressed for time to do anything substantial, and I am somewhat averse to reviewing in any case. I do want a bit of time to myself.

I am glad you are appealing for catholicity of judgment particularly when the parochialism of many of the Montrealers is being so blatantly exhibited under the name of cosmopolitanism. Klein tells me that they are falling out with each other already, Anderson claiming headship disputed by practically everyone else.

You know Dean Neville of Western Ont.[338] He came up to see me last week about a couple of men he needed. He said you had recommended Sirluck for one midway position. I strongly endorsed Ernest as he is the one I like & admire best of all the present grads. If I had my way & authority I'd snap him up for Vic but things are settled otherwise. Neville may ask A.J.M. Smith[339] to take the headship, if he can get more for him than he is getting at Lansing which is about $4000.

Do try to get up here in January or any time when you can spend a few days. There's the hell of a deal of news to be given sotto voce and I love the evenings when you are given an easy chair and a table to put your feet under. Rich experiences these!!

Love to Peggy & yourself.

Ned.

TO CARL KLINCK

Jan. 7, 1946

Dear Carl:

Our heartiest New Year greetings to yourself and wife.

---

337 Pratt had been asked for a contribution (in French) to a special number of the Quebec journal *Gants du Ciel* 11 (Spring 1946) on English Canadian writers, and wrote a brief article on Dorothy Livesay (61–5; *EJP: PAA*, 80–4). Brown was also preparing a contribution, referred to in the following paragraph.

338 K.P.R. Neville (b. 1876), professor of classics and registrar at the University of Western Ontario (1917–47), was also dean of arts (1927–47).

339 Smith was professor of English at the University of Michigan, Lansing.

I think a paragraph or two on the Canadian-Soviet Friendship Council might be appropriate.[340] I have been working for many years to promote friendship between Canada and Russia just as I have worked to promote good will between Canada & the U.S.A. Good neighbourliness and mutual trust and decency are all we have left.

It is not quite true that the Ambassador himself came to our family party, but last year (or I should say the year before last) the Chief Secretary of the Soviet Legation and his colleagues were our guests, and similarly a month or so ago the new successor came with some of his friends to a party which preceded the great rally at the Maple Leaf Gardens at which the Dean of Canterbury spoke.[341]

It might be interesting to mention briefly such facts though I do not think it necessary to publish the poem of dedication.[342] It might be referred to but not printed.

There is one other point that I forgot to state. In your references to the Witches Brew I should prefer to the passage you quote the one on page 245 (Macmillans)[343] –

Close to the dunnest hour of night, …

…

Weary from Hades, that dry land.

I think the use of kippered hocks of centipede[344] is a little too much of a strain.

Or

better still if you can work it in without too much revision of the context – Calvin's remarks on p. 254:

---

340 Pratt is making additional suggestions for changes to the typescript of the book that Klinck and H.W. Wells had written. (See the letter to Klinck, 21 November 1945 [p. 368].) Pratt had been a member of the Canadian-Soviet Friendship Council since its inception on 22 June 1943, but would distance himself from the organization shortly after this letter was written, following the revelation of an active Soviet spy ring in Canada.

341 The anecdote is repeated with embellishments in *Edwin J. Pratt*: 'Gay, friendly and witty, they warmed the heart of their host, captivated his wife, toasted their respective countries, and stayed for dinner' (44). 'The Dean of Canterbury' was Hewlett Johnson, known as the 'Red Dean.'

342 'A Victory Message and Pledge of Friendship from the Canadian People to the U.S.S.R.' written at the invitation of the Canadian-Soviet Friendship Council and read by Pratt at the rally at Maple Leaf Gardens. A specially printed broadside was presented to the secretary of the Soviet embassy (see Lila Laakso, 'Descriptive Bibiliography,' *EJP: CP* 2.440, B10).

343 *CP1*.

344 In the right margin, Klinck notes 'my pages / 33–34.' The recommendation to use 'Weary form Hades, that dry land' was adopted (see *Edwin J. Pratt*, 47).

If I had known etc.[345]

That judgment contains the core of the mad extravaganza as regarded by a rationalist.

I think this is all. But don't fail to write me for any suggestions. You never get on my patience. It is a delight for me to talk about the whole business.

Ned.

TO WILLIAM ROSE BENÉT

Feb. 3, 1946

Dear Bill:

This is to say 'Happy New Year' to you and your wife, and also to thank you on behalf of my daughter Claire for the delight she had in reading Steve's 'Twenty-five Short Stories'[346] with your grand introduction. Claire has been in bed sick for three months with osteomyelitis, which has necessitated several bone operations, and the tedium and pain has been mitigated by those stories. Vi read your appreciation aloud to the two of us the other night. It is so full of the warmth of brotherly kindness, and the style is a joy. The Devil and Daniel Webster[347] I had read before but I got an added kick with the genius-inspired ending – 'I'm not talking about Massachusetts or Vermont.' Claire received the book as a Christmas present from one of her girl friends who was rhapsodic over Steve. You and Steve stand for vital masculine literature. I hope the tide is turning against the blood-drained aesthetes with their arrogance and snobbery.

I have been invited to give the Morris Gray lecture-recital at Harvard this year. It is to be on the 27th of February, and I may take advantage of the trip to run on to New York for a few days immediately after. I should love to see you again. I shall give you a ring probably from the Prince George Hotel. The Times writers like Adams, Laube, and Lissner,[348] and the Columbia men like Wells and Brebner[349] have been so kind to me, and have asked me to look them up.

---

345 In the right margin, Klinck notes 'revised / J[.....] 4/46.' Klinck heeded Pratt's advice and quoted this passage by Calvin in the published version of the book (*Edwin J. Pratt*, 43-4).

346 (Garden City, NY: Sun Dial Press, 1943) by Stephen Vincent Benét (1898–1943) had been published posthumously.

347 First published in 1936, it is perhaps Stephen Benét's most popular short story.

348 Donald Adams, Clifford Laube, and William Lissner wrote for the *New York Times*.

349 Henry W. Wells and Bart Brebner of Columbia University.

The Collected Poems is going fairly well, slowly but steadily. I hope the sales don't let Knopf down too much. About one thousand have sold since last April, which is good from my standpoint. You started all this good work for me and I have always been so grateful to you.

May good health attend you both,

As ever,
Ned

TO VIOLA AND CLAIRE PRATT

[New York, N.Y.]

Saturday am [3 Mar. 1946]

Dearest ones:

Your letter of Wednesday eve. just came. I suppose you got my telegram and card. Everything is going swimmingly so far. The Harvard occasion was successful. The place was filled with many standing. I stayed with the Bushes and met one splendid fellow, Ted Spencer,[350] a man as likeable as Wells.[351] Packard, the man in charge of poetry readings on the phonograph,[352] took two disks of my readings. I am to get a complimentary presentation, and if they turn out well they may be marketed.[353]

I spent yesterday with Henry & Katharine.[354] They put on a tea for me at the Columbia Friendly Tea Room where thirty men of the English staff assembled. Following that I spent the evening with the Benéts[355] – just the three of us for dinner. The Denisons[356] came in afterwards till midnight. Today I have lunch with

---

350 Theodore Spencer (1902–49), American poet, professor, prolific critic and editor, especially of Shakespeare.

351 Henry W. Wells.

352 Associate Professor F.C. Packard Jr was the editor of Harvard Vocarium Records, a subsidiary of the Harvard Film Service.

353 The Harvard phonograph discs, which were marketed on a small scale, feature Pratt reading a selection of his poetry. In something of a discographic curiosity, they give his name as Edward J. Pratt and the date as 1949.

354 Henry Wells and his wife.

355 William Rose Benét and his wife Marjorie.

356 Merrill and Muriel Denison.

Clifford Laube of the Times,[357] and in the afternoon I shall be with Henry followed by dinner and an opera. He got the tickets by a fluke – the rush is tremendous.

Just now I telephoned Nellie,[358] gave her your message about Frayz[?]. She says they have stopped making it. Tomorrow she and Carl and Peggy[359] are coming to the Prince George for evening dinner with me.

Tuesday morning at 11, Henry wants me to lecture on the Titanic to his class which I shall do. Then in the afternoon I shall probably spend a few minutes with Knopf,[360] and at 8:30 pm. I leave for 21[361] and you & Cayke. Bless your dear heads and hearts.

Love,
Ned

TO WILLIAM ROSE AND MARJORIE BENÉT

March 17, 1946

Dear Bill and Marjorie:

This is St Patrick's Day and I thought I should celebrate it by dropping a note to the two of you. It is a note of thanks for your hospitality, for your dinner, the initial snort, the bass (I have been trying to remember the adjective and all I can recover is ribbéd, corrugated, flutéd, delvéd. Oh, by Christopher, I got it STRIPÉD with a huge accent on the second syllable! but the subtle distinction between the accented variety and the unaccented I am still cudgelling my brains to unravel – My Lord, what a parenthesis)! and then the evening with the Denisons and all the lovely, perfumed, smoky conversation. God bless you ye merry host and hostess. Marjórie, you looked more youthful than ever and that's saying a lot, a charming and brilliant hostess you are. Here's a rouse to ye both.

Love,
Ned Pratt

---

357 *New York Times.*
358 His sister, Nellie Pratt.
359 Carl and Peggy Klinck.
360 Alfred A. Knopf, Pratt's American publisher.
361 21 Cortleigh Blvd., Pratt's home address.

TO VIOLA AND CLAIRE PRATT

Tuesday am. [9 Apr. 1946]

Dearest Vi and Claire:

It is 90° in the shade today but I am told to thank heaven that it isn't 110. It is not so bad as I brought light inside wear.

I was met at the Airport by Father Dwyer[362] and whom do you think else, Father Edmund McCorkell.[363] He is here for a month supervising Basilian affairs. He referred to you last night in his introduction of me to the Philosophy Club. Do you know that I have given four addresses already. As soon as I arrived I had to speak to 300 men in the St Thomas College – out under the trees and then at night to the Philosophy Club of about 50. At the end we had refreshments and when we got back to St Thomas, Father McCorkell, Father Dwyer, Father Lynch and Father Harrigan[364] spent two hours till midnight in my room telling stories. This morning just after breakfast I spoke to the St Agnes College – 300 girls and nuns – then immediately after to another 300 girls in another convent. I am now in my room preparing for a broadcast which must be given over the local station at 10:30, a quarter of an hour readings, etc. That will make three performances today. Tomorrow there are two more and on Thursday night in the big auditorium of San Jacinto College I have to make the main address. The tickets are selling well I am told and I am enclosing a copy of one of the papers.[365] You will recognize Father McCorkell if not Father Dwyer & myself.

It is all very pleasant and the Texas hospitality is wonderful. I expect to leave Friday evening getting into Toronto Saturday afternoon as there are several delays.

Much love to you sweethearts.
Father Ned.

362 Wilfred Dwyer, a Basilian father, was a Canadian posted temporarily to Houston.

363 A former professor of English at St Michael's College, Toronto, and principal of St Thomas More College, Saskatoon, McCorkell was superior general of the Order of Basilian Fathers.

364 Lynch and Harrigan, both American Basilians, were members of St Thomas College.

365 A newspaper article.

TO EARLE BIRNEY

Victoria College
Toronto, Ont.

April 14, 1946

Dear Earle:

As soon as I returned from my trip yesterday Vi greeted me with the announcement that you had won the Governor-General's.[366] Both of us decided to celebrate your triumph with a good drink, Vi with tea, Ned with a sailor's snort of navy rum, a concentrated remnant from last summer. Boy, we are glad that you won it, and that you are getting your deserved recognition somewhat earlier in the game than would have been possible fifteen or twenty years ago. I am glad that a double-header came your way.[367] You will probably have to put your port and starboard bows into a sea of jealousy caused by a lot of adolescent farts down your way,[368] but ride above them all. There is no one in Canada whose success gives me more satisfaction as I have been with you from the start, prodding you on to greater activity.

I have just come back from Texas, of all places. A Poetry Group of Houston sponsored an annual celebration in connection with the alumni of a college, and invited me down for a poetry-recital, guaranteeing plane passage and return plus an honorarium. I could not understand how any organization could justify such expense – a trip across a continent and back for one address, yet they paid the shot of four hundred dollars, $200 for expenses and 200 for fee. I was there for three days and spoke to some institutes and schools as an extra. I gave them the Titanic as the main item. That meant a series of five trips during the last two months, Rochester, Buffalo, Harvard, Columbia and Houston. If this sort of thing had come ten years ago, how welcome it would have been. That is why I think you should take every opportunity of enlarging your public platforms and radio and magazines. You have the goods and they should be displayed and

366 Birney won the annual award for poetry for his book *Now Is Time* (Toronto: Ryerson,1945).

367 He had won his first Governor General's Award for Poetry in 1943 for *David and Other Poems* (Toronto: Ryerson, 1942).

368 Since returning from overseas, Birney had been with the CBC's International Service in Montreal. Here, and in the last sentence of the letter, Pratt is referring to the poets associated with the small magazines *Preview* and *First Statement*. In his 20 April reply, Birney comments: 'I have much that I want to talk over with you, including an account of a recent session I had with Anderson, Smith and Frank Scott' (Birney, FRBL).

sold in the highest market of all, the spirit. I talked a bit about your work in all the centres I visited and to reporters who wanted to know what is happening in Canada. You are my white hope and it is a pleasure to introduce you, because you have something to say to the people and not to a coterie of constipated arses.

Our love to you, Esther and Bill.[369]

Ned

TO E.K. BROWN

April 23, 1946

Dear Ed:

Your letter just came. Yes, I had a grand time in Texas, spent a week there, and though I was scheduled to address the main audience on Thursday night, I was made to speak 12 times during the interval.[370] The hospitality was unparalleled. Father McCorkell's visit happened to coincide with mine and together we were fêted almost all over the state. I gave them both the *Titanic* and *Brébeuf* at the same recital, with an interlude by a violinist from Dallas.

I just heard from Arthur Woodhouse that Daniells & Birney are for B.C.[371] I agree with you that Sirluck would be the ideal for Manitoba had he his degree and a little more experience. Ernie is as you know, a great admirer of yours. You can count on him.

When I was at Harvard, Bush[372] said that your Victorian Book[373] was highly esteemed, but they were short of copies through manufacturing difficulties. I found Bush and Spencer[374] grand fellows.

By the way I sat next to Ruth Irwin (daughter of Bill Irwin of Chicago – theology)[375] at the Senior Dinner this year and she rhapsodized about your lecturing

369 Birney's wife and son.

370 He was actually there four days and spoke ten times.

371 Roy Daniells, then at the University of Manitoba, and Earle Birney, with the CBC in Montreal, had both received appointments to the Department of English at the University of British Columbia.

372 Douglas Bush.

373 An anthology, *Victorian Poetry*, which Brown had edited in 1942.

374 Theodore Spencer.

375 William A. Irwin (1884–1967), a graduate of Victoria College, was professor of Old Testament Studies at the University of Chicago and the author of several books, most notably *The Old Testament: Keystone of Human Culture* (1952).

powers at Chicago. She said you were head & shoulders above them all for transmitting enthusiasm. Do you remember the kid? She is President of her year.

I go to Queen's this summer from July 3 to August 20, but I shall be taking some week-end runs to Toronto. If you come here – let me know and I shall try to time my presence with your visits. Quite a few of the boys will be here lecturing to the veterans and we might have a presentable gathering.

This is just a note. Next time when there is any special news I shall write at greater length.

Vi would be glad to see Peggy and begorra so would I; and the kid too in person would receive a welcome. If you can arrange to come after the third week in August so much the better. The back of the heat is generally broken by then.

Affectionately
Ned

TO VIOLA PRATT

[Kingston, Ontario][376]

July 3, 1946

Lovins Vi:

I sent off a card yesterday from the General Post Office and telephoned at 3 pm. as the line was busy earlier. The trip was a bit uncomfortable but I got a seat in the smoking compartment after we left Oshawa. It was the most crowded journey I ever took; hence the advice to the two of you dears is 'never travel on a holiday.' However, we got in just a little late – a few minutes after 8 daylight[377] and Mrs Cartwright had my old room ready – the little room overlooking the library. She is not very well, has arthritis with pains and swellings and yet has to earn her living as clerk in the Highways Dept. She makes out licenses for cars etc., works from 8:30 to 5. I told her she didn't need to make my bed as all I have to do is to pull a coverlet over me at night and pull it back in the morning. My meals are the same as before. I go over to the Queen's restaurant you remember for breakfast and lunch and then out to the Cataraqui Golf Course for dinner. Some of my old friends have died. Both Noble and Walter Steacey. I got a shock

---

376 He was teaching at Queen's University summer school.

377 Daylight saving time.

when I went in to Steacey's store to call on Noble and Herb told me he died last October. I hadn't heard anything about it.

The hours here are going to be easy. Scott Thomas of Acadia[378] and I divide one course and for the first half the subjects run parallel, one class at 8 the other at 11. I offered to toss him for the eleven hour but he said he would rather have the 8 & have it over. So I don't have to keep the alarm wound up. I got up this morning at 8:30 and now after breakfast I am going over my notes for the 11 session. It seems I have only 1 hour a day until the middle of the term when possibly I may have a second.

I don't know yet what the size of the classes will be or how the registration compares with the previous years. All I know is that they have a veterans course which they didn't have previously.

Letters are coming in and telegrams about the CMG.[379] One funny incident occurred yesterday when I went into the Faculty Room. Two or three fellows were gathered there and our old friend Marcel Tirol the Frenchman[380] (he of his 'Sooreroous' fame) exclaimed – 'Oh here is Pratt. Congratoolasheions on your hon*ór*. It was a nice leetle hon*ór* I hear you receeved. What was it preciselee?' I said CMG. and he said 'Well for the lands sake whoever would have thought it?' The other chaps roared, and Tirol rebuked them with 'What are you amuséd at?'

Harrison[381] is away up at the lakes somewhere. I haven't seen Clarke[382] yet but I am glad he is here for I shall have some company. I like him. I may see MacKinnon[383] today.

Well do you know darling Vi I will be back on Friday week. I shall get in about 10 I think and go back on Sunday at 4. It breaks the trip nicely. I hope you don't go gadding about too much on the highways, and don't bother too much about dust in the house.

When I hear from MacLeans[384] I shall let you know immediately. Best of love again & again to you and Cayke pie.

Ned

---

378 H.F. Scott Thomas (1897–1947), a graduate of the universities of Toronto and Johns Hopkins, was a member of the Department of English at Acadia University from 1927 until his death.

379 Pratt had been named a Companion of the Order of St Michael and St George in the Dominion Day Civil Honours List.

380 A professor of French at Queen's. ('Sooreroous' refers to his pronunciation of the name of Professor J.A. Surerus of the German Department at Victoria College.)

381 G.B. Harrison, head of the English Department.

382 George Herbert Clarke.

383 M.M.H. (Murdo) MacKinnon.

384 The context is unclear.

TO WILLIAM ARTHUR DEACON

Summer Session
Queen's University
Kingston, Ont.

[10 July 1946]

My dear Bill:

Your letter[385] is characteristic in your generosity and warmth of friendship. The two men in Canada who have meant most to me in literary stimulation are (academically) Pelham Edgar and (in the broad public field) your esteemed self. Whatever the Canadian Authors' Foundation[386] may develop into, I trust that, whenever your retirement comes, the Foundation will regard you as its foremost beneficiary. I have consistently preached the debt Canadian writers owe to you and I feel sure the debt will be honoured in due time.

I am writing Birney along the lines you suggested in your letter.[387] I had a chat with him before he left and I emphasized the importance of preserving the golden mean of letters and avoiding the rasping edges of intolerant extremes. I think his year in Montreal showed him that the local coterie there were interested only in themselves and that their screaming abuse at everything and everybody gone before them was only a bit of inflated exhibitionism. They pretty well sickened him – I mean the Anderson, – Layton – Souster gang.[388] They may grow out of it in time. In the meanwhile the new Canadian P.M.[389] may reap the sincere poetic labours of *all* the 'groups.' I think he appreciates the fact that the history of literature in its permanent form is a combination of tradition and experiment

385 Of 6 July.

386 Established in the early 1930s mainly through the efforts of Pelham Edgar, its purpose was to provide financial assistance to older authors in straitened circumstances. By 1946 its name had been changed to Canadian Writers' Foundation.

387 Deacon, national president of the CAA, was trying to persuade Earle Birney to edit *CPM* and was seeking Pratt's support.

388 Pratt shared Birney's resentment of the elitism of some of the young Montreal poets, although his antipathy is usually directed at the poets associated with *Preview* – "the Anderson Scott Page Ruddick gang" (see his letter to A.J.M. Smith, 28 January 1944 [p. 276]). The addition of Layton and Souster here may indirectly allude to the merging of Anderson's *Preview* with John Sutherland's *First Statement* to form *Northern Review* in 1945.

389 *Canadian Poetry Magazine.*

and that between the two there should be mutual respect. As you say, team play counts as much here as it does in the field of sport competition.

I believe in Birney. He has exceptional intellectual talents. He is maturing and mellowing and his editorship, if he accepts it, will cover the young as well as the more established writers. I shall give him every help by way of advice and friendly practical cooperation. We have great days ahead of us Bill and nothing gives me more unalloyed delight than your Presidency of the C.A.A. You are worthy of the highest honours and I say this not merely out of a profound love and loyalty to you but out of an objective appreciation of your gifts.

I wish also to pay tribute to good old Sal who so well sustained your book-page when you were heavily involved in patriotic duties during the last six years.[390]

We shall have a reunion in the Fall.

Very affectionately,
Ned

TO JOHN M. GRAY[391]

The Summer School
Queen's University
Kingston, Ont

July 13, 1946

My dear Jack:

Many thanks for your telegram and letter. I appreciate as much as ever your good wishes and all the evidences of your friendship. And it will be a pleasure to be identified with you officially in the future.

Regarding the Wells manuscript[392] I regret, as you do, that it has to be refused, after the work done on it by Wells and Klinck. Wells might revise it in

---

390 Deacon's wife Sally had filled in for him for more than three years. From November 1942 to January 1946 Deacon, as a full-time member of the Wartime Prices and Trade Board, had been responsible for the rationing of paper in Canada.

391 John Morgan Gray (1907–1979), born in Ontario, educated in Canada and in England, joined Macmillan of Canada in 1930 as a travelling salesman (Educational Department). During the next ten years he occupied several other posts in the firm. After service in the Second World War, he rejoined the firm and in 1946 was made its president. In 1978, he published his autobiography, *Fun Tomorrow: Learning to Be a Publisher and Much Else*. He and Pratt were good friends for many years.

392 Of *Edwin J. Pratt: The Man and His Poetry*.

accordance with the critical suggestions but I scarcely think he will do so. He might try an American publisher but I think the chances over there are slim. Nevertheless, Wells has in mind several articles upon my work, one long chapter in a book called The Social Emphasis in Contemporary Poetry which he has submitted to the Chicago Press.[393] He gives me full and sympathetic treatment. Did you see his article in College English for May,[394] I think. It is very quotable. He is one of the best supporters and interpreters I have in the U.S.A. and personally I am sorry for the rejection though I understand the publisher's and readers' points of view.

For Canada E.K. Brown could do a splendid thing as his name ranks ace high in the academic world and is growing fast in the public field. Could he not be approached. Klinck's biographical chapters were simply grand but he could turn them into articles I imagine.

I was glad to get at the St Martin's selection[395] because I am convinced that there will be a big sale through the Canadian schools for years to come. Hundreds of teachers of English have been my students over the last 25 years. I shall be delighted to cooperate with Mr Knights[396] as soon as I get back to Toronto which will be by the middle of August. Would you ask him to take a look through *Brébeuf* and advise me on what selections he thinks appropriate. The poem is on the list suggested by the Committee.[397] I thought I would take the highlights of the poem and link them together by prose narrative to make a continuous story.

I am assuming that the ms. should be ready by this fall in order that the book should be in the hands of teachers by the early fall of 1947. Would Mr Knights give me approximate dates?

I am also assuming that I am doing the work on the usual 10% royalty basis, and that the book would be approximately 65 cents which would govern to some extent the size of the volume. How is the paper situation shaping up? Any better?

I want also to thank you for your marvellous dinner at Winston's.[398] Vi and I were delighted. As Ernie Sirluck remarked – 'That fellow is a host of the first strain.'

Affectionately,
Ned

---

393 This chapter never materialized.

394 'Canada's Best-Known Poet: E.J. Pratt,' *College English* (May 1946): 452–6.

395 Pratt's *TSP* was published in the Macmillan series 'St Martin's Classics.'

396 A Macmillan editor.

397 The Education Committee. See the letter to Claire Pratt, 18 April 1945 (p. 331).

398 A fashionable Toronto restaurant.

TO CLAIRE PRATT

Queen's
152 University Avenue
Kingston Ont

Monday [15 July 1946]

Dearest Claire:

Who should I see this morning on my way to a lecture but Lorne Pierce. In the course of our conversation he asked me what you were doing. He knew you had been at the Copp-Clark[399] plant and wondered if you might not prefer a Ryerson Press connection.[400] I said I thought you might consider some editorial work and he told me the Publishing House was contemplating revising all their Readers for the High Schools, that there would be a big job running over many months. He said he would be glad to offer you a part time editorial job where the work might be done at home and in the libraries, substituting stories and essays and poems for those already in the texts and adding more. I thought the plan would appeal to you and he is going to make you an offer in the fall. I imagine it will develop into something permanent and yet allowing for intermissions.

Naturally I said nothing about the 'Johnston-Everson,'[401] but that wouldn't interfere with Pierce's proposition as each would be part time and you could handle both I am sure. It would also give you a chance at selecting which alternative suited you best. I like the Ryerson idea better don't you, that is, at first glance as it is editorial work, but you can decide for yourself later.

Love,
Father

399 A Toronto publishing firm.

400 Apart from summer work at Ryerson Press (which also served as the United Church Publishing House), Claire did not work for the company. (See the note to 'at work in the Wesley Bld.' in the letter to Viola Pratt, 19 July 1945 [p. 355].)

401 Claire had had an offer of a part-time job with the public relations and publishing firm of Johnston, Everson, and Charlesworth.

TO EARLE BIRNEY

August 16, 1946

My dear Earle:

How are you, old top? I have just returned from Queen's and intend taking a holiday by loafing around the premises.

Deacon wrote me a letter suggesting that I get in touch with you about the C.P.M.[402] Of course, you know how strong I have been for your editorship right along. In fact, all of us feel you are the only man that can take hold of it and make it a going concern.

Personally I am through with all kinds of editorship[403] having done my bit. I couldn't accept any responsibility now as I have to cut down on activities somewhat. But I would suggest as the Ontario (regional) Editor either Norrie or Sirluck. Sirluck is going to put on a seminar in Canadian lit. and I am sure would like to cooperate. Either he or Frye would do fine. I suppose Cox might act in Quebec. He knows the field down there.

I am glad you are back in academic life. It's your milieu certainly, and for the future nothing better.

Kindest regards to Esther &Bill.
Ned

TO PELHAM EDGAR

August 16, 1946

My dear Pelham:

Your letter was forwarded to my Queen's address and back to Toronto. I returned from the summer session only yesterday. Vi and Claire came to Kingston for the last few days and we returned together.

402 See the letter to Deacon, 10 July 1946 (pp. 379–80).

403 Deacon had written on 10 August to report on his negotiations with Earle Birney about new directions for the *CPM* under his editorship. Birney wanted Pratt to be *CPM*'s associate editor for Ontario: 'I like his plan for regional representation and you will be doing the Association a service by accepting' (Deacon, FRBL).

The first thing I did when I arrived was to go out to the York Downs and see if I could collect a few golf balls. I could get only one new ball when I was at Kingston for the whole six weeks. The pro said they were absolutely extinct – all but a few Campbells.[404] I had to play with some old ones I brought from Toronto. So I ran out to see Billy Freeman[405] and he would allow me but one, and when I said I wanted some for you he allowed me one more. It is a famine really. I am sending you six, three good and three durations.[406] That's scraping the barrel.

You mentioned enclosing a cheque. I didn't want payment. In any case you forgot to put the cheque inside; so don't bother: accept the six such as they are, and don't slice or hook into the rough.

My game is 9 holes, but I play a constant 44 – not so hot but comfortable and leisurely without the old time blasphemy.

I am glad you struck such an ideal spot for yourself, Dona & Jane.[407] You escape the torrid weather. We have been lucky here, the temperature never rising above the high 80's and these comparatively rare.

Things are pretty dull in the city. The staff at Vic are away. Brown[408] is on the Pacific Coast and De Beaumont[409] is somewhere, and I don't care. Only Woodside & Frye[410] pop in and out.

Vi and Claire are fairly well. Claire is taking up painting – pastels & waters – and showing some talent. I hope it develops as she needs a hobby, dear girl. I am going out for 9 holes tonight after 6. Claire will sit down outside & sketch while I draw trajectories of variable contours and direction.

The U.C.[411] has increased professorial pay – the top men getting $500 more than last year. Vic has no prospects as money simply won't come in. No benefactor will leave a clause in his will for the College. If it weren't for the influx of students I don't know what we would be doing, with our interest rates halved. We are safe for two years apparently but after that – Eh, what?

---

404 A popular brand of golf ball.

405 The golf professional at the York Downs Club.

406 An inferior ball for use during the 'duration' of the War. Few top quality golf balls were being manufactured, the plants that made them and other sporting goods having been converted to war production.

407 Edgar and family were on holiday at Cavendish, Prince Edward Island.

408 Walter T. Brown, chancellor of the University of Toronto.

409 Victor de Beaumont, born (1884) in the United States and a graduate of Columbia University, was head of Victoria College's French Department (1940–9).

410 Moffatt Woodside and Northrop Frye.

411 University College.

I shall be looking forward to your Leacock paper.[412] I haven't written anything for six months.[413]

The best to the three of you.
Ned.

TO EARLE BIRNEY

[20 August 1946]

TORONTO ONT 20

PROFESSOR EARLE BIRNEY

ACADIA CAMP UNIVERSITY OF BRITISH COLUMBIA VANCOUVER BC

WROTE LETTER LAST WEEK FEELING I SHOULD NOT RESUME EDITORIAL WORK HOWEVER LIMITED BUT REVISED DECISION ON RECEIPT OF YOUR LETTER[414] STOP WILL SERVE AS MASTHEAD ASSOCIATE BECAUSE OF YOURSELF STOP HAVE NOT A SINGLE SHORT POEM AVAILABLE BUT WILL BACK YOU SPIRITUALLY AND OTHERWISE

NED PRATT

TO CHRISTOPHER AND HELEN MORLEY[415]

Sept. 16, 1946

Dearest Chris and adorable Helen:

You blessed us with your presence – Chris and his Imperial jointress – and your letter to Bill[416] was read to my family punctuated with rounds of laughter and applause.

---

412 'Stephen Leacock,' *QQ* (Summer 1946): 173–84.

413 Not strictly true. He had written some of 'Behind the Log.'

414 In his letter of 17 August 1946, Birney had written 'I need your name for its prestige and to feel I have your moral support,' promising that he would not 'call on you for a tap of work beyond sending me the occasional poem' (Birney, FRBL).

415 American journalist, novelist, essayist, and poet Christopher Morley (1890–1957) was a mathematics professor at Haverford College, and one of the founders of the *SRL*. He is best known as the author of the novel *Kitty Foyle* (1939).

416 Morley had written an account of his visit with Pratt on 3 September in a letter to William Rose Benét and sent a carbon copy of the letter to Pratt.

Thanks Chris for your reference to 'No 6000.'[417] I made enquiries at the C.P.R. office and found you were right. In fact, '6000 tons of caravan' was a typographical error, and in the Nova Scotia High School text-book where the poem was first printed the line was 2000. I am so glad you brought it to my attention, as I am now preparing a text of my own verse for the Canadian High Schools & Collegiates and they have asked for this poem amongst others. It has been authorized by the Dept. of Education.

You (the both of you) were greatly beloved by the party here. Some of them looked upon you as a god almost before you came and after you left you both were compounded of the loveliest divine and earthly essences. God bless you and Helen, and cause his face to shine upon you and give you peace and the everlasting warmth of friendship.

Vi & Claire send their love to you.

Affectionately
Ned.

TO M.M.H. MACKINNON[418]

Oct. 23, 1946

---

417 In the letter to Benét, Morley said that having read Pratt's railway poem 'No. 6000' (*EJP: CP* 1.257), and having travelled on a train pulled by one locomotive engine, he doubted whether it could singly pull '6000 tons of caravan,' as in Pratt's poem in his *CPA*. Pratt's explanation here is not quite accurate, nor is his account of the matter in a postprandial talk on *TLS* in 1952 when he says that 'by some error the printer … inserted 6,000 tons as the load the engine pulled' (See *EJP: OHLP*, 149ff). When the poem was first published in the *CNR Magazine* (December 1931), the load was given as 2000 tons. This was the version he supplied to Lorne Pierce and C.L. Bennet, who were editing the *Canada Book of Prose and Verse* (Book VI), and the tonnage there and in all subsequent editions of the book was 2000. (This is the 'anthology for students' Pratt refers to in his talk.) However, Pratt himself made the change (as well as other minor revisions) to 6000 tons when the poem appeared in *MM* in 1932. What prompted him is unknown, but it was *not* a typographical error. Nor is there any other revision of the poem. In all three editions of *Collected Poems*, the higher tonnage stands, and the 2000-ton load appears only in the school-text versions of the poem. In fact, by 1946, loads of 4000–6000 tons were common in the United States, if not in Canada.

418 M.M.H. Murdoch ('Murdo') MacKinnon (b. 1917) had recently taken up a position teaching English at the University of Western Ontario (1946–64).

Dear Murdo:

The poems in the Collection[419] as suggested by the Teachers' Committee are: –

- Titanic
- Cachalot
- Ice-Floes
- Brébeuf
- No 6000
- Submarine
- Old Eagle
- Putting Winter to Bed

and probably the new naval poem 'Behind the Log' which is now completed. Not the Witches' Brew! The size of the book is limited.

Thanks for your interest, my good old friend. It looks as if there might be a yearly sale for it.

Ned.

Are you loaded with work? Take it easy.

TO LORNE PIERCE

Oct. 28, 1946

My dear Lorne:

Have you come across the poetry of Anne Wilkinson[420] at all? She has remarkable promise, but has not published anything up to date. I went through some

---

419 The selection then in preparation and later published as *Ten Selected Poems* (1947). (See the last paragraph of his letter to Claire Pratt, dated 18 April 1945 [p. 331].) A committee of high school teachers had initiated the project and suggested the book's contents. The final selection included 'Dunkirk' and 'To Angelina, an Old Nurse' in addition to the poems listed here.

420 Toronto-born Wilkinson (1910–61) published two books of poetry, *Counterpoint to Sleep* (Montreal: First Statement, 1951) and *The Hangman Ties the Holly* (Toronto: Macmillan, 1955). She also wrote *Lions in the Way* (Toronto: Macmillan, 1956), the story of the family of Sir William Osler from which she was descended on her mother's side. She was a founding editor of *The Tamarack Review*.

of her verse and I think it is very good indeed. I have advised her to send it on to you to see what you think of it.

Mrs Wilkinson is the young wife of Dr Rob. Wilkinson of the Dept. of Surgery in the U. of T. and she is the daughter of Mr & Mrs Boyd[421] who have wide and influential connections in this city.

Ned Pratt

TO EARLE BIRNEY

Nov. 26, 1946

Dear Earle:

It was grand to hear from you. I have thought of you scores of times and intended writing to congratulate you on your September issue … but time slips in …

I liked it very much – its new stamp – Roy's[422] third sonnet particularly, the light delicate *Abracadabra* of Dorothy,[423] *Steelyards* (tip top) of Bruce[424] and all of Warr's,[425] especially *The Heart to Carry on* and the *Eagle Sorrow*. I am glad that Roy is going back to verse after his academic abstinence period. Lord, how we wish we had more time for things we like to do.

I have a suggestion to make about circulation and donation. Why shouldn't a form asking for donations accompany the subscription form. Every subscriber ought to be solicited for funds. I am sure you would get a fair percentage responding. I told Deacon that now is the time for a campaign seeing that the magazine is in such capable hands as yours. It must not slip this time.

---

421 Wilkinson was the daughter of Mary Elizabeth Osler and George Sutton Gibbons. Her father died in 1919, and her mother married Dr Edmund Boyd in 1926.

422 Roy Daniells.

423 Dorothy Livesay.

424 Charles Bruce (1906–71) served for many years with the Canadian Press in Canada and the United States. He published several books of poems, and his *The Mulgrave Road* (Toronto: Macmillan) won the Governor General's Award for 1951. He is probably best known for his novel *The Channel Shore* (New York: St Martin's, 1954).

425 Bertram Warr (1917–43) was attending the University of London when he was drafted into the Royal Air Force in 1941. He was killed in action at the age of twenty-five. He published little verse in his short lifetime, but in 1950 his best poems were published in *In Quest of Beauty: Selected Poems* (Carillon Poetry Chap-Books).

Regarding my own work, I haven't done anything except the *Skeena* poem[426] which I have just finished in its last revision. I have put a lot of time on it to get the sense of something more than a mere story. I have worked in the asdic principle of the echo as a kind of symbolism of man forever calling out to the rocks and getting back the echo of his own voice. I worked out the scientific data with my friend Lachlan Gilchrist in Physics here[427] and with an asdic operator who located three V-boats during the war.

(The Department of Education in Ontario is very keen that it should be used as a text in the High Schools, to be added to the Titanic, the Cachalot and other poems.[428]) I am preparing the text of the others now for next September, but I am wondering about its prior publication. Macmillans would bring it out separately in a book, but I feel that a poem of 500 lines is too short for a book, and it is too long for a magazine though I feel that the Star Weekly might take it though I don't like such a medium.

I am sending it along to you for extracts if you feel that the selections can be tied together by a prefatory note. I don't care about the financial side. The regular rate suits me fine, but I hesitate to impose anything of disproportionate length. Perhaps a hundred lines might be worked in or a little more or a little less. In any case you are welcome to any portion you think practicable, or, if impracticable, you can return the poem. Either way will satisfy me.

I regard the work as much more satisfying than 'They Are Returning' which was occasional only – depending for part of its value upon the tread of boots back to Canada. This, however, is not occasional at least from my point of view, and it wasn't done in a hurry like the other poem. Well, old dear, do what you like. I should love to have an old-time evening with you. Remember me to Esther, Roy, Garnet, Bill, Jack.[429]

As ever, Ned.

I am sending the poem surface mail. You ought to get it in a week.

---

426 The poem he would name 'Behind the Log.'

427 Professor of physics at University College, Toronto

428 In the left margin of the letter Pratt wrote 'Very confidential at present till released.' (See the letter to M.M.H. MacKinnon, 23 October 1946 [p. 387].)

429 Esther Birney (Earle's wife), Roy Daniells, Garnet Sedgewick, and Bill Robbins. Jack is unidentified.

TO EARLE BIRNEY

Dec. 13, 1946

Dear Earle:

I was so glad to get your letter today with its appreciation of the poem[430] and I am very grateful for your points of criticism which I think is quite valid.

In respect to publication there are two or three matters which deserve mention.

(1) The Macmillans want to bring it out as a separate book but as I intend spending some time revising the poem in the early spring (when lectures relax) it will be a *fall* publication. Hence there will be no trouble about priority.
(2) The C.B.C. have asked for the poem and have consulted with Merrill Denison in regard to its radio dramatisation. They want it on the air this coming New Year's Day – a one-half hour presentation, but as the radio script will abridge here and retain there there shouldn't be any difficulty. I am told that a radio performance works up interest in the published appearance.
(3) I am satisfied with the June issue of the C.P.M. if you want the poem in its entirety. I should prefer that date to March as I am now revising the poem – expanding it to perhaps another forty lines, and revision always takes me a hell of an amount of time – more than the original construction. In fact it is a remarkable coincidence that I was doing just what you suggested in your letter. I was retouching the conclusion in precisely your terms and I was making more of the asdic operator[431] who is so vital to the scene. I feel that he is too sparsely handled in the first copy. I want to show that Kelvin[432] and Doppler[433] are behind him in getting that echo.

I shall send you the revised copy in plenty of time if you still think the magazine could carry such a long load. I own the copyright till next September when

430 On 9 December 1946, Birney had written, 'My only criticism … is that the poem is too short. In creating a "dying fall" at the end I think you have left out something that I, at least, wanted – an evaluating story in terms of humanity both the dead and the survivors, and the meaning of their deeds. I feel that you have taken on an action so enormous that the human figures tend to get lost in the spectacle, as they do not in the "Roosevelt and the Antinoe"' (Birney, FRBL).

431 See the note to 'asdics' in the letter to E.K. Brown, 27 July 1945 (p. 355).

432 British scientist William Thomson, Lord Kelvin (1824–1907), was noted for his work on electric oscillations, which formed the basis of wireless telegraphy.

433 Austrian physicist Christian Johann Doppler (1803–53) discovered the 'Doppler effect': the apparent change in frequency of sound waves and light waves in accordance with the relative velocity of the source and the observer.

Macmillans take over, and therefore I shall not allow the poem to be published even in extracts until after June.

The very best to you, Esther
& Bill.
Ned.

TO WILLIAM ARTHUR DEACON

21 Cortleigh Blvd.
Toronto

Monday am. [early 1947]

Dear Bill:

Will you let me know any further details about that Montreal representation or rather misrepresentation?[434] Did the Sproule[435] group print my name in connection with their rump Parliament? I knew nothing about their secession and certainly was not approached to speak at any one of their meetings. Should I write Gwethalyn[436] or would you do it at my request?[437]

I have a piece of news for your Fly leaf[438] if you would be kind enough to put it in. Claire has started a mail-order book business called the Book Truck operated from the house, 21 Cortleigh.[439] She has made connections with the Publishers and will use the house for a store room. She is making up a mail order list and will be soliciting purchases by correspondence exclusively.

As ever
Ned.

---

434 A faction of the Montreal branch of the CAA, mostly members of the poetry group under Dorothy Sproule, had resigned from the branch and formed a small, short-lived independent association. It had been falsely reported that Pratt had agreed to address the group. Deacon was then national president of the CAA.

435 Dorothy Sproule.

436 Gwethalyn Graham was a Montreal novelist, author of the best-selling *Earth and High Heaven*, which had won the 1944 Governor General's Award for fiction. Active in the Montreal branch of the CAA and an opponent of the secessionist movement, she was one of Deacon's three vice-presidents of the CAA.

437 This paragraph is bracketed and marked 'confidential' in the left margin.

438 Deacon's column in the *Globe and Mail*.

439 Claire's mail-order book business, later renamed 'The Claire Pratt Book Service,' operated from 1946 to 1950.

TO EARLE BIRNEY

Jan. 2, 1947

Dear Earle:

The radio production[440] came off well and quite a few responses are coming in already. I tried to get a plug in for the C.P.M. but the Producer was scared of plugs. However, Deacon gave it the first paragraph in his fly-leaf and was most enthusiastic over the presentation.

I think though that quite a bit of work has to be done on it yet, and much in accord with your suggestions. I am finding the character expansions very stimulating to myself. When I get it all finished I'll send it to you and if you find it too long we can work together upon any necessary excisions. I have by the way got in touch with the actual asdic operator on the Skeena that night.

I have heard several favourable comments on your January issue, and quite a lot of adverse criticism of Anderson's[441] meaningless imagery. He has a fund of images all right but little power of direction & application. That mixture of social criticism and surrealism is just oil and water, and is getting tiresomely out-of-date, in spite of the assumption of modernity.

Still you are wise in your catholic attitude of editorial approach. Did you see Sandwell's[442] short notice in the Bookman? I am writing O'Brien[443] to the same effect.

Ned

TO PELHAM EDGAR

Jan 13, 1947

Dear Pelham:

Your John (and mine) crackled from the page.[444] He was indeed electrically alive. I can hear his volleys yet in your house.

440 Of 'Behind the Log.'

441 Patrick Anderson.

442 B.K. Sandwell.

443 Arthur H. O'Brien, born (1865) and educated in Toronto, was a lawyer by profession who acted as legal counsel for the CAA for many years.

444 Edgar had sent him a letter he had received from John C. Robertson, long since retired as dean at Victoria College. Robertson had complained about the paucity of his pension from the college and its inadequacy to meet his recent expenses.

I ran in to see Sissons[445] about the proposed new deals in Victoria finance. S. is our senior man on the staff and he presented the case to the Council[446] for general rehabilitation. The Board[447] last year gave us a 5 percent bonus and that will be repeated this year with possibly an increase. Several recommendations were made – (1) that the Vic salaries be moved up to approximate those at U.C.[448] That recommendation will certainly be rejected. Nothing higher than the ten percent will be considered, and that won't become effective till next summer: (2) that the superannuation time be 70 (65 + annual appointments as at U.C.). Brown[449] is irrevocably opposed to it and has intimated to Sissons that if there is any change it will be retrogressive. Sissons appears to B. to be arguing for Si here: (3) that the Pension be increased in proportion to the advance in the cost of living. All the staff recognize that this claim is indisputable. What the Board will do remains to be seen. Sissons informed me that during the last two years (since he passed 65) the Pension Fund was drawn on to supply $1800 of his $5000, and that, if any of us go beyond the 65, such will be the practice.

Brown countered Sissons' personal opinion, that retirement should be advanced to 70, with the realistic contention that the University must more and more become a young man's institution. Sissons struck a shoal with every tack.

I have a feeling that Robins[450] and I will be given some extension. My case comes up next July, and Robins's the year following as he is one year younger.[451] I have no complaint against Brown personally. He allows Vi to help me with the flood of essays and pays her 35 cents per. It amounts to pin money. Robins[452] gets another $200 for his Library work.

It is the Pension matter which is our gravest consideration. I don't see how a fair-minded Board can keep it where it is.

Robertson's letter is informative but he is not in your plight nor in mine prospectively. He must have saved a good deal over his lifetime, getting top pay and being conservative. Grant[453] has been earning good money for twenty years and his wife is well off. And hospital expenses! Who does not have them? In *one* year I paid out over a thousand dollars for Claire – one year only. And you have to provide for dear little Jane.

---

445 Charles B. Sissons (1879–1965) was professor of ancient history at Victoria College, author of *Edgerton Ryerson: His Life and Letters* (Oxford: Oxford University Press, 1937, 1947) and *A History of Victoria University* (Toronto: University of Toronto Press, 1952). An ardent mountaineer, he was president of the Alpine Club in 1920–2.

446 Faculty Council.

447 Board of Regents.

448 University College.

449 Walter T. Brown, president of Victoria College.

450 J.D. Robins.

451 Born in 1882, Pratt was actually two years older than Robins.

452 Robins, professor and head of the English Department, was also chief librarian.

453 Grant Robertson, son of J.C. Robertson, taught Greek at Victoria College.

I shall pass on to you anything I hear from time to time. In the meantime my love to Dona, Jane and a big slab to yourself. Hoping you are over the bloody phlebitis.

Ned

TO JOHN M. GRAY

Jan. 28, 1947

Dear Jack:

Here is the script[454] revised for the present. It has to be expanded somewhat yet but this ought to be enough to give Macdonald[455] and New York and London[456] an idea of the book. As I have difficulty in typing, could someone type out a few copies and let me have two or three? There is a great deal of interest developing in the poem all over Canada and I think we can do something with it in a big way. I hope Macmillans in N.Y. and London will share in the marketing. I know you will do your best. The C.B.C. will do a lot of publicity for us a few weeks before its appearance. Scott[457] and Morrison[458] are very keen about it. Too bad you are going to be out of the city on my birthday Stag, Feb. 15. Frank[459] is coming anyway.

The best,
Ned.

---

454 Of 'Behind the Log.'

455 Grant Macdonald, who was illustrating the book.

456 The American and British Macmillan Companies.

457 James Scott (b. 1916), at various times professor of English, literary editor, author, and political organizer, was in the Talks and Public Affairs Department at the CBC.

458 Hugh W. Morrison (b. 1908), a graduate of Oxford (Rhodes Scholar) and director of Talks and Public Affairs at the CBC 1938–42, was currently working in public relations in New York. In 1948, he would return to Canada as director of the CBC International's Latin American Service.

459 Frank Upjohn of Macmillan.

TO ELLEN ELLIOTT

Feb. 19, 1947

Dear Ellen:

It's too bad that Knopf refused 'Behind the Log' but the N.Y. Mac's[460] may take it. It is a bit small in size but the illustrations may help to swell it out. Besides it will be larger when I have finished it. Knopf sold over one thousand of the 'Collected' but as he expected to get rid of his 3000 (which was the first edition) he is disappointed. Follett[461] told me that they intended keeping it on their shelves indefinitely as they believed in it and there was a library sale which was fairly steady if it was slow. I am afraid that we can't compete with *Forever Amber*[462] and such sellers. We are at a disadvantage. However, let us hope. I have been looking over the reviews (of the Collected Poems) from the American Press and apart from two[463] the reception has been all that I could desire. Yet the sales are thin. We always live in the future.

No need to answer this note.

Ned.

TO EARLE BIRNEY

March 18, 1947

Dear Earle:

O'Brien[464] has just telephoned me about sending the script pronto. I have been working like hell at it to give it shape and human intensity. The poem is developing a lot because of the introduction of a number of characters other than the

460 The American branch of Macmillan Publishing.

461 In the Sales Department of Alfred A. Knopf Inc.

462 A popular, mildly risqué novel by the American writer Kathleen Windsor.

463 He is probably referring to reviews by Babette Deutsch in the *New York Herald Tribune* (29 July 1945), who described his major narratives as 'all unhappily too long-winded and verbose to be … touching or exciting … Mr Pratt says too much and says it too emphatically'; and by Winfield Scott in *Poetry* (September 1945), who saw little to commend in Pratt's work, finding it dull, old-fashioned, and lacking excitement.

464 Arthur H. O'Brien.

asdic operator, buffer, stoker, captain, etc. It is going much beyond the limits of a magazine poem so I am sending a new script containing one or two amplifications which you can use instead of the original. O'Brien says the poem should not go beyond fifteen pages or 500 lines (circa). I feel, too, that there might be criticism of such space allotted to one person. I am sending it to you within ten days deadline, if that is O.K.

I had to argue the case with Macmillans who will bring out the book (with Grant Macdonald illustrations[465]) by next fall. They wondered if too much market attention to the magazine would interfere with the book sales, but I had decided on the C.P.M. before I submitted the m.s. to the firm. They now agree. I think that eventually, say in three months, I shall have something that won't be too bad. Your suggestions have helped a lot – a most fruitful directive.

Do not reply to this note, as my longer letter plus m.s. ought to reach you before the end of March. In the later letter I have some ripping stories ('don'tyerknow') which will tickle the palate I hope.

Love to Esther & Bill
Ned.

465 Grant Macdonald (1909–87), a graduate of the Ontario College of Art, was one the Navy's official war artists. Perhaps best known for his portraits of actors, he portrayed other celebrated subjects, including Pratt.

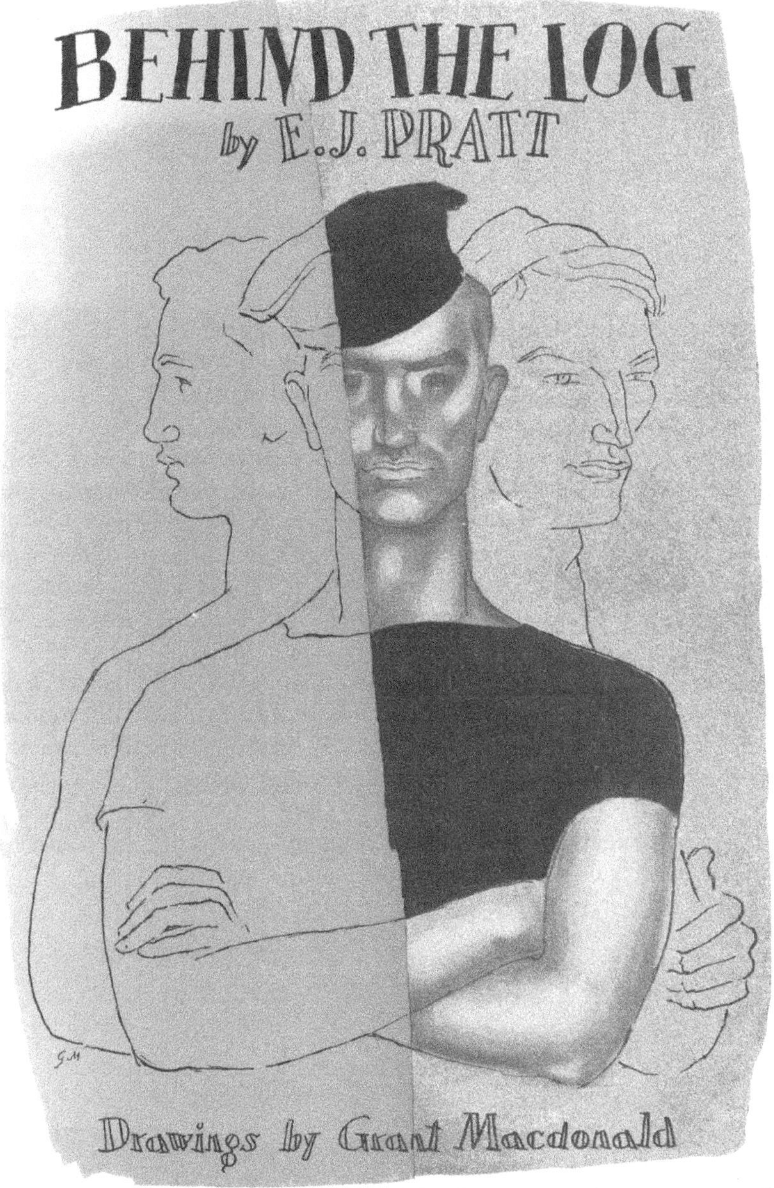

Behind the Log (Macmillan 1947) was designed and illustrated by war artist Grant Macdonald.

Please don't quit CPM. for a year. I had a talk with Deacon. We all hope you'll hold on for another year.

TO EARLE BIRNEY

March 23, 1947

Dear Earle:

It is now late Sunday night and I have just finished typing with one finger the revised Behind the Log. I have been acting on your most valued suggestions and I feel that there is quite a bit to be done. My last draft calls for close to a thousand lines and it may be some time into the summer before I get it finished for Macmillans. I expect to go to Ottawa to get the 'low down' on the Convoy Briefing.

O'Brien intimated that the poem should not go beyond five hundred lines as there should be room left for other contributors in the same issue.[466] Five hundred is the approximate figure. Hence, I have been working to condense the poem to manageable length. I brought it down to 560 and now I have indicated in the margin how another 40 lines may be excised. See page 2 for the account of torpedoes symbolised. Page 4 for the Arctic description. And page 6.

I have altered some of the poem and put my main weight on the concluding sections which strike me as the best of the job. I hope you like the direction I am proceeding, because it is along that line I shall do my elaborations this summer. I have five or six individual characters to go in but I haven't their sweaters on yet. It will take time.

I hope you do not leave the C.P.M. for some time, as I cannot see a successor to you. He may turn up in a year perhaps.

All good luck,
Ned

---

466 See the letters to Birney, 27 November 1946 (*EJP: Web*) and 18 March 1947 (pp. 395–7).

TO EARLE BIRNEY

April 9, 1947

Dear Earle:

You are always helpful in your suggestions. It is too late though to do much revision for the magazine. I shall have to content myself for leisurely and careful expansion and transposition during the months ahead.

I think, however, you had better make a couple of small changes[467] – '*were* answering' instead of *was* on page 5. And how about 'merely heroic memories by morning.' *Merely* gets rid of the repetitive *only*.

I wonder if *bursting* would do for the first *loaded*.

'Empire Hudson, leader of port wing
Bursting with grain.'

It avoids the second *loaded* which I had overlooked. If, however, you have sent the stuff forward let the changes slide.

I shall have to take more time in the redistribution of the cargo,[468] though I feel strongly that I ought to excise the four lines – 'Hundreds of trucks …' to 'thousand planes' and follow up 'others deep with freight,' with 'Twelve columns – stations.' This would read logically and get rid of the catalogue – What do you think?

If it appeals to you and there is time do it, will you?[469]

I like Bill Robbins' grand medley of Butler, Pope, Dryden, Byron et al.[470] We need a lot of that sort of thing today. Congratulate Bill upon a superb bit of fun and incisive mockery.

Love to Esther & boy,
Ned.

B.C. will be taking the poetic lead from U of T. More power to you anyway. Please cut Dr in front of my name for successive issues. Just E.J. Pratt.

467 These changes were made.

468 In his letter of 28 March 1947, Birney had approved Pratt's plan to introduce more characters, but also suggested that 'the catalogue of cargoes seems perfunctory & the phrasing montonous (e.g. "loaded" used twice in four lines). Isn't it enough to bring in the cargo when the individual ship comes into the action – leave names & cargo-details until then.'

469 Again, the corrections were made.

470 'Canadiad,' by William Robbins, published in *CPM* (March 1947).

TO FRANK UPJOHN

[May 1947]

Dear Frank:

Here is the complete draft[471] though spelling, punctuation will have to be gone over.

Should Grant Macdonald have this, do you think? He may need the elaborated account. I hope G.M. doesn't do *all* his illustrations as portraits. The ships need attention too.

I shall have to write a short Foreword giving my acknowledgements to the Navy. I am going to Ottawa tomorrow for two or three days at the invitation of the Naval Board. A bang-up dinner at the Chateau tomorrow night with all the frills – well! – nearly all!

Ned P.

TO JOHN M. GRAY

June 4th, 1947

Dear Jack:

I have split up the Norwegian's speech into a medley.[472] The English intrusions taken together with the Danish master's interpretation should make the drift clear enough. I think the foreign masters are necessary to give a complete account of the straits into which the Admiralty was forced in the early years of the war when all possible ships were requisitioned. They had Russians too later on.

You do not need to reply to this. You can substitute this page for the one you already have.

We must arrange for a lunch or dinner soon.

As ever,
Ned

471 Of 'Behind the Log.'

472 Pratt is still making revisions in the manuscript of 'Behind the Log.'

TO W.E. COLLIN

June 28, 1947

Dear W.E.

Every October Victoria College arranges a series of lectures on Canadian literature, one a week for the month. It is our custom to invite an out-of-town guest to give the first of the four. Last year A.J.M. Smith gave an address on pre-Confederation poetry, and the year before Pelham Edgar spoke on Scott, Lampman and the others.

We are inviting you this year to give the opening lecture on French-Canadian poetry. Could you come? We would pay expenses and a small honorarium, I think it is $25.00. If you can do it, I should like to be host at a dinner for you, very informal indeed, but very cordial.

Personally, I should be keen to see you again after such a long absence.

Yours sincerely,
Ned Pratt

TO VIOLA PRATT

Friday am. [18 July 1947]

Dearest Vi:

I have just written out the 'Foreword' finally, I hope. Would it be too much to have it typed and one copy put in Hibbard's[473] script, attached to the pages. I am sending the other pages so you can make any comparisons, in case of illegible letters and words.

You might then return the other two copies to me so I can put them in my books – the original will go into the Macmillan's hands for printing.

I think it is all finished now though I may come across a word or two which will need changing.

473 Captain James C. Hibbard, D.S.C and Bar, later vice-admiral, was senior officer of the escort during the action described in 'Behind the Log.'

What lovely weather we are having? I should like to see this all the summer. I shall come home next Friday evening. That helps to break the trip.

Lovingly,
Ned.

TO ALBERT G. HATCHER

July 31, 1947

My dear Bert:

Thanks again for your warm invitation to Newfoundland.[474] I should be delighted to go but I think, as Cal does, that a year from now would be more suitable. A series of lectures is likely to come off a poor second in competition with an organized Concert programme.

Cal made a tentative, very tentative, suggestion to me when he was in Toronto some months ago. He wanted me to visit the 'old country' before very long and deliver a few addresses or recitals, one to the Kiwanians (or Rotarians), one as a broadcast, and possibly two or three others which might be sponsored by societies or institutions. A trip of such length could be justified (apart from the pleasure of the visit itself) by a series of lectures, and he wondered if the Memorial College would undertake such sponsorship. It gives me great satisfaction to know that you initiated or at least approved the suggestion.

I think I could manage to get away during the last week in September 1948 and stay for the first few days of October. It would mean delaying my University work here but that could be arranged if I knew sufficiently in advance.

During the time in St. John's I could give three lectures (excluding the two special ones) or subjects relating to my own work, say, provisionally, 'Poetry of the Sea,' 'The technique of the dramatic narrative,' 'the *Titanic* as a study in Irony,' or kindred subjects which would let me to work in some readings and some references to Newfoundland life.[475] This could all be straightened out with a bit of discussion.

With kindest personal regards,
E.J. Pratt

---

474 Hatcher had initially invited Pratt to address the graduates of Memorial University College at the May convocation. Pratt had declined in his letter of 7 April 1947 (*EJP: Web*), but suggested that he would be pleased to come at a later date.

475 In his letter to Viola Pratt, 6 July 1947 (*EJP: Web*), Pratt tells her he is preparing 'the Nfld. skeletons of lectures.'

TO JOHN M. GRAY

Summer School
Queen's University
Kingston,

Sunday [10 Aug. 1947]

Dear Jack:

Thanks for your note about Grant.[476] I had an hour with him yesterday and found him most congenial. It was a surprise to know that he was the officer who took me over the Puncher the aircraft cruiser at Halifax two years ago.

His drawings are splendid and just what I want. I suggested a couple of changes – one being the cutting out of the submarine in the picture showing the asdic operator listening. I pointed out to him that the asdic worked only with *submerged* objects. He saw that and is complying. The portraits are tip-top. I hope the expense isn't too great as I have memories of Sclater's sale failures.[477] You must go according to your estimates, of course, but I trust the book can be manufactured at 2.00 at most.

I shall do my best to sell the book in as unobtrusive a manner as possible. I have received four invitations already and wherever possible I should like to have the books at hand generally at the book stores and occasionally I hope at the lecture halls wherever signing is requested.

Russ Locke[478] wants me to speak to his group of men (two hundred of them) in Toronto late October. It's in Timothy Eaton Church. There is Peterborough on Oct. 20, the Detroit Modern Language Association where upwards of 1000 professors attend in Dec., and yesterday, the enclosed came along.[479] I shall make 'Behind the Log' the theme on all and later occasions, so the stimulation through lectures should mean some promotion. Also I have to speak in the Chapel of Victoria on it the last week of October and I imagine our Book Bureau could palm off a few sales.

If this book doesn't sell I won't bring out another. It is true that Knopf was disappointed in his American sales of the Collected but still over a thousand sold and the book, he tells me, will be held in stock indefinitely as the critical journals, barring a few of the '*aesthetic* variety' are referring to it fairly frequently

476 Grant Macdonald.

477 William Sclater's book, *Haida*, published by Oxford University Press.

478 Russell Locke, a brother of Clark Locke (see the note to 'Clark and Nora Locke' in the letter to Claire Pratt, 4 November 1944 [p. 302]), was a Toronto lawyer and judge.

479 An invitation to address the Ottawa Rotary Club.

and in warm terms. By the way Benét[480] wrote me last week. He wonders when the 'Navy poem' will be out. He has often referred to it. I hope N.Y. Macmillans will represent it on some terms or other.

I thought the English sale of the Collected wasn't too bad for a Canadian, and considering the appalling conditions over there. Still, it is U.S.A. that's most important.

I shall be coming in next week for good, remaining in Toronto till the term opens. I'll be seeing you. Glad you're in the York Club.[481] We'll have many an evening together.

As ever
Ned.

TO HELEN O'REILLY[482]

August 21, 1947

Miss Helen O'Reilly,
Macmillans,
70 Bond Street
Toronto.

Dear Helen:

I have been shuffling through my papers and have discovered a few things of interest.

Will you pass on the Modern Language invitation[483] to the appropriate source and send it back to me later? Upwards of a thousand teachers and professors will attend this Conference though I don't flatter myself that such a number will listen to me. However, my lecture is for the general membership and a fair audience can be anticipated. *Behind the Log* will be my subject. Will you tell Mrs. Patterson[484] that I shall notify her, through you, of any American lectures that may be impending. You might send her a copy of the enclosed letter.

Here are some of Hibbard's letters. In another letter he stated something like this – '"Behind the Log" has succeeded wonderfully in recreating the

---

480 William Rose Benét.

481 In a letter to John Gray, 29 November 1946 (*EJP: Web*), Pratt says he has nominated him for membership.

482 The replacement at Macmillan for Ellen Elliott, who had recently resigned.

483 See the fourth paragraph of the letter to John Gray, 10 August 1947 (p. 403).

484 Of the New York office of the Macmillan Company.

atmosphere and main course of the action in the first wolf-pack battle of the North Atlantic.' Captain J.C. Hibbard, senior escort officer in command of the convoy known as S.C.42.

You might ask him if he would O.K. this statement or amend it or add to it. It will be on the cover.[485] An acknowledgement of his help will be made in the Foreword.[486] He likes a bit of taffy, etc., etc. A lot of general interest is being developed in the event and the publication.

I am sending one of Knopf's pamphlets. The ticked sentences[487] might be used with the New York Times account and Morgan-Powell's[488] and Deacon's[489] according to space. You will know what is best here.

Anything else of interest that comes my way I shall send along.

Yours sincerely
E.J. Pratt

Excuse my one-finger typing.

TO CLAIRE PRATT

21 Cortleigh Blvd.
Toronto, Canada

[late Aug. 1947]

Dearest Cakes[490]:

I spent most of the day at Macmillans. Gray invited me in to a meeting of the sales staff & called on me to give a pep-talk. I told them the story but I am not sure it had any sales pep. At least I didn't sniffle and sneeze as an unmentioned

---

485 The quotation from Captain Hibbard appears on the back inside of the dust wrapper.

486 The acknowledgment of Hibbard's assistance reads as follows: 'For use of his Log and the Report of Proceedings, and for his personal narrative, I am deeply indebted to the commanding officer of H.M.C.S. *Skeena*, Captain James C. Hibbard. D.S.C. and Bar, R.C.N., who as senior officer of the escort was in command during this sixty-hour action off Cape Farewell."

487 On the back cover of the completed dust wrapper, the *New York Times* review, and E.K. Brown's review in *UTQ* are quoted.

488 Samuel Morgan-Powell's review of *CP1*: 'New Edition of Poems by E.J. Pratt,' *Montreal Star*, 4 November 1944, 22.

489 W.A. Deacon's review of *CP1*: 'Pratt's Definitive Edition Symbol of Poetic Leadership,' *Globe and Mail*, 21 October 1947, 21.

490 Claire was in Cleveland. See letter to Viola and Claire Pratt, 7 August 1947 (*EJP: Web*).

person did on a previous occasion. I told them about Spinney[491] and how the English R.N.[492] officers liked the episode. Grant Macdonald has done a fine job.[493] The book will be out by late October.

Love.
Father.

TO HELEN O'REILLY

21 Cortleigh Blvd.

Tuesday am. [9 Sept. 1947]

Dear Helen:

The wrapper material[494] is perfect. I made some slight emendations as indicated in our telephone conversation. I hope the Naval Board passes on Hibbard's comment favourably. If there is a hitch there I wonder if Admiral Grant[495] would offer a statement.

There is no need to answer this note. I shall be in touch with you soon.

Lor' bless you.

E.J.P.

TO EARLE BIRNEY

Sept. 30, 1947

My dear Earle:

You will have to excuse any typographical errors in this missive because I have just come [from] a glorious party (I had almost said 'farty') and am feeling on the top of the world for a few hours. I should love to have you and the family

---

491 A character in *BL*, a young classics student who had joined the navy as a rating, a sailor with specialized training.

492 Royal Navy.

493 On the illustrations for *BL*.

494 The dust jacket for *BL*. See the letter to O'Reilly, 21 August (p. 405).

495 Vice-Admiral Harold W.T. Grant, born (1899) in Halifax, held commands in both the Canadian and British navies, serving at sea during the Second World War before being appointed chief of the naval staff in Ottawa in 1947.

here for a session so that all inhibitions could be released and the flow of soul continue uninterrupted. God bless you and Esther and Bill. By the way I have made a vow not less sacred than the vows of Brébeuf, namely, that not one of the children of my dearest friends should ever come to want while I have a quarter in my pocket. I have made the vow in respect to Pelham's daughter, Jane. He was one of my truest friends, loyal throughout life. The poor bugger didn't save up much in the tenure of his office and now, though he has a College pension, yet he is in undignified quarters, living in one of Currelly's houses near Port Hope. He tells me that he is reduced to a kitchen. I am going to motor down to his place soon with a hamper. Bill will come under the same codicil as Jane and as earnest of the pledge I am sending this little note for him to deposit into a safety box as a start.

Now to get down to business, there are several things I want to say. The C.P.M. printing[496] was excellent and I received more than a hundred letters of appreciation. You probably received as many of disapprobation, and I don't give a damn.

Second: I had a party the other night with Knox, Sirluck, Bissell, B.K. Sandwell (whom I love and shall always love) and several others, and we spent some time talking about the future of Canadian poetry. I claimed as I have maintained for some years, that you were our white hope, that no one, particularly in the Montreal 'faction,' was even within light-years of your constellation. I had your Now is Time[497] and leafed it through. We agreed on the main quality of your work, but differed on individual poems. I had always held up *David* in your former volume as the masterpiece though I must say that *Joe Harris*[498] was so close a rival that I could not maintain an argument with much force against one who would pick the latter as a winner. B.K. said that he was very proud that it appeared in the Saturday Night. The poem simply tears me up just as *Hands*[499] does. That last poem is worth more to me than all the bilge that has appeared in the Northern Review in many a moon, or in the general run of contemporary verse. Sirluck liked *Anglosaxon Street*[500] best of all your work. I differed, as did the others, but as I was not familiar with Old English I didn't pursue the point. However, the whole room was full of your friends, all well-wishers for your future.

Third: Frank Scott was here last week and, though I did not see him, Norrie[501] told me the gossip about the Montreal egomaniacs. Scott and two or three others have resigned, leaving the running to Sutherland, Harrison, Layton[502] and

---

496 Of the abridged version of 'Behind the Log,' published in the Spring number of *CPM*.

497 Birney's second book of poems, published in 1945 by Ryerson Press.

498 A poem in *Now is Time*.

499 A poem in Birney's first collection *David and Other Poems* (1942).

500 A poem in *Now is Time*.

501 Northrop Frye.

502 John Sutherland, John Harrison, and Irving Layton.

the rest. The crux was the onslaught on Finch,[503] but it was only the climax of a series of attacks on *all* non-Northern Review satellites. They had exterminated Roberts, Lampman, Pickthall,[504] and Duncan Campbell Scott (this last was atrocious in its venom). Why they jumped the ditch and got after Finch, I suppose it was on account of the timeliness (pardon) of the production. Sometime ago I wrote Scott telling him that he and his co-adjudicators knew nothing about criticism. I expounded to him that criticism etymologically (you see I have spelled the word correctly) meant discrimination, a winnowing of the good from the chaff, and those bastards were out for wholesale slaughter, allowing nothing good in Canada before the appearance of their smutty forms. Look at the dismissal of D.C. Scott, as if his sixty years of writing meant nothing in this country. Probably the sheet will die, but not before you and I are swept into the limbo, for we are next on the Gestapo or N.K.V.D.[505] blacklist.

Fourth: I hope you will keep on with the C.P.M. for a while yet until a suitable successor is found.

Fifth: (You will note by this time, unless you have been out to a joint, how logical I am). Paul Arthur asked me recently if I would contribute to a new magazine[506] which a young group are forming, and be a supporter. He is an able youngster, the son of an old friend, Eric Arthur in Architecture here. He asked for a poem and a message. I told him that I had not written a short poem for two years and did not see any chance of doing so for months to come, in view of the great deluge of students and the work involved. He asked me then if I would go on the masthead. That I refused because I was on the C.P.M. I might, however, write a message of encouragement, etc. etc. He said that he had approached you. His magazine wouldn't conflict with ours because it was prose and verse. I guess it is all right: the more interest generated in poetry throughout Canada, the better for the craft. This brings me to my

Sixth: Earle, I haven't a line as yet, but if the Muse warbles into my cochlea during the next two months, I shall send something, though you must return it if it isn't suitable. The note may be that of a hermit-thrush or a crow, God knows. We shall see.

---

503 A highly critical commentary by John Sutherland in *Northern Review* (August-September 1947) on the awarding of the Governor General's Medal for poetry to Robert Finch's *Poems* (1946) and on Birney, E.K. Brown, and Leo Cox, who judged the competition.

504 Charles G.D. Roberts, Archibald Lampman, and Marjorie Pickthall

505 The Russian secret police, later the KGB.

506 *Here and Now*, which published four numbers between December 1947 and June 1949. Pratt contributed a brief foreword to the first number.

Seventh: I haven't seen the fall number of the C.P.M. yet, but I have the same doubt about Wells' and Klinck's book[507] as you have. I am embarrassed over a biography as people say – 'So, Ned, you're not dead after all.' Still, I cannot argue over anything so kind in its general attitude: hence I shall say no more.

My love to Esther and Bill,

Affectionately,
Ned

TO EARLE BIRNEY

Dec. 3, 1947

Dear Earle:

You asked me to submit some verses for 'Outposts.'[508] I have just finished *Lake Success*[509] after working at it for two weeks or more. It is the only poem I have done since Behind the Log. And it isn't likely that I shall have any more for some time. You know best what kind of contributions you need for your purpose, and if you find that it is unacceptable, do not hesitate to return it. I shall understand.

Behind the Log is having a good advance sale, a thousand before publication. It is being released this week and Simpson's Book Department is giving me an autographing party on Saturday. I hope you will like the complete poem with its dramatic sketches most of which have been suggested by your good self.

My love as usual to Esther, Bill,
and you.
Ned.

---

507 *Edwin J. Pratt: The Man and His Poetry* by H.W. Wells and Carl Klinck had been published by Ryerson Press in May 1947.

508 A British journal. Birney had been asked to edit a Canadian issue.

509 First published in *Outposts* 10 (Summer 1948), it was published as 'Summit Meetings' (*EJP: CP* 2.186) in the second edition of *CP2*.

TO A.J.M. SMITH

Jan. 6, 1948

My dear Arthur:

It was grand to see you and your lovable Jean at the Convention.[510] You and the Canadian group made the visit a holiday for Vi and me.

I am sending along a copy of the 'Collected' which is a Second Edition.[511] You will notice that the 'Witches Brew' is reduced by about fifty lines from the original as it appeared in the Selwyn & Blount English Edition.[512]

I have two or three extra minor alterations – Instead of the sub-caption – 'In celebration of a fifth wedding anniversary' I have substituted – 'An account of a nightmare' which has more meaning than the former. And wherever ¶ is in the margin please make space to indicate *paragraphic* space.

When you write Macmillans suggest that you are re-arranging your Anthology[513] and would like to put in the Witches Brew, hoping that the *Cost* wouldn't be prohibitive et cetera. Gray may take it up with me and I'll do my best to lower the amount. Let me know what he says.

Most affectionately
Ned

You may keep this copy.

N.

---

510 The MLA conference in Detroit. (See the letter to John M. Gray, 10 August 1947 [p. 403].) Jean was Smith's wife.

511 His *CP1* was reissued in 1946.

512 He is mistaken. 'The Witches' Brew' as it appears in *CP1* has exactly the same lines as in the first edition of the poem. He may be confusing it with 'The Great Feud,' which was reduced by about fifty lines from its length in *Titans* (1926).

513 Smith was preparing a second, revised edition of his anthology *The Book of Canadian Poetry*, first published in 1943. 'The Witches' Brew' was included.

TO A.J.M. SMITH

Feb. 14, 1948

Dear Arthur:

I have just sent off a copy the 'Log' as it is quite possible that the other went astray in the New Year's rush.

Thanks for the inclusion of the W.B.[514] It was wise to subtract the other two[515] as some criticism might come in on account of undue proportion.

The W.B., of all my productions, depends most on caprice of taste, some people liking it enormously, others thinking it just tomfoolery and not worthy of print. One woman wrote Eayrs years ago protesting against symptoms of insanity in poetry – a Montreal dame who wrote deadly serious evangelical poems.

The Log is going well, getting fine reviews in general. Louis MacKay thought that the speeches of the Masters and others were prosaic.[516] That may be so but I intentionally did not venture to depart too much from the naval idiom. Any man who spent some of his days below deck would recognize the lingo. Certainly the RCN fellows did. I appreciated Louis' article for, despite his strictures on form it was sympathetic generally as Louis has always been to me. Birney and Sirluck like the poem best of all I have done for it is most daring in treatment. The printers let me down a lot, for after I had corrected the page proofs they dropped words, broke up speeches, omitted punctuation, and botched rhythms in many places. A second edition will have to take care of this.

What about another book of poetry from you? E.K. thinks it is high time for another. I present you to classes here with marked success.

Love to Jeannie.
Ned.

514 'The Witches' Brew' was included in the second, revised edition of Smith's *Book of Canadian Poetry* (1948).

515 'Silences' and 'The Old Eagle' were dropped from the second edition.

516 In a review of the poem 'The Feeling of Growth and Experiment Found in Pratt's Latest Work,' *Saturday Night*, 31 January 1948, 18.

TO EARLE BIRNEY

March 26, 1948

Dear Earle:

What a thrill I got yesterday when I read through your book,[517] most of the poems for the second time, and what a thrill when I discovered the dedication. I hadn't seen it the first time. Indeed it was only in the car on our way down town that Vi mentioned it. I said, 'I didn't see that!' So when I got back near midnight I took another look and sure enough there it was. I am proud to have such a volume of sterling poetry dedicated to me. There is no poetry written in Canada equal to it. I have stated that again & again privately and publically. In comparison with it, the stuff of those Northern Review fellows is bullshit. No wonder they talk about shit (their own) so much. They are good judges of that commodity considering their familiarity with it. They roll over in it like bitches on a lawn.

I think that Vancouver has stolen the spotlight in Canada for poetry – what a crew you have there now – Roy, Bill, Louis[518] and yourself. Louis has a marvellous satirical gift and I hope he goes on cultivating it. But as for yourself, Vi's remark last night struck the keynote – 'Earle has a mind as well as feelings, and a capacity to blend them.'

Love to Esther & Bill,

With brotherly love,
Ned.

Here is the latest story I got from my brother Cal who is here from Newfoundland as a guest of the Canadian Club. A fellow from Gushue who is in much demand as a radio speaker in Nfld, made a heated address against Confederation two weeks ago. He was half-tight and became more and more irresponsible as he proceeded towards his peroration which was as follows. 'If you bastards, who want Confederation down here in Newfoundland,[519] wish to get your asses burned you

517 Birney's third book, *The Strait of Anian* (Toronto: Ryerson, 1948), was dedicated to 'Ned Pratt.'

518 Roy Daniells, William Robbins, and Louis MacKay.

519 Led by former newspaperman and broadcaster Joseph R. Smallwood, the campaign of words that brought Newfoundland into Confederation with Canada in 1949 had been going on for many months. (See the letter to Smallwood, 25 April 1948 [p. 413].)

must be prepared to sit on the blisters.' That went right through the mike to all Nflders and one thousand letters came from the ladies in protest and another 1000 from the men, of congratulations.

Ned.

TO JOSEPH R. SMALLWOOD

Victoria College

25 April 1948

Dear Mr Smallwood:

It is a pleasure to record my personal wish that Newfoundland should 'come in.' As far as my connection goes, I find that such a wish is shared by the great majority of Newfoundlanders living in Canada. My one qualification is that the Terms should be attractive to the Island and that mutual trust and good will should be the basis on which the whole arrangement is effected.

Yours sincerely,
E.J. Pratt

TO E.K. BROWN

April 27, 1948

Dear Ed:

Strange as it may seem, but I have spent most of April in bed – an infected foot probably the result of a bout with the flu. The germ must have hit the instep inside as there was no abrasion. The doctor doesn't know when it will clear up – some weeks yet in any case. He wants me to give it all the rest possible though I have to get up for a few hours occasionally.

I would have written you at length otherwise, telling you how much Vi and I enjoyed your Arnold.[520] We read every sentence of it – so beautifully clear is the

---

520 *Matthew Arnold: A Study in Conflict*, published by the University of Chicago Press that year and dedicated to Pratt.

account of the conflict between disinterestedness and practicability – this moving by slow approaches and the immediate impulse to let the philistine have it direct to the pants. The book has opened up a new Arnold to me as I have dwelt generally on his sweetness and light. That claptrap passage is immense. His bile must have been working overtime when he wrote it. The conflict illustrates the contrast of style. Doesn't 'Docile echoes of the eternal voice' sound like the first line of a Wordsworthian nature poem? And then the conclusion of chapter five!!

Your notes too are most illuminating.

We are in the thick of exams. In a few days the first batch of my 200 papers will be sent up and I expect to have a few dizzy spells.

I go to Queen's again in July. Wallace[521] wrote me a most cordial invitation. But before going there, I may go to Southeastern State College in Oklahoma to give a poetry recital or two. It is a long way to go but it helps to expand one's 'American' constituency. I shall probably give *Brébeuf* and *Behind the Log* as two lectures.

When are you coming back? I shall be here till July 1, with a few intermissions.

Brébeuf was put on the air a little while ago[522] and it got a wonderful write-up by Archer in Montreal – I should say a talk-up as Archer devoted a quarter of an hour to it in 'The Listener Speaks.'[523] The C.B.C. is wonderfully pleased about the warmth of his references. The broadcast came at the perfect hour – 8-9 Wednesday (pm).

Well, here's toasting your Arnold and its wide circulation. Love to Peggy and family.

Ned

I am still basking in that dedication. I told Pelham[524] about it. We both agree that you could be the Arnold of this generation but possessing even more 'flexibility,' though God knows there are enough backsides to kick which would defy all the strategy of an Olympian.

521 R.C. Wallace, principal of Queen's University.

522 A dramatic reading of *BB* with musical accompaniment by Healey Willan was broadcast by the CBC, 17 March 1948.

523 Music critic Thomas Archer wrote for the Montreal papers and occasionally the broadcast media. His comments on the *BB* broadcast were aired on 19 March in a CBC series devoted to critiquing radio programs called *The Listener Speaks* (alternately hosted by Archer and playwright John Coulter).

524 Pelham Edgar.

TO WILLIAM ARTHUR DEACON

May 6, 1948

My Dear Bill:

I have just sent off my 'yes' to the National Secretary.[525]

I am amazed at the vast amount of time you put into the work of the organization. You have been the most sacrificial member of the C.A.A. has ever had, speaking from the commercial angle. I trust that when June is through you can get down to your own writing and your pet projects. You deserve a good store of leisure in which you can indulge your self-interests a bit.

There are a few points I want to mention in connection with the June meetings. Jack Gray informs me that I am scheduled for Thursday the 10th at nine p.m. That is all right for me but I shall have to return Friday as I have a number of Commencement addresses to give in mid-June, two in the U.S.A. It will have to be a matter of rushing to Ottawa and back. The College with its enormously increased activities is absorbing most of my energy nowadays.

I have been indoors now for a month with a flu-infected foot which is very slow in clearing up. It has caused quite a limp. I get out a little but under medical advice to rest the right instep as much as possible. I hope to get to the Branch[526] meeting a week from Friday. The trouble is a bit better than it was a week ago and I hope in two weeks or so to be walking fairly normally. (Strictly confidential.)

You do not need to reply to this note as I know your present preoccupations. I shall keep in touch with Jack Gray about Ottawa. I have found Jack a prince of a fellow. He admires and likes you, which is another point to his credit.

Kindest regards to Sal and family,
Ned

525 He had agreed to address the annual convention of the CAA in Ottawa in June. He repeated the paper on 'Science and Poetry' which he had given to the MLA in Detroit in December 1947.

526 The Toronto branch of the CAA.

TO VIOLA PRATT

152 University Ave.
Kingston, Ont.

Wednesday am. [7 July 1948]

Dearest Vi:

Your (or my) bag came yesterday, so now I can shave in peace and solitude instead of going down town. Fortunately my first lectures (on Shakespeare) were in the note books I carried in the other and larger bag.

I have a small class of less than twenty which suits me perfectly. The room is small. I don't have to lift my voice. There are four sweet nuns who sit in the front row and take voluminous notes. I hope to goodness all my facts are right if my opinions aren't. It is the real gospel you know.

It is much easier than I thought it was going to be. The term work will be light and I may have it done in class which makes it more leisurely for me.

I asked Mrs Cartwright about your coming up as last year – She said it would be perfectly all right. We shall get all our meals out. Breakfast and lunch at the Queen's, and dinner at the Club.[527] Let me know when you expect to arrive and where you stop so I can meet you. Claire will have her schedule soon I suppose.[528]

What a thunderstorm we had on Monday night – the worst I ever knew in the East! I have seen its parallel out West but never in these parts. It knocked down a heavy branch of the tree in front of our door and Mrs Cartwright was frightened by the continuous lightning. Then it came on again yesterday afternoon, almost as bad. Did you have it in Toronto?

Today is cool and bright – just perfect for me and for lecturing. This morning I saw Grant Macdonald at Queen's Restaurant. He is teaching at the school – so is Carl Schaefer.[529] I haven't seen many of my friends yet though in a day or so I'll be with some of them at the Club.

527 The Queen's Restaurant and the Cataraqui Golf Club.

528 For a holiday trip she was planning with friends to Montreal and elsewhere in the province of Quebec. (See the postcard to Claire, 9 July [*EJP: Web*].)

529 Born in Ontario, Carl Schaefer (1903–95) studied at the Ontario College of Art with painters Arthur Lismer and J.E.H. Macdonald. He first painted Ontario agrarian scenes, but later focused on starker subject matter in a more aggressive style. He was an official war artist with the RCAF and later taught at the Ontario College of Art and Queen's University.

My golf clubs are merely a handicap at present as I am determined not to play until the foot gets better. It is about the same as it was two or three weeks ago, perhaps a wee bit improved.

Much love to you dear and to Cayke. I shall drop a line to her in a day or two.

Lovingly,
Ned.

TO PELHAM EDGAR

Dept. of English
Queen's Summer School
Kingston

July 13, 1948

Dearest Pelham:

I am deeply sorry you are laid up in that fashion.[530] Peggy[531] told me before I left Toronto that you had considerable trouble with your arches and had to get around in a wheeled chair for a time. Too bloody bad that the cause is circulatory but I understand that there is a lot of vicarious action going on among the veins and that huge blockings can take place without permanent damage. Dear old boy, I know that feeling of getting out to a golf course and watching those beautiful trajectories without the capacity to emulate them.

My bloody foot is about the same as two months ago. It is indeed better than it was during the first two weeks of April when the devil hit the nerve governing the instep turn. Then the foot was red and swollen. The inflammation and swelling is gone but the pain is always there when I bend the toes. And during the last month other pains (or aches I should call them for they are dull) have developed in the right thigh & hip changing their location somewhat, so it looks like genuine rheumatism. It isn't arthritis because the joints are not infected, but I wake up at night with aches that feel like cramps. They last a

---

530 Edgar suffered from phlebitis in his legs. He died in September 1948. (See the letter to E.K. Brown, 20 November 1948 [p. 422].)

531 Margaret Ray, librarian at Victoria College.

few minutes. I take aspirin and they subside for a time, then call out again at 3 am. or 4 am. or 5 am. etc. etc. etc. Nothing acute but boringly insistent if you know what it means. It may be something like yours, except that it doesn't interfere with my standing or slow walking provided I put the pressure on the heel (right) rather than on the toes.

My chief involvement is psychological. I was sure last spring that I could play a few holes in July & August at the Cataraqui Golf Course, though Fletcher Sharpe[532] wasn't so sure. He said a climb up a hill might put me back where I was at the beginning. But by God I took my clubs to Kingston and yesterday I made the great adventure as Barber[533] called death when the poor departed blighter visited me in 1923 when I was in bed with a heart[534] – you remember.

Pelham, Dona, Jane sweethearts all – I couldn't stand those fellows (with whom I had often played in Kingston) executing their celestial curves in their first drive at the tee. I simply couldn't stand it, so I went into the locker room, got a caddy and came with a Byronic limp to the first tee. I was last of the four. Like O'Casey at the bat, I was magnificent before I struck. Foot or no foot, rheumatism or no rhuematism, immortality or no immortality, I wasn't going to let the game down or my colleagues. I struck and the god damn ball went up in the air with a curve that boomeranged it back to the first tee to the consternation of three ladies on the bench. Convulsions seized both legs and feet. Still I persisted and I wound up at the first hole with a ten, and at the third hole I resigned & returned to the locker room to get what cheer the quarters provided.

But – but – Pelham – listen! Today I am no worse!! I am going out again until by the middle of August I can play my nine – but all by myself & the caddy. There is much to be thankful for. There is still the odd lecture to be given and the odd line to be scrawled. Bless you & Dona & Jane. May Victoria College be good to us all and allow us to indulge in reminiscences in the days to come without fear of bailiffs.

Love,
Ned

P.S. I haven't seen Percival's book[535] yet but one friend told me you had written a beautiful chapter.

532 A Toronto physician.

533 Probably Rev. F.L. Barber of Victoria College.

534 See the note to 'heart convalescence' in the letter to Deacon, 27 April 1923 (p. 22).

535 *Leading Canadian Poets*, edited by W.P. Percival (Toronto: Ryerson, 1948). In fact, Pratt had read Edgar's chapter on his work in proofs sent to him by Lorne Pierce. (See the letter to Pierce, 7 June 1948 [*EJP: Web*].)

TO VIOLA PRATT

152 University Ave.
Kingston

Monday pm. [9 Aug. 1948]

Dearest Vi:

I have just had a lunch with George Herbert[536] and he has mapped out almost a week of engagements.

Tomorrow evening we go out to dinner, and spend the rest of the time at MacNeil's recording poems on his machine. Thursday he, Kyte[537] and I have an evening 'yarning.' Friday we go to see Schull's[538] play 'The Bridge' following a dinner. Gundy[539] has something either Saturday or Sunday at his place, so the time will pass quickly.

Last evening I had a group out at the Club for tea & toast (not so well done). I asked the Alexanders but I saw that Mrs A. preferred that I ask Peter.[540] It was a mistake on my part that I didn't ask him first but I got around it by saying that I wanted the Alexanders represented, and she was delighted that I asked Peter. He is a very fine chap, quite modest and intelligent. I had the Edinboroughs[541] too and the party was very pleasant. I am being asked back for dinners – Grant Macdonald wants me at his place before I leave.

If Peter comes to Toronto next year we must have him up occasionally. Mary Winspear[542] gives us the use of her wagon. She is very sociable and less blue stockingish than formerly.

---

536 G.H. Clarke.

537 E.C. Kyte, retired librarian at Queen's University.

538 Joseph Schull (1906–80), primarily a historian and biographer, also wrote verse and plays, mostly for radio.

539 H. Pearson Gundy, one of Pratt's former students, had been professor of English and head of the department at Mount Allison University. In 1948 he was head librarian at Queen's.

540 Their son.

541 Arnold Edinborough (b. 1922), assistant professor of English at Queen's (1947–54), became editor of the Kingston *Whig-Standard* (1954–8) and of *Saturday Night* (1958–62). He later purchased *Saturday Night*, serving as its president and publisher (1963–70) before becoming a contributing editor on culture for the *Financial Post* (1970–90).

542 A former student of Pratt's and Claire's former teacher at St Clement's School, Toronto, she operated a girls' school she had founded in Montreal. She had been teaching at Queen's summer school.

Today my class in the Refresher Course[543] went over after the lecture and saw three students at work under Schaefer and Masson.[544] Schaefer had one picture of two apples with clouds behind them. I think that Claire could beat him a dozen times over. And Masson's picture of the dock and derrick was not a whit better than Claire's. I should be willing to wager that if a critic saw Claire's picture, either of the boats or of the fence, and then compared it to Masson's, he would give the edge to Claire's. And one visitor was then bargaining for the Masson picture at $100.00. Claire could put on an exhibition by and by with successful results I am perfectly convinced.

Tomorrow the Refresher Course go out to Johnson's[545] house for lunch and I give the lecture there instead of in the College. Johnson is a school teacher, a veteran of the war, and a member of the class.

I hope you got back in due time Sunday afternoon – I shall be happy to be back with you next Thursday week.

Much love
Ned.

TO M.M.H. MACKINNON

Aug. 26, 1948

Dear Murdo:

It is difficult to give a settled judgment on that Short Story Quarterly[546] as there are many thorns in the bush. The idea is splendid but what about the financing?

The matter should be brought before a number of literary people first so it could be mulled over in their minds. Lorne Pierce, W. H. Clarke, and the U of T

543 An academic upgrade course for returning servicemen and for teachers to 'refresh' their knowledge of the subject.

544 Carl Schaeffer and Belgium-born artist Henri Masson (1907–96). Masson had lived in Ottawa since 1921. Trained as an engraver, he was influenced by the Group of Seven but was largely self-taught as a painter. By the mid-1940s, he was able to support himself through his art.

545 Unidentified.

546 MacKinnon had asked Pratt's advice about a quarterly that he and some colleagues at the University of Western Ontario were considering starting up.

Press might offer some practical advice. I shall moot it here and there if you wish and sometime when you come to Toronto we might have a chin about it.

I should like to see you get in on the short story business as actual creative writing. That's a long term proposal possibly. Scholarly entrenchment is, I think, the first consideration and if you feel the urge about Milton, why not go ahead and get it behind you?

Speaking to George H. Clarke[547] this summer, I found that all the Canadian Quarterlies were simply with their nostrils above water. The market is so limited. However, let's give it some thought in the days ahead.

The best,
Ned.

TO EARLE BIRNEY

Sept. 28/48

Dear Earle:

Did you see the enthusiastic review of Anian in a recent issue (two weeks back) of the Saturday Review of Literature N.Y.[548] It warmed my heart for two reasons –

(1) It was your book.
(2) The Americans are waking up to you.

Affectionately
Ned.

---

547 Clarke was editor of *QQ*.

548 The review of Birney's book of poems, *The Strait of Anian* – 'Clearing the Brush and Brambles' by Gustav Davidson – appeared on 21 August 1948.

TO E.K. BROWN

Nov. 20, 1948

Dear Ed:

Yes. Pelham[549] died nearly two months ago, I thought surely the news would have been disseminated widely, and to think that you and Ernest[550] had not heard of it.

He had been sick for several months with a clot in the right leg which blocked the blood to the foot and it looked last June as if the foot would have to be amputated. But he came to Toronto, received special treatment and it was good. He wrote me when I was at Queen's reporting progress,[551] and he seemed quite optimistic though he knew it would be a year at least with a stick or crutches. The day before he died Bert Proctor, Alan Barr and I, together with two or three others of his cronies, were to leave on a motor trip to Port Hope to spend the day with him. It began to rain and we postponed the visit.

Suddenly the end came. He was out on the verandah in the sun when he said to Dona: 'I feel queer' – *just queer* 'in the head.' No pain at all. She brought him in to his bed and he passed away in five minutes.

We got the news and Dona asked for his friends as pall-bearers – Malcolm Wallace, Bert Proctor, Alan Barr, Stewart Wallace,[552] Lorne Pierce and myself. He was buried in the St. James Cemetery.

I spent the day with Dona and Jane and ever since I have been behind a scheme (mainly through Victoria College) to provide a fund for Jane's education. It is at present confidential but things look promising. I have been asked to draft resolutions of regret, which I have done and am still doing for Boards and Clubs etc., but his death is a tremendous gap. He loved you and me particularly.

I have been going over his books and letters. The Library is interested. Dona will stay on at Port Hope. R.R.l, Port Hope will reach her. She would appreciate a letter.

I am so glad that we got him to give a course of lectures at Vic last winter. He was very successful. He supplied for Fisher[553] as you probably know.

549 Edgar.

550 Sirluck.

551 See Pratt's response to Edgar's letter, 13 July 1948 (pp. 417–18).

552 Head librarian at the University of Toronto library; historian, author or editor of many historical works, including, as editor-in-chief, *The Encyclopaedia of Canada* (1935–8).

553 Joe Fisher.

Yes I saw Deacon's review[554] and was very vexed. Vi said it wasn't a review at all but just an old time expression of his animosity to Universities in general. It wasn't personal, but just off the track. I wonder if he read it. I haven't seen Deacon for two months or more but his last remark was about the '*windy line* of approval' which was handed out to me by a Columbia Professor (in that biography).[555] It is true that the treatment is open to criticism, but he called it a lousy book. I thought Klinck's introduction was good, but I couldn't say much as it was too personal, and it was on the whole kindly as also was Wells.' Still the fault was that it was written by two '*professors*.' I was hoping that the breach was being healed but it breaks out from time to time.

I had an unfair attack made on Behind the Log by a fellow named Weaver,[556] one of the Varsity editors and I think an Endicott protegé.[557] He misquoted with, I think calculated falsification, an article appearing in the Montreal Standard by Shalto Watt.[558] I didn't reply as I never do anyway. On the whole the book got a good reception and an odd vilification doesn't disturb me, provided it comes from a second rate or third rate source. Any book can be damned if only the worst or weakest passages are printed for illustration.

To come to other matters – who's on the horizon for Western[559]? The Dean wrote me last week asking me to suggest a name for Head of the English Dept. Klinck evidently doesn't want administration.[560] Would Bill Robbins of B.C. suit, or Malcolm Ross? The Dean wants a man in the forties at least, so there wouldn't be too much of the 'youth among youths.' You know they are nearly all recent graduates there.

Well, the best as always, old chap. I hope it won't be too long before we smoke & chat together.

Ned.

---

554 Of Brown's *Matthew Arnold: A Study in Conflict* (1948).

555 Wells and Klinck's *Edwin J. Pratt: The Man and His Poetry* (1947).

556 As a student, Robert Weaver (1921–2008) wrote for *Varsity* magazine. He went on to become founder and editor of the *Tamarack Review* (1956–82) and anthologist of short stories both broadcast (in the CBC's *Anthology* series) and in print, including *Canadian Short Stories* (Toronto: Oxford University Press, 1960, 1968, 1978, 1985, 1991), *The Oxford Anthology of Canadian Literature* (1973, 1981), and *The 'Anthology' Anthology: A Selection from 30 Years of CBC Radio's 'Anthology'* (Toronto: Macmillan, 1984).

557 See the note to 'Endicott' in the letter to Arthur L. Phelps, 26 October 1922 (p. 17).

558 A Montreal journalist, for some years posted to Ottawa as a member of the House of Commons press gallery.

559 The University of Western Ontario.

560 Klinck was appointed head of the department and served many years in the position.

VI Knockings at the Door, 1948–1953

There are so many … things to take up a chap's energy … knockings at the door, etc.
– E.J. Pratt to E.K. and Margaret Brown, 16 January 1951

TO WILLIAM ROSE AND MARJORIE BENÉT

January 1, 1949

Dearest Bill and Marjorie:

A Happy New Year to the both of you sweethearts. This is just a new year's aberration. I want to thank you for your gorgeous party, one of the most pleasant I have ever had anywhere. It was the high light of my visit.[1] Those are the events I look forward to in the years ahead when travelling restrictions relax if they do. I was so glad to meet Donald Adams whom I knew only by correspondence.[2] It was nice to see Mike Sullivan[3] again. He called in to see me at the Queen's University, Kingston, Ont. last summer and I took a great liking to the chap. He came for me on Thursday night to address the Poetry Society of America. I met there a number of people whom I knew only by name.

Vi, Claire and I are talking about a motor trip to the New England coast next August, and if we go, we shall certainly look you up. The best that the gods can give to you, dears.

Yours affectionately,
Ned.

1 Pratt had attended the annual meeting of the Modern Language Association in New York.
2 See the letters to J. Donald Adams, 14 June 1945 and 28 November 1947 (*EJP: Web*).
3 A.M. Sullivan was a New York journalist. He had written a generally favourable review of *BL* for the *SRL* (15 May 1948).

TO LORNE PIERCE

January 24, 1949

My dear Lorne:

I should be glad to offer the poem entitled *Newfoundland* in the revised form as it appears on 165 in the Collected Poems.[4] It is the only substantive poem that I have written on the country itself and as it is in the form of an ode, it might suit your purpose. I haven't anything quite new and as I am working twice as hard as at any other time of my life I cannot see any leisure ahead.

The feeling against Confederation is running so high down here[5] that I wouldn't touch the issue (or comment on its benefits etc. etc.) with a pole as long as from Gander Air Port to London and back to Ottawa. In my addresses I steer clear of it as I am no economist anyway. That is the reason why a poem like *Newfoundland* would be much preferable to a Foreword which, to have any teeth in it at all, would have to refer to the union, the future and so on.

I shall be back in Toronto after ten days. They arranged a schedule here for me three times as big as formerly agreed on.

As ever
Ned.

---

4 Like other publishers, Ryerson Press was responding to the possibility of Newfoundland joining Confederation with a thematic collection, *This is Newfoundland*, edited by Ewart Young. As the most prominent Newfoundlander living in Canada, Pratt was asked – as he recalls in his letter to Pierce of 13 April 1949 – to contribute 'a prologue poem of 100 lines' (p. 430). The poem he offers here was previously published in *NV* (*EJP:CP* 1.99). However, on his return from Newfoundland, he composed two other poems for the occasion of his country's entry into Confederation, 'Newfoundland Calling' and 'Newfoundland Seamen' (*EJP: CP* 2.186–8 and 188–9). See the letter to E.K. Brown, 28 April 1949 (p. 433).

5 Pratt was in Newfoundland for a ten-day visit during which he was to make the address at a Burns Night celebration. (See *EJP: MY*, 399-401, and the letter to Leo Cox, 4 May 1949 [pp. 433–4].)

TO VIOLA AND CLAIRE PRATT

Monday morning [24 Jan. 1949]

Two dears:

Talk about a schedule and the way it grows. If it weren't for Cal's firm jaw I'd be at it from crow-time to cat-time if you know what I mean.

The plane got in to Torbay quite late as there was a delay at Sidney. Cal, who was at the airport missed me because of the delay at the customs. A cab took me or rather deposited me at Waterford Bridge Road after it had disposed of five other passengers at various Hotels. That was past midnight. All day Friday the telephone rang – Would your brother speak at the Prince of Wales Academy? at the Library? at A, at B? at C? – to which Cal said 'impossible. One body can't be at two or three different places at the same time.'

I refused to speak before the Burns Night as that's what I came down for.[6] Saturday evening Jim & Minnie came up to dinner with Jean and Gertrude (Uncle Art's daughters). We reminisced till midnight. I told them your story about Nellie, May and Dr Butterick. It was funny but not quite so side-splitting as you make it.

Minnie looked so frail, so thin. Jim is in good health or fair health.

I spent much of my time Saturday and Sunday in reworking the lectures in view of what Cal thought they would like. I went down town to Cal's premises, saw Sclater's old store,[7] Bannerman Park, the Royal Stores and many other places. Later Saturday afternoon Cluny, Harold, & Campbell Macpherson[8] came up for an hour. Cluny is quite deaf and looks ten years older than his real age. Then on Sunday the stage was set for a midday dinner for the Governor[9] and Clarke Burchell.[10] Agnes had prepared a chicken dinner when the Governor's

6 Pratt had been invited by the St Andrew's Society to preside at the annual Robbie Burns dinner. See the third paragraph in the section headed 'Nature of Research' in his letter to the chairman of the Humanities Research Council (p. 429).

7 The dry-goods store where Pratt had worked between 1897 and 1900 was a favourite source of anecdotes. See the letter to E.K. Brown, 2 May 1942 (p. 266), and *EJP: TY*, 53–5.

8 Pratt's cousins.

9 Sir Gordon MacDonald was governor of the colony of Newfoundland. He would soon be replaced by the first lieutenant governor of the new Canadian province, Sir Albert Walsh.

10 Nova Scotia native Charles J. Burchell had been appointed high commissioner for Canada in St John's in 1941.

Secretary (his own son) telephoned to say all three of them, dad, mother & son were down with the flu and high temperature, that the Governor was so disappointed but intended going to bed so that he might be fit for the dinner on Monday night. If he wasn't so fit he would telephone all his guests that the function was off. It is now Monday noon and he hasn't telephoned, so it looks as if it is on, though I cannot see that the danger of contagion is over in six hours. Agnes suggests I get hold of a gas mask if I have to sit anywhere in the vicinity of the old boy. Still we had the dinner yesterday with the Burchells. Charlie is a fine breezy chap.

Sunday night Cal took me to Jim's at 8:30 where we reminisced till 10:30. Minnie had a cold chicken repast for us while Daphne and Gweneth waited on the table. All the boys were there – not their wives as it was a Pratt reunion. Jack – Art & Max. Artie who is 6 ft. 3 with a mass of black hair sat there without a word for the two hours – shy I suppose. Jack I like a great deal and Max too.

Today I go to Cal's and Art's afternoon tea 4.30 to 6. Then we hustle back and I have to wrestle (this is the word) with tails, a vest, a new shirt and stiffer collar, white tie and the whole diabolical complex – that is *if if* the governor's temperature is down.

Tuesday night of course – that's the main responsibility, but thank goodness it is at least prepared and I think I'll enjoy it, if I can measure up to 50 percent of the advertising.

Wednesday – the nuns, priests at the Littledale Convent, followed by a less bashful audience at Burchell's.

Thursday Rotary and something at the Library. Then another broadcast[11] and on Friday the Memorial College a long address and then the return Saturday with the plane at Torbay back to Toronto where I ought to arrive after midnight. Won't I be glad to be back with you sweethearts?

Agnes stays in most of the time, going to bed about 9 and getting up about ten. She says she is feeling better, the last two weeks particularly.

Jim is delighted with your picture Cakey[12] and Max is enthusiastic talking about it a great deal. I told Jim that his three pictures were very much approved by us all. Really his painting hobby has added to his health immensely and to his spirits which were always inclined to be somewhat low.

11 'Highlights in My Early Life,' CBC (27 January 1949). See *EJP: OHLP*, 3-5.

12 James ('Jim') Pratt had taken up painting on retirement. He encouraged an interest in art in his own branch of the family; his grandson is prominent Newfoundland painter Christopher Pratt.

Bless you and love you Vi and Cakey. Everything is fine here – hospitality wonderful as you might expect, but there is no substitute for the both of you. All are concerned about your rheumatism and hoping for speedy recovery.

Most lovingly,
Father Ned.

TO THE CHAIRMAN OF THE HUMANITIES RESEARCH COUNCIL

[Spring 1949]

Dear Mr President[13]:

I shall endeavour to place my Work in Progress under the three headings indicated in your letter.

(1) Nature of Research

I am very keen on the attempt to put into verse the account of the last expedition of Sir John Franklin and his crew. This has been in my mind for several years and the magnitude of the task is most challenging (1) because of the sparseness of data regarding the catastrophe and (2) (resulting from (1)) the degree of imaginative reconstruction based on probability and conjecture.

(2) Expenditure

Out of an appropriation of $275.00, there has been expended up to date $175.00. I realized from the first that, apart from expenses for a trip to the vicinity of the North Pole, I should have to get in touch with navigators, explorers, & sealing captains familiar with the formation and the demolition of ice. I should have to plunge into archives wherever material, direct or oblique, might be found. To that end I went to Ottawa and to Montreal, to the latter place particularly because

13 Maurice Lebel (1909–2006), professor of Greek literature at Université Laval in Montreal, was the current chairman of the Humanities Research Council. In 1948 Pratt had successfully applied for a small grant for research on the ill-fated expedition of Sir John Franklin to the Arctic in 1845–7. This was his reply to the Council's request for a progress report on his project.

the 'Atlantic Guardian'[14] is published there under the editorship of a group of Newfoundlanders familiar with the early history of Northern exploration.

In addition to this I made my visit to Newfoundland last January ostensibly to propose the toast to Robert Burns under the auspices of the St Andrew's Society. I thought now was the time to kill two birds with the same stone. I stayed in Nfld for ten days and interviewed friends of the famous Bartlett family, particularly those who knew Captain Bob Bartlett of the Peary expeditions.[15] I am against putting in a bill for this trip inasmuch as the St Andrew's group financed me in Toronto with the air ticket (return), but as they failed to allow for other expenses such as a stay over in Montreal and 'incidentals' in Nfld, I feel that a small item for 'petty account' might be included in the aforementioned $150.00. All this is given [..] again[?]. To hell with the [....]. You will understand.

I have done quite a bit of typewriting, in fact damaged my own typewriter to the amount of $10.00 repairs exclusive of the ribbon and paper cost. My daughter and wife have helped me in secretarial work in the accompanyment of several annotations[?] of journals [.....] of the whole Franklin expedition.

I have bought a small filing cabinet but as it may be used for other purposes at some future date I am not charging it to the account. There is also the matter of entertainment of men who have been helpful to me, but as such an expense might not get past the auditors I am simply dismissing it with a supercilious gesture.

Hence (2) might be specified as following: Travel $100.00. Travel and hotel expenses, secretaries & charges for [...], etc. 75.

(3) Stage reached in Project.
  (a) Amassing and arrangement of relevant materials
  (b) Periodic brooding over the subject especially over the effect of blizzards on the human constitution.
  (c) Consideration of the Arctic nights and the pictorial nature of the Aurora Borealis.
  (d) An attempt at a description of a drunken dinner on the Erebus and a New Year's celebration on the Terror.[16]

---

14 A small monthly (subtitled 'a Magazine of Newfoundland'). Established in 1945, it merged with the *Atlantic Advocate* in 1957.

15 Captain Robert Abram ('Bob') Bartlett (1875–1946) – the most famous member of the seagoing Bartletts of Brigus, Newfoundland – had accompanied Robert Peary on his 1898, 1906–7, and 1908–9 expeditions in search of the North Pole. Pratt stayed in Newfoundland for seven days (not ten), and there is no evidence that he conducted interviews with friends of the Bartlett family.

16 Franklin's two ships.

NB. Project has not yet reached the verse-stage, and the more it is considered the greater it appears requiring probably all my spare time in the next two or three years. I hope to take a trip to the west next summer going north from Winnipeg or Edmonton. May I remark that I tried to find a passage to the North about three years ago and would have had it, if a colonel, by claiming priority, had not requisitioned my berth. I do not wish the balance of the present[?] appropriation. When I get more [.....] [.......] in a year or two I may reopen the matter if the Humanities[17] [.........] [......] has not become bankrupt.

With best personal regards,

Sincerely yours,
Ned Pratt

TO LORNE PIERCE

April 13, 1949

My dear Lorne:

You are of course welcome to the short poem Newfoundland Seamen if you can work it in though I guess it is a bit late now.

When you wrote me in Newfoundland for a prologue poem of 100 lines,[18] I knew I couldn't accomplish it because a poem of that length would take at least a month or more of my time, and the time was not available. When I got back to Canada St Laurent asked me for a short poem which he could in extract fit into his broadcast.[19] That one of three stanzas took me three weeks of my spare

---

17 Humanities Research Council.

18 See the letter to Pierce 24 January 1949 (p. 425). Pierce had requested a contribution to Ewart Young's anthology in honour of Newfoundland's entry into Confederation, *This is Newfoundland.*

19 Prime Minister Louis St Laurent's address on the entry of Newfoundland into Confederation' was broadcast on 1 April 1949. The first stanza of 'Newfoundland Seamen' was used as the prelude to his promise that 'In becoming a province of Canada, you in Newfoundland will not lose your own identity, of which you are all so justly proud':

> This is their culture, this – their master passion
> Of giving shelter and of sharing bread,
> Of answering rocket signals in the fashion
> Of losing life to save it. In the spread
> Of time – the Gilbert-Grenfell-Bartlett span –
> The headlines cannot dim their daily story,

time between lectures, etc. I think it is the better of the two I wrote and possibly the best I have done in a couple of years. St L. read the first verse: so did Brockington in his Confederation broadcast.[20]

You are at liberty to use it if you wish as I possess the copyright completely.[21] If it does not suit or if it is too late, just return it. I shall understand.

Yes, I am going to Queen's again this summer. I love the peace and you are sky high in the esteem of the grads & staff. I know it. They talk about you on numerous occasions. You are their most brilliant and distinguished alumnus.

Regarding the Nfld book I could refer you to a fine young writer named Harrington[22] who does a lot of work for the Broadcasting C. of Nfld, now merged with the CBC. Michael Harrington – I think you once published a chapbook of verse of his.

He writes well; knows the country and could do the job effectively. He is the best of the younger writers who hasn't got in the slough of obscurity and obscenity.

Try him out as the job is far beyond my time possibilities. I wish I had time to do a spot of verse on my own, but the deluge of students will continue for another year.

By the way, one of the Queen's staff remarked in an enthusiastic conversation about you – L.P. is about the '*whitest*' man I have ever known.[23]

Affectionately
Ned.

(over)

If you choose the poem for your book, and feel the penmanship is somewhat illegible, I will do it over.

N.

Nor calls like London! Gander! Teheran!
Outplay the drama of the sled and dory.

20 Also on 1 April 1949, as president of the Canadian Broadcasting Corporation, Brockington spoke on Confederation and the merging of the CBC and the Newfoundland Broadcasting Corporation.

21 The poem appeared as a holograph under the title 'Newfoundland Sailors.' (Hence Pratt's reference in the postscript to his handwriting.)

22 Born and educated in St John's, Michael F. Harrington (1916–99) was a broadcaster, teacher, and editor and columnist for the St John's *Evening Telegram* (1959–83). His books of poetry include *Newfoundland Tapestry* (Dallas: Kaleidograph Press, 1943), *The Sea Is Our Doorway* (Toronto: Ryerson, 1947), and *The Modern Magi* (St John's: Harry Cuff Publications, 1985). *Going to the Ice* (St John's: Harry Cuff Publications, 1986) contains stories of the seal hunt. (See the letter to Harrington, 27 August 1943 [*EJP: Web*].)

23 From an archaic slang meaning of the word 'white': 'Honourable; square-dealing' (*OED*).

TO E.K. BROWN

April 28, 1949

Dear Edward:

It was fine to hear from you. I wish you could come up this late spring or early summer – at least before I go to Queen's. They have invited me there so heartily that, though I thought I should take the summer off, I decided to accept. Wallace was so gracious: so was Harrison.[24]

Nobody is taking G.B.'s place,[25] so Alexander[26] tells me. Economy I suppose, though ill-advised. The R.M.C.[27] at Kingston wanted a principal and I understand quite a number of instructors and professors. I heard that a Ph.D. of last year at Toronto, Peter Fisher, was given the principalship.[28] Quite a job for a novice. I haven't had it confirmed yet. A.S.P.[29] would know but I haven't seen him. I heard also that both Birney and Daniells applied either for that or the Headship of English. Still an unconfirmed rumour! Something is happening at Q.U.[30] A tremendous cut in the budget.

Yes I followed the Birney, Child, Gibbon controversy.[31] I intended cutting out the selections and forwarding them to you, but I thought you would be getting the Saturday Night.

Had dinner with Sandwell last week. He has an unbounded admiration for you and hopes you will never give up your Can. literary connections.

Criticism is in a bad way here and I don't see anyone to take your place by many a mile. Reid Mac[32] is assuming the rank but I fear his preciousness, and I

---

24 Principal R.C. Wallace and G.B. Harrison, chair of the English Department.

25 Harrison was leaving Queen's to go to the University of Michigan.

26 Henry Alexander.

27 Royal Military College.

28 Peter F. Fisher (1918–58) had been appointed head of the English Department at RMC, not principal. His study of Blake, *The Valley of Vision*, edited by Northrop Frye, was published in 1961 by University of Toronto Press, after Fisher's death by drowning.

29 A.S.P. Woodhouse.

30 Queen's University.

31 *Saturday Night* (5 April) had published acrimonious letters by Philip Child and Birney (pp. 16–17): the former defending, and the latter attacking the CAA. J. Murray Gibbon, the object of Birney's critical remarks, responded in a letter published on 19 April (p. 22). (Child, bursar of the CAA and professor of English at Trinity College, had won the Governor General's Award in 1949 for his novel *Mr Ames against Time*. Gibbon, now publicity manager for the Canadian Pacific Railways, had been the first national president of the CAA from 1921 to 1923.)

32 See the note to 'Reid MacCallum' in the letter to Claire Pratt, 7 February 1945 (p. 314).

prefer a man drawn from the 'English' infantry. 'Here and Now'[33] has been importuning me for verse but until recently I had nothing. I submitted a short poem on 'Displaced Persons' which they accepted readily. I hope it looks well in print.

Confederation with Nfld made insistent demands on me for verse. I wrote two, one indifferent, the other good (I think).[34] St Laurent quoted from the latter in his broadcast[35] and wrote me such a cordial letter of thanks. Brockington also at night quoted it – '*Newfoundland Seamen*.' I steered clear of the political issue as is my custom.

McGill is giving me a D.Litt. on May 30, and Bishop's a D.C.L.[36] on June 12. The former I prize and the other also though I imagine McG. counts more.

I am in the midst of 145 papers, and shall write at greater length when I get through.

The bloody Northern Review sweeps Canada off the literary map, except themselves.[37] Callow quasi-literates they are.

Love to Peggy and family, Ernie and Lesley.[38]

Vi is still in with rheumatoid arthritis. The summer may help.

TO LEO COX

May 4, 1949

My dear old Leo:

It was good to hear from you after a long absence.

I have had a pretty busy winter and spring, though not so much with my writing as my engagements on the public platform. I shall have to curtail them in the future. The most interesting was a week's trip to Newfoundland to speak at the Burns Night affair in St John's. I was nearly wined – or at least dined – off my feet, including a formal banquet at the Governor's house. (No wine there,

---

33 See the note to 'a new magazine' in the letter to Earle Birney, 30 September 1947 (p. 408). Pratt's poem 'Displaced Persons' was published in the last number, June 1949.

34 The 'indifferent' poem was 'Newfoundland Calling,' first published in the Toronto *Star Weekly* (26 March 1949).

35 See the note to 'St Laurent asked me for a short poem' in the letter to Lorne Pierce, 13 April (p. 430).

36 Doctor of canon law.

37 See the note to 'the onslaught on Finch' in the letter to Earle Birney, 30 September 1947 (p. 408).

38 Sirluck.

since the old boy, an Old Country Methodist, is a strict temperance man.) But I was treated to a pretty good spread in my honour with 25 guests chosen from the upper crust of the local gentry. All in all, a splendid time.

I may have a chance to see you in June, or rather at the end of May. I go to Montreal on the 29th to get an honorary degree at McGill on the next day and have to make a speech, I think. And again on June 12 I go to Bishop's Univ. for another. That is my last engagement before I go to Kingston, except for a trip to the University of Michigan in Ann Arbor on June 29 to lecture on Canadian literature mostly poetry. I'll mainly read – some of the better work. In spite of all the side-tracking and squabbles about our poetry I foresee a brilliant future for poetry in this country, with such bright stars getting brighter in the firmament every year as Birney, Smith, Klein, Roy D,[39] Dorothy L,[40] and newcomers like young Gustafson, Doug LePan,[41] and 'Louie' Dudek.[42] I am not so hopeful of Canadian criticism, however – there are too many hacks engaged in calculated falsification and all too often vilification. More than ever we need good, honest, forthright criticism. Every artist worth his salt does. There are one or two bright lights here and there, mostly in the academic field, though even there the field is small. Outside the academic circle it is, of course, infinitely worse, with the newspaper boys trying to outdo themselves in dishing out platitudes, empty-headed mouthings and judgments distorted by personal prejudices.

Well, old chap, so much for my letting off a little steam. I really must make a strong point of seeing you when I am in your historic burg next month. Let's try to get together for a good chin.

My very best to you,
Old Ned.

39 Daniells.

40 Livesay.

41 Douglas LePan (1914–98) was educated at the universities of Toronto, Harvard, and Merton College, Oxford. After the Second World War he joined the diplomatic corps, leaving in 1959 to teach at Queen's University and the University of Toronto. He published his first book of poetry, *The Wounded Prince*, in 1946, and won Governor General's Award in 1953 for his second collection, *The Net and the Sword* (Chatto and Windus), and in 1964 for his novel *The Deserter* (McClelland & Stewart).

42 Louis Dudek (1918–2001) was a professor of English at McGill and sometime member of the *First Statement* group. His first book of poems, *East of the City* (Toronto: Ryerson), appeared in 1946. In 1952, he founded Contact Press with Raymond Souster and Irving Layton, and in 1953 was a driving force behind the little magazine *CIV*/n, founded and edited by Aileen Collins. He published many books of verse, as well as influential studies and anthologies of modernism and Canadian literature.

TO EARLE BIRNEY

June 30 [1949]

Dear Earle:

I had a good time with your poetry last night in the lecture hall. I singled out you, Roy, L.A. MacKay & Klein.[43] As Louis has become an 'American'[44] I had to rest my hopes for the Canadian future on the three of you. You were particularly my boast because you have more 'variety' than any one on the horizon – lyricism, satire, background description, etc. etc. I paid a lot of attention to your relatively shorter pieces – Hands, Dusk, Slug, Steve and Joe.[45] Joe still hits me with a terrific impact. 'David' is a triumphant piece of work but it must not be allowed to shade down the best of your shorter productions.

I had a great audience. Rice[46] asked me to give an hour on Can. poetry and the response to you fellows was genuine and enthusiastic. I left out myself as being an embarrassment, but after the lecture I was asked to read from a few poems – the Titanic & the Roosevelt particularly. This was done in another room – a lounge, and more informal. An enterprising young chap in charge of a 'poetic workshop' who is planning on getting poets to come to Ann Arbor to give recitals took your name & address. You may be hearing from him in the fall.

The interesting feature of this Summer School is the emphasis on the cultural relationship between Canada and the U.S.A. There is a special dept. devoted to it, and it will be heard from in the future.

There is a chance for us to break in as never before.

How is your novel[47] coming along?

Love to you, Esther & Bill.

Affectionately
Ned.

43 Roy Daniells, Louis A. MacKay, and A.M. Klein. Pratt had delivered a guest lecture 'on Canadian stuff' at the University of Michigan.

44 In 1948, MacKay had moved from the University of British Columbia to take up a position in the Classics Department at the University of California. He became a naturalized US citizen in 1954.

45 The full titles are 'Dusk on English Bay,' 'Slug in Woods,' 'For Steve,' and 'Joe Harris'

46 Unidentified.

47 *Turvey: A Military Picaresque*, which was published later that year.

I am dropping a note to Roy.[48] I haven't heard from him in three years. I hope he has got over his stomach complaints.

Remember me to Garnett,[49] Bill Robbins & Grant[50] and the others.

TO VIOLA PRATT

Monday a.m. [4 July 1949]

Dearest Vi:

I reached 152[51] at 9:30 as the full train was delayed. Mrs Cartwright was there with her one cat Pat – 14 years old and very rheumatic. I got the whole story of how *Mikey* died, how a new kitten was brought in to replace him, but as Pat arched his back and snarled, Mrs Cartwright had to dispose of the three weeks old future hope.

I rang up Alexander[52] to find out the schedule. I have English 5 at 9 a.m. till the second half of the term when the Refresher[53] comes on.

It is simply stifling today with the humidity – middle nineties too, but it does look like rain. Kingston hasn't had any rain since May, not even the passing showers.

I asked Mrs C. about the room and she said she would be delighted if you could come again, preferably in August as that is the lightest month for her work during the year. How about blending the Douglases[54] with the Cartwrights – sounds like a whisky blend – come here first, then take a short trip to the Lake, as long as is needed for the minerals, then back to 152 and return home to Toronto together.

I have been thinking of the Eastern trip[55] too. Don't worry about it. If the invitation comes in good form you might combine all excursions. But as we

---

48 Roy Daniells.

49 Garnet Sedgewick.

50 Unidentified.

51 152 University Avenue in Kingston, Ontario – the rooming house where he stayed when teaching in the Queen's University summer school.

52 Henry Alexander, now head of the English Department at Queen's University, replacing G.B. Harrison, who was moving to the University of Michigan at Ann Arbor.

53 An English course designed for teachers to 'refresh' their knowledge of the subject.

54 George V. Douglas, a geologist at Dalhousie University, and his wife had invited Viola to their summer place near Gananoque, near Kingston.

55 Viola had also been invited by W.H. Clarke and his wife Irene to join them on a motor trip to the Maritimes.

shall have the big one out West[56] which will be a real voyage you don't need to be too particular.

We can talk it over this week-end. I am joyful at the thought of going back so soon and seeing your sweet self. We shall have to begin making plans about future summer vacations – sea-side? Perhaps?

Much love,
Ned

TO VIOLA PRATT

152 University Ave.
Kingston, Ont.

Monday a.m. [25 July 1949]

Dearest Vi:

Both letter and card came this morning from Ingonish Beach dated July 20. I am so glad that you are feeling better. I do trust that the arthritis will find its cure.

I have just returned from Toronto. Carl Schaefer drove me there on Friday. I got in just in time for dinner. Claire & Daphne[57] had a steak for me – not bacon and eggs. I took Daphne out for a movie on Saturday night – the Forbidden City[58] – when Claire was at Adele's[59] wedding and party. The MacEwens[60] took Claire and brought her back. Then on Saturday I took both of them out to lunch at York Downs where I showed Daphne all the scenic beauties of the place much to Claire's amusement of course.

On Sunday after a late breakfast or brunch Carl called for me, but before leaving I showed him some of Claire's pictures. He liked them particularly the fantastic ones like the tree which looked like a totem pole with a witch's head. He urged her to develop that fantastic vein and restrain the 'representational' side. Of course that's the vogue. But it was something for Carl to show quite a bit of enthusiasm. The big flower like a huge tulip attracted him. It is interesting to discover how artists have their own special likes. He didn't think much of

---

56 The trip he was planning to research his Sir John Franklin poem. (See the letter to the chairman of the Humanities Research Council, Spring 1949 [pp. 428–30].)

57 His niece, Daphne Pratt, daughter of his brother James, was visiting.

58 Possibly *Forbidden* (1948), a British thriller starring Douglass Montgomery and Hazel Court.

59 A friend of Claire's – called 'Dilly' in the letter to Claire, 22 October 1944 (p. 297).

60 Friends of Claire's from her university days.

Payne, but he thought Dorothy Austin was an excellent artist and thoroughly good teacher.[61]

Daphne looks well though a little worried I thought. I don't know just what she will do. She is spending most of her time in thinking things out. I hope she doesn't make a false move which will be irrevocable.

This Wednesday I start the Refresher Course. Last Friday Douglas[62] came in to see me and told me that they had received a letter from you saying that you intended paying them a visit. I don't suppose you will have much time. It would be nice to spend some time here at 152 for I think that the cottage won't be too comfortable. We are not so young as we were – at least I'm not, and swatting flies & mosquitoes through the night is not quite the same pastime as golf or reading inside screened doors.

Best regards to the Clarkes.

And much love
Ned.

TO CLAIRE PRATT

152 University Ave.
Kingston, Ont.

Thursday a.m. [28 July 1949]

Dearest Kako:

Here is a drawing which mother sent me of the harpoon and boat they use in killing swordfish,[63] I wrote her commenting on this new development of interest in subject matter and technique.[64]

---

61 Payne and Austin were Claire's art teachers.

62 George Douglas.

63 He had enclosed a page from Viola's letter containing a crude sketch of a small boat with a long bowsprit (or jibboom), a 'pulpit' and 'harpooner' (labelled) on its tip, and a projecting 'harpoon' (also labelled).

64 In his letter to Viola Pratt, 27 July (*EJP: Web*), his analysis of Viola's drawing is more succinct: 'Your drawings are superb in the classic purity of the harpoon point, in the modeling of the steel, in the representation, at least, of the intention of the harpooner to get that sword fish, and in the ensemble. I couldn't escape the idea that you were by the sea and that's just where I should like to be at this hour with its 90 degrees.'

(1) The boat is drawn in proper perspective. It has four sides as all boats should have – I mean all decent boats. It has a prow and a stern in the orthodox descriptions noted in woodcuts and copper engravings of the 'sixties and 'seventies of the last century. There is no question either that the lowest horizontal line is the waterline seen by an observer who is not short-sighted and who is situated on the starboard side. All the lines are clear – there is no mysticism or symbolism about them – up to a point that is.
(2) On the very top of the jibboom is a *pulpit*. Why they call it a pulpit is very significant. It is above the deck considerably, as a pulpit is above the auditorium, much above it as the good old Scotch pulpits used to be in days when Calvinistic clergymen handed down hell to their congregations. It is situated between earth and heaven, that is between the sea and the skies.
(3) The double lines going up to the pulpit, I think, represent stairs or a ladder somewhat reminiscent of Jacob's ladder – that is the Jacob who wrestled with the angel and wouldn't let go. If I am correct here, mother must be given a great deal of credit for Biblical knowledge and, what is more – credit for the application of the Scripture to daily life on the part of the people who go down to the sea in ships. I have had some knowledge of pulpits myself. I know whereof I speak and it is just here where my critical appreciation of this new phase of modern art has a solid foundation.
(4) I feel a little dubious about the two marks | | under the pulpit. My first idea was that they were the legs of the preacher dangling over the puplit on a very hot day which made standing quite wearisome. Be that as it may or be that as it may not, the sitting position of a harpooner is quite realistic until he sees a whale or a swordfish.
(5) The long line representing the harpoon is so vividly drawn that it could be the spear of Michael the archangel about to charge Satan in the P. Lost.[65] Or it could be the strong arm of Justice as there is a classic purity in the line, a fatalistic determination in the intention of the harpooner which when combined with the former quality makes a superb blend of the barbaric and the Christian.
(6) You will, dear Cayke, probably have noticed that there is a slight bend in the middle of the line. I refuse to believe that such is not part of the craftsman's (or craftswoman's) design. It is a phase of modernistic art which would occasionally forfeit the correctness of a ruler to the feeling of glorious improvisation – a heaven-sent spontaneity which you yourself my dear daughter have so triumphantly evidenced in the sharks you

65 *Paradise Lost.*

> have drawn and in that tree which is rapidly becoming my favourite in your collection. There is something implacable about that half-human face at the top of your tree. There is likewise something uncompromising in that instrument of destruction, the harpoon.

I loved that little drawing of mother's. She was probably pulling my leg gently. I am returning the gentle pull.

Richest love from Father

TO CLAIRE PRATT

152 University Ave.
Kingston, Ont.

Aug. 3, 1949

Darlin' Cayke:

Your card came today and I am drawing this bow at a venture, hoping that you'll get it at the G.D.[66] in St. John.

Everything is going along as well as the eighties will allow it. In a few moments I'll be off to the links or at least to the Club for dinner.

Principal Wallace telephoned me this afternoon asking me if I would speak to a Club of his next Thursday week on Newfoundland. I shall probably give them a talk on Nfld. lingo.[67] You know, 'Any arn dis marn?' or the 'congregational side' of the shirt.

The lectures are swimming along with I fear the slow crawl stroke. Most of the students are superannuated teachers who have stood the burden and the heat of the day a long time and now are taking Refresher Courses. God help them, or rather God help me.

I hope you are finding things convenient and comfortable on your way. You have the three most delightful companions one could wish on a voyage – bless 'em.

---

66 General delivery.

67 According to the script of his 'talk,' 'Any arn dis marn?' (as a Newfoundland fisherman's wife might ask of him on his return from his nets) meant 'Any herring this morning?' – to which he might reply, 'No, dere ain't any arn dis marn. Might as well be narn as arn, cause if dere arn dere nar a bit big.' The same script explains that 'the congregational side' of a shirt was the visible outside of the starched front of a 'Sunday shirt.'

Mother will be coming back next week and will hasten to Toronto to get ready for the Western trip, though I should be hearing from George Johnston about the trip soon. Possibly there is mail awaiting me at 21 Cortleigh.

Apart from lecturing and golfing I am spending my evenings as a bat-exterminator.[68] Mrs Cartwright has taken up verse. She comes in with a poem either on bats or humming-birds. Both objects of interest are to be found in the house and back yard. The hummers drive their needles into the trumpet vine flowers. I am collecting Mrs C's effusions on them.[69] She at least has no difficulty in rhyming bat with Pratt. I tell her that she can get off to a good start.

Love to you and the girls,
Father.

TO EARLE BIRNEY

152 University St.
Kingston, Ont.

Aug. 10 [1949]

Dear Earle:

Two lovely surprises came my way this week –

(1) Your friendly letter with its two fine poems in your genuine hand. You certainly have struck out an individual style. I could tell your stuff, call out to it and it would come to me like a terrier. You have ability to burn over and above what you can use, and, as I have told you often, it is a pleasure for me to hold you up in my traveling lectures as what Canada has in promise and achievement.

(2) Last night I happened to be at a party of Queen's people and at 10:15 we turned on the dial.[70] Your reading of Brébeuf was grand, and that of the

68 See the letter to Viola Pratt, 27 July (*EJP: Web*).

69 One of Mrs Cartwright's 'effusions' has been preserved, a limerick 'On the Occasion of the Killing of a Bat at Kingston, August 1949':

> There once was a frolicsome bat
> Was chased by a poet named Pratt
> Who showed his technique
> When with never a squeak
> He laid the bat flat on the mat.

70 Birney gave a series of poetry readings on CBC that summer entitled *The Poets Look at Canada*.

Esquimau was an example of what a good radio voice could do with sounds. The recital was an incantation. I wonder if you know how good it was. Then someone interjected – 'I hope Birney reads one of his own' and along came your 'Pacific.'[71] I was thrilled. So were they all. Jack Vincent is the live wire here at Queen's. He has managed, against years of resistance to Canadian poetry, to put on the syllabus a course in it, and he has a class through the regular session of 150 – both prose and verse. He is a regular and Queen's may open up through his activities. His future is bright here as Harrison[72] has gone to Michigan and Roy[73] is being superannuated next year. The colonial complexes are being resolved I think, or I hope.

I am delighted to find that your novel[74] has come along. I have a hunch it is good. If I were fifteen years younger I might take a flyer at fiction, but I'll stay with verse now. In two years time I get out of Vic as our tenure is five years shorter than U.C.[75] I have ceased hoping that an income might result from verse. Though I have no complaint about sales and the critical reception, which in the U.S.A. & England has been generally fair, is most encouraging (Day-Lewis I understand is quite enthusiastic),[76] yet the royalties, after all, do not much more than supply tobacco and rye for my friends. I have a steady though modest sale and I get lectures here and in the States as a by-product, more renumerative than the direct royalties. In two years I shall go down to a pension less than $2000 annually, so I shall have to try to find a few perquisites.

I notice that you read one of Bourinot's poems. Arthur is a pretty good fellow personally and can occasionally pull off an attractive piece of work. He still keeps my name on the masthead just transferring it from yours though he didn't ask permission.[77] I shall keep it there for a year though I'll suggest its removal as I don't contribute anything except the odd short poem at his insistent request. He has requested me to go to Ottawa in October and give a recital for funds. I

71 'Pacific Door,' a poem in Birney's *The Strait of Anian* (1948).

72 G.B. Harrison.

73 James A. Roy of the English Department at Queen's University.

74 *Turvey* (1949).

75 Victoria College had been considering strict enforcement of retirement at sixty-five, with a three-year extension for older faculty. (See the letter to Pelham Edgar, 13 January 1947 [pp. 392–4].) Pratt's birth year having been recorded erroneously as 1883, he was now 'officially' in his sixty-sixth year, but was actually sixty-seven.

76 Cecil Day Lewis (1904–72), Irish-born British poet, novelist, and literary critic, Poet Laureate from 1968 until his death. After the war he was a senior editor with Chatto and Windus. It is not clear how Pratt knew that he was 'quite enthusiastic.'

77 Bourinot was then editor of *CPM*, having succeeded Birney. Birney had listed Pratt on the masthead as a contributing editor (see the telegram to Birney, 20 August 1946 [p. 385]), and Bourinot had continued the practice.

said yes after some deliberation for he must be up against it as I was when I was editor and as you were. He may be able to do something with it.

Last week came a circular from the Northern Review asking me for contributions and (inferentially) for donations. I haven't subscribed for three years because I don't like their persistent sniping at all Canadian poets who have made a bit of success. The prospectus looked more reasonable. I have written some half-a-dozen shorter poems this summer and I am debating now whether I shall open contacts. I do not know who the Editorial Committee are. It was not stated in the circular. We certainly need magazines not committed to precious poops which are about all most of the versifiers are capable of emitting from their Viscera nowadays.

I miss Pelham[78] a lot. I was with him just before he died. He loved you as he loved me and Norrie.[79] Two or three of my closest friends have left the springboard recently and haven't returned, and two or three others of the old poker days have coronaries.

How is U.B.C.? I had a sweet letter from Bill Robbins last week. I got greatly attached to him. How I wish the boys could foregather. Give my best to Garnett & Roy.[80] I use Garnett's Irony[81] in the class-rooms. That Othello is magnificent. It stirs me every time I read his 'play of irony' foreshadowing the conclusion. He is so stimulating. I remember lovingly even his mannerisms – God bless 'im.

I go back to Toronto next Wednesday. Vi is still suffering from her rheumatoid arthritis which struck her last December. Her doctor advised her to spend 90% of her time lying down which, of course, her energetic nature won't allow her.

Love to you, Esther & Bill

Affectionately
Ned.

78 Pelham Edgar had died in September 1948.

79 Northrop Frye.

80 Garnet Sedgewick and Roy Daniells.

81 Sedgewick's book *Of Irony, Especially in Drama* (London: Oxford University Press, 1935, 1948, 1960; rpt University of Toronto Press, 2003).

TO VINCENT MASSEY

[Sept. 1949]

Dear Mr Massey:

This is to vouch for John Sutherland,[82] Editor of the *Northern Review*, a Canadian magazine published in Montreal. He is hoping to secure some support for this little magazine devoted to the arts. As his present list of guarantors and subscribers is inadequate for its continuance, the magazine may have to fold up this year. It has been running for several years mainly through the personal efforts and expenditures of Sutherland himself. It has been a heroic attempt to keep the little magazine floating and it would be a pity to see it go under. Sutherland wants to know if anything can be done through the Royal Commission and he asked me simply to give him an introduction.

I hesitated at first to bother you in the midst of your manifold duties and, besides, I imagine the briefing is over now. However, this note is to attest his name and position should he write to you in reference to the magazine.[83]

With every good wish,
E.J. Pratt

TO E.K. BROWN

Oct. 21, 1949

Dear Edward:

We are looking forward eagerly to your visit.[84] Vi was saying two days ago – 'We must put on a real dinner & evening for Peggy & Ed. Get hold of the date and reserve it.' Then Arthur W.[85] telephoned that you would have as your best

82 The letter was written to Massey as chairman of the Royal Commission on National Development in the Arts, Letters and Sciences, generally known as the Massey Commission. It began public hearings in August 1949, concluding in July 1950.

83 Sutherland submitted a lengthy brief to the commission in November 1949. (The brief was published in *The Making of Poetry in Canada: Essential Articles on Contemporary Canadian Poetry in English*, ed. Louis Dudek and Michael Gnarowsky [Toronto: Ryerson, 1967], 66–79.)

84 To deliver the annual Alexander Lectures.

85 A.S.P. Woodhouse.

opening Thursday evening. That suited me, particularly because the load of lecturing would be off your shoulders leaving you free to enjoy perfect relaxation. Arthur also stated that you might be coming alone, though he wasn't sure. Vi & I would love to have Peggy and a mixed dinner at the York Club. Will you let me know the circumstances so I can get busy on the invitations. If you come alone I shall have about ten men at the Y.C.[86] If there are any special friends you would like, let me know. I had in mind a selection from the following: – E.K., Ned (*musts*, the latter executively unavoidable!!), B.K. Sandwell (a great admirer of yours), Ed Corbett, Arthur Woodhouse, Mazzoleni (a real lad), Sid Smith, Knox,[87] Father McCorkell or Shook (I am quite fond of both and they are good boys especially after dinner), Bissell, one of Child, McGillivray or Barker or Roper, Dunn, Rouillard (French), Grant (English, quiet but fine).[88]

Would you pick out ten of this group who, you would think, would be most compatible? Or substitute any others?

If Ernest[89] comes, he, of course, would be most welcome. I mentioned it to him last summer. Convey this to him. Later on I shall drop him a line. At present, I am up to my ears with engagements. Just returned from Queen's having received an L.L.D. but had to deliver the Convocation address as a *Penalty*. A big joke in this which I shall relate to you later.

Love to family

from Vi and myself. Vi is still with that arthritis – our hope is in cortisone but that takes so much time.

Ned.

---

86 York Club.

87 R.S. Knox.

88 Philip Child, J.R. MacGillivray, and Arthur Barker (professor and head of English, Trinity College, Toronto), Gordon Roper (a professor of English at Trinity College), Charles Dunn (a professor of English at University College), C. Dana Rouillard (a professor of French at University College, author of *The Turk in French History, Thought and Literature, 1520–1660* [Boston: Harvard University Press, 1936]), and Douglas Grant (associate professor of English at University College and the editor of *The Poetical Works of Charles Churchill* [Oxford: Oxford University Press, 1956].

89 Ernest Sirluck.

TO RALPH GUSTAFSON

Oct. 21, 1949

My dear Ralph:

I have just returned from Queen's, Kingston,[90] and found your letter. Hence this delay.

I should only be delighted to hand on a warm recommendation.[91] I believe you would justify the Foundation in every respect and shall say so in detail. Would you let me have a list of your activities, prizes, etc.etc. I know most of them, of course, but I should like them particularized to give concreteness to the letter.

I would suggest that in writing the secretary you state a theme for your most substantial poem in your proposed collection – that is, if you intend more than a number of relatively short lyrics. It helps the managing secretary to give definiteness to his presentation to the Board. Still it is not absolutely necessary as LePan got his fellowship mainly on proposed lyrics.[92]

My recommendation may possibly be qualified by the fact that I am doing one for Northrop Frye of Victoria College. He wants to get a year's leave of absence for a work on Shakespeare's comedy. However there are several Guggenheims for Canada and yours ought not to clash with Frye's as his is criticism and yours creation. The Foundation, I understand, favours historical and critical research – that is as judged by previous awards. So if you can convey the impression of doing some underbrushing, it would be to the good. A.J.M.S. worked this to his advantage and he did a grand job.[93] Keep this idea under your hat – it is a bit of personal advice.

I shall stress both your critical and creative talents in which I profoundly believe. This is independent of my deep affection for you. I wish you every success.

---

90 He had received an honorary doctor of laws degree at Queen's University's fall convocation.

91 Gustafson was applying for a Guggenheim fellowship. (See the note to 'your Fellowship' in the letter to A.J.M. Smith, 29 March 1941 (p. 203).

92 Douglas LePan had been awarded a Guggenheim Fellowship in the field of 'Poetry' in 1948.

93 In 1941, A.J.M. Smith had received a Guggenheim Fellowship in the field of 'Literary Criticism' to complete *The Book of Canadian Poetry* (1943).

If you think that Frye would be competitive (as he is my colleague with his masterly *Blake* behind him[94]), have another supporter up your sleeve. But, in any case, count on me.

I should love to see you and have a York Club dinner for you.

Sincerely,
Ned

TO CLAIRE PRATT

Christmas 1949

Dear Cayke:

Towards your private account (annuity instalment) with love from Father H M O M. (Have Mercy on me) of the Order of GC (good cheer) Division S.E.C. Society for the Extermination of Crows, S.F.G.B.E. (Society for Going to Bed Early).

Father in Sympathy

TO EARLE BIRNEY

Feb. 17, 1950

Dear Earle:

It was a pleasure to get a line from you apart from the 'official' invitation.[95]

I deliberately set apart a few nights during the last month to try to get the pressure of hydrogen[96] off my chest. I couldn't get away from the idea and I knew the only release (if one may call it such) was through verse. You know only too well how these things get hold of one.

---

94 *Fearful Symmetry: A Study of William Blake* (New Haven, CT: Princeton University Press, 1947). Pratt was correct, as Northrop Frye was awarded a Guggenheim Fellowship in 1950.

95 Birney had asked him for a poem to include in a Canadian number of *Poetry Commonwealth*, which Birney was editing. Pratt's 'Myth and Fact' appeared in the journal in the spring of 1951.

96 In January Pratt had been shocked by US President Harry Truman's announcement that the United States would develop a hydrogen bomb.

I managed to produce four relatively short pieces,[97] two of which I am holding back for revision as I am not sure of their quality. I put most of the time at 'Myth and Fact' and the 'Moon'[98] (in a satirical vein). You are welcome to one of the two if it suits the columns. Will you let me know which one, as soon as possible, and return the other. I have had several requests recently for poems. Bourinot[99] has written three times but I haven't the material available. I may send him a short one, for my name still stands as a contributing editor taken over from your mast-head. I am asking him to remove it as I am on four magazines (a Newfoundland one, too)[100] and the correspondence with it has become a nuisance.

I hope to have more time next year as this is my last year at the College[101] – our retiring time being earlier than at U of T.[102] It is possible I might get part-time lecturing here but the salary or pension is pitifully small.

My love to you, Esther & Bill and the boys at the Dept.

Ned.

I trust Turvey is smiling exultantly and not sardonically at the sales.

TO MARJORIE BENÉT

May 11, 1950

My dear Marjorie:

I learned only yesterday of Bill's passing[103] and the news came with the same shock as if a brother of mine had gone. Of all my New York friends he was the dearest. He meant so much to me personally and as a literary friend and sponsor.

97 Besides 'Myth and Fact' and 'The Unromantic Moon' (*EJP: CP* 2.193 and 250), Pratt had written 'The Good Earth' and 'Cycles' (*EJP: CP* 2.193 and 195).

98 'The Unromantic Moon.'

99 Bourinot had written as editor of *CPM*. Pratt sent him 'The Good Earth,' which was published in the Summer 1950 number.

100 The Newfoundland magazine was *Atlantic Guardian*. (See the note to 'the "Atlantic Guardian"' in the letter to the chairman of the Humanities Research Council, spring 1949 [p. 429].) The others, besides *CPM*, were *Saturday Night* and *Liberty*.

101 See the note to 'In two years time I get out of Vic' in the letter to Earle Birney, 10 August 1949 (p. 442).

102 He means University College; Victoria College was a member of the federated University of Toronto.

103 William Rose Benét died in New York City on 4 May 1950.

My richest experiences at New York were at your house with him and your own sweet self. I shall never forget your hospitality. My heart is profoundly moved by your loss and I send you my tenderest sympathies. My family add theirs, for when I 'broke the news' last night it cast deep shadows on them, for they seemed to have known the two of you personally from my constant references to you.

God bless you,
Ned Pratt

TO VIOLA PRATT

152 University St
Kingston

Monday morning [3 July 1950]

Dearest Vi:

Everything has gone exactly by schedule. The train came in on time – the same taxi at the station (Amey's), arrival at 152 at 8:45, Mrs Cartwright there to hand me the key, a dish of strawberries and cream, unpacking of the suitcases, bed at ten, breakfast at the Queen's[104] with immediate recognition by the proprietor, who didn't have to be told to bring orange juice, one egg & bacon and toast a bit on the burnt side, followed by coffee.

George Herbert[105] called and will call again this afternoon about five to go to his place for the evening.

I do not go to the course today as the knee still pains[106] and I won't play till it is much better. I hope it clears up in reasonable time as I shall miss the bit of golf.

Mrs Cartwright talks about selling her house within the year. She has had a strenuous time of it with no holidays and her blood pressure is 260, a fearful reading. Other than that she looks about the same.

Tomorrow morning I start in at 10 going straight to 12. That suits me better than the earlier hours last year. I saw Edinborough who teaches 'speech.' Alexander is away in England for the summer. Mrs A & Peter[107] are staying here at their house.

---

104 Restaurant.

105 G.H. Clarke.

106 That spring he had experienced rheumatism in his left knee.

107 The Alexanders' son.

I am going to take a run over to the Union and see what they offer by way of lunches or dinners. It wasn't open last year.

The registration is up – more than a hundred above last year's. It's now 800 odd. I don't know how big my class will be. All the returns won't be in for two or three days.

I spent the time on the train going over the Alchemist[108] and trying to jot down a lot of train-squiggly notes. The work can do double time, as I said.

The weather is lovely today – about 70 and sunny.

Take care of your sweet self and don't do too much work in too short a time. There is a secret in that sort of doing things.

Much love to you & Cayke.
Ned.

TO VIOLA PRATT

Thursday [6 July 1950]

Darlin' Vi:

Your letter came and I was sorry to find that the squirrel had eaten the lemon off the lemon tree. When I get back I'll scare off the squirrels with the popgun which is more effective there than with the crows.

I shall be leaving here a week from tomorrow night and it will be a joy to be back with you for it gets lonely here though the lectures do occupy one's time. All the afternoon I spend on the sofa in the library with my back bunched up against two pillows and with one pillow under my knee and another one on the other knee to prop up my note book and two Elizabethan books. I can work in this beautiful cool weather. It suits me perfectly.

Mrs Cartwright works from 8 to 5, comes home, dozes till 7, has her slight dinner all by herself and then works for three hours at her license accounts.[109] She is aging somewhat. Her operation which I thought was slight was more serious, a growth which had to be removed – a tumor as far as I could find out. It hasn't reappeared yet after six months. She ought to give up her heavy job and live with her sister but she says she doesn't know how to part with her

---

108 A comedy by Ben Jonson (1610). Pratt was teaching a course in Elizabethan and Jacobean drama.

109 Mrs Cartwright worked for the Motor Vehicle Licencing Bureau.

house. She simply deifies it. The dogs still bark on either side but not quite so persistently as last year.

I see Douglas[110] is lecturing here in the Session. I am going to get in touch with him as soon as I can talk intelligently on ranges.[111]

I told you Ross is here, Malcolm Ross a full professor. I haven't seen Vincent yet. I mentioned to Ross that Vincent will try to coax him up in his plane. Ross replied that he had no intention of going to heaven yet by that means. I wouldn't go up for anything and wonder why a man should take up that kind of hobby.

Keddle & Shea, the Insurance Co[112] sent on the nominal cheques to Floss, Claire & Cal & Ag. Will you post Floss's to her and I'll send Cal his. It is formal only to relieve the Co. of further obligation. The cheques of course are genuine.

My dearest love to you Vi
Ned.

TO VIOLA AND CLAIRE PRATT

152 University
Kingston, Ont.

Thursday [27 July 1950]

Dearest Vi & Claire:

Your letters and cards have been coming in regularly but what happened to mine. I sent two to Washington c/o General Delivery but your card from Williamsburg said you did not receive anything from me. I sent the first one regular mail as I felt sure that it would get there first as I wrote on Saturday. Then the next by air. I hope you get this – just to say how d'ya do? like hearing a voice.

I am so glad that you are having a good time – and what scenery you are passing through. I am quite prepared to believe that Washington is, as Claire says – the most beautiful city in the world – a big claim indeed.

---

110 See the note to 'the Douglases' in the letter to Viola Pratt, 4 July 1949 (p. 436).

111 Mountain ranges. Pratt was doing research on the geology of the Rocky Mountains in preparation for writing 'Towards the Last Spike.' Douglas was a geologist.

112 In June, the Pratts' car – with E.J. Pratt driving and with Viola, Claire, his sister Floss, his brother Calvert and wife Agnes all passengers – had been hit from behind by a driver attempting to race a traffic light. No serious injuries or damage had been incurred.

I mentioned yesterday in my card that I had started my Refresher, and fortunately, it is just the size I hoped for – close to 20. And I had a very pleasant surprize. When the class was finished a man came up that looked to me to [be] a Newfoundlander. Why he should look so it is hard to describe – but there he was. He had come up specially from Montreal, where he and his wife live, to attend the course. He was none other than Scammell – the author of the Squid Jiggin' Groun.'[113] He had also composed two or three other rough salt water ballads just as rough and tough as the Squid one, had them all set to music by himself and then put on gramophone records. I told Jack Vincent about him and we are all going to Jack's house on Sunday night to hear them played. Scammell hasn't a gramophone and is glad to find a place where they can be played. Miss Winspear is coming too. Scammell put himself through three years at McGill on the royalties from the disks. He looks like Walter Knight, talks like him, and acts like him – our carpenter Walter.

I suppose you will be leaving tomorrow or next day. When you said Friday did you mean as soon as that – this week. If so, I wonder if this air mail will reach you.

Love to the both of you.
Ned.

TO CLAIRE PRATT

Saturday a.m. [9 Sept. 1950]

Dearest Cayke:

Here we are in Vancouver having arrived yesterday morning. It is now 9 a.m. with breakfast finished and the forenoon before me to get some work done by the time Belle and Thora and George arrive for lunch. George Dalmage[114] (Thora's husband) is a gov't geologist here and though I do not know him

113 Arthur R. Scammell (1913–95) was born in Newfoundland, educated at McGill University, and for many years taught high school in Montreal. He wrote 'The Squid Jiggin' Ground' (1929) while still in high school. *My Newfoundland: Stories, Poems, Songs* (Montreal: Harvest House, 1966) is a collection of his work.

114 Thora was a friend of Viola's. Belle was the Dalmages' daughter.

personally I am inviting him to tap his knowledge in connection with mountain strata and fossils.[115] Some of the questions will be as follows:

(1) Would fossils be discovered in the midst of the mountain tunnels several thousand feet below the summit?
(2) Are they found along the river beds?
(3) What makes the Kicking Horse River so chalky white, a dirty chalky? (Note specially – the nearest thing I can compare it to is the colour of a foul mixture doctors give to patients when said doctors want to diagnose said patients in respect to trouble along the digestive tract. It consists of a quart of milk containing a dissolved calcium compound which under the X-ray shows up the shadows of things like ulcers etc. etc. etc. I took it once when I was going through my fourth year at Vic and under the impression (fortunately without foundation) that I had something wrong with the gastric juices. May I add just here to lengthen this addendum that I never had the impression or sensation before or since.) Well the Kicking Horse River looked like that concoction and if I can find out the medical name I shall so describe it.
(4) Do wild big-horn goats drink of this vile unnatural product? Does it act like a poison on grizzly bears when they descend the mountain side thirsty after a deadly bout with cougars?
(5) What was the nature of the sea-life from which the fossils were formed. The trilobites, crinoids, brachiapods – Did they just float around like jelly fish grabbing anything within reach? Did they have any sensations, any social life such as dancing, cavorting, in other words did they ever descend into such low form of activity as meditating in the night watches or worse still, did they sing in chorus, that is, did any poetic strains ever emanate from their gelatinous strings?
(6) Why do so many of the mountain peaks look like embalmed Egyptian mummies? – they are so placid, recumbent, never troubled with the cawing of crows or the squawling of tom-cats.
(7) Do they ever snore? Are avalanches a kind of snoring or a variety of swearing?

Well to move from these low planes to higher and more ethereal realms, I may say that your mother has just gone down to the shore with a party gather-

115 In preparation to write 'Towards the Last Spike.' For a review of the knowledge gleaned from this conversation, see the letter to Claire Pratt, 10 September (pp. 454–5).

ing shells, while I stay here in this room gathering wool as it will take me a day or two to get over those four sleepless nights on the train and then to gather my thoughts. You may observe that my aforesaid 7-point classification does not reveal any supreme philosophical or poetic heights.

Well, how are you getting along chick? I hope you are having some parties. Make sure that you get long leisurely week-ends to sleep them off. I shall be here at the Hotel till Friday a.m.; then the address will be the Royal Alexandra Hotel at Winnipeg from Monday, Sept. 18 to Thursday, Sept. 21 7:30 p.m.

Most lovingly,
Fossilized fanciful Father

TO VIOLA PRATT

Sunday [10 Sept. 1950]

Dearest Vi[116]:

One day more has gone and I spent most of the time making an abstract of the Post's article[117] (which I found more informative and suggestive on a second reading) and an elaborate account of Dalmage's[118] geological information. Between him and Douglas[119] I have quite a stretch of fact which I shall have to beat into some shape later on.

In the afternoon I called on Sage[120] who is inviting me to the Faculty Club on Tuesday where I expect to meet a few of the University chaps. I tried several times to get hold of Robbins.[121] He is in town but was not at his house. On Tuesday night I expect to be with Birney and some of the 'authors anonymous.' I guess they will be a keen gang of youngsters worth knowing. Tomorrow I shall see Major[122]

---

116 She had gone to visit her brother, Ralph Whitney, in Red Deer while Pratt stayed in Vancouver to research 'Towards the Last Spike.'

117 Unidentified.

118 See the letter to Claire Pratt, 9 September 1950 (pp. 452–3).

119 George Douglas.

120 Walter Noble Sage (1888–1963), long-time chair of the History Department at the University of British Columbia. He was a noted historian of the west coast region and in a position to provide Pratt with advice about his research for 'Towards the Last Spike.'

121 William Robbins.

122 Unidentified.

and try for something else, and it is quite possible that I shall try a quick trip to Victoria – but only if information is available there and nowhere else.

I got back to the Hotel today about five and I have been at the writing pad right up till now which is about eight o'clock.

I shall drop Claire a line before I turn in tonight.[123]

I think the trip is going to be quite valuable for I am loaded with information about the Fraser River which I shall check up along the Route on Friday morning. For instance, Lytton in the Coastal Range is where the Fraser from the North meets the Thompson from the East. A few phrases from Blake[124] can be made texts: – 'the sea of mountains,' and 'lost in the gorges of the Fraser,' etc., etc. They will put dynamic in the story I hope.

I have also learned what muskeg is exactly – a lake of water over which vegetation has grown particularly caribou moss (the food of caribou) and – what I had hoped for – it covers the pre-Cambrian rock – so it can be made part of the 'lizard,'[125] perhaps a leg or a flipper such as an alligator might have. This lizard I expect will be fearfully and wonderfully made, perhaps grotesquely made, before the beast is finally carved out.

With the trip finished, it will be a matter of assembling data from historians, geologists, miners and books. You and I will have to go over your rocks in the furnace room.

Well, I'll be glad to see your dear self on Saturday. It was lonely when you left. I hope you had a restful trip. Don't fail to make yourself comfortable. I am glad that the trip is going to be no longer than it is because I am impatient to be back with you at our own home at 21.

My deepest love to you.
Ned.

123 See the letter to Claire Pratt, 10 September (pp. 456–8).

124 Liberal politician Edward Blake (1833–1912) was the second premier of the province of Ontario (1881–2) and subsequently the leader of the federal Liberal Party (1880–7), during which period it was twice defeated by the Conservatives under John A. MacDonald. He was known for giving extremely long-winded and elaborate speeches.

125 Pratt had already decided that a huge geological reptile would be a primary mythopoeic form in his proposed 'railway poem.' In it the 'reptile' is described as 'A hybrid that the myths might have conceived, / But not delivered' (ll. 870–952).

TO CLAIRE PRATT

Sunday [10 Sept. 1950]

Cayke duck:

You might be interested to know what a trilobite looks like. It lived about a billion years ago in the sea when the Rocky Mountains were under the sea. The Rockies by the way are not volcanic as was once supposed, but rather great plains under the water which were thrown up in tremendous folds thousands of feet high. On the top of them and in the middle of them where the tunnels are bored there are millions of low forms of sea life which have died and left their impressions in the petrified mud. Every time a pick-axe goes to work on mountain or canyon numerous crustaceans and softer fish are unearthed. The trilobite is like a crab. I shall give evidence of my draughtsmanship by drawing one from a verbal description given me by Mr Dalmage[126]:

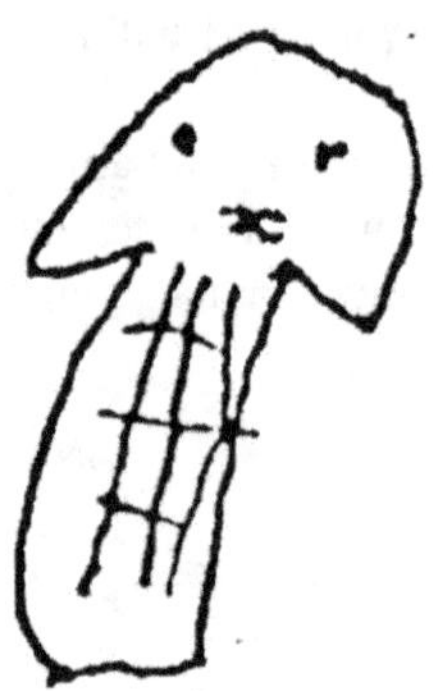

Almost human isn't it? I have known people whose faces resembled that. I could mention a few but my artistic modesty forbids elaborating on the resemblance for if you knew whom I had in mind you would say that I was seeking a compliment on my achievement. Suffice it to say that I have looked like that occasionally when a poem went bad or when I was turning over in bed vainly trying to get to sleep on the CPR.[127] Those vertical lines represent plunges from a

126 See the letter to Claire Pratt, 9 September (p. 452).

127 Pratt had not slept well on the train trip west. See the letter to Claire Pratt, 9 September (p. 454).

horizontal position when the train rounded a sharp curve in the Kicking Horse canyon. The eyes indicate vacancy and the mouth impatience for the morning and breakfast.

I shall now draw a crinoid:

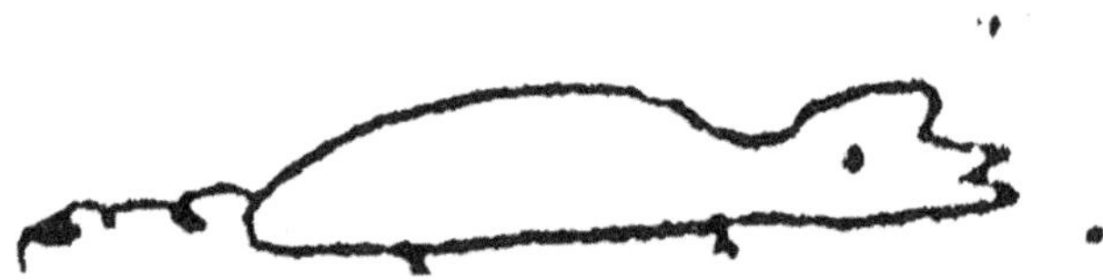

This might at first glance look like a frightened duck with a piglet's tail, but nothing could be further from the truth. Symbolically it is a fish and one must use the imagination for the abstract to find its significance. I know some art galleries where this would be hung up as a triumph.

The brachiopod is a clam or close to it – a real bivalve with hairs on its legs so fine that when it is seen in the mountains only the magnifying glass can reveal them. Outside to the eye (if a person could have lived in those times to see it) it would be just an ordinary clam like this:

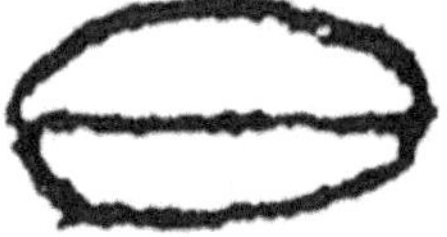

See the horizontal lines making it a bivalve but inside it would be like this:

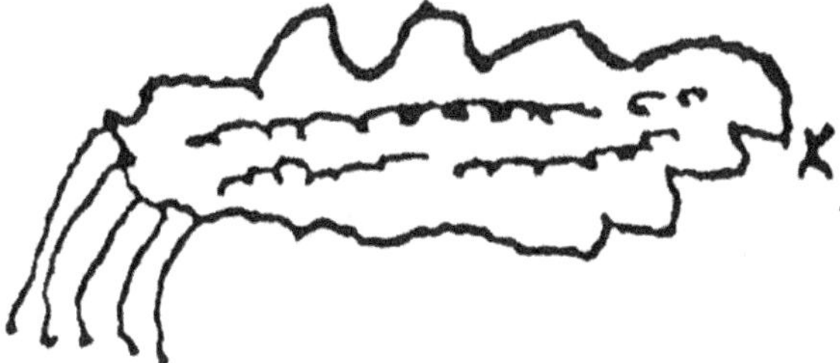

The humps indicate the gelatinous movement of the clam in search of sea-weed. The tails (I have shown only five for space considerations though the hairs are numerous really). The beak X is not a beak but only intended to be such – a bit of marine symbolism known only to sailors who have the gift of second sight or possibly third sight which may be credited to me at midnight. Ponder over this Cayke for it is important as it may be the beginning of a new school of art.

Lovingly
Father

TO ROY AND LAURENDA DANIELLS

Sunday 17th [Sept. 1950]

My dear Roy and Mrs Roy[128]:

Here I am at the Hotel Saskatchewan staying a day with my cousins prior to going to Winnipeg on the night train.

It was a joy to be with you the other night and the lady of the house even exceeded in charm and loveliness my anticipation which was very high to begin with.

The three hours went like three minutes. The warmth was enough to melt the Selkirk snows. It was good to meet people I hadn't known before this trip – the Andrews pair – I had known her mother Mrs Grant,[129] and Geof[130] himself must be a pippin on the administrative side. He struck me as a brilliant and delightful chap. Sorry though I didn't see Larry[131] though I looked into his office twice. Will you remember me to him, as an old friend of Varsity days.

I expect to arrive in Toronto on the 23rd where I shall give a glowing account of the Daniells team. You have a Department of English second to none in this 'broad Dominion.' The Reeds[132] are grand and what a nice fellow W. Gage[133] is.

---

128 Daniells had married Laurenda Francis in 1948.

129 The former Maude Perkin (1880–1963) was the widow of William Lawson Grant (1872–1935), long-time head master of Upper Canada College, Toronto.

130 Geoffrey Clement Andrew (1906–87), a graduate of Dalhousie and Oxford universities, was a professor of English and executive assistant to the president of the University of British Columbia.

131 Norman MacKenzie (1894–1986) – universally known as 'Larry' – was a graduate of Dalhousie, Harvard, and Cambridge universities whom Pratt had known since he was a professor of international law at the University of Toronto (1926–40). He served as president of the University of British Columbia from 1940 to 1944.

132 Unidentified.

133 Walter Gage (1905–78) was a professor of mathematics at the University of British Columbia. He was appointed dean of administrative and inter-faculty affairs in 1948 and served in a number of other administrative positions before becoming president (1969–75).

My love to you everlastingly and Roy may your poetic pen still continue to flourish!

Ned.

The baby is wonderful and so is Jane.[134] Caress the both of them for me.

TO CLAIRE PRATT

Sunday morning [17 Sept. 1950]

or just after noon hour Daylight Saving Time.

Dearest Cayke:

We arrived in Regina about ten a.m. today. At Calgary all the Whitney family[135] met me at the station yesterday morning – Ralph, Ernestine, Ann, Oran and the two little boys (one with spectacles, the other without). We drove around the city, visited the zoo, saw all specimens of the saurians, including Tyrannosaurus rex about the size of three elephants, some done in plaster or cement, others under glass in their petrified skeletons. Rex had a tail bigger than his body – thirty feet long and many feet thick. I wondered how he navigated in his era. All animals were there, leopards, mountain lions, and African lions, grizzlies and polars, gazelles, wild boars in real life. Then we drove along the Bow River where so many of the dinosaurs were dug up from a depth of 1500 feet. They were with us all day (I mean the Whitneys not the dinosaurs). For dinner all of us went to the Palliser Hotel for a good meal – eight hungry monsters including the little monsterlings whose appetite was a good illustration to me of how the great saurians became extinct because of the failure of the food supply on their part of the globe. I was glad to see them all. Ernestine is lovely and Ann is the pick of them all. The youngsters are very bright.

I got a lot of information from Ralph about fossils and mountain structure, supplementing what I got from the Provincial geologist – Dalmage, the husband of Thora – Vi's friend. There is a lot to learn yet and today I learned something about drilling into hard rock from Karl.[136] His father worked on the Rockies and knew a great deal about sandslides etc.

---

134 The Daniells children.

135 The family of Viola's brother Ralph from Red Deer, Alberta. Viola rejoined Pratt in Calgary to travel with him by night train to Regina.

136 Karl Whitney, Viola's brother from Francis, Saskatchewan. She returned with him to for a brief visit, Pratt staying for the day in Regina.

We had lunch – the five of us – at a restaurant. A Mr Buchanan drove Karl & Rita down to Regina. We spent two or three hours together. One amusing incident happened. The clergyman – a Methodist – was to drive us but since the train was late and he knew he couldn't get back to his morning Sunday service, we had Buchanan as a substitute. I learned that the minister's name was Walker[137] and he told Buchanan that he was a class-mate of mine in 1911. I tried to recollect and the man came back to my memory and here is what I said to Buchanan (and the others in the car): 'Yes, I remember him – a most fastidious probationer, so fastidious that a speck of dust on his clothes would send him into convulsions. He stood out above all of us rough fellows by his immaculate grooming and we hesitated to touch him for fear of contaminating him.' I was rattling on like that while the smile on Buchanan's face developed into a grin and then into a lusty laugh which made him slow down his motor-car. Then to stop me from committing myself too far he remarked – 'You know, or perhaps you don't, that Walker is my son-in-law. He married my daughter 4 years ago.' I tried to get out of it as best I could by saying he was greatly respected by his class-mates for his cleanliness and his artistic tastes etc.etc. and Buchanan let me out by remarking, 'My son-in-law is still exactly as you describe him. He goes into the pulpit with all of his ministerial apparel absolutely perfect – collar exactly suiting his shirt and his throat and his broadcloth coat looking as if it came out of a bandbox.' For five minutes I was silent going over in my mind what I had said. Well, so far so good.

Then all of them went back to Francis and I am here in Regina for the day. I telephoned 'Pop' Knight Weaver[138] and shall run up at 5 p.m. to see them. When I get back to Toronto I shall go to bed for a week to make up for 9 nights on a train.

Lovingly Father.

---

137 Earl H. Walker.

138 A daughter of Pratt's uncle, Allan Knight, who had settled in Regina long ago. Her given name was Charlotte.

TO VIOLA PRATT

Monday a.m. [18 Sept. 1950]

Dearest Vi:

I have just got to Winnipeg and finished my bacon and one egg with toast and coffee at the coffee shop. This is such a unique experience that I thought I ought to mention it first.

After you left Regina yesterday I went to my room and telephoned Pop.[139] Lincoln Weaver came down for me and I spent most of the afternoon there. Roy, the son, and his wife came in and we regaled one another about Nfld days. Pop had about one hundred photos some of them forty years old. I had to see each and pronounce favourable on each though in some cases the faces were indistinguishable. I looked like a Labrador retriever, thin and gaunt, something meant to be a terrier but went astray in the growth.

It was nice to see Karl and Rita and Buchanan, and a pleasure to have them for lunch.

My plans for the day are to go to see Stanley,[140] Graham[141] and Chester Duncan,[142] besides telephoning arrangements with whatever CPR official I can reach.

I have written some of my Vancouver friends and have to write others still. I really needed one more week to get my work thoroughly done but I think I can supplement it in Winnipeg.

I have a fine room in the Royal 492 quite inexpensive. The Birneys were delighted with your craftsmanship. Esther would rather have that little bowl than all the new furniture coming into the house put together. Your pottery makes lovely presents, something special and unpurchasable.

139 His cousin Charlotte Knight Weaver (nicknamed 'Pop'), married to Lincoln Weaver.

140 Pratt had known Carleton Stanley when he was president of Dalhousie University. Following his retirement from Dalhousie in 1945, he moved to Winnipeg, where he joined the English Department at United College, teaching there until 1953.

141 Reverend William Graham was president of United College (formerly Wesley College and later the University of Winnipeg) from 1938 to 1955.

142 Duncan (1913–2002) was a professor of English at the University of Manitoba from 1943 to 1978. He was a pianist and composer and, from the 1950s on, a broadcaster known for his commentaries on arts and culture for the CBC. Some of these are recorded in a collection of autobiographical essays, *Wanna Fight, Kid?* (1975).

Will you keep your eyes open for any kinds of trees, flowers, moss etc. that the CPR tracks might go over in their first laying. I don't know what use I can make of them yet but I am sure that they will be helpful some time.

Give my avuncular blessing to Karl & Rita's children and children-in-law. Tell Rita she looks younger than she did fifteen years ago. All the Whitneys keep their youthfulness – you most of all.

I shall drop another line to Claire today.[143] Much love.

Ned.

TO E.K. BROWN

Friday 17th [Nov. 1950]

Dear Ed:

I have just been re-reading your 'Rhythm'[144] and I had to write to tell you again how superb a piece of work I think it is. As I also remarked before I think, it is the highlight of the Alexander series so far. Everyone around here thinks so.

I am still busily pressing on with my railway saga when I can. It is still hard to say what it will develop into by the time it is finished – probably in a year's time. The curious thing about it is that its nature seems to be changing all the time. As I said to one of the chaps the other day when he asked me about it, 'You know, this thing is turning more and more into a protracted "Great Debate."' I've come to the conclusion that the C.P.R. was built not so much by the chaps who did the technical and physical work, indispensable as they were, but by the fellows with the gift of gab, the talkers and the wranglers and argufiers. 'In the beginning was the Word' – and so to the end, to the last spike. Does that strike you as a perverse way of viewing the thing? I sometimes take a cockeyed view of things, as you are well aware. But I think I am sound on this. Do you by chance have any book or books that might be relevant to the subject?

---

143 See the letter to Claire Pratt 18 September (*EJP: Web*).

144 Brown's Alexander lectures had been published as *Rhythm in the Novel* (Toronto: University of Toronto Press). See the letter to Brown, 7 December 1949 (*EJP: Web*).

Are you still keeping on with the Willa job[145]? I imagine so. I am looking forward immensely to reading it. I know it will be another superb masterpiece.

My best to you and Peggy
and family.

Affectionately,
Ned.

TO JOHN M. GRAY

December 2, 1950

Dear Jack:

Just a note to thank you for a good time the other evening. 'A jolly time was had by all.' I went over the CPR script[146] so far, and find that I was close to my estimate, that the thing is about half finished – more than 500 lines.[147] One never knows, of course, what its extent will be when finally finished. There is a hell of a lot of ground to cover – in more senses than one.

Yours
Ned Pratt

TO E.K. AND MARGARET BROWN

Jan. 16, 1951

Dear Edward and Peggy:

Thanks very much for the book on the Canadian millionaires.[148] It is going to be of help in some aspects of the project – when I can get time to plunge into the

145 Brown was writing a biography of the American novelist Willa Cather (1873–1947). Unfinished at his death in 1951, *Willa Cather: A Critical Biography* was completed by Leon Edel and published by Random House in 1953.

146 'Towards the Last Spike.'

147 He underestimates the length of the completed poem: 1,626 lines.

148 Unidentified.

job. There are so many fiddling things that take up a chap's energy, as you well know; chats, knockings at the door, parties, etc. etc.

I was hoping to see you at the M.L.A. in N.Y. but you didn't turn up. I saw Frye for only a minute and Arthur Woodhouse for about the same length of time, but didn't hear their papers. I had planned on a lot of things but had to return a little earlier than I expected. Two evenings were taken up with my sister who is a nurse in Brooklyn and one dinner with the Van Dorens and Brebner.

That was a lovely dinner on Yorkville St.[149] It was good to be with you both, bless you.

My Irish good wishes go with
you for the New Year.
Ned.

TO JOHN SUTHERLAND

Jan. 25, 1951

My dear John:

You have done yourself proud in this number – one of the best of them all. I particularly like your 'decade' analysis.[150] It is incisive and comprehensive. I was glad to see Horwood[151] this time (as at other times) in your pages. He is an exceptionally able fellow and lays the shillelagh around him like a real gladiator. He is a genuine critic, generous enough to bestow appreciation on what he likes and honest enough to drive in the sting when required. Personally I feel grateful for his kind comments – that would be but human and natural – but I also feel respect for him for the way he tore *Brébeuf* up. All of us need the cracks as well as the caresses and that is the only way we can have a discriminating critical literature.

---

149 The Pratts had dined with the Browns during a visit they had made to Toronto late in the summer of 1950.

150 A reference to Sutherland's essay 'The Past Decade in Canadian Poetry,' published in *Northern Review* 4 (December 1950–January 1951).

151 The same number of *NR* included an essay by Harold Harwood: 'Number Ten Reports.' See the note to 'William Noble' in the letter to William Noble (Harold Horwood), 2 November 1944 (p. 300).

By the way how is the mag. faring? It may be hard to parallel the larger donations of last year.[152] I am enclosing $15.00 for 1951-2. I would have repeated last year's amount but this is my final official year at the University and shall find myself on the *retired list* in June with its heavily reduced stipend.[153]

Another point – Try to get some leisure for your own verse. The best of luck to you and your wife and all your interests.

Sincerely,
E.J. Pratt

The cheque is unconditional of course. If you are writing Horwood convey him my compliments.

TO EARLE BIRNEY

Feb. 10, 1951

My dear Earle:

Don't worry about the Commonwealth issue.[154] It's just the luck of the navy and must be accepted. No one anticipated Monteith's[155] sickness. He may be more ill than we know. In any case I can make use of the poem. Your liking it is of more value to me than Monteith's acceptance had that been possible.

Our family listened in on your 'Gawain'[156] for the whole hour. We were thrilled. It was a superb piece of work. I have been telling it to the C.B.C. fellows and all and sundry. You were magnificently equipped to re-tell the tale with your knowledge of that period and above-all with your poetic gift which is all the time growing. You head your own generation in this country (and I could go farther afield if I were drawn into an argument on the point). Vi was

---

152 *NR* had conducted an appeal for donations in the summer of 1949. See the letter to Earle Birney, 10 August 1949 (p. 443).

153 See the note to 'In two years time I get out of Vic' in the letter to Earle Birney, 10 August 1949 (p. 442).

154 See the note to 'the "official" invitation' in the letter to Birney, 17 February 1950 (p. 447). Birney had submitted Pratt's 'Myth and Fact' in 1950. It was published in 1951.

155 Lionel Monteith, editor of *Poetry Commonwealth*.

156 A radio adaptation by Birney of the medieval romance *Sir Gawain and the Green Knight* was presented by the CBC from Vancouver on 3 January 1951.

breathless with the beauty of the story as you fashioned it, and directed me, *nay*, *commanded* me to tell you in my next letter.

Only today we were talking about starfish and she was reminiscing on that afternoon[157] which was such a delight to her. Bless you and dear Esther and Bill. How I wish I were near enough to chortle the latest story going its rounds into your receptive ear.

Much love.
Ned.

TO MARGARET BROWN

April 30, 1951

Dear and beloved Peggy:

It is very hard to express our sorrow and the depth of our sympathy for you so soon after the blow.[158] Vi and I were really stricken by it when we read the account in the morning paper. It is unnecessary for me to say how much I loved Edward. He was a brother and his passing could not have affected me more deeply if he had been one of my family of blood brothers. And our sorrow is blended with a sense of admiration both for you and for him. The way you stuck it out during the last two years when you knew the shadow was over you was heroic.

I did not go to the telephone the other evening when Vi called you. I thought I might choke if I said anything. Our love will be constantly with you.

Very affectionately,
Ned Pratt

157 During the trip to British Columbia to research 'Towards the Last Spike,' Viola had gone with Birney on a seaside expedition. See the letter to Claire Pratt, 9 September 1950 (pp. 453–4).

158 E.K. Brown had died in Chicago on 23 April at the age of forty-six.

TO RALPH GUSTAFSON

May 11, 1951

My dear Ralph:

I have just finished your 'Moment of Visitation' and am delighted with it – such poems as *The Atlantic Shore*, *New Testament* and *Philosophers* (to cite my favourites) burn on the pages.[159]

My congratulations for the many honours you have received and deserved.

And I must not fail to mention the *Pigeon*[160] which was referred to by Tom Allan over the C.B.C. (Wednesday Night).[161] He said it was one of the best stories he had read in years. I knew the story from the Northern Review and remembered the eerie effect it had on me at the time. My wife and daughter were most impressed by it. In fact I got out the N.R. copy yesterday and read it with a lump in my throat. How wonderfully you worked up the suspense and what an inevitable ending! Give us some more stories as well as poems. The strings vibrate.

When are coming up this way again? I'd love to see you.

Affectionately
Ned Pratt

TO IRVING LAYTON

May 16, 1951

Dear Mr Layton:

Thank you very much for your complimentary copy of 'The Black Huntsman.'[162] I am already acquainted with several of the poems published in First Statement

159 Titles of poems which Gustafson had sent to Pratt.

160 A short story, later published in Gustafson's *The Vivid Air: Collected Stories* (Victoria, BC: Sono Nis Press, 1980).

161 He apparently means Ted Allen, the pseudonym of journalist, novelist, playwright, and broadcaster Allan Herman (1916–65). He had served in the International Brigade in the Spanish Civil War and with Dr Norman Bethune's blood-transfusion unit and is best known as co-author with Sydney Gordon of *The Scalpel, the Sword: The Story of Doctor Norman Bethune* (Boston: Little Brown, 1952; rev. 1971).

162 Layton's third book of poems, published by the author in 1951.

and its Montreal successors. I remember the third stanza of 'Compliments of the Season' and commented on the vividness of its second line. And the 'Newsboy' I remember 'Danubes of blood wash up his bulletins.' This poem is my favourite in the collection.

I like the poems of the calibre of *Proof Reader* and the *Swimmer* and *Poet Killed in action.*

Go to it.

Yours sincerely,
E.J. Pratt

TO VIOLA AND CLAIRE PRATT

152 University Ave.
Kingston, Ont.

July 3, 11 a.m. [1951]

Phone no. 5181

Dearests:

Train on time last night, retired at 9:30 roused myself at 8, went to the University Union for breakfast at 8:45 and found that breakfast would not be served till 8 on Wednesday on account of repairs, sauntered over to the famous Queen's,[163] was welcomed by the proprietor (Christopher) who greeted me with the salutation 'Ah, has he come for his orange juice, eggs sunny-side up, crisp bacon, very-well-done toast, marmalade and two cups of coffee.' 'Right you are,' I said, said I, 'You haven't forgotten me.' 'Ah no, my friend, 'Chris replied – 'Who could forget an appetite like yours and your individual taste.'

That was a good beginning. I went over to Queen's and found two hundred students at least lined up for registration. I found that my hour is from 9 to 10, quite satisfactory. I couldn't learn how many had registered for the Refresher Course, as some may apply late, but I shall have about thirty for English 5.

After that I went down to Princess Street and purchased the following articles:

(1) 2 small jars of Nescafé as the coffee at Queen's has fallen arches.
(2) Stamps.

---

163 Restaurant.

(3) Health Salts.
(4) Gillette Blades.
(5) A bottle of Parker's Ink.
(6) Chewing gum.

Now at 11 a.m. I am back in my digs, same place exactly.
Several items of information may here be mentioned:

(1) The dog next door named Tatters went to his eternal rest last winter to the satisfaction of the neighbours. R.I.P.
(2) Counteracting this heavenly dispensation, a tom-cat belonging to Miss Austin[164] roams the stately University Ave. all night – so Mrs Cartwright informs me, and pays special attention to houses numbered 152 and 154. Mrs C interviewed Miss Austin complaining – 'Can't you keep the cat in at night?' 'Oh dear no,' saith Miss Austin. 'The cat needs as much fresh air as you do.' Miss A now has two dogs and this cat. Heaven has not yet decided to intervene on behalf of humanity. Mysterious are the ways of Providence. However I should prefer the cat to Tatters so the blessings associated with mortality are divinely graded.
(3) George Herbert Clarke is here for the summer-so I shall see a good deal of him.

My job this afternoon will be preparing the first lecture so as to start off fairly well.
The blessings of Earth and High Heaven upon your darling heads.

Much love from finicky Father
and how-do-you do hubby to
beloved Vi and Cakes.

164 Margaret Austin, sister of Dr L.J. Austin. (See the note to 'John Austin' in the lettter to Viola Pratt, 4 July 1940 [p. 183]). Queen's University's historian Herb Hamilton described her as 'the only woman in the world who could walk down the street holding two dogs on a leash, knit a sweater, and read a book all at the same time, and know all that was going on about her.' (*Queen's! Queen's! Queen's!* [Kingston: Alumni Association of Queens University, 1977], 63).

TO VIOLA PRATT

152 University Ave.

Thursday a.m. [5 July 1951]

Dearest Vi:

I suppose by the morrow you will be jaunting off to the North[165] after lunch. I hope the rain isn't as bad in Toronto and environs as it has been here. I never saw such floods in three days in my life. They started with a cloud burst Tuesday night with thunder and lightning and they have been continuous ever since. Even now at 8:30 a.m., the roads are flooded and it is still coming down. I wonder if it is advisable for you to take that trip. If the rain is general the roads will be in a fearful condition. In Kingston opposite the University Union one couldn't walk across as the water is up above the hubs of the motors. Hadn't you better make inquiries about the traveling? The outlook for the day is bleak.

I started yesterday with English 5. I have a class of about thirty – a good class and easy to lecture to. I don't know yet what the registration in the 'Special' Course is.

I saw Glad Phelps and Art[166] yesterday. They are counting on us taking that week-end trip at the end of July. Do you still feel like it? You can come back on the Sunday evening train or as Glad suggests you could stay over for a week and then come back with me to Toronto. Do what you feel like doing. The transportation is the difficult thing as there is no bus service from Kingston to Chaffey's Locks. Perhaps we could take a taxi from Kingston. Glad is writing you. Art comes in every Tuesday to do the BBC. broadcast from the Whig Standard radio.[167]

I think I am going to like the work here. I have been out to the course only once and then was driven back by a thunderstorm. I don't like being away from you my sweet for long, but I think that between your coming to Kingston and my trip to Toronto, the time won't seem too long. Are the blackberries blackening? I am now off to Queen's for my bacon and eggs and the distinctive toast.

Much love to you and Cakes

165 To visit a friend at her cottage in Algonquin Park.

166 Gwald was the sister of Arthur ('Art') Phelps. The Phelpses had taken a summer cottage at Chaffey's Locks, approximately 40 kilometres north of Kingston.

167 Phelps had a regular program on BBC called *Letter to Scotland.*

TO PHYLLIS WEBB[168]

152 University Ave.
Kingston, Ont.

July 19, 1951

Dear Miss Webb:

My apologies for the delay in answering your letter[169] but it had to be re-addressed from Toronto to Queen's University where I am giving a Course in the Summer Session.

My first book *Newfoundland Verse* was published by the Ryerson Press 1923. I had been writing several years submitting poems to various Canadian and English magazines and Lorne Pierce suggested the publication of a collection, mainly sea poems. I was fortunate in having a number of lyrics and narratives printed in the *London Mercury* and the *Manchester Guardian* as well as in the Canadian periodicals like the *Bookman*, the *Saturday Night* and the University Quarterlies; fortunate too, in that Professor Alexander of the University of Toronto who was compiling a High School anthology of verse, decided to include the *Ice Floes* in that collection. Hence the Ryerson Press Editor thought he would take the risk.[170]

The volume sold only moderately well, taking two years to exhaust an Edition of one thousand copies.[171] This was followed by *The Witches' Brew*, a Bacchanalian fantasy which was published first in England by Selwyn and Blount, to whom I was introduced by Professor George Gordon of Oxford and Sir John Squire of the

168 Poet and broadcaster Phyllis Webb was born (1927) in Victoria, BC, and studied at the University of British Columbia and McGill. She first published her poetry alongside poems by Eli Mandel and Gael Turnbull in *Trio* (Montreal: Contact Press, 1954). She has since published many volumes of verse, including *Selected Poems: The Vision Tree* (Vancouver: Talonbooks) which won the Governor General's Award in 1982, and has taught creative writing at the universities of British Columbia and Alberta, and the Banff Centre for the Arts.

169 She had sent him a long letter addressed to a number of Canadian poets, requesting data for 'a short study on the ins and outs of poetry publication in Canada during the past 20 years or so.'

170 This paragraph is full of inaccuracies. In 1922, Arthur Phelps had suggested to Lorne Pierce that Ryerson publish a collection of Pratt's poems. None of his poems were published in *LM*, the *Manchester Guardian*, *Saturday Night*, or any university quarterly before *NV* appeared in 1923. 'The Ice-Floes' was published in Alexander's *Shorter Poems* (Toronto: Timothy Eaton Co., 1924).

171 This is an accurate statement, though his publisher's contract for *NV* had called for a first printing of 2,500 copies.

London Mercury. Five hundred copies were printed and John Austen, a London artist did the illustrations. The book did not sell very fast but the Macmillans of Canada under Mr Hugh Eayrs became interested and bought out the unsold copies and then published under their own imprint a Canadian Edition. Eayrs also went over to the Ryerson Press and negotiated for the copyright of Newfoundland Verse, taking over about two hundred copies not yet sold. This was the beginning of my connection with Macmillans who published all my work afterwards.

The next publication was *Titans* 1926 – two poems, *The Cachalot* and *The Great Feud*. The former was printed in the *Canadian Forum* just after it was written, the latter being too long for a periodical appearance. *Titans* also was slow selling: it didn't reach a second edition.

The next was *The Iron Door*, a personal ode in memory of my mother. It had a trade edition of five hundred and a special one of a hundred copies. It took two years to sell out. Then the Macmillans issued a small edition – Verses of the Sea – which was taken up by some of the High Schools.

But my first break came with *The Roosevelt and the Antinoe*, a narrative of a sea rescue. The American Macmillans brought out their own edition while the English House took the Canadian plates. Approximately three thousand were sold. In the meantime several anthologies included poems – short lyrics and one long extract from the *Roosevelt*, the burial service. The *Titanic* followed with a sale of one thousand in two years – slow going for a time. Likewise *Many Moods* (a collection of shorter verses) and the *Fable of the Goats*, each one thousand copies.

I had now grown accustomed to a one-edition frame of mind. By selling out, barely selling out, the Macmillans neither made nor lost, and certainly I had abandoned all intention of purchasing a ticket for a Miami vacation. All I needed was a book that would break the jinx of a single edition. It came with *Brébeuf and His Brethren* which struck five editions in Canada and the United States. *Dunkirk* also had five. *They Are Returning* went back to one, and likewise *Behind the Log*.[172]

The radio was now helping circulation. *Brébeuf* was set to music by Healey Willan, was put on the air twice and once in Massey Hall Toronto under Sir Ernest MacMillan with the Toronto Symphony Orchestra and the Mendelsohn Choir.

Anthologies and school texts became a great medium for publicity, and last year the *Titanic* was printed in full along with *The Ancient Mariner* and the *Death of Arthur* for matriculation students in Ontario.[173] It took nearly twenty

172 He has not mentioned *Still Life* (1943) and the Canadian and American editions of *Collected Poems* (1944 and 1945 respectively).

173 The booklet was entitled *Poems for Senior Students* (1950).

years to get the feel of a royalty cheque that would buy a new washing machine for my wife and mend some plaster cracks in the ceiling. Miami still must wait.

I am now engaged on a long poem in blank verse, the subject being the building of the First Canadian Transcontinental. The title is *Towards the Last Spike*. I hope to have it finished by November of this year in time for publication next spring. I have my fingers crossed and Macmillans have crossed both fingers and toes. At any rate it is great fun whether it turns out to be a flop or a success.

If there is anything further you would like to know, please feel free to write me. I shall be at the above address till August 14, after that Victoria College, Toronto.

Here's wishing you every success,

Yours sincerely,
E.J. Pratt.

Some further information may be gathered from E.K. Brown's book On Canadian Poetry (Ryerson's).

TO VIOLA PRATT

152 University Ave.
Kingston

Tuesday [24 July 1951]

Dearest Vi:

Your card came today and I am greatly relieved that Ted Ridding discovered the *real* cause of the stalling. If the car isn't satisfactory keep at him till it is perfect.

Things are going a little better here now. Not that the youngsters do not still continuously reach high A from 8 a.m. till 7 p.m. but I can get out of the radius by going to the Faculty Room at the Union until it is time to march out to the 9 holes. And then Mrs Minnis[174] has returned from Ottawa whither she went to restore her nerves, and on returning I think she must have read the riot act over the cats. She was against having a cat in the house from the first, but she tolerated one. Now she was informed by Mrs Cartwright that there are three, the last one being Miss Austin's abominable Tom who came over on Saturday

174 A neighbour, otherwise unidentified.

afternoon and, taking advantage of the Whalley[175] absence to the Lake for a few hours, got into the cellar with the two others and couldn't get out. Do you recall my saying that Dr McNeill[176] and I thought the screams inside the house were those of youngsters! Well, when it got too bad, McNeill, Mrs Cartwright and I went over armed with panfulls of water to throw over them thinking the quadrupeds were in the alley-way between the two houses. We couldn't see them but imagined they were under the verandah. Along came Edinborough. I explained the situation to him and he readily agreed to use an umbrella. The four of us marched like Sennacherib's army, that is like wolves upon the feline fold, but found no visible signs of the enemy though the audible manifestations were beyond all measurement. Now as Mrs Minnis knows about it, we expect another war this time to end all wars. I shall keep Headquarters at 21 Cortleigh informed of later manoeuvres.

Miss Austin's dog has developed his belligerency in a most curious way. He not only runs out after the automobiles when they stop at the corner but he bites the tires. I hope one blows up on him. Still Miss A takes him in after 10 p.m.

I have just finished my examination paper and I am now running over to Miss Healey[177] to give it to her. I thought I'd do it now and not have to rush it at the end.

Well, my sweethearts, take things easily. I shall be home on Friday following this one. I am spending some time with Clarke[178] & McNeill over the week-end and there is an academic function Saturday evening that Wallace has asked me to attend. They want me to speak at a Sunday evening meeting but I have refused.

Much love
Ned.

---

175 George Whalley (1915–84), born in Kingston, educated at Bishop's and Oxford universities, and author of several books of verse, scholarly essays, and criticism. At the time, he was an associate professor of English at Queen's University.

176 [*sic*]. William E. MacNeill.

177 Secretary in the Department of English at Queen's University.

178 G.H. Clarke.

TO LEONARD W. BROCKINGTON[179]

[Sept. 1951]

Dear L.W.:

What a grand affair from 1 to 5:30 under the canopy on the lawn! And now I am content about John Masefield.[180] I always loved that man and his work. His *Everlasting Mercy* in the *English Review* was my introduction and I think I read everything he wrote right up to the present. Dauber, Reynard the Fox, Good Friday, his numerous ballads are still on my shelves together with the finest piece of English writing that came out of the first World War, Gallipoli. The critics agree on that. My brother Art (a sergeant in the Newfoundland Regiment) was with the rearguard in the battle and years after the War referred to the authenticity of Masefield's account and the power of its expression.

I had the temerity to send him an early poem of mine (the Cachalot) and I shall never forget the kindness of his reply and the fruitful suggestion that I expand the conclusion by a few lines to deepen the thunder of the whale's forehead against the side of the ship. Masefield's phrase was 'before death blurs the edges.'

I had the honour of meeting him three times – at Hart House with Malcolm Wallace, at Macmillans with Hugh Eayrs, and after his lecture in Massey Hall.

If you are writing him please extend my regards and admiration. Tell him too that I have read 'Consecration'[181] and Aug. 1914[182] to thousands of students over the thirty years of my teaching at the University of Toronto.

Yours affectionately,
Ned.

Perhaps Mr Masefield might be interested in a recent Newfoundland poem,[183] one of a nostalgic scene of my homeland. I can still hear the sea gulls screaming.

179 See the note to 'Brockington' in the letter to Ellen Elliott, 28 October 1940 (p. 199).

180 Brockington was a friend and correspondent of the English poet. He had written Pratt an account of a recent visit he had paid Masefield at his home in Oxfordshire.

181 The prologue to Masefield's early book, *Salt-Water Ballads* (1902).

182 'August, 1914,' a poem in Masefield's *Sonnets and Other Poems*.

183 Probably his 'Newfoundland Seamen' written in 1949.

TO ANNE WILKINSON

Sept. 24, '51

Dear Anne:

I had a pleasant hour or two over the week-end reading 'Counterpoint to Sleep.'[184] It certainly justifies expectations and more. Let me point out some of the qualities of special interest.

(1) Summer acres: phrases picturesque and musical –

eyes – wired – willow
heart – boughed – cedar
ears – tied – tattle of water

(2) Winter Sketch[185]:

'black extravagance of night,' good
but 'crystal christen Christ' is uneuphonic because of excessive gutteral alliteration.

(3) Folk Tale[186] – 'the clear etceteras of a kiss' – fine, full of implied associations.

'pools of pupils,' 'polar pull of blood' – excellent alliteration because, though you keep the same consonant, you give variety by changing the vowel sound four times. This is good craftsmanship.

(4) Anxiety: 'octave' etc. I like the language & image.
(5) Lake Song: Hopkins – wimple the beach.
(6) I know not what to do, love: made for a musical setting.

I like the whole of 'The Great Winds' with its subdued ending. Also the Psycho-Neurotic.[187]

---

184 Published in the New Writers Series (no. 8) by First Statement Press in 1951.
185 The full title of the poem is 'Winter Sketch, Rockcliffe, Ottawa.'
186 'A Folk Tale / With a Warning to Lovers.'
187 'Poem of Anxiety.'

May I make two suggestions for the future?

(1) a little simplification of the content wouldn't injure the verse. Some of the poems are very compressed owing to remoteness of allusion and imagery – a very common feature of present-day writing indeed, but there is a swing against too much ambiguity.
(2) Work out further that delightful vein you have of playing variations on old themes.

'I know not what to do love' I have mentioned.

The Lord Randall variant[188] is wonderful with its genuinely ballad characteristic of the dramatic surprise at the conclusion. It reminds me not only of Randall but of Edward: –

'Why does your brand sae drop wi bluid
Edward, Edward?
.....
The curse of hell frae me sall ye beir
Sic counseils ye gave to me O.'

I should like to see the return of Song and ballad to our poetry today, and, dear Anne, I think you can do a lot to that end.

I notice your book is in Tyrells, and I am going to order some near Christmas time to hand to my friends.

More power to ye,
Ned Pratt

TO MARGARET BROWN

Oct. 10, 1951

Dear Peggy:

Will you reserve either Tuesday or Thursday Oct. 23 or 25 for dinner with us – whichever one suits you. Then Vi wants you for a lunch, too.

188 'After the Ballad, "Lord Randall, My Son."'

After our dinner we can talk over the Library and letter mutualities.[189] I have something extremely funny about a letter of mine which happened to get into 'wrong' hands[190] – something you and Edward would appreciate.

We can go over Mrs Bond's list[191] and make our selections of Canadiana.

I shall call for you at the Palace[192] to take you up to our house on the day you choose.

In the meantime Scott & Pratt letters in abeyance. I shouldn't like to have poor Lorne hurt as Scott can be both unkind and unjust at times.[193]

Love from both of us.
Ned

You may drop me a card about the choice of dates.

TO JOHN SUTHERLAND

Nov. 15/51

---

189 Margaret Brown had asked Pratt's advice about purchases of Canadian titles for the University of Chicago Library and the disposition of letters in her husband's collection, mainly those from Duncan Campbell Scott and Pratt.

190 See the note to 'Dear Mrs Parsons' in the letter to Mrs Horace Parsons, 22 September 1925 (p. 61) for the probable reference.

191 Mrs Bond was the librarian in charge of the Poetry Room at the University of Chicago Library. E.K. Brown had left most of his large collection of books to the Poetry Room. Anxious to add to it, she had made a list on which she had consulted Mrs Brown, who in turn was seeking Pratt's advice.

192 The Alexandra Palace Hotel.

193 Lorne Pierce had asked Margaret Brown for Duncan Campbell Scott's letters to Brown for the Canadiana collection he was giving to Queen's Library. As some of the letters contained uncomplimentary references to Pierce himself, Mrs Brown had asked Pratt's advice. Scott's letters were finally deposited in the Public Archives of Canada, and a selection was edited by R.L. McDougall in 1983 in *The Poet and the Critic: A Literary Correspondence between D.C. Scott and E.K. Brown* (Ottawa: Carleton University Press). Mrs Brown kept Pratt's letters for some years after his death. In 1969 she provided copies to David G. Pitt for his biographical research, and later deposited most of the originals in the Pratt Collection at Victoria University, Toronto.

Dear John:

Thanks for your letter and your kind suggestions about broadcasts and articles. It warms me to be so appreciated and I am not over-sensitive to criticisms. I learn a lot by them and feel grateful.

I do not think there will be any difficulty about a reprint of one of the longer poems or a substantial portion.[194] The Great Feud is quite long, but when the time comes I will take the matter up with Macmillans so as to avoid any consideration of royalty. They own the copyright of all my publications but I am sure they would waive the claim for an article.

But before taking action I should like to submit a manuscript which I have been working at for two years in spare time. It is called *Towards the Last Spike*, an objective poem on the First Canadian Transcontinental – objective in the sense that it is neither pro nor con politically. It is a new experiment in that [it] is a symbolic treatment of an historical subject. It is now in the hands of the Macmillan editors and will be a March or April publication 1952.

If I can get a second typed copy I'll hand it along in a few days so that you may pass your scrutiny over it.

My lecture on the Titanic is not in print. If I can find my notes I'll arrange them in some order and slip them to you. Perhaps within a week I can let you have both.

I am sorry you find it so hard to raise the necessary funds for the N.R.[195] If you go absolutely broke, (or just before that becomes imminent) notify your personal friends. I am sure that an ordinary sense of decency on their part would safeguard you against *personal* loss. You have been doing a national service, almost single-handed, and, I think, without parallel in the publication of little magazines.

---

194 Sutherland was writing a substantial critical essay on Pratt for *Northern Review*. He wished to accompany it with 'The Great Feud' and had written asking Pratt's permission and help securing copyright permission. See the letters to Sutherland, 25 February and 15 March 1952 (pp. 484–7 and 487–8).

195 *Northern Review*.

You do not need to reply to this until after you hear from me in regard to the matters aforementioned.

The very best to you,
Ned Pratt

TO JOHN M. GRAY

Thurs. [29 Nov. 1951]

Dear Jack:

Three phone-calls naught availing, herewith a brief reply to yours of the 26th.

I appreciate your remarks, which do not surprise me greatly.[196] The ending gave me trouble and raised doubts of my own. I agree it needs more work though I am dubious about a 'recap.' What it needs is a stirring coda of some sort to bring the thing to a crashing finale. I am not so sure that the other parts are so bad as you suggest, though the 'omelette' is probably a bit overdone. I'll see what I can do.

Yours,
Ned Pratt

TO 'K'[197]

[late 1951]

Dear K:

I am sending along 'The Mechanical Bride'[198] for you to glance at. Some of the ads are exceedingly funny. I don't know what you can find in it or whether you might consider writing an article on it. I sent the book to Mark Van Doren and

---

196 Gray had written him about his readers' reports on *TLS*. All agreed that the poem's ending – originally at line 1594 – was 'something of an anticlimax.' They also felt that 'the Lady of British Columbia' lines (in which Sir John A. Macdonald woos British Columbia as if she were a coquettish woman) and an incident involving Edward Blake, in which Pratt made use of a rather graceless 'omelette' metaphor, were below his usual standard. He agreed to delete the 'omelette' but not 'the Lady' section. And he did write thirty-one new lines to end the poem.

197 Unidentified.

198 The recently published book by Marshall McLuhan, subtitled 'Folklore of Industrial Man,' discusses the power of the advertising media to influence the public consciousness.

Mark was exceedingly interested and amused. McLuhan[199] disclaims the [....] of himself as a communicator. He is a teacher of English literature at St Michael's with a flair for philosophy and psychology. Would you pass on the Bride to Jack[200] to see if he is inspired. We should get him on the list of New Liberty as a possible contributor. He is an eloquent speaker, a little abstruse at times, but he can gear up a production in a wink in fine style. When Jack returns I shall make up a lunch at Burwash Hall for the four of us.

Yours,
Ned.

TO ARTHUR PHELPS

Jan. 2, 1952

May all the blessings that the Deities and their prophets bestow upon mankind descend upon the Phelpses -- among those personages I include Yahweh, Allah, Mohammed, Confucius, Budha and other luminaries.

Yes Art, I was delighted to get the little book from McClelland & Stewart.[201] I chuckled and chuckled over the reminiscential phases. They made the past come back deliciously. And the one of Morley[202] is just as finely written – The others, too, are full of Phelpsian turns of phrase and Puckish whimsicalities that have made your household tones a part of Canadian radio music.[203]

The reason why I deferred acknowledging the book was that Vi wondered if you and Lal could come to Toronto for a visit, stay with us, of course, and also '*here's the catch*' if you would address the University Women's Club of Toronto.

199 Marshall McLuhan (1911–80), later celebrated for his studies of media and communications including *The Gutenberg Galaxy: The Making of Typographical Man* (Toronto: University of Toronto Press, 1962), *Understanding Media: The Extensions of Man* (New York: McGraw Hill, 1964), and *The Medium Is the Message: An Inventory of Effects* (New York: Random House, 1967). He was then a young associate professor at St Michael's College, Toronto.

200 Jack Kent Cooke, owner of the journal *New Liberty*. (See the note to 'Jack Kent Cooke' in the letter to Earle Birney, 20 November 1952 [p. 515]). Pratt was on the journal's editorial committee.

201 *Canadian Writers* (Toronto: McClelland & Stewart, 1951). The book included commentaries on E.J. Pratt, Morley Callaghan, Thomas Haliburton, R. W. Service, Frederick Philip Grove, Merrill Denison, Archibald Lampman, Thomas Raddall, Stephen Leacock, Hugh MacLennan, L.M. Montgomery, W.O. Mitchell, French Canadian writing in translation, A.M. Klein, and Earle Birney.

202 Morley Callaghan.

203 An allusion to his long-running radio series *Neighbourly News*.

Could you make a planned trip to Toronto coincide with the time and delivery of said address? After the speech we would put on a cocktail party at the House, and then after the other guests depart, we should indulge in far-off memories – another variety of indulgence. Vi will write to you.

I am writing McClelland[204] who told me that he intended bringing out the book in hard covers next Spring.

Neddie

TO CLAIRE PRATT

Friday, Jan. 30, 1952

Dearest Cayke:

Your letter of Tuesday the 27th just came.[205]

First the financial situation.

The first thousand was made up of two amounts of $700 + 300. You needed 600.00 you said in your message. Well I slipped along an extra hundred making it 700.00. Then later thinking that you needed more I added the other 300.00. It came out of my account which is quite flush. The royalties etc. have been very substantial.

Then I thought you might as well have one of those two 1000.00 bonds. They are bearer bonds and did not need any signature. Mr Adam suggested that instead of selling one of them the Royal would telegraph the First National Bank of Boston the thousand dollars in cash for you, and the Royal would hold the bond in its possession as security. That would save all the trouble of coupon clipping and negotiation in your case.

There is yet the other thousand bond which is in the vault and you can draw on it in an emergency should one arise.

I am right in the throes of getting out a text for Macmillans.[206] Mother is trying to decipher my writing for the typewriter. I must have everything in Miss Eayrs' hands by Monday – Miss A-h- -h- -s s, if you know what I mean.

---

204 Jack McClelland, then general manager of McClelland & Stewart.

205 See the letter to Claire, early January 1952 (*EJP: Web*).

206 *TLS.*

I shall write again in a day or two. Enclosed is a letter which came unsealed to the house.

Father

TO HIS FOURTH YEAR STUDENTS

[24 Feb. 1952]

Dear Class:

Your gift is delightful. It is lovely to look at and I know it will be delicious to the taste. I haven't yet torn off the cellophane cover, as my wife says your tangible message of sympathy must stand for a few days on the centre of the mantlepiece for visitors to admire. This is rather tough on me as my mouth is watering for that pear and grapefruit and all the other things suggestive of Miami. The gift has turned February into summer, and when my family decide that the time has come to bring the contents into full sunlight there will be an appropriate ceremony, the chief feature being a toast to the class drunk in the very Canada Dry now reposing in the lower left corner of the box.

Well, a word now about my accident. Last Friday week,[207] precisely at 10 pm, I was crossing Cortleigh Crescent into Cortleigh Boulevard (the street on which I live). As the street was very slippery following the snow storm I thought I would take the centre of the road instead of the sidewalk. There was my mistake. One second I was walking erect, dignified, chin up, professional, in fact pure Greek in the symmetry of my pose and locomotion, and the next second I was angular, out of proportion, my centre of gravity lying decidedly outside my base of support; in other words I was earth-bound ending up in a condition of extreme gloom, my left shoulder fractured.

For a period which I could not calculate, my mind was occupied with the following maze of considerations:

(1) I observed that there was no person on the street who could report the indignity of my position.
(2) I was thankful that it was my shoulder not my neck which was broken.
(3) I was thankful also that I had enough anatomical sections intact to enable me to collect and hold together the other fragments until I reached my

207 15 February 1952.

house which luckily was only fifty yards away.

(4) My spirit of thankfulness, however, was modified by inward agitation vainly trying to find language strong enough to do justice to the event. Having spent so much time with you in the presence of Hardy was fortuitous. I tried a few of the more vehement oaths – *Crass Casualty, It, Unconscious Principle, the President of the Immortals*, the Brute and Blackguard who made the world and the *Brooding Fate*. I rejected them all as too abstract. I wanted something I could get my teeth into, something I could hit with my right fist and I found it in a very concrete individual, namely the Head of the Department of Street Clearing at the City Hall who neglected to put sand or cinders on that treacherous corner. What I said about him cannot be written down. But this spate of invective was of meagre support in keeping my mind off the pain of the fracture.

And now I am in my house for another two or three weeks.[208] With all the bandages on me I look like a dromedary. At least my pose can scarcely be said to be photogenic. In the meantime, my dear students, I shall toast you in Canada Dry and offer up a prayer that all the good angels both pagan and Christian will hover over you with their heavenly wings and preserve you from falling.

With esteem & affection
E.J.P. X his mark

TO JOHN SUTHERLAND

21 Cortleigh Blvd.
Toronto

Feb. 25, 1952

My dear John:

Excuse these straggling pencil marks as I am in doors with a cast on my left shoulder. I fell last week and broke the shoulder blade which will keep me in cast and sling for a month yet.

---

208 He was in a cast and sling for nearly six weeks, but was back in class by the end of February.

I would not be human if I did not feel grateful for your wonderful tribute.[209] It is refreshing to discover the novelty and variety of the treatment. Your definition of 'heroic' presents a valid differentiation. Criticism generally is obsessed with the Beowulf conception in dealing with the traditional struggles. I hope I am not so immodest as to stretch my own work alongside the historical landmarks, but, if any comparison is made on qualified grounds, it is certainly time that *mere* glorification of strength was never my intention. As you imply, terror in the presence of power is a concomitant, and it would be a strangely lop-sided interpretation which excluded the outcroppings of the social sympathies. Frye (who by the way is one of your admirers) emphasized the terror factor to balance the power.[210]

This article is the first one to make use of material of which I was more or less unconscious as a shaping force. It is only now in retrospect that I can feel the influence of two works which had to be thoroughly studied – The 'Principles of Psychology' by Wm James,[211] and 'Immediate Experience' by Wundt.[212] And I might add a third – James' 'Varieties of Religious Experience.'

There are several pages of this essay that moved me tremendously – pages 14-18 particularly. That figure of 'the slow withdrawal of consciousness from someone who is dying' belongs to the pageant of poetry rather than of prose. It is magnificent.

I had this problem in the 'Titanic.' I had to select from the reports of two Commissions of Inquiry just those facts which, while safeguarding historical objectivity, would impart a unified psychological impression. The extremes of human behaviour were exhibited on that deck – self-control at one end, and at the other fear on the verge of panic. The impulsive rush to the boats on the part of a few and the action of the stoker had to be balanced by the conduct of the engineers and bandsmen and of individuals like Ida Straus. I realized the danger of elaborated comment which would sentimentalize these fine elements in human nature, so I tried to give them as much condensation as possible.

Your analysis of the reason-instinct antithesis is masterly. You have made explicit to me what, in part, was only subconsciously implicit in my tackling the 'Great Feud.' The 'Titanic' and the 'Feud' are, in my opinion, the most successful

---

209 Sutherland had sent him a typescript of the essay he had written for *Northern Review* on E.K. Brown (in *On Canadian Poetry* [1943]).

210 He is probably referring to Frye's 'La tradition narrative dans la poésie canadienne-anglaise,' *Gants du Ciel* 11 (printemps 1946): 19–30.

211 William James, American philosopher and psychologist (1842–1910).

212 Wilhelm Wundt (1832–1920), German physiologist and psychologist, generally regarded as the father of experimental psychology.

things I have done, more so than Brébeuf which I find on re-reading to be too simple and homogenous through the dominance of the martyr-motif. Besides, it has too much of factual over-burden.

How right you were about the 'Witches Brew.' I had been drifting continually in Newfoundland Verse, but in this fantasy I discovered that the tiller was geared to a rudder, but such a discovery took some time.

Suggestions.

(1) Page 2. A slight qualification may be in order here. As far as I know, the important american anthologies like Untermeyer's[213] and Sanders and Nelson[214] do not include the work of any contemporary Canadian.

I have appeared in a few recent anthologies across the Line, but they have been special and topical and not comprehensive: such as 'The Eternal Sea,' 'Religious Poems of the World,' 'The Questing Spirit,' 'The Literary Tradition.'[215]

(2) Page 8. The Titanic sank in 1912.

(3) The order of composition was:
(1) The Witches Brew (2) The Cachalot (3) The Great Feud.

It is, however, quite true that (3) was inchoately in my mind as a possible theme before the Cachalot was completed.

(4) Page 36. The final formal induction[216] took place, but I decided against entering the 'active' ministry, preferring a classroom to a pulpit.

---

213 Louis Untermeyer (1885–1920), American poet, critic, editor, and anthologist. Pratt is probably referring to his *Modern American Poetry since 1900* (New York: Henry Holt, 1923).

214 *Chief Modern Poets of England and America*, 3rd ed. (New York: Macmillan, 1943).

215 His recollection of recent American anthologies in which his poems appeared was somewhat imperfect. The following is a complete record of his publications in American anthologies during the previous five years: *The Eternal Sea: An Anthology of Sea Poetry*, ed. W.M. Williamson (New York: Coward-McCann, 1946) ['The Way of Cape Race' and 'Sea-Gulls']; *The Questing Spirit: Religion in the Literature of Our Time*, ed. Halford E. Luccock and Frances Brentano (New York: Coward-McCann, 1947) ['To an Enemy']; *World Literature*, ed. Arthur Christy and Henry W. Wells (New York: American Book Co., 1947) ['The Man and the Machine']; *College Book of English Literature*, ed. James Edward Tobin et al. (New York: American Book Co., 1949) ['The Way of Cape Race'].

216 His ordination to the Methodist ministry in June 1913.

May I keep the script for a few days. My wife wants to read it again at greater leisure. By the way the Feud is her favourite too. She found in your exposition just the interlinear significances she had been groping for.

Page 41 (balance of power) is about as fine a piece of writing as I wish to see anywhere. I wonder if you realize how good it is.

Again my thanks, and my apologies for this inadequate scrawl.

Yours with kindest regards
Ned Pratt

TO JOHN SUTHERLAND

21 Cortleigh Blvd.
Toronto

March 15, 1952

Dear John:

Thanks for your letter which I am answering right away.

Macmillans, of course, possess the copyright[217] and they might release *The Great Feud*. If you wrote Gray,[218] suggesting your purpose, he would consult me and I'd back up your scheme naturally. If he had a copy of your article, it would impress him tremendously. I want him to release it to you without a permission fee, as you cannot afford that, and the advertising value of the issue would far outweigh the fee. Should he demand a fee, I would make this agreement with you. Though Macmillans have the control, yet they hand over royalties to me less 10% for collection. I would personally hand back this fee to you. So you wouldn't be out. This would be confidential obviously.

Collins is bringing out an anthology this spring of contemporary verse[219] and they are including the whole of *Dunkirk*. They paid $50.00 for the right and Macmillan passed it on to me.

I do not think Gray would publish in a single edition the three – *Titanic*, *Cachalot* & *Feud* – as the 'Collected Poems' contains those poems and the volume

---

217 See the note to 'a reprint … or a substantial portion' in the letter to Sutherland, 15 November 1951 (p. 479).

218 John M. Gray.

219 This anthology never appeared.

is selling well. It would indeed be an advantage to do so especially with your introduction, but I doubt its feasibility, particularly as *Towards the Last Spike* is appearing next week[220] under the Macmillan imprint and the firm intends to put all its weight of publicity on it. The poem is a semi-realistic, semi-symbolic account of the building of the First Canadian Trans-Continental, and it was written over the last two years.

I am enclosing a glossy print of Forbes' portrait. Hope it works out all right. Still apologizing for this unsteady hand.

Kindest regards,
Ned Pratt

P.S. When your issue appears I want 50 copies sent straight from your office to addresses which I shall furnish. I shall cover the expense with a $25.00 cheque.[221] My brother[222] who read your introduction also wants 50 copies. You may bill him direct for $25.00 and he will remit promptly.

More anon
P.

TO FATHER V.J. GUINAN[223]

March 22, 1952

Father V.J. Guinan, C.S.B.
President
University of St. Thomas
Houston 6, Texas

My dear Father:

Your kind letter brought back vivid memories of my visit to Houston several years ago.[224] It was a delightful journey for me in that I made real friends among

---

220 Though originally scheduled for March, publication of *TLS* was delayed until June.

221 Since the special issue of *Northern Review* devoted to Pratt was double (February-March and April-May), the cost was $1.00 a copy. But Pratt and his brother confirmed their original orders for fifty copies each.

222 Calvert.

223 President of the University of St Thomas in Houston, Texas. He had invited Pratt to give several lectures or readings both at St Thomas and at meetings of the Southwest Writers' Conference in Corpus Christi.

224 Pratt's previous visit had been made in April 1946. (See the letter to Viola and Claire Pratt, 9 April 1946 [p. 374].)

the staff of St. Thomas. All of you set out to make things comfortable for me and hospitable to the last degree.[225] It will be a pleasure to renew the friendships.

I sent off a telegram of acceptance yesterday, but there is just one qualification which I discussed with Father McCorkell. I like giving lectures, but Floor discussion is a bit uncongenial, partly because an ear infection this winter has made me slightly deaf, and partly because controversy from the Floor has always been a nervous exaction for me. I don't mind small groups where there is a sit-around intimacy and informality and everyone is at ease. Would Mr Tatton[226] consent to this limitation?

In addition to my main lecture, I could substitute for any prospective participant who for some reason or other couldn't make the Conference. Or I could do my part in filling gaps with poetry-readings.

As for Houston, I should gladly place myself at your disposal for as many 'talks' and lecture-recitals as desired, inside or outside your city, the same as on the previous trip. The dates mentioned suit me admirably. I would go by train arriving in Houston Monday 26th or Tuesday, whatever is convenient to you.

I remember going with Father Dwyer and Father McCorkell to Galveston and to some other town where I spoke to the Seminarians for Monsignor (?)[227] and also to the party at the house of the *Decorator* where I read for a few minutes. It was all most pleasant for me.

Here is a list of subjects to choose from:

1. 'The Titanic.' I gave this with readings at Houston. Would it be appropriate for the address at the Conference? It takes about three-quarters of an hour.
2. 'Brebeuf and His Brethren,' a poem on the Jesuit Missionaries to the Huron territory in the 17th Century. This was also given in your city. I should prefer a leisurely treatment of the 'Titanic' if the audience at Corpus Christi were largely secular.
3. 'Heroism on the Sea,' a new lecture with readings.
4. 'Pitfalls in Verse Composition' – largely humorous (I hope) from my own efforts.
5. 'Rescue of Life without thought of gain,' or more briefly 'Risk without counting the cost.'

225 A rough draft of this letter follows this sentence with the words 'even though it was Lent and I couldn't ask for any Irish stew.'

226 John M. Tatton, British by birth and a graduate of Cambridge University, was a member of the Senate of the University of St Thomas. He was a well-to-do rancher as well as a musician and poet. He had proposed that Pratt address the Writers' Conference in Corpus Christi.

227 The name Pratt could not recall was that of Monsignor James Fleming, the Rector of St Mary's Seminary at LaPorte, Texas.

6. 'Newfoundland Life and Idiom' – a new lecture, now in preparation, illustrating quaint habits and modes of speech (essentially Irish).
7. 'Readings of Miscellaneous Poems.'

I shall be glad to hear from you and accept any suggestions. By the way, do I need to bring a dinner jacket with black tie? I have a dark-business suit (light in weight) and with white soft shirt. That's what I wore last time.

With kind personal regards,

Yours sincerely,
E.J. Pratt

Sorry I cannot type, as I have a broken shoulder from a fall. It is getting better.
P.

TO F. DAVID HOENIGER[228]

May 5, 1952

Dear Dave:

It was good to hear from you. You can certainly use my name anytime you like for a reference.[229]

I met Hunter[230] only once and that was when I was 'down' to Newfoundland three years ago, proposing the toast to Robbie Burns on St. Andrew's night.[231] I don't know what qualifications he expects by way of degrees, and what

228 Born in Germany (1921), Hoeniger completed his BA and MA at Victoria College and his PhD at the University of London in 1954. After teaching at the University of Saskatchewan (1946–7), he was appointed to the Department of English at Victoria College, where he remained until his retirement in the early 1990s. He published many scholarly works on Shakespeare, including the Arden edition of *Pericles* (1963).

229 On leave at the time, and a permanent appointment at Victoria unconfirmed, Hoeniger was seeking a post at Memorial University of Newfoundland.

230 A.C. Hunter (1890–1971), British-born and a graduate of the universities of London, Oxford, and Paris, was professor and head of English at Memorial University, vice-president, and dean of arts and science.

231 Actually it was a Burns' Night (25 January) celebration, sponsored by the St Andrew's Society.

competition there will be. I know the competition is terrific in Canadian universities generally, but one can only enter the race.

As you know I am retired now (apart from two lectures a week which may end this year). John[232] goes on the emeritus list next year, though he will be giving special lectures for three years after that as far as he can predict.

I have had a trying time this winter with a broken shoulder. I fell on the ice last February, smashed the right shoulder,[233] which was followed by bursitis, a most painful inflammation which persists and may persist for months yet according to the doctor. I am taking cortisone and shock wave treatment. But it is goodbye to golf for the summer I fear.

I hope you are in good condition yourself.

The best of luck to you.
Ned Pratt

TO VIOLA AND CLAIRE PRATT

[Houston, Texas]

Wed. [28 May 1952]

How are you dears?

First day in Houston. Address and banquet tonight. Tomorrow I put on royal regalia and attend Mass at 10, and at night 7:30 I line up with the Convocation Procession. Then Friday I take a trip by motor with the Rev. Fathers along the shore. On Saturday Corpus Christi[234] with autographing (such as it is) at 3 p.m. Weather thundery and warm.

Love, Ned.

---

232 J.D. Robins.

233 A curious error: he had broken his left shoulder. (See the letters to his fourth-year students, 24 February, and John Sutherland, 25 February [pp. 483–4 and p. 484].)

234 He was to spend several days there at the Southwestern States Writers Conference. (See the letter to Father V.J. Guinan, 22 March 1952 [pp. 488–90].)

TO VIOLA PRATT

Friday am. [6 June 1952]

Dearest Vi:

I have just got in and am expecting Claire (who left a note of welcome on the breakfast table) in about an hour.

The first night from Corpus Christi I had a roomette with not enough room to stand up without calling the porter to release the spring and put it back during the night. Last night I was managed to finagle a one-passenger bedroom which was infinitely better, though it was quite late before it was available.

I got your notes at the Writers' Conference though there was no reference to my cards which I sent every day. Probably they didn't reach you early enough. I sent a small box of cigarettes to Nellie from Corpus Christi.

I shall tell you all about the Conference later. It was most enjoyable with hospitality belonging to the 'deep south.' The Texans are wonderful. Mr & Mrs Tatton[235] were my hosts and they wouldn't let me buy a meal or a cigar. Tatton (Jack) always managed to get in ahead of me.

I brought back $150.00 net with me, room at the Driscoll Hotel being $10.00 a day. Everything was very expensive – even a shave costing a dollar. But Tatton paid all transportation.

I notice on the table a letter to Claire with the suggestion that you might need an extra fiver or so. By all means make arangements for a single bedroom[236] in plenty of time. It was only by the merest chance I got one on my return and that was on the train. I had my order in for more than a week but there was no space. Fortunately the purchaser of Bedroom D couldn't go at the last moment. On a long trip one needs it. See to it that you get the reservation in lots of time, and have plenty of quarters for tips in carrying suitcases and meals. Do not deprive yourself on your holiday. I hope you *see* 20 Questions.[237] Go to the theatres and take trips. Make the most of it all. I am going down to the College this afternoon to get what I expect to be a heavy correspondence. I am anxious to see what they intend doing about Banff.[238] If it weren't such a long distance away! I hope

235 See the note to 'Mr Tatton' in the letter to Father V.J. Guinan, 22 March 1952 (p. 489).

236 On the train home from New York, where Viola was visiting Nellie Pratt.

237 The popular radio show originating from New York. Viola and Pratt's sister Nellie planned to attend a performance as members of the audience.

238 With Sir Ernest MacMillan (music) and Frederick Haines (painting), he had been invited by the University of Alberta to receive one of its new National Fine Arts Medals for 'contributions to the cultural progress of Canada.'

the 'provision' Frank McDowell alluded to is generous.[239] But I would be perfectly happy to stay at home with you and present you with a dish of raspberries every day for a week or so.

I have reserved $50.00 in American money for Claire should she whimsically decide to go to New Hampshire. If she doesn't, she can change it into Canadian.

I am enclosing a $20.00 bill to eke out your meagre existence. Later on I shall send more but don't try to economize too much.

Bless your sweet heart. I shall roast a duck for you crisp and brown some day.

In my next letter I shall tell you the funniest story of the Corpus Christi convention[240] which had all the delegates laughing at me, even the Chairman referring to it in his introductory remarks. Nellie too will enjoy it, because it was straight unadulterated absent-mindedness – not so bad as going on to the platform without my trousers[241] but almost as funny.

Much love,
Ned.

TO LORD BEAVERBROOK[242]

[early June 1952]

Dear Lord Beaverbrook:

May I congratulate through you the University of New Brunswick upon the excellent literary output of the Department of English.

Pacey's recent publication on Canadian culture[243] is a credit to the Institution.

Yours respectfully,
E.J. Pratt

---

239 A public relations officer with Canadian National Railways, McDowell had promised to make 'provision' for reduced fares for the Pratts so that they could afford to attend the ceremony.

240 See the letter to Viola Pratt, 9 June 1952 (p. 495).

241 This he appears to have absent-mindedly done in the early 1930s, arriving late for a recital and hurriedly removing a mackintosh to find he had failed to don his pants.

242 New Brunswick politician and newspaper magnate William Maxwell (Max) Aitken (1879–1964) was raised to the peerage in 1917. He had not attended university, but was a generous benefactor of the University of New Brunswick and served as its chancellor (1947–1964). Beaverbrook dictated a response, dated 11 June 1952, after being briefed on Pratt's identity and credentials (as indicated in a typewritten notation on Pratt's letter). It reads in part: 'Although I can of course claim no credit whatever for the good work done by the department of English, I am delighted to receive your congratulations.'

243 *Creative Writing in Canada: A Short History of English-Canadian Literature* (Toronto: Ryerson, 1952). See the letter to Pacey, 8 June 1952 (p. 494).

TO DESMOND PACEY

June 8, 1952

Dear Des:

I am sending this article[244] along to you which came from an Ottawa friend. I am proud of an old student – glad to have your criticisms as well as your generous appreciation.

It is not often that I use my 'hifalutin' stationery but I gave his Lordship the works last week[245] – congratulating him on 'his' University, particularly on the contribution to scholarship which you are making.

More power to your elbow.

Deep regards to Mary.[246]

Ned Pratt

Will you send me back the enclosed article when you have read it.

Excuse scribble as the injured arm still aches.

TO VIOLA PRATT

June 9, 1952

Vi dear:

Your letter came today and I hope you can get a bedroom and be comfortable on the train. I hate to have you stay up all night. You'll arrive exhausted I'm afraid.

244 Unidentified.

245 See Pratt's letter to Lord Beaverbrook, early June 1952 (p. 493). Pacey wrote to David G. Pitt (18 April 1967): 'That spring … in Toronto I read a paper called "Areas of Research in Canadian Literature." Pratt was most enthused over the paper, and that evening he was at a party at Claude Bissell's home and was quite high. (Incidentally, that is the only time I saw Pratt visibly affected by alcohol …) He told me that he had decided to write Lord Beaverbrook [Chancellor of the University of New Brunswick] and tell him what a wonderful fellow I was. "I'll give him the works, Des. I'll write the letter on my special stationery with C.M.G.'s and D. Litt's, etc. and I'll blow you up so high the Beaver will endow your chair at $25,000 a year or some fantastic sum!" Ned was so nearly drunk that night that I believed he would forget all about the letter to Beaverbrook – but his letter to me of June 8 indicates that he did write it. Beaverbrook wrote me a note saying he had heard great things of my work, but needless to say he did *not* endow my chair!'

246 Pacey's wife.

I spent the afternoon with Malcolm[247] golfing though my shots were terribly off since the ache is fairly continuous. One good result of going to Marko's[248] is the increased flexibility, but the ache is very little better. He told me that would take a longer time. So I must draw on my Methodist patience and Newfoundland fortitude.

I do hope you are having a good time. When we listened in on 20 Questions last Saturday night we were thinking of you and wondering if we could detect your and Nellie's laugh, but we weren't sure.

One funny thing happened at Corpus Christi that had the whole Conference laughing at me in a good-natured manner. Tatton took me to a part of the Hotel for a lunch and when it was over, a reporter kept me half-an-hour getting a column on Canada, poetry, Newfoundland. Tatton left, so I went to the elevator to go to my room 906 for a nap preceding the afternoon speech. I had a little trouble with my key but it didn't bother me much as the key was bent anyway. I heard an angry female voice inside shouting – 'Where are you trying to go anyway?' I didn't think it was the room maid as she would scarcely shout in that tone. I said this room is 906, isn't it?' She replied just as angrily as ever, '*Yes*, it is 906 all right, but it is my room, not yours, so get the hell out of this.' I said, 'My key is 906.' She yelled, 'So is mine 906 but it is my room.' I looked at my key, turned it upside down to see if 9 and 6 inverted would be 6 and 9. But no it was still 906 and I shouted my key is 906 and that's my room. I was there last night and I am staying here until Wednesday morning.' 'Like hell you are – over my dead body.'

Then I went to the elevator operator, showed him the key and he remarked, 'This is not the Hotel Driscoll, it's Hotel Eagle adjoining by a very narrow passage.' Well, the story got around the 350 delegates and became the laugh of the occasion, so much so that when the Chairman (a publisher) introduced me to the audience he began, 'This is a Canadian-Newfoundlander who has the talent of breaking into the wrong room.' I wondered if that person in Eagle Hotel was one of the delegates. I never found out. But the argument at the door was certainly a scene. It was made more real as 906 was at the left corner from the elevator – the same parallel passage etc as the Driscoll set-up. When I went to the cashier to pay my final bill on Wednesday morning she said 'Oh, you're the Canadian who goes into the wrong room. It's a wonder you're alive. This happens sometimes and always there's a bump on the head.' So far, so good.

I got a letter from the Alberta University President[249] who is expecting me to come in person for the medal. I haven't replied yet, till I get all the circumstances. If Macmillans come through as Gray said – it ought to be a good trip. It is August 17.

---

247 Malcolm Wallace.

248 Dr Jacob Markowitz.

249 See the note to 'Banff' in the letter to Viola Pratt, 6 June 1952 (p. 492).

Blessings on your head dear one. I shall be glad to see you back. There'll be much to talk about. Darn this pen. I hope you can make out the writing. Love to Nellie and a great deal to yourself.

Ned.

TO WILLIAM ARTHUR DEACON

21 Cortleigh Blvd.

June 15, 1952

Good old Bill:

You have always been a regular – a true loyal friend and I love you for your constant friendship.

We have struck a little snag in the award business.[250] Since hearing from you I have received a letter from Stewart saying that he couldn't make it on June 28, London.[251] Accordingly, the medal will be given during the last week of the Banff School, probably August 14, Thursday. As he is going to make some contribution to the transportation expenses, I shall go (otherwise I couldn't afford it). I shall take Vi along for a holiday on my own.

Now about London on June 28th. I think that Vi and I will go for the banquet returning on the Saturday as we are pressed for time. As the Award will be announced there but not presented I suppose it would be wise to be present. I hope I do not have to make two replies – one at London, one at Banff, unless it is the same reply.[252]

---

250 See the letters to Viola Pratt, 6 June (p. 493) and Deacon, 18 June (*EJP: Web*).

251 The original plan was for the National Fine Arts Medal for Literature, like the Governor General's Awards, to be presented at the CAA conference in London the third week of June. However, President Stewart of the University of Alberta was unable to attend, and the ceremony was postponed to mid-August, with the winners being announced at the CAA banquet on 28 June.

252 Deacon replied (19 June 1952):

> It doesn't really matter what you say or do on June 27 at [the CAA] dinner. At that moment it is what you have done in past 30 years that matters. But you are wise to attend. This is the No. 1 honor; and we, your fellow writers dreamed it up and wish a chance to applaud. It became apparent that something special was needed for people at the top; and the award is only to be made when a worthy recipient is in sight.
>
> At Banff the atmosphere will be different [than the announcement in London in June]. They will want a set address; and I hope it will be a variant of Science and Poetry. You are the best judge of that. Whatever you decide to do, I'll be glad of a carbon copy of the Banff speech in advance. Too little of it will be on the wires. I'd like my report longer. Thus I shall get three separate whacks over a period of seven weeks, which should increase sales [of *TLS*].

I wrote Stiling[253] saying that my contribution at the banquet might be the reading of a few unpublished short verses, possibly a half-dozen taking up ten minutes. That would avoid a repetition of acknowledgement in both cases. I don't know what Stewart expects of me. He said nothing in his letter. In any case, I shall send you in plenty of time the mim,[254] short as it may be, and you can take a sentence or paragraph as you wish.

I am fully appreciative of this honour.

With affection
Ned.

TO LORNE PIERCE [READER'S REPORT ON RONALD HAMBLETON'S *OBJECT AND EVENT*]

Excuse penmanship: the arm is still aching.

[Summer 1952]

This is worth publishing[255] though I have qualms about the market for a type of verse which savours so much of the material in the *Partisan Review*[256] and *New Directions*.[257] R.H. aims at originality of expression which is to the good. He achieves *novelty*, at least in language, and he will be noted as one of the *avant garde*. There are many good lines and passages. I only wish they were more sustained and that the poems as a whole could convince the mind as the individual fragments undoubtedly do. I shall put down my impressions, my criticisms as well as my appreciations.

The Tour starts out well with striking images to the woman and the Bank's stony face; to the argosies; to the banker shaving. The line: 'And all he had to borrow were his thoughts' is excellent. So is his picture of the city 'feathered with morning.'

---

253 Frank Stiling (b. 1897), professor of English at the University of Western Ontario, which was hosting the 1952 CAA conference, was president of the London branch of the CAA (later national president), and chairman of the board of the Governor General's Awards.

254 Short for 'mimeograph.'

255 Pierce had asked Pratt to provide a reader's report on the manuscript of Ronald Hambleton's *Object and Event*, which Ryerson Press was considering (and which they published in 1953). Hambleton (b. 1917) worked as a journalist in print, radio and television. His poems were first published in the anthology *Unit of Five* (also including poems by Louis Dudek, P.K. Page, Raymond Souster, and James Wreford), which he edited for Ryerson Press in 1946. After *Object and Event*, he published a brief biography of Mazo de la Roche: *Mazo de la Roche of Jalna* (Toronto: Hawthorn Press, 1966).

256 An American journal of literature and politics, published quarterly (1934-2003).

257 An American publishing firm, and the journal of the same name (1941–), which published avant-garde and modernist verse.

The second paragraph is weak – 'Some you can see with *there*[?] generation … empty past.' Unnecessarily vague. The same applies to the ambiguity in 'Slicing our airy food.'(5).

Page 8. *The Mountains* is good, but why *mechanician*? (9)

11. *The Nightingale and the Rose* is another example of metaphysical ambiguity which has become a stale vogue.
13. *The Criminal* is a refreshing bit of poetic imagery, crisp and apt. The last line is superlative. So with *At the Asylum*.
15. Striking final stanza in *The Forsaken Man*.
19. *Lost* has no significance for me. It is not enough to claim that it has significance for the author.
29. Attractive description in *To Music*.
31. 'Not projects outward, etc.' is ugly and strained.
33. *The River* is a fine poem where R.H. has found a golden mean between extreme facility and an irritating obscurity. This is one of his best. We can follow the course of the stream in spite of its eddies.
38. *Sunscape* is too imitative of Hopkins.[258] The craze for ellipses has outrun its function.

Nevertheless taking the poems by and large, I think they are worth the imprint.

P.

TO RALPH GUSTAFSON

July 9, 1952

Good old Ralph:

It was just like your dear generous self to write such a spontaneous letter. Praise from you is praise indeed. I value your appreciation as I love your personality.

The Reviews have been enthusiastic[259] and I hope the sales by the Fall will be encouraging.

Sutherland's article[260] was more than I expected by way of approval of the earlier work. Something must have got hold of his insides. He was most generous.

---

258 Gerard Manley Hopkins.

259 Reviews of *TLS*, which had been published on 2 June.

260 In *Northern Review*. See the letter to Sutherland, 25 February 1952 (pp. 485–7).

When are you coming up to Toronto again so I can order a porterhouse for you in company with the good lads? We miss your fine critical mind and creative spirit in these parts. I didn't get down to New York to the M.L.A.[261] this time as I had a broken arm[262] followed by bursitis which still cramps my legibility (as you can observe). I have been taking treatment twice a week for six months. But I still am able to enjoy an evening with my boon companions and no one would be more welcome than your thoroughly human lovable self. Do let me know if you can make it next fall after the term opens.

My love to you,
Ned.

Note – Bursitis doesn't disturb digestion, assimilation or elimination, thanks be.

TO A.J.M. SMITH

July 15, 1952

Dear Arthur:

My congratulations to Queen's that they managed to secure your services.[263] The place is lucky to have you.

I would have written you before but a broken shoulder (which still pains when I write) prevented a lot of correspondence.

I am sending you a copy of the 'Spike.' I hope you will like the debates between Blake and Sir John A[264] and the clutching of the Highland Cream when Sir John wanted to drown his sorrows. I trust I made him pie-eyed when Stephen[265] came for more money.

Affectionately
Ned.

Excuse illegibility.

---

261 The Modern Language Association held its meetings in late December.
262 He did not break his shoulder until mid-February.
263 Pratt had quit teaching summer school at Queen's University, and Smith had been hired to replace him.
264 Edward Blake and Sir John A. MacDonald.
265 George Stephen, president of the CPR.

TO KARL SHAPIRO

July 25, 1952

Dear Mr Shapiro:

I appreciate the honor of your request to submit a poem for your October issue.[266] I am enclosing *Myth and Fact* but should you feel that the 'album' might be too heavily weighted on the serious side, *The Unromantic Moon* is offered as a substitute.[267] Both are new poems and I think the best of the few short ones I have on hand. I hope they reach you before the deadline. You letter came *via* Montreal,[268] which accounts for the delay.

I understand perfectly that there can be no guarantee of publication. Having done some editorial work in the past (not in *Northern Review* by the way), I realize the difficulty of acceptance. I can see the Missouri deluge threatening to swamp you already, and many otherwise presentable poems must be turned down through limitations of space and possible monotony of themes and structures in the general contents. So if you find the enclosed verses unavailable, do not add to your burden of correspondence by returning them. I have carbon copies.

May I say just here a word about the delight and stimulation your own poetry has given me for the last ten years. Nims[269] and I spent many an hour reading it, and discussing it, and presenting it to our classes in the University of Toronto. When your *Person Place & Thing* came out, I found it fresh and original. Likewise your V-Letter. Later I read to my classes such poems as *The Puritan* and that deeply moving *Mongolian*. The latter still haunts me, partly I suppose, because before I joined the staff in English at Victoria College, I spent two or three years teaching Psychiatry and demonstrating in clinics. The Mongolian

---

266 A fortieth anniversary of *Poetry: A Magazine of Verse*, of which Shapiro had been appointed editor in 1950. (See the note to 'Shapiro' in the letter to George Dillon, 30 May 1942 [p. 228].)

267 'The Unromantic Moon' appeared in *Poetry* 82 (June 1953): 143. 'Myth and Fact' was not used. (See the letter to Shapiro, 27 August 1952 [pp. 508–10].)

268 Having been sent a copy of the special Pratt issue of *Northern Review* by John Sutherland, Shapiro had addressed his letter to Pratt in care of Sutherland at his Montreal address.

269 American poet and academic John Frederick Nims (1913–99) spent most of his career as a professor of English literature at the University of Notre Dame. Pratt had gotten to know him when he had been a visiting professor at the University of Toronto in 1945–6. See the letter to Claire Pratt, April 1945 (pp. 327–8).

face[270] was not more poignant than the face of the mother who brought the son to the clinic, vainly hoping that 'something might be done for him.' Your poem made the face actually visual.

Well, here's luck to your Issue – and may there be no moaning to worry you following the rejection slips.

Yours sincerely,
E.J. Pratt

TO JOHN SUTHERLAND

July 25, 1952

Dear John:

The letter from Shapiro[271] was an invitation to submit a poem for an 'album' of verse celebrating the 40th anniversary of *Poetry*. Though he made no reference in his brief statement to N.R. or to your article, I feel sure that your interest in my work must have occasioned the invitation.

The poems for his album are, all of them, to be short, one page preferably and to be the result of individual solicitation. I looked over the very small batch I have on hand; had my doubts on some of them, but finally selected one which might satisfy the Editor.

Your review of the 'Spike'[272] made fine reading and was characteristically honest. As I have frequently told you, your criticism, like your appreciation, has always been welcome and helpful. I realize that the climax, despite the sledge hammer, didn't have the punch of the Great Feud or the Titanic. Neither the hammer nor the lizard had the claw of the iceberg.

I am very grateful that you liked Sir John's reach for the whisky. In fact, when I read from the 'Spike,' I concentrate upon the conflict between the sedate and

270 Until the 1960s, the term 'Mongoloid' or 'Mongolian' was used to describe people with Down syndrome (originating in an 1866 study by Dr John Langdon Down which likened the facial characteristics associated with the condition to those of Asian or 'Mongolian' peoples). The term is now considered offensive, but both Shapiro and Pratt were using accepted scientific terminology.

271 See Pratt's reply to Shapiro's letter, 25 July 1952 (pp. 500–1).

272 Sutherland had sent him a copy of the review of *TLS* he had written for *Poetry*. It appeared in the September 1953 issue, pp. 350–4.

soporific Blake and the mercurial John A. It allows characterization of which I have made sparing use in the past.

I am also pleased that in your 'Spike' review you made that representative preface. I hope Shapiro prints it though he may demur at the length (certainly not the *style*). However, you have done me a great service in bringing my work to his attention. I can't thank you too much for that.

The double issue has met with a good deal of enthusiasm. Macmillans, particularly, are loud in praise of it. I trust that their ad becomes a permanent feature.

More anon.
Ned Pratt

TO JOHN SUTHERLAND

21 Cortleigh Blvd.

Aug. 8, 1952

Dear John:

I should have replied at once to your recent letter but there were two reasons for the delay. One was that my wife and I were in the midst of packing for our trip to Alberta (the Banff School of Fine Arts) where I have to make an address in acknowledgement of a medal from the University of Alberta. As MacMillan (Music) and Haines (Painting)[273] cannot be present, extra duties rest on me. We leave tomorrow night and the presentation takes place on August 14th, and we hope to return by Aug. 23. The other reason is that I want to go through both your article and review in a leisurely and concentrated manner on the trip, so as to reply to your queries as fully as possible.

You have done such a magnificent piece of work in the article that you have left very little for me to add. It is a profound and original analysis, and a wonderful tribute as I have said before.[274]

I shall write you on my trip out so my letter may reach you early next week. I must do some rummaging in my memory to bring back the conflict just before the '20s, when, on one day in a classroom, we were soaked with German Positivism plus theories on the subconscious and on the next day in the same

---

273 Sir Ernest MacMillan and Frederick Haines (painter, art teacher, former principal of the Ontario College of Art) had also been chosen to receive medals.

274 See the letter to Sutherland, 25 February 1952 (pp. 501–2).

classroom another lecturer gave us huge doses of Thomas Hill Green's Idealism – the Plato-Kant-Hegel development. 'Creative Evolution' or God in nature and man was the 'antidote' to Darwin's naturalism, though the serum worked on some of us and not on others. Those were exciting years, stimulating, and soul-searching, for we didn't want our Theism to crack. (More of this later).

Further back still, the same cleavages existed between 'orthodox' Methodism with its literalism and the more liberal interpretations by way of allegory. Many of those explanations were shed later, not because we *solved* the problems; we simply *forgot* them. But one major problem remained – the assignment of evil (physical and moral) to its place in a Universe presumably governed by a God of compassion and love. This was expressed in thousands of 'testimonies' at Methodist revival meetings – 'God does not *ordain* evil; he simply permits it. He doesn't prevent disaster; he enables us to triumph over it.' Hence acceptance or submission became a high note – hard indeed to sing. You have graphically covered the idea in your treatment – the first time it has been done in any estimate of what I have written.

I'll amplify this on my journey to Banff.

Gratefully yours
E.J. P.

TO JOHN SUTHERLAND

Canadian Pacific Railway
en route (and in motion)

Aug. 11, 1952

Dear John:

There are two terms you refer to in relation to the Titanic[275] which enter the core of the poem – 'peak' and 'claw.' You have explained them so incisively that I had to read through the poem again to discover the degree of their relevance.

It is astonishing how much a critical reader will bring to the surface what had been but dimly implicit in the thought of a writer. Part of a critic's job is to perform this interlinear task. It is the emphasis on the 'peak and claw' antithesis which strangely and powerfully moved me – your reference to the combination

275 He is referring to Sutherland's essay 'E.J. Pratt: A Major Contemporary Poet,' *Northern Review* 5 (February-March, April-May 1952): 36–64.

of *exaltation* and *terror*, the constructive and destructive elements in nature and life. As with the iceberg, so with the ship – the parallelism is there. One might enlarge it into the relation between Evil and Good in the Universe, between chance and purpose.

Before you elaborated this point, I held the 'claw' only loosely in my mind as a symbol of the subconscious, though Wundt, Freud, James[276] and D.H. Lawrence (Fantasia)[277] must have been working underneath. The 'peak,' like the proud run of the ship, was a visible and conscious process, but the 'spur' was invisible – a depth-hidden symbol which had not only discarded the last 'touch' of the peak but assumed in the darkness an utterly malevolent function.

It is very natural to move over on to theistic ground, but I did not do so directly, as I do not like too much philosophical didacticism in a poem. I leave that to the reader who may wish to work it out for himself. But I think it is implicit in the contrast between the disaster itself and the courage exhibited by the engineers, the Band (playing fox trots), Ida Straus and the lad.[278] Those ideas are at any rate *latent* without being too much underscored. Those descriptions are brief but, I imagine, they serve to indicate the qualities of compassion and sacrifice to which you refer. So, more lengthily, is the account of the ape as distinct from the dinosaur[279] – reason versus the pin-point brain of the Saurian.

Again, one could hardly fail to be moved by the sight of a Newfoundland lifeboat pulling out in an attempt to save the crew of a wreck. If the effort were fruitless, it would not mar but accentuate the heroism and compassion, though it would deepen the sense of tragedy. I did not refer to the numerous steps taken afterwards to preserve life on ships as a result of the Titanic's loss. That's another matter outside of the scope of the poem, though again to be chalked up to the credit of man on his constructive and humanitarian side. That phase of 'creative evolution' is emphasized in Green's *Prologomena*,[280] though I did not need a knowledge of such a work to realize the essentials.

To come back to James' *Varieties*.[281] I was impressed by his own confession that his theistic beliefs were very thin and unsatisfactory to an audience largely favouring providential or paternalistic qualities in God. He calls his own attitude an 'over-belief' which you mention in your quotation – that subconscious welling up of something within us which baffles formulation. Not that he accepts

276 William Wundt, Sigmund Freud, William James.

277 Lawrence published *Fantasia of the Unconscious* (New York: Thomas Seltzer) in 1923.

278 The wife of the American millionaire Isidor Straus chose to stay with her husband when offered a seat in a lifeboat, and the 'boy of ten' gave up his seat to 'a Magyar woman and her child.'

279 An allusion to 'The Great Feud.'

280 *Prolegomena to Ethics* by British philosopher T.H. Green (1836–82).

281 *Varieties of Religious Experience: A Study in Human Nature* (London: Longmans, Green, 1902).

dogmatically (or rationalistically) an orthodox or evangelical position – not at all, but he is not far from the Methodist emphasis on the phrase – 'I have *felt*.' That sounds mystical, but it is an ineradicable element in the nature of many people, sailors sharing it to an unusual degree. Without wishing to sermonize, I find it expressed in Job's statement – 'though he slay me yet I will trust in him; and it helps, at least *emotionally*, to resolve the dualism in the interest of theistic unity. Such a feeling may not be present at the time of the announcement of a shipwreck, but it asserts itself in the subsequent groping for a faith. (With some people.)

I feel that myself at times, though my themes have largely been realistic and tragic where the dualism is paramount.

I don't know that I can add much more to this statement, for the subconscious groundwork is tremendously operative though darkly present to the so-called rationalist.

And now, my good friend, many thanks for your interest. I shall be back in Toronto about Aug. 23, and any correspondence with you will be welcomed most heartily.

Pratt.

Your issue[282] is on the stalls of the leading bookstores, prominently displayed.

P.

Addenda.

You will be interested to know that the 'Titanic' last year was placed in the 'longer poems' for Matriculation Students (in Ontario),[283] the other two being *The Ancient Mariner* and *The Death of Arthur*. It was my first substantial 'break' in royalties, as 11000 students *had* to take it. The Ont. Dept. of Education for the first time decided to put on one long Canadian poem as a text.

Incidentally, my telephone rang often from teachers who asked about the poker game and its significance. And my reply was:

(1) the parallel between a game of chance *within* the ship and the chances *outside* of the Titanic hitting that spur, is the irony of coincidence;
(2) the game ending with a player calling for water and ice – which was most instantaneously handed by the iceberg through the port-hole of the cabin. It was but an illustration of the irony which enveloped the ship.

P.

282 The double issue of *Northern Review* devoted to Pratt: 5 (Feb-Mar, April-May 1952).
283 The collection was titled *Poems for Senior Students* (Toronto: Macmillan, 1950).

TO A.J.M. SMITH

[Banff, Alberta]

Aug. 12, 1952

Dear old Arthur:

Although I was on the C.P.R. Sunday when your 'critical speaking' was on the air,[284] I had no less than four letters today when I arrived at the Cascade Hotel. All of the correspondents spoke enthusiastically of your 'matter' and delivery. One former student took notes by shorthand and gave me extracts.[285]

I am indeed grateful to you for your publicity and affectionate estimate of the last book. Indeed, I have had more fervently appreciative reviews through Canada on the Spike than I have ever had all my life, but the most valued is that of your dear self.

I am at Banff to receive the University of Alberta medal on Thursday night. Since Sir Ernest MacMillan and Fred Haines are away I have to make the acknowledgement. I wish you were here to enjoy the Banff scenery. Vi is here and wishes to send her love to you & family.

Most affectionately
Ned

Will be back in Toronto by the 23rd of August.

TO CLAIRE PRATT

[Banff, 13 Aug. 1952]

Dearest Cakie:

We got in yesterday morning uneventfully, went to the Cascade Hotel where we shall remain till Friday morning. Then we go to a suite in the Arts School.

The three nights trip on the train (I must confess) did not produce much slumber in the profound sense of that term, but we hope to make it up under

284 On 10 August Smith had broadcast on the CBC radio series *Critically Speaking* reviews of *TLS* and Sutherland's *Northern Review* essay.

285 See the letter to Claire Pratt, 13 August 1952 (p. 507).

less 'rocking' conditions. The word 'rocking' does not imply the cradle idea. Rather it is used in the pugilistic sense when a boxer 'rocks' his opponent back on his heels or crashes him against the ring posts. My head is slightly aching from the train jolts around corners plus starting and stopping the way the inexperienced drivers on the Toronto street cars do it. However, we are recovering by means of the Banff scenery.

Tomorrow night I have to give my 'spiel.' I think it will be quite gaseous and vapoury.

I hope you enjoyed the Buffalo trip and that you got back on Sunday before dark.

Don't bother about looking for more raspberries. There are none left. I snitched the last one precisely at 6 p.m. Saturday.

And as for bacon and eggs, don't worry about that kind of larder. Since Sunday morning till now I have devoured 24 rashers of bacon and a dozen eggs; so I need a respite. It will be quite satisfactory to peer into a refrigerator vacuum on Aug. 23 for once.

We had a letter from Dorothy[286] containing some excerpts from A.J.M. Smith's (Critically Speaking) address last Sunday night. They were very encouraging.

Mother and I weighed in yesterday. The four days trip accounted for three pounds and two ounces respectively – mine 159, hers 110 and those 2 ounces. By the time I return you won't know who it is coming down the stairs, Winnie[287] or yours faithfully and ponderously. The Banff air has something to do with it I think.

I wish you could be here to paint Cascade Mountain with its great avalanche furrows through the spruces. The mountain is just at the end of the main street of the town.

We visited the museum and the three things which attracted my attention most were a cougar, a bald-headed eagle, and (would you believe it?) a gigantic *crow*. I gazed fondly (though with mixed feelings) at the crow stuffed double its normal size and murmured reflectively, 'thank Heaven its cawing days are over.' There was, however, a slight strain of nostalgia which I am almost ashamed to confess, but I think it was mainly the thought of 21 Cortleigh Blvd. which I shall be glad to see again and your sweet self.

Father a long distance off and
in a reminiscent mood.

286 Dorothy Sigmund.

287 Winnie Fitzpatrick, the woman who came as needed to do housework for the Pratts.

TO EARLE BIRNEY

August 27, 1952

My dear and beloved Earle:

I have just sent off a credential for you to J.B. Marshall of the Awards Committee.[288] I have said that as a combination of scholar and creative writer there is no one in Canada to surpass you, and a number of other statements equally genuine from my heart. I do trust you get the scholarship.

I am sending along a copy of the Spike. I hope you and Esther will like Sir John A's inebriation and Blake's debates with that red-nosed gentleman.

Affectionately,
Ned Pratt

TO KARL SHAPIRO

August 27, 1952

Dear Mr Shapiro:

This note is by way of apology.

Quite a long time ago Lionel Monteith of *Poetry Commonwealth* invited Earle Birney (Canadian scholar and poet whose fine work you may know) to be the guest editor of a Canadian number. Birney asked me to submit a poem. I gave him a choice of one out of three. He chose 'Myth and Fact,' but later he informed me that *Poetry Commonwealth* was in straitened circumstances, and it was very doubtful that the Editor would bring out the number. The Little Magazines were folding up one after another.

The poems were not acknowledged by P.C. Now this morning through the mail the Spring number of *1951* arrives containing 'Myth and Fact.' As two years went by without any communication from the English Editor, I naturally assumed that the issue had gone the way of the numerous 'little' fellows. Birney was convinced of this and suggested that I would be free to place the poem elsewhere if I wished. In fact, Monteith says in his Editorial that with this issue P.C. closes up.

288 Birney was applying for one of the recently instituted Canadian Government Overseas Awards.

So now I am hurrying along this information to you in case you have decided on the publication of 'Myth and Fact.' If you have not, there is obviously no problem. You may have chosen 'The Unromantic Moon' which is more recent and free. If you have not done so, there is no difficulty either. I shall understand.

There are two or three other points. As P.C. has a very limited circulation, I am wondering if the non-acceptance of a prior publication, however small the output, is an inexorable rule. I own the copyright of 'Myth and Fact,' and since I am relieved of any obligation both by Birney's letter and by the fact that no payments are made to contributors, it is still available subject to the discretion of the Editors. I fear, however, that the rule holds.

Again, inasmuch as I have through the last two years been preoccupied with a long poem, my supply of short verses has been slim. Only 'Myth and Fact' and 'The Unromantic Moon' have satisfied me from my own private point of view.

I hope this has not caused you embarrassment. As I said in my previous letter, whatever decision you reach will be acceptable to me.[289]

Yours sincerely,
E.J. Pratt

TO RAYMOND GUSHUE[290]

[12 Sept. 1952]

RAY GUSHUE PRESIDENT OF MEMORIAL COLLEGE
STJOHNS NFLD
WILL GLADLY DELIVER ADDRESS AT INSTALLATION[291] STOP AIR LETTER FOLLOWS IMMEDIATELY REQUESTING INFORMATION ABOUT ORDER OF PROGRAM LENGTH AND NATURE OF SPEECH SUITABILITY OF THEME AND SO FORTH.

E.J. PRATT

---

289 Shapiro chose 'The Unromantic Moon' for *Poetry* (June 1953).

290 Born in Newfoundland, Gushue (1900–80) was a graduate of Dalhousie University, a lawyer by profession, and former president of the Salt Codfish Board. He was president of Memorial University from 1952 to 1966.

291 Gushue had invited him to address a special convocation on 8 October 1952 called for the purpose of the installation of himself as president and Lord Rothermere of Hempsted as chancellor of Memorial University.

TO RAYMOND GUSHUE

Sept. 13, 1952

Dear President Gushue:

This letter follows my telegram of last night. It may be too early to have the following questions answered since your programme may not be completely determined.

(1) In what order do the speeches come? I imagine the Chairman of the Board comes first. Does he introduce both Chancellor and President? Naturally, both reply.
(2) Does each official university delegate speak for his university?
(3) At what place in the programme do I come in?
(4) Would fifteen or twenty minutes be approximately my prescribed time? I can shape the speech to less than that if the ceremonies require brevity.
(5) Would a subject such as the 'function of a university' with prefatory remarks about the historic nature of the occasion be acceptable? It is not necessary to publish the title other than an 'address.' That gives me leeway.

If anything else occurs to you would you kindly let me know?

May I personally congratulate you in advance on the choice of the Board! Cal and I are both delighted. I have a homebred interest in the cultural future of the *dear old Island*.

By the way, Sid Smith spoke so warmly about you and your student days.[292] Sid is one of my closest friends.

Yours very cordially,
E.J. Pratt

292 Smith and Gushue had been at Dalhousie Law School together.

TO CLAIRE PRATT

[St. John's, Newfoundland]

Friday Oct. 10, 1952

Dearest Cakie:

Though the impress on the top is the Senate I am writing from Waterford Bridge Road.[293] I am sending it airmail so that it may reach you by the time you arrive as you are due to leave this afternoon.

I telegraphed mother the morning after I got here and followed it up with a letter and I am leaving here on Sunday a.m. getting into Toronto by evening.

The trip altogether has been enjoyable though marred by the sickness of Jim who is in hospital here and exceedingly depressed. And Calvert[294] is in hospital at Montreal. Mary[295] telegraphed today that they had located the germ but further tests had to be made. He is feeling fairly comfortable considering the circumstances.

And then Harold Macpherson[296] is in the same hospital as Jim. He is suffering from spinal trouble which may be tubercular. Poor fellow he has to be flat on a board with his head lower than his body for four months. I went in to see him yesterday and shall again tomorrow.

The pleasant side of the trip is its hospitality. I had to give the Installation address on Wednesday. The next day I had to speak to the dear sweet nuns at the Mercy Convent. Most of them were Irish and if, as they said, I had kissed the blarney stone, then they had swallowed it for I was blessed off my feet. They wanted to meet me in Heaven. I replied that I had no wish to have a hurried meeting preferring to meet them again on solid ground like St John's. It was about the same as three years ago. Today I spoke to the Prince of Wales Academy (the successor to the old Methodist College) and I gave them the *Titanic* for an hour. They managed to stand up or rather sit up against the gruelling. Tomorrow I have the day off with Cal followed by a stag at Hal's[297]

293 His brother Cal had been appointed to the Senate in 1951. While in St John's, Pratt was a guest at Calvert's house on Waterford Bridge Road.

294 Cal's son, Calvert Junior.

295 Calvert Junior's wife.

296 Pratt's cousin.

297 Harold G. Puddester (1905–80), married to Pratt's niece Gwenyth (his brother James's daughter), a lawyer by profession, was a judge of the Supreme Court of Newfoundland.

with some notables like Sir Albert Walsh, Chief Justice;[298] Charlie Hunt,[299] Sir Leonard Outerbridge[300] and others. It looks overwhelming from the judicial point of view so I have to behave myself to keep out of the clutches of the law. To secure this I am staying within doors at Cal's, dining on partridge, not a terribly hard imposition.

The joke is this. Cal had informed his friends that his brother would give anything for a partridge or a brace of them. As a result about ten brace have been sent up to the house. Cal's strategy was to put the whole business on me. One meal or two were enough, but he is putting the rest in the deep freeze for the fall – a very ingenious transaction (which he admits). Poor Ned needs a partridge and his friends unknown to each other send the birds to the house thinking in the transparent infancy of their hearts that I am consuming all of them. We are laughing together at the ruse.

Rose[301] is doing the cooking – good soul.

I am wondering how you are getting along. I suppose that you will get this letter just about the time you arrive. I hope you will have a grand trip and will enjoy the convention. It will be a pleasure to see you again on your return. Do not economize too much and prejudice your comfort. Take all the conveniences, bless you.

Nfld is so hospitable that I am putting on the bacon (or the partridges and Devonshire cream) on my ribs. I have added five pounds but feeling fine though I am making a dent in the sidewalks when I go out. Would you believe this?

Poss[302] left today for Toronto. She will get in tonight. She couldn't manage to change her reservations so as to go back with me. The passengers are numerous.

With the greatest love,
Father

298 Walsh (1900–58), a lawyer, served as a member of the commission that governed Newfoundland from 1934 to 1949. He was head of the delegation that signed the Terms of Union between Newfoundland and Canada, and the province's first lieutenant governor (April to August 1949), before being appointed chief justice and chairman of the Board of Regents of Memorial University.

299 A lawyer by profession and director of several commercial enterprises, Hunt (1886–1954) was celebrated as a public speaker and debater.

300 A lawyer by training, Outerbridge (1888–1986) had abandoned the law for commerce and was director of several large commercial firms. Knighted for service on the home front in the Second World War, he was lieutenant governor of Newfoundland from 1949 to 1957.

301 Calvert's housekeeper. His wife Agnes had died in the summer of 1952.

302 Pratt's sister Florence.

TO EARLE BIRNEY

[Oct.1952]

Double Congratulations old boy![303] Just got back from the Installation of the Nfld University, and heard of the Fellowship. Delighted beyond measure.

Sorry I didn't hear the broadcast[304] as I was in transit, but I am deep in your Vancouver poems.[305] You have a grand future.

Blessings on you all from Vi,
Claire & Old Ned.

TO GEORGE JOHNSTON[306]

Nov. 13, 1952

Dear George:

Your letter with its kind remarks made grand reading. It is always a pleasure to hear from you.

We have had a melancholy term at Vic. Joe's[307] death was, as you can readily imagine, a terrible loss both as lecturer and personal friend. I can't yet get used to his not sauntering into my office every day or so for a chat. And Ruth Jenking is in hospital for a heavy operation. That means that the work of both of them has to be divided up between the rest of us.

Though Robins[308] and I are now on the 'retired' list, we have been called back for *special* lecturing – *special* but the schedule is as heavy as ever.

303 He was congratulating Birney on the September publication of his *Trial of a City and Other Verse* (Toronto: Ryerson, 1952) and on winning a Canadian Government Overseas Award. (See the letter to Birney, 27 August 1952 [p. 508].)

304 Birney had read some of his poems in a CBC broadcast from Vancouver.

305 *Trial of a City and Other Verse.*

306 (1913–2004). Born in Ontario, Johnston was a former student of Pratt's at Victoria College who taught English at Mount Allison (1947–50) and Carleton (1951–79) universities. His first book of poems, *The Cruising Auk* (Toronto: Oxford University Press, 1959), was followed by six more and several volumes of translations from the Old Norse.

307 Joseph Fisher.

308 J.D. Robins.

I wish we had you here. In fact, a year ago, I mentioned you to Joe but he said he understood you were quite happy at Carleton. The College appointed this fall as lecturer a Vic grad and Harvard Ph.D. David Knight.[309] In a year or two both Robins and I will be definitely *emeriti* and I don't know what the prospects will be. Norrie[310] is now acting Chairman[311] and a grand fellow he is.

We are out for 'a living endowment' of $50,000 – a big deficit in view of the-decrease of enrolment. The last of the returned men graduated a year ago, so we have dropped from 2400 to 1100.

I am glad you liked 'The Spike.' I had to make it a bit rough in spots wherever the subject matter required granite. The book has received the best reviews yet forwarded to me. The first edition is about exhausted and a second is in sight.

I hear glowing accounts of your Ottawa lectures mainly from Ottawa students attending Queen's. I gave up Queen's last summer and A.J.M. Smith took charge. I hope to have more time during the summers for my own personal work. I trust also that you will find time for your poetry, but lecturing does make inroads into private interests.

So you are to have a 'fourth.' Give my best regards to Jeanne (if I may so call her). Let me know results later will you.

Ned Pratt

TO EARLE BIRNEY

Nov. 20, 1952

Dear Earle:

This is a rush note.

First, I want to thank you for your kind references to the Spike – the appreciations and the helpful advice.

Second, Do you want to make a bit of money when you are circulating through Western Europe?[312]

---

309 Born (1926) in Toronto, educated there and at Yale University (not Harvard), he spent his teaching career at Victoria College, apart from a year (1965–6) at the University of Ibadan, Nigeria. He published a novel, *Farquharson's Physique and What It Did to His Mind* (London: Hodder and Stoughton; New York: Stein and Day), in 1971.

310 Northrop Frye.

311 Of the Department of English.

312 See the letters to Birney, 27 August and October 1952 (pp. 508 and 513).

Perhaps you may have heard that the *Saturday Night* has changed ownership and the new proprietor called me up to give him the names of the best writers in Canada. Naturally, I gave your name, and he wants to know if you would send articles upon the European situation – anything of interest to Canadians. The new man is Jack Kent Cooke[313] and he has already got Hugh MacLennan as an occasional contributor and Robertson Davies as the book editor. He hopes to have Lister Sinclair,[314] Bart Brebner and you; and others.

I don't know how much he pays. That's a matter for later negotiation. He is concerned principally with prose though I imagine the ratio of verse will be about the same as under the former sponsorship.

Would you do it? I am assuming you are still in Vancouver. If so, would you send me a line air-mail pronto, and tell me when you will be in Toronto on your way to Europe, so we could have lunch together. If you can't make the personal visit will you write him – Jack Kent Cooke, Publisher, Consolidated Press, Richmond and Sheppard, Toronto. It will be a good connection for you later on when you return as well as when you are journeying. I don't know who the new general editor is at present as things are *confidential.*

With much affection
Ned.

TO HENRY W. WELLS

Friday a.m. [early Dec. 1952]

Dear Henry:

Many thanks for your note with its kind remarks about the Spike. It has been going well, thanks be, and on the whole been well received by the reviewers.

I would love to visit New York again and see all my friends there, but I see no prospect of doing so in the immediate future. I spent a week in Newfoundland in

313 Hamilton-born entrepreneur Jack Kent Cooke (1912–97) engaged in enterprises ranging from radio, television, and publishing to professional sports. In 1948, he and Roy Thomson purchased the Canadian edition of *Liberty* magazine, renaming it *New Liberty*; and in 1952, he purchased the Consolidated Press, whose holdings included *Saturday Night*. In 1960, he became an American citizen to skirt legislation prohibiting foreign ownership of American media. At various times, he owned the Washington Redskins, the Los Angeles Lakers, and the Los Angeles Kings.

314 (1921–2006). Radio dramatist, script writer, and director, for many years attached to the CBC in Toronto.

October. I was invited down there to address convocation of the Newfoundland Memorial University which was installing a Chancellor and President. I had a grand time if somewhat strenuous. I spoke on the function of a university in the mid-twentieth century – sat on the platform with two Knights of the realm,[315] a Lord of the British House,[316] a bishop and an archbishop,[317] the new President, and Premier Joey himself,[318] who sat right next to me. Afterward, at night, I banqueted with the lords and ladies and other celebrities and rolled home (by car of course) around 11 p.m. I also spoke at some high schools, mostly Catholic – on account of Brébeuf.

Thanks again. If you come this way let me know and we'll have a repast together.

Greetings of the forthcoming season to you and yours.

Affectionately,
Ned Pratt

P.S. The book,[319] I hear from Lorne,[320] is still going fairly well – favourable comment still being heard from time to time. P.

TO JOHN SUTHERLAND

[late 1952]

Just a note to appreciate Roy Campbell's comments.[321] I have to thank you for bringing my work to his attention. I have often said that of all contemporary

---

315 See the notes to 'Sir Albert Walsh, Chief Justice ' and 'Sir Leonard Outerbridge ' in the letter to Viola Pratt, 10 October 1952 (p. 512).

316 Viscount Rothermere of Hemsted, who was installed as chancellor.

317 Anglican Bishop P.S. Abraham and Roman Catholic Archbishop P.J. Skinner.

318 Joseph R. Smallwood.

319 Klinck and Wells, *Edwin J. Pratt: the Man and His Poetry* (Toronto: Ryerson, 1947).

320 Lorne Pierce.

321 Born in South Africa, Campbell (1901–57) lived much of his life in Spain, where he was a bullfighter and served with General Franco's forces in the Spanish Civil War (1936–9). He published several books of poetry and autobiographical works. Sutherland had sent him a copy of his *Northern Review* essay, the text of 'The Great Feud,' and Forbes's portrait of Pratt. Campbell had been greatly impressed, replying (in part):

> I think Pratt is a very fine poet indeed. He can think and he uses the vernacular naturally to simplify complicated ideas by means of unusual images, whereas most moderns use an obscure literary jargon to disguise the excruciating triviality of the few apophthegms that serve them in the place of ideas. I was impressed as much by the portrait as by the poem and extract quoted. He has a very human and amusing face quite apart from being

writers he is the poet with the highest flight of imagination – so far ahead of Spender and MacNeice,[322] et al. His 'Terrapin' and 'Flowering Rifle'[323] left me breathless with excitement. Never before had the heroic couplet been so brilliantly sustained, and the imagery is beyond praise. I was introduced to his work by Squire of the 'London Mercury' when I was in England in 1924. I wanted very much to meet Campbell but our paths didn't cross.[324] Some day perhaps. If you know his address convey my compliments to him, will you?

Pratt

TO CLAIRE PRATT

21 Cortleigh Blvd.
Toronto, Ont.

Jan 15/53

Dearest Cayke:

We were delighted that you got in on time without customs and immigration officialism.[325] I stay in the house during the mornings to get the mail and take a good long look at your most artistic calligraphy. In fact, the contents inside, as much as we appreciate them, (and there is no doubt whatsoever of such appreciation) takes second place to the masterly way you end t's and p's and c's. Cortleigh should certainly be spelled Co*u*rtleigh to accord with the flourish which looks as if it came from Buckingham Palace.

Which brings me to a second point.

Cal has just written saying that he wants 1000 copies of *Magic in Everything* which appeared in Mayfair last month.[326] He wants to send a copy to 1000 of his friends and clients everywhere. I think he puts too high a value on the poem but

---

ornamental – and there is a great deal of humour in the work. I have ordered his books … and am looking forward to reading his work in big chunks. His imagery is superb (quoted with permission of Campbell's literary executor, Francisco Campbell Custadio).

322 Stephen Spender (1909–95) and Louis MacNeice (1907–64), British poets.

323 Books of Campbell's poetry: *The Flaming Terrapin* (London: Jonathan Cape, 1924) and *Flowering Rifle: A Poem from the Battlefield of Spain* (London; Toronto: Longmans, Green, 1936).

324 Pratt finally met Campbell in November 1953. See the letters to W.A. Deacon, 29 October 1953 (*EJP: Web*) and Claire Pratt, 5 November 1953 (p. 544).

325 Claire had moved to Boston and was searching for employment.

326 (*EJP: CP* 2.197). A Christmas poem he had written for the magazine *Mayfair* (December 1952). His proposal here materialized in a four-page Christmas card (1 leaf folded, using recto and verso, front and back) bearing both an abridged version of the poem (reduced from 114 to 45 lines) in Pratt's hand, small and neat, and illustrations and decorations by Claire.

still many misguided Newfoundlanders have been talking to him and wanting to get the verbiage. Well, here's the point.

I should like to write it out in long hand as I did the other and shorter 'Mother and Child.'[327] This would take four pages the size of this one, leaving a wide margin on the right hand side for illustrations.

Would you do the illustrations for me on Father Christmas etc. etc. etc.? As much as you like. Then I would get your printer to run off a thousand. Cal is very anxious to get something like this for his next Xmas present – strictly on a commercial basis in which you and I would be paid adequately. There would be plenty of time.

Only one thing has to be cleared up and that is copyright. Mayfair might agree to the thousand offprints with suitable acknowledgement. The poem took two pages of the magazine. The condition here of course would be that illustrations must go in the margin and such illustrations would have to be done extra. I should rather write out the poem in longhand and leave myself free for space. I haven't telephoned the Editor yet and there may be conditions attached. But I am writing you ahead to see if you would do your part. You would have as much latitude as you like in interpretation – the old boy with the whiskers, the reindeer, the open fire-place, the stockings, the bells, the youngsters, the madonna and so on, following the thread of the 100 lines. It would be signed by me and the illustrations by you. We could also use it as our own Xmas card. This is just a feeler – more to come later. Your 12th day[328] is constantly getting appreciation – a wonderful work of illustrative art.

I am enclosing Bush's note to give you the address whenever you manage to get up his way.

Much love
Father (still sneezing)

327 (*EJP: CP* 2. 295). A Christmas poem he had written for Viola Pratt's young people's paper, *World Friends* (December 1936). The poem in Pratt's hand illustrated by Claire had been used on a Christmas card a year or so earlier.

328 A Christmas card illustrating the Twelve Days of Christmas, which Claire had designed around 1950, had been reproduced in the *Globe and Mail* along with designs by a number of other artists.

TO CLAIRE PRATT

Feb. 4, 1953[329]

Dearest Claire:

Your letter just came and I am answering it at once. We found the transcripts and all the necessary documents in the house. They look most encouraging. We think you are wise in making your decision.[330] That banging of the typewriter is only a study or exercise in cacophony.

I have already dropped a note to Miss Cécile de Banke of Wellesley as I had to Doug Bush some time before to be on the look-out for a visit from you. You remember Cécile, don't you? She would have some influence at Wellesley, I'm sure. You mention a donship or tutorship or perhaps at first a 'coach-ship.' And a year studying would get you in touch with the staff. Besides, the longer vacations would leave you time for a 'spot of travel' particularly to Toronto – which the other position might not allow you.

Ditch that doggone typewriter deeper than plummet did ever sound[331] or keep it for personal use.

Don't worry about finances.

I looked into that bond matter again and found that it was sold and the proceeds sent to the First National. First I clipped the coupons which had matured and then the Bank rook possession of the bond (not as security but in exchange for the $1000 approximately). I messed up the explanation over the telephone to you, partly because I was a bit excited at hearing your silvery tones, and partly because my mind was on my uproariously sneezing *conch* (sea-shell to you).

The other $1000 is in the vault which may be treated in the same way when you need it.

We have now in the Bank vault $8000.00 four thousand of mine and four of mother's. Mine you may have whenever necessary.

329 Double underlining of the number '4' emphasizes that it is Pratt's birthday.

330 Claire was still searching for work and had turned down a position as a typist.

331 Prospero's words in *The Tempest* when he resolves to give up his magic: 'I'll break my staff, / Bury it certain fathoms in the earth, / And deeper than did ever plummet sound / I'll drown my book' (V, i, 54–7).

As I see your income it stands thus:

(1) $900.00 from annuities yearly.
(2) $300.00 through us to you as I explained in the last letter.
(3) *Jack* (hiatus) *Kent* (hiatus) *Cook*[332] is paying me $1200.00 a year till I decide to drop my connection. You may have at least half of that. By the way, whenever you pronounce Jack's full name give it all its essential and emphatic dignity as one might say *Elizabeth the Third.*

The house at 21 is now almost clear of all mortgage debt. My income next year will be nearly what it is this year. I am mentioning this because it is highly probable that we may take the odd trip to Mass. USA. to see a blue-eyed dragonette and by that I don't mean Ruth[333] in that description (if you can gather my ulterior meaning).

So don't worry or tax your physical energies too much. A part-time job fulfills all requirements, doesn't it?

Further advice:

(1) Don't pound the keys too hard.
(2) Try to sleep after hearing a symphony
(3) This above all, don't sneeze too much. One in the family is enough at that sort of unease.
(4) Let me know what else you need at any time.

Scrawlingly
Father.

'A happy birthday to *me*.' Both of us sang that song this morning. – Mother used her best soprano on 'to you' and I varied it with a basso profundo 'to me.'

332 'Jack' and 'Kent' are underlined twice, while 'Cook' – a misspelling of Cooke's last name – is underlined four times. Cooke was the new owner-editor of *Saturday Night.* (See the letter to Earle Birney, 20 November 1952 [p. 515].)

333 Ruth Stauffer.

TO CLAIRE PRATT

21 Cortleigh Blvd.

Feb. 9, 1953

Dearest Cayke:

I sumptuously repasted on cheddar[334] last night before retiring. So did Mother, after which we placed the remainder (I should call it the *remnant* we ate so much) in the refrigerator, having wrapped said cheese in saran according to instructions. I also took due notice of the whereabouts of the wayside store, the connection of Henry Ford and Lafayette, and Longfellow with grist mills, Martha & Mary chapels and cheese.[335] Every time I think of you I shall think of cheese – magnificent and Miltonic conception.

Mother wrote yesterday about Radcliffe[336] and wondered if it were a sound decision to take up college studies after a lapse of ten years.[337] The doctorate is a gruelling business especially the Orals. If it followed immediately on the B.A. it would be different, but even then it would take three years, and the teaching, if it were offered, is a nervous and physical exertion.

Have you inquired if Radcliffe or Wellesley[338] have a course in Commercial Art. That would be delightful as you have an unquestioned vein for that, and later there is bound to be some work. Perhaps Boston has a number of such schools. What do you think of the suggestion? Don't be in too much of a hurry but canvass the situation thoroughly.

I remember how teaching at Vic in my first year put me in bed all through April.[339] Questions came from all quarters of the room on points on which I was ill-informed, coming straight from Philosophy to English. It was only after three or four years I felt at home on the job. Think it over in any case.

---

334 Claire's birthday present to him.

335 References in Claire's most recent letter.

336 A women's liberal arts college in Cambridge, MA – sister institution to Harvard University. The two consolidated in 1999.

337 She contemplated resuming her postgraduate studies, abandoned in 1945 when her health failed.

338 A women's college in Wellesley, MA.

339 It was actually his third year on the staff of Victoria College in which he had spent April (1923) 'in bed.' (See the note to 'heart convalescence' in the letter to W.A. Deacon, 27 April 1923 [p. 22].)

'Magic in Everything' (Mayfair) is going to be written in long hand and if you will do the illustrations it would be fine.[340] I am sending you a copy of the printed material so you can get the idea and later on the handwritten stuff. I think some of the illustrations ought to be comedy and whimsical which you do perfectly. I am enclosing the Currelley letter. Your 12th day has got people excited.

Yours till the cheese lasts
and afterwards.
Father

TO ROY WILES[341]

Feb. 13, 1953

Dear Mr Wiles:

I thought 'In Quest of the Humanities' might be a suitable title for the address.[342]

I should prefer not to have the address mimeographed and distributed for I shall be preparing a *speech* not an *article* – two distinct things from my point of view. To do the second would require more time than I have at my disposal with the pressure of work ahead. Besides, the address which I shall prepare for the H.A.[343] may be given elsewhere after the May meeting and I should like to keep myself free for that purpose. I could, however, send Dr Tracy[344] a synopsis of the argument if he could use it in a report.

Yours sincerely,
E.J. Pratt

---

340 See the letter to Claire Pratt, 15 January 1953 (pp. 517–18).

341 (1903–74). Born in Nova Scotia and educated at Dalhousie and Harvard universities, Roy Mckeen Wiles was a professor of English at McMaster University. He was a member of the Humanities Research Council (1948–55) and president of the recently formed Humanities Association of Canada. He had invited Pratt to address the association's annual meeting during the sessions of the Learned Societies held in London, Ontario, in May.

342 See the letter to Wiles, 9 February 1953 (*EJP: Web*).

343 Humanities Association of Canada.

344 Clarence Tracy (1908–88), born in Ontario and educated at the University of Toronto and at Yale, was a professor of English at the University of Saskatchewan. The author of a number of scholarly works, he was secretary-treasurer of the Humanities Association (1952–4).

TO CLAIRE PRATT

Friday [20 Mar.1953]

Cayke dear:

We have practically secured our new duplex apartment[345] and the place looks better each time we see it. I suppose Mother told you about the basement – commodious, dry and acceptable in every way.

As soon as the agreement is signed Pash[346] will put 21 Cortleigh up for sale and the interest on the capital will nearly pay the rent of the apartment. Cal was up at the house last night and thinks that the National Trust would arrange for at least 5% on the capital.

Work will be at a minimum and there is a 'dear little den' where I can scribble at will. No snow to shovel, a man looks after two duplexes. The garage is big. The only 'disadvantage' (?) is that I shall have to open and shut the door and I have never been initiated into doing that sort of thing. There is a small garden where I can put a steamer chair and have a snooze in the middle of the day.

We are both delighted. We shall have a 'bee' on the day of removal. Besides ourselves, Pash, Poss, Muriel, Winnie will help place whatever furniture is not sold. Unfortunately my big chair in the den at 21 will not find room, but a chesterfield will take its place.

In a week or so when I get rid of lectures I shall send you your draft on the coupons due now.

Clare Hincks wants me to be Chairman of a Committee on Mental Hygiene[347] – no writing or work – but just Chairman. An honorarium goes with it. So everything is *hunky-dory*.

Much love
Father.

Our affectionate regards to the Buckleys.[348]

345 47 Glencairn Avenue. See the letter to Claire Pratt, 1 May 1953 (pp. 526–7).

346 Ida Pashley.

347 See *EJP: MY*, 457-8.

348 Claire's old friend Ruth Stauffer and her husband Elery Buckley, with whom Claire was living (temporarily) in Concord, MA.

TO CLAIRE PRATT

21 Cortleigh Blvd.

Sunday [29 Mar. 1953]

Hello Cayke:

This is a little addendum[349] to say 'How do you do?'

I am off on Wednesday to give an address to the Faculty of Queen's Annual Dinner.

I had prepared a speech which, according to the suggestion of Dr Tracy,[350] should be in a 'festive' not a 'research' mood, which suits my mood all right.

But now I am revising it because George Herbert Clarke died on Friday[351] and I must make some references to him. He was 81, and it wasn't unexpected.

It will be nice seeing Queen's again to renew old friendships. I may pay a visit to the ham and eggs restaurant – just to get the smell.

Next week I go to Windsor as I told you and I'll be there for 2 nights. But as it is the same speech – 'Newfoundland Reminiscences' – there is no extra work entailed beyond the telling of the Universal Lung Healer and how I came to Toronto on the proceeds of the sales.[352] The President of Assumption College[353] – the Reverend Father LeBel – asked me to tell it. Can you beat it?

Love,
Father

349 Pratt added this note to a longer letter by Viola.

350 Herman Lloyd Tracy (1897–1986), head of classics at Queen's University.

351 In her letter, Viola Pratt elaborates: 'He was having a shower bath, and the water was too hot. He was scalded. I don't know how much – but he had weak heart anyway – so I suppose the shock was too great.'

352 In 1900, Pratt and Willis Pike concocted a mixture which they sold in the outports, earning over $300. The story of the swindle was published in the St John's *Daily News* ('A Northern Holiday,' 23 August 1906). (See *EJP: TY*, 78–80.)

353 A co-educational undergraduate college in Windsor, Ontario. In 1956, it became Assumption University and, in 1962, the University of Windsor.

TO CLAIRE PRATT

Saturday am. [11 Apr. 1953]

Dearest Cayke:

I am writing this at the York Club following dinner. Mother went to the Heliconian Club and I came here. I shall pick her up in the Chev about 1:30.

I have *just* returned from the *Assumption College, Windsor,* and the Graduation Dinner, followed by speeches, was like a play in a Gayety theatre. I sat next to Bishop Nelligan[354] who, everytime I told a tall story, would pass me a cigar right in the presence of the audience. The audience smiled at the cigar as much as at the story. Well by the time I finished, I had eight cigars each one covered with aluminum – expensive cigars.

As most of my stories were Newfoundland-Irish they suited the moods of the students and staff. Then the Chairman, Father LeBel (who, by the way, I had in my graduation class twenty years ago) called on Bishop Nelligan to make a 'few remarks.' All his remarks were stories of his Irish experiences in Dublin. Here is one of them. He was being driven by a Dublin cabby through the city just after the Rebellion of 1916 when so much damage was done to the buildings of the city. Nelligan noted six statues and asked the cabby what they represented. The cabby replied – 'Oh, the 12 apostles.' But, said the Bishop – 'there are only six.' The answer immediately was *Day-shift*.

I then handed him back one his cigars – which convulsed the graduation class. I had been asked to tell the story of the Patent Medicine – Universal Lung Healer – you remember. I had said that the medicine at least couldn't do any harm, and no complaints of any significance had come to Cal after I had left for Toronto. Nelligan then said – 'Dead men make no complaints.' I then passed him over another cigar and by the time he had finished his speech the whole eight had been transferred to him. I am sure that in a year's time or so when my speech and his are forgotten, the students will talk about the bandying of cigars between us. The whole evening was more funny even than Queen's.

I spent three days there – Wednesday to Friday – and the Basilians were wonderful. I told them about Father McCorkell[355] and the lake trout your mother

354 Charles L. Nelligan, born (1894) in Prince Edward Island, was made bishop of Pembroke in 1937 and military bishop of the Armed Forces in 1939. He was professor of History, French, and theology at Assumption College.

355 See the note to 'Father Edmund McCorkell' in the letter to Viola and Claire Prattt, 9 April 1946 (p. 374).

cooked for him on that Friday night when Currelly, Edgar, Binyon,[356] Eayrs[357] and one or two others repasted at our place on Tullis Drive – the evening when Edgar pushed his finger through the buzzer filled with tar and grease. Do you remember that?

I got in about 11:30 last night, and Hazel[358] had just left for the North.

There was one sad bit of news when I arrived. Mr Watkins[359] had died of a thrombosis on Wednesday. Mrs Myles[360] took us out to the funeral parlour this morning. He had been ailing for some time, as one might imagine from his haggard look and thinness. He was 69 years but had worked day and night as you know, and worrying about his business I think.

Best love,
Father.

TO CLAIRE PRATT

47 Glencairn Ave.

Friday May 1, 1953

Dearest Cakes:

We are getting settled in 47 quite nicely and finding the six rooms capacious for our needs. We haven't sold 21 yet though Pash and Doris[361] are working valiantly. Just as soon as the deal is closed I shall write you pronto.

We may have to put off our Boston trip for some time because May is going to be a month crammed with engagements and work of all kinds. After June 6 things will be comparatively quiet and we shall probably be able to put in a week. A lot depends on Pash too as she will be 'Johnny' or 'Mary' on the spot trying to negotiate 21. Selling a house is an indefinite business anyway, like getting up in the morning if you know what I mean.

Our telephone was put in yesterday and we managed to retain the old number Hu.8 -1041. Lucky, wasn't it?

We have been so busy at the house and at moving that we haven't been out anywhere. And I have 80 papers to examine in 2b, whereas last year I had none.

---

356 See the note to 'Laurence Binyon' in the letter to Lorne Pierce, 11 April 1928 (p. 81).
357 Hugh Eayrs.
358 Mrs Hazel Joliffe, a friend of the family.
359 A neighbour on Cortleigh Boulevard.
360 Another neighbour.
361 A friend of 'Pash' (Ida Pashley) and fellow real estate agent.

I haven't untied the bundle yet though the '*provisional*' time is May 1 for sending them back. But we know what 'provisional' means. I start today in real earnest.

I have also to get up a paper on the 'Humanities' to read at London, Ont. towards the end of May.[362] I have refused other requests as I want a bit of time for my own work.

I shall be writing again in two or three days.

Bless you dear.
Father

TO JOHN SUTHERLAND

May 12, 1953

Dear John:

Apologies for the delay, but the eye strain is still with me. I managed, however, to read the Campbell poems.[363] They are immense – no fading of the old form in which I take such delight. Is there anyone on the other side of the Atlantic equal to him? I think not.

And that last paragraph of your editorial[364] is magnificent. I like its affirmation, its outlook.

Sorry I haven't one poem to hand over to you. I have a number of projects in 'mind' – just waiting for the recuperation of a holiday. I may go to Newfoundland this summer if plans are favourable.

By the way I gave an address at Assumption College last month and talked about you and Roy Campbell to Father LeBel. He is strong for Roy and the tour. I hope he reads your editorial.

I am slipping along a small cheque for your list. Please make it *anonymous*.

Keep after Marshall McLuhan.

The very best,
Ned Pratt

---

362 An address to the Humanities Association of Canada. See the letters to Roy Wiles, 9 and 13 February 1953 (*EJP: Web* and p. 522).

363 Sutherland had sent him some poems he had received from Roy Campbell, for whom Sutherland was attempting to arrange a Canadian recital tour.

364 In the spring number of *Northern Review*.

TO CLAIRE PRATT

Tuesday a.m. [19 May 1953]

Dearest Cayke:

Your letter and card came this morning, and weren't we glad to get them?

So the Rouillards arrived with the suit-case and cushion. They have become great friends of ours. I have Dana to my stags.

Don't worry too much about the 'Slaughter-House'[365] and the Spelling.[366] If odd jobs come as they come for free-lance that is all right. It allows some time for leisure and a spot of travelling about. I hope you will get a satisfactory apartment with all conveniences and comforts.

What a life the Buckleys[367] are living? It isn't life at all but straight killing drudgery. I don't know how Ruth can stand up under the strain.

Tonight I have to attend a dinner at Wymilwood[368] in advance of the U. of T. degree.[369] I made it a condition that I was not to make a speech. 'Oh,' said Bennett,[370] 'you might make a few remarks if you like.' All I am going to say is that I have taught for more than thirty years. Taking ten lectures plus addresses as the average per week, that means 300 per year, and if my mathematics serves me right that means 10,000 for the 30 years and odd. What a strain on the larynx of the speaker and what punishment for the ear-drums of the listeners. So why should I now add to the double strain, etc., etc., etc.? 'Bunk,' say I.

However, it will likely be a jolly party.

I haven't heard how Cal is getting along. I expected a note from him today. It looked like a heavy operation but he wrote in his natural good spirits, and expected to be out in reasonable time.

We are getting used to the apartment, but would be more pleased if the house were sold and yielding 5% on the equity. Pash is optimistic.

---

365 Term used by the family for a book about the Chicago abattoirs that Claire was editing at Harvard University Press.

366 Claire was also editing a spelling text for Ginn and Company. See the letter to Claire, 11 May 1953 (*EJP: Web*).

367 Ruth (née Stauffer) and Elery Buckley.

368 A women's residence at Victoria College. University dinners were often held in its capacious dining room.

369 Pratt was to be awarded an honorary degree at the 1953 convocation.

370 Harold Bennett (1890–1973), professor of Latin at Victoria College since 1932, held several administrative posts there (registrar, dean, acting president) before being appointed principal in 1951.

We shall keep you informed about everything. There will be a draft for you as soon as Peggy sends the cheque for the library books.[371] I understand it will be substantial.

Blessins on yer,
Father

TO CLAIRE PRATT

Toronto

Friday [5 June 1953]

Dearest Cayke:

Well, the house is sold at last. Pash came in to tell us that an owner of a bowling alley put in an offer of $25,000.00 with a deposit of $1250.00. We accepted it and got in touch with Mac Burden[372] to do the negotiation. The new owner's name is Cherney. So it's good-bye to 21.

[ ]

We shall be rushing about next week getting the small mortgage paid off and the signatures on the dotted line. We expect to leave here on Friday the 12th getting into Cambridge Saturday night. Could you arrange for a double room for us in a Cambridge Hotel? We would stay there for the following week. We have to be back in Toronto on the 24th which would mean that we should leave on the 22nd at least.

It will be lovely to see you and paint you – I mean draw you for I am going to take up art without lessons or agony. It will be fine impressionism – great sweeping lines making hair to look like seaweed, and the eyes to have the glare of Medusa. 'French without Tears.' You remember.

Love,
Father

---

371 Margaret ('Peggy') Ray; Pratt was selling part of his library to Victoria College.

372 The Pratts' long-time lawyer. See the note to 'Mac' in the letter to Viola Pratt, 22 June 1924 (p. 39).

TO MARGARET BROWN

47 Glencairn Ave.
Toronto 12

June 9, 1953

Our dear Peggy:

This is certainly a belated acknowledgement of Willa[373] but we have been in the throes of moving from our house at 21 Cortleigh to a small apartment at 47 Glencairn about three blocks north of Cortleigh. We are hardly settled yet, storing eighty cartons of miscellaneous things mainly in the basement in addition to 'placing' the heavy furniture brought over by Rawlinson.[374] We love Willa with her friendly smiling face looking right out from the cover, and the biography is a masterpiece as one might assume it would be from Edward. He is in my thoughts continually. He has meant so much to me during the 25 years of our deep friendship. No two brothers could have been linked together by closer bonds. And you, dearest Peggy, are just as much in our hearts.

What human variety Edward gave Willa! She is full of flashes and facets. I hope the book is selling well.

I am sending you a copy of the 'Last Spike.' It is going pretty well in Canada. The C.B.C. presented portions of it some time ago and now, bless you, it is being broadcast in no less a place than Scotland through the B.B.C. I guess the oatmeal passage caught the Scots. Last week it won the Gov. General's Award which greatly heartened me as it would, I imagine, have given pleasure to Edward.

We expect to go to Newfoundland next month for a holiday but chiefly to be with my beloved brother Cal who has been in the Royal Victoria Hospital in Montreal for five weeks with a heavy operation. Poor fellow lost his wife two years ago, and his son Calvert had been in the same hospital for a month. Both are improving, though slowly.

Vi is adding a message on the next page. If you come up this way again, no one will receive a more sisterly welcome.

Bless you,
Ned

373 E.K. Brown's *Willa Cather: A Critical Biography* (New York: Knopf, 1953) was published posthumously. (See the note to 'the Willa job' in the letter to E.K. Brown, 17 November 1950 [p. 463].)

374 The moving company.

TO CLAIRE PRATT

47 Glencairn Ave.
Toronto 12

June 25/53

Dearest Cayke:

We got back on Tuesday evening safe and sound. Today I went down to the Stratford Festival agency and got three tickets for Wednesday evening July 15th (Richard III). Fine seats. We thought R III would be best as most of the other tickets were sold and away back in the theatre, and the accommodation overnight was difficult to secure. We would leave Toronto on Wednesday morning and get into Stratford nice and early. I am to hear from the agency soon as to the motel we are to occupy – as near to the theatre as possible. We would return then on Thursday morning. The manager said there was no hotel accommodation left, but the hotel proprietors were looking after the guests.

We sent a night telegram to Cal last night that we would be leaving on August 1 by air and spend most of August in Nfld.[375]

It will be grand to have you with us for a couple of weeks or until we go to Nfld.

Lovingly,
Father

TO CLAIRE PRATT

47 Glencairn Ave
Toronto 12
Ont.

Sunday [27 June 1953]

Dearest Cayke:

It was good to hear your chimes over the phone yesterday though I was in the next room. It was a sweet tinkle with a charming undertone.

375 The telegram read as follows: 'Just received your letter of the tenth today on return from Boston to visit Claire. Our earliest flight from Toronto to St John's is August 1 as we must be in Toronto July 31 since Claire will be visiting us from July 13 to end of month. We can stay in Nfld through most of August. Keenly anticipating being with you. Ned.'

We are at home today though your mother expects to go visit with Mary Eddis at 4 o'clock to see Hazel.[376]

Would you kindly buy me a pair of ear-stoppers and bring them with you when you come home in July (the pen is beginning to scratch and I am borrowing your mother's). Not that the noise here bothers me much for I am getting used to it but occasionally a motor-horn at night awakens the city. The enclosed will buy the stoppers. If there is any left over you can put it down to the credit of the radio.

We went out to York Downs the other evening for dinner. It is lovely out there. I shall see to it that you will be shaded under the elms several times while you are getting inspiration for some Michael Angelo lines etc., etc.

Your York Downish father.[377]

376 Her friend Hazel Joliffe.

377 Viola added a note, which reads in part as follows: 'I asked your father to tell you all the news. I see he hasn't told you much. He didn't mention the very swish C.A.A. party and dinner at which he received the Gov-General's Gold Medal for *The Last Spike*, and which was the occasion of his picture in the paper – nor that we went to *Le Moulin Rouge* last night and were entranced by it ... Yesterday I was at a trousseau tea for Barbara Hincks who is to be married next month, and is going to live in Bourlemanque. Afterwards I drove past our house and saw a television aerial atop it. Who would have thought that 21 Cortleigh would inaugurate T.V. on our section of the street.'

VII Accepting the Years, 1953–1955

I miss the students … but one must accept the years.

– E.J. Pratt to Earle Birney, 2 November 1954

TO CLAIRE PRATT

c/o C.C. Pratt
Waterford Bridge Road
[St John's, Newfoundland]

August 4, 1953

Dearest Cayke:

I suppose you got into Cambridge before we arrived at St John's. Wasn't it a bit of a shock to hear the clerk shout out through the loud speaker – 'Passenger Pratt wanted at the Customs' Office.' I thought of all things like smuggling, false returns or straight neglect, but your reappearance was reassuring. I hope you had a good trip and that the 'black magic'[1] wasn't run down completely when you tried to start the motor.

We are living in the lap of luxury here. Rose[2] had a roast turkey (cold) for dinner at 8 p.m., followed by raspberries and Devonshire cream.

1 Claire referred to her car as 'B.M.' and her father enjoyed thinking of what the initials might stand for. (See the letter of 14 February 1953 [*EJP: Web*].)

2 Calvert Pratt's housekeeper.

Then yesterday Ewart took us down to Bally-haly Golf Club for lunch. Today we have lunch at Yvonne's[3] and dinner at Gwenyth's.[4] Jim came up to see us last night. He looked far better than I anticipated though his forebodings were as dismal as usual. Cal is improving fast and is almost normal in activity. Yesterday afternoon after the Club lunch, Cal and little Calvert (the grandson) went fishing. It was the fulfilment of six months of expectation. The little fellow promised me one trout if he should catch two. To the disappointment of grandad and grandson they didn't get a bite but they had the satisfaction of boiling the kettle anyway. They are to go again after our trip around the island.

We leave here tomorrow afternoon at 5 and arrive at Corner Brook Thursday at 3, where we stay till the following Tuesday. The whole trip takes three weeks and we plan to leave St. John's about the 28th of August.

The weather is a bit muggy, heavy thunderstorms occurring after three weeks of a dry spell.

You should see the raspberry patch in Cal's garden – enough berries for the household and all the neighbours. Our 21 Cortleigh patch would need a microscope to see it in comparison. The whole place is wonderful – flowers, shrubs, trees, lawns, fountains – everything. The famous South Side Hills are just made for you and your paints. I could almost draw them myself – at least to distinguish them from whales for the sake of the observer.

When you write, address c/o C.C. P.[5] Waterford Bridge Road and mail will be forwarded though it will take some time in transportation. Oho! my pen is running dry and I haven't any Parkers 51 in the house.

Much love
Father away off

TO CLAIRE PRATT

[Cornerbrook, Newfoundland]

August 7, 1953

---

3 Yvonne (née Rorke) was Ewart Pratt's wife.

4 Pratt's niece, James Pratt's daughter. (See the note to 'Hal' in the letter to Claire Pratt, 10 October 1952 [p. 511].)

5 Calvert C. Pratt.

Dearest Cakes:

We got your letter before we left St John's and were so glad you had no further mishaps (customs, etc.). Too bad, however, that you had that ride to the hospital with Beverley. It must have been as troublesome for you as for her. We hope that there have been no further untoward effects since.

We are now at Corner Brook and the motor trip along the Humber today rivals the Rockies (except for snow caps). Mother used up all her films. She is now trying to fit a new one in the camera – a difficult job for which she is getting very little *valuable* assistance from me. There is no lack of *willingness* on my part I can assure you. It is lack of knowledge plus lack of mechanical ability, my fingers being all thumbs, often exhibited by other men in the changing of diapers if you know what I mean. Do you remember the story of Pelham Edgar in that connection? (It cost Pelham $25.00 to call in Alan Brown.)[6]

Tomorrow we are invited to a cabin about sixty miles away. We shall spend the week-end fishing for grilse, a species of small salmon. I hope to have more finesse with that operation than with the aforementioned camera.

The hotel where we are staying[7] is wonderful. It overlooks the Humber and high hills on the other side. Fred Bugden[8] was here and brought back one of his best pictures. The forest is mainly soft woods – spruce mainly – the source of pulp for the paper plants. The town produces about 1000 tons a day. Cal has interests here so it is a combination of business and pleasure. For me it is a more complicated interest – sight-seeing, motoring. and napping being the major ones.

Before we left St John's we had a reunion at Hal Puddester's[9] and I heard a beautiful story which I must tell you. Perhaps you may have heard a variant of it. A certain man who was rather fed up with living decided to jump from the seventh storey of a hotel. When he was making the preparatory exercise of leaping an Irish policeman arrived on the pavement and called out to him in the most pleading tones –

'Don't jump.'

'Yes, I'm going to jump.'

'Please don't for the sake of your poor old father.'

'I have no father.'

6 Professor of Pediatrics at the university and consulting physician at the Hospital for Sick Children. Edgar's 'story' is not revealed.

7 The Glynmill Inn in Corner Brook.

8 A Corner Brook business acquaintance of Calvert Pratt.

9 The husband of Pratt's neice Gwenyth, daughter of his brother James.

'Then don't jump for the sake of your poor old mother.'
'I have no mother.'
'Then don't for the sake of the *Holy Virgin*.'
'I never heard of the Holy Virgin.'
'Then jump, you bloody Protestant.' Finis.

You can imagine what an intellectual evening and spiritual feast we had.

Excuse my handwriting as my fountain pen has run dry and I am using a scratching hotel pen. More anon.

Rambling Father

TO CLAIRE PRATT

47 Glencairn Ave.
Toronto, Ont.

August 26 [1953]

Dearest Cayke:

We got in last night (or I should say this morning since the watch showed 2:30 a.m.). Pash,[10] the dear old thing, met us at the airport and drove us home. We found the vestibule full of letters and magazines but we opened only the most important correspondence and then tumbled into the cots.

Our trip was wonderful mainly in its scenery and in the quaint people at the wharves when the Northern Ranger[11] stayed long enough for us to go ashore. We have gathered a bin-ful of stories. I shall give you one.

The captain, Cal, your mother and I were invited to the home of the Norrises[12] for an hour or so and Mrs Norris told me of an Anglican bishop that came to the port to preach. The janitor couldn't get the stove to work and as it was a very cold day he valiantly went to the Roman Catholic priest and asked him if he would lend him the stove in the chapel and some coal – anthracite. The priest was very friendly and duly the stove was installed. But the anthracite plus the bad chimney sent up an awful smoke and when the Bishop arrived he couldn't preach, couldn't breathe. All he could say was 'I can't preach in this

---

10 Ida Pashley.

11 The Canadian National Railways coastal steamer in which they travelled from Corner Brook up the Great Northern Penninsula and along the coast of Labrador to Hopedale, and then down the east coast of Newfoundland to St John's (11–23 August).

12 Unidentified.

smoke. This is a nice way to treat your Bishop.' To which the janitor replied – 'Well, what could you expect with a Catholic stove and *anti-Christ* coal?'

Our stay at St John's after the trip was very short on account of the steamer being held up by fog and storm. However, we managed to see most of our friends and relatives. We motored to Topsail to the summer house of Ches Pippy[13] who gave me for your stamp collection a wonderful lot of rare stamps. When we have them classified we shall give you an accounting. We thought it best to keep them in the house rather than send them through the post to you as they might get crumpled or mutilated. Some of the stamps are very old and valuable.

The plane trip from Moncton to Montreal was bumpy because of a thunder storm but we came through it with no other discomfort than loss of sleep.

I am spending this day answering correspondence now long in arrears. Enclosed are two cards for you, the only first-class mail addressed to you.

Just the day before we left St. John's I had to give a 15-minute broadcast on the trip – meant only for the Newfoundland Division.

Love and everything else.
Father.

TO CLAIRE PRATT

47 Glencairn Ave

Friday [4 Sept. 1953]

Dearest Cayke:

Today is Friday. Mother and Ruth Jenking are going to the C.N. Exhibition and I'm going down to the College to arrange books and things and make ready to occupy Kay Coburn's[14] office for the year. She is going to England in two weeks on her Coleridge business. My office is to be jointly occupied by David Knight[15] and Ken Kee.[16] Things are changing all over the place all right.

---

13 A prominent St John's businessman, director of numerous commercial firms, noted for his community interests and philanthropy.

14 See the note to 'Kay Coburn' in the letter to Pelham Edgar, 21 February 1945 (p. 317).

15 See the note to 'David Knight' in the letter to George Johnston, 13 November 1952 (p. 514).

16 Kenneth Kee (b. 1922), graduate of the University of Toronto, taught English at Victoria College until his retirement. He edited Macmillan's College Classics *Geoffrey Chaucer: A Selection of His Works* (1966).

The latest piece of news is that Clare Hincks has asked me to be Chairman of the Toronto Branch of the Mental Hygiene Committee.[17] I told him I would be a heck of a chairman but he assured me that all I had to do was to hold dinners at the York Club with 'influential' friends who might become patrons and donors for the Committee – men like Brockington, J.S. MacLean, Cal (when he comes to Toronto), Sid Smith and the like.

I made a fine collection of stories when I was in Nfld and some of them I shall tell at the opening dinner early in October. How to relate them to Mental Hygiene is a problem in ingenuity. The stories are crazy anyway, so they are relevant in that respect.

Mother's pictures of Nfld scenes and people came out very well indeed. I think she is sending you some.

So it is economics, is it?[18] I hope it won't be too taxing on you. I hope also you know more about the subject than I do, for to me it is a matter of making out tax returns – complicated enough!

Get as much rest as you can and take care of your eyes.

Lovingly,
Father

TO CLAIRE PRATT

47 Glencairn Ave.

[15 Sept. 1953]

Dearest:

Your letters arrived yesterday.

I have just sent off a letter to Cal asking him to be present at a Ned Pratt-Clare Hincks dinner on Oct. 9. Those who are coming enthusiastically are J.S. McLean (Canada Packers),[19] Jimmie Stewart (General Manager of the Bank of Commerce),[20] Eve Holmes (Manager of the Toronto Branch of the same

---

17 [*sic*] The board of the Toronto branch of the Ontario division of the Canadian Mental Health Association.

18 Claire had returned to postgraduate studies in Boston.

19 James Stanley McLean (1876–1954) was the first president of Canada Packers. He was a patron of the arts and a generous contributor to hosipitals and medical charities.

20 Stewart (b. 1894) was made general manager of the Bank of Commerce in 1947, director in 1949, and president in 1952.

bank),[21] Sir Ellsworth Flavelle, Dick Meech (of Loblaws), Malcolm Wallace, Arthur Meighen,[22] Ray Birks[23] whom I coached in Ethics away back in 1911 – in 'Ethics' (no less). He is now a big Corporation Lawyer. Cecil Cannon (of the Board of Education)[24] and about a dozen others. We are to have Fillet Mignon and Roast Beef plus Yorkshire Pudding, Peach Melba and Coffee. If you were here I'd put a little of the 'Melba' in my pocket for you and a cup of Nescafé contingent on safe transportation.

More anon
Father

TO CLAIRE PRATT

47 Glencairn Ave.
Toronto 12

Sept. 27, 1953

Dearest Cayke:

We have just been home one month and it seems like last week.

This is Sunday and we have remained in the house all day, but we are not going to waive the wonderful privilege of attending Church tonight. The privilege, of course, means to shake hands with Dr Short[25] at the end of the series, thus keeping up the appearance of Sabbatical respectability.

---

21 Evelyn Holmes (b. 1892) joined the bank in 1911 and served in various posts including chief inspector and manager of the Windsor branch, before his appointment in 1943 as manager of the Toronto (Main) branch.

22 Meighen had served as prime minister in the 1920s and was appointed to the Senate in 1932. Meighen later settled in Toronto as a Bay Street financier.

23 A graduate of Victoria College and of Osgoode Hall, Birks (b. 1893) was a partner in the law firm of Briggs, Frost, Birks and Langdon, Toronto.

24 A graduate of Queen's and Toronto universities, Cannon (b. 1898) held many administrative posts in the Ministry of Education and was deputy minister (1951–6).

25 Reverend Dr John Short was minister of the Pratts' church, St George United. He had just succeeded Willard Brewing. (See the note to 'Dr Brewing' in the letter to Claire Pratt, 4 November 1944 [p. 303]).

Last night we had a unique experience. We were invited over to Dorothy and Douglas Henderson's to meet Mr & Mrs Roland Hayes[26] and a group of people. Hayes didn't sing but he told us some of his remarkable experiences when he was on a continential (European) tour in 1926 about the time when Nazi-ism was growing so frightfully.

He was scheduled to sing in Berlin and the papers of the city announced that they didn't want him in Germany. People went to hiss him and for 10 minutes he stood at the piano silent while the hisses went through the roof and all the properties of the stage fell down around him by design. He waited till the hisses and boos stopped and then he started to sing one of Schubert's songs in perfect German accent. He went on singing quelling the crowd, conquering them in fact, and when he finished his program people came up and carried him on their shoulders amidst wild acclaim. If you come across him at Brookline ask him to tell the story. It riveted me and your mother.

Ernie Hunter,[27] the minister of Trinity Church, was present last night and we listened in on CFRB to his sermon this morning. He told the story superbly weaving it into his text on the 'necessity of inner spiritual reserves.' There were other stories too that were most dramatic. Hayes is a wonderful fellow.

Love,
Father

TO CLAIRE PRATT

Monday [12 Oct. 1953]

Canadian Thanksgiving Day

Not quite 10 a.m.

Duck:

Your uncle Cal came in last Friday and I gave a stag for him at the York Club with about twenty guests – the number I wanted to get on the Board of the

26 A popular concert tenor, Roland Hayes (1887–1977) was the first African American singer to receive international acclaim. He wrote and published an autobiography entitled *Angel Mo and her Son, Roland Hayes* (Boston: Little, Brown, 1942). (See the letters to Claire Pratt, 28 October 1953 and 9 November 1944 [*EJP: Web*].)

27 See the note to 'Ernie Hunter' in the letter to Claire Pratt, 11 May 1945 (p. 332).

Toronto Branch of the Ontario Division of the National Health Association of Canada.[28] This runs me out *of ofs*. Said association pays the – shot of the dinner.

Cal and Clare Hincks were the guests, Clare making the main speech expounding the aims of the association, and my job now, as Chairman of the Board, is to get the consent of the twenty members of the stag to become members of the Board. As I told you before, I get a monthly stipend.[29] I think I'll make a heck of a Chairman, presiding over the transaction of business, but I may throw them off the track by telling them stories of my connection with Abnormal Psychology in the U. of T. before I went over to Victoria to examine other 'patients.'

After dinner we repaired to the main sitting room to talk about our early experiences and tell jokes.

Cal is off to New York now, returning on Thursday for two or three days.

Tonight we have Thanksgiving dinner at Floss's. Marjorie and Alice Fenwick[30] are calling for us in their new car. I have eaten a hearty breakfast, so I shall have a very light lunch to make room for the turkey – get me?

Nora Cochrane phoned last night. She expects a letter from you some time soon.

I also got a nice letter from Cécile de Banke acknowledging Ruth's review of her Shakespeare book[31] which delighted her no end. It appeared in the Canadian Forum.

Tomorrow night is Charter Night[32] and I have to give an address at the dinner preceding the function – subject, *Newfoundland*. It will be mainly stories, reminiscences, etc.

We have been working at the house, getting chairs in shape. Pash upholstered one.[33] Your mother painted the four white kitchen chairs and I sandpapered one. We are now putting books in order. On Sunday we drove down to my office (Kay Coburn's) and classified mine, some of which Peggy will buy.[34] Distribution (ha-ha!) soon.

---

28 [*sic*]. The National *Mental* Health Association.

29 Of $100.00.

30 Daughters of the Reverend Mark Fenwick. See the note to 'Mr Fenwick' in the letter to Viola Pratt, 27 July 1944 (p. 283).

31 Ruth Jenking's review of de Banke's *Shakespearean Stage Production, Then and Now* (New York: McGraw-Hill, 1954), in *CF* (July 1953).

32 An annual event, marked by a dinner and other observances, to commemorate the granting of a charter to Victoria University in 1841.

33 Ida Pashley. See the letter to Claire Pratt, 23 September 1953 (*EJP: Web*).

34 Peggy Ray, Victoria College librarian. The college was purchasing part of Pratt's library. (See the letter to Claire Pratt, 19 May 1953 [p. 529].)

I am enclosing Carol's[35] letter. She made out a million or less to send them along to her friends.

More later,

Lovingly,
Father.

TO CLAIRE PRATT

47 Glencairn Ave.
Toronto 12

Oct. 24, 1953

Dearest Chuck:

I wonder if this letter will have to be forwarded to your new address. You were on the point of leaving when you wrote last. We hope you will find your new quarters comfortable and that you will have help placing your furniture, etc. Is it on the ground floor in a general apartment building? How far is it from the Press? Don't buy your winter coat yet. If you can manage to get away for Christmas holidays come up for we want to give you for a present a good light fur coat, either a short like your mother's or a longer one. Make no mistake about it – I'll be there at Sellers-Gough[36] to see if it fits and is warm ha-ha! Your mother's is a dandy. When she put it on the other day I felt like walking three paces behind her – she was so regal in the muskrat and I felt like a squirrel.

We had a stag party last night at the York Club. Clare Hincks was host and the guest of honour was Dr Rees, President of the International Association for Mental Health.[37] It was a smart affair and after Rees had spoken I had to tell the story of my early connection with the Mental Hygiene movement and of my experience with a murderer in the Don Jail. I was dispatched there by Dr C.K. Clarke[38] to get his I.Q. which was forty-five. I laid it on a bit I must confess though embroidery was not necessary.

---

35 Carol Cassidy.

36 A Toronto furrier.

37 Pratt may be referring to the International Committee for Mental Health (ICMH) or the World Federation of Mental Health (WFMH), of which John Rawlings Rees (1890–1969) was founding president.

38 Charles K. Clarke (1857–1924), one of Canada's first psychiatrists, served in several Canadian mental asylums before being appointed superintendent of the Toronto General Hospital in

I have now my twenty members of the Toronto Branch of the Ontario Division of the National Association for Mental Health – what a formidable name. Your Uncle Cal is on. Dick Meech, the President of the Canadian Bank of Commerce (Jimmie Stewart), Sid Smith (as Patron), Ellsworth Flavelle are among the list who have accepted.

When I stand up with my gavel at the first meeting in January I am going to hit the table with a resounding whack, though as Chairman I fear I shall be ridiculous.

Jack Kent Cooke had a party last evening at the Royal York for all members of his staff – about 300. I was swamped by the members but found a few congenial souls in the Advertising Business – and in the Editorial world. They certainly made me feel at home. After that came Clare's[39] dinner and the experience, to say the least, was exciting.

John Gray (of Macmillans) has given me a big ms. to edit on Newfoundland.[40] Your mother and I are going to reconstruct it and he offers a good fee.

Last week the B.B.C. sent me a cheque for *The Last Spike* which, as I told you, was put on at the Edinburgh Festival. They made a dramatized version of the poem which, unfortunately, was not heard in Canada. They may send me the records. They particularly emphasized the effect of oatmeal on the Scotch blood resulting in such Canadian personages from Scotland like Sir John A. Macdonald, Angus, Lord Mount Stephen, Strathcona.[41] It was good fun to show how oatmeal developed gorse on the eyebrows and thistles on the beards. Strathcona's eyebrows looked like a full-foliaged precipice.

By the way, do you have anything equivalent to the Ontario Motor League in the U.S.A.? Don't hesitate to put on every help and security.

Phone whenever it is convenient, especially on Sundays about 10 a.m. or 9:15 p.m. Your voice sounds like Bach's Mass in A Minor – marvellous!, though as you know Handel's Dead March in Saul is my favourite.

With much love
Your Mental Health Father
E.J. Pratt

1911. He was co-founder with Clarence Hincks of the Canadian Mental Health Association in 1918. Toronto's Clarke Institute was named for him.

39 Clare Hincks.

40 Leo English's *Historic Newfoundland*. See the note to 'the Macmillan ms. of English' in the letter to Claire Pratt, 29 January 1954 (p. 553).

41 John A. Macdonald, Richard Angus, George Stephen (Baron Mount Stephen), Lord Strathcona (Donald Smith) were all participants in the building of the CPR and characters in *TLS*.

TO CLAIRE PRATT

47 Glencairn Ave

Thursday [5 Nov. 1953]

Kakie dear:

This is just a little note to tell you about Roy Campbell, the famous S. African poet now living in Portugal. I have always been a great admirer of his work and I was asked to go down to Montreal to act as his Chairman Monday night. Then last night I was again his Chairman in Toronto at St Mike's. He was wonderful, talking about his experiences – deep-sea diver, octopus-killer (with his bare hands), bull-fighter in Spain and a marvelous writer of verse. As I had to make my introduction brief I typed it out and am sending it along.[42] Will you return it later?

Hoping you are finding the new quarters comfortable.

Father.

TO CLAIRE PRATT

47 Glencairn Ave
Toronto 12

Sunday a.m. [8 Nov. 1953]

Dearest Cayke:

The bazaar is over at last. I was the only man in the house with about one hundred women and wasn't I glad when Cal came in to open the function! You should

42 In his introduction Pratt began by speaking of the pleasure and honour of introducing a man whom, though he had not met him in the flesh until then, he had long known through his writings. He went on to say: 'When I was in England in the early twenties I came across … his *Flaming Terrapin* … I read the book and found it a great aesthetic experience, well worth I thought a trip to England. The poem was so full of power, so charged with original metaphor – and, I may say, an undercurrent of philosophy which never obtruded itself, that I could not wonder if the young man of about 20 years could keep up this pace in his later development. So I followed his career and I found his early promise amply justified. Book after book appeared and the pace was not only sustained but increased. I do not know where his Pegasus will go in the future but I have the conviction that it will soar out of sight. When I read his *Flowering Rifle*, it was like a high-voltage current going through me … I read other of his works with the same

have seen the multitude of dolls. Ina[43] sent over a half dozen, then another half-dozen, then twenty-four more making 36 all told. I had to turn my back to get away from the fixity of glare. Every eye (72 of them) was on me.

Cal opened the show with a few felicitous remarks saying that down in Newfoundland they sold everything but their souls and the reason why they didn't sell them was that they were all assigned to heaven beforehand. After it was over I pulled him away and went down to see Clare Hincks and there and then I sold him a doll for $3.65 which made one less. Ina took back about two dozen of them to be marketed at the next bazaar. What an afternoon. Still they made $400.00 for Talents,[44] which was most gratifying. Marjorie Keyes[45] is going to buy something or other later, having decided to do so when she saw the distressful look on my face during the description of the little beauties.

Today it is quiet and necessarily so for the period from 2 to 6 p.m. was an ordeal. Pash and Marion[46] dressed up like Santa Claus. Pash had a black moustache about a yard wide which swept things off the table, and I was kept busy picking the darned things up.

Mrs Malcolm Wallace and Bea[47] came along and bought a cake so soft that it nearly broke before they managed to get in the car.

No more bazaars for a long time.

Pity me.
Father

---

excitement.' (The script of Pratt's slightly different introduction delivered in Toronto is reprinted in *EJP: PAA*, 285-7.) Writing to Sutherland next day, Campbell commented: 'I had a wonderful time with Ned in the chair last night.'

43 Ina McCauley.

44 The Talents Service Club was founded in January 1952 by Dorothy Knight, Ida Pashley, and Marian Whytall; Claire Pratt was one of twelve charter members. Members were called on to use their 'talents' to raise money for people who were in need but could not appeal to any established agency for assistance. The club was a great success, growing to about thirty-five members, with Eddie Cantor serving as its honorary president.

45 Dr Clare Hincks's secretary and later his second wife.

46 Ina Pashley and Marion Whytall.

47 Malcolm Wallace's daughter.

TO CLAIRE PRATT

47 Glencairn Ave
Toronto 12

Wednesday [11 Nov. 1953]

Dearest Cayke:

How are you getting on with your apt.? Are you having help in hanging up the tapestries, arranging tables, chairs, and making proper display of flora on the mantelpiece, etc. etc. etc.?

On Monday evening the Board of Regents gave me an official retirement dinner. Brockington proposed the toast and I had to wag my head and tongue for 30 minutes in acknowledgement. Ethel Bennett[48] presented your mother with a bouquet of roses. Frye made a fine speech – very heart-warming. Laure Riese had a supper for a dozen of us in her room afterwards. Malcolm Wallace lost his overcoat in Burwash Hall and hasn't recovered it yet. He left his hat in one room and coat in another. The hat stayed put but the coat vanished.

Love
Father

TO LEOPOLD MACAULAY[49]

47 Glencairn Avenue

[15 Nov. 1953]

Dear Leo:

Would you convey to the Board on behalf of my wife and myself our deepest appreciation for the evening of the 9th of November. From the first handshake to the last, the program was marked by the utmost cordiality and affection. We

48 The wife of Harold Bennett, principal of Victoria College.
49 Chairman of Victoria College's Board of Regents.

shall never forget the dinner; the Chairman's remarks; the speeches of Norrie Frye and Leonard Brockington; the toast and the ringing response to my address; the floral presentation to Vi by Ethel Bennett; the laughter and comments, and the final 'Jolly good fellows' sung miraculously in key, were all expressions that warmed our hearts. Long live Victoria, and our love to everyone again.

Vi and Ned Pratt

TO DESMOND PACEY

Victoria College

November 18th, 1953

Dear Des:

Some of the late Pelham Edgar's friends would like very much to have Allan Barr's excellent portrait of him purchased for Victoria University.

Dr. Lorne Pierce has offered to head the subscription list with $100.00, and has asked me to convene a Committee for the purpose of soliciting contributions from former colleagues and students of Dr. Edgar.

The Fund will be known as The Pelham Edgar Portrait Fund, and contributions from $5.00 to $25.00 will be appreciated.

It was Dr. Edgar's wish that this portrait would be hung in Victoria University. It is an excellent likeness and is considered one of the finest examples of portrait painting in Canada.

Those of us who were his colleagues or students and remember him with affection have welcomed this opportunity to do something tangible to honour his memory. Your name has been suggested as one who might like to be considered in this category, and I am writing, therefore, to give you an opportunity to contribute, if you wish to do so.

In the event that we are unable to reach our objective, contributions will be returned to the donors.

Cheques should be made payable to Margaret V. Ray, in Trust, The Library, Victoria University, and should be earmarked for *The Pelham Edgar Portrait Fund.*

Yours sincerely,
E.J. Pratt

TO LORNE PIERCE

Thursday pm
[26 Nov. 1953]

Hello, you old cetacean:

I will be charmed to have you in my cove tomorrow evening at eight or earlier to see your Taurian dome and hear you spout.

Farewell to any school of mackerel or squid that may happen to be around. Your capacity for deglutition, I know, is enormous. I may warm you up with a little of 'Witches Brew' in tangible and gustatory form.

Welcome
Ned

TO CLAIRE PRATT

47 Glencairn Ave
Toronto 12 Canada

Friday [27 Nov. 1953]

Dear Cakye:

I finished up the collection for Pelham's Portrait today. We managed to raise $600.00 chiefly among his old friends. It was hard getting it in dribbles of 5.00 mainly. So by Xmas time we'll hang it in the Library. Peggy[50] is arranging the event and ceremony. My job is to draw aside the curtain after Lorne Pierce has pronounced the 'Eulogium.' Allan Barr[51] is down on his uppers and the 600 will come in useful, but after that he is dependent on commissions which come rarely.

Mother is out attending the 50th anniversary of the U.W.C.[52] One act of the performers is to have a cheer-leader going on the double leading ten women in shorts – most of them are between 50 and 60 years – What a show!

Father

50 Margaret Ray.
51 The painter of Edgar's portrait.
52 University Women's Club.

TO CLAIRE PRATT

47 Glencairn Ave

Monday a.m. [7 Dec. 1953]

Dearest Cayke:

[ ]

We are planning a Christmas dinner which will make your Thanksgiving affair look like a seal-flipper stew cooked on a Greenland glacier. There will be no cheese soufflés by the way – I have other culinary plans in my mind, assisted of course in execution by your mother's intentions.

So the Slaughter House book[53] is out. I am a little vague about both title and contents. Is Slaughter house a nickname for a phase of the meat-packing industry? Or is it a nickname without any other meaning than that it nearly killed you in editing it? Or is Slaughter the name of a man, and house added just as we might add the word to a famous man, e.g. the Osler or Churchill book? These are incidental things to you of course, but to me they are of paramount significance.

Mother is just shouting out not to forget to ask you if you need more envelopes for your Christmas cards. If you do, she can easily get them at Wesley Buildings.

Last night we had supper at the Daykins[54] with the MacLarens and the Harknesses.[55] Most of the conversation afterwards consisted of Newfoundland stories particularly the one relating to the action of Sir Humphrey Walwyn[56] pouring a bottle of screech down the throat of a salmon – most edifying!

We are getting our Xmas cards out in time – how about a hundred enveloped and stamped. That eases the rush around the '20s.

Cheese soufflé to you.

With love,
Father

53 See the note to 'the 'Slaughter-House' in the letter to Claire Pratt, 19 May 1953 (p. 528).

54 Kathleen and Hume Daykins were friends of the family.

55 Friends of Viola Pratt. Otherwise unidentified.

56 A retired admiral of the Royal Navy, and former governor of Newfoundland (1936–46).

TO THE AWARDS COMMITTEE OF THE ROYAL SOCIETY OF CANADA

[15 Dec. 1953]

The Awards Committee
of the Royal Society of Canada,
Ottawa

Dear Sirs:

Dr. C.F. Klinck is applying for an emolument[57] from the Royal Society and I have much pleasure in endorsing his application.

Since he has forwarded his academic credentials there is no need for me to re-state them, but I can testify to his ability and industry. I know from personal contact with his staff in his English Department that he is held in the highest esteem as an administrator, teacher and scholar. Moreover his research and writing have been considerable in spite of the fact that he has wedged them in during his managerial duties as Head of the Department. An extended period assured by a scholarship would, I am sure, result in production that would justify a favourable decision by the Awards Committee.

Yours sincerely,
E.J. Pratt

TO CLAIRE PRATT

47 Glencairn Ave.

[20 Jan. 1954]

Dearest Claire:

I didn't get a chance to see the skunks.[58] The letter was addressed to your mother and I didn't recognize the handwriting. She says the drawings are very fine and she sent them off before I returned from the College. More power to you though I must say that the subject was scarcely attar of roses.

57 'Profit or gain arising from station, office, or employment; dues; reward, remuneration, salary' (*OED*).

58 Illustrations by Claire for her mother's magazine, *World Friends*.

I am feeling fine again now, have spent most of the day at the College in Kay's office.[59] I had lunch with Malcolm Wallace in the York Club. He is gloomy as ever, quite, quite bored. He says he gets up at 9, finishes breakfast at 10, reads the Globe & Mail; finishes that at 11, answers his correspondence at 12; has lunch, then meditates or looks at the [..]e [...]s most of the afternoon; goes curling sometimes in the evening and so to bed.

He is waiting now for the spring and will resume golfing if I do. If I don't he'll repeat the winter round. It was good, however, to see him and talk about the old days.

Our house is very warm and satisfactory and, as you know, very convenient to the car line.

Last night I addressed the Newfoundland Group of the Library Association on the Titanic – my first lecture since November. I didn't feel tired and the audience seemed very interested. The CBC put it on for the Ontario schools a month ago and now they contemplate putting it on over the network on the Wednesday Night Program. It seems to go with the students the best of all my work – the notes are voluminous.

Our love to you
Father

Glad you received the 500.00 draft. Excuse my pen, it is running dry.

TO CLAIRE PRATT

47 Glencairn Ave.

Monday [25 Jan. 1954]

Dearest Cayke:

Your letter of the 22nd just came and I am answering it immediately. Mother has gone down to the U.W.C.[60] to introduce today's speaker. She makes about two introductions a week in addition to offering thanks at the end.

Yes, the unveiling went off all right except for the light. I wrote Dona to tell her that the portrait would be hung in the reading room of the Library and

59 He was using Kay Coburn's office.
60 University Women's Club.

now Wilf James[61] says he is going to remove mine from the dingy quarters of the second floor of the College and put it opposite Pelham's – which satisfies me no end. Some visitor guided by Irving[62] through the Victoria halls recently remarked that the 'gallery' looked like a collection of 'tortured misspent personalities.' I shall be glad to be out of it.

We gave the Fryes a buffet supper Saturday night. Nineteen persons came – all of my English Department. After the supper we put a number of Newfoundland records on the gramophone – '*The Squid Jiggin Ground*,' the *Kelligrew's Soiree*, 'We rant and roar like true Newfoundlanders.' They were funny and Ruth Jenking almost split her sides at the quaint idioms.

I forgot to mention in my last letter that Harriet Rouillard[63] is going to Boston early in February. She goes by train and will take a little parcel for you.

We are quite thrilled over the prospect of an exhibition next summer.[64] We think the house will be the best place as the vacation will empty the College anyway. When things get ripe we can get the invitations out.

Ewart[65] was up here recently on business. We had lunch with him at the King Edward. Your Uncle Cal may be here in early Feb., but he is not sure as he may have to go to England. That travelling business doesn't appeal to me ecstatically.

We are having a mild spell after zero weather last week. The quicker the winter goes the better I'll like it. However, there has been on the whole an astonishing lack of snow. The Telegram reporter rang me up last week to find out if I thought snow beautiful. I said it is beautiful on trees but hellishly awful in a driveway. She actually put in the comment which had people laughing and telephoning. There are two points of view, perhaps more.

With much love,
Father
(of the Basilian Order).

61 Wilfrid C. James, graduate of Victoria, chairman of the college's Board of Regents (1942–51), then bursar and secretary of the board.

62 John A. Irving (1903–65), professor of ethics and social philosophy and department head at Victoria since 1945. He published many scholarly articles and several books, most notably *Science and Values: Explorations in Philosophy and the Social Sciences* (Toronto: Ryerson, 1952).

63 See the note to 'Rouillard (French)' in the letter to E.K. Brown, 21 October 1949 (p. 445).

64 Of Claire's woodcuts and sketches.

65 His nephew.

TO CLAIRE PRATT

47 Glencairn Ave
Toronto 12, Canada

Friday am. [29 Jan. 1954]

Dear:

Poss[66] just telephoned to say that George Harris[67] passed away yesterday. He had been sick for years as you know, practically bed-ridden, and Lottie's stroke made it hard for her to give him the attention required. Poss doesn't know what Lottie's plans are. I suppose she will stay in Grand Bank where most of her friends are, paying occasional visits to St John's governed of course by her health. That will be her problem for the next few weeks and months. We had been expecting this outcome for a long time

Your Boston snow struck us the day before yesterday – the biggest fall for the year. It snowed for a solid 24 hours, but fortunately we have a man who does the shovelling. He does it for the estate. That is one important advantage over 21 Cortleigh.

I am in the house alone this morning, your mother having gone down to the U.W.C. to attend a meeting.

The Macmillan ms. of English on Newfoundland[68] proceeds apace. I have 200 pages done and there remains only 80 more. The ms. is exceedingly interesting though it needs quite a bit of revision. It is full of 'the tempestuous Atlantic,' 'the brave and gallant heroes,' 'his soul took flight to his immortal rest,' 'and God or Fate executed his eternal vengeance' (on the pirate) etc. He writes as if the early 19th century, but the material is original and at times fascinating.

[ ]

I am having my birthday stag a week from tomorrow (Saturday). It will be much the same gang at the York Club – Knox, McLuhan, Goudge, Corbett et al.

66 His sister Florence.

67 Husband of Pratt's sister Charlotte, Harris (1879–1954), a Grand Bank businessman and graduate of Mount Allison University, was active in Newfoundland politics in the 1920s. He had been a strong supporter of J.R. Smallwood's Confederation campaign in 1947–8.

68 Leo E.F. English (1887–1971), curator of the Newfoundland Museum (1946–60) and amateur historian, published several works on Newfoundland, but Macmillan rejected the book referred to here – *Historic Newfoundland* – as requiring major revision. The Newfoundland Department of Tourism published it in 1955.

After dinner we do nothing but chin, chin, chin till we have exhausted all the stories. I enjoy such an evening and the boys say such stags are the highlights of existence.

I hope your snow storms are over. Boston must be the centre of snow hurricanes. Why I can't imagine.

With much love,
Father

TO CLAIRE PRATT

Wed. a.m. [3 Feb. 1954]

Dearest Chuck:

(Do you remember that was the salutation which Macbeth gave to Lady M. in the letter. No further context implied of course.)

I am alone in the house today, your mother having gone down to Mrs Auger's[69] for lunch.

Cal wrote from St John's on Monday enclosing a letter 60 years old from Mrs Spurgeon just after Spurgeon's[70] death. You remember Jim was called after Spurgeon though he didn't use the name for fear the St John's school boys would laugh [at] it. That was Cluny Macpherson's suggestion – 'For goodness sake, don't have them calling you *Spurge*.'

His news from Newfoundland is not very optimistic. He finds himself very tired when he walks any distance, and I am writing him today giving advice – 'Never fight fatigue. As soon as you feel tired, sit or lie down until recuperated.' Cal has come up to Ottawa not merely to attend the Senate but to get a rest from business. I don't know whether he can make it to Toronto or not. I am having my birthday stag on the 6th and I hope he can come. You know that George Harris died last week and perhaps Floss will go to Nfld early in March to be with Lottie for a time.

---

69 Widow of C.E. Auger. See the note to 'Auger' in the letter to George Herbert Clark, 12 January 1932 (p. 94).

70 Charles H. Spurgeon (1834–92), the celebrated Baptist preacher of the London Tabernacle (England), had been a personal friend of Pratt's father. Pratt's brother Jim had been baptized James Charles Spurgeon.

Then Calvert[71] is down with diphtheria of all troubles. Cal says it is probably the only such case in Nfld, and little Cal has scarlet fever. That in addition to Jim's illness and Minnie's[72] frailty looks like a casualty list of the Pratt tribe. Still Jim seems to be better somewhat and I supppose the anti-toxin can clear up Calvert's ailment.

We are fine here. Mother is wonderful – in tip-top shape and I am getting over the flu though the leg muscles are still weak – not serious however.

Our car has been in the garage nearly all the winter except for brief runs to keep the battery in shape. When I try to start her every few days, the motor sounds like the moan of dying swans.

Brockington[73] sent us a year's pass to the Odeon. We shall try to make more use of it than last year as the Hyland Theatre is an Odeon and only a few blocks away by street car.

Let me know if you are in need of funds for running expenses. They will be remitted pronto.

Love
F.

TO CLAIRE PRATT

47 Glencairn Ave.

[6 Feb. 1954]

Dearest Cayke:

Your two letters came at once.

The proof of the skunks[74] also invaded the house and I actually backed away from them, they were so realistic. The white tails looked like mainsails in a nor-easter storm, but I couldn't make out if that mushroom was moving away from the skunkies or the opposite. Both parties, in any case, diverged. It is really a beautiful job you've done. I am sure that this issue will attract a lot of attention – more than usual.

---

71 Pratt's nephew.

72 James Pratt's wife.

73 Leonard W. Brockington was president of Odeon Theatres.

74 Claire's illustration to be published in *World Friends* magazine. See the letter to Claire Pratt, 20 January 1954 (p. 550).

I told you about the scarf and how Miss Waugh[75] (I think it was) turned around and wondered if I was a flamingo, a peacock or Fred Astaire waltzing down the street. It is so warm and colorful and all the more so because I have been wearing colorless thin nylons up-to-date. They are so anaemic compared to that neck wrap.

Did I tell you that the party we gave to the Fryes was in honor of his invitation to give a series of lectures at Princeton University.[76] The Princeton class of 1932 established a lectureship and Frye is the first to receive an invitation. He is to be away for five months.

The new fellows on the staff in English are Knight, MacLure[77] and Kee, none of whom you know. Kay Coburn is away in the U.S.A. and later is going to England.

Tomorrow is Sunday and we have invited Dick Meech up to dinner. Cal was to come but Dr Norman advised him to go the Western Hospital for a check-up. He has been feeling tired, but he doesn't think that there is any particular trouble that a rest won't fix up. He may remain in Toronto for a week. It is probably a fatigue-aftermath of his operation in Montreal last Summer. It is hard to keep him resting – 'idling' he calls it. I was expecting him to be at my stag tonight in the York Club, but that is now impossible. I telephoned him an hour ago and he was quite cheery, going over a blue-print for a cruiser-yacht as he plans to take a coastal trip this coming Summer.

Well, long may the skunkies flourish their fluffy tails!

Love
Father

TO CLAIRE PRATT

47 Glencairn Ave

Feb. 10, 1954

Dearest Cayke:

Your A magical[?][78] was excellent. I read it through the second time and liked it as much as the pictures which is saying a lot.

---

75 Unidentified.

76 The four lectures which Frye gave in Princeton in March 1954 were published as *The Anatomy of Criticism: Four Essays* (Princeton: Princteon University Press, 1957).

77 Millar MacLure, a recent graduate of the University of Toronto. His later scholarly works include a study of George Chapman and a critical edition of Christopher Marlowe's poems.

78 Something she had written and illustrated.

I have just telephoned Cal and he seems to be improving though it will mean three more weeks before he can get out of the Western. They caught him just in time – he had been working away as if he had no operation last June in Montreal. It takes some time to get over an ailment which keeps one in bed for nearly two months. However, they managed to diagnose the case this time before any permanent damage had been done to the heart. We go in to see him every second day.

Your flamingo scarf is so warm that when even it is around the neck it warms my feet, and helps the mild arthritis in the knees. I didn't know colour could radiate so powerfully or be transferred from one sense to another.

I had my birthday party last Saturday night at the York Club. Ten men of the University College English Department came to it and when I got home at midnight I found another party at Bridge – mother, Mrs Barfit, Mrs Lacey, Mrs. Leslie and Ina. They didn't leave till after one. What a gang! I stayed in the den till they departed, one hour of waiting and I thought I was the late one getting in at 12.

I see you are having jollification down your way.

[ ]

I suppose Mother told you that Karl[79] is in the Regina hospital again – same kind of clot so Rita says. He has had an unfortunate time of it poor chap.

I haven't heard how Calvert and son[80] are getting along recently, but no news is good news. I am writing Lottie today. I don't know just what she will do now.[81] Floss is going down in March to be with her for a while.

Mother, Kathleen Daykin and I are going to the Alumni lecture on Dylan Thomas in a few minutes. The lecturer is Millar MacLure, our new Assist. Professor in English.

The best of everything to you.

Lovingly
Father

79 Karl Whitney, Viola's brother.

80 Cal Pratt's son and grandson. See the letter to Claire Pratt, 3 February 1954 (p. 555).

81 His sister's husband had recently died. (See the note to 'George Harris' in the letter to Claire Pratt, 3 February 1954 [p. 554].)

TO CLAIRE PRATT

47 Glencairn Ave

Feb. 25, 1954.

Dearest Syllabub:

'Economics' is a loveless thing, God wot! How did you get railroaded into that science for editing? What a mess I would have made of it if I had been in your place! I know you would like to get into the literary or artistic field. Perhaps the next book will be in it.

We are looking forward to the visit after Easter very much.[82] The Belleview Hotel seems quite satisfactory. Whatever you do by way of tickets will be agreeable to us. We start with *Carmen*. As this is a holiday for us, get the best things going. But don't start us going before 10 a.m. There are bed and breakfast to be considered and an hour or two meditating Plato-wise through the window.

No, no you must not be out one simolio. It's our treat – that's the original understanding. Don't draw on your reserves.

Cal and Karl are improving.[83] We got a letter from Rita this morning which reports progress.

Your mother's anniversary[84] went off splendiferously. One would think it was Christmas by the way the mantelpieces are littered with cards. I suppose she told you about the wrist-watch with the chain bracelet which does not have to be clasped or unclasped. Chris and Vo Love[85] sent her a plant from Simpson's flower shop.

On Saturday Art Phelps speaks to the U.W. Club[86] and we are putting on a tea at our house afterwards. This means I have to stay home all day preparing sandwiches, soufflés and trifles, with Winnie[87] helping out of course. I am studying cook books now with more concentration than I ever put on Pauline Eschatology,[88] Lord help his humble servant! I need his help considerably. But it will be all over Saturday evening and then I can go to bed.

---

82 He and Viola were planning to visit Claire in Boston.

83 See the letters to Claire Pratt, 3 and 10 February 1954 (pp. 554–5 and 556).

84 Her birthday on 22 February.

85 Christopher Love was an associate professor of English at Victoria College. Vo (short for Viola) was his wife.

86 The University Women's Club.

87 Winnie Fitzpatrick, the Pratts' cleaning lady.

88 St Paul's doctrine of 'last things,' the subject of Pratt's doctoral dissertation in 1917.

In a few minutes I take your mother to Irene Clarke's[89] for lunch. Then she goes to the Granite Club to address 200 dames on poetry for ten minutes.

It's about time now.

Lovingly,
Father

TO CLAIRE PRATT

47 Glencairn Ave.

March 2, 1954

Dear:

This is the second day of March and the month came in like a roaring lion and is still roaring with two inches of snow. But the next month is April anyway.

I am staying in this morning doing correspondence and answering telephones for your mother who has gone down to the Wesley Buildings. Winnie has just come and is sweeping the snow from the front door and the walk.

I suppose your mother told you about the shindig we put on for Art and Lal.[90] There were about fifty in all Saturday afternoon, and on Sunday the four of us had midday dinner at the University Women's Club.

I get down to the College (to Kathleen's office) every day and in the afternoon I run over to see Cal. He is improving gradually though I think it will be another three weeks before they allow him to leave the Western. He is in fine spirits and not having any distress.

Lottie managed to write a letter to Poss[91] last week. She is in her house with her nurse and feeling the shock of George's passing very much. It was a real shock though partly expected. Mary (Calvert's wife) is not too well. It is likely she may have to go to Boston soon for an examination. I don't think the St John's doctors are too clever at diagnosis. They send many of their patients to Montreal and Boston for clinical treatment.

Art Moore is not yet back at Victoria. It is over a month now. Every spring he comes close to collapse through overwork.

---

89 Wife of William Henry Clarke.

90 Arthur Phelps had delivered a talk at the University Women's Club. See the letter to Claire Pratt, 25 February (p. 558).

91 Florence Pratt.

It will soon be your birthday and we were wondering what we would send which would not have you go to the Customs House for appraisal and clearance. You know the way I can cut that Gordian knot. I am sharpening my scissors already, bless your sweet heart!

Your stories[92] are grand. We read them together and you are getting a good deal of acclaim from the readers. The clarity and simplicity of those Bible episodes are refreshing. It seems to me that between the Press, and art, and writing you don't have much reserve time, but make sure of your sleep and cat-naps.

With much love,
Father

TO CLAIRE PRATT

47 Glencairn Ave.

March 31, 1954

Dearest Claire:

I shall begin by referring to your questions and points in your newsy 6-page letter this morning.

(1) Re Stratford. There was some confusion at first in the ads. The final line up is (a) *Measure for Measure*, (b) *The Taming of the Shrew*, and (c) *Oedipus Rex*. Not a very exciting prospect especially since Guiness[93] isn't coming. I think James Mason[94] is on the cards. And I don't like *Measure for Measure*; never did. It was Knox's[95] decision to out it on the University curriculum. However, I shall try to get tickets and accommodation from an agency.

(2) Yes, I remember Uncle Harry Archibald,[96] a looney if there ever was one. He slept in the next bedroom to mine at the Methodist College Home and used to snore himself hoarse – in fact so hoarse that Holloway (our Principal)[97]

---

92 Claire had written and illustrated some Bible stories for a special issue of Viola's *World Friends*.

93 Alec Guiness had played the title role in Shakespeare's *Richard III* during the first season of the Stratford Shakespeare Festival in 1953.

94 James Mason (1909–84), the British-born film star, played the title role in the Stratford Festival's production of *Oedipus Rex* in 1954.

95 R.S. Knox.

96 Archibald (1883–1969), graduate of McGill, was a businessman in Harbour Grace, Newfoundland, and later its mayor. He was the uncle of Mary, wife of Pratt's nephew Calvert.

97 English-born Robert Holloway (1850–1904), a professional photographer and science aficionado, was principal of the Methodist College from 1874 to 1904. Pratt was his student in 1900–2.

could not make out a word from his laryngeal answers. A kindly disposed fellow though!

(3) When do they expect the baby[98] to reach 8 pounds? You say another two months. Yes, I daresay cannibals grow as fast as that.

(4) No, Chris[99] hasn't bought the car yet. He needs more time to decide. Besides he has to take a Canadian Road test. He drove in England but not here.

(5) That hymn is something to remember – what morbidity.

(6) I hope those books or mss on semantics[100] don't get you down.

(7) The *Titanic*. It is on tonight at 7:30 C.B.C. network. We are having dinner with the Lamberts. R.S.L.[101] is Supervisor of programmes and we'll hear the broadcast on his radio. They are ponying up 100 simolios. I'll let you know when Macmillans collect it for me.

The University of Syracuse broadcast is local I think. The time hasn't yet been determined. I imagine you won't get it in Boston.

(8) Do the 'animals' at the office bark or bite? What a nest! Perhaps Thomas Mann[102] had such things in mind with that glorious and ineffable effusion on a carcass.

Well, there are the eight points. I shall think of some (between the lines) next time I write.

Lovingly,
Father

TO CLAIRE PRATT

47 Glencairn Ave

May 7, 1954

Dear Cakie:

[ ]

---

98 Reference obscure.

99 Christopher Love.

100 A reference to Claire's work as an editor for Harvard University Press.

101 Richard S. Lambert (1894–1981) was supervisor of educational broadcasts for the CBC (1943–59). He was also an adviser on radio to UNESCO.

102 German novelist and critic (1875–1955), author of such celebrated works as *Buddenbrooks*, *The Magic Mountain*, and *Joseph and His Brethren*. The allusion here is unidentified.

Your card came this morning announcing your cup of coffee. We enjoyed the trip[103] very much and the return voyage was all that could be desired. Pash and Muriel[104] met us at the airport and Pash drove us right here. Service *par excellence.*

Next week is going to be very busy for the two of us. I have to address the feminine galaxy of the University Club on the Pleiocene Armageddon.[105] I am trying to find some connection of theme. It suggests Amazons though such a thing of course couldn't be further from my mind. They are like a bevy of turtle doves – at least that's how I imagine them before I hear their cooing.

Cal is here for a few days. He spent a few hours with us last evening and may come up again before he goes to Montreal. He looks much better.

We had a letter from Poss[106] who says Lottie is improving. We don't know how long she will stay in Grand Bank, probably until she can be sure that the nurse will continue her work there.

Love from
Uncle Harry Archibald[107]

TO CLAIRE PRATT

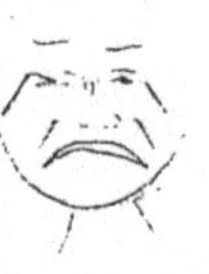

47 Glencairn Ave.
Toronto 12 Ont.

Monday [10 May 1954]

---

103 Their recent visit to Boston. See the letter to Claire Pratt, 25 February 1954 (p. 558).

104 Ida Pashley and (possibly) Muriel Denison.

105 'Pleiocene Armageddon' is the subtitle of Pratt's 'The Great Feud,' on which he was to address the University Women's Club.

106 Florence Pratt had gone to stay with her sister Charlotte following the death of her husband. See the letter to Claire Pratt, 29 January 1954 (p. 553).

107 A joking reference to an uncle to Mary, wife of Calvert Pratt Jr. (See the note to 'Uncle Harry Archibald' in the letter to Claire Pratt, 31 March 1954 [p. 560].)

Dearest Cayke:

You may wonder why the above hieroglyphics[108] should appear in this letter. Well, here's the explanation.

You said in your telephone message yesterday that I shouldn't become so money-conscious. – Lor' help me. I said I had a surplus of fifty-cent pieces around the place and I pitched one at your mother. It hit her, and she retaliated by taking it and biting it so hard that it split a tooth. Then she took the ruptured coin and fired it at a couple of starlings in sheer vexation. No (2) is an attempt to show how she looked when the episode was over – an expression one-half homicidal, one-half suicidal. No (1) is myself deeply penitential, my ears out, my left eye glued over against the nose, my mouth drawn down like a moustache trying to appear villainous but in *deep* remorse over the loss of the coin. You'll have to come back to set things right because I went into a deep huff, refusing to dry the dishes and so on.

Touching the matter of the hospitalization,[109] don't for a moment think of anything but a private room with all comfortable accessories. Uncle Cal adds his own pressure to this urgency.

By the way he had a good night last night. Dr Norman took us out to the Lambton Golf Club for dinner and such a dinner, such a relaxation! Cal and I took sirloin steak and mushrooms. Egg-plant,[110] a vicious vegetable I indignantly rejected and asked for a double heap of mushrooms. So did Cal. But do you know what happened? Cal was continually directing my attention to things outside the window, notably a rabbit on the lawn. I didn't realize that all the time he was diverting my interest he was helping himself to my mushrooms though he had a prodigious supply himself. There was a near fight over it. However, all quarrelsome feelings were ended when I discovered later that the fun did him so much good and your mother laughed herself almost into hysterics.

So much for the present.

Love,
Father as lazy as ever

God bless you.

---

108 A reference to the two crude drawings at the head of the letter of (more or less) human faces, which have been numbered 1 and 2.

109 Claire had decided to enter hospital in New York later that year for treatment on her spine, still affected by the legacy of the severe osteomyelitis.

110 One of Claire's favourites.

TO JOHN SUTHERLAND

47 Glencairn Ave.
Toronto, Ont.

May 12, 1954

Dear John:

I am glad you got the honorarium[111] and I'll do my best to collect data for you. But two things have gone beyond recall. I have no copy of *Demonology* or *Rachel.*[112] The latter is no good anyway. I think I can secure *Clay* (which was never published – simply typed). I think it is pretty stuffy. *Pauline Eschatology*[113] is available somewhere and contains much of the material of Demonology. I shall send you the book soon. As it was an academic exercise, I was under imaginative restraint – you know the nature of doctorates.

Best regards to yourself
and Audrey.[114]
Ned.

TO CLAIRE PRATT

47 Glencairn Ave.
Toronto 12 Ont.

May 14, 1954

Dearest:

Your cherished letter came just now and as mother is down at the Wesley Buildings I thought I'd write first. How we enjoyed our trip to Boston to see you and your friends! We plan from time to time to take that trip.

111 Funding from the Humanities Research Council to support research for the study that would be published as *The Poetry of E.J. Pratt: A New Interpretation* (Toronto: Ryerson, 1956).

112 'The Demonology of the New Testament in Its Relation to Earlier Developments, and to the Mind of Christ,' Pratt's MA thesis (1912). Neither it nor the early, privately printed, *Rachel* had 'gone beyond recall.' Typescripts of both are in the Pratt archives at Victoria College.

113 Pratt's PhD thesis (1917).

114 The former Audrey Aikman, Sutherland's wife.

Keep that toaster. If it smokes and burns – that's all right with me. You know that I like bread brown with its autumnal tints.

Too bad it rained when your clothes were hanging out. Don't put them on wet.

Last night we went to the annual dinner of the Toronto Branch of the C.A.A. Bill Deacon gave the valedictory address covering forty years of editorial experience. Mazo de la Roche gave the vote of thanks. After that we went to the Deacons' (darn this pen) for a party which lasted till midnight.

The broadcast (15 minutes on Wednesday night) came off all right. Dr Short of our church wrote a lovely letter about the 'Old Eagle' which ended the programme.

Margaret Lacey[115] telephoned to get your address. She is writing you.

With the greatest of love,
Father fingering with
a scrawly pen instead
of a typewriter

TO CLAIRE PRATT

47 Glencairn Ave.
Toronto

May 17, 1954

Dearest Claire:

[ ]

We are getting along as usual. Your mother and her friend went out yesterday (Sunday) to a dinner group – about 15 miles from here. I remained in all day browsing and drowsing as always. John Sutherland of the *Northern Review* (Montreal) has been given a fellowship from the Humanities Research Council to bring out a book on poor me by the end of 1954.[116] He has written for an account of Pauline Eschatology as a background. The world, flesh and the devil, body, soul, spirit, the last Judgment, the division of the goats from the sheep. I say to myself '*Poor fish.*' I'd rather be that than a goat anytime.

Love
Father

---

115 Daughter of Alexander Lacey of the French Department at Victoria College, she had been a close friend of Claire from childhood.

116 The book, *The Poetry of E.J. Pratt: A New Interpretation*, was published by Ryerson in 1956.

TO JOHN SUTHERLAND

47 Glencairn Ave.
Toronto 12, ON.

May 21, 1954

Dear John:

Excuse this delay but I have been trying to locate magazines, etc. which are hard to find on account of our change of residence from 21 Cortleigh Blvd to the above.

However, I managed to get a copy of *Pauline Eschatology* and *Clay*. I could not get hold of the M.A. thesis on Demonology but much of that material was incorporated in P. Eschatology.[117] I do not list P.E. in the volumes published as I don't care much for it since the subject was not of my choosing and I did not feel free to handle it in my own way, there being so many academic restrictions attached to it. Clay, likewise, was not published. I liked it when I wrote it but later I thought it was very loose in construction. The only parts I still regard as passable are the lyrics interspersed – at least some of them. Two or three were included in *Newfoundland Verse*. The others remain unpublished. The only significance the poem (so-called) possesses is that it did represent a lot of philosophical speculation current at the time in the University of Toronto. Much of it is abstract and wooden as I see it now. It was mainly an account of the difference between Intuitionalism and Rationalism.

Rachel is gone beyond recovery. It was written in a flat Wordsworthian (Michael) style[118] and printed privately by my friends in New York. It was a story of a mother (Rachel) who lost her son at sea and has a Newfoundland background. One section of it – the concluding part – is in Nfld Verse as a *fragment*. Similarly the fragment from *Clay* is printed in the same volume.

I didn't find my characteristic vein till *The Witches' Brew* which, by the way, is on the University of Toronto curriculum (English Department) this year. I never believed it would reach that distinction and I am still a bit nervous about its subject matter. Norrie Frye was strong for it which counts a lot with me. I would have preferred the *Cachalot*, but I had nothing to do with the selection, now being Emeritus.

117 His doctoral dissertation, published by Ryerson in 1917.
118 On the model of Wordsworth's 'Michael: A Pastoral Poem' (1800).

The seance you refer to was the result of a request from the widow of a good friend who died at St Catharines, Ont., many years ago.[119] I should prefer not to have it mentioned as there was so much doubt about its authenticity, and I didn't follow up the 'meetings.'

I have about a dozen short poems unpublished in book form, some of which you have seen. I haven't written much because of eye-strain which I referred to some time ago. It makes reading and writing difficult. I may get down to it again if the condition improves.

The 'Titanic' seems to be most acceptable today. It has been on twice in Poems for Senior Students in Ontario High Schools, and twice on the air, first in Ontario; then last week dramatized by the C.B.C. over the Canadian network. The Great Feud is also in demand for speeches, etc.

I can't locate those magazines. E.K. Brown wrote a lot on the various volumes in the spring numbers of the U. of Toronto Quarterly and L.A. MacKay wrote a long review in the Canadian Forum about ten years ago. The Manchester Guardian wrote a lengthy review of the *Roosevelt and the Antinoe* about the time of its publication. C.P. Scott wrote it – 21 May 1954 heartening review.

By the way did I tell you that your N.R. issue[120] came in for more enthusiastic accounts given personally to me, commenting upon the strength and maturity of your style. There is nothing like it in Canada for incisiveness and originality, it was claimed. This brings me to the last point of your letter – the relation between Methodism and Calvinism.

As you know my father was a Methodist minister, born in England, came to Nfld as a probationer staying there till his death. My mother was the daughter of a sea-captain and the ancestry away back was English.

Have you access to the two big volumes called *The Book of Newfoundland*[121] edited by Premier Smallwood? In the Second Volume there are two articles, one on Methodist evangelism in Nfld. and one on the Presbyterians. If you can't find this volume in Montreal I shall send my copy to you.

Calvinism and Predestination didn't take much root in the island. Methodism with its salvation *free to all* flourished. Predestination from Eternity was displaced by the doctrine of Repentance which remitted all sins through faith in Christ. And if a man relapsed into sin the same route to Salvation was still

119 Pratt had attended several spiritualist seances in 1928 at the invitation of Jenny O'Hara Pincock. (See *EJP: MY*, 46–50.) At the time he was quite convinced of their 'authenticity,' and arranged for other such sessions at his own house in Toronto.

120 A reference to the special Pratt number of *Northern Review* in 1952.

121 Joseph R. Smallwood, editor (St John's: Newfoundland Book Publishers, 1937).

open through Repentance. The Methodists had their affinity with the milder Arminianism,[122] though I must say that the preaching was about as drastic as the Calvinistic, the unrepentant sinners finding their way to the bottomless pit where the fires burned just as fiercely, and the repentant ones could look forward to the joys of Heaven. Free Will was a basic fact. Let me know if you can find the second volume, the Methodist argument written by Rev. Levi Curtis,[123] the Presbyterian by Dr Fraser.[124]

Enough for now
Ned.

Excuse the scribble

TO CLAIRE PRATT

47 Glencairn Ave.
Toronto 12 Ont.

May 22, 1954

Dear:

These are the last of the one dollar Simolios though mother has another one which will be sent in the next letter. Thank heaven I am rid of the alien notes. The fervor of this expression springs from the long look of the grocers and butchers which I have mentioned already.

Yesterday there arrived from Jack Kent Cooke a letter expressing gratitude for my help with Saturday Night. I had done nothing but leave my name on the editorial board of three. I hadn't written a word for the paper and I wanted to get off. Instead of that he retained it and sent me a cheque for $600.00 (semi-annual). I was bowled over. I shall pass over from my current account that $400.00 which takes care of the September premium which Miss Elizabeth MacKay (née) so

---

122 Named after Jacobus Arminius (1560–1609), a Dutch religious reformer, Arminianism emphasized free will in opposition to the extreme determinism of Calvinism's doctrine of predestination.

123 Curtis (1858–1942) was a prominent Methodist (later United Church) clergyman, for many years superintendent of schools in Newfoundland

124 N.S. Fraser (1864–1953) was a St John's physician who at various times held most of the major posts in medical administration in Newfoundland. The article in *The Book of Newfoundland* on the Presbyterian Church in Newfoundland was co-written by N.S. Fraser and Robert A. Templeton.

fondly dangles before her roving eyes. I shall simply transfer the premium from my Current to your Savings.

Another nice thing happened yesterday. The B.B.C. asked the C.B.C. for a repetition of my broadcast (poems) and they are paying extra for it. It must have taken on in spite of some elongated S's which made me a bit nervous, though it appears the listeners were not conscious of the siren notes. I thought the reproduction would sound like a dozen fire-reels outside the building and happily it didn't.

We are spending May 4th at York Downs with the Phelpses, Dalys[125] and perhaps with others. Dinner at 7. We are not playing golf so there will be no dubbing or fanning.

Love,
Father.

By the way, has Uncle Harry Archibald[126] left for Nfld, being fed up with the Boston brand of humour?

TO CLAIRE PRATT

47 Glencairn Ave.
Toronto 12 Ont

May 23, 1954

Dearest artist, editor, entertainer, etc.

Your letter took just two days to get here – May 19 to 21 – isn't that nice?

Planets for Pearls.[127] There couldn't be a more beautiful substitute, if there had to be a substitute in that shell picture. There is always some subjectivity in art anyway.

About the car – I hope you get a new one because no matter how good a 'second' is there is bound to be some undesirable quality even if it is a matter of mileage.

---

125 Roland O. and Marion Daly. A graduate of the University of Toronto, Daly was a Toronto lawyer. He and Pratt were fellow members of the York Downs Golf Club and had been friends since their undergraduate days.

126 See the note to 'Uncle Harry Archibald; in the letter to Claire Pratt, 31 March 1954 (p. 560).

127 The phrase describes an etching by Claire of an oyster shell with a pearl in the centre, the whole having, to quote her, 'a rather cosmic ambience' (letter to David G. Pitt, 3 August 1987).

You told us that you wanted a smaller car as it increases parking facility and other things. Would your service man give sound disinterested advice? He ought to know.

We found our Chev (power drive) splendid and Chris says it runs like a charm but it really was too big for the garage at 47.[128] It is a satisfaction not to be bothered with it now we have the subway which takes us to Bloor in 7 minutes. In fact as soon as I get on the train I close my eyes for a 'quiet doze' and immediately I see Bloor St. on the walls. It is a drowsy ride, quite nerve-soothing. Another point. Do you intend to get one before you come up in August?

We are spending May 24 at York Downs. I think I mentioned that pleasant and sublime fact. The Dalys[129] are coming and perhaps Clare Hincks if he feels better. He is in one of his periodic and blackest depressions. He has always had them – a kind of manic-depressive condition, which makes him averse to activity or social gathering. This one has lasted longer than usual, but when he is well he is on top of the world.

I am now writing this note to the accompaniment of one of your tobacco brands (Drum). It fills the house with fragrance different from the attar of roses if you know the significance whereof I speak.

This is Sunday and we are lazing around the place. The temperature is 70° and it is sunny – a perfect May day. I have just finished breakfast consisting of orange juice, bacon and egg, two slices of brown toast and marmalade, one glass of skim milk, and all washed down with coffee stiffened by Nescafé, which makes me ready to fight the world, flesh, the devil and (if you will pardon the addition) yourself. No one has been spanked yet in the house – a highly exceptional omission.

I think it is time to stop just here.

Lovingly,
Father

TO CLAIRE PRATT

47 Glencairn Ave
Toronto 12 Ont.

Thursday [27 May 1954]

128 Glencairn Avenue.

129 Roland O. and Marion Daly.

Dearest Cayke:

I sent off a card last night to state that the W.M.S.[130] had begun their meetings and the big World Friends was exhibited.

Mrs MacLean[131] gave an account of the Special Features of the magazine and she said that among the best she had seen in a long time were the splendid Biblical stories from that 'talented Claire Pratt.'[132] The comment met with applause from the audience – about a few dozen or so. I felt like getting up and shouting 'Sennacherib'[133] but as most of them wouldn't know their bibles despite their missionary training (ha, ha!) I desisted.

I am now at the office answering letters and doing odd jobs. Your mother has gone home and I'll follow in an hour or so. She goes to Hamilton tomorrow to attend a lunch and give an address, staying over night to attend a meeting of the University W. Club,[134] so I shall be alone.

Sometime toward the end of June she goes to Quebec as a Club representative spending three or four days and I may run down to Boston to see you and to fill in that interval. If I go, I shall travel by train, stay over at the Belleview and see a few shows, attend a few dinners with you and discuss the nature of the universe and such minor problems so easy of solution. It would be grand just to see you and perhaps nail up a shelf or two just to show you how straight I can drive a nail.

I haven't played any golf yet mainly because the car is sold and Malcolm Wallace has given the game up altogether. He gets so vexed at his bad drives and high (terrifically high) scores that his wife cannot stand his profanity when he reaches home. I told him to take a good nap when he gets home before he talks golf. If I felt like that after a poor game I'd hide myself in a cow-shed and moo my despondency off.

Last week we had dinner at the Club with the Dalys and the Phelpses – I think I told you – and we told all the stories we could remember. The place is wonderful under the trees. This I guess I never mentioned to you, *or did I?*[135]

Next week will be easier as the Boards[136] (the two of them) will have finished their business transactions.

Lovingly,
Father

---

130 Women's Missionary Society.

131 Unidentified.

132 See the note to 'Your stories' in the letter to Claire Pratt, 2 March 1954 (p. 560).

133 King of Assyria who defeated Hezekiah, King of Judah, and laid seige to Jerusalem (2 Kings 18.7–19.37).

134 University Women's Club.

135 In fact, he had mentioned this dinner engagement repeatedly. (See the letters to Claire Pratt of 22 and 23 May 1954 [pp. 569 and 570].

136 Church boards of which Viola was a lay member.

TO CLAIRE PRATT

47 Glencairn Ave
Toronto Ont.

Sunday am. [30 May 1954]

Dearest Claire:

Your newsy letter came yesterday and I am answering it now even though I may give you a ring about 5 p.m. today – just for a chat.

Julia's book[137] certainly has a characteristic title. She must eat, drink and cough murder. '*Made for Murder*' undoubtedly will catch the eye of the blasé wayfaring man looking for something to pass the railroad time. It will be difficult for her to surpass the bloody nature of that title for her next. Perhaps 'Damned ye shall be' or 'Give him another shot in the throat, Jock' might serve.

That Belarussian project[138] looks awful. Why don't they give you something exciting?

What a visitor, just as you were sitting down to dinner! Why didn't you hand her some of that dandelion stuff to put her to sleep. If it is on its way to being chloroform you might patent the vile stuff and sell it to hospitals and anaesthetists. There's money in that sort of thing if you knew how to work it. Make certain it is all disposed of by the time we get down to Allston[139] or we'll never get back except on stretchers. I thought I went the limit years ago when I made that fermented grape juice but you have out-played me at my special game. If that widow doesn't use it up, send the rest to Alice.

Mother came back from Hamilton last night after a pleasant and successful trip. X X X Oh, you have just rung up and told us about your car, the Plymouth. We are glad you have a new one because the second class ones do sometimes have defects.

I am sending you the last of the single dollars. How glad I am to get rid of these things.

[ ]

It is quite likely that I shall spend that week-end with you when Mother goes to Quebec. I shall let you know the exact dates later on.

---

137 Julia McGrew had written the murder mystery *Made for Murder* (New York: Rhinehart & Company, 1954) with Caroline Fenn under the pseudonym Fenn McGrew.

138 In 1954, Belarus was part of the USSR. The reference is to an editorial job that Claire had been given at Harvard University Press.

139 The Boston suburb where Claire was now living.

Well, sweet sleep over

that dandelion.
Father

TO CLAIRE PRATT

47 Glencairn Ave.
Toronto 12, Ont.

Wednesday [9 June 1954]

Dear Cakie:

It was so pleasant to hear that warbling of the hermit thrush last night. It was a coincidence that your mother was just raising the receiver to call when you called.

The arrangements[140] are fine. You do what you like so long as you don't have too much bother mucking around. The Bushes[141] and the Havelocks[142] are O.K. with us for one evening; but I should like to have at least two dinners at the Bellevue as I stated in my last letter. I'll bring along enough 'Kale'[143] to cover all expenses and a bit left over for you for Plymouth gas, etc. etc.

If there is anything you would like me to take with me let me know. I am bringing a painting of Dr A.P. Coleman's[144] for you – a lovely picture of Marjorie Pickthall's house. I would bring her desk[145] but it is four feet high and I would have to carry it on my slender shoulders – so that's out of the question. It seemed to weigh a ton when we carried it into the house that day.

Tomorrow afternoon I go to the C.B.C. to have a recorded interview with Ron Hambleton who is also having interviews with Healey Willan and Ernest MacMillan. The records are to be placed in the National Library of Ottawa. My

---

140 For his proposed visit to Boston while Viola was in Quebec.

141 Douglas Bush and his wife.

142 Eric A. Havelock, a former member of the English Department at Victoria College, had moved to Harvard University in the 1940s.

143 Paper money.

144 Arthur P. Coleman (1865–1939), a graduate of Victoria College, and for many years professor of natural history and geology there. He was a brother of Helena Coleman (1860–1953), who published several books of verse between 1906 and 1937. Crippled by polio, she and her brother acted in loco parentis for Marjorie Pickthall. (See the note to 'Majorie Pickthall ' in the letter to Duncan Campbell Scott, 18 January 1918 [p. 10].)

145 Helena Coleman had inherited Pickthall's desk on her death in 1922. When Coleman died in 1953, she left the desk to Claire Pratt, who later donated it to the Edith and Lorne Pierce Canadiana collection in Queen's University Library.

interview is already done and I think I served up a lot of eyewash about my early days and so on.[146]

Yesterday I spent most of the morning, getting clothes out of the cupboards, putting them up on the line, and then spraying them with flytox. You mustn't, however, get the notion that your mother didn't have a hand in the business. She did – but I did the most work, at least so it seemed to me. There is to be another day at it. Would it were over!

Now I go down to the Bellevue by taxi when I get in, so you can get in touch with me in the afternoon.

Love,
Father, soon on his way to
Boston

TO CLAIRE PRATT

47 Glencairn Ave
Toronto 12, Ont. Canada

4 p.m. in the shade of the maples,
writing on this pad which is
supported by a board.
Temperature 88° with the promise
of cooler tomorrow!!
So help me!! [11 June 1954]

Dear:

We are indeed having a run of hot weather, 85° and the coolest place is at 47 with a breeze. Mother is inside reading the Star[147] having come back from a

146 Following preliminary interviews (see the letter to Claire Pratt, 2 June [*EJP: Web*]), a written outline had been prepared for the interview to be broadcast as part of the series *An Experience of Life* (22 January 1955). His remark about 'serv[ing] up a lot of eyewash' was not intended to be taken seriously. Ronald Hambleton wrote: 'Every word broadcast on the CBC had to be written out beforehand, which meant that he and I had to meet several times to work out the script, and only after it satisfied both of us … did we sit in front of a microphone … to record it … He was a serious collaborator at every step and didn't let me fudge anything he told me in our preliminary discussions' (letter to David G. Pitt, 14 November 1988). The text of the broadcast interview appears in *EJP: OHLP*, 41–7.

147 *Toronto Daily Star.*

futile effort to negotiate a building for the U.W. Club.[148] Bob Fennell wanted $90,000 for his house, which would have to be enlarged in any case.

Tonight we go down to the Royal York to join a party which the Bannermans[149] are giving in connection with the Trade Fair.

We phoned Pash[150] yesterday to see if she and Marion[151] would be going through Boston on their trip which will begin early next week. Pash said if they go through Boston she will take a carpet for you, so you will not have to buy one. We are going also to suggest that she take along that little folding table. It depends of course upon the car space. We hope she can do it, as the table is most convenient.

I am bringing Dr Coleman's picture of Marjorie Pickthall's house. It will go into my suitcase all right.

This morning we went to the funeral of Mina Brown.[152] She had been sick for several months. It was sad to see Walter looking so feeble and strained. Their son MacRae and his wife, and the sister were there. The burial is taking place at Lakefield, the home of the Browns. Walter, nevertheless, is better than he was two years ago. He can talk now in sentences whereas [at] first he had to pause between words. He is also hearing better.

Excuse this incredible penmanship: the board is so shaky, and I am writing with a 39 cent pen.

Hurrah for next Friday afternoon – Can you make this out?

Lovingly,
Father in the shade

The interview yesterday went across tolerably well I think. The CBC is satisfied.

---

148 University Women's Club. Eventually, the building at 162 St George Street was extended.

149 Glen Bannerman was a former student of Pratt who worked in advertising in Toronto and later in the federal government.

150 Ida Pashley.

151 Marion Whytall.

152 The wife of Walter T. Brown. He had had a stroke and died later that year. (See the note to 'Brown' in the letter to Pelham Edgar, 15 August 1940 [p. 195].)

TO CLAIRE PRATT

Thursday [24 June 1954]

47 Glencairn Ave.
Toronto 12 Ont.

Dearest:

We telephoned last night just to tell you that I got in all right without any roomette cramps.

Now I am down at the office cleaning up some correspondence. Tonight we are going down to the Art Club to meet 'celebrities.' I asked Vida Peene[153] who they were and she said it was a secret which couldn't be revealed – probably the Stratford group – at least that's my guess.

Mother is down at the Missionary Board all day – the regular June meeting – a bore in my opinion.

I am bringing home two volumes of *Osler's Life* for her to gather her material.[154] The Banting account was most dramatic as you may imagine and she has it half done. Osler will be interesting of course, but Penfield, though he is a great neuro-surgeon, will be more difficult as the stuff is so technical.

It was most delightful to be with you for four days. It was one of the happiest short holidays I ever had. I suppose you have your fan by now. The weather in Toronto was only 4° less than Boston and today it is slightly over 80°. Make certain you get a portable and easily handled fan so you can turn it on the chesterfield when you are taking your siesta.

Is your hand getting better? I hope it isn't giving you any trouble.

So you are going by car and boat to Nantucket. I trust everything will be smooth and convenient in spite of the 4th of July. Say 'hello' to Melville and Moby Dick for me. I think there is a jaw bone of a cachalot in one room of the museum, and a presentation of Melville's photograph (by his daughter) in another room. If you find conditions satisfactory, paint or draw one tooth and I'll compare it with the one I have when you come up. It may not be as beautiful as

153 Hamilton-born Vida Peene (1898–1978) was a graduate of the University of Toronto and the Ontario College of Art, and a 'practical patron' of the arts in Canada, especially the visual and performing arts. She was director of the National Ballet of Canada (1955–8), a member of the Canadia Council (1957–61), president of the Dominion Drama Festival (1962–4), and director of the Canadian Music Centre (1964–70). She was awarded the Order of Canada in 1970.

154 Viola was writing a book on three celebrated Canadian physicians. The book, *Famous Doctors: Canadian Portraits*, was published by Clarke Irwin & Company in 1956.

your shell, but a very dramatic subject. Just imagine thirty-six of them getting around a whaleboat in a fight.

My best respects to all the friends you introduced me to and my love to you.

Father

TO CLAIRE PRATT

47 Glencairn Ave.
Toronto 12 Ont.

Sunday [27 June 1954]

Dearie:

We have just finished 'brunch,' the result of my late Sunday morning getting up, and partly the result of an anticipated big dinner this evening at the McLuhan's 8 p.m. at the Chaumière on Charles St. East.

The enclosed needs an explanation. I thought I had put all my American money in a box on my return, when yesterday I discovered that this bill had been concealed in my key folder (purse) in my right pocket. For several days I wondered what made that pocket so warm. Was it a burning match? Or the sun's rays shining on my right side, for the temperature was 92°, almost equal to that of the home of the bean and the cod? No, it was indeed a twentier wedged in between the house key and the office key. I was beginning to speculate upon the nature of spontaneous conflagration and thought I had made a scientific discovery of the first magnitude. Well, here it is – sufficient, I hope, to defray most of the expenses of Nantucket.

By now you will be at Rye Beach.[155] Give my warmest regards to the girls despite the fact that you will have returned by the time you receive this letter. What a paradox!

Today is sunny and cool – about 70 compared with yesterday's 84. Our church is closed up for the summer. A disastrous disappointment to me naturally, as my piety suffers when I don't get my regular doses of clerical intonations, etc. etc. etc. But still, I shall recover I guess.

I have resumed my dish-washing and drying and hanging out clothes. I am told on the highest feminine authority that my housekeeping is 99% perfect.

---

155 In nearby New Hampshire.

Winnie does the other work Tuesday while your mother writes the life of Banting. It's a dog's life to be sure.

Brockington has at last consented to make a ten-minute speech at the World Congress in Toronto of the Mental Health Movement in August. I have to arrange for dinners and lunches and offer grace. It will be the third week. I have tickets for the Stratford Festival for you and others on Wednesday the 11th and I am planning for the shade of the elms at York Downs for you and your friends anytime during the whole month. The meals will be almost as good as the Statler's.

Well, use up this enclosure for your convenience and comfort.

Much love,
Father

TO CLAIRE PRATT

47 Glencairn Ave.
Toronto 12, Ont.

July 1, 1954

Dearest Claire:

We got back from Stratford yesterday. The Clarkes (Bill and Irene) took us as guests.

We saw *Measure for Measure* Monday evening and *The Taming of the Shrew* Tuesday. Most people were agreed that the performances were not up to last year's standard. James Mason as Angelo was a bit disappointing as the audience couldn't hear him when he turned to one side to speak to the actress. He seemed rather distressed by his part and Mavor Moore[156] who acted as the counsellor to Angelo, told me that Mason wasn't up to scratch.

I notice also by this morning's paper that Brooks Atkinson[157] criticized Tyrone Guthrie[158] for making The Taming of the Shrew too much of a burlesque. For

156 James Mavor Moore (1919–2006) was a Canadian a playwright, actor, radio and television producer, as well as a professor at York University (1970–84) and chairman of the Canada Council (1979–83).

157 A celebrated New York critic, mainly of dramatic productions.

158 (1900–71). The British-born theatrical producer who was the first director of the Shakespearean Festival Theatre in Stratford, Ontario. He was knighted in 1961 for outstanding service to the theatre.

instance, one of the actors jumped into the melée with a Shell Flytox as a weapon. Imagine spraying the Chancellor with Flytox. There were many other farcical features. Bob Christie[159] came in as the pedant with an umbrella, stood on the edge of the parapet brandishing it and dancing while the audience felt sure he would fall down the fifteen feet. Indeed, he nearly did so but managed to sit down on the edge to save himself. Then Bob, nose now a fiery red – all right, but why eight inches long.

Measure for Measure was better as the Duke and Pompey (the clown) did their parts well. Still people remarked that Mason, however good he might be on film, was no substitute for Guiness of last year. Moreover, the tent was not filled, there being at least 100 seats not taken up.

After the final performance we went to the reception given by Tom Patterson, the originator of the Festival idea.[160] That lasted two hours, and we got back to the Hotel by 2 o'clock. A bit exhausting taking it all in all.

Today is Dominion Day, a general holiday, and we are staying home, listening to Churchill's speech at Ottawa[161] and other speeches on the national event. Churchill naturally was cheered to the echo everywhere he was seen or heard. His humour sent audiences into stitches. Knowing his liking for cigars (10 long ones a day) the audience responded with a gale of laughter when he remarked that he and Ike[162] came together to smoke out their differences. It was delightful.

Last night the (R.O.) Dalys took us out to York Downs for dinner. You have heard of the place no doubt. They picked up Judge Barlow[163] and his wife. We sat under the trees till 10 following a lavish dinner. I had my usual steak and your mother her usual salad (awful diet I *says*). She may write you tomorrow and give you the calorie constituents.

With much love
Father

159 Robert Christie (1913–96), Toronto-born actor and director. After some years on the British stage, he returned to Canada, where he performed in many roles both in 'live' theatre and in radio and television.

160 Harry Thomas (Tom) Patterson (1920–2005) was a British-born Stratford, Ontario, businessman whose initiative and enterprise were the primary impulses behind the inauguration of the Shakespearean Festival at Stratford in 1953.

161 Winston Churchill, visiting the US in June, was invited to Ottawa by Prime Minister St Laurent. He met the federal cabinet, gave a press interview, and addressed the Canadian people during the Dominion Day observances.

162 President Dwight D. Eisenhower.

163 Frederick H. Barlow, educated at the University of Toronto and Osgoode Hall, was a judge of the Supreme Court of Ontario from 1942 to 1961.

TO JOHN SUTHERLAND

47 Glencairn Ave.
Toronto 12, Ont.

July 26, 1954

Dear John:

Thanks for your letter with its kindly references. You may indeed keep the books until you are finished with them. *Verses of the Sea* is a little collection now out of print and I think all of them have been culled from the other books. It was published by Macmillans for a school text. If I can locate a copy I shall send it along. It has an introduction by Sir Charles Roberts, who, strong for archaeological history, couldn't swallow the dinosaur.[164] He ignored the explanatory passage regarding dates, the moon, stegosaur, etc. However, the introduction was kindly and helpful.

The best,
Ned

TO RAYMOND GUSHUE

47 Glencairn Ave.
Toronto 12
Ont. Canada

August 23, 1954

Dear President Gushue:

I think that our good friend Sid over-rated my influence with the moneyed people of Toronto.[165] In fact, the only one he mentioned in that list[166] whom I knew is J.S. McLean. I never met Eaton, or Tory or Taylor and I never exchanged any

164 A reference to 'The Great Feud.'

165 Sidney Smith, president of the University of Toronto, had suggested Pratt to Gushue as a possible Toronto contact for a fund-raising drive being undertaken by Memorial University of Newfoundland of which he was president. He had written Pratt to sound him out.

166 Smith had given Gushue a list of 'moneyed' Torontonians whom he thought Pratt knew and could intercede with. All were presidents and/or directors of major business firms, and

conversation with Edgar Burton. I recently tried out J.S.M. in the interest of the National Health Movement[167] but couldn't get a cent. Besides, Victoria College is in the throes of a campaign for badly needed funds and I imagine that all the tycoons that Sid mentioned will soon be approached.

There is a further consideration. My daughter has to undergo a serious spinal operation in Boston which will necessitate the presence of my wife and myself for at least three months this Fall.[168] If Sid could stand that Luncheon,[169] and I were in Toronto, I should be glad to be present. Otherwise I think that the best procedure would be to write an explanatory letter to the 'prospects' and then on your arrival in Toronto you might get in touch with them.

When it comes to gathering in funds I fear I am a weak reed. My good wishes in any case.

Yours sincerely,
E.J. Pratt

TO CLAIRE PRATT

47 Glencairn Ave.
Toronto 12

Friday [8 Oct. 1954]
11 a.m. just 1 minute
after you phoned

---

included, besides J.S. McLean (see the note to 'J.S. McLean' in the letter to Claire Pratt, 15 September 1953 [p. 538]), John David Eaton (president of the T. Eaton Company), J.S.D. Tory (a prominent Toronto lawyer), E.P. Taylor (president of Argus Corporation), and Edgar Burton (president of Simpsons Limited).

167 [*sic*]. The National *Mental* Health Association.

168 Claire was living in Boston, but her surgery was to be performed in New York. Pratt may have anticipated a prolonged stay with her there, but his one visit was limited to three days. Viola spent several months with Claire, as later letters indicate.

169 Gushue had suggested to Pratt 'a luncheon arranged through you' at which 'the invitees' would be primed and pumped. There is no evidence that Pratt attended such a luncheon. Gushue subsequently wrote (16 September 1954) to thank him for the 'frank way' in which he had replied.

Dearie:

[ ] Both of us will go to New York either together or separately later on, depending on circumstances.[170]

Well, the summer is about over now and our York Downs annual dinner next Monday (Thanksgiving) will close the dining room. I may go out to the dinner and bring in my clubs for the year. Most of my friends have left the Club, retired, or in exchange for another such as Lambton[171] and I think that, like Malcolm Wallace, I'll just become a non-playing member but reserving the rights of entertainment at dinner. Malcolm wants me to take up bowling and curling with him. I may do so but it will be a vast difference just watching a curling stone slide down the rink for a mere piffling sixty feet and surveying a golf ball rising in its trajectory straight towards the pin 200 yards away; that is, of course, if a dub doesn't alter the trajectory. I'm optimistic just now.

On Tuesday evening we have Charter Night celebrations.[172] Dinner first then the presentation of prizes. Chancellor Lester Pearson will preside and the speeches will be delivered by the following celebrities in order of executive standing: Art Moore, Hal Bennett, and the punning Archie.[173] You'll be hearing from us again soon. Mother will write tomorrow.

Excuse penmanship as I am writing with a 39 cent pencil-pen.

Love,
Father

TO DESMOND PACEY

Oct. 20, '54

Dear Des:

Many thanks for your monograph which reached me yesterday. You were most magnanimous in your paragraph on my work[174] and I also appreciate your criticism wherever it appears.

---

170 Claire was to enter hospital in New York for surgery and treatment on her spine.

171 Lambton Golf Club.

172 Marking the anniversary of the establishment of Victoria College.

173 Arthur Moore was the current president of Victoria College (1950–70), and Harold Bennett was his predecessor (1949–50); F. Archibald Hare was a member of the French Department.

174 'English-Canadian Poetry, 1944–54,' *Culture* 15 (1954): 258.

The whole article is well-balanced, discriminating, and incisively written. I am glad you gave young Reaney[175] a 'leg-up' because there's talent in that fellow. I think he beats the Montreal group as he is not so warped by prejudice. He hasn't their stridency – that 'you must listen to me' sort of thing.

Personally, I haven't written anything worthwhile since the 'Spike' two years ago, mainly because my right eye has played out and is under constant treatment by an oculist. I find it difficult to read.

The College has given me a room to hang my coat and hat up, so to speak. It is nice to be near students even if I don't lecture now. How Anno Domini catches up with one but the inevitable must be accepted with grace.

Incidentally I have learned to realize the difference between a poem written for radio and one meant for publication. You rightly refer to 'They Are Returning' as journalism. It is just that: when I saw it in print I knew that radio success is a different matter from that which attends publication in book form. I see how facile it looks.

Excuse illegibility in this letter of appreciation.

Kindest regards to wife.

Yours warmly,
Ned Pratt

TO CLAIRE PRATT

47 Glencairn Ave.
Toronto 12

Sunday [24 Oct. 1954]

Dearie:

We just got your telephone conversation with your statement that you wouldn't be in the cast till next Tuesday or Wednesday. It was good to hear your voice as always.

---

175 James Reaney (1926–2008), an English professor at the University of Western Ontario, had won the Governor General's Medal for poetry with his first book, *The Red Heart* (Toronto: McClelland & Stewart, 1949). He went on to publish many works of drama and poetry, winning a second Governor General's Award in 1958 for *A Suit of Nettles* (Toronto: Macmillan) and a third in 1962 for the poetry volume *Twelve Letters to a Small Town* (Toronto: Ryerson) and his first book of plays, *The Kildeer and Other Plays* (Toronto: Macmillan).

Cal just phoned. He is on his way back to Montreal, Ottawa and parts east. Now mother is phoning Aunt Nellie for a chat. And Edith Wilkinson[176] phoned to say that she is picking us up at the Rosedale stop on the subway to go to the Minklers[177] and from there to the Granite Club for lunch.

The guests are Mr & Mrs C.P. Snow[178] the novelists from England. They are in love with Canada – hospitality everywhere. We saw them at a little party at Macmillans. John Gray had all the *Snow* books on the shelves – ten of them. We liked the pair very much. Your mother sat next to Mrs Snow at the U.W. Club[179] lunch and found her delightful.

Last night I went to the Arts & Letters Club to hear Eric Aldwinkle[180] speak on his trip to Russia.[181] Twelve of us were invited. I declined because we knew that we would be shown just what they intended to put on exhibit. Only two went, Aldwinkle and Varley, but Varley took so much of vodka that in Aldwinkle's description Fred was out like a light. What he saw and learned was zero. They always had a couple of interpreters who not only interpreted but took photographs of Eric & Fred at every turn. They had the feeling that all movements were watched and transmitted to the authorities. What they wanted most was to see the inside of the homes of the people. This they were refused. Instead of that they were shown the Kremlin and the museums and public buildings particularly their fine university.

---

176 Wife of Bertie Wilkinson, professor of medieval history at the University of Toronto. Both were British-born.

177 Frederick W. Minkler (1903–70), inspector of schools, later director of education in North York and chairman of the first board of governors of Seneca College of Applied Arts and Technology, Willowdale, Ontario.

178 Charles Percy (later Lord) Snow (1905–80), British scientist and academic, best known for his novel sequence, *Strangers and Brothers*, and his controversial Rede Lecture in 1959, 'The Two Cultures' (later published as *The Two Cultures and the Scientific Revolution*) in which he lamented the gap between science and the humanities. His wife, Pamela Hansford Johnson, was also a novelist, author of *An Impossible Marriage*, *The Unspeakable Skipton*, *Cork Street, Next to the Hatter's*.

179 University Women's Club.

180 Aldwinkle (1909–80), who came to Canada from England in 1922, was a graphic designer, printmaker, painter, illustrator. He had been a war artist with the RCAF and was a designer of medals and seals whose work included the Great Seal of Canada.

181 The trip was sponsored by the Canadian-Soviet Friendship Council, of which Pratt had been an enthusiastic supporter prior to Igor Gouzenko's defection in February 1946. (See the note to 'Conventions' in the letter to William Rose Benét, 13 August 1944 [p. 289].) However, the Cold War was now in full force. Fourteen prominent Canadians – including Pratt – were invited on a cultural exchange, but only six accepted the invitation: Aldwinkle and Varley as well as puppeteer Michelain LeGendre, poet Charles Lemoine, and journalist Pierre St Germain and his wife.

I went to the A. & L. Club with Hume Daykin[182] and Arthur Daly.[183]

The Daykins are taking us to the Symphony on Tuesday night and we are taking them to the York Club for dinner.

We may phone on Wednesday evening. If you can't answer perhaps the nurse will do so for you.

Good luck and love.
Father

TO DESMOND PACEY

Victoria College
Toronto, Ont.

Oct. 29, 1954

Dear Des:

Your kind, exhilarating letter was most welcome.

I shall try to answer your question about *The Great Feud* as fully as I can,[184] if you will forgive the discursiveness since I am just jotting down the impressions as they occur to me.

It is quite true that strength and courage and heroic qualities generally, like rescue attempts with sacrificial effort, have always made the deepest impression on me. Occasionally it would seem that strength and courage are being displayed for their own sake, but I think such is comparatively rare. *The Cachalot* might here be taken for an example and the cat in *The Witches' Brew* though the latter was for me a matter of straight fun or a fantasia to let off steam.

But certainly the launching of the *Roosevelt* boats from the blocks to rescue the British sailors was an effort of will, courage and skill whose absolute purpose was benign. Similarly, the episodes which remain in my memory concerning the *Titanic* are those dealing with Ida Straus, the boy of ten, the Engineers in

---

182 Kathleen and Hume Daykins were friends of the family.

183 Richard Arthur Daly (b. 1886) was a Toronto broker and director of numerous commercial firms, active in community philanthropic and cultural enterprises, brother of Roland O. Daly (see the note to 'the Dalys' in the letter to Claire Pratt, 23 May 1954 [p. 569]).

184 Pacey was writing a book of critical essays on major Canadian poets, including Pratt, and had written to ask him questions about some of his poems. *Ten Canadian Poets* was published in 1958.

the hold, the Band and so forth. Brébeuf stood for heroic faith, however much a Protestant might disagree with the creed.

My own profession of faith was expressed in *The Truant*, a comparatively late poem (which, by the way, Norrie Frye considers the best thing I have done). It is an indictment of absolute power without recognition of moral ends. It was written at the height of the Nazi regime. You were right in your guess reference to [it] in your letter.

Now for *The Great Feud*.

This of course was written after the First World War and before the Second. I have called it a Dream though it might appropriately be termed a nightmare. What might happen in a Second war or a Third, though naturally the A-Bomb and the Hydrogen type were not forming their terrible mushrooms. It is an Armageddon between the inhabitants of the land and those of the sea. It is an attempt to give a picture of some stage in the evolutionary struggle for existence, of how near to extinction a race might come if the instinct of aggression were given absolute rein. I put it away back millions of years before the appearance of man upon the earth. The scene is in Australasia on a 300-mile coast line joining Australia and Malay, one of the most fertile regions of the world and the great nursery for life on land and sea. The fish are represented as half-blindly and dumbly conscious of *hostility*[185] on the part of the earth. In the first place they have lost large numbers through the lure of emigration to unknown regions. Many have adventured on the muddy flats to develop lungs and flippers and feet and have been destroyed. Many have been attacked on the shoreline by beasts of prey; many have been seized by birds and they have become possessed by a desire for revenge, to get back at a foe which, in the natural order of things, is out of reach. The main idea of the Feud crystallizes around a boundary question. Both sides claim possession of the shoreline and some justification is given by the ambiguous nature of the shoreline through the flow and recession of the tides. 'This is mine,' says the sea. 'Some of my nationals are here and have occupied territory.' 'No,' says the land, 'we were here first.' Patriotic feelings are appealed to with equal and fiery insistence. Life for life exacted.

But here is the practical problem. As the land animals have to be united for the conflict against the fish, the carnivores have to refrain from eating flesh until the time came for the attack upon the marines. This meant that the land carnivores had to become vegetarians in that supreme interval covered by the *entente cordiale*. I had no trouble with the herbivores naturally, for plants, grasses and herbs were ready at hand, but the carnivores had somewhat hard going

185 Underlined twice for emphasis.

on rice and celery and rhododendrons, etc. Still, they agreed to try it out and there wasn't anything wrong in making carnivores vegetarians for a short while because it had the effect of increasing their rage and hunger when the hour came for their onslaught on the fish. It was an orthodox point of grand strategy, and it gave me a chance of injecting a chuckle of humour into the poem which might have been too ghastly and grim without it.

The volcano Jurania is the ironic Spirit brooding over the whole scene and preparing us for the general catastrophe.

Now I wanted two individual protagonists. I asked myself and biologists – What would be one of the oldest forms of life possessing great strength but little intellect and the answer was the dinosaur; so I selected Tyrannosaurus Rex. With his pin-point brain, he could lay around him magnificently and his low primitive intelligence wouldn't discern which were his allies, which his foes, so he attacks both. I had in mind, perhaps feebly, the idea of human allies changing sides over a period.

Then what was the highest point reached at that time in evolution? Obviously, the anthropoid ape. You ask me which was the hero, which the villain? I really didn't have in mind a villian-hero composition. There might be elements of both in Rex and the ape. The former starts the panic, the latter controls it and directs the organized beasts. Intelligence in the ape could not prevent belligerency and destruction. A gas-chamber today is the result of an unusual intelligence. As you say, cunning and skill and hate couldn't be more deadly than a primitive beast's rush on its prey. And certainly torture is a human product.

I tried to portray both Rex and the ape sympathetically at the conclusion. Suicide for the former and frustration accompanied his exit and pity could be evoked for him.

But why should the ape be allowed survival. A logical point. The Darwinian hypothesis in mind, where would we be if she died? Collin deals with that. But she struggles back, horrified at what had taken place. What happened to her after she returned to her brood? Well, that's another story and I had inflicted enough horror on my readers as it was.

John Sutherland got one thing from the poem, another writer might get something different. For me it was an allegory of war in its final or near-final stage. John did something which was of deep concern to me in that he brought out the studies from my philosophical course where we were imbued with Freud, James, Wundt and theories of the subconscious.[186] One never knows in any expression what may come up from the well-springs. This can be over done,

186 See the letters to John Sutherland, 25 February and 11 August 1952 (pp. 485–6 and 504).

of course, and several times after I read his analysis, I remarked to myself – 'Did I have that in mind when I wrote?' 'Perhaps not explicitly,' I thought. Still it can't be brushed aside completely.

But to come back to your point. Strength for its own sake has not been uppermost in my mind – that is to say, mere glorification of power. Concentration camps may come from it, as the world knows.

I hope, Des, that I have done something to answer your questions. Forgive handwriting as I am notoriously illegible.

A personal point again! On Wednesday night I go to New York for a week to see my daughter Claire who is in Hospital for spinal treatment. The cure may mean almost a year in a complete cast. It's the result of polio. Vi and I take turns visiting her.

My kindest regards to yourself
& Mary.
Ned Pratt

TO CLAIRE PRATT

47 Glencairn Ave.
Toronto 12 Ont.

Oct. 29, 1954

Dearest Claire:

Your letter just came – the one written last Tuesday – so we were glad that your penmanship didn't suffer from the cast. That you can write at all is a blessing. I have just written a note to Henry Wells in answer to his nice letter. Mother will write Peg[187] answering *her* breezy and voluminous letter. She must be a whirlwind. Perhaps a later hurricane (which the Lord forbid) will be named after her. What a personality! I shall be glad to see her. I expect to get a room at the Hotel so as to be near you. I have bought my ticket C.P.R. for Wednesday night at 8, getting in about 8 or 9 Thursday morning.

Mother is spending the day at the Wesley Buildings and this evening we are having dinner at the Park Plaza with Murdo MacKinnon who is also inviting as his guests the Fryes and the Alexanders (Queen's).

---

187 Peg Durand, a friend whom Claire had met through Shirley Freshman. She lived near the hospital where Claire was a patient.

Did I tell you that Kay Coburn is trying to get an allocation from the J.S. McLean Foundation.[188] I have written Malcolm Wallace and Norman McLean[189] to enlist their support as executors of the estate. The allocation required is $8000.00. She always inquires about you.

I have the old George Locke room as an office though its privacy is somewhat disturbed by the frequent entrance of Edith Honey[190] and her assistants. It seems that all they do is to take a book from a shelf and put it in another position on the same shelf. However, the room is fairly satisfactory.

With much love,
Father

TO CLAIRE PRATT

47 Glencairn Ave.

Sunday [31 Oct. 1954]

Dearest Claire:

We have just finished phoning you and I am 'penning a short epistle.'

You would have been interested in the party last night. Two weeks ago a woman named Mrs Parker telephoned us an invitation out to her place for an evening's chat. Your mother thought the name was Jane Parker – a former student of mine. She was going to have a number of my old students. I imagined it was 2T6[191] and I looked up the list of the year and found a Janet Parker. 'That's the girl,' I said. Then she phoned yesterday to say her husband would call for us in his car bringing Marshall and Mrs McLuhan. We didn't want to give ourselves away in our ignorance and we waited until Parker[192] gave *himself* away in the conversation. He talked about Varley, Schaefer and Lawren Harris.[193] I

---

188 Established by J.S. McLean in 1945 to support the arts, education, health, and conservation. See the letter to Claire Pratt, 15 September 1953 (p. 538).

189 J.S. McLean's son and a director of the foundation.

190 Librarian.

191 The class of 1926.

192 Harley Parker, a close friend of Marshall McLuhan, with whom he later collaborated on a book, *Through the Vanishing Point: Space in Poetry and Painting* (New York: Harper & Row, 1968).

193 Frederick Varley and Lorne Harris (1885–1970) were members of the original Group of Seven; Carl Schaefer (1903–95) had studied with Arthur Lismer and J.E.H. Macdonald at the Ontario College of Art, but was known for his southern Ontario landscapes.

remarked to myself – 'Ah, ha! an artist.' Then he remarked, 'It's a hobby, for I teach for a living.' Oh, I ruminated – a teacher in the High School. 'Well, you have two months in the summer for your hobby.' 'No, I have four months.' Hence a University man. After his many references to architecture I thought he belonged to that Faculty. No, he didn't. He was a teacher in the College of Art.

Then who was Janet – if that was her name? I kept mum until I came to the home and the person [who] met us at the door was Mary Gibson Parker, my student of 4T0 (Class of 1940). We saw Margaret Avison looking as wan and chalk-like as ever, Isabel Fraser[194] and several others. It was all cleared up now and we spent the evening until 2 a.m. which accounts for drowsiness this morning.

Margaret Avison said she would love to come and see you when you got to our home, and talk over old times. Parker himself I had never met before though he claimed we did meet at McLuhan's three years ago.

That's the daily news.

I am looking forward to Thursday, thankful that Peg has a room for me, and what a delight to see you. I am going to read to you anything you can get from the Library or anything you wish me to bring down. I shall practise up my graceful gestures and intonations to get the correct sense of poise and emphasis – understand.

Much love,
Father

TO EARLE BIRNEY

Victoria College
Toronto

Nov. 2, 1954

My dear Earle:

It was a delight to get your letter this morning. Here's wishing you triumphant success in your forthcoming novel.[195] Your Turvey grins at us from the top shelf of my den. I think you brought off both a psychological and a literary masterpiece in that work. You are the only one in this country who is hitting the high spots in prose and poetry alike.

---

194 A librarian at one of the Toronto libraries.
195 *Down the Long Table* (Toronto: McClelland & Stewart, 1955).

I was interested in the Auden affair.[196] Imagine fourteen hundred students craning their necks from the gallery beams to get a sight of a person who is 100% intellectual! When ability and publicity go together there's no limit.

I was so glad to know your *David* was prescribed for the Senior students in the Ontario schools. I had the good fortune in having the *Titanic* on five years ago and again the year before last. In *texts* is the only way to start a savings account. The general market, though good in its way, doesn't change nickel into gold.

Your North-star West[197] still thrills me as does the old Saturday Night funeral ceremony.[198] B.K. S.[199] often refers to it when we get together. Auden couldn't do as well I feel sure.

Victoria C. has given me a room to hang up my coat and hat and get my mail. I miss the students though but one must accept the years.

I haven't done anything poetically since the Spike, one reason being that the sight of my right eye troubles me and is in constant need of treatment from the oculist – drops seven times *every* day to maintain a stubborn level. The other reason is more important. Claire is in hospital in New York. She had been working at Harvard Press – editorial work – but she found that the spinal curvature resulting from polio of earlier years was increasing. We knew that the best surgeon in the U.S.A. was Dr Cobb of the Hospital for Special Surgery. He has her now in a cast prior to the operation which may be within a couple of weeks. We were staggered at the description of the spine. It must be straightened first through pressure of the preliminary cast; then the operation in two or three sections at intervals of months when a bone must be grafted onto the spine – rather two or three bones. It will take ten months perhaps a year during which time she must remain horizontal. After the first operation she comes back to the flat for six months on a stretcher, then returns for further treatment. It is her own decision, plucky little youngster and the doctor says it is absolutely necessary as braces are simply makeshifts and cannot hold back the progression of the curve. So you see what we are up against. The fee of the surgeon is $2500.00 and the private room is $20.00 per day, but when the thing is over and successful, all that will be a minor affair. To have her straight as she was at ten years of age will be heaven on earth.

196 The poet W.H. Auden had given a lecture-recital at the University of British Columbia in October.

197 Based on a flight from Montreal to Vancouver in a Trans-Canada Airlines North Star plane, published in *Trial of a City and Other Verse* (1952).

198 Unidentified.

199 B.K. Sandwell, long-time editor of *Saturday Night* (1932–52).

Vi has just come back from N.Y. having spent a week with her and I leave tomorrow night to spend a time. So we'll alternate our trips. Fortunately she has an aunt – my sister – living in Brooklyn. She is a nurse and will visit her very often. One thing I feel sure of is that she is in good hands and starts in relatively good health otherwise.

Well, that's enough of my troubles and now I'll write Esther and tell her a couple of stories as a counter-irritant for myself and to give her a laugh.

Here they are. Pass them on.

Affectionately
Ned

TO ESTHER BIRNEY

[2 Nov. 1954]

My Dear Esther:

I heard two good stories yesterday from my bank manager at Yonge & Bloor.

A group of doctors arrived at the Pearly gates and demanded that St. Peter let them in. The Saint replied that there was no need of doctors 'up there.' They departed, but one returned with the claim that he had done nothing but good while on earth and he didn't see why he should be rejected. Peter replied – 'Just what is your specialty?' Answer – 'I am a psychiatrist.' 'Oh,' said Peter – 'mental eh?' 'Yes.' 'Well I think we can make use of a psychiatrist here.' He whispered into his ear, 'Do you know that we have had a little trouble with God recently. He has got the idea that he is George Drew.[200] Come in.'

The other story I heard in Newfoundland when I was down there a year ago. A friend of my brother Cal, named McIntyre,[201] was quite fond of bridge but he couldn't stand the chatter from his friends at the game. It was about the time that radio sets were being installed in Nfld, and McIntyre had to listen to the boasts of his three friends which infuriated him.

---

200 Former premier of Ontario (1943–8) and current leader of the federal Conservative Party (1948–56).

201 Unidentified. When Pratt told the same story in a letter to the Birneys dated 5 February 1954 (*EJP: Web*), the protagonist was Sir Tasker Cook.

(1) I turned on the dial last night and got New York.
(2) I turned on mine and got San Francisco.
(3) I turned on mine and got London, England.

Mac jumped up from the table, flung his cards down and left the room grumbling – 'I turned my ass to the open window last night and got *Chile*.'

Our love to you. Vi is well, and the rest of the news you can get from Earle.

Little Neddie

P.S. As we shall be in New York a lot, any message you and Earle send should be addressed to Victoria College as mail will be forwarded from there. The house at 47 will be mostly unoccupied.[202]

TO DESMOND PACEY

Victoria College
Toronto, Ont.

Nov. 11, 1954

Dear Des:

Apologies for pencil writing. My fountain pen has gone dry.

First let me say that your letters are always welcome. Write for anything that will help. I regard it an honour to get your interest.

Let me also take up your points one by one.

(1) *The Brew*

I must confess that the only 'didacticism' I had in mind when I scribbled that fantasy was to get away from the dead seriousness of Newfoundland Verse which, apart from ten or a dozen short poems, has little merit. I wanted to strike a new vein which generally has persisted till the present with sufficient variation (I hope) to break the monotony of tone. It was a complete departure for me. I wasn't conscious of a 'rebel' position. Over-piety was present indeed here and there, but I didn't bother about it. Edgar and I (as soon as I entered Victoria) took the position that if people let us alone we would let *them* alone. We abhorred interference, being individualists like yourself.

---

202 The house was actually unoccupied for only a few days, when his one visit to New York in November briefly overlapped with a visit there by Viola.

It is true that the fish had no moral law. They were products of evolution – the Holy Script hadn't appeared. So it was an objective position. Probably you are right that 'primitivism' underlay my ideas though I wasn't conscious of it, and you may be right that, as one critic pointed out, I was 'thumbing my nose at academic just-so-isms.' It looked crazy when it appeared, one theological professor claiming that it was the 'daftest' thing he ever read. Another seriously approached the Chancellor with the question – 'What did Pratt mean by the poem?' Bowles,[203] generous soul replied – 'Mean? He meant nothing. It was just "let her go Gallagher." He had to get something out of his system.' Another, quite rightly, I think, said it was an 'anti-maple psychosis' which had taken hold of Canadian writers. The Edinburgh Scotsman reviewed it as an advertisement of the brands, another Scotch paper claiming that it was a temperance pamphlet in disguise. But some took it for what it was, a fantasy, saying that the grin never left his face from beginning to end.

I never believed that it would be placed on the U of T.[204] curriculum as prescribed reading. Anyway it is there for better or worse. To have a lot of interpretations is better than to have none at all. At least some people became interested and controversial. It certainly wasn't written for a Sunday School paper, and I have never been a consistent Sabbatarian any more than yourself. But it was fun having people coming to me and talking about the scurrilous nature of the subject. Why the Cat? Well, to hell with the Cat. It disappeared in the Irish Sea – appropriate place!

Still, I cannot dispense with the primitive streak, strive as I may. And this brings up the next point.

I was brought up with 'turning the other cheek' and 'Go with him twain.' Noble indeed but was it practicable? It was my father's creed. The Fable of the Goats is pacifistic but the argument was between *two* individuals and not *two* hosts or races although they are in the background. The problem of concession is easier to solve when one stretches out his hand and says 'let's forget.' When a nation is aroused it isn't so easy. I must say that the matter of reconcilation has always been present in my mind, and perhaps this poem is an attempt at its expression.

Then why the change? I do not profess to be able to solve it. Could a man see another maltreat a child and not interfere even by force? I had this idea in the *Autopsy on a Sadist*. The concentration camps, the a[..]s, the tortures, etc. etc., couldn't go without protest. And the bombs on the children in London while

203 Richard Pinch Bowles.
204 University of Toronto.

the bombers escaped by air unseen! Perhaps there is a solution to it all, but it is beyond my comprehension and to offer a formula was beyond my scope. Possibly Ghandi had it – I don't know. But at least I honoured him.

May I say just here that it was Psychology with its emphasis on experience – Wundt, James,[205] and others – and not Pure Abstract Reason that most impressed me in undergraduate days. I found more fighting in the latter than in the former.

The best to Mary.

Affectionately,
Ned Pratt

TO VIOLA PRATT

47 Glencairn Ave, Toronto

Thursday a.m. [11 Nov. 1954]

Dearest Vi:

'My heart to thy sweet voice' etc. That's how I felt when I heard your *notes* over the phone yesterday. I thought first I would telephone the Hotel first but on second thought decided on the Hospital hoping to catch you before you returned to your room. I caught you in time.

I found the house *as I left it*[206] – no dishes to wash, if you know what I mean. I had dinner with Poss[207] last night, and today I have lunch with the McLuhans. One would think they were a brother and sister, phoning up to see how I am getting along and you and Claire. I am having dinner again tonight with Poss. So I am well looked after.

I suppose you spent most of your time at the Hospital. It's too bad I didn't get a chance to see Dr Cobb but his activities prevented it. Next time may be more favourable.

Hincks telephoned a couple of times. If possible, I want to reserve *November 18*, Thursday, for a meeting of the Ontario Division of the C.M.Health[208] as the lack

205 William Wundt and William James. See the letter to Pacey, 29 October 1954 (pp. 587–8).
206 He had just returned from his visit with Claire in New York.
207 Florence Pratt.
208 Canadian Mental Health Association.

of a quorum cancelled the last one and at least I can count myself one of the number. That's about all I am good for. But the really important one comes in December. So I can make *Cal's* arrival tally with the meeting. He can bring in some of his friends. Clare is quite keen on that, and I must justify my membership and my stipend somehow, being President. God save the mark!

The Macmillans sent me a cheque for *Erosion* and *Sea-Gulls* to be used in anthologies. Let me know when you want a draft in advance and don't go depriving yourself in the least. That's what the money is for – to bless you and Cayke. You said that Claire was getting along as well as might be expected.

Note: your letter of Tuesday just came through the door per the whistling warbler. Both the whistler and the letter were most welcome.

I haven't moved out of the house except for meals and provisions. I shall soon get at the Browning business[209] which is due about the middle of December – about 14 minutes of notes and 16 of readings all of which will be done by John Drainie,[210] thank heaven!

By the way what does MU stand for as a telephone section? I have forgotten the full name. I know the Beckman[211] – ELdorado 5-7300. This is in case I have to telephone.

I am sending the first class mail – the second class can wait.

Much love to you dear. I shall write Cayke tomorrow and try to reproduce the bird-calls of the postman.

Ned

TO CLAIRE PRATT

47 Glencairn Ave.
Toronto Canada

Tuesday am. [16 Nov. 1954]

My Dear:

I have a couple of stories to tell you which Currelly related to me a few days ago.

---

209 He was preparing a script on Robert Browning's 'Andrea del Sarto' for an Ontario school broadcast.

210 Radio announcer and actor associated with the CBC.

211 The New York hotel where Viola was staying.

The Head of the Methodist Church named Carman[212] who, because of his autocratic ways, was known as Bishop Carman when he visited St. John's to preside over the Methodist Conference. He was a disciplinarian and quite rude, clamping down on interrupting clergymen.

One timid soul, who was known never to speak at the General Assembly, managed to summon up enough courage to get on his feet when Carman was presiding. His remark was 'Mr Carman, I sometimes think' and Carman's rejoinder before the poor soul could get through his statement (which probably wasn't very profound) – 'Do you?' He sat down immediately. Later on, feeling the importance of his idea, he rose again and said – 'Mr Chairman, I have an idea,' to which the Bishop curtly answered – 'Keep it, brother.' The minister kept silent for the rest of the session, having the sympathy of the audience but the neglect of Carman.

I thought I'd hand this on to you. Pass it on to your mother as I didn't tell her in my letter.

Here's hoping for a rapid healing,
love.
Father

TO VIOLA PRATT

47 Glencairn Ave

Wednesday a.m. [17 Nov. 1954]

Dearest:

Claire's letter just whisked through the door and I am answering it at once and also dropping you a line with some enclosures.

Winnie was here yesterday and cleaned up everything in true Winnie[213] fashion. She even washed the clothes and ironed them. I told her she didn't need to come next Tuesday as I am out nearly all day, but she could turn up in two weeks time. By that time you may be back with your little white cap or your scarcely less attractive (probably not even scarcely) red cap plastered on the back of your finely moulded poll.

---

212 Albert Carman (1833–1917) was general superintendent of the Methodist Church in Canada from 1883 to 1915. He had been a bishop of the Methodist Episcopal Church.

213 Winnie Fitzpatrick.

I told you I was at the Dalys' the night before last and at Poss's last night for a stew. I am putting on weight I think.

This afternoon Hal & Ethel Bennett are having a 3 p.m. tea and I'll turn up.

I saw Charlie Leslie[214] yesterday on Bloor St and he passed me with just a nod as if he were in the depths of melancholia. Something has happened. Chris[215] says he resents his transference from Vic to Emmanuel and Irving's[216] headship. But that's conjecture. Charlie has asked for a year's leave of absence on grounds of health. It's too bad isn't it?

I am preparing to get at my Andrea del Sarto' and have that off my chest. The contract calls for first and second drafts, as they are very finicky with High Schools – Grades XI-XIII.

Jim[217] wrote a nice letter almost in the old style though I could detect notes of personal complaint. He is taking up sketching again which is good. He was inquiring mainly about Claire. I saw Dr John McDonald[218] yesterday and he reaffirmed his belief in Cobb[219] and said that if the first four days following the operation passed without temperature, infection could be ruled out. The antibiotics have made vast strides. The doing of the first the operation low down was very sound he thought.

I am sending this to the Hotel as I know you like to get in there with a letter in the box.

Very much love,
Neddie

TO JOHN SUTHERLAND

47 Glencairn Ave
Toronto 12 Ont.

Wednesday [17 Nov. 1954]

Dear John:

Apologies for not immediately answering your letter but I have been in New York visiting my daughter who is in hospital for a complete spinal fusion, the result of

214 See the note to 'Leslie' in the letter to Claire Pratt, 13 December 1944 (p. 310).
215 Christopher Love.
216 See the note to 'Irving' in the letter to the Claire Pratt, 25 January 1954 (p. 552).
217 His brother.
218 A Toronto surgeon and friend of the family.
219 Claire's surgeon, Dr John Cobb.

polio some years ago. She will have to remain in a cast for more than a year, poor little girl. Vi is with her now and I shall go down again soon.[220] Our visits will alternate. My eyes are still bothering me as you may infer from this script.

Glad you are coming to Toronto. I think it is a good venture.[221] If I hear of an apartment I'll let you know, but since my retirement I have been living in a little flat on the outskirts of the city.[222] Either Father Shook or Marshall McLuhan might be successful in locating something near St Michael's. I looked up the Globe & Mail but prices are not stated. Unfortunately the costs are high anywhere. We are paying $135 a month on a two-year contract. We may leave when the time is up.

The dog accommodation may pose a problem. Our contract prohibits one but there may be one available.

It will be good to see the both of you.

The best,
Ned Pratt

TO VIOLA AND CLAIRE PRATT

47 Glencairn Ave.
Toronto Ont.

Saturday pm [20 Nov. 1954]

Darling Vi and Claire:

Here I am in the house this mild Saturday afternoon penning a note to the twa o'ye.

I had lunch at Floss's, heard a few records which Peggy[223] put on – Oklahoma and Don Cossacks and others, then decided to embark for 47.

I saw Hal Bennett on the way down the stairs. Ethel[224] is staying in a lot, on account of so many student parties she has had.

---

220 He often talked of making, indeed of having made, a second trip to New York to visit Claire, but there is no evidence that he actually did.

221 Sutherland was planning to register as a student at St Michael's College, University of Toronto. He had attended Queen's and McGill briefly in the late 1930s and early 1940s, but illness had intervened.

222 47 Glencairn Avenue was actually a duplex house and, while situated well north of the city centre, was hardly on its 'outskirts.'

223 Margaret Ray.

224 Harold Bennett's wife.

Cal phoned this morning just before his trip to Newfoundland. He had spent an hour or so with Brockington in the Hotel lounge at the Windsor.[225] L.W.B. is off by plane to Scotland to deliver a St Andrew's address. Can you beat it? How he travels around with all his infirmities[226] surpasses my understanding. He told Cal he was going the rounds as long as he could last – rather ominous it sounded.

Today I got a cheque for $16.00 from the Harvard Vocarium.[227] Hitherto it has been between 3 and 5 dollars a year for record royalties which makes me think the Victoria order of 30 sets is included, but I'm not sure. I hope it is altogether American.

Hincks is on his way to New York and probably will run in to see Claire. His financial efforts seem successful for the Toronto Branch. Arthur Daly came through with $250, a handsome sum. My cheque for entertaining and signing papers (imagine it!) will soon come. Clare is on the top of his psychological world.

Love to the two of you. I shall telephone tonight.

Neddie boy

TO DESMOND PACEY

Victoria College
Toronto

Nov. 25, 1954

Dear Des:

Sorry for the delay but I had been in New York for a time and must go again shortly.[228]

The questions now are harder to answer.

(1) I admired (and still admire) the Carman, Lampman, Roberts, D.C. Scott group. But, as far as I know, there was no *influence*, for I reacted in the early '20s against the landscape prepossessions, regarding 'scenery' mainly as backdrop to human endeavour.

---

225 The Windsor Hotel in Montreal.

226 Leonard Brockington was severely crippled.

227 Harvard Vocarium Records was the commercial label of the phonograph disks made of him reading his poems when he visited Harvard University in 1946. (See the note to 'they may be marketed' in the letter to Viola and Claire Pratt, 3 March 1946 [p. 372].)

228 See the note to 'I shall go down again soon' in the letter to John Sutherland, 17 November 1954 (p. 599).

I think highly of Roy C.[229] and Masefield. The sweep of the former fascinates me yet though the *Cachalot* & *Great Feud* were written before I read Campbell.[230] I think the similarities are largely coincidences. Influences are hard to track down, aren't they? Fantasy with an underlying purpose has always had a hold on me.

(2) Nationalism was never very strong. The only poems which might be called 'Canadian' are *Brébeuf* and certainly the *Spike*. The subject is tremendously dramatic, and I had-the additional advantage of being able to *go over the ground*.
(3) As Canadian poetry had its fill of pastoral and amorous treatment, I got a bit fed up with it. As you say, I didn't feel drawn to it. I abhor sticky sonnets particularly.
(4) You are never a 'bloody nuisance.'

Kindest regards,
Ned Pratt

TO VIOLA PRATT

Saturday am.

[18 Dec. 1954]

Dearest Vi:

Your letter (Wednesday) just came, following a phone message from Clare Hincks who has just arrived. He told me that he saw the both of you and that you were over your cough and Claire was progressing. I hope the wound heals fast.

Pash came in this morning with the Clarke frame[231] and I wrote out the Sea-Gulls. She is coming back on Monday at 11 when we shall go to South Drive.

The cards have come in literally by the hundreds. I suppose I shall keep them, as they are the conventional ones. George Johnston sent us Meighan's book on Shakespeare[232] – a wonderfully fine piece of book craft.

---

229 Roy Campbell.

230 Not strictly true. He had read Campbell in London in the summer of 1924. See the letter to John Sutherland, late 1952 (pp. 516–17).

231 Ida Pashley was having Claire's woodcut of seagulls and a holograph of Pratt's poem 'Sea-Gulls' framed for W.H. ('Bill') and Irene Clarke.

232 'The Greatest Englishman of History,' a reprint of an address to the Canadian Club in 1936.

Last night I had dinner with the MacCrimmons,[233] and what an array of guests – Dr & Mrs Emlyn Davies of Westminster, Fred & Mrs Gullen[234] and three others besides Judge & Mrs Smiling.[235] The turkey was 25 pounds and after dinner we spent two hours telling stories, Davies very prominent in his reminiscences on Lloyd-George[236] – F.E.D. Smith,[237] Sir John Simon[238] and British celebrities. Some of the stories couldn't be told from a pulpit certainly, but the house rang with laughter. Davies has a deep tremendous voice and when he laughs it is like an earthquake. Elsie[239] sends her love to you and Claire. She rings up quite frequently and I relay the news.

Today I have lunch again with Cal and tomorrow with Floss. I shall obey all your instructions. The $15.00 for Floss through Peggy[240] from you and Claire, $5.00 for Winnie[241] and the milkman and postie will not be forgotten.

I am being looked after very well by my friends though I miss you very very much. I shall certainly go down after the 'third'[242] which you say will take place after Xmas. Isn't it too bad that Dr Cobb is unwell. I trust he is better now.

I sent the 'Collected,' I hope in time for Xmas. I marked it first class mail and stamped it accordingly.

Your W.M.S.[243] cheque came. I suppose I should keep it here till your return or should I send it on for your signature and then put it in your account. Possibly I had better wait till the end of the year and send the two together, or retain them, whatever you think best.

Yes the Titanic lecture was well received though I imagine Chris and Vo[244] are naturally a bit exuberant and inclined to exaggerate. Fortunately I had it

233 Family friends.

234 Emlyn Davies (b. 1897) was attached to the Defence Research Department in Ottawa; Frederick C. Gullen (1882–1961) was a Toronto judge.

235 [*sic*]. Facetiously or not, he refers to Judge Percy E.F. Smily (b. 1890), appointed to the Supreme Court of Ontario in 1946.

236 British Liberal politican David Lloyd-George (1863–1945) was prime minister of the United Kingdom from 1916 to 1922, heading a coalition government during and after the First World War.

237 Frederick Edwin Smith (1872–1930), first Earl of Birkenhead, was a British politician and lawyer known as a skilled orator. He was a close friend of Winston Churchill.

238 John Allsebrook Simon (1873–1959) was a long-serving member of the British parliament, serving at various times as home secretary, foreign secretary, and chancellor of the exchequer.

239 Elsie MacCrimmon.

240 Margaret Ray.

241 Fitzpatrick, the cleaning lady.

242 Of Claire's surgeries.

243 The Women's Missionary Society was Viola's employer as editor of *World Friends* magazine.

244 Chris and Viola Love.

written out and could sit down as in a class-room. An hour of it I find very exhausting afterwards, but the experience doesn't come often.

Kay Coburn is still trying to find funds from various foundations to get her Coleridgeana into Vic. It is uphill work.

Has Claire enough reading material? Bruce Mackinnon[245] asked. I suppose Henry Wells will keep her supplied with the kind she likes.

Bless you sweetheart, and bless Cayke.

Love always
Ned

TO VIOLA PRATT

Sunday am. [19 Dec. 1954]

Dear:

It was sweet to hear your voices last night. I may phone again tonight at 6:30. When you phoned me before twice I was at (1) the Flenley dinner[246] (he is retired now) and (2) at the MacCrimmons.'

I have just finished my breakfast of one slice of toast, one 'delicious' apple and two cups of coffee. That's enough as I go to Poss's for mid-day dinner with Cal.

Three parcels have come which I decided not to open until Christmas – one from Karl & Rita,[247] one from the Shahoffs[248] and one from Mrs Gordon Keyes[249] of Weston. But I am sending on Hager's[250] letter & picture and in another letter I am enclosing a couple of cards for Claire.

We have had very moderate weather, no rain and little snow though the sidewalks are quite slippery. The temperature hasn't gone below 25 and not above 40, almost a record for December – so far.

People have called up by phone, Mrs Turnbull – there are three of them and I'm not sure which one but she said she had been away with her daughter and had not returned till yesterday.

---

245 Unidentified.

246 For historian Ralph Flenley (1886–1969). See the letter to Claire Pratt, 14 December 1954 (*EJP: Web*).

247 Whitney; Viola's brother and sister-in-law.

248 Dorothy Sigmund and her husband.

249 The former Mary Ferguson, one of Claire's classmates. Her husband, Gordon L. Keyes (b. 1920), a member of the Classics Department at Victoria College, was its principal in 1976–81.

250 Hager Whitney.

I have just phoned Ina[251] who said that Nan[252] had to go to a nursing home on Poplar Plains Road. She had lost her speech and the use of her right arm and leg but was slightly improving. Ina said she had to get her into a 'home' as she (Ina) was losing her nerves herself. In fact it was a most distressful conversation with Ina crying instead of talking, poor girl. She had had three nurses each day and she had to look after them, answer the door and the phone, etc. until she almost collapsed. She is feeling a little better since and getting some rest and sleep. She sends her love to you and Claire.

Coming back to domestic affairs, I bought a Porterhouse at Henley's and put it in the Refrigerator in case Cal should come up and have a stew. I took a little of it yesterday but frying it made such a smoke in the house I decided to put it back and make a stew out of it, Cal of course helping when he arrives. I have some onions and I'll get a few potatoes tomorrow when I am through with the parcel delivery. Pash[253] is taking me around. Her Clarke framing is splendid.[254] And the more I look at Claire's Seagulls and waves the more I see in the picture. It is a real present on the grand scale. Cayke, you're a wonder!

How is Dr Cobb getting along? Or do you not hear any news? Isn't it too bad that he should take sick?

I haven't been at the College office for a week and haven't seen any of the staff. Anyway the holidays have begun and the crowd won't be back till the second week in January.

Dear, if you need any more money let me know and I'll send a draft for any amount required.

Blessings on you both.
Ned

By the way, I think I'll send this by air and the enclosed pictures by regular mail. I think there's a day's difference at least. Your air letter written Wednesday got here on Saturday.

251 Ina McCauley.
252 Ina McCauley's sister.
253 Ida Pashley.
254 See the note to 'the Clarke frame … Sea-Gulls' in the letter to Viola Pratt, 18 December 1954 (p. 601).

TO CLAIRE PRATT

47 Glencairn Ave
Toronto, Ont.

Friday [24 Dec. 1954]

Dearest Claire:

Merry Christmas to you Sweetheart! Julia[255] phoned up to say that she was going to be in New York next week. She is calling here tomorrow to pick up a couple of small parcels sent as presents. It will be nice for you to see her especially when your mother is coming home for a spell. Julia belongs to God's feminine peerage if there is such a body, and you're in there too.

I forgot to mention a small item in connection with that steak dinner which Cal & I had. As you know by this time I intended a stew but he thought it was a waste of good food to stew a Porterhouse. I complained that I had fried a portion of the steak the evening before and it raised such a helluva stink that I thought the Mars[..]s[256] would ring up and object. 'Oh no,' says Cal, 'I can fry it beautifully.' Well, he did and we sat down to supper and the fumes became intolerable – worse by far than from my frying. 'There,' I said, 'you're worse,' when he turned his head towards the toaster and found that I had failed to take out the plug. The two pieces of toast were cinders and Vesuvius was pouring up towards the roof. He had me there. I put on two more pieces and told him to watch it himself. All things went well after that to the strains of 'Men of Harlech.'

Last night we had another scoff.[257] He brought up a delicatessen chicken and the following items: – Is your French good enough to interpret these?

(1) a tin of condensed Bouillon Écossais (Scotch broth)
(2) one of Soupe Crème de Champignons (mushroom)
(3) " " Crème de Tomatoes (more obvious)
(4) " " Chivers Olde English Marmalade
(5) a lot of biscuits etc.

255 Julia McGrew.
256 The neighbours.
257 A Newfoundland word for 'a good feed.'

I am putting on weight – a little. Only the firmest determination on my part makes it [a little].[258]

In an hour or so I go down to the Royal York to have a snack with him. Then we proceed to a film of 'Two Years before the Mast,' Dana's masterpiece.[259]

Today I received a $400 cheque from Brendan[?][260]which I am putting away for you. Let me know anytime when you want American funds or whether you prefer the amounts to be placed to your credit at the Royal Bank here.

A great deal of love for you
and Julia
Father

Pash and I are going out to the airport to meet Mother when I know the exact plane flight.

TO CLAIRE PRATT

47 Glencairn Ave.
Toronto

Thursday [30 Dec. 1954]

Dearest Cayke:

Your card just came – the fastest mail delivery yet.

I am alone today as your mother is over with Ina.[261] She stayed with her last night as Ina is somewhat distraught over the passing of Nan so suddenly.[262] Mother will be back this afternoon as soon as a housekeeper comes.

Christmas is over and in two days New Year will be on us. We are putting on a dinner for Cal Saturday, and Poss and Peggy[263] are coming, Cal leaving for Ottawa the following day. He is much better in back and leg, though *better* and *worse* oscillate – something he has learned to expect now. Still it is much improved as against the condition two months ago.

---

258 An arrow is drawn to 'a little' in the previous sentence.

259 The 1946 film starring Alan Ladd was based on the the popular account of 'the life of a common sailor at sea as it really is' by American author Richard Henry Dana, Jr. The plot was based on his experiences during a two-year sea voyage from Boston to South America and around the Cape Horn to California (1834–6).

260 Unidentified.

261 Ina McCauley.

262 See the letter to Viola Pratt, 19 December 1954 (p. 604).

263 Florence Pratt and Margaret Ray.

Our Christmas presents consisted largely of chocolates, cakes, socks and cigars – the latter being enough to last me and Winnie's[264] father for months to come. Oh, I forgot the cards, about 200 of them not yet opened.

So they are allowing you a draught of beer. Good! Is it Budweiser, the beer that made Milwaukee famous or Pilsener? Marko[265] said that beer possesses rich vitamins and [is] all right except behind a wheel. Fine in bed. So there you are.

Tonight we go to the Barfoots'[266] for supper and on Friday we go to Pash's[267] for dinner – Cal, Mother, Father, Poss, Peggy and others. We are being well fed. I am buying a Porterhouse roast at Henley's tomorrow. Cal phoned up to say it must not be fried – miserable memories of smoke and huskiness, etc.[268] We live and learn.

I think I told you that all turned up at the Hincks dinner[269] and every resolution concerning the 1955 budget was passed unanimously. You know the kind – Senator Pratt moved or Bertie Proctor, seconded by Bill Zimmerman or Leo Macaulay, the chairman (humble me) not calling for votes, but pronouncing 'approved unanimously.' I spent an hour yesterday at Hincks' office signing papers authorizing the making out of cheques. By the way it was passed unanimously that the Bank of Commerce be the bank for deposits. What else could we do, seeing that Cal was a director. As my financial experience was so limited, I contented myself with sitting in the chair and telling the odd story that had no relevance to the business in hand.

I am told that I am to get $100 a month for pronouncing grace at dinner and telling yarns. So if you have any more stories such as that on neurotics & psychotics, etc., pass them along, and I will credit you as the source.

Ever lovingly,
Father

TO CLAIRE PRATT

47 Glencairn Ave
Toronto Canada

New Year's Day[270] [2 Jan] 1955

264 Winnie Fitzpatrick.
265 Jacob Markowitz.
266 Friends of Viola.
267 Ida Pashley.
268 See the letter to Claire Pratt, 24 December 1954 (p. 605).
269 The annual dinner meeting of the Toronto branch of the Mental Health Association of Canada.
270 Actually, 2 January as Pratt recounts the New Year's dinner and the tea the next day.

Darling:

A happy New Year to you.

We had our New Year's dinner last night with your Uncle Cal, Peggy and Floss as our guests. Mother and I went out to select our Sirloin Roast Friday. Uncle Cal said he liked the 'black outside' best so I gave him that. You should have seen me glaring at the roast when I started to carve in mid-Victorian style with my serviette (napkin to you) tucked down my collar and vest. I went at it as if I were knocking down a penguin, half in sorrow and in anger. We devoured everything. Then we went in and listened to Carmen on the long-playing record and some of Mozart & Handel.

Your mother will go down soon and I will go a little later for I *must read* Elsie Dinsmore[271] to you – just to get the darned female off my mind. I used to read it when you were sick in Toronto and I have the nostalgia to start it again. I am going to read by the hour in your room – so look out!!!

We shall be phoning you again tonight probably after we return from Baile[?]'s tea. We may go to church *or we may not*. I have to prepare a speech for the graduation dinner in Hart House and that's on my mind and requires some preparation. I don't like to think that I am recounting stories I told in Vic two or three years ago, so I have to think up some new ones, actual or apochryphal.

I was so glad to get an account of Dr Cobb's letter to you. He must be a wonderful fellow, all that Sallie & McDonald[272] said about him, as the best surgeon on the continent – McDonald said 'in the world in his field.'

Bless your sweet face and everything about you.

Your loving father
Ned

By the way the Collected Edition is in constant demand. Isn't that swell?

TO CLAIRE PRATT

47 Glencairn Ave.
Toronto Canada

Wednesday am [5 Jan. 1955]

---

271 The Elsie Dinsmore books was a lengthy series written in the late nineteenth century for young girls by Martha Finley. Moralistic tales, they were favourite Sunday school library fare.

272 Dr John McDonald. See the letter to Viola Pratt, 17 November 1954 (p. 598).

Hello Mees, Mees, Mees:

How are you darling? We heard your voice last night and we shall telephone again tonight.

Mother has just gone downtown and I am left as the sole occupant of 47 Glencairn. I may go down this afternoon to get a suit from Eaton's special sale. Tomorrow both of us are invited to the National Club as the guests of good old Dick Meech – luncheon.

I was down at the College yesterday and had lunch with Norrie and Lord Surerus,[273] the latter coming in after Norrie and I were through our soup. His lordship spoke pontifically about things near, remote and sundry if you know what I mean.

John Sutherland, Editor of the *Northern Review* (Montreal), has come to live in Toronto. He wants to teach and is going to take his B.A. at St Michael's.[274] He and his wife are occupying a small flat. The magazine has a limited circulation and cannot support them. Father Shook is taking a great interest in John, especially as he is a converted Roman Catholic, a very devout one too. He is granted two years on his course and I am sure that there are two subjects in which he cannot fail – Composition and English Literature. I am having lunch with them at Burwash Hall on this coming Saturday. I guess he will be a teacher of English in a Separate School.[275]

Ken MacLean has an Easter term of leave of absence – much I guess to his Lordship's disgust, as the English Dept. has had several leaves of absence through the last three years.

Nora Cochrane dropped (or rather sailed in) yesterday to wish us a happy New Year. She wanted to get the latest news on you and she gave us the latest news on herself – which is private editing plus two days at the Press per week. I think she is cute. She devoured most of Dick Meech's cake and a fair quantity of Jimmie Norman's[276] wine (home-made) which tasted like treacle flavoured with lemon and soda. She told us all about her annuities and insurances and her rosy prospects, and her increased avoirdupois[277] (which she says she cannot avoid).

Cal went to Ottawa on Sunday. He will be back sometime next week to attend the meeting (or meetings) of the Bank of Commerce,[278] for which he gets

273 Northrop Frye and J.A. Surerus. See the note to 'Surerus' in the letter to Claire Pratt, 14 March 1945 (p. 324).

274 The Roman Catholic college forming part of the University of Toronto.

275 In Ontario, a Roman Catholic parochial school.

276 Dr James Norman, the family doctor.

277 'Weight; degree of heaviness' (*OED*).

278 Senator Pratt was a member of the board of directors of the bank.

$300.00 per attendance. Commerce pays well. He seems in good health apart from arthritis, which I suppose is there for keeps.

Well, we are looking forward to seeing your sweet face (hang this ball pen for smudges).

By the way dear, if Peg's[279] voice is so stentorious, add another foot of space between telephone & ear. It will help. One has to learn these little artifices & gadgets. I'll phone tonight, bless you.

Father

TO VIOLA PRATT

47 Glencairn Ave
Toronto

Friday [14 Jan. 1955]

Dearest Vi:

It was sweet to hear your charming voices last night. I shall telephone again tonight.

So Claire doesn't know yet when the *third*[280] comes off. You will let me know the time, of course.

If you need any American notes call on me and I'll send them by mail.

Clare Hincks is starting off the New Year with a bang (bingo, bendix[281]). I signed some more papers this morning and soon I'll get my monthly cheque. Marko[282] and Nat Benson may collaborate in speaking and play writing for the Committee[283] and on the 17th February I have to read Angelina[284] as my part

279 Margaret Durand.

280 Surgical procedure.

281 The Bendix Corporation – and engineering firm – made everything from hydraulic braking systems and computers to home washing machines. In American naval slang, the phrase 'all ahead Bendix' meant 'beyond maximum possible ship's speed.'

282 Jacob Markowitz.

283 A committee preparing a fund-raising entertainment on behalf of the Toronto branch of the Canadian Mental Health Association.

284 His poem 'To Angelina, an Old Nurse' (*CP* 1.249–52).

of the programme at the Margaret Eaton School of Expression (McGill St.) in company with Lady Eaton,[285] Edward Johnson,[286] Clare Hincks and others. As Lady Eaton was once a nurse she might see the humour of the old girl. I haven't to make a speech – just to read – that satisfies me.

Things are moving along here in even tenor.

I'll be phoning at 8:30 tonight.

Bless the two of you. Your cards came today & yesterday.

Much love.
Ned.

TO VIOLA PRATT

47 Glencairn Ave

Saturday am. [22 Jan. 1955]

Dearest:

Your letter of Wednesday evening came this morning with the whistler's[287] compliments.

I was so glad to hear your voice twice yesterday. That the third operation is over[288] is wonderful. Won't it be grand when after a few days the immediate effects are worn off and she can reply in her bright and courageous voice to the telephone message. I seem to live for those intervals with the both of you.

Here is the news in writing:

(1) [ ]
(2) I am enclosing Mrs Mitchell's letter. I thought the scrawled Mrs was a Mr, so I opened it. You can reply as you see fit. She is a friend of Evelyn MacDonald.[289] The job looks formidable, so don't overtax yourself in these critical times.

---

285 Flora Eaton, widow of Sir John Eaton, former president of the T. Eaton Company, was active in many cultural and philanthropic organizations.
286 Canadian-born tenor (1878–1959), a leading performer at the New York Metropolitan Opera (1922–35) and its general manager (1935–50).
287 The postman, who invariably 'whistled while he worked.'
288 Claire's operation had taken place on Friday morning, 21 January.
289 A friend of Viola.

(3) I am being looked after well – lunch today with George Johnston at the York Club, after which I shall try to reach Floss's place to see how that Hambleton interview[290] comes off. I don't think it is enough to make the angels sing though the archangels may weep. It is really old stuff. Tonight I go to MacLuhan's for dinner, and tomorrow, Sunday, at 2, Floss is cooking a chicken to add another 500 calories to my increasing girth.
(4) I think I told you that Ewart took me to the hockey match and if he can find the time on his return we are going to the Skating Capades which is my favourite out-door pastime though it doesn't come very often.
(5) The plasterer comes on Monday. He may have to come a second time to put on a coat of paint. I will put down a lot of newspapers to take the dust and drips, then Winnie[291] can clean up on Tuesday. Things are going well though nothing can take the place of seeing your face and the news of Claire's recovery. Tell Nellie she is a gem of 'the purest ray serene.'
(6) *The driver's licence*. Here the time is put back to Jan 21. So if you send me yours signed I can post the two together. We may have to take short runs in the future so we mustn't be in a position to explain to a cop that we have only the 1944 licence. Nothing is needed on your card but the name. I can fill in the particulars.
(7) *Claire's licence*. I don't know what the regulations are there in Boston[292] but Elery or Shirley[293] would know. They say that if the applications are not in on time a new test must be undergone. That would be a bother.
(8) Wasn't it nice to have Clare Hincks in again. I am writing Henry and Katherine[294] soon and telling them how grateful I am for their attention.

My, but this letter with its numbers looks like a seed catalogue.

Abundant love to you.
Ned

290 Part of the CBC series *An Experience of Life* (22 January 1955). See paragraph 4 in the letter to Claire Pratt, 9 June 1954 (pp. 573–4).
291 The cleaning lady.
292 Claire planned to return to Boston when she was well again.
293 Elery Buckley; Shirley Freshman.
294 Henry and Katherine Wells.

TO VIOLA AND CLAIRE PRATT

47 Glencairn Ave.

Friday morning [28 Jan. 1955]

Dears both:

Just got your letter Vi written on the 26th. Everything is fine here, including the bacon and eggs which I have devoured an hour ago.

It will be wonderful to have you home.[295] Will you let me know Vi when you get in so I can meet you at the station.

Clare Hincks is counting very much indeed on my taking part in his meeting at the Margaret Eaton Hall on Thursday, Feb. 17th. He has me on the list with Edward Johnson, Lady Eaton and two or three others. It is just a reading for about 10 minutes. I told him about the possibility of Claire's return sometime close to that date. Naturally if you and she return that evening I'll cancel my performance. If Claire came on the 15th or say the 19th, I would go down to N.Y. and come back with you and then wedge in my job on the 17th. I feel I should be with you in any case but if Dr Wilson[296] allows the earlier or later date, so much the better. I haven't done much for the Mental Health organization beyond the odd dinner and as I have been put on the payroll at $100 a month, this task would be a little contribution. I shall phone tonight or tomorrow night and get your view.

Yes I did phone Kathleen MacDowell and she told me that both the girl and the boy were manic depressives and the mother (I've forgotten her name) is in bed herself so that Phil[297] has to shoulder the burden of the three. What some people have to go through. Perhaps Kathleen is exaggerating a bit as I haven't heard a whisper from anyone else.

Well, it will be lovely to see you.

Love to two o' ye as always,
Ned.

295 Viola Pratt travelled to Toronto on 4 February to prepare for Claire's arrival, returning to New York on 11 February. Her datebook records Claire being transported from the Toronto train station by ambulance on Tuesday, 15 February.

296 Dr Phillip Wilson, Jr, had taken over Claire's case during Dr Cobb's illness. In her datebook for 1955, Viola Pratt records Dr Cobb's letter of recommendation on 13 January, and Dr Wilson's first meeting with Claire on 15 January, and the 'third' surgery on Friday, 21 January.

297 Philip Childs, who taught English at Trinity College.

TO VIOLA AND CLAIRE PRATT

47 Glencairn Ave.
Toronto 12

Jan. 30 [1955]

Beloved ones:

Here I am on Sunday morning just finished scrubbing out the bacon-and-egg pot. I haven't much housework to do as I have most of my meals at Floss's. Was there last night and I go again this late afternoon.

I got a letter from my old friend Father LeBel asking me if I would go to Windsor to attend the opening meeting of their new University. It was Assumption *College*. He has invited six people to come (including Watson Kirkconnell) and receive a D. Litt. I can't very well refuse as it won't be held till June, and the College has had me four times in the past with their generous honoraria.

There isn't much news going. How glad I shall be when the both of you are back. I telephoned Mr Free who manufactures Hospital beds. He said that he would install one at any time as soon as we clean out the room. He will get all the particulars from you so as to make the bed similar to the N.Y. one. It is a satisfaction to know that there will be no difficulty on that score.

Peggy went out to her country house last Sunday and found it in a terrible shape, doors and windows open. She got out again today as the job of fixing is a long and tiring one.

Did you know Soper of St George United[298]? He died in hospital a few days ago. He was the brother of the Hanna Soper and I stayed with when we came to Toronto first.

Jessie Norman[299] is improving though she had a troublesome time of it at first.

Love to you always
Ned

298 Reverend Samuel H. Soper (1882–1978), born in St John's and a classmate of Pratt's at Victoria College, served as a United Church missionary in China from 1912 to 1929. Invalided back to Canada, he later served as minister of a number of circuits in Ontario.

299 Wife of Dr James Norman

VIII As Good as Any Old Horse My Age, 1955–1964

I have my ups and downs, but of late have been ... as good ... as any old horse my age.
– E.J. Pratt to Henry W. Wells, 6 December 1956

TO LEO COX

47 Glencairn Ave.

April 16, 1955

Dear Leo:

Thanks for your note. It was nice to hear from you, old friend, even if the missive was brief.

No, I don't expect to be in your city for some time. I have greatly cut down on my speaking and travelling in recent months. It puts more of a strain on me than I can comfortably take these days. We had our daughter Claire in hospital in New York for six months having spinal fusions and other treatments done. She is home now but still in bed until the healing is complete, which means anywhere from another six months to a year or more. That has been an extra strain as you can imagine. But one of these days I may run down to see all my old friends in Montreal. If you should come this way do not fail to call me up and drop in to see me if you possibly can.

With fond memories of times past, and my love to you,

Ned

TO HENRY ALEXANDER[1]

47 Glencairn Ave

June 6, 1955

My dear Henry:

It was a delight to have a chat with you the other evening and reminisce about old times at Queen's. I miss those summer sojourns in Kingston very much, especially my old friends and my favourite golf course. But it was very pleasant to relive some of the old times in conversation. I was sorry we could not have got together again. Perhaps I'll pay a visit to the old town during the summer.

The Learned meetings[2] seem to have gone very well. I only attended a few – found it too tiring to sit through a lot of long-winded dissertations. But I enjoyed meeting and chatting with some of the chaps I hadn't seen in months, in some cases years.

All the very best to you.
Ned Pratt

TO LOUIS DUDEK

Victoria College
Toronto

June 18, 1955

My dear Louis:

Your *Europe*[3] with its heart-warming inscription was forwarded to me from the College.

1 See the note to 'Alexander' in the letter to Pelham Edgar, 7 August 1944 (p. 283).

2 The Learned Societies of Canada was a conclave of scholarly associations, led by the Royal Society, which had met at the University of Toronto during the last week of May and first week of June 1955. The annual event is now called the Congress of the Humanities and Social Sciences and meetings alternate between eastern, western, and central locations.

3 A sequence of ninety-nine poems recording his responses and impressions evoked by a voyage to and travels in Europe, published in 1954 (Toronto: Laocoön Press).

I read it *twice* and was delighted with it – 'twice,' because the condensation of the language demanded renewed application to unravel the meaning and discover the aptness of the similes. Here, I thought, is something which combines the cerebral and the visceral. You may know that I have a special fondness for the latter as it is so basic to impulse and action.

The most primordial thing in the world is the sea and you made it sweep over me until I nearly went down for the *third* time.

And then, your use of resounding proper names struck my solar plexus. Besides this, the desolation of Europe and the sense of an unnamable future brooded over me. May I indicate a few passages, lines and words which specially held my attention.

I love the name *Stephanie.*

Cellophane, dollar bills of green, Donald Duck villages, the *tamed moment of eternity.*

An *ice-floe* could look like a seagull's wing granted the distance.

Sky-sperm; 'the sea salmon that dies in the mountains.' Simple statement but superb and in a sense tragic.'

'luxurious ermine and leopard coat.'

Poem 10 is grand; so is the conclusion of 12.

'The conqueror sea revelling in its strength' is a simile faithful to its source. Its indifference (20) to the Lilliputians – to the entertainment, etc.

'The landscape weeping like a watery Turner.'

47 is a fine study in contrast.

'The sea carving the architraves of the ragged rocks.'

I think 70 is the finest poem in the volume with 84 a close second, though 91 with its particularity of the number of shells on Reims – 'the Euclidean cemeteries' makes me doubtful of the priority of the other two. I saw the poem in the Canadian Forum and it haunts me yet.

I could go on. The sea-imagery is so tumultuous that it makes Anderson's[4] vaunted 'flow' sound like a stricture-piddle.

I am glad that McGill has you in the English Department.

A personal remark here. I haven't written a line since 'The Last Spike.' Reasons: – my right eye has played out on me and (2) my daughter has to be in bed with a polio aftermath for a year, which absolutely destroys concentration for me.

4 Patrick Anderson.

Should you come to Toronto in the fall, let me know in advance so I can get the gang together with you in the festivities.

The best.
Ned Pratt

TO MARGARET (MRS E.K) BROWN

47 Glencairn Ave.
Toronto 12
Ont.

July 24, 1955

My dear Peggy:

We were so sorry to have missed you. We tried to reach you by telephone several times at the Park Plaza but could make no contact. The phone girl said she would leave a message but probably you had left.

We had planned to have a party at the York Downs Golf Club for you, but Claire who was in the Hospital for a spinal fusion had developed a tumor which threw all our plans out. She is being operated on tomorrow and we are keeping our fingers crossed. She will have to remain at the '*General*'[5] for several weeks. This new development arising before the spine was healed has had a most depressing effect on us. We have the best surgeon in Toronto taking care of her but our minds will be clouded till she is definitely out of the woods.[6]

We would dearly love to have seen you. Perhaps in happier days we can reunite. Vi sends her love to you.

Affectionately,
Ned.

---

5 General Hospital.
6 Claire's tumour proved to be benign, but she remained in hospital for a month.

TO RONALD G. EVERSON[7]

47 Glencairn Ave.
Toronto, Ont.

August 14, 1955

Dear Ron:

The whole thing was wonderful – cheque, lunch, poems, and your mediating generous self. I shall see to it that the expenditure will count well. There are two magazines that will be helped by it.[8]

Your verse makes 'the Montreal group' stuff appear anaemic. I saw the *Milking* poem in the Atlantic[9] and I am glad that such a fine exclusive magazine accepted both.[10] Keep on at it and give us similar fresh original images and phrases – 'the tail lopping a timothy,' 'Stuns the farm to drowsiness,' 'a deep nap of sidewalk plush,' 'the long bones of the elms' and so forth.

Good luck old chap and my love
to you.
Ned

Claire is improving though it has been a long grind. She comes home next Thursday we hope, and though the cast may yet remain on for a year, it will be a comfort to have her under our own roof.

7 Everson (1903–92) was a lawyer, partner in the public relations and publishing firm of Johnston, Everson, and Charlesworth. His verse appeared in magazines in the 1920s, and his first book of poetry, *Three Dozen Poems* (Montreal: Cambridge Press), appeared in 1957. He subsequently published several more books and pamphlets, and his poems appeared in numerous magazines and anthologies. Pratt had encouraged him to write and provided detailed notes on his verse in a letter dated 7 February 1952 (*EJP: Web*).

8 In a letter to Pitt (1 May 1967), Everson explained that 'Ned ran an unofficial Canada Council, using his own money and bits from some others of us, to help deserving unknown poets and shaky little magazines.' (See the letter to John Sutherland, 29 September 1955 [p. 621].)

9 'After Evening Milking,' *Atlantic Monthly* (February 1955).

10 His 'Looking for Firewood' would appear in the July 1956 issue of *Atlantic Monthly*.

TO JOHN SUTHERLAND

47 Glencairn Ave.
Toronto 12
Ont.

Sept. 29 [1955]

Dear John:

The exposition[11] is marvelous. I read it through twice and so did a few of my friends. All of us thought that the style was of the finest order. Naturally, I was predisposed towards it because of the enthusiasm and generosity of the treatment. But apart from that, even if it had been on another subject, I would have been exhilarated.

My brother Calvert C. Pratt of St John's, Newfoundland said – 'Put me down for 100 copies when it is published.' He intends contributing two copies to each of the 28 libraries in Nfld. and taking the balance for personal gifts. You can use that as an initial bargaining point with your publisher. I hope Macmillans will undertake it. It shouldn't be too expensive. I mention Macmillans for two reasons: (1) they are my publishers, (2) they are, I think, cheaper than Ryersons and besides that, Ryersons didn't sell out the Edition done at Columbia University by Wells and Klinck.[12] I don't know what reaction Gray (Macmillans) will have but the relatively small size of the book ought to keep the expense down. I had a chat with Pierce recently. He is a grand fellow, willing to take a gamble but his superiors have the last word and the commercial element is strong with them. Pierce admires your work in the N.R.[13] It is a strong corrective to the awful stuff that is being poured out by the C.I.V.[14] I have never met Layton but is he as bad as his writing?

Viola (my wife) said that this critique is the only thing she has come across in Canada where the sub-conscious areas are explored to render up valid meanings. That is true.

---

11 Sutherland had sent him a typescript of his prospective book on Pratt's poetry: *The Poetry of E.J. Pratt: A New Interpretation*, published the next year by Ryerson.

12 *Edwin J. Pratt: The Man and His Poetry* (1947).

13 *Northern Review*.

14 A 'little magazine' edited by Aileen Collins. Its title was actually *CIV/n* (code for 'civilization'), from a remark in a letter from Ezra Pound to Louis Dudek, who worked on the magazine: "Civ/n is not a one man job." First published in 1953 in Montreal, it ran for only seven issues, publishing verse by Layton, Leonard Cohen, Eli Mandel, and many other new poets.

Another thing! How is the N.R.? And what are your future plans? I referred to your work and the difficulties you were labouring under. The little group responded with small contributions amounting altogether to $50 which I am enclosing.[15] No one was prosperous but all were unanimous in their respect for you and your writings. They preferred to remain anonymous, so if you compile a list again, just print $50 (anonymous). There are no strings attached. If unfortunately you cannot bring out another number, the amount is for past services.

Personally, I am restricting my articles now because of severe eyestrain which needs constant medical attention, the pressure hinders concentration on writing. In any case, I am retired from the College having reached the age limit.

The best.

Ned Pratt

P.S. I forgot to mention two points:

(1) The *Mauritania* had several knots of speed ahead of Titanic though the owners were hoping the big ship might come close to the other.[16]
(2) Possibly a little change in the beginning of the Postscript[17] might lessen the ammunition of a few 'intellectuals' or 'obscurantists' who claim there are no ideas in the poetry. They like to think they have a following. This was pointed out to me by a friend. Still, I leave that matter with you as you see fit.

TO EARLE BIRNEY

47 Glencairn Ave.
Toronto 12, Ont.

Nov. 8 [1955]

Dear old Earle:

Your Down the Long Table[18] is a gorgeous bit of autobiographical analysis. Vi and I are reading it now. Your poetry, and Turvey and this put you in the

15 See the note to 'two or three magazines will be helped by it' in the letter to Ronald G. Everson, 14 August 1955 (p. 619).
16 A reference to a statement by Sutherland in his chapter on the *Titanic*.
17 Sutherland's brief conclusion of his book on Pratt.
18 Birney's second novel, just published by McClelland & Stewart.

driver's seat in Canada as far as variety of gifts are concerned. And you got a grand road ahead of you yet.

How you managed to concoct those names of the inquisitors is a triumph – Reksky, Arnup, Sather, Dirty Dirkin and countless others probably had their prototypes.

I anticipate great sales for this book.

Here is a story for Esther.[19] Hand it on to her.

Affectionately
Ned.

Am sending the Star review of your book.

TO ESTHER BIRNEY

[8 Nov. 1955]

Dear Esther:

Here is a recent one I think you'll enjoy. 'A young ordained minister was sent up to the Porcupine to take his first charge with the advice to pay especial attention to the spiritual welfare of the miners. He went to the Foreman of a Section and urged him to come with his gang to the church to hear his first sermon. They came expecting to sit at the back of the church, but to their dismay they were ushered to the front row of twelve seats on the explicit orders of the minister.

When the minister saw the twelve faces and the twenty-four eyes glaring at him malignantly, he got very nervous and when the time came for the sermon he became utterly inhibited in speech. He forgot the sermon and the text, but he remembered one incident. He couldn't see the congregation – no people but those twelve damn miners. So he shouted out (addressing them), "What did Moses say when he came down from the mount?" No answer. Again, louder this time, "I say what did Moses say when he came down from the mount?" No answer. Again the third time (still with his eyes on the foreman), "*What did Moses* etc." The foreman couldn't stand it any longer and yelled out – "Look it here, bloody reverend, I'll stand sucker for the bunch, What the hell *did* he say?" The minister had a stroke and had to be carried out.'

Bless you, Ned.

---

19 See the letter to Esther Birney, 8 November 1955 (below, p. 622).

TO CARL KLINCK

47 Glencairn Ave.

June 13, 1956

Dear Carl:

Tell Reg[20] I am honoured in having his interest in my verse.

I never expected that *Rachel* would ever see print. I wrote [it] in 1917 and read it to a group of friends. A man named *Alf Good*[21] asked to go over the ms. and the next thing I knew he had a limited number printed in New York in soft covers and without the name of either printer or publisher. It was distributed just among friends.

I didn't think much of the poem upon a re-reading a year afterwards and decided not to include it in Newfoundland Verse, except its conclusion. Later on I omitted it from the Collected Poems. It is very imitative of Wordsworth at a low level, though I think that conclusion in N.V. has some good lines.

I cannot find a copy anywhere – which doesn't make me weep anyway. A possession of it might do so.

Give my most cordial greetings to Reg and take a good share of affection for yourself and Margaret.

Vi and Claire send their regards.

Ned.

TO SISTER DOROTHY MARIE DOYLE[22]

July 10, 1956

20 Reginald E. Watters, professor of English at the Royal Military College, and Klinck were preparing their *Canadian Anthology* (Toronto: Gage, 1955, 1966, 1974), and had asked Pratt for bibliographical data on *Rachel* to include in their list of his books.

21 An insurance agent whom Pratt had met through his friend Robert S. LeDrew (see the note to 'poor old Bob' in the letter to Arthur Phelps, 18 September 1918 [p. 13]). LeDrew, who thought very highly of the poem, had interceded with Good to have it printed. When Pratt included lines from 'Rachel' in *NV* he dedicated them to the memory of R.S. LeDrew, who had died in 1919.

22 Sister Doyle had written an MA thesis at the University of Ottawa entitled 'The Epic Note in the Poetry of Edwin John Pratt,' and sent Pratt a copy for his comment. The following year she began a PhD dissertation entitled 'The Poetic Imagery of Edwin John Pratt.' See the letters to Sister Doyle of 21 July 1957 and 7 April 1958 (pp. 635–7 and *EJP: Web*). She later became an English professor at St Francis Xavier University, Antigonish, NS.

My Dear Sister:

The delay in replying to your 'epic note' is due to my absence from the city for a few days.

You have done a wonderful piece of analysis and I feel honoured by its scope and, I may say, by its friendly treatment. It is the kind of attention I like – both critical and appreciative. I am glad that you placed 'Brébeuf' at the top, as it is my favourite, for the story took hold of my soul. It has always been my belief that a life without a faith is the most miserable form of existence imaginable. Brébeuf, as the martyr, is one of the most dramatic and ineffacable characters of history.

Your manuscript warmed my heart. When do you wish it returned, as I should like to re-read it?

Yours cordially,
E.J. Pratt

TO SISTER DOROTHY MARIE DOYLE

July 25, 1956

Dear Sister:

There is no need to worry over a few type errors in your manuscript. I make more myself when I pound the typewriter. It is a pleasure for me to read your letters and have your enthusiasm.

You ask about symbolism and imagery.[23]

The central idea to me was to get hold of a symbol which at the time of the Crucifixion represented the very limit of shame in the eyes of the pagan world, but later became the transcendent glory of the Christian theology and experience, namely, the *Cross*. I had to end on that note.

It was necessary to work in correlative ideas such as the singing of 'the Gloria' by the Fathers, their comradeship, their willingness to face their martyrdom, their complete renunciation of material gain and such like considerations; and, technically, for dramatic purposes, a rather extensive description of the lull before the storm broke. When I took a trip to the Martyrs' Shrine near Midland

---

23 She had inquired about imagery and symbolism in *B*, already looking ahead to her proposed doctoral dissertation.

I found a spring of clear cool water with water cress at the bottom; I wondered if Brébeuf saw it.

You also ask about the recording.[24] A few years ago I was invited to Harvard University to give a couple of lectures. One was on 'Brébeuf.' They asked me to give a recording of 'Brébeuf' and shorter poems, which I did. Victoria College bought one hundred copies and is ordering more next October. The Librarian may be in touch with you after the summer holidays.

The very best to you,

Yours sincerely,
E.J. Pratt

TO JOHN SUTHERLAND

47 Glencairn Ave.
Toronto

Monday 13th [Aug. 1956]

My dear John:

Your book[25] is a masterpiece of analysis, not so much on the ground of its personal subject-matter, but for its wonderful style. I never had anything written about my work equal to it in the probing of backgrounds. I had to read it twice to discover sources and influences which had hitherto escaped me or had been forgotten through the years. The way you brought in my early Newfoundland experiences was almost miraculous. And my University days became fresh again. James[26] was at my side; and, though I could scarcely have recalled a sentence from *Demonology*, *Eschatology*,[27] and all the other '*ologies*, you made those investigations sweep over me – such was the strength you imparted to the subconscious process. But what amazed me most was your parallel classifications of terms and expressions! I was honoured no end by your attention to detail – significant detail. How often, indeed, does the word *cross* (higher and

24 See the note to 'they may be marketed' in the letter to Viola and Claire Pratt, 3 March 1946 (p. 372).
25 Sutherland had sent him an advance copy of *The Poetry of E.J. Pratt: A New Interpretation*, just off the press.
26 William James.
27 His masters thesis and doctoral dissertation.

lower case c) appear! Even in the 'Cachalot' it stands side by side with *royal*, *monarch*, *pain*, etc. The apocalyptic vision holds the horizon in your treatment as it does now in mine.

Before I came to the *Great Feud* I wondered what would happen to the dinosaur. Yet he suffers not only pain and humiliation but the arduous passage up a steep hill before he commits himself to the sea. The parallel almost blinded me with its force.

But I must not fail to underline your mode of writing. That expression, 'conjuring a continent out of a couplet' was itself poetry at a very high level. Vi and I read it and conversed about it for many minutes. She was ecstatic, and it hit my ear like a Mozartian phrase.

We shall cherish the book. We are ordering many copies from Ryersons for Christmas presents.

Our love to you John and to dear Audrey.[28]

Ned.

TO CARLYLE KING[29]

Victoria College
Toronto, Ont.

August 15, 1956

Dear Carlyle King:

I am writing this for two reasons:

(1) Your article on G.B.S. in the current *Queen's Quarterly*[30] is the finest piece of biographical revelation I have seen in the Quarterly for years. I have lectured on Shaw for a long time and admired both his sparse encomiums and disembowelling wit. Your account is the best I have seen of the combination. It is so eminently readable for a quarterly.

(2) The second reason is personal. I have always refrained from responding to reviews and articles upon anything I have done myself, but your article in

---

28 This was Pratt's last letter to Sutherland, who died on 1 September 1956.

29 King (1907–88) had taught in the English Department in the University of Saskatchewan since 1929 and was head of department (1949–64). For many years he was active in the CCF, forerunner of the New Democratic Party, serving as president of the party (1945–60).

30 'GBS and Music,' *QQ* 63 (Summer 1956): 165–78.

the Canadian Forum[31] warmed my heart beyond measure, because conflict between 'heart and brain' has consistently been with me, though it has been neglected in favour of the 'story' element. As you may know, Frye has often emphasized that collision.

May Heaven bless you,
Ned Pratt

TO RALPH GUSTAFSON

47 Glencairn Ave

Sept. 19, 1956

My dear Ralph:

It is always grand to get a word of appreciation from a man like yourself whom I admire and love. You have ever been a great friend of mine and (apart from it) when you come to Toronto I shall put up a real 'stag' for you at the York Club with your friends to 'circle' you at the dinner table, if the geometry of the room allows the 'circling.' You have a lot of admirers in this city.

My wife and I took a long look through our shelves last night but could not find a single copy of Verses of the Sea, the reason being, I suppose, that most of the poems were included in the *Collected Edition* eight years ago. I haven't written one thing of value since 'Towards the Last Spike' three years ago. If you haven't a copy I shall gladly send one to you! I am sending a copy of 'Poems for Senior Students in High Schools,'[32] just published. It may sound a bit ridiculous, but the book contains only two poems – Chaucer's *Prologue* and the *Roosevelt and the Antinoe*. As it was authorized by the Board of Education 20,000 copies were sold by Macmillans at once and this helped to pay our grocery bill, since I retired from Victoria College on a pension. I wonder if good old Geoff has been turning over in his grave at the companionship. The students have to take the book willy nilly and since Macmillans own the copyright, they and the Board have to shoulder the responsibility of disturbing Geoff's dust by the proximity.

---

31 'The Mind of E.J. Pratt,' *CF* (April 1956): 9–10.
32 [*sic*]. *Poems for Upper School 1956–57*.

I am delighted that you are returning to poetry. You have a fresh note unsurpassed by anyone writing. And then your novel![33] I trust M. & S.[34] have enough sense to put their weight behind it.

Blessings on you.

With much love,
Ned

TO CLAIRE PRATT

47 Glencairn Ave.
Toronto, Ont.

Wednesday, the 26th [Sept. 1956]

Dearest Cayke:

Here I am at the table, having finished the breakfast dishes without damaging a cup or glass. Your mother is doing a bit of washing – the left-overs from yesterday.

We were so glad to get a phone message from you Monday evening[35] and possibly tonight we shall be hearing from you again. It is grand to hear your voice.

Ruth[36] and your mother went to the Royal Alex last night to see Romeo & Juliet with the Little Vic Players.[37] They heard every word though they were in the gods.[38] The acoustics of the theatre are perfect. I stayed home and who should come in but Margaret.[39] She had a thousand snaps (more or less) which, when the hour (one whole hour) was finished, had me on the floor just slumped with inertia. It was a matter of – 'Oh but you should see this one – this rock was as slippery as glass – we fell off it and got soaked,' and so on and so on and so on. By George it was an awful evening. I sneezed all the way through with a real hayfever. This

---

33 Entitled *No Music in the Nightingale*, it was never published.

34 McClelland & Stewart.

35 Claire was now well enough to have returned to her work at Harvard University Press in Cambridge, MA.

36 Probably Ruth Jenking. See the note to 'Ruth Jenking' in the letter to E.K. Brown, 4 November 1941 (p. 214).

37 A Victoria College troupe.

38 The upper gallery of a theatre.

39 Probably Margaret (Lacey) Tansley. See the note to 'Margaret Lacey' in the letter to Claire Pratt, 14 May 1954 (p. 565).

prolonged the exhibit. I don't want to see another snap whether of a lake or of an elephant with a camel's neck and a rat's tail. However, she's a nice kid.

This is just a note. I shall write you again soon (as soon as I get over the photographic agony).

Much love,
Sneezing Father

My love to dear Shirley.[40]

TO CLAIRE PRATT

47 Glencairn Ave,

Oct. 22 [1956]

Dearest Cayke:

I am putting these points down seriatim so I won't forget them:

(1) Your 'bountiful' letter just came.
(2) Your mother got your two prints.
(3) Do you recall the time when the '26 gang[41] came in last year and Ruskin (Ruck) Thompson (the practical joker) threw the elastic lizard or salamander into the wash basin unknown to Helen Lloyd who was to do the washing? Well last Saturday night we had our '26 Reunion, the biggest we have had, 50 in all. I tried to burlesque myself. I took Hamlet and worked in all of the 50, at least the '26 section of them. Ruck was one of them and I called him up to the platform to receive his mark which was 50. Each person had a Shakespearean name in the middle. So I called, 'Thompson – *Ruck Salamander Thompson*, will you please come to the platform.' He came up and I said, 'You have a short essay – only "Hamlet, or what came up the drain."' They howled. You didn't see the serpent or salamander, did you? It was devilishly natural – wriggling along. No wonder Helen (who wasn't in on the trick before) screamed. [ ] Your mother was in the front row with Helen and Ruth Wilson. I whispered to them that they had to cry. Your

40 Shirley Freshman.
41 Pratt had been honorary president of the Victoria College Class of 1926 for many years. Individuals named in the letter were members of the class and friends of the Pratts.

mother (whose name was Viola Volumnia) dried Helen's tear with a big red bandanna hanky. It was all good fun.

My love, we'll be glad to see you when you decide to come. I am re-arranging your bed-room after your mother arranged it. I like things perfect, as you know.

Much love.
Father.

TO CLAIRE PRATT

[Ottawa, Ontario]

Friday a.m. [26 Oct. 1956]

Dearest Cayke:

Here we are at the Chateau,[42] having survived three hours of entertainment (roast-duckling and speeches) last night. Your mother has just gone over to the Parliamentary Library and I am in my room sending off a brief record of the occasion. Our air trip was on the split-second time – good weather and everything favourable. We leave by air today at 4 o'clock, getting in to Toronto about 6:30.

Lester Pearson gave a very fine speech mainly on the Freedom of the Press plus its responsibilities. I never saw him in better form. His wife Marion (a former student of mine)[43] looked quite fatigued. One would think she had gone through Nato[44] instead of Mike or she may have been listening to an old speech.

Ian and Marion[45] are coming to the Chateau to have lunch with us today. I may call up Claude Bissell who is now President of Carleton College.[46] I saw Doug LePan and several of my old friends. More than one hundred attended the banquet.

So you think you'll move by van.[47] We shall be so glad to see you. Let us know your schedule so we may be on hand to help in the moving of the furniture.

Your mother addressed the letter to you.

Love,
Father

---

42 Château Laurier.

43 Pratt taught Mrs Pearson, the former Maryon Elspeth Moody of Winnipeg, in 1920.

44 The North Atlantic Treaty Organization was at the time deeply involved in the worsening Suez Canal dispute. Pearson as minister of external affairs was Canada's chief representative.

45 Ian Whitney, son of Viola's brother Ralph, and his wife Marion.

46 It officially became Carleton University in 1957.

47 Claire was moving back to Toronto from Cambridge, MA.

TO CLAIRE PRATT

47 Glencairn Ave.
Toronto 12
Ontario

Oct. 29, 1956

Dearest:

I am enclosing 'Mike' Pearson's speech[48] or at least a part of it which brought down the house at the dinner last Thursday evening. He made it up himself. I would have sent it last Friday but I had to wait to get our own copy at 47.

I am also sending two letters which perhaps need answering before you return.

Our house is like a church basement meeting.[49] As many as ten come in to tie those infernal knots and to exchange views on everything under Arcturus. I put on the Star programme last night – the Sunday night programme[50] – to drown out the chattering but it was no use when Pash and Marion[51] got arguing with the rest of the bevy. They left about eleven p.m., and then I managed to settle down with two pillows and three blankets to make sure I was in bed.

Let us know when you expect to get back but don't hurry on the highway.

Armand Whitehead and his wife took us out to dinner yesterday away beyond Richmond Hill. All of us met at the St. George's Church where we had a delightful sermon from Dr Short. He told one story which your mother claimed was meant for my ears. Short had had a busy week and was very tired on Sunday night but he had to keep an appointment on Monday at 10 a.m. So he telephoned a friend in whom he had absolute trust to wake him by telephone at 9 which would give him an hour to dress and breakfast. Imagine having the telephone waking him up at 9. Your mother whispered – 'Ah, that's meant just for you.'

Lovingly,
Father

48 See the letter to Claire Pratt, 26 October 1956 (p. 630).

49 The members of the Talents Service Club were preparing for another bazaar. See the note to 'Talents' in the letter to Claire Pratt, 8 November 1953 (p. 545).

50 A radio programme of music sponsored by the *Toronto Daily Star*.

51 Ida Pashley and Marion Whytall.

TO DESMOND PACEY

Nov. 12, 1956

Dear Des:

Thanks for your grand article.[52] It is a superb bit of analysis – the sort of thing I like (1) appreciation and (2) helpful criticism.

I agree with most of your judgments. You may have noticed that I discarded in the *Collected* edition most of those heterogeneous verses in *Newfoundland Verse*. To me now they appear very amateurish.

I am so glad you like the three of my favourites – the *R & A*,[53] the *Titanic* and *Brébeuf*. In fact I put so much energy into the last one that I developed a severe chronic eye-strain which certainly interfered with the later composition.

Poor John Sutherland. I didn't know that he was writing his book until two weeks or so before his death.[54] To give him credit he was the first critic who tried to get inside those years I spent in Psychology. Some of his conclusions are far-fetched such as the representing of the dinosaur as a phase of Christ, but John did insert a 'caveat' at the beginning that he was going beyond the 'conscious intention,' a perilous excursion indeed. And, again, though I had to teach Wundt, I hated Wundtianism and its mechanisms. You properly place that period in its proper orientation.

Thanks for letting me see your article. I should have answered before but this is my first day out, having wrestled with a bug for two weeks.

My love to Mary, yourself
and family.
Ned Pratt

52 The chapter on Pratt that Pacey had written for his projected *Ten Canadian Poets*. (See the letter to Pacey, 29 October 1954 [pp. 585–8].) Pratt, it seems, was not aware that it was a chapter for a book rather than an article for a journal.

53 *Roosevelt and the Antinoe*.

54 This, as we know from his letters to Sutherland and others, was untrue. Pratt had responded to Sutherland's enquiries and seen a draft of the analysis (see the letters of 12 May and 21 May 1954 [pp. 564 and 566–8]), although he did not receive a copy of the book until about two weeks before Sutherland's death on 1 September (see the letter to Sutherland, 13 August [pp. 625–6]). It is curious that Pratt should have felt it necessary to make this denial. In the draft of his letter, Pratt is much more explicit in his explanation of why Sutherland may have felt that his interpretations of Pratt's poems, particularly 'The Great Feud,' had been endorsed by the author. (See "Textual Notes," pp. 723–4.)

TO HENRY W. WELLS

47 Glencairn Ave

Dec. 6, 1956

My Dear Henry,

It was good to hear from you after a long silence and to know that you are keeping hale and hearty. I have had my ups and downs, but of late have been quite on top of the world healthwise, without an ache or a pain and as good an appetite as any old horse my age (75 now), and sleeping each night like a cherub in bliss. What more can a body ask?

No, I'm not doing much writing now. I gave up verse about four or five years ago. I still do a few talks now and then. Vi is the chief writer in this household now and she is very good at it. I sometimes give her a helping hand.

Yes I still recall those visits[55] with great pleasure. They were good times. If you ever come up this way again be sure to call me and we'll have a meal and a round together for old times sake.

Compliments of the coming Season to you.

Affectionately,
Ned.

Give my best regards to Bart[56] when you see him.
N.

TO RALPH GUSTAFSON

47 Glencairn Ave.

[21 Mar. 1957]

My dear Ralph:

I am sorry that you have struck this snag[57] as your troubles with publishers have been many and complicated.

55 To New York in the 1940s.

56 Bart Brebner.

57 Gustafson had written on 19 March, enclosing a letter from Alfred A. Knopf which stated that the firm considered itself the holder of the American copyright to all of Pratt's poems published in *CPA*. Gustafson commented: 'In the light of their definition, author's copyright becomes meaningless.'

I have not been able to locate the contract but I assumed that the possession of copyright gave the owner the right to dispose of the contents as he wished, but apparently it isn't so. I have a vague recollection that, as far as American anthologies are concerned, Knopf offered to collect the fees for the selections and pass them on to me. This happened in only a few instances. The selections were brief and Knopf promptly handed the amounts to me. I think $10.00 was usual, but it is years since I have heard from the Firm. A.J.M. Smith's anthology was published before the Knopf negotiations were made, hence he had to deal only with the Canadian Macmillans. In both cases the royalties and permission costs were given to me, though Macmillans (legally, I imagine) might have retained the income.

There are two possibilities here:

(1) The Penguin selections could be abbreviated, for at present they are very generous.
(2) I should be very happy indeed to go 50 – 50 on the permission costs with *Penguin* and for that matter with Macmillans too, for I appreciate the extent of those publishing rivalries. (This would be confidential of course.) Macmillans' deduction is 10% for collection.

I realize the delicacy of this situation for you but please accept No 2 if it helps out. After all something should be written off for publicity, and you have been a peach throughout all our relationships (overlook the possible mixture of metaphor here).

If there is anything further to clear up, don't hesitate to ask me. The mere getting of a letter from you is worth a lot.

Bless you,
Ned
E. J. Pratt

TO DESMOND AND MARY PACEY

47 Glencairn Ave

[May 1957]

My dear Des and Mary:

Blessings on the both of you for your hospitality.[58] It was grand to be with you.

---

58 He had been in Fredericton to receive an honorary degree. See the letter to Desmond Pacey, May 1957 (*EJP: Web*).

By the way, Des, whom should I meet on the train, as it left Kingston for Toronto, but Lorne Pierce who was most enthusiastic over your forthcoming book.[59] He described it as the finest piece of critical prose to come out of Canada and was proud that Ryersons had it.

I enjoyed my trip to Fredericton though the two nights going and coming were sleepless. But the days made up for it, and the entertainment – the entertainment!!

My love to you and

your sweet family.
Ned.

TO IRVING LAYTON

47 Glencairn Ave.
Toronto 12

June 9, 1957

Dear Irving:

I know I am going to have a lot of fun reading through your volume of verse.[60] Thanks for the complimentary copy with its good wishes. It may take me some time to get through it as I am having trouble with my right eye which cannot be corrected through glasses.

Congratulations on the Foundation Award.[61] I just came across the note. More power to your brain and general anatomy.

Yours sincerely,
E.J. Pratt

TO SISTER DOROTHY MARIE DOYLE

47 Glencairn Ave

July 21, 1957

59 *Ten Canadian Poets* published by Ryerson Press in 1958.

60 *The Improved Binoculars: Selected Poems*, introduction by William Carlos Williams (Highlands, NC: Jonathan Williams, 1956; 2nd ed., 1957).

61 A Canadian Foundation Award of $4,000.

Dear Sister Dorothy Marie:

Your letter was forwarded to me from the College by a roundabout route – hence the delay in answering.

I have no objection whatever to your task; in fact, I am honoured by your interest.[62]

First, I may point out that Sutherland brought out many facets in my work of which I was unaware (or but *dimly* conscious) at the time of writing, but of which I could see the partial truths after re-reading his book. He did plough back into the past to uncover the unconscious processes, and I was amazed at the skill with which he did his microscopic analysis. It is true that the microscope was unduly active when it played upon the squid and the cachalot but it brought into brilliant focus the concluding pages of *Brébeuf*. Leafing through the 'Collected Poems' recently, I was astonished at the numerous references to Christ, the Cross and the symbol of grace. Personally, I derived more exaltation from the dying moments of Brébeuf than from anything I ever selected as a subject.

Before answering your question about Nature, may I mention some poems which are undercurrents of my convictions.

(1) 'Before an Altar'	page 95 (Collected Poems)
(2) To an Enemy	95
(3) The Empty Room	96
(4) The Iron Door	212
(5) Old Age	226
(6) A Legacy	227 (In memory of my mother)
(7) The Highway	228
(8) The Decision	228 (To a dear student of mine)
(9) The Truant	309

'The Truant' is an elaborate symbol of human resistance to a pagan god of power divorced from all moral considerations. It was written at the height of the Nazi regime. The *Panjandrum* is personified Power without kindness, mercy and love. The *Truant* is a Christian who defies this giant of Might and is willing to prefer pain and death to submission. The poem ends on the Rood, the sublimest symbol of sacrificial love.

62 She had asked how he felt about her writing a dissertation on his poetry for the PhD degree at the University of Ottawa. (See the note to 'Sister Dorothy Marie Doyle' in the letter to Doyle, 10 July 1956 [p. 623].) The dissertation was completed in 1958.

Nature

Perhaps the *Titanic* may be chosen as the most complex example. The ship itself may be taken as a protagonist of the story provided other factors are taken into account. It is an illustration of beauty, grace, magnitude and power but it also possesses a 'flaw' imposed upon it by its builders – the ambition of the White Star Line to make the 'perfect ship' and to that end she ran at top speed through the floe-ice though warned of the danger by other ships. The *flaw* was the belief in her invulnerability. Nature in the existence of an iceberg proved how *overweening* the hubris was. The Iceberg struck at the 'Achilles heel.' See page 114.

The Roosevelt and the Antinoe had to contend with nature in the form of the greatest storm on the Atlantic recorded in years. There is no apparent evidence of a flaw in the traditional sense. It is a straight contest between human courage and devotion and the terrific sea. Two lives indeed were lost but under no 'hubris.'

In the 'Great Feud' nature gives the finishing blow to the battle in the action of Jurania, the volcano, but the poem is a *dream* of an Armageddon. I think John Sutherland forced the religious issue in this allegory,[63] though his treatment was superb.

The Ice-Floes is a simple struggle between sailors and the elements.

I trust this will be of some help.

Yours most cordially,
E.J. Pratt

TO THE CANADA COUNCIL[64]

47 Glencairn Avenue
Toronto, November 11, 1957
The Canada Council – Category 10
Ottawa, Ontario

Dear Sirs,

Mr. Ralph Gustafson is applying to the Canada Council for a full term fellowship in order to pursue work in poetry and fiction, and I have the greatest pleasure in supporting his application.

---

63 Sutherland in his *The Poetry of E.J. Pratt: A New Interpretation* (1956) had seen *The Great Feud* as a Christian allegory in which Tyrannosaurus Rex symbolizes Christ. At the time of the book's publication, Pratt had thought the interpretation 'fantastic nonsense.'

64 The Canada Council had been established by an act of Parliament in March 1957. Gustafson was entering its first competition, applying for a 'special' fellowship for 'scholars and workers of distinction in the arts.'

I have been familiar with him and his writings for nearly fifteen years, and I do not know anyone in the whole Canadian field more able in respect to versatility. It has always been a delight to watch his performance measure up to his project. He is as good a critic as he is a creative artist – a bird of rare plumage nowadays.

Again with pleasure,
Yours sincerely,
E.J. Pratt

TO EARLE BIRNEY

47 Glencairn Ave Toronto

Dec. 7, 1957

My good old Earle:

Thanks for your sweet note of concern. Let me hasten to say first that Dudek's diagnosis was over-pessimistic.[65] There was no coronary and no angina.

I had what the doctors call tachycardia – a very fast pulse – 150 beats per minute which wore me down a lot. I went to the Hospital. Nothing organic – purely functional and nervous strain on the heart but serious enough to keep me in the house for last month where I am now.

The pulse has slowed down under digitalis but it has left me weak – too weak to get out of doors. I trust I can get out by the new year.

Bless you & your family and my benediction covers any stray cat or dog you may have in the house.

Lovingly
Ned

TO DAVID G. PITT

47 Glencairn Avenue

---

65 In a letter dated 28 November 1957, Louis Dudek had written Birney that Pratt had had 'a serious heart attack.'

Toronto, February 2, 1958

Dear Mr Pitt:

I have had a letter from Cal, who tells me that you have kindly consented to undertake the editing of the proposed book of Newfoundland poems,[66] and has asked me to send my list of selections which you may alter as you please. I am enclosing my list with this letter,[67] and am sending in addition a copy of *Magic in Everything*,[68] and a few hitherto unpublished poems.[69]

In regard to a title for the book, I would like to suggest 'Here the tides flow' – the first line of the poem *Newfoundland* which might be the opening section. A sub-title could be added – 'Poems of Newfoundland by E.J. Pratt,' and I would like the book dedicated to my fellow-Newfoundlanders.[70]

Since *Brébeuf and His Brethren* is much too long to be printed in its entirety, I am enclosing a list of parts which should form a collected whole, and which I should like as the final poem in the book.

If there is any other assistance which I can offer you, please let me know.

With kindest regards
and best wishes,
Sincerely yours,
E.J. Pratt

---

66 In December 1957, Senator Calvert Pratt heard David G. Pitt's contribution to 'Profile of a Canadian Poet' – the CBC's 'radio birthday party' on the occasion of Pratt's seventy-fifth (actually his seventy-sixth) birthday. He suggested that Pitt edit a selection of his brother's poems for Newfoundland readers, particularly students, and shortly thereafter proposed the project to John Gray of Macmillan of Canada. Gray asked Pitt to edit the book.

67 Pratt's list included most of the poems in Pitt's tentative table of contents. (See the letter to David Pitt, 18 February 1958 [p. 641].)

68 The copy of the poem sent to Pitt was in the form of a Christmas card used by Macmillan of Canada on the occasion of its fiftieth anniversary, December 1955. (See the note to 'Magic in everything' in the letter to Claire Pratt, 15 January 1953 [p. 517].)

69 'The Unromantic Moon,' 'Mother and Child,' and 'Newfoundland Calling.' Only the last was included in *Here the Tides Flow*.

70 On the advice of John Gray, neither the suggested subtitle nor the dedication were used in the book.

TO DESMOND PACEY

47 Glencairn Ave.
Toronto 12

February 18, 1958

My dear Des:

I should have written you before this but I have been under the weather for some time and spending three weeks in bed. Hence excuse the wobbly scrawl. Neuritis set in all through my left foot necessitating a wheel chair in the house.

Nevertheless I must send a word of congratulation upon your new book.[71] Lorne Pierce is jubilant over it. He sent me a copy and I have read and re-read it. It is truly magnificent in style and content. I am honoured in the lovely dedication and in the kindly treatment of myself, critical and appreciative – a blend I like.

Did you hear the Sunday account of the book by Louis Dudek[72] who said that your book would stand on his bookshelf for years? He was enthusiastic.

It is good to have the Ryerson gang firmly behind it. Many people have telephoned me in admiration of your appraisals. I trust the book will have an enduring sale. Pierce thinks it will.

I should write at greater length but my hand is shaky with neuritis.

My love to you and Mary and
the whole family.
Ned.

TO DAVID G. PITT

47 Glencairn Avenue.

Toronto, February 18, 1958.

Dear Mr Pitt:

Thank you for your fine letter. I should have answered it before, but I am still a bit under the weather.

---

71 *Ten Canadian Poets* (Toronto: Ryerson Press, 1958).
72 Dudek had reviewed the book in the CBC series *Critically Speaking.*

I shall deal with your questions numerically:

1. The pencil markings in *Magic in Everything* have no significance.
2. Our lists have a close similarity. Your additions are welcome. I should, however, prefer to leave out 'The Passing of Jerry Moore.'
3. I am glad you included 'Putting Winter to Bed,' and particularly 'Inventory of Hades.'
4. All your suggestions on page 2[73] are excellent.
5. Keep the biographical study to a minimum. Benét's introduction contains the relevant elements, all but the reference to Irish whisky. Keep that out, for heaven's sake, or I'll be up on the carpet. Have you seen Pacey's *Ten Canadian Poets* (Ryerson Press) just out?
6. Tentative: My first long poem written 40 years ago[74] was never published. A few friends of mine got together, and, unknown to me, privately printed 500 copies in New York for personal and non-commercial distribution. It doesn't bear my name and I never bothered about retrieving it. My wife has only one copy and she had a printer run off a second. It is the most 'Newfoundland' poem I ever wrote, and I was amazed to find that it was delivered over the radio by Arthur Phelps on my birthday. People have written in hoping to get a copy but I should rather have it published first in your Newfoundland collection if it is published at all. As a first long poem it is a bit amateurish and if you thought it advisable, you might edit it. I leave the matter of inclusion in your capable hands.
7. An erratum. There is a typographical mistake in 'Silences.'[75]

   'And silence in the growth and struggle for life,' should be
   'And silence in the struggle for life.'

8. An important exclusion: Please do not put in 'The Fable of the Goats.' It is laboured, ambiguous and bathetic. Exclusion, moreover, makes room for 'Towards the Last Spike.'

---

73 On page 2 of his letter (8 February), Pitt had suggested including 'carefully selected extracts' from 'The Cachalot,' *Titanic*, *DK*, and 'a fairly large portion' of *TLS*. He also suggested that he write prose 'bridges' linking the selections from *BB*, 'so that the sense of the narrative will not be lost.'

74 *Rachel*, of which he enclosed a photostatic copy. The poem was included in full in the book.

75 Pitt passed on his amendment to John Gray of Macmillan, but the poem was published in *HTF* without the change and as it appeared in both editions of *CP* (1944, 1958).

I leave everything to your editorial judgment.

Sincerely,
E.J. Pratt

TO CLAUDE AND CHRISTINE BISSELL

47 Glencairn Ave.
Toronto 12

Feb. 20, 1958

Very dear Claude & Christine:

The deep love of the Pratts goes with this brief acknowledgment. I could write longer but my hand is still shaking after two months in doors, as you can readily see. I am thankful to say that there is nothing organic in my condition, – all the x-ray plates were negative. But the trouble was a very acute neuritis in my left foot which at present prevents me from walking.

Claude, how glad we were when we got the news of your appointment.[76] To have the two of you 'fluttering' through the halls next fall will be a tonic to us all. But be sure to keep your hair brushed and tell Christine to preserve her lovely blue eyes for the more mature and observant graduates. God bless the two of you.

Affectionately,
From Vi and Ned.

TO A.J.M. SMITH

47 Glencairn Ave
Toronto 12 Ontario

Feb. 26, 1958

---

76 Bissell had been appointed president of the University of Toronto.

Dear old Art:

Your article in *Tamarack*[77] gave me the 'lift' of the week. It was actually therapeutic for I have been in doors and a good deal of the time in bed for three months with severe neuritis in the foot which has meant a wheel chair. (Could you believe it?). I suppose the bloody thing will disappear in Nature's own laggard time, giving me a chance to put some legibility into my penmanship (see?).

I have been dipping into your *Seven Centuries of Verse*.[78] What a mine of poetry. I should have acknowledged this before but my shaky hand wouldn't obey my will.

My love to you and Jeannie, and Vi is calling out 'Send them mine too Ned.'

Affectionately,
Ned.

TO RALPH GUSTAFSON

47 Glencairn Ave.
Toronto

Feb. 27, 1958

My dear Ralph:

I am still indoors with that confounded neuritis, three months of it now.

It is wet and blustery (and snowy), a perfect correlation for your sonnet.[79] The sestet is simply magnificent, Ralph! Lear, Owen, Mozart, Constanze present a sounding lead that plumbs the depths of poignancy.

I have read through your Penguin Introduction.[80] It is fine, very fine. What a job you are doing for Canadian writers. We are all in debt to you.

When you and dear Betty come again, bless us again with your presence. We loved Betty as we love you.

Ned, Vi, Claire

---

77 'A Garland for E.J. Pratt: The Poet,' *Tamarack Review* 6 (Winter 1958): 65–71.

78 A substantial anthology of poetry, British and American, edited by Smith and published by Scribners (1947, 1957, 1967).

79 'On Such a Wet and Blustery Night,' a sonnet referring to Mozart's burial in Vienna. See Gustafson's *Collected Poems* (Victoria, BC: Sono Nis, 1987), 62.

80 Gustafson had sent him the preface to his new Penguin anthology, published as *The Penguin Book of Canadian Verse* later that year.

TO CLAIRE PRATT

47 Glencairn Ave.
Toronto 12

April 5 [1958]

Dearest, darlingest sweets:

Excuse pencil because ink couldn't do justice to the above salutation.

When the enclosed arrived we thought it wise to open the letter as it might have contained information about your reservation.

Well it has been a long 24 hours since you left but the trip[81] is only for a week which is a consolation. We have spent much of the time before the T.V. which gave us a most thrilling experience today as the most dangerous shoal on the Pacific Coast (near Vancouver) known as *Ripple Rock* was blown up under two million pounds of High Explosive.[82] It had the appearance of an atom-bomb (mushroom shape). The Rock has been responsible for dozens of shipwrecks.

Your mother has just answered a buzz at the front door – Vicki Turnbull[83] with a Bermuda Easter lily.

I am in the midst of marking the Bowater articles[84] – an awesome collection of stylistic patterns and homicidal moods. May heaven forgive me for taking on such a job. I am resigning when I get in my report.

That's the news up to date.

Lovingly,
The Reverend Pratt
(God help him).

TO EARLE BIRNEY

47 Glencairn Ave.
Toronto 12
Ont.

April 19 [1958]

81 Claire had gone on a holiday trip.

82 On 5 April 1958, the notorious hazard in the channel of British Columbia's Seymours Narrows was cleared by one of the largest non-nuclear explosions ever recorded.

83 A friend of the family.

84 He had agreed to judge entries in a contest sponsored by the Bowater Corporation, operator of a paper mill in Corner Brook, Newfoundland.

Dear old Earle:

Excuse pencil but the hand (as well as the foot) is still gesturing with neuritis.

It's a grand job you did,[85] done lovingly! I have read it twice: so did Vi who is delighted with it.

I wish I could have found an article written by no less a critic than C.P. Scott, Editor of the Manchester Guardian, on the *Roosevelt and the Antinoe*.[86] It was equal to Benét's, though on one poem only. As you may remember, Scott was regarded as the Dean of publishers and editors in the early 30's.

I shall be looking forward to the publication of the Carleton group of essays.

I should write at greater length but the neuritis isn't letting up.

affec.
Ned

TO DAVID G. PITT

47 Glencairn Ave.
Toronto, Ont.

May 21 [1958]

Dear David:

Thanks for the final Table of contents for the Newfoundland collection.[87] I like it very much, including the proposed excerpts from the 'Spike.' As you know it was almost my last poem, my very last long poem. Although it is not really connected with Newfoundland it should be of interest to students in NFLD where railways have been almost as important as the sea. You are doing a fine job.

I apologize for the typewriter but it is sometimes easier to use for me than holding a pen in my arthritic fingers.

Best regards and good wishes.

Yours sincerely,
Ned Pratt.

---

85 In an essay entitled 'E.J. Pratt and His Critics' which Birney had read at Carleton University in the lecture series known as 'Our Living Tradition' (published in *Our Living Tradition*, ed. Robert McDougall [Toronto: University of Toronto Press, 1959]).

86 Scott's review of *RA*, 'An Epic of the Sea,' *Manchester Guardian*, 5 August 1930. Comparing Pratt with Masefield, Scott gave the poem its most enthusiastic review in the British press. (See the second-to-last paragraph and the note to 'P.C. Scott' in the letter to Hugh Eayrs, 9 July 1932 [p. 99].)

87 *Here the Tides Flow*. See the letter to Pitt, 2 February 1958 (p. 639).

TO JOHN M. GRAY

47 Glencairn Ave
Toronto

June 14, 1958

Dear old Jack:

Thanks for the munificent cheque.[88] It was manna from heaven.

The books[89] came today. They look lovely. As for the great John Milton, may I say that if we meet in the empyrean and he objects to the company, I'll give him a Newfoundland kick in the posterior and send him down to Pandemonium to keep company with the rest of the black-winged archangels. He may be a great bastard but still a bastard. I am blushing already.

Ned.

TO JOHN M. GRAY

47 Glencairn Ave

June 25 [1958]

Dear Jack:

I managed to find a copy of an unpublished recent poem called *Newfoundland Seamen* which should go in.[90] I discussed it with Norrie.[91] Is it too late to insert it? I think the appropriate place ought to be immediately after *Come Away, Death* in the section – From *Still Life and Other Verse*.

As ever,
Ned

---

88 A royalty cheque for the sale of *Poems for Upper School 1956–57*, containing 'The Roosevelt and the Antinoe' and Chaucer's 'Prologue to the Canterbury Tales,' prescribed for Ontario high school students in 1956–7 and 1957–8. (See the letter to Ralph Gustafson, 19 September 1956 [p. 627].)

89 *Poems for Upper School 1958–59*, which contained *Titanic* and Milton's *Paradise Lost*, Book I.

90 In *CP2*, which Northrop Frye was editing. The 'recent poem' submitted here had actually been written in 1949 and published as 'Newfoundland Sailors' in *This Is Newfoundland*, edited by Ewart Young (Toronto: Ryerson, 1949).

91 Northrop Frye.

TO WATSON KIRKCONNELL

47 Glencairn Ave.
Toronto 12
Ont.

Feb. 8, 1959

Dear Kirk:

Thanks for your Christmas greetings, and your 'free Alexandrines' which I greatly enjoyed. You are the most versatile writer in Canada, and I always admired you even from the Winnipeg days.[92]

I'd write you at greater length but my arthritis is hitting my fingers as it does my hands. Still I feel better and I'm getting out a bit.

Affectionately,
Ned.

TO CLAUDE AND CHRISTINE BISSELL

47 Glencairn Ave.
Toronto 12

Dec. 2 /59

Claude & Christine (loved ones):

Bless your sweet hearts for your note of congratulations.[93]

Claude, your writings (speeches) in the Star[94] are magnificent and statesmanlike.

Christine – Did you see Lotta Dempsey's[95] reference to you in the Star the other evening – 'Tall, dark, and handsome'? She told only half the truth.

Bless you again.

With love,
Ned

92 Kirkconnell had taught at Wesley (later United) College in Winnipeg (1922–40). The college later became the University of Winnipeg.

93 Possibly on the occasion of his receiving the Civic Award of Merit from the mayor and council of the city of Toronto on 24 November 1959. The proceedings were televised.

94 *Toronto Daily Star*.

95 A journalist, former editor of *Chatelaine* magazine, she wrote a regular column for the *Toronto Daily Star* from 1958 to 1981.

TO DAVID G. PITT

47 Glencairn Ave.
Toronto 12
Ont.

Jan. 2, 1960

Dear Mr Pitt:

Thank you very much for your Preface.[96] It covers the ground beautifully and I appreciate it.

I'd write at greater length but the arthritis in my fingers is a handicap. I wish you great success in the sale of the book.

Yours sincerely
E. J. Pratt

TO RONALD G. EVERSON

47 Glencairn Ave.

Jan. 20 [1960]

My dear Ron:

These are delightful poems – full of striking metaphors.[97] That 'blood-red, hunt-coat autumn' is perfect as an image, apt and original. 'Ancient-Briton groundhog,' 'squid-suck.' The Montreal Incident[98] is very moving.

Ron: there is no poet I would rather see succeed in a big way than your dear self. Congratulations on the Poetry acceptances.

I'd write more but my arthritis precludes legibility. Still indoors with the damned complaint.

Most affectionately,
Ned

96 On 22 December 1959, Pitt had sent him a typescript of the preface he had written for *HTF*.

97 Everson had sent him copies of six poems just accepted for publication by *Poetry* (Chicago), where they appeared in the September 1960 issue.

98 A poem entitled 'Incident in Montreal.'

TO DAVID G. PITT

47 Glencairn Ave.
Toronto, Ont.

February 11 [1960]

Dear David:

Many thanks for your note and especially the birthday wishes.

I too enjoyed the visit and the hour or two we spent together, especially the reminiscing [about] the distant past. Make what use of my recollections that you wish – when the time comes.[99]

Best wishes for all your projects.
Sincerely,
Ned.

TO A.J.M. SMITH

5 Elm Ave. Apt 7
Toronto 5
Ont.

Aug. 13, 1960

My dear Art:

A friend of mine sent me your Oxford book[100] two days ago and I simply thrilled at the loving dedication. It was so good of you my affectionate buddy.

I have been kept in doors for nearly two years with arthritis in the left foot springing from a thrombosis in the leg below the knee. It is a hell of a disease and almost universal isn't it? It hits the hands too as you can probably see by this scrawl. But my love for you remains as constant as ever.

---

99 On 23 January 1960, Pitt visited 47 Glencairn Avenue and broached the idea of writing his biography. Pratt consented on condition that it not be published until he was 'dead and gone.' The two-volume biography appeared as *E.J. Pratt: The Truant Years 1882–1927* (1984) and *E.J. Pratt: The Master Years 1927–1964* (1987).

100 *The Oxford Book of Canadian Verse* (Toronto: Oxford University Press, 1960), which Smith had edited and dedicated to Pratt.

Vi sends her love too.

That introduction in *Oxford* is masterly. The old fire is still there and the 'natural force unabated.'

Always
Ned Pratt

TO DAVID G. PITT

5 Elm Ave. Apt. 7
Toronto 5

Sept. 22, 1960

Dear David:

My apologies for the penmanship. As you know my arthritis is still troublesome.

About a picture for the book – it is not really necessary. But I should think it could be arranged. I have had many photos taken in the past and several portraits painted. The best of these is one Ken Forbes did nearly twenty years ago, but it has been used a number of times. Professor Fairley[101] did one away back, but I never liked it and gave it away to someone.[102] A friend said I looked like Beelzebub and he was probably right. If you really want to put one in, I'll get Vi to dig up a half-decent photo[103] and send it down to Jack Gray of Macmillans.

I hope this will be satisfactory.

My best to you.

Sincerely yours,
Ned Pratt

---

101 Barker Fairley.

102 Fairley's portrait of Pratt (oil on wood panel, 1939) eventually came into the possession of Northrop Frye. It is reproduced in its original 'wine-dark and plum-colour' in *Barker Fairley Portraits*, ed. Gary Michael Dault (Toronto: Methuen, 1981), and is used, in black and white, as a frontispiece in *EJP: CP* 1. In a letter to Pitt (2 October 1967) Fairley, who believed the portrait 'caught the essence of the man,' confirmed that Pratt himself 'never liked it.'

103 The photograph finally settled on as a frontispiece for *HTF* is by Ashley & Crippen Photographers in Toronto. It was also used in *CP2*.

TO SISTER DOROTHY MARIE DOYLE

5 Elm Ave. Apt. 7
Clifton Manor Apts.
Toronto 5

Nov. 10, 1960

My dear Sister:

I should have replied before this but I have been somewhat ill with arthritis and had to suspend correspondence to some extent.

I am sorry that there is no recording of the *Titanic*. I have read it over the air a few times for the C.B.C. on their school programmes. As it was a national broadcast it is just possible that a Maritime station may have made a record, but if so it didn't come my way.

It was very heart-warming to hear from you again. You have been most encouraging with your appreciation.

May God bless you and your work.
E.J. Pratt

TO DAPHNE PRATT HOUSE[104]

5 Elm Ave. #7
Toronto 5

Feb. 19 [1961]

My dear Daphne:

Thanks for your delightful letter. I appreciated it so much.

104 Daughter of his brother James. Born (1916) in St John's, she was for many years a nurse in Newfoundland.

The T.V. presentation[105] was so funny that my ribs are still cracking. We had a dozen or so in the apartment to watch it, including Floss who couldn't stop laughing for an hour after the show was over.

Convey my love to your mother and Bill[106] and reserve a big chunk for your sweet self.

Uncle Ned.

TO JOHN T. STOKER[107]

Toronto 5

April 12, 1961

Mr J.T. Stoker
Secretary to the Senate,
Memorial University of Newfoundland,
St. John's,
Newfoundland.

Dear Sir:

It is indeed a great honour to receive the invitation to be present at your Fall Convocation and to have the Honorary Doctorate bestowed upon me. There is no gift I should rather prefer, for my beloved Newfoundland is ever in my heart and mind.

Unfortunately, my chronic arthritis (now lasting for several years)[108] has prevented all forms of travelling near and remote.[109]

105 A television interview with Pratt conducted by J. Frank Willis. Filmed in Edwards Gardens, Toronto, in late summer 1960, it was telecast by the CBC in the *Close Up* series on 7 February 1961.

106 Daphne's husband, William John House (1920–63).

107 John T. Stoker, professor of French at Memorial University of Newfoundland, was also secretary of the university senate. He had invited Pratt to receive an honorary degree at a special convocation celebrating the university's move to a new campus situated on the northern perimeter of St John's.

108 In the margin opposite these words, Pratt had written 'confidentially just here.'

109 On receiving Pratt's reply, the university senate voted to award him the degree in absentia. However, Premier J.R. Smallwood, chief organizer of the celebrations, refused to accept

Would you convey my love to all the staff of Memorial University and my congratulations on its expansion.

With sincere affection,

Yours,
E. J. Pratt

TO CHARLES L. BENNET[110]

5 Elm Ave. Apt. 7
Toronto 5

June 11, 1961

Dear Bennet:

It was a joy to hear from you. Yes, I remember the steak that wafted its fragrance to the nostrils of the dear Evangeline.[111]

Names come crowding in on opening your letter – Dougald Mac[112] (my Lord, what a height when he wore his busby in a procession!), Henry Munro,[113] and, among others, a man whose nickname sounded like that of a golf-club.

Bless you forever C.L.
Pratt

Pratt's regrets and wrote him several letters passionately urging him to be present at 'the greatest assembly of distinguished Newfoundlanders ever seen.' As a result, Pratt changed his mind and on 31 July sent Smallwood the following telegram: 'Thanks for overwhelming invitation. Mrs Pratt and I will be delighted to attend.' (See the letters to Raymond Gushue, 20 August and 12 September 1961 [pp. 654 and 654–5].)

110 See the note to 'Bennett' [*sic*] in the letter to Hugh Eayrs, 9 July 1939 (p. 98).

111 The incident referred to occurred in the summer of 1931 when Pratt was teaching in Halifax. One weekend Bennet drove Pratt to Grand Pré to view the celebrated statue of Evangeline and visit the nearby chapel. Pratt had brought a bag of kindling and a large steak, and proceeded, to the great astonishment of Bennet and other visitors to the shrine, to make a fire and cook the steak in the shadow of the historic statue.

112 See the note to 'McGillivary, the stately Dugald' in the letter to Viola Pratt, 8 July 1933 (p. 108).

113 See the note to 'Munro' in the letter to W.A. Deacon, 11 July 1931 (p. 92).

TO RAYMOND GUSHUE[114]

5 Elm Avenue, Apt. 7

Toronto 5, August 20, 1961

Dear Dr. Gushue:

Since writing to you saying I did not feel able to attend the Memorial University ceremonies, I had a most persuasive letter from Mr. Smallwood explaining that reservations were being made for travel on the Vanguard,[115] and that everything would be as easy and comfortable as possible. I should have written you immediately when I had reversed my decision, but I thought the Premier would have been in touch with you.

If my health permits, I shall be very pleased to attend the ceremonies, and to receive in person the degree the University is so kindly conferring on me. I hope that every success will attend your preparations for this memorable event.

Very sincerely yours,
E.J. Pratt

TO RAYMOND GUSHUE

5 Elm Avenue, Apt. 7

Toronto, September 12, 1961

Dr. R. Gushue,
Memorial University,
St. John's, Nfld.

Dear Dr Gushue:

I am extremely sorry that for health reasons I have again had to change my mind about coming to Newfoundland. A day or so ago I had a severe fall which has

114 See the note to 'Raymond Gushue' in the letter to Gushue, 12 September 1952 (p. 509).
115 The Newfoundland government had chartered a Vanguard aircraft from Trans-Canada Airlines to transport invited guests to St John's.

aggravated the arthritis from which I suffer to such an extent that any kind of travel is at present quite out of the question. I hope you will forgive me for disarranging your plans again, through unforeseen and unavoidable circumstances.[116]

Very sincerely yours,
E.J. Pratt

TO MARGARET FURNESS MACLEOD

September 27, 1961

Dear Mrs. MacLeod:

How kind of you to send me a message of congratulation[117] which I very much appreciate. I too have happy memories of evenings spent at your home, of your generous hospitality and of the discussions we had together. What would we be without our memories?

I am hoping to get a copy of the July number of 'The Evangelical Christian' to read your article on *Our Family Bible*. I think you are quite wonderful to be continuing with your writing.

My wife joins me in kindest regards and best wishes.

Sincerely your friend,
E.J. Pratt

116 Memorial University conferred the degree on him in absentia. President Claude Bissell of the University of Toronto wrote Pratt on his return: 'We were terribly sorry that you were not able to be present, but I can assure you that your name was often on our lips and your spirit was powerfully present' (12 October 1961).

117 On receiving the Canada Council Medal (and $2000 in cash) for 'distinguished contributions to the cultural life of Canada.'

TO ALAN CRAWLEY

5 Elm Avenue, Apt. 7

Toronto 5, [Sept.] 1961

Dear Alan:

Thank you very much for your kind letter of congratulation, and for your cordial words in regard to the bestowal of the award.[118] I appreciated hearing from you more than I can say, as it is old friends who now mean the most to me.

We too have taken to apartment life, which we find much to our taste. However, at present a bout of arthritis is seriously restricting my activities to a temporary arm-chair existence.

With kindest regards to your wife and to you, and again many thanks.

Sincerely yours,
Ned Pratt

TO H. PEARSON GUNDY

5 Elm Ave. Apt. 7

Toronto 5 [24 Oct. 1961]

My very dear Pete:[119]

It was a joy to get your warm-hearted letter and to have the memories of fifteen years ago revived. My unqualified recommendation of you to Wallace[120] was my *one good* deed for that year.

118 The Canada Council Medal. See the note to 'a message of congratulation' in the letter to Margaret Furness MacLeod, 27 September 1961 (p. 655).

119 H. Pearson ('Pete') Gundy (see the note to 'Gundy' in the letter to Viola Pratt, 9 August 1948 [p. 419]) was collecting the letters of Bliss Carman to edit for publication. He had written asking whether Pratt had any letters from Carman, or copies of letters he had written to Carman. Gundy's edition was published by McGill-Queen's University Press in 1981.

120 R.C. Wallace (see the note to 'Wallace's four lectures' in the letter to Hugh Eayrs, 27 March 1934 [p. 123]) was principal of Queen's University in 1946 when Pratt recommended Gundy's appointment as head librarian of Queen's University Library, a post he still held in 1961.

Dear old Carman – I was quite fond of him. I was one of the two (the other being Professor J.W. MacMillan)[121] who passed around the plate for him in Hart House when I organized a dinner and lecture-recital for him. I do not know how much he netted but I did notice a few crisp one-dollar bills covering the dimes. I said as I squeezed the amount into his hands – 'Bliss, this will at least buy you a new hat.' By the way, this is a rather significant remark, considering what the old hat looked like. Pete, do you remember Carleton Stanley?[122] He was sent out to pick up Bliss's hat just before leaving. He was gone for a considerable time and then sent for me. 'Ned,' he remarked, 'I'm not certain about this hat, but I think it must be his; it smells like him.' I passed on the quip verbatim and Bliss roared over it.

I met him a number of times with Roberts and Lorne,[123] and became very much attached to him. He could sniff a joke a mile off, and he could eat so hearty a dinner that one might imagine he didn't expect another meal for a month.

By the way, I could refer you to a woman who has made a special study of both Roberts and Carman, who in fact has written the biography of Roberts with copious references to C. Miss Elsie Pomeroy,[124] 211 College St, Toronto. She is an ex-school teacher and is a mine of information about the group. Also Desmond Pacey of the English Dept. of the University of New Brunswick, Fredericton.

As for my own letters and correspondence generally, I haven't preserved a syllable – not a letter. I have never had a 'proprietary' interest in my own compositions apart from my manuscripts of poetry and all these have been taken over by Vic[125] under contract (although a somewhat loose one). Sorry, Pete. I am not doing any writing nowadays on account of chronic arthritis which affects the hands as you can infer from this indecipherable scrawl.

My love to you,
Ned.

121 John Walker Macmillan, a Presbyterian cleric, professor of sociology at Victoria College (1919–32). An avid golfer, he may have been the subject of Pratt's 'Jock o' the Links' (*MM*, 44; *EJP: CP* 1.289).

122 See the note to 'Stanley' in the letter to Hugh Eayrs, 9 July 1932 (p. 98).

123 Charles G.D. Roberts and Lorne Pierce.

124 Elsie M. Pomeroy (1886–1968) was a close confidante of C.G.D. Roberts during the last fifteen years of his life. Her book, *Sir Charles G.D. Roberts: A Biography*, was published by Ryerson Press in 1943.

125 Victoria College.

TO SISTER DOROTHY MARIE DOYLE

5 Elm Avenue
Toronto 5

April 17, 1962

Sister St. Dorothy Marie:

That was one of the sweetest letters written to me in a very long time. I was indeed honoured to have *Brébeuf* coupled with *The Faerie Queene*, *Sorhab and Rustum*,[126] et al, in your 'epic core.'[127]

Thanks for the Frost enclosure[128] and your lovely reference to *Putting Winter to Bed*. I am still savouring the beauty of phrases like 'the feminine administrative technique.' You do write endearingly.

I have just transmitted your *oramus*[129] to my beloved wife. She reciprocates it heartily.

May God bless you forever and
ever dear sister.
E.J. Pratt

TO VINCENT D. SHARMAN[130]

[1962]

126 A narrative poem by Matthew Arnold.

127 She was using his poems in a course she was teaching at St Francis Xavier University.

128 In her letter of 11 April 1962 (EJP, VUL), Sister Doyle writes: 'The recent news reports concerning Robert Frost have brought the glory of your epic poems to the forefront of my thought … I am enclosing in my letter a couple of clippings the recent press carried.'

129 Latin for 'let us pray.'

130 Sharman was writing an MA thesis on Pratt's poetry ('Patterns of Imagery and Symbolism in the Poetry of E.J. Pratt') at the University of British Columbia. Sharman went on to teach English at Nipissing University College in North Bay, Ontario, and published on Pratt, Leacock, and Thomas McCulloch.

Dear Mr Sharman:

Thank you very much for your kind and interesting letter.[131] It is gratifying to know that one's work is understood.

You have expressed exactly what I meant to convey in the conclusion of *The Roosevelt and the Antinoe*, and indeed in the whole of the poem: man's unremitting struggle with nature, and his indomitable courage in pitting his strength against hers, no matter how great the odds. The whole of the gallant rescue was ready made for my purpose, and every detail was as accurate as careful research and re-enactment could guarantee.

Sincerely yours,
E.J. Pratt

TO FATHER J. STANLEY MURPHY[132]

January 10 [1963]

Dear Father Murphy:

How nice of you to send Birthday greetings and your copy of the *Basilian Teacher* with its kind references to myself. The *Order* has always been dear to me; I count among its members some of my closest friends, I might say my buddies. God bless Father McCorkell, & LeBell and all the wonderful Fathers, too many to mention. May Assumption thrive in grace and numbers.

Affectionately yours,
E.J. (Ned) Pratt

P.S. My wife adds her blessing (more efficacious than mine)
E.J.P.

---

131 Sharman had sent his interpretation of the closing lines of *RA*, requesting comments. This letter is Pratt's reply.

132 Head of Assumption College (which had become the University of Windsor in 1956.

TO RONALD HAMBLETON

[7 Feb. 1962]

Dear Ron:

I felt pleased and honoured by the performance last night.[133] The parts were so well co-ordinated by you and the individuals who read it did it excellently – real artists in enunciation, tone and variation of emphasis. My wife and I were delighted. A few years ago you thrilled us in the same way;[134] so our indebtedness to you and your colleagues is a double one. God bless you old chap. We love you and yours.

Most affectionately
Ned Pratt

TO RAYMOND GUSHUE

5 Elm Avenue, Apt. 7
Toronto 5, Ontario

February 10, 1963

Dear Dr Gushue:

Will you please accept my sincere thanks for the birthday telegram you sent on behalf of Memorial University.[135] I am very proud to be counted among its alumni, and send best wishes for its continued success.

Sincerely yours,
E.J. Pratt

133 On 6 February 1963, the radio series *CBC Wednesday Night* had marked Pratt's eightieth birthday on 4 February with a special program in his honour. He was actually eighty-one years old.

134 CBC had also hosted a 'radio birthday party' when Pratt was seventy-five (actually seventy-six). See the letters to David G. Pitt, 2 February 1958 (p. 639) and Earle Birney, 6 February 1958 (*EJP: Web*).

135 On 4 February, Pratt had celebrated his eightieth brithday (actually his eighty-first).

TO LEO COX

Feb. 11 [1963]

Dear old Leo:

You are a prince among men. Your royalty and nobility sing in every word of your letter which just came in the post. I had to reply at once even if briefly – my arthritic hands don't work a pen very well. Glad you enjoyed the broadcast.[136] Thanks so much.

My love to you.
Ned

TO DOUGLAS AND HAZEL BUSH

[Feb. 1963]

Dear Douglas and Hazel:

Thanks for Birthday congratulations, though 80th has a frosty sound, to paraphrase the immortal Will (I hope).[137]

Bless the two of you.

Ned Pratt

Doug: We have heard the chimes at midnight together.[138]

---

136 See the note to 'the performance last night' in the letter to Ronald Hambleton, 7 February 1963 (p. 660).

137 He is recalling Worcester's words in Shakespeare's *1 Henry IV*: 'Ay, by my faith, that bears a frosty sound' (4.1.128).

138 An echo of Falstaff in *2 Henry IV*: 'We have heard the chimes at midnight, Master Shallow' (3.2.231).

TO DAVID G. PITT

[Feb. 1963]

Dear David:

Thanks for your lovely card with Signal Hill, the Narrows, the Harbour, the ships and all the sweep of the nostalgic memories. I am honoured by those signatures.

Give my love to the staff and students of Memorial University. I hope the Tides flow gently over them.[139]

Yours affectionately,
E.J. Pratt

TO A GRADE FOUR CLASS[140]

[Feb. 1963]

Dear little friends in Grade 4:

Your letters with the hugs and kisses (X O) have given me great pleasure – also your paintings of frost on the window panes. I enjoyed them all – both the objective and non-objective art.

Thank you very much. I shall always keep these little art treasures.

Yours affectionately,
E.J. Pratt

139 He was responding to a birthday card (with a panoramic view of St John's harbour), signed by the first-year students at Memorial University who were reading his poems in the anthology *Here the Tides Flow*, edited by Pitt.

140 The grade 4 pupils at Havergal College in Toronto, whose teacher, Viola Love, was a friend of the Pratts (see the note to 'Chris and Vo Love' in the letter to Claire Pratt, 25 February 1954 [p. 558]), had sent him greetings on his recent birthday. Viola Love writes: 'The girls very much enjoyed his poems, Frost, Mother and Child, Sea-gulls, The Shark, in the anthology we were using and, because they felt that through me he was a friend, there was a spontaneous decision to send birthday greetings' (April 1982).

TO WILLIAM ARTHUR DEACON

[14 Mar. 1963]

Dear Bill:

I was glad that my brother Cal was here from Ottawa and had the chance to read your heart-warming article in the A & B.[141] It was another evidence of the unwavering loyalty existing between us for more than thirty years. That's what gives immortality to friendship. When we returned to the house we talked long and tenderly of our associations, for richer for poorer, in sickness and in health (to paraphrase the sacred ritual). God bless you & Sal and the rest of the family. Vi calls out – give Sal a second blessing for me. There will always be a second loaf of bread for the Deacon clan when the flour turns to dough.

Yours
Ned.

TO SISTER DOROTHY MARIE DOYLE

[Mar. 1964][142]

Dear Sister:

Your very sweet letter to me, to my wife and daughter is much appreciated. The Sisters have always been very dear to me. I admire their work and sacrificial service. My memories of Antigonish are very sweet.[143] May God bless you and the fold generally.

Yours very cordially,
E.J. Pratt

141 'Laureate Uncrowned: A Personal Study of E.J. Pratt,' *Canadian Author and Bookman* 38 (Spring 1963): 2, 20.

142 The letter is undated, but Sister Dorothy assured Pitt that it was written 'just one month before he died.' It is probably the last letter he wrote. He died on 26 April 1964.

143 She had written him from Antigonish, where she taught at St Francis Xavier University. He had visited the town and university while teaching in Halifax in 1933.

Appendix

Some Letters by Viola Pratt

Written towards the end of Pratt's life when he could write few letters himself and shortly after his death.

TO WILLIAM ARTHUR DEACON

November 12 [1962]

Dear Bill:

Your letter was the most heart warming thing that has happened to Ned during his two months illness.[1] I have read and re-read it to him – and when I finish he says 'Good old Bill – those were the peak days' and then he recalls some of them. Thank you very much.

Ned is still very alert in his mind and his sense of humour and ability to avoid clichés are as strong as ever, but his body is very thin and frail – and I am afraid he is growing steadily weaker. Thoughts and memories of friends tried and true are of unspeakable comfort.

Love to you both,
Vi

1 He had suffered cardiac and other complications.

TO A.J.M. SMITH

[Dec. 1962]

Dear Arthur:

I was hoping that Ned might be able to write a line of thanks himself for your *Collected Poems*,[2] a copy of which we are very proud to own. I have always loved your 'Phoenix'[3] and you were wise to use it for your jacket cover.

Ned says to tell you that he is never disappointed when he reads a poem of yours or becomes acquainted with a new one, and I feel the same. They are very satisfactory [...] – and your harp has many strings. Thank you very much for sending us a copy. It is pure joy to read your poems for their melody.

Ned is slowly getting better but is still very thin and frail.

Ned and Claire join me in wishing you and Jeanie a very happy Christmas.

Sincerely,
Vi Pratt

TO SEVERAL CORRESPONDENTS[4]

March 23, 1964

Dear

The C.B.C. have just sent Ned a great batch of letters written to him in their care after his February 1961 broadcast. We are terribly sorry and embarassed about this[5] and hope you will understand.

Ned has been very ill for many months and I have been attending to his correspondence. He was delighted to have your letter and of course remembers you very well. He has asked me to send you all of his best and to thank you for taking the trouble to write such a charming letter which has lost nothing over the passage of the years when it remained sealed in its envelope.

2 Published that year by Oxford University Press.

3 Smith's first book of poems, *News of the Phoenix and Other Poems* (1943).

4 With a few minor variations, this letter is typical of replies Viola Pratt wrote to nearly a score of well-wishers who had written to Pratt care of CBC following the 1961 broadcast. (See the letter to Daphne Pratt House, 19 February 1961 [pp. 651–2].)

5 About the three-year delay in responding to their letters.

The broadcast was taken in the summer at the Edwards Gardens and Ned spent most of the time in between reminiscences swatting mosquitoes and brushing caterpillars off his lap.

Kindest regards,
Sincerely,
Viola Pratt

TO A.J.M. SMITH

3 May [1964]

Dear Arthur:

Thank you very much for your kind letter. Claire and I are bereft *indeed*, but Ned was so alive and vital that his bright spirit seems to surround us. Ned had been very ill for many months and finally his heart could no longer stand the strain. But his mind was clear until the very end and he did not suffer any pain. [ ]

Sincerely,
Vi Pratt

TO LEO COX

May11 [1964]

Dear Leo Cox:

Thank you very much for your kind letter. It is indeed a consolation, in this time of unbelievable loneliness and grief, to know that so many people in so many places are grieving with us.

Ned often spoke of you as one of his good friends – and as a good poet too. He had been frail and tired for a long time but his mind was gay and clear to the last minutes and his glowing spirit seems to surround and sustain my daughter and me.

Will you thank your wife, too, for sending her sympathy.

With kind regards to you both.

Sincerely,
Viola L.Pratt

TO M.M.H. MACKINNON

May 20 [1964]

Dear Murdo:

I am sorry I didn't see you and Earle in Convocation Hall[6] – but I am glad you were there. I really didn't see anyone, and am only gradually finding out who came.

It was good of you to write Claire and me and to reminisce. As you say, I don't think anyone ever knew all the things Ned did, and I was being continually surprised by some new story or escapade.

Please don't feel badly that you didn't see Ned lately. He was very, very frail and tired and was waiting till he was better to see his friends. He never wanted to see anyone when he was sick – but only a few days before he died he said, 'As soon as I get up I am going to give a bang-up dinner at the York Club.' His mind was clear and gay until the very end, and his courage high. His patience was remarkable – never once did he complain about anything. It was a rare privilege to see his constant composure.

I hope you and Elizabeth will come to see us. Our friends are wonderful but life without Ned is strange and unreal.

Affectionate regards from Claire and me to Elizabeth and you and your boys and girls.

Vi

TO MARGARET (MRS E.K.) BROWN

3 July [1964]

Dear Peggy:

I have just received your letter and I must apologize for not having written you, but I had so many hundreds of letters to write and I thought you would probably hear some other way. I have *thought* of you a great deal – as I have thought of all those whose lives touched Ned's closely. Ned always considered Edward one of his choicest friends – and you too were a favourite of his.

You know all about the loneliness and grief attendant upon the death of one's best loved – and it is an incredible experience. I scarcely left Ned night or day

6 Pratt's memorial service was held in Convocation Hall at the University of Toronto on 28 April 1964.

during the sixteen months he was really incapacitated, but I only wish I could have had him forever. Though he was very weak and frail and tired, his mind was alert and gay and his courage high until the very end – so that his radiant spirit still seems to surround and comfort us.

Claire is with me and has been marvellous. Ned's brother Cal, the only remaining brother and our great standby, died in November (we did not tell Ned) so we had a very great many things to do and decisions to make ourselves. Claire is taking a two-month leave of absence[7] in August and September, and we plan then to go to Newfoundland and England.

I would love to see you, Peggy, and hope you may be contemplating a trip to Toronto soon.

Thank you very much for your understanding letter. We did have a perfect life together, and all my memories of Ned are wonderful.

Affectionately always,
Vi Pratt

TO EARLE BIRNEY

July 7, 1964

Dear Earle:

Thank you so much for your kind and interesting letter. You said all the right things about Ned, regarding whom scarcely anybody has reached the depths and heights of his being. I cannot remember of him anything but the finest, and the separation is almost unbearable.

Though Ned was so frail and weak and tired for a long time, he never lost his patience nor his courage, nor his lovely mind, and his radiant spirit which is still here to comfort us.

You said you had been asked to take part in a CBC radio memorial – let us know when. They never tell us. I cherish memories of happy times with you and Esther. Will see you one of these days.

Claire is taking leave of absence in August and September. We plan to go to Newfoundland and England. Claire is very tired but we both are reasonably well.

Love,
Vi

---

7 Claire was employed as an editor with McClelland & Stewart.

Abbreviations

The following volumes have so far appeared in the *Collected Works*, being published by University of Toronto Press:

EJP: CP	*E.J. Pratt: Complete Poems*. Edited by Sandra Djwa and R.G. Moyles; introduction by Sandra Djwa. 1989
EJP: OHLP	*E.J. Pratt: On His Life and Poetry*. Edited and introduced by Susan Gingell. 1983
EJP: PAA	*Pursuits Amateur and Academic: The Selected Prose of E.J. Pratt*. Edited and introduced by Susan Gingell. 1995

In addition, an electronic gathering of manuscript material, facsimiles of printed books, illustrations, audio recordings, a detailed timeline of Pratt's life and works and extensive notes, is available on the World Wide Web:

EJP: Web	*The Hypertext Pratt* (www.trentu.ca/pratt)

Works by Pratt

BB	*Brébeuf and His Brethren*. Toronto: Macmillan, 1940 / Detroit: The Basilian Press 1942
BL	*Behind the Log*. Drawings by Grant MacDonald. Toronto: Macmillan, 1947
CP1	*Collected Poems* [Canadian edition]. Toronto: Macmillan, 1944
CPA	*Collected Poems* [American edition]. Introduction by William Rose Benét. New York: Alfred A. Knopf, 1945
CP2	*Collected Poems*. Second edition. Edited and introduced by Northrop Frye. Toronto: Macmillan, 1958

DK	*Dunkirk*. Toronto: Macmillan, 1941
FG	*The Fable of the Goats and Other Poems*. Toronto: Macmillan, 1937
HTF	*Here the Tides Flow*. Department of English, Memorial University of Newfoundland / Toronto: Macmillan, 1962
ID	*The Iron Door: An Ode*. Toronto: Macmillan, 1927
MM	*Many Moods*. Toronto: Macmillan, 1932
NV	*Newfoundland Verse*. Toronto: Ryerson Press, 1923
RA	*The Roosevelt and the Antinoe*. Toronto and New York: Macmillan, 1930
Rachel	*Rachel: A Sea Story of Newfoundland in Verse*. New York: Privately printed, 1917
SL	*Still Life and Other Verse*. Toronto: Macmillan, 1943
SPE	*Studies in Pauline Eschatology*. [Doctoral dissertation, University of Toronto.] Toronto: William Briggs, 1917
TAR	*They Are Returning*. Toronto: Macmillan, 1945
Titanic	*The Titanic*. Toronto: Macmillan, 1935
TLS	*Towards the Last Spike*. Toronto: Macmillan, 1952
TSP	*Ten Selected Poems*. Notes by E.J. Pratt. Toronto: Department of English, Victoria College / Macmillan, 1947
VS	*Verses of the Sea*. Introduction by Charles G.D. Roberts; notes by E.J. Pratt. Toronto: Macmillan, 1930
WB	*The Witches' Brew*. London: Selwyn & Blount 1925 / Toronto: Macmillan, 1926

Works about Pratt

EJP: MY	David G. Pitt. *E.J. Pratt: The Master Years 1927–1964*. Toronto: University of Toronto Press / St John's, NL: Jesperson Press, 1987
EJP: TY	David G. Pitt. *E.J. Pratt: The Truant Years 1882–1927*. Toronto: University of Toronto Press / St John's, NL: Jesperson Press, 1984

Letterhead (in order of first use)

LH1	Victoria College [with crest]
LH2	Victoria College / Toronto, Canada
LH3	[Victoria College crest] Victoria College / University of Toronto / Department of English Literature / E.J. Pratt
LH4	The Residence / Victoria College / Toronto 5, Canada
LH5	Victoria College / Toronto 5, Canada
LH6: *CPM*	*Canadian Poetry Magazine*

LH7	Victoria College / Toronto
LH8	[Victoria College crest]
LH9	*Victoria College / University of Toronto // E.J. Pratt, PhD, DLitt*
LH10	5 Elm Avenue, Apt. 7 / Toronto 5, Ontario'

Journals

AV	*Acta Victoriana*
CB	*Canadian Bookman*
CF	*Canadian Forum*
CPM	*Canadian Poetry Magazine*
DR	*Dalhousie Review*
LM	*London Mercury*
NR	*Northern Review*
QQ	*Queen's Quarterly*
SRL	*Saturday Review of Literature*
UTQ	*University of Toronto Quarterly*

Dictionaries

DNE	*Dictionary of Newfoundland English.* Edited by G.M. Story, W.J. Kirwin, and John D.A. Widdowson. 2nd ed. Toronto: University of Toronto Press, 1990
OED	*Oxford English Dictionary [Online].* Oxford: Oxford University Press, 2008

Archival Collections

Acadia	Acadia University Library (Wolfville, Nova Scotia)	
	Kirkconnell	Watson Kirkconnell papers
BRBR	Beinecke Rare Book Room and Manuscript Library, Yale University (New Haven, CT)	
	Benét	William Rose Benét papers
CAML	Charles D. Abbott Memorial Library, University of New York at Buffalo (Buffalo, NY)	
	Abbott	Charles D. Abbott papers
	Contemporary Manuscripts Collection	
CUL	Concordia University Libraries	
	Layton	Irving Layton Collection
FRBL	Thomas Fisher Rare Book Library, University of Toronto (Toronto)	

	Birney	Earle Birney papers
	Deacon	William Arthur Deacon papers
	Hambleton	Ronald Hambleton fonds
	Hardy	E.A. Hardy fonds
	Moore	Dora Mavor Moore fonds
	Smith	A.J.M. Smith fonds
LAC	Library and Archives Canada (Ottawa)	
	Bourinot	Arthur S. Bourinot fonds
	Clay	Charles Clay fonds
	Denison	Merrill Denison fonds
	Eggleston	Wilfrid Eggleston fonds
	Dudek	Louis Dudek fonds
	Klein	A.M. Klein fonds
	Macbeth	Madge Macbeth papers
	MacDonald	Wilson MacDonald fonds
	Pacey	Desmond Pacey fonds
	Scott	Duncan Campbell Scott fonds
	Webb	Phyllis Webb fonds
McGill	McGill University Library, Rare Books and Special Collections (Montreal)	
	Barnard	Leslie Gordon Barnard papers
	Lighthall	William Douw Lighthall papers
MMLM	Mills Memorial Library, McMaster University (Hamilton, ON)	
	Copp Clark	Copp Clark fonds
	Everson	R.G. Everson fonds
	Macmillan	Macmillan Company of Canada
	McRaye	Walter Jackson McRaye fonds
	Reynolds	Ella Julia Reynolds fonds
MUNA	Memorial University of Newfoundland Library (St John's, NL)	
	Hatcher	
	Miller	Phebe Florence Miller papers
	Pratt	E.J. Pratt Letters
NYPL	North York Public Library (Toronto)	
	MacTavish	Newton MacTavish Collection
PABC	Provincial Archives, British Columbia (Victoria, BC)	
	Perry	Martha Eugenie Perry papers
QUA	Queen's University Archives (Kingston, ON)	
	Clarke	George Herbert Clarke fonds
	Crawley	Alan Crawley fonds

	Gundy	Henry Pearson Gundy fonds
	Pierce	Lorne Pierce fonds
	Woodcock	George Woodcock fonds
RHRC	Ransom Humanities Research Center, University of Texas (Austin, TX)	
	Costain	Thomas Bertram Costain
	Knopf	Alfred A. Knopf, Ltd.
Trent	Trent University Archives (Peterborough, ON)	
	Smith	A.J.M. Smith fonds
UBCL	University of British Columbia Library, Special Collections (Vancouver, BC)	
	Brown	Audrey Alexandra Brown fonds
	Dalton	Annie Charlott Dalton papers
	Daniells	Roy Daniells fonds
UC	University of Chicago, Special Collections Research Centre (Chicago)	
	Poetry	*Poetry* Modern Poetry Manuscript Collection
UCAL	University of Calgary Library, Special Collections (Calgary, AB)	
	Ross	Malcolm Ross fonds
UML	University of Manitoba Library (Winnipeg, Manitoba)	
	Livesay	Dorothy Livesay fonds
	Phelps	Arthur Phelps fonds
UNB	University of New Brunswick Archives and Special Collections (Fredericton, NB)	
	Beaverbrook	Lord Beaverbrook papers
	Pacey	Dr. William Cyril Desmond Pacey fonds
	Roberts	Sir Charles G.D. Roberts fonds
USKL	University of Saskatchewan Library (Saskatoon, SK)	
	Gustafson	Ralph Gustafson Literary Papers
	Pratt	The Pratt Collection (E.J. Pratt)
UTLA	University of Toronto Library Archives & Records – Private Records	
	Markowitz	Jacob Markowitz fonds
UWL	University of Waterloo Library (Waterloo, ON)	
	Pincock	Maines Pincock Family fonds
UWO	University of Western Ontario, Special Collections (London, ON)	
	Collin	William Edwin Collin fonds, Regional Collection
VUL	Victoria University Library (Toronto)	
	Edgar	Pelham Edgar Papers
	Gullen	Augusta Stowe-Gullen fonds, Emmanuel College

	CP	Claire Pratt fonds
	EJP	Edwin J. Pratt fonds
	VLP	Viola Leone Whitney Pratt fonds
Wellesley	Wellesley College Library (Boston, MA)	

Private Collections

In some cases, letters in private hands were transcribed by David G. Pitt on-site from the original document, or from recordings; in others, photocopies were provided.

Bennet	James Bennet
Bissell	Claude Bissell
Brown	E.K. Brown
Margaret Brown	
Bush	Douglas Bush
Cox	Leo Cox
Davies	Robertson Davies
Doyle	Sister Dorothy Marie Doyle
Dwja	Sandra Dwja
Givens	Imogen Knister Givens
Gray	James M. Gray
Harrington	Michael F. Harrington
Kennedy	Leo Kennedy
Klinck	Carl Klinck
MacKay	Louis MacKay
MacLeod	Margaret Furness MacLeod
McCauley	Ina McCauley
Phelps	Arthur L. Phelps
Pitt	David G. Pitt
Procunier	Edwin Procunier
Sutherland	John Sutherland
Audrey Sutherland	
Wells	Henry W. Wells
Whalley	George Whalley
Wiles	Roy M. Wiles
Wornell	Abel C. Wornell

Textual Notes

I Peregrinations, 1903–1925

The Editor, *The Collegian* (Sept. 1903). United Church Archives (St John's, NL). Published.

Barbara Brett (22 Sept. 1904). Pitt. Handwritten, plain paper.

Willis Pike (26 Jan. 1908). Procunier. Handwritten, LH1.
6 as usual. I saw him *altered to* as usual

The Reverend Charles E. Manning (8 July 1908). United Church Archives (Toronto, Ontario). Handwritten, plain paper.

Viola Whitney (5 July 1917). EJP, VUL. Handwritten, letterhead: 'University of Toronto / Toronto, Canada / Department of Philosophy.'
8 typewriting] type-writing
9 Kapuskasing] Kap-uskasing

Duncan Campbell Scott (18 Jan. 1918). Scott, LAC. Handwritten, letterhead: 'University of Toronto / Toronto, Canada / Psychological Laboratory.'

Arthur Phelps (9 Aug. 1918). Phelps, UML. Handwritten, plain paper.

Arthur Phelps (18 Sept. 1918). Phelps, UML. Handwritten, plain paper.

Arthur Phelps (21 Sept. 1918). Phelps, UML. Handwritten, plain paper.

Arthur Phelps (late Apr./early May 1922). Phelps. Transcribed by Pitt from tape-recorded reading.

William Arthur Deacon (18 Sept. 1922). Deacon, FRBL. Handwritten, LH3.
15 MacKenna has *altered to* McKenna had

Arthur Phelps (26 Oct. 1922). Phelps, UML. Handwritten, plain paper.

Lorne Pierce (16 Jan. 1923). Pierce, QUA. Handwritten, LH2.

William Arthur Deacon (27 Apr. 1923). Deacon, FRBL. Handwritten, LH2 with address crossed out and written over.

Lorne Pierce (16 May 1923). Pierce, QUA. Handwritten, LH3.

Lorne Pierce (23 May 1923). Pierce, QUA. Handwritten, LH3. 'Corrigenda' on separate page.
24 Some of them *altered to* Some or most of them
24 my own *altered to* mine own
24 as [....] *altered to* the case
24 'subtle *altered to* 'subtlety

Lorne Pierce (24 May 1923). Pierce, QUA. Handwritten, LH3.

William Arthur Deacon (19 June 1923). Deacon, FRBL. Handwritten, LH3.

Lorne Pierce (23 Nov. 1923). Pierce, QUA. Handwritten, LH2.
27 intervened] inter-vened
27 as prolonged delay *altered to* as the prolonged delay
28 Department – then] Department then
28 [.....] me? *altered to* gave all

Lorne Pierce (1 Dec. 1923). Pierce, QUA. Handwritten, LH2.
29 many letters *altered to* many personal letters
30 a few picked *altered to* a few outside picked

Lorne Pierce (5 Apr. 1924). Pierce, QUA. Handwritten, LH2.

Lorne Pierce (12 Apr.. 1924). Pierce, QUA. Handwritten, LH2.
33 Dr Davies *altered to* Dr Trevor Davies

Viola Pratt (23 May 1924). VLP, VUL. Handwritten, letterhead: 'CANADIAN PACIFIC /on board / Montclare.'

Viola Pratt (5 June 1924). VLP, VUL. Handwritten, plain paper: 3rd page of 4 missing.

Viola Pratt (10 June 1924). VLP, VUL. Handwritten, letterhead from the King's Head Hotel, Barnard Castle.

Viola Pratt (22 June 1924). VLP, VUL. Handwritten, letterhead: 'St. Enoch Station Hotel / Glasgow, C.I. / 192 / ...'

38 last [...] *altered to* last from
40 mother, Mrs *altered to* mother, Mr & Mrs

Viola Pratt (29 June 1924). VLP, VUL. Handwritten, plain paper.

40 m[..] *altered to* circa
41 three bisks *altered to* nine bisks
41 means I *altered to* means a
41 glad of? *altered to* glad to
42 Floss o[..] *altered to* Floss returns

Viola Pratt (2 July 1924). VLP, VUL. Handwritten, letterhead: 'Queen's Hotel / Keswick. / ... / Manageress / Mrs. MacWilliam'

44 health, th[.] *altered to* health, not
44 If you ca[.] *altered to* if you get
44 lectures ab[...] *altered to* lectures from

Viola Pratt (3 July 1924). VLP, VUL. Handwritten, letterhead: 'Furness Abbey Hotel / Furness Abbey / Lancashire / 199 / ...'

45 Supper of roast *altered to* Supper of cold roast

Viola Pratt (16 July 1924). VLP, VUL. Handwritten, plain paper.

46 car ten *altered to* car for
46 had erected *altered to* had been erected
46 Tha? *altered to* Knox & Davis
46 I write *altered to* I will communicate
46 [..] *altered to* to your most
46 highness *altered to* Highness

Viola Pratt (21 July 1924). VLP, VUL. Handwritten, plain paper.
47 1833] 183
47 Dr Johnson's *altered to* Dr Samuel Johnson's
47 his ho *altered to* his room

Viola Pratt (24 July 1924). VLP, VUL. Handwritten, plain paper.
48 saw a copy *altered to* saw a original copy
48 and Wm Nash *altered to* and Nash

Viola Pratt (30 July 1924). VLP, VUL. Handwritten, plain paper.

Lorne Pierce (7 Aug. 1924). Pierce, QUA. Handwritten, letterhead: 'The Grafton Hotel / (opposite maple's) / tottenham court road / london, w.i, 192/ ...'
51 sure to[..] *altered to* sure those

Viola Pratt (23 Aug. 1924). VLP, VUL. Handwritten, letterhead: '[crest] / Hotel Empress, / Bournemouth / ...'

Viola Pratt (29 Aug. 1924). VLP, VUL. Handwritten, plain paper.
54 hope will for *altered to* hope will not

Viola Pratt (5 Sept. 1924). VLP, VUL. Handwritten, Arthur Pratt's letterhead: '"Terra Nova," / Lynmouth Road, / Aigburth, / Liverpool. // Tel. Garston 210.'

Lorne Pierce (24 Sept. 1924). Pierce, QUA. Handwritten, LH2.

Lorne Pierce (18 Dec. 1924). Pierce, QUA. Handwritten, LH2.

Saturday Night (Apr. 1925). Published (with letters by other correspondents) in *Saturday Night*, 25 April 1925 under the heading 'Is Carmen Supreme?'

William Arthur Deacon (4 May 1925). Deacon, FRBL. Handwritten, LH2.
59 Fox's w[..] *altered to* Fox's appreciation

William Arthur Deacon (10 Aug. 1925). Deacon, FRBL. Handwritten, plain paper.
59 could exe *altered to* could be executed

William Arthur Deacon (18 Aug. 1925). Deacon, FRBL. Handwritten, LH2: 'Victoria College' scored out and replaced with 'Bobcaygeon.'

Mrs Horace Parsons (22 Sept. 1925). Pitt.

II A Taste of National Acclaim, 1925–1932

Mrs Horace Parsons (29 Oct. 1925). Pitt. Handwritten, plain paper.

William Arthur Deacon (Oct. 1925). Deacon, FRBL. Handwritten, LH2.

Arthur Phelps (3 Jan. 1926). Phelps. Transcribed by Pitt from tape-recorded reading.

Austin Bothwell (12 Mar. 1926). EJP, VUL. Handwritten, LH2.
64 make a *altered to* make it a

Arthur Phelps (8 Apr. 1926). Phelps. Transcribed by Pitt from tape-recorded reading.

William Arthur Deacon (3 June 1926). Deacon, FRBL. Handwritten, LH2.

William Arthur Deacon (7 June 1926). Deacon, FRBL. Handwritten, LH4 with 'Residence' and 'Victoria College' scored out and replaced with '25 Tullis Drive.'
67 on the shelves *altered to* on one of the shelves

William Arthur Deacon (9 Sept. 1926). Deacon, FRBL. Handwritten, plain paper.

Arthur Phelps (9 Nov. 1926). Phelps, UML. Handwritten, LH2.

Lorne Pierce (2 Jan. 1927). Transcribed by Pitt from tape-recorded reading.

Arthur Phelps (18 Jan. 1927). Phelps, UML. Handwritten, LH2.

Lorne Pierce (20 Jan. 1927). Pierce, QUA. Handwritten, LH2.
71 extravagance *altered to* extravaganza

Lorne Pierce (15 July 1927). Pierce, QUA. Handwritten, plain paper. On envelope, Pierce's Toronto address ('233 Glen Grove Ave. / N. Yonge Street / Toronto') is crossed out and replaced with 'Delta *Ont.*'
72 judgement that it *altered to* judgment that the ode
72 publish it in *altered to* publish it over

Lorne Pierce (4 Aug. 1927). Pierce, QUA. Handwritten, plain paper.
73 I have often s[i]g *altered to* I have often stated

Lorne Pierce (10 Aug. 1927). Pierce, QUA. Handwritten, plain paper.
74 came to Toron *altered to* came to Victoria College
74 1917. Associate Professor. *altered to* 1917. Now
74 Visits *altered to* Visited

William Arthur Deacon (27 Aug. 1927). Deacon, FRBL. Handwritten, plain paper. Typescripts of *The Iron Door* and 'Cherries' enclosed.
75 last Spring, one *altered to* last Spring, once
75 going on, the *altered to* going on, on the
76 Hardyesque type – *altered to* Hardyesque type (or Bertrand Russell type) –
76 the reflection of *altered to* the reflection on
76 would publish on *altered to* would publish it on
77 two Editions an *altered to* two Editions a limited

Lorne Pierce (2 Oct. 1927). Pierce, QUA. Handwritten, letterhead: 'Canadian Pacific Railway / en route.'
78 West. I *altered to* West. And I

Charles G.D. Roberts (15 Dec. 1927). Roberts, UNB. Handwritten, LH5.

Harriet Monroe, *Poetry* (Chicago) (6 Feb. 1928). Poetry, UC. Handwritten, LH5.

Lorne Pierce (5 Mar. 1928). Pierce, QUA. Handwritten, LH2.
80 in which she st *altered to* in which she says

Lorne Pierce (11 Apr. 1928). Pierce, QUA. Handwritten, LH5.
81 and the closin *altered to* and the practical closing

Raymond Knister (6 Oct. 1928). Givens. Handwritten, LH5.

Lorne Pierce (12 Dec. 1928). Pierce, QUA. Handwritten, LH5.

Pelham Edgar (6 Aug. 1929). EJP, VUL. Handwritten, LH5. On first sheet, 'Victoria College' and 'Toronto 5' are scored out and replaced with 'Bobcaygeon, Ont.'
85 cordially] cordialy [*sic*]
85 oath of discipline in *altered to* oath of discipline etc. in

William Arthur Deacon (11 Oct. 1929). Deacon, FRBL. Handwritten, LH5. Across the top of the page, Pratt has written '*The Rooskell* [*sic*] *and the Antinoë*.'
000 E *altered to* Ned

Lorne Pierce (Oct. 1929). Pierce, QUA. Handwritten, LH5.

William Arthur Deacon (21 Oct. 1929). Deacon, FRBL. Handwritten, LH5.
87 Mechanisation' *altered to* Mechanization,' Page 2

Pelham Edgar (17 July 1930). EJP, VUL. Handwritten, LH5.

Newton MacTavish (15 Dec. 1930). MacTavish, NYPL. Handwritten, LH5.
91 chat with you *altered to* chat with each

Audrey Alexandra Brown (30 Jan. 1931). Brown, UBCL. Handwritten, LH5.

Newton MacTavish (3 June 1931). MacTavish, NYPL. Handwritten, LH5.
91 June 3, 1930 *altered to* June 3, 1931

William Arthur Deacon (11 July 1931). Deacon, FRBL. Handwritten on stationery from 'Halifax Club / [crest].'
92 July 11, 1931] July 11, 1913
92 fact of sm *altered to* fact of having the ocean smell

William Arthur Deacon (17 July 1931). Deacon, FRBL. Handwritten on stationery from 'Halifax Club / [crest].'
93 enjoy it here *altered to* enjoying the trip here

George Herbert Clarke (12 Jan. 1932). Clarke, QUA. Handwritten, LH5.
94 gone to the *altered to* gone to Chicago
94 Poetry recital th[?] *altered to* Poetry recital in the

Lorne Pierce (13 Jan. 1932). Pierce, QUA. Handwritten on the bottom of a letter from Pierce on Ryerson Press letterhead, dated 12 January 1932.
95 the house was *altered to* the house has remained

Lorne Pierce (30 Jan. 1932). Pierce, QUA. Handwritten, LH5.

George Herbert Clarke (6 Feb. 1932). Clarke, QUA. Handwritten, LH5.

George Herbert Clarke (30 June 1932). Clarke, QUA. Handwritten, LH5.
97 Eggeleston *altered to* Eggleston

Hugh S. Eayrs (9 July 1932). Macmillan, MMLM. Handwritten on plain paper.
98 given me for *altered to* given me a[?] ticket for
98 common pass them. I[?] *altered to* common pass them on.
99 He is regarded as *altered to* He is regarded (or was) as

Pelham Edgar (26 Aug. 1932). EJP, VUL. Handwritten, plain paper.
99 you have swea *altered to* you have survived
100 term but she *altered to* term but Claire
101 If I had a brea *altered to* If I had a big break

William Arthur Deacon (4 Sept. 1932). Deacon, FRBL. Handwritten, plain paper.
102 a little gi *altered to* a little fresh-air girl
102 contents of the Re[..] *altered to* contents of the approaching
103 200 lines [..] *altered to* 200 lines each
103 which is partly re *altered to* which is partly descriptive, partly reflective

O.J. Stevenson (5 Sept. 1932). Copp Clark, MMLM. Handwritten, plain paper.
104 of a Dog' – might] of a Dog' might

Hugh S. Eayrs (5 Sept. 1932). Macmillan, MMLM. Handwritten, plain paper.
105 and you as [..] *altered to* and you as to

III Prospect and Promotion, 1932–1939

Katherine MacTavish (Dec. 1932). MacTavish, NYPL. Handwritten, LH5.
106 time later yo *altered to* some time later would you

William Douw Lighthall (13 June 1933). Lighthall, McGill.

Viola Pratt (8 July 1933). VLP, VUL. Handwitten, letterhead: 'Halifax Club / [crest].'
108 or tomorrow] or to-morrow
108 *in time underlined twice*
109 to see w *altered to* to see how

Viola Pratt (25 July 1933). VLP, VUL. Handwritten. letterhead: 'Halifax Club / [crest].'
109 hint to [.] *altered to* hint – 'What

Claire Pratt (28 July 1933). EJP, VUL. Handwritten, letterhead: 'Halifax Club / [crest].'

Lorne Pierce (20 Aug. 1933). Pierce, QUA. Handwritten, plain paper.

William Arthur Deacon (31 Oct. 1933). Deacon, FRBL. Handwritten, LH2.

William Arthur Deacon (5 Nov. 1933). Deacon, FRBL. Handwritten, LH2.
113 night I *altered to* night aloud

William Arthur Deacon (16 Nov. 1933). Deacon, FRBL. Handwritten, LH2.
113 Literary C *altered to* Literary Section
114 S *altered to* Immediately

George Herbert Clarke (29 Nov. 1933). Clarke, QUA. Handwritten, LH5.

An Unknown Correspondent (Dec. 1933). EJP, VUL. Handwritten draft in notebook.

F.R. Scott (3 Jan. 1934). Djwa. Handwritten, plain paper.

F.R. Scott (9 Jan. 1934). Djwa. Handwritten, LH5.
118 submitting three *altered to* submitting two

F.R. Scott (16 Jan. 1934). Djwa. Handwritten, LH5.
118 going t *altered to* going over

F.R. Scott (23 Jan. 1934). Djwa. Handwritten, LH5.

Hugh S. Eayrs (24 Feb. 1934). Macmillan, MMLM. Typewritten, LH5.
121 find that students *altered to* find that the students
121 This is a book *altered to* This (the Broadus) is a book

Hugh S. Eayrs (27 Mar. 1934). Macmillan, MMLM. Typewritten, letterhead: 'Victoria University.'
124 Redvers Dent. *altered by hand to* Redvers Dent?
124 caht *typed over and replaced with* chat
124 adption *typed over and replaced with* adoption
124 pwerfu *typed over and replaced with* powerful
124 on Grand Pré.] on Grand Pre.
124 too] two [*sic*]

F.R. Scott (6 June 1934). Djwa. Handwritten, LH5.
125 afterward *altered to* after which

F.R. Scott (19 Sept. 1934). Djwa. Handwritten, LH5.
126 However, he] However, he he

Leo Kennedy (24 Oct. 1934). Kennedy. Handwritten, LH5.

F.R. Scott (7 Nov. 1934). Djwa. Handwritten, LH5.
127 $200 or $300 *altered to* $200 or $250

F.R. Scott (30 Nov. 1934). Djwa. Handwritten, LH5.
129 co-operate] cooperate

F.R. Scott (10 Dec. 1934). Djwa. Handwritten, LH5.
130 $25 *per double underlined*
130 $25 *per altered to* $25 per poem

William Arthur Deacon (8 Apr. 1935). Deacon, FRBL. Handwritten, LH2.
131 concentrated, to *altered to* concentrated, so as

F.R. Scott (13 Oct. 1935). Djwa. Handwritten, LH6: *CPM.* Underscoring may be by recipient.

George Herbert Clarke (25 Oct. 1935). Clarke, QUA. Handwritten, LH6: *CPM.*
133 so I will be ce *altered to* so I will be sure

Wilson MacDonald (20 Nov. 1935). MacDonald, LAC. Handwritten, LH6: *CPM.*

F.R. Scott (29 Nov. 1935). Djwa. Handwritten, LH5.

Dorothy Livesay (5 Dec. 1935). Livesay, UML. Handwritten, LH6: *CPM.*

Charles Clay, *Winnipeg Free Press* (14 Dec. 1935). Clay, LAC. Handwritten, LH5 with 'English Department' added above the address.
136 glad if you *altered to* glad if, when you
136 Board. I *altered to* Board. We

F.R. Scott (20 Dec. 1935). Djwa. Handwritten, LH6: *CPM.*
137 impression will *altered to* impression which will be

George Herbert Clarke (28 Dec. 1935). Clarke, QUA. Handwritten on plain paper.
137 Victoria College, [.....] *altered to* Victoria College, Toronto

F.R. Scott (14 Jan. 1936). Djwa. Handwritten, LH5.
138 in spite of the critical *altered to* in spie of the warm and cordial critical

George Herbert Clarke (22 Feb. 1936). Whalley. Handwritten.

F.R. Scott (23 Feb. 1936). Djwa. Handwritten, LH5.

George Herbert Clarke (27 Mar. 1936). Clarke, QUA. Handwritten, LH6: *CPM*.

Ina McCauley (8 May 1936). McCauley. Handwritten, LH5.

Viola Pratt (7 July 1936). VLP, VUL. Handwritten, plain paper.
143 the way, [...] *altered to* the way, so you

Lorne Pierce (12 July 1936). Pierce, QUA. Handwritten, plain paper.
145 goodwill [..] *altered to* good will is

Viola Pratt (16 July 1936). VLP, VUL. Handwritten, plain paper.
145–6 It is cute wa *altered to* It is cute the way

Viola Pratt (20 July 1936). VLP, VUL. Handwritten, plain paper.
147 Aug 1 to 20 *altered to* Aug 1 to 21
147 cool and ref[..] *altered to* cool and refreshing

Viola Pratt (24 July 1936). VLP, VUL. Handwritten, lined paper (foolscap from an examination booklet).
148 Let wor *altered to* Let her work
148 the time a C[..] *altered to* the time a little

Viola Pratt (27 July 1936). VLP, VUL. Handwritten, plain paper in pencil.
149 wrote dis *altered to* wrote diplomatically
149 take a [...] *altered to* take a drink

Viola Pratt (6 Aug. 1936). VLP, VUL. Handwritten, plain paper in pencil.

Viola Pratt (10 Aug. 1936). VLP, VUL. Handwritten on plain paper.

Eugenie Perry (2 Sept. 1936). Perry, PABC (copy in EJP, VUL). Handwritten, LH5.

Hugh S. Eayrs (18 Nov. 1936). Macmillan, MMLM. Handwritten, LH5.

Eugenie Perry (1 Dec. 1936). Perry, PABC (copy in EJP, VUL). Handwritten, LH6: *CPM.*

E.K. Brown (3 Feb. 1937). Margaret Brown. Telegram: 'Canadian Pacific Telegraphs.'

Lorne Pierce (16 Apr. 1937). Pierce, QUA. Handwritten, LH6: *CPM.*

George Herbert Clarke (15 May 1937). Clarke, QUA. Handwritten, LH6: *CPM.*

Pelham Edgar (13 June 1937). EJP, VUL. Handwritten, LH6: *CPM.*

Eugenie Perry (21 July 1937). Perry, PABC (copy in EJP, VUL). Handwritten, LH6: *CPM.*

Claire Pratt (29 July 1937). CP, VUL. Handwritten, LH6: *CPM* with the header crossed out.

Claire Pratt (7 Aug. 1937). CP, VUL. Handwritten, LH6: *CPM* with the header crossed out.
160 [ ] = *half of the first sentence has been blocked out by the recipient*

Lorne Pierce (13 Sept. 1937). Pierce, QUA. Handwritten, LH5.

George Herbert Clarke (18 Oct. 1937). Clarke, QUA. Handwritten, LH5.

F.R. Scott (3 Nov. 1937). Djwa. Handwritten, LH5.

George Herbert Clarke (12 Jan. 1938). Clarke, QUA. Handwritten, LH5. Erroneously dated 1937.
163 19th Century *altered to* 19th Century poetry

George Herbert Clarke (28 Jan. 1938). Clarke, QUA. Handwritten, LH5.

J.R.M. Butler (18 Feb. 1938). Pacey (copy in EJP, VUL). Handwritten, LH5.

Charles G.D. Roberts (5 Apr. 1938). Roberts, UNB. Handwritten, LH5.

Leo Cox (10 Apr. 1938). Cox. Copied by Pitt from the original.

Ina McCauley (2 May 1938). McCauley. Handwritten, LH6: *CPM.*

William Arthur Deacon (Spring 1938). Deacon, FRBL. Handwritten, plain paper. Undated but filed by Deacon with his 1938 correspondence.

E.K. Brown (31 May 1938). EJP, VUL. Handwritten, LH5.

Earle Birney (early 1939). Birney, FRBL. Handwritten, LH5.

Arthur Phelps (1939). Phelps, UML. Handwritten, LH5.

George Herbert Clarke (7 Feb.1939). Clarke, QUA. Handwritten, LH5.

Madge Macbeth (16 May 1939). Macbeth, LAC.

IV Historical Fact and Epic Construction, 1939–1944

Claire Pratt (13 July 1939). EJP, VUL. Handwritten, LH5.

Claire Pratt (20 July 1939). EJP, VUL. Handwritten, plain paper.
174 how should *altered to* how you should

Claire Pratt (28 July 1939). EJP, VUL. Handwritten, LH5.

Claire Pratt (1 Aug. 1939). EJP, VUL. Handwritten, LH5.

George Herbert Clarke (Aug. 1939). Clarke, QUA. Handwritten, LH5.

Members of the Canadian Authors Association (30 Sept. 1939). Deacon – CAA Records, FRBL. Typed, plain paper.
179 broadcast had been *altered to* broadcast has been

Madge Macbeth (15 Jan. 1940). Macbeth, LAC. Telegram: 'Canadian National Telegraphs.'

Leo Cox (27 Mar. 1940). Cox. Handwritten, LH5.

Lorne Pierce (7 June 1940). Pierce, QUA. Handwritten, LH5.

Ellen Elliott (7 June 1940). Macmillan, MMLM. Handwritten, LH6: *CPM.*

George Herbert Clarke (21 June 1940). Clarke, QUA. Handwritten, LH5.

Viola Pratt (4 July 1940). VLP, VUL. Handwritten, LH5. Written from Kingston, Ontario, where Pratt was again teaching Summer School.

Pelham Edgar (19 July 1940). EJP, VUL. Handwritten, LH5 with the address scored out.

Claire Pratt (19 July 1940). EJP, VUL. Handwritten, LH5.
186 July 20 *altered to* July 19

Viola Pratt (22 July 1940). VLP, VUL. Handwritten, LH5.

Viola and Claire Pratt (23 July 1940). VLP, VUL. Handwritten, LH5.

Viola Pratt (29 July 1940). EJP, VUL. Handwritten, LH5.
190 Monongahela.' I] Monongahela.'; I

Earle Birney (7 Aug. 1940). Birney, FRBL. Handwritten on plain paper.
192 free of clichés:] free of cliches:
192 Joshua simile] Joshua simile'
192 sent me two [....]ems *altered to* sent me two poems

Viola Pratt (7 Aug. 1940). VLP, VUL. Handwritten, plain paper.
193 ago, Ro *altered to* ago, Mrs
194 reviews of Brébeuf,] reviews of Brebeuf,

Pelham Edgar (15 Aug. 1940). EJP, VUL. Handwritten, plain paper.

E.K. Brown (9 Oct. 1940). EJP, VUL. Handwritten, LH5.

Ellen Elliott (28 Oct. 1940). Macmillan, MMLM. Handwritten, LH5.
198 M *altered to* Campbell-MacInnes

F.R. Scott (4 Dec. 1940). Djwa. Handwritten. LH5.

Ralph Gustafson (16 Jan. 1941). Gustafson, USKL. Handwritten. LH5.

Ralph Gustafson (31 Jan. 1941). Gustafson, USKL. Handwritten, LH5.
200 Forum, which *altered* to Forum, 'The Radio in the Ivory Tower,' which

Ralph Gustafson (5 Feb. 1941). Gustafson, USKL. Handwritten, LH5.

Watson Kirkconnell (19 Mar. 1941). Kirkconnell, Acadia. Handwritten, LH5.

A.J.M. Smith (29 Mar. 1941). Smith, FRBL. Handwritten, LH5.

A.J.M. Smith (8 Apr. 1941). Smith, FRBL. Handwritten, LH5.

Ralph Gustafson (15 May 1941). Gustafson, USKL. Handwritten, LH5.

Father Stanley Murphy (14 July 1941). CP, VUL. Handwritten. LH5.

George Dillon (5 Aug. 1941). Poetry, UC. Handwritten, LH5.

Pelham Edgar (8 Aug. 1941). EJP, VUL. Handwritten. LH5.
208 Were *altered to* We are
208 treatments two *altered to* treatments twice

George Dillon (26 Aug. 1941). Poetry, UC. Typed, LH5.

A.J.M. Smith (17 Sept. 1941). Smith, FRBL. Handwritten, LH5.

Miss Udell (19 Sept. 1941). Poetry, UC. Handwritten, LH5.
211 [large check in the left margin beside the request to charge his account for extra copies and a renewal of his subscription.]

Margaret Furness MacLeod (22 Sept. 1941). MacLeod. Handwritten, LH5.

Ellen Elliott (7 Oct. 1941). Macmillan, MMLM. Handwritten, LH6: *CPM.*
212 1942 *altered to* 1941

A.J.M. Smith (8 Oct. 1941). Smith, FRBL. Handwritten, LH5.
213 criticism *altered to* critical reviewing

Leo Cox (3 Nov. 1941). Cox. Handwritten, LH5.

E.K. Brown (4 Nov. 1941). EJP, VUL. Handwritten, LH5.

Leo Cox (late Nov. 1941). Cox. Handwritten, LH5.

Ellen Elliott (2 Dec. 1941). Macmillan, MMLM. Handwritten, LH5.

A.M. Klein (23 Dec. 1941). Klein, LAC. Handwritten, LH5.
217 Dec. 24 *altered to* Dec. 23
217 original g [.] *altered to* original a product

Cécile de Banke (24 Dec. 1941). Wellesley. Handwritten, LH7.

Ralph Gustafson (17 Mar. 1942). Gustafson, USKL. Handwritten, LH7.
219 that Dunkirk sonnet *altered to* that the Dunkirk sonnet

Ralph Gustafson (13 Apr. 1942). Gustafson, USKL. Handwritten, LH7.

E.K. Brown (20 Apr. 1942). Letter: EJP, VUL. Handwritten, LH7. Enclosure: Pitt. Handwritten, LH7.

Enclosure:
221 1.] I.
221 that Light appeared *altered to* Light, 'Overheard by a Stream'
221 in the Fo *altered to* in the Canadian Forum
223 4.] (4)
223 to the human *altered to* to bring in (with the more severe elemental and heroic qualities) the human idiosyncrasies
224 O'Dowd but wo *altered to* O'Dowd but should

E.K. Brown (21 Apr. 1942). EJP, VUL. Typed, plain paper; handwritten draft (*MS1*), LH7. The typist had some difficulty reading Pratt's handwriting.
224 April [21]] April 19
225 Father Sally *altered to* Father Lally
225 The [blank space] contined *altered to* The Relations contained
225 Roosevelts *altered to* Roosevelt's] Roosevelt's *MS1*
225 Then on the B. and his *altered to* Then in the B. and his] Then in the B. & his *MS1*
225 NED] Ned. *MS1*

E.K. Brown (22 Apr. 1942). EJP, VUL. Handwritten, plain paper.
225 Shrine is *altered* to Shrine at Midland is *altered to* Shrine near Midland is
225 The Decision *altered to* The Decision (1928)
225 Sea-Gulls *altered to* Sea-Gulls (1932)

E.K. Brown (2 May 1942). Pitt. Handwritten, LH7.
226 at 15, was *altered to* at 15 in St John's Newfoundland, was

Ralph Gustafson (2 May 1942). Gustafson, USKL. Handwritten, LH5.

Watson Kirkconnell (6 May 1942). Kirkconnell, Acadia. Handwritten, LH5.

E.K. Brown (May 1942). Margaret Brown. Transcribed by Pitt from tape recording, 1969.

George Dillon (30 May 1942). Poetry, UC. Handwritten, LH5.

Claire Pratt (early June 1942). EJP, VUL. Handwritten, plain paper.
229 got 76 *altered to* 77
229 You made 220 *altered to* You made 150

Lorne Pierce (9 June 1942). Pierce, QUA. Handwritten, LH5.

Lorne Pierce (20 June 1942). Pierce, QUA. Handwritten, LH5.

Leo Cox (28 June 1942). Cox. Handwritten, LH5.

Eugenie Perry (2 July 1942). Perry, PABC (copy in EJP, VUL). Handwritten, LH5.

A.J.M. Smith (15 July 1942) . Smith, FRBL. Handwritten, LH5.

George Dillon (26 Aug. 1942). Poetry, UC. Handwritten, LH5.

Pelham Edgar (1 Sept. 1942). EJP, VUL. Handwritten, plain paper.

A.J.M. Smith (2 Oct. 1942). Smith, FRBL. Typed, plain paper, with handwritten postscript: 'Forgive type errors. I thump the typewriter with one finger.'
237 permission coss [*sic*], *altered to* permission costs
237 the Uiniversity [*sic*] expense *altered to* the University expense
238 theu [*sic*] refuse *altered to* they refused
238 [.]alcom [*sic*] *altered to* Malcolm
238 He leathes [*sic*] *altered to* He loathes
238 that the production *altered to* that the early production
238 generated by *altered to* generated, by
238 It ss [*sic*] so remote *altered to* It is so remote
238 sshieved [*sic*] *altered to* achieved
238 no expemse [*sic*] *altered to* expense
239 A saw-oo [*sic*] *altered to* A saw-off

A.J.M. Smith (15 Nov. 1942). Smith, FRBL. Handwritten, LH5.

Ralph Gustafson (18 Nov. 1942). Gustafson, USKL. Handwritten, LH5.
240 Macmillan's] Macmillans [*sic*]

Cécile de Banke (21 Nov. 1942). Wellesley. Handwritten, LH5.

A.J.M. Smith (30 Nov. 1942). Smith, FRBL. Handwritten, LH5.

A.J.M. Smith (7 Dec. 1942). Smith, FRBL. Handwritten, LH5.
243 extant [....] *altered to* extant with
244 MacInnes'] McInnes'
244 Schools found *altered to* Schools form
244 referring to farts *altered to* referring, indirectly but obviously, to farts
245 think you have in[?] *altered to* think you have as

George Herbert Clarke (12 Jan. 1943). Clarke, QUA. Handwritten, LH7.

Leo Cox (12 Jan. 1943). Cox. Handwritten, LH7.

Pelham Edgar (16 Jan. 1943). Edgar, VUL. Handwritten, LH5.

M.M.H. MacKinnon (26 Jan. 1943). Pitt. Handwritten, LH7.

A.J.M Smith (16 Feb. 1943). Smith, FRBL. Handwritten, LH5.

A.J.M Smith (24 Feb. 1943). Smith, FRBL. Handwritten, LH5.
251 claimed he was *altered to* claimed he (MacD.) was

Merrill Denison (5 Apr. 1943). Denison, LAC. Handwritten, LH7.
252 when he flings *altered to* when in his mind he flings
252 London co *altered to* London didn't

Lorne Pierce (29 Apr. 1943). Pierce, QUA. Handwritten, LH7.
253 that is J. R *altered to* that is J.R. Robins.

E.K. Brown (11 May 1943). EJP, VUL. Handwritten, LH5.
254 [...] you *altered to* Still, you

A.J.M. Smith (13 May 1943). Smith, FRBL. Handwritten, LH5.
255 age, an[.] *altered to* age, and

A.M. Klein (9 June 1943). Klein, LAC. Handwritten, LH5.

Malcolm Ross (22 July 1943). Ross, UCAL. Handwritten, LH5.

Ellen Elliott (17 Aug. 1943). Macmillan, MMLM. Handwritten on plain paper.
257 The 10 poems *altered to* The 14 poems
257 exactly 1000 *altered to* exactly 1050
257 with a *Collected*] with a '*Collected*

Watson Kirkconnell (8 Sept. 1943). Published in *The Canadian Author and Bookman* (Dec. 1943).

William Rose Benét (9 Sept. 1943). Benét, BRBR. Typed, LH5.
259 the Benét brothers] the Benet brothers
260 'Witches] 'Wiches [*sic*]
261 intended merely] intended merely / intended merely
261 steamer towed a whale *altered to* steamer towed in a whale

E.K. Brown (14 Sept. 1943). Pitt. Handwritten, LH7.

E.K. Brown (20 Sept. 1943). EJP, VUL. Handwritten, LH5.
263 from a desk *altered to* from a reading desk
263 symphony of Brébeuf] symphony of Brebeuf
263 Dale as Brébeuf.] Dale as Brebeuf.

Ellen Elliott (27 Oct. 1943). Macmillan, MMLM. Handwritten, LH5.
264 Benét's influence] Benet's influence

A.J.M. Smith (30 Oct. 1943). Smith, FRBL. Handwritten, LH5.
265 case of MacDonald] case of Macdonald

Ellen Elliott (1 Nov. 1943). Macmillan, MMLM. Handwritten, LH5.
266 Benét is reviewing *Brébeuf*] Benet reviewing *Brebeuf*

E.K. Brown (3 Nov. 1943). EJP, VUL. Handwritten, LH5.
266 William Rose Benét] William Rose Benet
266 Cachalot. Benét] Cachalot. Benet
266 after leave *altered to* after leaving
266 as well. Leave[?] *altered to* as well. There

A.J.M. Smith (8 Nov. 1943). Smith, FRBL. Handwritten, LH5.

Ellen Elliott (11 Nov. 1943). Macmillan, MMLM. Handwritten, LH5.
268 Since Benét's review] Since Benet's review
268 'Still Life' simply] 'Still Life simply

A.J.M. Smith (5 Dec. 1943). Smith, FRBL. Handwritten on plain paper.

E.K. Brown (6 Dec. 1943). EJP, VUL. Handwritten, LH5.
269 Benét was] Benet was

William Rose Benét (15 Dec. 1943). Benét, BRBR. Handwritten, LH5.

Cécile de Banke (15 Dec. 1943). Wellesley. Handwritten, LH5.
272 the Saturday Night *altered to* the Saturday Night of Toronto

John Sutherland (5 Jan. 1944). Audrey Sutherland. Handwritten, LH5.

Ralph Gustafson (6 Jan. 1944). Gustafson, USKL. Handwritten, LH5.

V Steering between Extremes, 1944–1948

Margaret Furness MacLeod (25 Jan. 1944). MacLeod. Handwritten, LH5.

A.J.M. Smith (28 Jan. 1944). Smith, FRBL. Handwritten, LH5.
275 volume of verse *altered to* volume of Canadian verse
276 (newspaper critics) very] (newspaper critics very
277 the new, the traditional] the new the traditional
277 Ruddick were [....] *altered* to Ruddick were mad
277 the ear of Benét] the ear of Bénét

William Rose Benét (10 Feb. 1944). Benét. BRBR. Handwritten, LH5.
277 Vi and I *altered to* Vi (Viola) and I

William Rose Benét (18 May 1944). Benét, BRBR. Handwritten, LH5.
279 extreme, perhaps] extreme perhaps

Ellen Elliott (7 June 1944). Macmillan, MMLM. Handwritten, LH5.

Alan Crawley (26 June 1944). Crawley, QUA. Handwritten, LH5.

Viola Pratt (18 July 1944). VLP, VUL. Handwritten, plain paper.

Viola Pratt (27 July 1944). VLP, VUL. Handwritten, plain paper.
283 so I shall have to] so I shall to
283 warming (or should] warming (, or should

Pelham Edgar (7 Aug. 1944). EJP, VUL. Handwritten, LH5 with address scored out.
285 specially by Maclean's] specially by Macleans
285 lines. Maclean's] lines. Macleans

Earle Birney (8 Aug. 1944). Birney, FRBL. Handwritten, LH5.
286 Anderson, Me[?] *altered to* Anderson, Shaw
286 with themselves as *altered to* with themselves as the
287 am a bit in[?] *altered to* am a bit excited
287 I may ma[?] *altered to* I may 'break

William Rose Benét (13 Aug. 1944). Benét, BRBR. Handwritten, LH5 with address scored out.
290 of the Goats (Governor *altered to* of the Goats 1936 (Governor
290 His Brethren 1939 (ditto)] His Brethren (do) *altered to* His Brethren 1939 (do)
290 (12) [......] of Newfou *altered to* (12) Still Life

Mrs Stagg (31 Aug. 1944). Knopf, RHRC. Typed, LH5.
291 about 'Brébeuf] about 'Brebeuf
291 this year, orchestra *altered to* this year (orchestra

William Rose Benét (15 Sept. 1944). Benét, BRBR. Handwritten, letterhead of the Prince George Hotel, 14 East 28th Street, New York 16, N.Y.

Jenny Pincock (30 Sept. 1944). Pincock, UWL. Handwritten, LH5.

Claire Pratt (2 Oct. 1944). EJP, VUL. Handwritten, LH5.

Claire Pratt (13 Oct. 1944). EJP, VUL. Typed, plain paper.
296 lecture on *Brébeuf*] lecture on *Brebeuf*
296 letter on Brébeuf.] letter on Brebeuf.

Claire Pratt (22 Oct. 1944). EJP, VUL. Typed, plain paper.
297 on his medical rounds] on his ron [*sic*] medical rounds
298 Cluny replied, 'Is] Cluny replied V [*sic*] Is

Claire Pratt (30 Oct. 1944). EJP, VUL. Typed, LH5.
298 Even if it is not like] Even if it is not lie [*crossed out*] like
298 abusrd [*sic*] *altered to* absurd
298 took up up *altered to* took up
299 the Presodent [*sic*] *altered to* the President
299 manufactured [*sic*] *altered to* manufacturer
299 [ ] = *6 line paragraph whited out*
299 of letter writer *altered to* of letter writing

Claire Pratt (25 Oct. 1944). EJP, VUL. Typed, LH5.

'William Noble' (Harold Horwood) (2 Nov. 1944). Published in *Protocol* (Nov. 1945).

Jenny Pincock (2 Nov. 1944). Pincock, UWL. Handwritten, LH5.

Claire Pratt (4 Nov. 1944). EJP, VUL. Typed, plain paper.
302 Sidney Smith] Sydney Smith

Claire Pratt (13 Nov. 1944). EJP, VUL. Typed. LH5.

E.K. Brown (15 Nov. 1944). Pitt. Handwritten, LH5.
304 Sidney Smith] Sydney Smith
304 at Queen's] at Queens
305 The S.R.L., the] The S.R.L. the

A.J.M. Smith (15 Nov. 1944). Smith, FRBL. Handwritten, LH5.

Claire Pratt (21 Nov. 1944). EJP, VUL. Typed, LH5. Poem appended on a separate sheet: typed, plain paper.
306 like you to] like tou [*sic*] to
307 answer Margaret's letter] answer Margaret,s [*sic*] letter
307 take an occasional] take and [*sic*] occasional
307 would suggest that] would sugge/gest [*sic*] that

Louis MacKay (7 Dec. 1944). MacKay. Typed, LH5. Handwritten closing.
308 of the 'Collected'] of the Collected
308 you my good old friend *altered to* you, my good old friend,
308 a very great] a verygreat

Claire Pratt (11 Dec. 1944). EJP, VUL. Handwritten, LH5.
309 people came, nearly] people came nearly

Claire Pratt (13 Dec. 1944). EJP, VUL. Handwritten, letterhead: 'The Women's Missionary Society of the United Church of Canada / Periodicals Department / 433 Wesley Buildings / ... / World Friends / Mrs. E.J. Pratt, Editor.'

Albert G. Hatcher (3 Jan. 1945). MUNA. Handwritten, LH5.

Charles D. Abbott (28 Jan. 1945). Contemporary Manuscripts Collection, CAML. Typed, LH5.
312 work sheets of *Brébeuf*] work sheets of *Brebeuf*

A.M. Klein (7 Feb. 1945). Klein, LAC. Handwritten, LH5.

Claire Pratt (7 Feb. 1945). EJP, VUL. Handwritten, LH5.
314 MacGillivary] McGillivary
314 telephone Saturday *altered to* telephone message Saturday

Charles D. Abbott (19 Feb. 1945). Contemporary Manuscripts Collection, CAML. Handwritten, LH5.

Claire Pratt (19 Feb. 1945). EJP, VUL. Handwritten, LH5.
316 the Brébeuf pageant] of the Brebeuf pageant

Pelham Edgar (21 Feb. 1945). EJP, VUL. Handwritten, LH5.
318 When the dinner *altered to* When Bert's dinner

Claire Pratt (25 Feb. 1945). EJP, VUL. Typed, plain paper
318 address on Brébeuf] address on Brebeuf
318 I have goti [*sic*] *altered to* I have got in

Henry W. Wells (26 Feb. 1945). Klinck. Typed, plain paper; handwritten closing.
320 getting extensive for *altered to* getting extensive currency for

320 the Brébeuf composition] the Brebeuf composition
320 to get inside Brébeuf.] to get inside Brebeuf.

Lorne Pierce (3 Mar. 1945). Pierce, QUA. Typed, plain paper. Envelope postmarked 'Mar 3/45.'
321 nothing of Benét] nothing of Benet

Claire Pratt (12 Mar. 1945). EJP, VUL. Typed, plain paper.
321 for the snorer)] for the snore)
321 would come trom [*sic*] *altered to* would come from
321 *beckoning, beckoning, beckoning* [Underscored by hand: (in sequence) single, double, and then triple lines]
321 glad to mett [*sic*] *altered to* glad to meet
321 Conacher] Conacker
321 Dr. Bouoher's [*sic*] *altereed to* Dr. Boucher's
321 ice_cream [*sic*] *altered to* ice-cream
321 on the Totanic [*sic*] *altered to* on the Titanic
321 was so full thaa [*sic*] *altered to* was so full that

Claire Pratt (14 Mar. 1945). EJP, VUL. Handwritten, plain paper.
323–4 the Brébeuf man] the Brebeuf man
324 the disc. Brébeuf] the disc. Brebeuf
324 Brébeuf's fault.'] Brebeuf's fault.'
324 taking Brébeuf.] taking Brebeuf.

Claire Pratt (27 Mar. 1945). EJP, VUL. Handwritten, plain paper.
325 sure I didn't).] sure I didn't.

Claire Pratt (31 Mar. 1945). EJP, VUL. Typed, LH5.

Claire Pratt (Apr. 1945). EJP, VUL. Typed, LH5; handwritten closing.
327 the etntr [*sic*] *altered* to the entertainment
327 rounede [*sic*] *altered* to rounded up
327 Farther Flahiff [*sic*] *altered to* Father Flahiff
328 told told stories [*sic*] *altered to* told stories
328 [ ] = *approximately 4 lines blocked out by Claire Pratt*
328 however[.] *altered to* however,
328 when you vome [*sic*] *altered to* when you come

William Rose Benét (17 Apr. 1945). Benét, BRBR. Typed, LH5.
329 Bill syas [*sic*] about *altered to* Bill says about

329 and the rest, tell] and the rest tell
329 vespers (Brébeuf] vespers (Brebeuf

Claire Pratt (18 Apr. 1945). EJP, VUL. Typed. plain paper.
330 with the Fryes] with the Frys
330 Margaret Gould] Margarat [*sic*] Gould
330 and we are] and We are
330 Goats, but I] Goats, butI [*sic*]
331 that side of it] thatside [*sic*] of it
331 namely, Brébeuf,] namely, Brebeuf,

Charles D. Abbott (7 May 1945). Contemporary Manuscripts Collection, CAML. Handwritten, LH5.

Claire Pratt (11 May 1945). EJP, VUL. Typed, LH5; handwritten postscript.
332 so wee [*sic*] started *altered to* so we started
333 fond of sid [*sic*] *altered to* fond of Sid
333 the dggree [*sic*] of *altered to* the degree of
333 of 2q [*sic*] Cortleigh *alteredto* of 21 Cortleigh
333 to give yout [*sic*] *altered to* to give you
333 not encose [*sic*] *alteredto* not enclose
333 somehow I omitted] somehow i omitted
333 weeks time of [*sic*] *altered to* weeks time or
333 Robert Hillyer] Robert Hillier

Charles D. Abbott (30 May 1945). Contemporary Manuscripts Collection, CAML. Typed, LH5; handwritten closing and postscript.
334 the next plenary *altered to* the next, plenary
334 at the Pierresis' *altered to* at the Perrys'
334 the meeting *altered to* the meeting again
334 heartbeatsn [*sic*] the *altered to* heartbeats; the

Pelham Edgar (31 May 1945). EJP, VUL. Handwritten, LH5.
335 The Naval Dept. *altered to* The Depat. of Naval Education

William Rose Benét (8 June 1945). Benét. BRBR. Handwritten, LH5.
336 Magazine next *altered to* Magazine (Canadian) next

Ellen Elliott (15 June 1945). Macmillan, MMLM. Typed, plain paper.
337 in MacLean's] in MacLeans
337 be piblished [*sic*] *altered to* be published
337 copy for yout [*sic*] *altered to* copy for your

Viola and Claire Pratt (23 June 1945). VLP, VUL. Handwritten, letterhead: 'Canadian National / Railways – Steamships – Airlines – Hotels – Telegraphs – Express.'

Ellen Elliott (24 June 1945). Macmillan, MMLM. Handwritten, letterhead: 'Halifax Club [crest].'
339 while Maclean's] while Macleans
340 Titanic, Brébeuf,] Titanic, Brebeuf

Viola Pratt (24 June 1945). VLP, VUL. Handwritten, letterhead: 'Halifax Club [crest].'

Viola Pratt (26 June 1945). VLP, VUL. Handwritten, letterhead: 'Halifax Club [crest].'

Claire Pratt (27 June 1945). EJP, VUL. Handwritten, letterhead: 'Halifax Club [crest].'

Pelham Edgar (29 June 1945). EJP, VUL. Handwritten, letterhead: 'Halifax Club [crest].'

Douglas Bush (1 July 1945). Bush. Handwritten, letterhead: 'Halifax Club [crest].'

Viola Pratt (1 July 1945). VLP, VUL. Handwritten, letterhead: 'Halifax Club [crest].'

Ellen Elliott (7 July 1945). Macmillan, MMLM. Handwritten, letterhead: 'Halifax Club' [crest].
349 newer and g[.] *altered to* newer and more
349 interested over r *altered to* interested over there

Viola Pratt (8 July 1945). VLP, VUL. Handwritten, letterhead: 'Halifax Club [crest].'
350 all the [...] *altered to* all the school

Viola Pratt (14 July 1945). VLP, VUL. Handwritten, letterhead: 'Halifax Club [crest].'
351 used by Co *altered to* used by the Commanding
352 have no de *altered to* have no need
352 first and I ha[..] *altered to* first and I have
352 the tumbling de[...] *altered to* the tumbling denizens

Henry W. Wells (17 July 1945). Klinck. Handwritten, letterhead: 'Halifax Club [crest].'

Viola Pratt (19 July 1945). VLP, VUL. Handwritten, letterhead: 'Halifax Club [crest].'

354 F *altered to* Thursday

354 and all C[..] *altered to* and all through

E.K. Brown (27 July 1945). Pitt. Handwritten, letterhead: 'Halifax Club [crest].'

Viola and Claire Pratt (27 July 1945). VLP, VUL. Handwritten, letterhead: 'Halifax Club [crest].'

358 broadcast on Brébeuf] broadcast on Brebeuf

358 even at Brébeuf.] even at Brebeuf.

Viola Pratt (28 July 1945). EJP, VUL. Handwritten, letterhead: 'Halifax Club [crest].'

359 just ree *altered to* just returned

Claire Pratt (1 Aug. 1945). EJP, VUL. Handwritten, letterhead: 'Halifax Club [crest].'

Pelham Edgar (2 Aug. 1945). EJP, VUL. Handwritten, letterhead: 'Halifax Club [crest].'

362 *Brébeuf*] *Brebeuf*

362 the general area. ¶ The volumes ... ¶ Parkman's two volumes ... ¶ I got the present flora of the Midland territory, assuming it was the same three hundred years ago.¶ The volumes *altered to* the general area. ¶ I got the present flora of the Midland territory, assuming it was the same three hundred years ago.¶ The volumes ... ¶ Parkman's two volumes ...

362 given me p *altered to* given me top priority

Ralph Gustafson (21 Aug. 1945). Gustafson, USKL. Letter: typed, plain paper; handwritten closing. Enclosure: handwritten, plain paper.

363 Penguin and your Poetry and Canada. *altered to Penguin* and your *Poetry and Canada.*

363 most prnounced [*sic*] *altered to* most pronounced

363 hard up it *altered to* hard up, it

363 returning the chheque [*sic*] *altered to* returning the cheque

363 That too is *altered to* That, too, is

364 use an except [*sic*] *altered to* use an excerpt
364 it is justy [*sic*] out *altered to* it is just out
364 if you fins [*sic*] *altered to* if you find
364 hitherto unpiblished [*sic*] *altered to* hitherto unpublished

Ellen Elliott (Nov. 1945). Macmillan, MMLM.

Carl Klinck (21 Nov. 1945). Klinck. Handwritten, LH5.
368 as the ori *altered* to as the first wording

E.K. Brown (19 Dec. 1945). Pitt. Handwritten, LH5.

Carl Klinck (7 Jan. 1946). Klinck. Handwritten, LH5. Klinck's handwritten annotations in the left margin indicate his processing of Pratt's suggestions (see notes below).
370 & the U.S.A.] & the US.A.

William Rose Benét (3 Feb. 1946). Benét, BRBR. Typed, LH5.

Viola and Claire Pratt (3 Mar. 1946). EJP, VUL. Handwritten, letterhead: 'Prince George Hotel / 14 E. 28th Street – New York 16, N.Y. / Charles F. Rogers, Jr. – *Manager*.'
372 with the Benéts] with the Benets

William Rose and Marjorie Benét (17 Mar. 1946). Benét, BRBR. Typed, LH5.
373 ribbed, corrugated, fluted, delved. Oh, by Christopher, I got it STRIPED *altered to* ribbéd, corrugated, flutéd, delvéd. Oh, by Christopher, I got it STRIPÉD [É is double underlined]
373 lovely perfumed smoky *altered to* lovely, perfumed, smoky
373 Marjorie *altered to* Marjórie

Viola and Claire Pratt (9 Apr. 1946). VLP, VUL. Handwritten, letterhead: 'ST. THOMAS HIGH SCHOOL / 4500 memorial drive / HOUSTON, TEXAS // basilian fathers.'
374 and nuns – then] and nuns then

Earle Birney (14 Apr. 1946). Birney, FRBL. Typed, plain paper.
375 Governor-Gne [*sic*] *altered to* Governor-General's
375 Both os [*sic*] *altered to* Both of
375 to celer [*sic*] *altered to* celebrate
375 somewhat earlu [*sic*] *altered to* somewhat earlier

375 annual celebrato [*sic*] *altered to* celebration
375 institutes and schhols [*sic*] *altered to* institutes and schools
376 I taked [*sic*] a bit *altered to* I talked a bit

E.K. Brown (23 Apr. 1946). Pitt. Handwritten, LH5.

Viola Pratt (3 July 1946). VLP, VUL. Handwritten, LH5.
378 in the house. W *altered to* in the house. ¶ When

William Arthur Deacon (10 July 1946). Deacon, FRBL. Handwritten, plain paper.

John M. Gray (13 July 1946). Macmillan, MMLM. Handwritten, plain paper.
381 look through *Brébeuf*] look through *Brebeuf*
381 assuming that the book *altered to* assuming that the ms.

Claire Pratt (15 July 1946). EJP, VUL. Handwritten, plain paper.

Earle Birney (16 Aug. 1946). Birney, FRBL. Handwritten, LH5.

Pelham Edgar (16 Aug. 1946). EJP, VUL. Handwritten, LH5.
384 weather . We] weather – We

Earle Birney (20 Aug. 1946). Birney, FRBL. Telegram: 'CANADIAN PACIFIC TELEGRAPHS / World Wide Communications.'

Christopher and Helen Morley (16 Sept. 1946). RHRC.

M.M.H. MacKinnon (23 Oct. 1946). CP, VUL. Handwritten, LH7.
386 1946] 1945 [The correct year is established by Pratt's reference to *Behind the Log* as 'now completed.' It had been barely begun in October 1945.]
387 Brébeuf] Brebeuf

Lorne Pierce (28 Oct. 1946). Pierce, QUA. Handwritten, LH7.

Earle Birney (26 Nov. 1946). Birney, FRBL. Handwritten, LH5.
389 High Schools, be *altered to* High Schools, to be
389 Titanic, the Cachalot] Titanic the Cachalot
389 welcome to it *altered to* welcome to any
389 can return it *altered to* can return the poem

Earle Birney (13 Dec. 1946). Birney, FRBL. Handwritten, LH5.
390 In respect fo *altered* to in respect to
390 time revising in *altered to* time revising the poem in
390 feel that he is so *altered to* feel that he is too

William Arthur Deacon (early 1947). Deacon, FRBL. Handwritten, LH5, address crossed out.

Earle Birney (2 Jan. 1947). Birney, FRBL. Handwritten, LH7.

Pelham Edgar (13 Jan. 1947). EJP, VUL. Handwritten, LH5.

John M. Gray (28 Jan. 1947). Macmillan, MMLM. Typed, LH7.

Ellen Elliott (19 Feb. 1947). Macmillan, MMLM. Handwritten, LH5.
395 the reviews from *altered to* the reviews (of the Collected Poems) from

Earle Birney (18 Mar. 1947). Birney, FRBL. Handwritten, LH5.

Earle Birney (23 Mar. 1947). Birney, FRBL. Typed, LH5. Enclosed typescript of *Behind the Log*. Annotation by Birney, indicating in the upper margin the number of pages allocated to each component of the June 1947 number of *CPM*, with a further breakdown in the lower margin. *BL* was allotted 16 of 44 pages.

Earle Birney (9 Apr. 1947). Birney, FRBL. Handwritten, LH5.
399 'Empire Hudson,] Empire Hudson,
399 grain.' ¶ It avoids] grain.' It avoids

Frank Upjohn (May 1947). Macmillan, MMLM. Handwritten, LH7. Enclosed ms.

John M. Gray (4 June 1947). Macmillan, MMLM. Typed, LH5.
400 requisitioned. The had *altered to* requisitioned. They had

W.E. Collin (28 June 1947). Collin, UWO. Typed, LH7.
401 on preYConfederation [*sic*] *altered to* on pre-Confederation

Viola Pratt (18 July 1947). VLP, VUL. Handwritten, plain paper.

Albert G. Hatcher (31 July 1947). MUNA. Handwritten, LH5.

John M. Gray (10 Aug. 1947). Macmillan, MMLM. Handwritten, plain paper.
403 Puncher the [....] *altered to* Puncher the aircraft
404 By the way Benét] By the way Benet

Helen O'Reilly (21 Aug. 1947). Macmillan, MMLM. Typed, LH5. Handwriten closing and postscript.
404 shucfling [*sic*] through *altered to* shuffling through
404 me lateer[*sic*] *altered to* me later
404 membersip [*sic*] *altered to* membership
404 succeded [*sic*] *altered to* succeeded
405 the main atmosphere *altered to* the atmosphere

Claire Pratt (late Aug. 1947). EJP, VUL. Handwritten, plain paper.

Helen O'Reilly (9 Sept. 1947). Macmillan, MMLM. Handwritten, LH5 with address crossed out.

Earle Birney (30 Sept. 1947). Birney, FRBL. Typed, LH5.
406 this misi [*sic*] *altered to* this missive
406 almost aaid [*sic*] 'faryy' [*sic*] *altered to* almost said 'farty
406 and am feeing [*sic*] *altered to* and am feeling
406 you and the family] you and thefamily [*sic*]
407 could be released] couldbe reeaaed [*sic*] *altered to* couldbe released
407 vows of Brébeuf,] vows of Brebeuf,
407 my dearest freends [*sic*] *altered to* my dearest friends
407 tenure of his iffice [*sic*] *alteed to* tenure of his office
407 undignified quarters,] undignified quaretrs [*sic*],
407 and several oshers [*sic*] *altered to* and several others
407 in the Montral [*sic*] *altered to* in the Montreal
407 Scott and] Scott and
408 Picth [*sic*] *altered to* Pickthall
408 Campbell Scott (this] Campbell Scott, (this
408 the timleliness *altered to* the timeliness
408 Scott telling tia *altered to* Scott telling him
408 Gestapo or n. *altered to* Gestapo or N.K.V.D.
408 for a poem and an [*sic*] message *altered to* for a poem and a message
408 asked me them *altered to* asked me then
408 on the mast head] on themasthead [*sic*]
409 affectionately *altered to* Affectionately

Earle Birney (3 Dec. 1947). Birney, FRBL. Typed, LH5.
410 for'tut [*sic*] *altered to* for 'Outposts.'

A.J.M. Smith (6 Jan. 1948). Smith, FRBL. Handwritten, LH5. Note in left margin: 'You may keep this copy. / N.'

A.J.M. Smith (14 Feb. 1948). Smith, FRBL. Handwritten, LH5

Earle Birney (26 Mar. 1948). Birney, FRBL. Handwritten, LH5.
412 to get your ass *altered to* to get your asses
413 one thousand of *altered to* one thousand ladies

Joseph R. Smallwood (25 Apr. 1948). Published in *The Confederate* (20 May 1948).

E.K. Brown (27 Apr. 1948). EJP, VUL. Handwritten, LH5.
415 probably give *Brébeuf*] probably give *Brebeuf*
415 Brébeuf was put] Brebeuf was put

William Arthur Deacon (6 May 1948). Deacon, FRBL. Typed, LH5.
415 been indoors] been in doors
415 fairly normalle [*sic*] *altered to* fairly normally
415 confidential.)] confidential).

Viola Pratt (7 July 1948). VLP, VUL. Handwritten, plain paper.

Pelham Edgar (13 July 1948). EJP, VUL. Handwritten, plain paper.
417 dull) had developed *altered to* dull) have developed
418 or 5 am. etc. etc.] or 5 am. et etc.

Viola Pratt (9 Aug. 1948). VLP, VUL. Handwritten, plain paper.

M.M.H. MacKinnon (26 Aug. 1948). Pitt. Handwritten, LH5.

Earle Birney (28 Sept. 1948). Birney, FRBL. Handwritten, LH5.

E.K. Brown (20 Nov. 1948). Pitt. Handwritten, LH5.
422 got the news in *altered to* got the news and

VI Knockings at the Door, 1948–1953

William Rose and Marjorie Benét (1 Jan. 1949). Benét, BRBR. Typed, LH5.
424 of you seethearts [*sic*] *altered to* of you sweethearts

Lorne Pierce (24 Jan. 1949). Pierce, QUA. Handwritten, letterhead: 'Calvert C. Pratt / Waterford Bridge Road / St John's, Nfld.'

Viola and Claire Pratt (24 Jan. 1949). VLP, VUL. Handwritten, letterhead: 'Calvert C. Pratt / Waterford Bridge Road / St John's, Nfld.'
425 Wales Academy? at] Wales Academy; at
425 said 'impossible. One] said 'impossible One
426 It is now Sun *altered to* It is now Monday
427 Wednesday night *altered to* Tuesday night
427 Won't I be [....] *altered to* Won't I be glad
427 Cal is delighted *altered to* Jim is delighted
427 I told Cal *altered to* I told Jim

Chairman, Humanities Research Council (Spring 1949). EJP, VUL. Handwritten draft, plain paper.
428 the three sections *altered to* the three headings
428 into verse an example *altered to* into verse the account
428 most challenging first *altered to* most challenging (1)
428 catastrophe and seco *altered to* catastrophe and (2)
428 of $275.00, the amount *altered to* of $275.00, there
428 $175.00. [.....] [...] [...] study 75.00 [..] [...]' *altered to* $175.00. I
428 from expenses pertaining *altered to* form expenses awarded[?] from *altered to* from expenses for a
428 Montreal, to the latter] Montreal to the latter
429 Guardian' a journ[...] *altered to* Guardian' is published
429 to this I took *altered to* to this I made my
429 family Rober[..] *altered to* family, particularly
429 I am putting *altered to* I am against putting
429 me in Toronto with transportation[?] *altered to* me in Toronto with the
429 such as a stay in *altered to* such as a stay over in
429 that a small [*half-line unintelligible*] *altered to* that a small item
429 My daughter and wife *altered to* My wife and daughter
429 subject especially project[?] *altered to* subject especially over
430 probably two or three years. *altered to* probably all my spare time in the next two or three years.

430 find a passage about *altered to* find a passage to the North about
430 if a colonel req *altered to* if a colonel, by
430 I do not wish any further approp *altered to* I do not wish the balance
430 [......] my dear / from with [....] and [......] *altered to* Sincerely yours,

Lorne Pierce (13 Apr. 1949). Pierce, QUA. Handwritten, LH7.
430 time was available. *altered to* time was not available.
431 but the se *altered to* but the deluge

E.K. Brown (28 Apr. 1949). Pitt. Handwritten, LH5.
432 I thought I would *altered to* I thought I should
432 your literary connections. *altered to* your Can. literary connections.

Leo Cox (4 May 1949). Cox. Transcribed by Pitt from the original.

Earle Birney (30 June 1949). Birney, FRBL. Handwritten, letterhead: 'Michigan Union /Ann Arbor, Michigan.'

Viola Pratt (4 July 1949). VLP, VUL. Handwritten, LH5.

Viola Pratt (25 July 1949). VLP, VUL. Handwritten, LH5.
437 on Sunday *altered to* on Saturday
437 a huge tui; [*sic*] *altered to* a huge tulip

Claire Pratt (28 July 1949). EJP, VUL. Handwritten, LH5 with address scored out.
439 (4) I feel a little] (3) I feel a little
439 (5) The long line] (4) The long line
439 (6) You will, dear] (5) You will, dear

Claire Pratt (3 Aug. 1949). EJP, VUL. Handwritten, LH5 with address scored out.

Earle Birney (10 Aug. 1949). Birney, FRBL. Handwritten, LH5 with address scored out.
443 It was stated *altered to* It was not stated

Vincent Massey (Sept. 1949). ejp, vul.

E.K. Brown (21 Oct. 1949). Pitt. Handwritten, LH5.
445 Ned (*musts*, the latter executively unavoidable!!),] Ned, (*musts*, the latter executively unavoidable!!)

445 B.K. Sandwell (a great admirer of yours),] B.K. Sandwell (a great admirer of yours)
445 Mazzoleni (a real lad),] Mazzoleni (a real lad)

Ralph Gustafson (21 Oct. 1949). Gustafson. USKL. Handwritten, LH5.
447 competitive (and altered to competitive (as

Claire Pratt (25 Dec. 1949). CP, VUL. Handwritten, LH7.

Earle Birney (17 Feb. 1950). Birney, FRBL. Handwritten, LH5.

Marjorie Benét (11 May 1950). Benét, BRBR. Handwritten, LH5.

Viola Pratt (3 July 1950). VLP, VUL. Handwritten, plain paper.

Viola Pratt (6 July 1950). VLP, VUL. Handwritten, LH5.

Viola and Claire Pratt (27 July 1950). VLP, VUL. Handwritten, plain paper.

Claire Pratt (9 Sept. 1950). EJP, VUL. Handwritten, letterhead: 'Hotel Vancouver / Vancouver, B.C.'

Viola Pratt (10 Sept. 1950). VLP, VUL. Handwritten, letterhead: 'Hotel Vancouver / Vancouver, B.C.'
455 about the Fraser River] about the Frazer River

Claire Pratt (10 Sept. 1950). EJP, VUL. Handwritten, letterhead: 'Hotel Vancouver / Vancouver, B.C.'
456 numerous really). The] numerous really. The

Roy and Laurenda Daniells (17 Sept. 1950). Daniells, UBCL. Handwritten, 'Canadian Pacific Hotels / [crest – a sheaf of wheat] / Hotel Saskatchewan / Regina, Sask.'
459 is Jane. Caress] is Jane Caress

Claire Pratt (17 Sept. 1950). EJP, VUL. Handwritten, letterhead: 'Canadian Pacific Hotels / [picture of hotel] / Hotel Saskatchewan / Regina, Sask.'
459 to me of how the great] to me of how the extinction of the great
459 hard rock from Ralph. *altered to* hard rock from Karl.
460 – five of us – at] – five of us) at
460 – a Methodist – was] – a Methodist) was

Viola Pratt (18 Sept. 1950). EJP, VUL. Handwritten, letterhead: 'Canadian Pacific Hotels / [picture of hotel] / Royal Alexandra Hotel / Winnipeg, Man.'

E.K. Brown (17 Nov. 1950). Margaret Brown. Transcibed by Pitt from tape-recorded reading.

John M. Gray (2 Dec. 1950). Gray. Transcribed by Pitt from tape-recording, June 1966.

E.K. and Margaret Brown (16 Jan. 1951). EJP, VUL. Handwritten, LH5.

John Sutherland (25 Jan. 1951). Audrey Sutherland. Handwritten, LH5.

Earle Birney (10 Feb. 1950). Birney, FRBL. Handwritten, LH5.

Margaret Brown (30 Apr. 1951). Margaret Brown. Handwritten, LH5

Ralph Gustafson (11 May 1951). Gustafson, USKL. Handwritten, LH5.

Irving Layton (16 May 1951). Layton, CUL. Handwritten, LH7.
468 of the Season' and] of the Season and

Viola and Claire Pratt (3 July 1951). VLP, VUL. Handwritten, plain paper.

Viola Pratt (5 July 1951). VLP, VUL. Handwritten, plain paper.

Phyllis Webb (19 July 1951). Webb, LAC. Handwritten, plain paper.
471 by *The Witches' Brew*] by *The Witches Brew*
472 *Antinoe*, a narrative] *Antinoe* a narrative
472 came with *Brébeuf*] came with *Brebeuf*
472 circulation. *Brébeuf*] circulation. *Brebeuf*

Viola Pratt (24 July 1951). VLP, VUL. Handwritten, plain paper.
474 saying that McNeill] saying that MacNeill

Leonard W. Brockington (Sept. 1951). EJP, VUL. Handwritten draft.
475 *Mercy* in which [....] John Masefie *altered to Mercy* in which *altered to Mercy* in the *English Review*
475 Dauber and *altered to* Dauber, Reynard

475 are together *altered to* are still on my shelves together
475 to send him a poem *altered to* to send him an early poem
475 at Macmillans, *altered to* at Macmillans with Hugh Eayrs,
475 admiration *altered to* admiration. Tell him too that I have read Consecration and Aug. 1914 to thousands of students over the thiry years of my teaching at the University of Toronto.

Anne Wilkinson (24 Sept. 1951). Smith, Trent. Handwritten, LH5.
476 'I know what *altered to* 'I know not what
477 is in Tyrell's] in Tyrell's

Margaret Brown (10 Oct. 1951). Margaret Brown. Handwritten, LH5.

John Sutherland (15 Nov. 1951). Audrey Sutherland. Handwritten, LH5.

John M. Gray (29 Nov. 1951). Macmillan, MMLM.

'K' (late 1951). EJP, VUL. Handwritten draft, plain paper.
480 along 'The Mechanical Bride'] along The Mechanical Bride'
480 I don't know if *altered to* I don't know what
481 disclaims the adj *altered to* disclaims the [....]

Phelps, Arthur (2 Jan. 1952). Phelps, UML. Handwritten, LH5.

Claire Pratt (30 Jan. 1952). CP, VUL. Handwritten, plain paper.

His Fourth Year Students (24 Feb. 1952). EJP, VUL. Handwritten draft, plain paper.
483 says the food-[...] *altered to* says your tangible message of sympathy must
483 suggestive of I could [..] *altered to* suggestive of Miami.
483 bring the contents of the box into *altered to* bring the contents into
483 ceremony, and expos *altered to* ceremony, the chief
483 reposing in the bot[?] *altered to* reposing in the lower
483 Friday week, at *altered to* Friday week, precisely at
483 I live). I was feeling o[.] the front[?] grand-[...] *altered to* I live). As the street
483 sidewalk. That was *altered to* sidewalk. There was
483 professional, then *altered to* professional, in fact
483 symmetry of my locomotion *altered to* symmetry of my pose
483 gravity decidedly *altered to* gravity lying decidedly
483 I *altered to* For a period

483 of my position or [.....] [..] [....] position. *altered to* of my position.
483 thankful that it was not my neck but my shoulder *latered to* that I had not brocken my back instead of my shoulder *altered to* thankful that it was my shoulder, not my neck
483 that hit first *altered to* which was broken.
483 intact to be able to collect the *altered to* intact to enable
484 was only a stone's throw *altered to* was only fifty
484 world and the one now a[...]th[..] [....]e did then *altered to* world and the *Brooding Fate*

John Sutherland (25 Feb. 1952). Audrey Sutherland. Handwritten, plain paper.
485 the 'Great Feud.'] the Great Feud.'

John Sutherland (15 Mar. 1952). Audrey Sutherland. Handwritten, plain paper.

Father V.J. Guinan (22 Mar. 1952). University of St. Thomas Library. Handwritten, LH5.
490 weight) with *altered to* weight) and with

F. David Hoeniger (5 May 1952). EJP, VUL. Handwritten, LH5.

Viola and Claire Pratt (28 May 1952). VLP, VUL. Handwritten, postcard; postmarked Houston, Texas, 28 May 1952.

Viola Pratt (6 June 1952). VLP, VUL. Handwritten, letterhead: 'THE BOOK TRUCK / 21 Cortleigh Blvd. / toronto 12, ont // Claire Pratt, mgr. / / hu. 1047.' 'THE BOOK TRUCK' is scored out.
492 dollar. But the *altered to* dollar. But Tatton

Lord Beaverbrook (early June 1952). Beaverbrook, UNB. Handwritten, letterhead: 'Victoria College / University of Toronto // E.J.Pratt, C.M.G., D. Litt.'

Desmond Pacey (8 June 1952). Pacey. Handwritten, LH7 (typed transcript in EJP, VUL).

Viola Pratt (9 June 1952). VLP, VUL. Handwritten, LH5.
495 but didn't bother *altered to* but it didn't bother
495 anyway?' I] anyway? I
495 yours, so go *altered to* yours, so get
495 person in Eagel *altered to* person in Eagle

495 she said 'Oh] she said Oh
495 the head.' So] the head. So

William Arthur Deacon (15 June 1952). Deacon, FRBL. Handwritten, LH7 with 'Victoria College' scored out and replaced by '21 Cortleigh Blvd.'

Lorne Pierce (Summer 1952). Pierce, QUA. Handwritten, LH5.
498 why *mechanician*? (9)] why *mechanician*? 9
498 13. *The Criminal*] 13. '*The Criminal*

Ralph Gustafson (9 July 1952). Gustafson, USKL. Handwritten, LH5.

A.J.M. Smith (15 July 1952). Smith, FRBL. Handwritten, LH5.

Karl Shapiro (25 July 1952). Poetry, UC. Handwritten, LH5.

John Sutherland (25 July 1952). Audrey Sutherland. Handwritten, LH5.

John Sutherland (8 Aug. 1952). Audrey Sutherland. Handwritten, LH5 with 'Victoria College' scored out and '21 Cortleigh Blvd.' written in its place.
503 over it.' Hence] over it. Hence

John Sutherland (11 Aug. 1952). Audrey Sutherland. Handwritten, letterhead: 'Canadian Pacific Railway / en route.' [Note: as Pratt plays on the 'en route' notation, this letterhead is duplicated in the text of the letter on p. 503.]
504 confession were *altered to* confession that his theistic beliefs were
505 an ineradicable in *altered to* an ineradicable element in
505 Students, the *altered to* Students (in Ontario), the
505 decided to put one *altered to* decided to put on one

A.J.M. Smith (12 Aug. 1952). Smith, FRBL. Handwritten, letterhead: 'The Cascade Hotel / Banff National Park / [picture of hotel] / BANFF, Canada.'

Claire Pratt (13 Aug. 1952). EJP, VUL. Handwritten, letterhead: 'Canadian Pacific Railway / en route' with 'en route' scored out.

Earle Birney (27 Aug. 1952). Birney, FRBL. Handwritten, LH5.

Karl Shapiro (27 Aug. 1952). Poetry, UC. Handwritten, LH5.

Raymond Gushue (12 Sept. 1952). MUNA. Telegram: 'Canadian National Telegraphs.'; date-stamped 12 September 1952.

Raymond Gushue (13 Sept. 1952). MUNA. Handwritten, LH5.

Claire Pratt (10 Oct. 1952). EJP, VUL. Handwritten, letterhead: 'The Senate / [crest] / Canada.'

Earle Birney (Oct. 1952). Birney, FRBL. Handwritten, LH5.

George Johnston (13 Nov. 1952). Johnston, LAC. Handwritten, LH5.

Earle Birney (20 Nov. 1952). Birney, FRBL. Handwritten, LH5.

Henry W. Wells (early Dec. 1952). Wells. Transcribed by Pitt from original.

John Sutherland (late 1952). Audrey Sutherland. Handwritten, LH5.

Claire Pratt (15 Jan. 1953). EJP, VUL. Handwritten, plain paper.
517 Toronto, Ont.] Toronto Ont.

Claire Pratt (4 Feb. 1953). CP, VUL. Handwritten, LH5.
520 this morning – mother. *altered to* this morning. – Mother

Claire Pratt (9 Feb. 1953). EJP, VUL. Handwritten, LH5.

Roy M. Wiles (13 Feb. 1953). Wiles. Handwritten, LH5.

Claire Pratt (20 Mar. 1953). EJP, VUL. Handwritten, LH5.

Claire Pratt (29 Mar. 1953). EJP, VUL. Handwritten, plain paper. Letter is 'an addendum' to a longer letter form Viola Pratt.
524 Reminiscences' – there] Reminiscences' there
524 Father LeBel – asked] Father LeBel asked

Claire Pratt (11 Apr. 1953). EJP, VUL. Handwritten, LH5.

Claire Pratt (1 May 1953). EJP, VUL. Handwritten, LH5 with 'Victoria College' scored out.

John Sutherland (12 May 1953). Audrey Sutherland. Handwritten, LH5.

Claire Pratt (19 May 1953). EJP, VUL. Handwritten, LH5.

Claire Pratt (5 June 1953). EJP, VUL. Handwritten, plain paper. Two lines have been excised.
529 Thursday *altered to* Friday
529 [ ] = *approximately 2 lines are blocked out*

Margaret Brown (9 June 1953). Pitt. Handwritten, plain paper.
530 settled yet, storing] settled yet storing
530 imagine, have given *altered to* imagine, have given

Claire Pratt (25 June 1953). EJP, VUL. Handwritten, plain paper.

Claire Pratt (27 June 1953). EJP, VUL. Handwritten, plain paper.

VII Accepting the Years, 1953–1955

Claire Pratt (4 Aug. 1953). EJP, VUL. Handwritten, plain paper.

Claire Pratt (7 Aug. 1953). EJP, VUL. Handwritten, letterhead: 'GLYNMILL INN / Corner Brook / Newfoundland.'
535 letter before you *altered to* letter before we
535 leaping a policeman *altered to* leaping an Irish policeman

Claire Pratt (26 Aug. 1953). EJP, VUL. Handwritten, plain paper.

Claire Pratt (4 Sept. 1953). EJP, VUL. Handwritten, LH5 with 'Victoria College' scored out.
537 and Ken Kees. *altered to* and Ken Kee.
538 Toronto), Sid] Toronto) Sid

Claire Pratt (15 Sept. 1953). EJP, VUL. Handwritten, LH5 with 'Victoria College' scored out, and the '5' scored out in 'Toronto 5' and replaced with '12.'

Claire Pratt (27 Sept. 1953). EJP, VUL. Handwritten, plain paper.

Claire Pratt (12 Oct. 1953). EJP, VUL. Handwritten, plain paper.
541 out *of ofs*.] out *of offs*.

Claire Pratt (24 Oct. 1953). EJP, VUL. Handwritten, LH5 with 'Victoria College' scored out, and the '5' in 'Toronto 5' replaced by '12.'

543 the beards. *altered* to the beards. Strathcona's eyebrows looked like a full-foliaged precipice.

Claire Pratt (5 Nov. 1953). EJP, VUL. Handwritten, LH7 with 'Victoria College' scored out, and '12' added following 'Toronto.'

544 bare hands), bull-fighter] bare hands) bull-fighter

544 return it later?] return it later.

Claire Pratt (8 Nov. 1953). EJP, VUL. Handwritten, plain paper.

545 period from 4 *altered to* period from 2

545 it nearly broke before] it nearly broke it before

Claire Pratt (11 Nov. 1953). EJP, VUL. Handwritten, plain paper.

Leopold Macauley (15 Nov. 1953). EJP, VUL.

Desmond Pacey (18 Nov. 1953). Pacey, UNB (copy in EJP, VUL). Typed form letter, LH5. Note in Pacey's hand: 'Sent $7.50 / D.P.'

Lorne Pierce (26 Nov. 1953). Pierce, QUA. Handwritten, LH5.

Claire Pratt (27 Nov. 1953). EJP, VUL. Handwritten, plain paper.

Claire Pratt (7 Dec. 1953). EJP, VUL. Handwritten, LH5 with 'Victoria College scored out, and the '5' in 'Toronto 5' replaced with '12.'

549 [ ] = *approximately 4 lines blocked out by recipient*

Awards Committee of the Royal Society (15 Dec. 1953). EJP, VUL. Handwritten draft, plain paper.

550 that would l[....] [....]t *altered to* that would justify

Claire Pratt (20 Jan. 1954). EJP, VUL. Handwritten, LH5 with 'Victoria College' scored out and the '5' in 'Toronto 5' changed to '12.'

Claire Pratt (25 Jan. 1954). EJP, VUL. Handwritten, LH5 with 'Victoria College' scored out and the '5' in 'Toronto 5' changed to '12.'

Claire Pratt (29 Jan. 1954). EJP, VUL. Handwritten, plain paper.

553 [ ] = *7–8 lines are blocked out*

Claire Pratt (3 Feb. 1954). EJP, VUL. Handwritten, LH7.
554 recuperated.' Cal] recuperated. Cal

Claire Pratt (6 Feb. 1954). EJP, VUL. Handwritten, LH5 with 'Victoria College' scored out and the '5' in 'Toronto 5' changed to '12.'

Claire Pratt (10 Feb. 1954). EJP, VUL. Handwritten, LH5 with 'Victoria College' scored out and the '5' in 'Toronto 5' changed to '12.'
557 [ ] = *approximately 4 lines are blocked out*
557 you that Karl] you that Carl [*sic*]

Claire Pratt (25 Feb. 1954). EJP, VUL. Handwritten, LH5 with 'Victoria College' scored out and the '5' in 'Toronto 5' changed to '12.'

Claire Pratt (2 Mar. 1954). EJP, VUL. Handwritten, LH5 with 'Victoria College' scored out and the '5' in 'Toronto 5' changed to '12.'

Claire Pratt (31 Mar. 1954). EJP, VUL. Handwritten, LH5 with 'Victoria College' scored out and the '5' in 'Toronto 5' changed to '12.'
560 Principal) could make *altered to* Principal) could not make

Claire Pratt (7 May 1954). EJP, VUL. Handwritten, LH5 with 'Victoria College' scored out and the '5' in 'Toronto 5' changed to '12.'
561 [ ] '*approximately 4 lines blocked out*

Claire Pratt (10 May 1954). EJP, VUL. Handwritten, plain paper.

John Sutherland (12 May 1954). Audrey Sutherland. Handwritten, plain paper.

Claire Pratt (14 May 1954). EJP, VUL. Handwritten, plain paper.
564 Toronto Ont. *altered to* Toronto 12 Ont.
565 to the Deacons *altered to* to the Deacons'

Claire Pratt (17 May 1954). EJP, VUL. Handwritten, plain paper.
565 [ ] = *approximately 9 lines blocked out by the recipient*

John Sutherland (21 May 1954). Audrey Sutherland. Handwritten, plain paper.
567 of the *Canadian Forum altered to* of the U. of Toronto Quarterly
567 wrote it – most *altered to* wrote it – a most

Claire Pratt (22 May 1954). CP, VUL. Handwritten, plain paper.
569 the Dalys] the Daly's

Claire Pratt (23 May 1954). EJP, VUL. Handwritten, plain paper.
569 Toronto Ont *altered to* Toronto 12 Ont

Claire Pratt (27 May 1954). EJP, VUL. Handwritten, plain paper.

Claire Pratt (30 May 1954). EJP, VUL. Handwritten, plain paper.
572 [ ] = *1 line blocked out by recipient*

Claire Pratt (9 June 1954). EJP, VUL. Handwritten, plain paper.

Claire Pratt (11 June 1954). EJP, VUL. Handwritten, plain paper.

Claire Pratt (24 June 1954). EJP, VUL. Handwritten, plain paper.

Claire Pratt (27 June 1954). EJP, VUL. Handwritten, plain paper.

Claire Pratt (1 July 1954). EJP, VUL. Handwritten, plain paper.
579 the Festival idea.] the Festival idea).

John Sutherland (26 July 1954). Audrey Sutherland. Handwritten, plain paper.

Raymond Gushue (23 Aug. 1954). MUNA. Handwritten, plain paper.

Claire Pratt (8 Oct. 1954). EJP, VUL. Handwritten, plain paper.
582 [ ] = *approximately 4 lines blocked out by recipient*

Desmond Pacey (20 Oct. 1954). Pacey, UNB (copy in EJP, VUL). Handwritten, LH5.

Claire Pratt (24 Oct. 1954). EJP, VUL. Handwritten, plain paper.

Desmond Pacey (29 Oct. 1954). Pacey, UNB (copy in EJP, VUL). Handwritten, LH1. Double horizontal lines are drawn in the margins of paragraphs 2 and 4, presumably added by Pacey.
587 where we imbued *altered to* where we were imbued

Claire Pratt (29 Oct. 1954). EJP, VUL. Handwritten, plain paper.

Claire Pratt (31 Oct. 1954). EJP, VUL. Handwritten, LH5 with 'Victoria College' scored out, and the '5' scored out in 'Toronto 5' and replaced with '12.'
590 person [who] met us] person meet us

Earle Birney (2 Nov. 1954). Birney, FRBL. Handwritten, plain paper.
590 47 Glen *altered to* Victoria College
591 own decision, plucky] own decision plucky

Esther Birney (2 Nov. 1954). Birney, FRBL. Handwritten, plain paper.
592 whispered into his ear, 'Do] whispered into his ear, Do
592 Come in.'] Come in.

Desmond Pacey (11 Nov. 1954). Pacey, UNB (copy in EJP, VUL). Handwritten, plain paper.
594 'Mean? He meant] 'Mean? 'He meant
594 his system.' Another,] his system. Another,
594 camps, the tortures *altered to* camps, the a[..]s, the tortures

Viola Pratt (11 Nov. 1954). VLP, VUL. Handwritten, plain paper.

Claire Pratt (16 Nov. 1954). VLP, VUL. Handwritten, plain paper.

Viola Pratt (17 Nov. 1954). VLP, VUL. Handwritten, plain paper.

John Sutherland (17 Nov. 1954). Audrey Sutherland. Handwritten, plain paper.

Viola and Claire Pratt (20 Nov. 1954). VLP, VUL. Handwritten, plain paper.

Desmond Pacey (25 Nov. 1954). Pacey, UNB (copy in EJP, VUL). Handwritten, plain paper.

Viola Pratt (18 Dec. 1954). VLP, VUL. Handwritten, plain paper.

Viola Pratt (19 Dec. 1954). VLP, VUL. Handwritten, plain paper.

Claire Pratt (24 Dec. 1954). VLP, VUL. Handwritten, plain paper.

Claire Pratt (30 Dec. 1954). VLP, VUL. Handwritten, plain paper.
607 famous or Pilsener?] famous or Pilsener.

Claire Pratt (2 Jan. 1955). EJP, VUL. Handwritten, plain paper.

Claire Pratt (5 Jan. 1955). EJP, VUL. Handwritten, plain paper.

Viola Pratt (14 Jan. 1955). EJP, VUL. Handwritten, plain paper.

Viola Pratt (22 Jan. 1955). EJP, VUL. Handwritten, plain paper.
611 [ ] = *approximately 3 lines blocked out by recipient*

Viola and Claire Pratt (28 Jan. 1955). VLP, VUL. Handwritten, plain paper.

Viola and Claire Pratt (30 Jan. 1955). VLP, VUL. Handwritten, plain paper.

VIII As Good as Any Old Horse My Age, 1955–1964

Leo Cox (16 Apr. 1955). Cox. Transcribed by Pitt from original.

Henry Alexander (6 June 1955). Whalley.

Louis Dudek (18 June 1955). Dudek, LAC. Handwritten, plain paper.

Margaret (Mrs E.K.) Brown (24 July 1955). Pitt. Handwritten, plain paper.

Ronald G. Everson (14 Aug. 1955). Everson, MMLM. Handwritten, plain paper.

John Sutherland (29 Sept. 1955). Audrey Sutherland. Handwritten, plain paper.

Earle Birney (8 Nov. 1955). Birney, FRBL. Handwritten, plain paper.

Esther Birney (8 Nov. 1955). Birney, FRBL. Handwritten, plain paper.

Carl Klinck (13 June 1956). Klinck. Handwritten, plain paper.

Sister Dorothy Marie Doyle (10 July 1956). Doyle. Handwritten, LH7.

Sister Dorothy Marie Doyle (25 July 1956). Doyle. Handwritten, letterhead: 'The York Club / Toronto 5.'

John Sutherland (13 Aug. 1956). Audrey Sutherland. Handwritten, plain paper.

Carlyle King (15 Aug. 1956). Pratt, USKL. Handwritten, plain paper.

Ralph Gustafson (19 Sept. 1956). Gustafson, USKL. Handwritten, letterhead: 'The York Club / Toronto 5' with 'The York Club' scored out and the '5 in 'Toronto 5' replaced with '12.'

Claire Pratt (26 Sept. 1956). EJP, VUL. Handwritten, plain paper.

Claire Pratt (22 Oct. 1956). EJP, VUL. Handwritten, LH7 with 'Victoria College' scored out and '12 Canada' added following 'Toronto.

629 [ ] = *1.5 lines blocked out by the recipient*

Claire Pratt (26 Oct. 1956). EJP, VUL. Handwritten, letterhead: '[image of hotel] / Chateau Laurier / Ottawa, Ontario'

Claire Pratt (29 Oct. 1956). EJP, VUL. Handwritten, plain paper.

Desmond Pacey (12 Nov. 1956). Pacey, UNB. Handwritten, LH8 (copy in EJP, VUL). Rough draft [*MS1*] in Newfoundland Centre, MUNA: written on the outside and inside of an envelope addressed to 'Professor E.J. Pratt, Ph.D., D. Litt., D.C.L., LL.D., F.R.S.C.' from 'The Bowater Awards for Journalism / 47 Wellesley Street East / Toronto (5) Ontario' and postmarked 20 October 1956.

632 Thanks for your grand article.] Your article is magnificient [*MS1*]

632 It is a superb bit of analysis – the sort of thing] It is the sort of thing [*MS1*]

632 discarded in the *Collected*] discarded in Collected Poems [*MS1*]

632 verses in *Newfoundland Verse*.] poems in N.V. especially the monologues & dialogues [*MS1*]

632 and *Brébeuf*.] and *Brebeuf*.

632 the later composition.] the later composition. You know what I mean, Des. Take care of your eyes; they are valuable beyond comparison. [*MS1*]

632 his death. To give him credit] his death though I visited him in hospital two or three times every week. I didn't know till afterward that he was racing against time to complete the book. I never knew a man who showed so much courage & patience under siege. As you may know, from being an unbeliever he became a R.C. and hence his interpretation may be coloured by his convictions. When a friend of mine asked me if I intended the dinosaur to represent Christ I first had an impulse to laugh at such a far-fetched comparison (to say nothing of the contrast), but John's dying condition choked the laugh. It is true that he mentioned his

purpose was to go beyond my conscious intention, and when I read the final Feud and the dinosaur's ascent up the cliff, his suffering, etc., I could see what he meant. He had at least a half-truth. To give him credit [*MS*1]
632 spent in Psychology.] spent in Psychology before going to Vic. [*MS*1]
632 Some of his conclusions are far-fetched such as the representing of the dinosaur as a phase of Christ, but John did insert a 'caveat' at the beginning that he was going beyond the 'conscious intention,' a perilous excursion indeed. And, again, though I had to teach Wundt, I hated Wundtianism and its mechanisms. You properly place that period in its proper orientation.] I hated the whole Wundtian business though I had to teach Wundt. That physiological (or mechanized) being is life was as abhorrent to me as Professor Blewett's Idealism a[...] the life of the spirit was attractive. But behind all this lies the idea of conflict. In spite of evolution, has the savagery of human warfare been much diminished? With Hitler out, the present Kruschoff [*sic*] trends give us much basis for optimism. It may be a long time before the Sermon on the Mount will conquer the totalitarian quest for power & conquest. The two things are in conflict, let us make no mistake about that. But what is there left to us but our devotion to Christ come what may? [*MS*1]
632 Thanks for letting me see your article. I should have answered before but this is my first day out, having wrestled with a bug for two weeks.] Des. – Most of this is confidential. I wouldn't hurt the feelings of Mrs Sutherland for anything – with genuine faith in *Christian* humanism as you adequately describe it. [*MS*1]
632 Mary & yourself] Mary & you [*MS*1]
632 P.S. By the way, where does your article appear? [*MS*1]

Henry W. Wells (6 Dec. 1956). Wells. Transcribed by Pitt from original.

Ralph Gustafson (21 Mar. 1957). Gustafson, USKL. Handwritten, LH7 with 'Victoria College' scored out and '12' added following 'Toronto.'
634 (2) I should] I should

Desmond and Mary Pacey (May 1957). Pacey, UNB (copy in EJP, VUL). Handwritten, plain paper.

Irving Layton (9 June 1957). Layton, CUL (copy in EJP, VUL). Handwritten, plain paper.

Sister Dorothy Marie Doyle (21 July 1957). Doyle. Handwritten, LH5 with 'Victoria College' scored out and '5' in 'Toronto 5' replaced with '12.'
636 pages of *Brébeuf*.] pages of *Brebeuf*.
636 moments of Brébeuf] moments of Brebeuf

The Canada Council (11 Nov. 1957). Gustafson, USKL. Typed, carbon – plain paper.

Earle Birney (7 Dec. 1957). Birney, FRBL. Handwritten, plain paper.

David G. Pitt (2 Feb. 1958). Pitt. Handwritten – in Viola Pratt's hand, plain paper.

Desmond Pacey (18 Feb. 1958). Pacey, UNB (copy in EJP, VUL). Handwritten, plain paper.

David G. Pitt (18 Feb. 1958). Pitt. Typed, plain paper.
641 in the gowth [*sic*] *altered to* in the growth
641 struggle oor [*sic*] life *altered to* struggle for life
641 do not print *altered to* do not put in

Claude and Christine Bissell (20 Feb. 1958). Bissell. Handwritten, plain paper.

A.J.M. Smith (26 Feb. 1958). Smith, FRBL. Handwritten, plain paper.
643 the 'lift' of] the 'lift of

Ralph Gustafson (27 Feb. 1958). Gustafson, USKL. Handwritten, plain paper.

Claire Pratt (5 Apr. 1958). EJP, VUL. Handwritten, plain paper.

Earle Birney (19 Apr. 1958). Birney, FRBL. Handwritten, plain paper.

David G. Pitt (21 May 1958). Pitt. Typed, plain paper.
645 from at *altered to* from the 'Spike'
645 Best regrads [*sic*] *altered to* Best regards

John M. Gray (14 June 1958). Macmillan, MMLM. Handwritten, plain paper.

John M. Gray (25 June 1958). Macmillan, MMLM. Handwritten, plain paper.

Watson Kirkconnell (8 Feb. 1959). Kirkconnell, Acadia. Handwritten, plain paper.

Claude and Christine Bissell (2 Dec. 1959). Bissell. Handwritten, plain paper.

David G. Pitt (2 Jan. 1960). Pitt. Handwritten, plain paper.

Ronald G. Everson (20 Jan. 1960). Everson, MMLM. Handwritten, LH7 with 'Victoria College' scored out and '12' added following 'Toronto.'

David G. Pitt (11 Feb. 1960). Pitt. Handwritten, plain paper.

A.J.M. Smith (13 Aug. 1960). Smith, FRBL. Handwritten, plain paper.

David G. Pitt (22 Sept. 1960). Pitt. Handwritten, plain paper.

Sister Dorothy Marie Doyle (10 Nov. 1960). Doyle. Handwritten, plain paper.

Daphne Pratt House (19 Feb. 1961). Pitt. Handwritten, plain paper.

John T. Stoker (12 Apr. 1961). MUNA. Handwritten, plain paper.

Charles L. Bennet (11 June 1961). Bennet. Handwritten, plain paper.

Raymond Gushue (20 Aug. 1961). MUNA. Typed, plain paper.

Raymond Gushue (12 Sept. 1961). MUNA. Typed, plain paper.
654 I am extrmmely *altered to* I am extremely

Margaret Furness MacLeod (27 Sept. 1961). MacLeod. Typed, LH10.

Alan Crawley (Sept. 1961). Crawley, QUA. Typed, plain paper.
656 find mich [*sic*] *altered to* find much
656 However at present *altered to* However, at present
656 a bout of arthtitis [*sic*] *altered to* a bout of arthritis
656 my acivities [*sic*] *altered to* my activities

H. Pearson Gundy (24 Oct. 1961). Gundy, QUA. Typed transcription of the original holograph letter on Gundy's letterhead: 'Queen's University / Kingston, Ontario // from the Librarian.'

Sister Dorothy Marie Doyle (17 Apr. 1962). Doyle. Handwritten, plain paper.
658 to have *Brébeuf]* to have *Brebeuf*
658 *Sorhab* [*sic*] *and Rustum*] *Sorham and Rustum*

Vincent D. Sharman (1962). Transcribed by Sharman in his thesis.

Father J. Stanley Murphy (10 Jan. 1963). CP, VUL. Handwritten, LH10.

Ronald Hambleton (7 Feb. 1963). Hambleton, FRBL. Handwritten, LH10.

Raymond Gushue (10 Feb. 1963). MUNA. Typed, plain paper.

Leo Cox (11 Feb. 1963). Cox. Transcribed by Pitt from original.

Douglas and Hazel Bush (Feb. 1963). Bush. Handwritten, LH10.

David G. Pitt (Feb. 1963). Pitt. Handwritten, LH10.

A Grade Four Class (Feb. 1963). EJP, VUL. Handwritten, LH10.

William Arthur Deacon (14 Mar. 1963). Deacon, FRBL. Handwritten, LH10.
663 to friendship. When] to frienship. When

Sister Dorothy Marie Doyle (Mar. 1964). Doyle. Handwritten, LH10.

Appendix: Some Letters by Viola Pratt

William Arthur Deacon (12 Nov. 1962). Deacon, FRBL.

A.J.M. Smith (Dec. 1962). Smith, FRBL.

Several Correspondents (23 Mar. 1964). VLP, VUL.

A.J.M. Smith (3 May 1964). Smith, FRBL.

Leo Cox (11 May 1964). Cox. Transcribed by Pitt from original.

M.M.H. MacKinnon (20 May 1964). MacKinnon.

Margaret (Mrs E.K.) Brown (3 July 1964). Margaret Brown.

Earle Birney (7 July 1964). Birney, FRBL.

Index

www.ingramcontent.com/pod-product-compliance
Lightning Source LLC
LaVergne TN
LVHW010354080826
844660LV00016B/971/J

* 9 7 8 1 4 4 2 6 5 0 2 3 7 *